ELLIOTT'S GOLF FORM 2001

Keith Elliott

This Edition First Published in 2000 by
Portway Press Limited
Halifax West Yorkshire HX1 1XE
Tel: 01422 330330 Fax: 01422 398017
E-mail timeform@timeform.com

Paperback ISBN 1 901570 22 3

Cover photographs
Front: Tiger Woods, Allsport
Inset: Ewen Murray

Printed and bound by
The Charlesworth Group
Huddersfield UK 01484 517077

ABOUT THE AUTHOR

Keith was first attracted to golf betting because, being a game played between the ears, he could apply to it much of his knowledge from the positive thinking, personal motivation and mental skills courses, workshops, and broadcasts that he had given for many years.

Through the nineties he has applied his statistical ability, analytical skills and knowledge of mental processes to sports betting. Indeed while working at the Liverpool Business School, he was the only University lecturer in the country who had permission to run a sports service from his professor.

He chose early retirement in late 1995 to focus on his sports betting, horse racing and positive thinking interests.

He is the author of 'How to Win At Golf Betting' and this is his seventh successive golf betting annual.

He currently runs Timeform's Sportsline Service.

He was BBC Radio Merseyside's Racing Correspondent for eighteen years. In September 1997 he was appointed, (and in September 2000 re-appointed), by the Home Secretary to be an independent member of the British Horserace Betting Levy Board where he has shown a passionate interest in all matters relating to punter protection.

Keith has been happily married to Tik for 34 years, has two sons Steven (22) and Martin (20), two cats and a Tranmere Rovers' season ticket!

Elliott's Golf Form has become an institution for those in the game who like to enjoy golf tournaments armed with some specialist knowledge.

It offers viewers of televised golf a unique insight into each tournament venue, and the form of the players taking part.

I use this carefully-compiled dossier mainly for research, but there is no doubt that Elliott's Golf Form has been a key part in the growth of sensible golf betting.

Whether you have the occasional flutter on the outcome of major championships, or have more regular wagers on week to week tournaments, this form guide will ensure you start with a good chance against the bookies.

I've been known to have the odd each way bet in the major events but some of my chums have fun with perm bets on weekend two balls, and yankees on tournament three balls.

If you are going to have a golfing bet step one must be to turn the pages of Elliott's Golf Form.

Good golfing, and good luck!

Ewen Murray

INTRODUCTION

Welcome to the seventh volume of Elliott's Golf Form. This year I would particularly like to thank.

Ewen Murray – A peerless golf analyst and superb commentator with a fine sense of humour it was a great moment when he agreed to write this year's Foreword, especially as I discovered he was a fan of the book.

Coral Eurobet – For becoming the first sponsors of the book and for increasing the total prize fund for the competition to over £1,500. So to Bob Scott, Trevor Beaumont, Sheena Denston, Colleen Gee, Simon Clare and John Wright a big thank you.

Nick Metcalf and Vanessa O'Brien from the European PGA – 25-year-old Nick's the key man behind the compilation of the European stats, a golfer (he's off 4) since he was 14, and a number cruncher extra-ordinaire while Vanessa, although born in Rome, has been a magician in helping the media for well over 100 months!

Nigel Townsend from Portway Press – Nigel is the tower of strength that enables this book to roll off the production lines just a few weeks after the season ends.

Readers and fans of this book – Particular thanks to Frazar Peterson, James Schumacher, A Graham, Kevin Vine, Lawrence Merlin (South Africa), Roy Williams, Gary Bennett (ex Tranmere Rovers), Mark Wills, Bill Smith, and Paudie O'Donovan (Limerick) who were the first ten readers to contact me after the last volume.

Family and Friends – To my wife Tik for her amazing work in producing this annual miracle, and to my two smashin' lads, Martin and Steven for all their help.

To Mike (tootles) Rad, Beryl, Stevie B, Meggles and the Pifs for their continued friendship; to Jim and Sandra, Bob and Rae for a great holiday, to Nick Lewis (ACR Aerials) for ensuring I have sky dishes everywhere, and to Ian McGregor who's different class!

This year also to Lorraine Rogers, John Aldridge and the Tranmere Rovers team for making that Wembley Worthington Cup Final such a memorable day as the tears ran into my face paint.

AN OPEN INVITATION – Your feedback really is welcome and important so do please feel free to contact me either :-

Write to	Keith Elliott, c/o Timeform Sportsline, Timeform House, Halifax, West Yorkshire, HX1 1XE
Fax me on	0151 608 4860
E-mail at	Kevapositive@BTInternet.com

I hope you enjoy the book and that it helps you to a profitable golf betting year in 2001.

CORAL EUROBET SPONSORSHIP OF
ELLIOTT'S GOLF FORM 2001

Over the years this in-depth golf betting guide has become the 'Bible' for every person who takes their golf seriously.

I probably speak for the whole betting industry when I say that Keith Elliott's opinions on golf are respected and feared. His analytical compilations of golfers from all tours I find unerringly accurate.

This anorak of the fairways not only has the ability to unearth golfers with the physical and mental attitude to win on tour he also shows skill, good judgement and patience in selection.

Within these pages, along with unrivalled analysis of the full spectrum of professional golf, there are champions and major winners to bet on. Hope you get enjoyment in finding them before we do!

So we at Coral Eurobet are really delighted to sponsor this book and trust that you will bet with us as often as possible.

John Wright
Golf & Sports Odds Compiler
Coral/Eurobet

ABBREVIATIONS and DEFINITIONS

ALBATROSS	3 under par eg. a two at a par 5...sometimes called a miracle!
ANZ	Australian New Zealand tour
BIRDIE	1 under par eg. a 4 on a par 5
BOGEY	1 over par
CUT	The reduction of a tournament field, usually at halfway. All the players who 'make the cut' receive a cheque and so are 'in the money'
DYM	A DYM player is one who is quoted by one bookmaker at odds that are at least double those quoted by another bookie e.g. a player is 66/1 with bookie A yet only 33/1 with bookie B. So by backing with bookie A you can Double Your Money
DRAW	Moving the ball right to left
EAGLE	2 under par eg. a 3 on a par 5
FADE	Moving the ball left to right
DC	Defending champion
DNP	Did not play
DOUBLE BOGEY	2 over par
GIR	Greens in regulation (ie 2 shots on a par 4: 3 shots on a par 5)
HTWAGB	How To Win At Golf Betting - my other golf book
IBC	Inspiration by comparison
JOLLY	The favourite.....as in the 'jolly old favourite'
MC	Missed the cut
M/L	The US Money list
MLD	Mental let down
NIC	Never in contention
O/M	The European Order of Merit
PAR	The regulation or expected number of shots to be taken on a hole or on a course
PMA	Positive Mental Association
PWW	Previous week's winner
PWW2	Winner in each of the two previous weeks
Q SCHOOL	Qualifying school for either the US or European tours. Held in November each year
R1	Round one of a tournament. The second round would be R2
ROOKIE	A player in his first year on the US or European tour

T3	Tied 3rd. The T shows that one or more players are tied on that position
TBA	To be arranged
TPC	Tournament player's course
TRIPLE BOGEY	3 over par
TYM	A TYM player is one who is quoted by a bookmaker at odds that are at least triple those quoted by another eg. a player is 125/1 with bookie A when 40/1 is the quote from bookie B. By backing with bookie A you can Triple Your Money (TYM)
Y2K	The year 2000
!	The exclamation mark next to a statistic is to illustrate that it is particularly surprising
50/1	The odds quoted throughout the book, unless otherwise stated, were the biggest available in the market at the time.

CONTENTS

GOLF BETTING 2000   PART 1

A very warm welcome to this year's Elliott's Golf Form. This time you will notice a number of changes which have been made in response to your faxes and e-mails.

The four key improvements are :-

*   At the end of each tournament you will find the names of the players whose player profiles refer to that particular tournament. In the past readers had to checkout all the players profiles every week, now that will no longer be necessary.

    The players referred to are those who, at this early stage, must enter into betting calculations for the particular 2001 tournament. They may be expected to do well or badly, to be noted in 3 balls or match bets, or on the spreads, or in the outright markets.

    It is a change that will ensure you quickly get the maximum benefit from the book on a weekly basis.

*   This year all the main players who missed the cut are listed whereas in the past only about eight were named in the punters' points section. This change makes this volume the biggest and most comprehensive yet.

*   Each tournament now has a special couple of initial sections — one for the tournament itself, another specifically for the course so that the nature and peculiarities of each track are made clear.

*   After each individual players' profile this year you will find a key stat. I believe this will prove to be a really major addition to your enjoyment of the book.

There are other changes too.

*   The punters guides are even more detailed than in the past.

*   A new symbol has been added to the players' profiles. 'V' is given to golfing virgins who are established tour players who have yet to have their first experience....of a tour victory.

*   All players whose odds are at least double with one bookmaker what they are with another are known as DYMs (Double Your Money) players. The DYMs are shown with one asterisk, TYMs (Triple Your Money) with two asterisks, and that rarity (please see the John Deere Classic) the QYM (Quadruple Your Money) with three asterisks.

*   Each tournament has now got the result with the top 5 positions for each of the last two years, not just the previous year.

Otherwise the book is essentially the same mix of statistical record, detailed analysis and betting predictions (plus those dreadful puns) as before.

A WARM WELCOME TO ELLIOTT'S GOLF FORM 2001.

CORAL EUROBET - THE BOOK'S SPONSORS

As you will appreciate after reading about the Sam Torrance dispute later in this chapter, Corals and I were in disagreement in December 1999. However, it's surely a sign of the high mutual professional respect between us that Coral Eurobet are now the first sponsors of Elliott's Golf Form.

I have referred to Corals' creative speciality golf markets in this book many times over the years so I'm delighted that their ace golf compiler and professional shrewdie John Wright has written the introduction to Coral Eurobet's sponsorship.

So from now on Coral Eurobet will be offering the prizes for our annual competition, and they've increased the total prize fund to a huge £1,500 worth of free bets. It's free, easy to enter, based on the US Masters so do enter - it's on page 26.

A WARM WELCOME TO CORAL EUROBET - THE BOOK'S SPONSORS.

ELLIOTT'S ELEVEN LAWS OF GOLF BETTING

Over recent years in this annual volume, and in 'How to win at Golf Betting' I have created and introduced all sorts of concepts, ideas and pointers that can be used for golf betting success. Indeed MLD, DYMs, IBCs, PMAs and nappy factors have become part of our vocabulary.

So this year I have blended some new thoughts and ideas with the existing toolbox of concepts created over the last six to seven years and put them together as ELLIOTT'S ELEVEN LAWS OF GOLF BETTING.

Now when academics try to make sense of the world and the people in it they come up with laws. First there are the laws of universal truth, those that are always true such as the law of gravity to which there are no exceptions as you'll be aware if you fall out of a window!

There are also the laws that are statements of tendency that point to the probable consequence of a change in one variable on another. The laws of supply and demand, and indeed all the laws in economics are like this. They state what will usually happen although recognising that there will be exceptions.

In golf betting we can establish various trends and links between variables that enable us to create the laws of golf betting which, like the laws in economics, are statements of tendency rather than of universal truth as there will be exceptions.

The Law of The Nappy Factor

In the Golf Form book published in 1995 I first put forward the idea of the 'nappy factor'. I wrote then that, "Becoming a father, especially for the first time and especially of a son, can really have a profound effect on any sportsman," and I referred to the sudden form improvement in different sports then of Paul Ince, Steve Davis and Boris Becker.

The point was taken up by the late Peter Dobereiner writing in Golf World (March 1996) who concluded that, "the accumulating body of evidence does seem to establish a connection between fatherhood and achievement."

There are countless examples from the 'golden oldies' to the present day:-

> Arnold Palmer, first child (daughter) born 1956: 1957 four wins and career takes off.

> Nick Price, first child (son) born 1991. Won eight tournaments in following twenty-six months!

> Greg Norman, son born 1985. Tops Money list 1986.

> Jack Nicklaus, first child (son) born 1961. Won 1962 US Open.

> Larry Mize, first child (son) born 1986. Won 1987 US Masters.

In the last year or so we have had a whole series of 'nappy factor' success stories. They include:-

> Darren Clarke, first child (son) born 1998. "My perspective on life now is completely changed." He has gone on to beat Tiger for the World Match Play in 2000.

> Jeff Sluman, first child (daughter) born 1998 then wins two of his next twenty tournaments.

> Tom Scherrer, first child (son) born 1999. He's handed Thomas William to hold after his first US tour triumph in the 2000 Kemper Open.

> Phil Mickelson, first child (daughter) born 1999. After his first-ever winless year 'Lefty' wins four times in 2000.

> Patrik Sjoland, seven weeks after his first child (son Hugo) is born, he makes his first 72-hole tournament victory in the 2000 Irish Open.

> Robert Allenby, first child (son Harry) born in late 1999. In 2000 he achieves his first (and second) USPGA tour wins.

> Ernie Els, first child (daughter) born 1999. In 2000 he wins in USA and posts three 2nd places in the majors. Just wait for big Ernie when (and if) a son arrives!

> Michael Campbell, first child (son) born 1999. Then he won the Johnnie Walker Classic ("my son Thomas has inspired me to this victory") in late 1999, three early season tournaments this year, and the 2000 German Masters to give him five wins in twelve months.

> Michael Clark, first child (son) born in 1999. He gains his 'shock' 200/1 first win in the 2000 John Deere Classic.

> Thomas Bjorn, first child (daughter) born in 1999. Makes every cut in the 2000 majors, finishing T2nd in the British Open and 3rd in the USPGA, wins in Europe and 'moves to a higher level'.

However the biggest boost for the Law of the Nappy Factor came in June 2000 in Milan at the World Conference of the European Association of Labour Economists. The main research findings presented there were referred to in a front page feature in the Independent on 19th June by Cherry Norton, the paper's Social Affairs Editor. They were:-

> Men's salaries rise by nearly 5% every time they have a child, with the 'fatherhood premium' being far greater for a son than for a daughter.

> Economists found that men whose first child is a son earn 8% more than men who father a daughter.

> Each second and subsequent son raises the father's earnings by 3% more than each second and subsequent daughter.

The research was based on data from 1968 - 1993 covering over 1,200 men.

So the nappy factor which I found works well in golf is, in fact, at work across the board in public, business and commercial life. I am now totally convinced that my original belief is correct!

It works in golf because a first offspring gives an extra incentive for a player to make his new child, especially his son, really proud of him. Of course, there will be exceptions and, of course, initially there may well be a 'disruption' factor that temporarily counteracts the 'nappy factor' itself. Nevertheless it is now crystal clear that the nappy factor really works as a predictor of golfing improvement and success. Indeed the sight of a tournament winner cuddling his first child, often a son, is now common on Sunday TV.

THE LAW OF THE NAPPY FACTOR STATES THAT A PLAYER WHO HAS BECOME A FIRST-TIME FATHER, ESPECIALLY OF A SON, WILL SHOW CONSIDERABLY IMPROVED, AND POSSIBLY WINNING FORM IN THE REST OF THAT SEASON, AND ESPECIALLY IN HIS FIRST FULL SEASON AS A FATHER.

The Law of the Ryder Cup

2001 sees the renewal of the Ryder Cup and doubtless we'll see plenty 'Battle of The Belfry' headlines. However, the battle against the bookies can be won as the final day does provide golf punters with a real opportunity as this Law clicks in.

There is a danger that the captain of either side will 'burn out' his star players over the first couple of days in an attempt to build up a solid lead. However come the singles on Sunday such players are 'running on empty'.

On Sunday oppose players in the singles who have played in all four 'rounds' on the first two days unless they are playing a player who has not appeared at all. Kept hidden, such a 'rusty' player (like Coltart in 1999) will lack confidence and may not beat even a tired opponent.

However if two players who have both played all four rounds on the first two days should meet in the singles there should be no bet.

Let's remember the players you will be opposing will be 'name' players and probably favourites, so the potential rewards are high.

This system in 1997 produced four wins (15/8, 7/4, 11/8 and 5/4) in five bets, and 1999 also four wins (5/4, 11/10, 6/5, 11/8) in five bets. Obviously there is also scope for perm bets.

So with an 80% strike rate recently and a LSP of 9.17 pts and a 91.75% return on capital, this Law could lead a bookie-battering Belfry in 2001.

Applying this Law to the newly created Coral Eurobet-sponsored Seve Ballesteros Trophy played between Great Britain & Ireland and Continental Europe at Wentworth this year we find that there were six qualifying singles resulting in three wins and three losses, leading to a 3½ point profit for a 6 point stake and a 58.3% return on capital.

The immense intensity of the Ryder Cup was missing so this law probably does not apply Nevertheless it did apply to a 'totally jaded' Monty who had been both captain and player in all Thursday's and Friday's games and was beaten in the singles by Seve at 9/2.

There was only one qualifying single in this year's Presidents Cup when 'burnt out' Ernie Els lost 4 & 3 to Davis Love.

Nevertheless I think the difference in intensity between the three events suggests that this law should be applied with confidence only to the Ryder Cup.

> THE LAW OF THE RYDER CUP STATES THAT IN THE SUNDAY SINGLES PLAYERS WHO HAVE PLAYED IN ALL FOUR PREVIOUS ROUNDS TEND TO UNDERPERFORM AND SO CAN BE OPPOSED UNLESS THEY MEET A PLAYER YET TO START OR ONE WHO HAS ALSO PLAYED IN ALL THE EARLY MATCHES.

The Law of Post-major Mental Let Down (MLD)

Whenever a player is in serious contention in one of the season's four major championships he will find that he suffers from both physical and mental tiredness the week after.

In his profile in 1998 I had suggested that, "Olly at Augusta should be your slogan for the 1999 US Masters", and Jose Maria obliged at 66/1. However two weeks later as a heavily backed 9/1 favourite for his national title, the Spanish Open, Olazabal missed the cut and admitted that since his Augusta victory he'd not practised and lost his focus in all the media hype.

This year David Toms, the promising 33-year-old American player, got into serious contention in his first British Open. He played alongside Tiger in the last pair in R3 before the pressure told in R4 on the back nine when he took 39 to finish T4th. He flew straight back to the States to play in the John Deere Classic, he 'lost' his clubs for two days, missed the pro-am and without a practice round went straight into the tournament as the worn out, underpracticed and wrongly priced 14/1 favourite!! He was the most opposable golf favourite of the year and probably of the decade. He missed the cut!

Thomas Bjorn, a superb T2nd at St Andrews in 2000, made a late withdrawal from the Dutch Open the following week when he realised just how much the British Open had taken out of him.

Yes, as with all these laws there will be exceptions and Vijay Singh provided a classic example in 1998 after he landed his first major, the USPGA. No MLD for the workaholic Fijian who went straight on in the Sprint International, his very next tournament to win again at 33/1 leading from start to finish!!

Nevertheless Vijay was an exception as I believe this law over a season can lead to a handful of carefully selected successful bets.

> THE LAW OF POST MAJOR MLD STATES THAT A PLAYER IN SERIOUS CONTENTION IN A MAJOR WILL PROBABLY SUFFER A SEVERE REACTION IF PLAYING AGAIN THE FOLLOWING WEEK.

The Law of The Tiger

Tiger Woods as we all know is a truly amazing golfer. He has revolutionised the game, started to rewrite the history books, and has led to every major (and many 'ordinary' tournaments) having 'without Tiger' markets. He has now surely established a record for breaking records!

However a look at his four major wins and his very next tournament are very interesting as they do show a pattern.

Major Success	Time Gap	Next Tournament	Position	Odds
Won 1997 US Masters	5 weeks	Byron Nelson Classic	Won	6/1 fav
Won 1999 US PGA	1 week	Sprint International	T37th	5/1 fav
Won 2000 US Open	3 weeks	Western Open	T23rd	15/8 fav
Won 2000 British Open	3 weeks	Buick Open	T11th	7/4 fav
Won 2000 USPGA	1 week	WGC NEC Invitational	Won	11/8 fav

Certainly after his first four majors Tiger really did suffer from severe mental let down after each triumph. Indeed his worst finishing positions in each of the last two years have both come immediately after a major triumph.

1999 The Sprint (T37th)

2000 The Advil Western Open (T23rd)

In 2000 it was surely obvious that having honed his game and his mental approach to such a high degree of intensity for both the US and British Opens that he would find it impossible to reproduce even 80% of his best when next he played, and so it proved.

He was a never dangerous T23rd in the Western Open three weeks after his Pebble Beach triumph, and T11th in the Buick Open three weeks after his British Open career grand slam victory.

By contrast in 1997 Tiger followed up his US Masters victory with another win in his next tournament. However he had taken a five-week break and he probably was not as mentally tired then as he was this summer when he achieved his unique place in golfing history by becoming the youngest ever to record a career grand slam.

By mid August 2000 it was clear that whenever Tiger had returned to play within three weeks following a major triumph he had not posted a top 10 finish.

Tiger then won the 2000 USPGA and then did something he'd never done before and only attempted once, namely to win the week after a major triumph. Following his narrow USPGA win over Bob May he won the World Golf Championship, NEC Invitational at Akron, Ohio.

So we now know that whenever Tiger has played within three weeks of a major triumph he's got a record that reads T37th-T23rd-T11th-Won.

It could well be that his win after this year's USPGA triumph came because he'd taken relatively little out of himself compared to Pebble Beach and St Andrews, and that he was more motivated for a World Golf Championship than for an 'ordinary' tournament.

Overall I believe Tiger's performances show a pattern that can lead us to the Law of the Tiger.

THE LAW OF THE TIGER STATES THAT ELDRICK WOODS CAN BE OPPOSED IN ANY 'ORDINARY' TOURNAMENT HE PLAYS WITHIN THREE WEEKS FOLLOWING A VICTORY IN ANY MAJOR.

The Law of Hilton Head

The Worldcom (formerly MCI) Classic held at the Harbour Town Golf Links at Hilton Head in South Carolina is well established as the first tournament each year after the US Masters.

The draining effect of being in contention in a major, as we have seen in the last two laws, can lead to severe mental let down (MLD) the next week, so players who have been in the heat of battle at Augusta cannot be expected to come on here and play really well.

In 1998 and 1999 this was well illustrated when only one of the eleven players coming to Hilton Head on the back of an Augusta top 10 made a top 20 finish. However, in 2000 the position was not so clear cut.

	2000 US Masters position	**2000 MCI position**
Ernie Els	2nd	T3rd
Tom Lehman	6th	2nd
Davis Love	T7th	T3rd
Nick Price	T11th	T39th
Carlos Franco	T7th	T15th
Vijay Singh	Won	T3rd

So it might appear that this year, with four players from Augusta's top 10 'in the frame', the 'Law of Hilton Head' was broken.

However Love (70-71) and Els (74 in R4) showed clear signs of fatigue in the later stages, and Singh (64 in R4) was never in contention despite his very fast finish.

Lehman, although 6th at Augusta, was never really in contention there so perhaps he was 'fresher' than the rest.

So I still believe the statement of tendency embodied in this law is valid.

THE LAW OF HILTON HEAD STATES PLAYERS WHO WERE IN SERIOUS CONTENTION AT AUGUSTA IN THE US MASTERS CAN BE OPPOSED IN THE WORLDCOM CLASSIC BECAUSE THEY WILL BE SUFFERING FROM SEVERE MLD.

The Law of The US Masters

After Tiger Woods's runaway record breaking 1997 US Masters win there have been modifications to the Augusta course in an attempt to make it 'Tigerproof'.

It now appears very difficult for a player to come from 'off the pace' to win as the halfway leaderboards show.

	Halfway score	**Final Position**
1998		
D Duval	5 under	T2nd
F Couples	5 under	T2nd

1999

J M Olazabal	8 under	Won
S McCarron	7 under	T18th

2000

D Duval	6 under	T3rd
V Singh	5 under	Won
P Mickelson	5 under	7th
E Els	5 under	2nd

As you can see the eventual winner was either 1st or 2nd, or T2nd, in two of the three years. Mark O'Meara was the exception in 1998 when he came from 'off the pace' and stole the tournament with his hot putter.

THE LAW OF THE US MASTERS STATES THAT THE WINNER AT AUGUSTA WILL USUALLY BE PLACED 1ST OR 2ND (OR TIED 2ND) AFTER THE SECOND ROUND.

The Players Law

The Players Championship, held each year in Florida at the TPC at Sawgrass, is viewed by the players as 'the fifth major' such is its prestige. Bruce Critchley, on Sky TV once memorably described the Sawgrass TPC as a, "cruel course on which some exciting things happen."

It is very difficult on this tough track to come from behind as it's not a 'catch up' course. Indeed it is an amazing fact that nine times in the last ten years the winner has been in the front 3, or tied 3rd after the first round.

This year Hal Sutton the 3 under par leader after the first round, was the latest example of an eventual winner who was high on the leaderboard after day one.

THE PLAYERS LAW STATES THAT THE PLAYERS CHAMPIONSHIP TENDS TO BE WON BY A PLAYER WHO WAS IN THE FIRST 3, OR T3RD, AFTER THE FIRST ROUND.

The Law of The Early Bird

No serious punter will bet on a team to win a cricket match, especially a limited-over one-day game, without knowing the outcome of the toss. It is an absolutely vital piece of information especially in dodgy weather conditions.

Similarly in golf, as I have stressed before, tee times are really significant. An early tee time gives a player a chance to get 'off to a flier' when the course, and especially the greens, are in their best condition, and so establish some momentum.

An early opening-round tee time has four key advantages.

> You play the course when it's at its best before the field trample all over the greens and make divots on the fairways.

> There's no hanging about waiting to play.

> If weather conditions are variable then usually (but not always) the poorer weather will come in the afternoon. This is especially true on the coast on links-type courses.

> A fast start can give the player real momentum, and the 'feeling' he's in with a real chance.

This Law has been well illustrated over the last two years in the Hawaiian Open where in 1999 John Huston and in 2000 Paul Azinger both had early tee times, both opened with 63 in R1 to give them the momentum to notch a runaway victory (by 7 shots in each case).

With two tee starts i.e. with some players off the 1st tee at the same time as others are off the 10th tee this advantage is slightly reduced as you play only half the course in mint condition before you meet the holes that the other early starters on the other half of the course have already played.

The interesting and grossly unfair thing about tee times is that the first out in R1 in the morning is also first out in R2 on the second afternoon so over the first two days (i.e. half the tournament) some players are given a built-in advantage and others a disadvantage and sometimes a massive disadvantage.

Like a sprinter at Chester races with an outside draw, a player with a poor pair of tee times has a built in initial disadvantage.

> HOW CAN WE USE THIS FOR PROFIT?

Firstly, in spread betting sell the finishing position of any in-form player with a good track record who has an early R1 tee time (say in the first six groups out). You can then buy him back after R1 so closing the position and taking a nice profit after he's done well in R1. You'll be surprised how often this simple easy to follow guide works, and even if the guy plays just OK you'll probably find you can close the position without a loss.

Secondly, whenever examining a match bet always compare the tee times. So often compilers create match bets before the tee times are known. A player with a good pair of tee times has been given a shot or two 'start' over his match opponent with a poor set of start times.

Thirdly, if you fancy a player in the outright market it will probably pay to delay your bet until after R1 if he has a poor R1 starting time.

Fourthly, note players who have done well from a late R1 tee time because they then have an advantage going early in R2 and they may be favourably priced in the outright market after the first round because the busy compiler hasn't noticed this fact.

Yes there will be exceptions, and the weather can play tricks as it did in R1 at the AT&T this year, yet there can now be little doubt that overall this law operates.

> THE LAW OF THE EARLY BIRD STATES THAT A PLAYER WITH AN EARLY TEE TIME ON THE FIRST DAY TENDS TO HAVE AN ADVANTAGE OVER HIS RIVALS WHO START MUCH LATER ON.

Please note that on tough tracks on which 'catch-up' golf is very difficult, as discussed in the Law of the US Masters and the Players Law above, this Law is of particular significance.

The Law of The Streaker

So often we find that a player who produces a blistering burst of birdies as he 'streaks' to a very low round is quite simply unable to reproduce that magic in his very next round. Anti-climax sets in and the dazzling performance is so often followed by an ordinary, or poor, or in some cases very poor round.

As Lee Janzen has said, "It's amazing how often guys on tour shoot 7 or 8 under one day, next day they shoot above par....it happens to everyone."

This year there have been countless examples, among them:-

American Tour

Nissan Open	>	Rocco Mediate tournament low rd 63 in R3 - then 74 in R4
Tucson Open	>	Stephen Ames tournament low rd 64 in R3 - then 76 in R4
Bob Hope Classic	>	Frank Lickliter 62 (R4) - then 74
	>	Brent Geiberger 61 (R2) - then 71
	>	Barry Cheesman 62 (R2) - then 72
Bay Hill	>	Davis Love 63 (R3) then 72
	>	Mike Weir 64 (R2) then 72
	>	Steve Flesch 65 (R2) then 74
	>	Wayne Grady 65 (R2) then 73
	>	John Huston 64 (R2) then 75

(So at Bay Hill only five players shot rounds of 65 or less, and in their following round they shot (on average) 9.4 strokes more!)

Players	>	Scott McCarron 67 (R2) then 77
	>	Fulton Allen 65 (R2) then 82
	>	Jeff Sluman 66 (R3) then 76
	>	Robert Damron 66 (R3) then 70 (very good)
John Deere	>	David Frost 62 (R2) then 70
	>	Kirk Triplett 62 (R3) then 70

European Tour - Rio de Janiero Open

Only four players had rounds of 8 or more under par, and on average their next round was 10.25 shots worse!

> Alistair Forsyth 62 (R2) then 75
> Padraig Harrington 62 (R2) then 71
> Peter Lonard 62 (R1) then 74
> Roger Chapman 64 (R2) then 71

This law can be turned to profit in three key ways.

Firstly, oppose such 'streakers' who will often be short-priced favourites in their next round 2 or 3 balls.

Secondly, if the 'streaking' was in R3 the player can be opposed in final-round outright betting.

Thirdly, you can 'oppose' the streaker in running in any relevant spread betting market.

So we can really profit from streakers who can't keep it up.

THE LAW OF THE STREAKER STATES THAT A PLAYER WHO HAS SHOT A VERY LOW ROUND WILL NORMALLY SUFFER A REACTION IN HIS VERY NEXT ROUND.

The Law of Home Advantage

Playing at home gives a real advantage to teams in football, rugby league and, of course, American football. However, being an individual sport, home advantage is sometimes forgotten in golf.

Yet there are clear advantages.

* knowledge, and a feeling of comfort that comes from playing on your local course
* an awareness of the peculiarities of the grass used on the course construction, especially on the greens
* feeling comfortable in the local weather conditions, especially the winds or/and heat.

If the player still lives locally then he has other advantages too.

* The absence of long travel, possibly including time zone changes
* The avoidance of hotels
* The comforts of home
* The extra concentration created when playing at home.

Not surprisingly, there is now mounting evidence that such 'home' advantage is really important as the following examples of 'home' winners over the last two years show.

2000	1999
Tom Lehman, Williams Challenge	Chris Davison, Vodacom Players (S.Africa)
Brad Lamb, Victorian Open	Jarrod Moseley, Heineken Classic
Tom Lehman, Phoenix Open	David Frost, South African Open
Lucas Parson, Greg Norman Holden	Tiger Woods, Buick Invitational
Phil Mickelson, Buick Invitational	Craig Spence, Australian Masters
Paul Gow, Canon Challenge	M A Jimenez, Turespana Masters
Jim Carter, Tucson Open	David Duval, Players Championship
Andre Stolz, ANZ Tour Championship	Paul Lawrie, The British Open
John Huston, Tampa Bay Classic	Mike Weir, Air Canada

This year in Australia after winning the Canon Challenge in Australia in late February at 25/1 Paul Gow said, "I'm in my own backyard and to win here is just a great feeling." For good measure another Sydney 'local' Kenny Druce was 2nd at 66/1.

Although born in Switzerland, Andre Stolz, 100/1 winner of the season-concluding ANZ Tour Championship, grew up in Canberra and had local knowledge of the course.

In America the first two desert tournaments went to local desert residents Tom Lehman (33/1 Phoenix Open) and Jim Carter (80/1 Tucson Open)

However 'home' advantage can persist even if a player has subsequently moved to live elsewhere. Phil Mickelson, an Arizona resident now, was born on the West Coast in San Diego where as a schoolboy he played the front nine of the Torrey Pines course three times a week. Not surprisingly he used his local knowledge to win the Buick Invitational for the second time in 2000.

Final conclusive proof came in late October with John Huston's 66/1* victory in the Tampa Bay Classic on the Copperhead course which he'd played well over a hundred times. "There's no question that having the home crowd made a big difference. I just had good Karma all week. Anytime you have familiarity it kind of gives you that sense of security." It was Huston's sixth win, and five have been in his native Florida.

Monty's very poor start in the 1997 Troon British Open and Rocca's nervousness in Italian Opens show that sometimes the 'pressures' of family and friends far outweigh any home advantage.

Nevertheless overall the law of home advantage as a statement of tendency really does work.

THE LAW OF HOME ADVANTAGE STATES ANY PLAYER PLAYING 'AT HOME' ON A COURSE WITH WHICH HE IS REALLY FAMILIAR HAS A CONSIDERABLE ADVANTAGE AND TENDS TO PLAY TO A BETTER STANDARD THAN HE DOES ELSEWHERE.

The Law of The Comeback Trail

Trying to find players with a special inner drive for success led me some years ago to highlight players who were on the 'comeback trail'. Golfers lose form because of illness, injury, a change of clubs or simply a descent into a 'comfort zone' of mediocrity.

However once such a player, with a previous solid winning record, recovers from injury, overcomes his illness or re-adjusts his mental approach he will show vastly improved and possibly winning form. Refocused, refreshed and rededicated he has a real incentive, an increased desire and an extra determination to succeed.

The 'comeback kids' in recent years have included:-

	Wins before winless run	Winless years	Wins on comeback trail
John Cook	6	1993,1994,1995	1996 (2 wins), 1997,1998
Hal Sutton	8	1996, 1997	1998 (2 wins)
Mark O'Meara	7	1993, 1994	Won 9 times since!
Lee Janzen	7	1996, 1997	1998 US Open
Nick Price	14	1995, 1996	1997, 1998
John Huston	3	1995,1996,1997	1998 (2 wins)
Steve Jones	4	1990,1995	1996 US Open, 1997 (twice)
Payne Stewart	9	1993,1994,1995	1999 (2 wins incl. US Open)

Paul Azinger	11	1996-1999 incl.	2000
Tom Lehman	4	1997,1998,1999	2000
Rocco Mediate	2	1994-1998 incl.	1999, 2000 (both at 100/1)

Last year I nominated four American players for success on the 'comeback trail' in 2000. Tom Lehman did me a nice early favour at 33/1 (!) when he won the Phoenix Open and with that one victory he brought together the Law of Home Advantage and the Law of the Comeback Trail.

Phil Mickelson had both his first winless year and his first child in 1999, so he combined with The Law of the Nappy Factor, and in 2000 he's posted no less than four wins at 20/1, 22/1, and 14/1 (twice)!

However, as usual this law is a statement of tendency to which there are, of course, exceptions. For 2000 I also suggested that Mark Brooks and John Cook would be potential comeback trail winners and neither has won.

Unlike the other laws, this is very much a subjective law. However, I was so convinced by the comeback factor that two years ago the CT symbol was introduced in the profiles in Part 8 alongside the name of players on the comeback trail.

For 2001 one player who will be very much on the comeback trail will be the sweet-swinging Steve Elkington who has had an illness-ravaged, winless eighteen months. Having lost power, drive and confidence he had hip surgery in August after which he said, "It's like being 15 again!" I know it's risky nominating a player with his record of illness, however I expect 'the Elk' to win on the comeback trail in 2001. His player profile develops the point and names the key tournaments.

Another will be David Duval who is now fully recovered from the back injury that affected him through the summer before it finally put him flat on his back in early August. In 2001 I expect Duval will have a mega season winning more than once and with a very good chance of landing his first major. As with 'the Elk', his player profile names the key tournaments for him next year.

> THIS LAW STATES THAT A PROVEN WINNING PLAYER WHO HAS A LONG WINLESS RUN BECAUSE OF INJURY, ILLNESS OR A CHANGE OF CLUBS WILL TEND TO SHOW VASTLY IMPROVED FORM ONCE HE GETS ON THE COMEBACK TRAIL.

THE AGONY AND ECSTASY OF GOLF TIPPING

The Four-Day Wait

If you've been to the races with casino clients you'll know that they find a 30-minute wait for the next 70-second, five-furlong dash all too slow. They like the regularity of the spin of the wheel and get bored quickly so what they must think of golf betting which can take four days for a result, and very occasionally a fifth I shudder to think.

It's that roller-coaster of emotions over those 96 hours, especially (hopefully) those 3 hours on Sunday evening, that makes outright golf betting unique and leads to both agony and ecstasy.

Agony! The losing 40/1 bet

Last year in his player profile I'd written that Padraig Harrington, "would be worth a bet to be a 'shock' 40/1 winner in May at the Belfry in the Benson and Hedges...." Early in that week I was surprised and delighted that 40/1 was on offer, so I gave him on my golfline as my No. 1 selection. By the 'off' he was 33/1 best and by Saturday evening with a round to go he led by 5 shots and was as low as 7/2 on.

He was disqualified before the final round on Sunday after it was spotted that he'd failed to sign Thursday's card. I, like countless clients, was speechless. The 40/1 bet, that had become 7/2 on, was a loser!!

In the event however I still believe golf is right to insist that 'rules are rules' and must be adhered to. However, Sunday 14th May will live long in my memory.

Ecstasy! The winning straight forecast double

Sunday February 20th 2000 was another memorable day as the Canon Challenge on the ANZ tour and the Portuguese Open ended.

'Down Under' 25/1 Paul Gow held off 66/1 Kenny Druce. Then later sheer ecstasy as in Portugal my No. 1 and No. 2 choice finished 1st and 2nd as 22/1 Gary Orr beat 28/1 Phillip Price to give a 1-2 in both tournaments. One client won over £13,000 on the each-way double.

The Australian result on a new Sydney course was especially pleasing as the Laws of Home Advantage and the Nappy Factor, as well as course form, applied to Kenny Druce, and Paul Gow had course and current form as well as having home advantage.

UNIQUELY AMONG BETS OUTRIGHT GOLF BETTING PROVIDES AGONY AND ECSTASY SPREAD OVER FOUR DAYS, ENDING ON A SUNDAY NIGHT.

THE DYM SYSTEM'S RECORD YEAR

If you're a regular reader you will be familiar with DYM, TYM even QYM players. If not then here goes:-

DYM A player whose price with at least one firm is at least double that on offer with another firm. Hence the DYM because you can Double Your Money with the bookmaker offering the top odds.

TYM Same principle but here a player has a price with at least one firm that is at least treble that on offer elsewhere so you can Triple Your Money with the best price firm.

QYM Same principle again although very rare when one or more firms offer four (quadruple) times the price on offer elsewhere. Please see 200/1 QYM 3rd placed Charles Howell in the John Deere Classic.

You can check off the DYM and TYM players from the Racing Post's pricewise tables each week so creating a short-list of players to consider for any tournament.

All such players are marked with an asterisk * (DYM), two asterisks ** (TYM) or three asterisks *** (QYM) in this book.

The logic of the system

1. When bookmakers all agree on a price the strong probability is that they have not all made a mistake, and so although you may select the winner you will not be on at a 'value' price.

2. However when there are variations in prices you can use your judgement to decide which bookmakers if any have made a 'rick'.

   For example, in this year's Madeira Island Open you could make a solid case for Ross Drummond.

> In the previous two years on this quirky course he'd finished T10th (1999) and T14th (1998).

> He was an experienced player in a tournament in which six of the seven winners had been 30-plus.

> He'd played well in a mini-tour event on his last start in Scotland.

   40/1 with a couple of firms he was a massive 100/1 with another two. So he clearly was an overpriced DYM, and I am not being wise after the event as he was an each-way selection of mine at that 100/1!

Alternatively, sometimes you will feel that the bookmaker with the low price about the DYM player is simply being ultra-cautious and the bookies with the bigger prices are correct and there's no 'value' to be had.

2000 record of the DYM system

This year, particularly on the European tour, the DYM system has achieved spectacular and unprecedented success.

> ten outright winners, the highest ever recorded

> the first two (the 'exacta') were both DYMs in an amazing seven tournaments.

The full record is:-

Tournament	DYM winner	DYM 2nd or T2nd
Johnnie Walker Classic	Michael Campbell 66/1	Geoff Ogilvy 100/1
Alfred Dunhill Champ.	Anthony Wall (TYM) 100/1	−
Heineken Classic	Michael Campbell 33/1	Thomas Bjorn 40/1
Holden International	Lucas Parsons 100/1	Peter Senior 66/1
Madeira Island Open	Niclas Fasth 66/1	Ross Drummond 100/1
Moroccan Open	Jamie Spence 33/1	Ian Poulter (TYM) 100/1
Spanish Open	Brian Davis 100/1	Marcus Brier 150/1
Wales Open	Steen Tinning 100/1	David Howell 50/1
Irish Open	Patrik Sjoland 100/1	−
Dutch Open	Stephen Leaney 66/1	−

There has also been success in 2000 on the USPGA tour

Tournament	DYM winner	DYM 2nd (or T2nd)
Nissan Open	100/1 Kirk Triplett	—
Shell Houston Open	100/1 Robert Allenby	100/1 Craig Stadler
BC Open	25/1 Brad Faxon	—
John Deere Classic	200/1 Michael Clark	3rd was 200/1 QYM: 4th 150/1 TYM
Pennsylvania Classic	100/1 Chris DiMarco	—
Tampa Bay Classic	66/1 John Huston	100/1 Carl Paulson
Southern Farm Bureau Classic	25/1 Steve Lowery	—

> THE DYM CLEAN SWEEP

The most staggering DYM triumph however came in late October in the Tampa Bay Classic when amazingly all the first five players were DYMs.

1	66/1	John Huston
2	100/1	Carl Paulson
T3	50/1	Frank Lickliter
T3	100/1	Len Mattiace
5	80/1	Joe Durant

> THE FULL DYM WINNER RECORD NOW READS

	European tour	US tour	Total
Six years 1994-1999 incl.	20	34	54
2000	10	7	17
TOTAL	30	41	71

> WHEN A NEW COURSE IS USED

There appears to be no 'form' so many feel that such tournaments should be treated cautiously. However it is clear that without a quick and easy to use course form book compilers do often offer real value.

This year, for example, there have been three new USPGA courses used for the John Deere Classic, the Pennsylvania Classic and the Tampa Bay Classic and guess what?....all three winners were DYMs and so were six of the players in the top 5.

The frequency of DYMs

DYMs tend to be most noticeable

> when compilers focus on a big televised tournament so neglecting another event in the same week. In August 2000 the West of Ireland Classic (same week as USPGA) and the Scottish PGA (same week as World NEC Invitational) are a couple of examples.

> Whenever there is a Bank Holiday Monday you can be sure DYMs follow. In 2000 in the first week of May on the Bank Holiday Monday compilers were at

home watching the London rioters trashing McDonalds and Churchill's statue. That week's French Open had twenty-three DYMs among the forty-four players priced 33/1 - 100/1 inclusive!!

Using the system

You will need

> The Pricewise golf table of the Racing Post

> A range of accounts so you can 'get on'

> An up-to-date knowledge of the changing nature of the two tours so you can 'prune' the long short-list that the DYM system will provide.

Pruning the short-list

The key skill in using the DYM system is in pruning the short-list. Here you can use some of the thirty-seven tips given in 'How To Win At Golf Betting' to each of the DYMs.

DYMs in other golf markets

Of course DYMs can apply to other markets. For example after the third round of the Dutch Open Stephen Leaney had a 4-shot lead. 2/1 on at Ladbrokes he was 11/10 against with Surrey. A classic DYM situation ....but which bookie was right?

Well Leaney had lost a lead when leading into the final round on only one out of eight occasions. Ladbrokes looked right and 11/10 looked big. He won again unchallenged by 4 shots.

REGULARLY USE THE DYM SYSTEM IN THE SEARCH FOR 'VALUE' BETS

MENTAL SKILLS IN GOLF

One of the initial attractions of golf betting to me was that essentially the game was played 'between the ears'. It was a game in which mental skills are vitally important.

However many think that mental skills are really obvious, just common sense. Jeff Hawkes on SKY television was dismissive of the use of sports psychologists when he asked, "How do they know what you're thinking?" Well Jeff, you tell them!!

One particular aspect is the principle that 'you move towards what you think about'. After all what do you think accident-prone people think about?

This was a mental skills principle not understood in 1999 by Tiger Woods yet well understood in 2000 by Hal Sutton.

In the 1999 US Open at the 3rd hole in the final round Tiger was very concerned with his distance control. "Don't let me hit it over the green," he told his caddie.....with his mind firmly fixed on "over the green".....guess what? He did just that overhitting the green....Tiger moved to what he had thought about.

By contrast, this year many players in practice for the Players Championship at Sawgrass were afraid they'd put their tee shots into the water by the island green at the 17th hole so they practised shots from the drop area.

Hal Sutton refused to do this. "That is preparation for a bad result. If you put four good swings on that tee you won't be hitting it from the drop area." Sutton moved towards what he thought about, i.e. four solid tee shots and that's precisely what he did......and he won the tournament holding off Tiger Woods for a memorable victory.

MENTAL SKILLS ARE NOT COMMON SENSE THEY HAVE TO BE LEARNED.

YOU MOVE TOWARDS WHAT YOU THINK ABOUT.

LET'S HAVE PRIZE MONEY IN £s NOT EUROS

If there's one practice that I'm sure must irritate you as much as it does me it is to find

* On the European tour website all the European tour players winnings are given in Euros

* That, "all players eligible for the European Ryder Cup team will receive one point for each Euro won in Ryder Cup ranking events."

* The Order of Merit table is given in Euros won.

So what politically correct nonsense lies behind this Euro only policy?

* Do the players get paid in Euros?

* Has the European tour media office been bombarded by requests to scrap the £ so we can use the Euro as the sole unit of account?

The answers are, of course, 'No'.

The current Euro-only policy results in confusion and misunderstanding as you can't make sense of what the tables mean, and it's no use working out the value of the Euro in terms of the £ as the new currency keeps depreciating!

So, come on European PGA, let's have the return of the £ (with if necessary the Euro equivalent alongside it). It will have one great value.....we will understand it.......and isn't it part of your role to keep us informed rather than in the dark?

LET'S HAVE EUROPEAN PRIZE MONEY GIVEN CLEARLY IN £.

IS GOLF STILL AN OASIS IN THE DESERT OF COMMERCIAL SLEAZE?

I have written many times in these pages of my conviction that golf by its rigorous maintenance of standards of behaviour and the strictest enforcement of rules is alone among all professional sports as a game to be truly proud of. It develops character, integrity and honesty.

Pro golfers do not go in for sledging, verbal abuse or gamesmanship. Indeed so often they genuinely offer tips to a rival on how his swing or putting stroke can be improved. Professional golf really is different.

However last year I wrote about the disgraceful scenes when Tom Lehman led the US Ryder Cup players as they danced all over the 17th green, and that concern was heightened this year when Sergio Garcia, in full view of the worldwide millions, was so annoyed with himself that he took an extra completely unnecessary couple of divots out of the fairway at the British Open as he hacked away in anger.

Now this was not the first time that the talented Spaniard had thrown his dummy out of the pram. His shoe-kicking and club-throwing antics on the 15th tee in the 1999 Cisco World Matchplay were disgraceful, and I pointed out in last year's volume in his player profile that, "perhaps after Brookline he subconsciously felt that lack of self control is now acceptable."

Yet what happened after his round in the Open? He was interviewed in a deferential manner as if his conduct was a blip to be quickly forgotten. Imagine what would have happened if he'd been a young footballer of the same age?

Golf has now created a 'culture of deference' in which everyone is a nice chap and criticism of behaviour must be non existent or muted. This is in total contrast to the 'culture of criticism' so prevalent in other sports, especially football.

Garcia's behaviour last year merited a ban from future tournaments and certainly in this year's British Open he should have been suspended for at least two months. If you disagree just notice how many young local golfers start to hack at the course in frustration from now on. After all, they'll think that if it's OK for wonderkid Sergio it's OK for them.

And, of course, this year we have seen golf's good name dragged through the mud as 'Into The Bear Pit' took golf 'into the cesspit'. Mark James's revelations that he had received and then 'binned' a good luck team message from Nick Faldo prior to Brookline 1999 created a really unsavoury spectacle with James, totally out of order, betraying secrets known only to him. Yes we've seen it in football memoirs, but golf is supposed to be different. Eventually and inevitably James was forced to resign as assistant to Sam Torrance.

Then in early October we had the disgraceful scenes during the Solheim Cup. Annika Sorenstam had chipped in, then the US players and Captain complained she'd played out of turn. Weak refereeing led to her playing again, missing and bursting into tears. They were scenes Ewen Murray put into context when he said that for the very first time he was ashamed to be a professional golfer.

Lehman, Garcia and the Solheim shame on course, then James off course. Golf really must get a grip and re-impose rigorously and immediately those standards of conduct that for decades made golf an oasis in a desert of commercial sleaze.

I do believe in deterrents and players must know that if standards either on-course or off-course are not maintained they will be severely punished and severely punished quickly.

PENALTIES FOR LOW STANDARDS OF ON-COURSE OR OFF-COURSE CONDUCT MUST BE SEVERE.

GOLF BETTING

Let's have a new golf superbet

I have always believed that punters like the opportunity of exercising their skill in trying to win a big prize for a small stake.

The popularity of scorecasts on televised premiership games in which you forecast both the first goal scorer and the correct score is a case in point.

In golf there is no simple, easy-to-enter, big-win-for-a-small-stake superbet.

The 'Three Off The Tee' bet

I suggest for the American tour a new superbet is introduced.

* Punters would select three golfers in 1,2,3 order.
* There would be three ways to win.
> For selecting the first three in the correct order
> A consolation prize if your No. 1 and No. 2 selections finish 1st and 2nd
> A consolation prize if your No. 1 selection wins.

With a minimum stake of £1, 50p would go on the 1, 2, 3 forecast; 25p on the 1, 2 forecast, and 25p on the No. 1 selection winning. Creating the odds for the first three, and the first two in the correct order would surely be relatively straightforward. Traditionally it's been the deduction of a point and then a straight multiplication.

Of course the stake per bet could be £2 with £1 for the 1, 2, 3; 50p for the 1, 2; and 50p win on your No. 1.

If you selected four players in a special four-player perm bet you would have staked £16 (at £1 unit).

> 24 bets on 1,2,3 forecast at 50p = £12
> 12 bets on 1,2 forecast at 25p = £3
> 4 win bets at 50p   = £1

Working out the 1, 2, 3 odds would probably involve deducting 1 point from the odds of each player and multiplying them together.

So 33/1, 40/1 and 80/1 would be a 32 x 39 x 79 = 98,592/1.

The 33/1, 40/1, 1-2 would pay 32 x 39 = 1,248/1 and of course the 33/1 winner would be included. All in all:-

£1 stake		£2 stake	
98,592 x 50p	49,296.00	98,592 x £1	98,592.00
1,248 x 25p	312.00	1,248 x 50p	624.00
33 x 25p	8.25	33 x 50p	16.50
	————		————
	£49,616.25		£99,232.50

So for a £1 stake almost a 50 grand payout; for £2 almost the magic 100 grand!!

The bet is clear, simple and inexpensive and it would surely lead to Jeremy Chapman giving his weekly 'Three Off The Tee' bet in the Racing Post and I'm sure I would do the same for my Sportsline clients.

So which firm will take up the challenge to develop, package and market this "Three Off The Tee" bet?

LET'S HAVE A NEW, BIG-ODDS SUPERBET ON AMERICAN GOLF.

Place-only betting

Last year I called on bookmakers to offer 'place-only' betting. At that time not a single bookmaker regularly offered place-only betting at 1/4 odds the first 5, although Stan James did offer place-only 1/4 odds the first 4.

Well this year there has been some progress. Nick King, then Sunderland's golf compiler, told me that my plea for place-only betting on these pages had triggered the firm's decision to offer place-only at their competitive 1/4 odds the first 5. Sunderland's Pat Densham had decided, "to give it a go this year."

Multi-Sports and Victor Chandler also followed suit with place-only betting at 1/4 odds the first 5.

Sadly things later changed as first Multi-Sports changed the place odds from 1/4 to 1/5 odds the first 5, and later Victor Chandler withdrew place-only betting altogether, as did Stan James.

So congratulations to Sunderlands (1/4 1-5) and Multi-Sports (1/5 1-5) who are currently the only place-only golf betting firms. So the challenge to golf bookmakers is simple: which firms will give golf punters regular place-only betting at their normal place odds?

THERE'S DEFINITELY A PLACE FOR PLACE-ONLY BETTING.

Big Mac gets no credit

I regard John McCririck and his wife Jenny ('the Booby') as friends. Big Mac is genuinely on the side of punters and this unique guy, believe me, is no fool because behind the extraordinary flamboyance and unique appearance is a very sharp mind.

However this year on Easter Saturday in the Racing Post he said, "I would love to see the day where there is no credit betting and you have to pay out before you bet.....I think credit betting is an anachronism now."

Sorry Mac you're bang out of order here....indeed your words sound like those from a director of the Big Three Bookmaking chains.

I fully realise bookies don't like credit accounts. As one senior guy told me, "We have to win twice as the punter must lose the bet and then must also pay-up, whereas with debit cards we get the cash in at once."

However surely the best thing from a punter's viewpoint is to have the maximum choice. So if you want to bet on credit, and can get a credit account I cannot see a single punter-friendly reason against you having such an account.

So c'mon Big Mac let's give credit where it's due.......to the punters.

LET'S KEEP GIVING PUNTERS THE CREDIT.

Internet betting

The mushrooming growth of internet betting is a matter of real punter protection concern especially when new-never-heard-of-them-before-dot com firms offer us odds. What are we to do?

My advice is clear and simple.

Firstly, make as many inquiries as you can regarding the business, its backers, its location and when it started. The question you must ask is simple....do you believe the firm will pay up on your winning bets?

If you've any doubt then don't bet.

Secondly, make sure the firm is in IBAS. However do remember that IBAS membership is in no way whatsoever a guarantee of a bookmaker's financial strength or its ability to pay on winning bets.

I really do fear that sooner rather than later an internet bookie will simply vanish. Make sure they don't take your money with them.

BE WARY OF NEVER-HEARD-OF-THEM DOT COM BOOKMAKERS.

GOLF BETTING DISPUTES

Bet only with an IBAS bookmaker

Last year I recommended that you bet only with a bookmaker who is registered with IBAS, the Independent Betting Arbitration Service. Should you have a dispute which you cannot resolve with your bookie IBAS offers independent adjudication which the bookie has agreed to accept.

So far in every single sports betting dispute that has been decided in favour of the punter the bookmaker has accepted the findings and paid up.

Last year however I stated unequivocally that it was disgraceful that a publicly available list of all IBAS bookmakers was not available. Indeed the book contained two blank pages to highlight this scandalous omission. Well the good news is that, following that pressure, a list is now available and can be obtained directly from IBAS (see page 40).

CONTACT IBAS TO GET A LIST OF IBAS-REGISTERED BOOKMAKERS AND BET ONLY WITH AN IBAS-REGISTERED BOOKMAKER.

Who arbitrates on golf betting disputes at IBAS?

Well I'm delighted to say that IBAS's latest signing, who will adjudicate on all golf betting disputes, is Jeremy Chapman the ace golf writer and golf tipster of the Racing Post.

I don't think he got a signing-on fee and I suspect he doesn't have an agent, however Chris O'Keefe, the energetic manager of IBAS, sure has made a really shrewd signing because Jeremy possesses all the key requirements - a thorough knowledge of betting and odds, a deep understanding of golf betting and a well merited reputation for integrity. He really is a very welcome addition to IBAS's arbitration panel.

I AM SURE JEREMY CHAPMAN IS BRILLIANT AT SOLVING GOLF BETTING DISPUTES?

Golf betting rules

One aspect of IBAS's work has become the prevention rather than just the resolution of disputes. Already IBAS has initiated an agreement for all major bookmakers to treat first goal scorer bets in football in a uniform manner. Last season for example there was one premiership match in which the first and last goal scorer did not score either the first or the last goal. (That is a brilliant pub quiz question.)

So can I appeal to IBAS to create a clear, comprehensive and thorough set of golf betting rules that all the major golf bookmakers can accept, and that all golf punters can see to be fair?

I have discussed this with Chris O'Keefe and know he's keen to make progress. With Jeremy on board let's hope there will be progress.

LET'S CREATE A UNIFORM SET OF GOLF BETTING RULES.

Spread betting disputes

Golf spread betting is both popular and expanding. In essence there are two key differences compared to conventional betting with conventional bookmakers.

1. All spread betting debts are recoverable at law whereas conventional gambling debts are not.

2. Because spread betting debts are recoverable and spread betting itself is so volatile the spread betting industry is rigorously controlled by the SFA, the Securities and Futures Authority. As a result it is much much more difficult to become a spread bookmaker than to become a conventional bookmaker.

If you have a dispute with a spread betting firm, as one South African reader of this book had this summer, you should :-

Firstly, put your complaint to the Compliance Officer of the spread company. The firm will give you his (her) name.

Secondly, if you are still dissatisfied you should write to the SFA Complaints Bureau, South Quay Plaza, 183 Marsh Wall, London, E14 9SR fully detailing the dispute.

Thirdly, if the Complaints Bureau is unable to resolve the dispute to your satisfaction you have the right to refer the issue to the Bureau's Consumer Arbitration Scheme if your claim is below £50,000. For this you have to pay a £50 fee.

So if you are a spread bettor I suggest you give the complaints Bureau a call and ask for the booklet that details the service that it offers. The telephone numbers are 020 7964 1482 or 020 7964 1000 or fax 020 7964 1001.

IF YOU BET ON THE SPREADS GET THE SFA COMPLAINTS BUREAU BROCHURE NOW.

The Sam Torrance dispute

Last year in this chapter I referred to Corals' odds on the player to be the next Ryder Cup Captain. The initial 5/2 about Sam Torrance from Corals was I suggested very generous, indeed I had made it a banker bet on my sportsline. The price collapsed quickly to 2/5 within 24 hours.

However after Sam Torrance was announced as the 2001 Ryder Cup Captain Corals stated that they would not pay out until September 2001 when the Ryder Cup started. I found that decision most unexpected as I knew the top executives there to be men of integrity.

So I contacted Corals who knew that if they did not relent IBAS would be brought in and that as their position was indefensible they would almost certainly lose the arbitration and face a PR disaster.

I put my thoughts in a letter to the Racing Post which was published as follows:-

---

CORAL PAY-OUT RULE UNFAIR

Keith Elliott believes Coral should pay out on Ryder Cup captain Sam Torrance.

Coral are a superb firm in the way their compilers create markets for golf punters.

Indeed, they uniquely offer punters chances to bet on which players will play in the Ryder Cup teams and who will be European team captain.

However, I believe very strongly that their decision not to pay out on the next European team captain (Sam Torrance) until September 2001 is completely indefensible.

I would like to make a few points.

1) When the odds were made and the firm faxed them, they did NOT stipulate that the bet was to be settled in 2001.

2) When credit clients placed bets on the telephone, they were not told about the 'wait until the Belfry' stipulation. I presume cash clients in Corals' shops also were not so told.

   Indeed, 'the contract' between firm and company was clear - it was the person who was to be the next European Ryder Cup team captain. Clearly the next captain is to be Sam Torrance.

   Those backing him win, those backing other runners lose.

3) Should Sam, for any reason, not captain the side at The Belfry, Coral can open up a new book on the successor to Sam Torrance as Ryder Cup captain.

   There need be no reason to invent the 'pay out twice' red herring.

4) Bookmakers really cannot be allowed to get away with a decision on the timing of payment which they themselves have made arbitrarily after the bets were struck.

5) I do realise that bets with Coral on players to make the Ryder Cup team are only settled when the player has been selected and plays.

   However, the delay between selection and playing is at most two months, not two years and, above all, the 'must be selected and play' stipulation has always been clearly stated at the outset to all punters and on all faxes Coral send out.

   There simply is not a comparison between the two different sets of Ryder Cup bets.

   So, I ask Coral quite simply to pay up NOW as by any dictionary definition Sam Torrance has been appointed as the next European Ryder Cup captain.

Keith Elliott
Independent Member
Horserace Betting Levy Board

It became apparent very quickly that Corals realised that the individual who had made the decision had made an almighty howler. So Simon Clare, their Public Relations Manager, turned the situation round brilliantly when Sam Torrance dressed as Santa Claus suggested that those who had backed him be paid out in time for Christmas. Nice one Simon!

In the event I was delighted, not least because Corals have always taken a lead, under ace golf compiler John Wright, in creating original golf markets and they are always the only firm to offer odds for players to make the two Ryder Cup teams.

I regard this episode as a one off. It could, I believe, have happened with any firm. However it shows that arbitrary unfair decisions will not be tolerated, and so they are much much less likely to be made.

> BOOKMAKERS MUST NEVER BE ALLOWED TO CREATE RULES AFTER BETS ARE LAID.

AND FINALLY, it's been another superb golfing year. In 1999 we had the images of Van de Velde without socks in The Open, Garcia without inhibition in the USPGA and Lehman without control at Brookline.

In 2000 we've simply had Tiger Woods smashing record after record after record. So often we under-appreciate sporting stars until we get older, reflect and compare. Let's not do that with this guy............your as yet unborn grandkids will be unlucky as they'll have to watch videotape, whereas we can enjoy him live on the TV and in the flesh......and my favourite quote from Tiger came when he told coach Butch Harmon how much he enjoyed scuba diving...... "because the fish don't know who I am."

Competition

GOLF BETTING 2001   PART 2

THE 2001 RYDER CUP

The 34th Ryder Cup will be held at the Belfry from 28th – 30th September.

Looking at the evidence from recent Ryder Cups we can draw three conclusions.

FIRSTLY, in every single one of the last seven Ryder Cups there has NEVER been more than 2 points between the sides.   Indeed in five of them there's not been more than a single point.

●   THE BET MUST BE TO 'BET TO FIGURES' ON EACH TEAM WINNING BY 1 OR 2 POINTS, AND ON THE TIE.

      THE ODDS IN 1999 WERE 8/5 USUALLY THEY'RE 11/10 - 6/5.

SECONDLY, America tends to have a side whereas Europe has a team, so it's not surprising that Europe's superior team play has given them a first-day lead.

However, by contrast, in the five Ryder Cups in the nineties US have won 58.3% of the points in the singles. Indeed Europe have only 'won' the singles once in the last seven.

●   SO IF YOU WANT TO BACK USA TRADITIONALLY IT HAS BEEN BEST TO DO SO AFTER THE FIRST DAY, AND DEFINITELY BEFORE THE SINGLES.

A punters' wealth warning

However things may be about to change. In the 1999 Presidents Cup the American team got off to a flier winning all the five foursomes on the first day. Indeed team spirit appeared to be very good indeed ("We were like one big family."—Tom Lehman). If that 'new' team approach is carried to the Belfry then the traditional poor US start may be reversed.

THIRDLY, The Law of the Ryder Cup was fully discussed in Part 1 and can lead to a tidy profit on the final day.

●   THE LAW OF THE RYDER CUP STATES THAT IN THE SUNDAY SINGLES, PLAYERS WHO HAVE PLAYED IN ALL FOUR PREVIOUS ROUNDS TEND TO UNDERPERFORM AND SO CAN BE OPPOSED UNLESS THEY MEET A PLAYER YET TO START.

WHO WILL WIN?

THE CASE FOR EUROPE

1.   The Belfry course

Let's be completely clear, one big advantage is the fact that Europe is playing at home and can 'adjust' the course to minimise the Americans' strengths. European captain Sam Torrance has already met with the course's joint designer Dave Thomas and agreed changes (a new bunker, extending old bunkers and a new strategically planted tree) to counter the length of Love, Mickelson, Woods and co.

2.   Playing at home

Apart from course knowledge the European teams will have all the 'home advantages' discussed in Part 1.

3.   The best European team is very strong

Monty, Clarke, Westwood, Parnevik, Jimenez, Olazabal, Bjorn, and Garcia are all proven in the States, and together with four from Harrington, Price, Johansson, Coltart, Orr and Fulke, they would make a formidable team.

THE CASE AGAINST EUROPE

1.   The best European team will probably not play

With so many of the best European players planning to play in America (or at least a lot more in the States) it is going to be very difficult for our best players to qualify on merit. This could well result in two or three 'weaker' players being included with say, Garcia, Jimenez or Olazabal competing for 'wild cards'. All in all, a few of Europe's best probably won't play.

2.   The Presidents Cup experience

This really is a bonus for the USA, especially as it seems to have improved both American team spirit and their understanding of foursomes and fourballs which have traditionally been their weakness.

The emergence of Stewart Cink and Kirk Triplett as a strong fourballs (Pl 1 Won 1) and foursomes (Pl 2, Won 2) pairing at this year's Presidents Cup was a massive plus for the captain, Curtis Strange, as both currently have enough points to make the team.

3.   The US now have a really strong potential team

Woods, Duval, Mickelson, Love, Lehman, Sutton and Furyk will form the 'Magnificent 7' backbone of an obviously strong team.

THE ODDS

After the Presidents Cup the US odds were cut so that the best prices at the time of writing are:-

EUROPE 15/8 (Corals)   USA 4/6 (Chandler, Hills, Ladbrokes)

TIE 9/1 (Chandler, Surrey)

THE VERDICT

Sorry....it all depends on whether the best European players can qualify. If they do it's going to be mighty close.

TIGER AND THE 2001 GRAND SLAM

Currently odds from 12/1 to 20/1 are on offer for Tiger to win every major in 2001. However I think it's a poor bet to make as it won't happen and it's dreadful value.

So why won't Tiger do a clean sweep in 2001? After all he dominates world golf, won three majors this year and won the other one in a canter in 1997. Furthermore he'll be going for it to create a unique record to seal his position as the greatest-ever golfer!

> Although he finished brilliantly this year (68-69) Tiger's record at Augusta since his 1997 victory is not earth shattering. He has a three-year stroke average of 71.5 after finishes of 8th (1998), T18th (1999) and 5th (2000). So he's not a 'cert' for the US Masters as the 'Tiger-proofing' at Augusta has worked well.

> In 2000 he knew both the St Andrews and Pebble Beach courses which suited him in so many ways. However he won't have such an advantage in 2001. Royal Lytham with its lucky bounces and afternoon winds will feature a field that will include some quality links players. Tiger will not find it easy defending his British Open crown.

> The USPGA with its wider fairways does enable good, if lesser-known, players to shine so it has not surprisingly usually produced close finishes. He may have won the US Masters by 12, the US Open by 15 and the British Open by 8, yet Tiger's back-to-back USPGA wins were by a single shot and after a play-off.

> Tiger is now a master of the media and handles himself so brilliantly yet can you really imagine the 2001 USPGA should he go there having won the first three majors with a chance of winning the Grand Slam?

Even Tiger might find that pressure a tad too much.

> In 2001 he will face a rejuvenated David Duval. No longer lifting weights, although still pursuing his fitness programme, I believe Duval will be a worthy adversary in the New Year and could well win his first major, possibly at Augusta.

> Tiger will occasionally insist on playing shots that could result in injury.

  * 2000 Buick Open. He hits a ball resting against a tree root.

  * 1999 Tour Championship. He hits 'through' a rock.

I do hope not, yet sooner or later Tiger could injure himself going for such high-risk shots.

> His dad's health has not been robust and if it should deteriorate (again let's hope not) then Tiger would obviously be affected. Let's remember, personal life 'problems' have so far not occurred to affect Tiger's game adversely.

SO OVERALL I think it's possible but very, very unlikely that Tiger will land the Slam in 2001. However the very fact that he's between 12/1 and 20/1 to do so is in itself a massive compliment to him.

20/1 is equivalent to just over 11/10 against for each major

12/1 is equivalent to just over 11/10 ON for each major

As you can see the lowest price, 12/1 is equivalent to 11/10 ON and the best odds equivalent to 11/10 against. Even 25/1 would only equate to 5/4 against.

20/1 TIGER FOR THE GRAND SLAM IS A POOR-VALUE BET

THE ANSWERS TO THE TEASERS

Who is the unknown Swede, who won in Sweden in 1999, and will be a real value bet at 125/1 in the 2001 Scandinavian Masters?

Henrik Stenson is a 24-year-old from the Swedish conveyor-belt of talent. This year he won on the Challenge tour in Sweden, he was T11th in the 2000 Scandinavian Masters (after four sub-par rounds) just 3 shots off 4th place and he was T2nd at 66/1 in the Top Scandinavian market, and in 2001 the tournament moves to the Barseback Club to which he is attached. So with 'home' advantage Henrik can be followed as a 125/1 outsider in the outrights, and also in the top Scandinavian market in the 2001 Scandinavian Masters.

Which American player who is 144th in the final round scoring averages is expected to gain his first win in 2001?

Four times this year up to mid September Frank Lickliter got into serious contention going into R4 and each time he shot a poor over par final round. However from 24th September he continued his good play and got into serious contention in three tournaments. However he then scored significantly better on Sundays.

	R4 Score	Average Score Serious Contenders	Scg Quotient (R4SQ)
> Texas Open	67	68.5	97.81
> Michelob	69	71.47	96.54
> Tampa Bay Classic	69	71.22	96.88

R4SQ gives Lickliter's score as a % of the average of all the serious contenders. So as you can see in his last three tournaments he's shot sub-70 rounds and each has been well below the average. This suggests that at long last he's become a solid R4 player when the heat is on.

Indeed he was my No. 1 pick for the Tampa Bay Classic (T3rd at 50/1) partly because of these researches. However they are well hidden in his 'bald' R4 scoring ranking over the last three years, viz 163rd (1998), 84th (1999) and 144th (2000 up to 24th October).

So with his obvious skill, his return to his old irons and his vastly improved (if well hidden) R4 scoring record Frank Lickliter must have a serious chance of notching his first win in 2001.

Which US Ryder Cup player has won all his singles games for his country without ever having to step onto the 17th tee?

Jim Furyk has played in two Ryder Cup and two Presidents Cup matches. His singles record is brilliant. He's won all his four singles against Sergio Garcia (4 and 3) and Faldo (3 and 2) in the Ryder Cup, and against Frank Nobilo (4 and 2) and Shigeki Maruyama (6 and 5) in the Presidents Cup. So with a 100% record Jim has still to step foot on the 17th tee in any singles match for his country.

He must be backed in the Ryder Cup singles at the Belfry in late September.

Which player must be backed in second round 3-ball betting, but only after he's shot 70 or over in the first round?

This year in the 'ordinary' tournaments on the European mainland Michael Campbell has opened with a round in the 70s eight times and then followed on SEVEN of those eight occasions with a round in the sixties for a R2 stroke average of exactly 68.

The last time was in the Volvo Masters when he shot 73 in R1. He then shot 67 in R2 to win his 2 ball by 4 shots at even money! So back 'Cambo' in second round 3 balls, but only when he has shot 70 or more in R1.

Last year's teasers

> M A Jimenez suggested as top European for the USPGA was a winning 22/1 bet in that market in the previous American major, the US Open.

> Mathew Goggin, the 'unknown' shock, long-odds outsider did not win although he was T3rd at 150/1 in the Greater Milwaukee Open.

> David Duval, suggested as an outright bet in running after R1 in the Memorial made his usual slow start (73) then went 69-68 before a 75 left him T25th.

> However Dennis Paulson tipped for a 'breakthrough win' landed the Buick Classic at 100/1.

THE 2001 MAJORS

THE US MASTERS

The 'Tigerproofing' at Augusta has certainly worked with Woods finishing T8th, T18th and 5th this year since his runaway triumph in 1997. His closing 36 holes this year (7 under par) were truly brilliant and he will understandably be a 'red-hot' favourite in 2001.

However DAVID DUVAL is my selection to win his first major. His putting was very good in the Presidents Cup, he's recovered from his back injury and his long game is in first-class shape.

If he can just get off to a solid start (please see his player profile) he must go close. After all in the last three years he's finished T3rd (2000), T6th (1999) and T2nd (1998) for a stroke average of 70.58, which is much better than Tiger's (71.5).

THE US OPEN

In mid June I expect TIGER WOODS will retain his national title. This year at Pebble Beach he hit 71% of his greens in regulation, an amazing 10% higher than anybody else, with his huge length enabling him to approach the greens with shorter clubs than his opponents. With his putting now first class I suggest you back Woods on 13th June as you'll then be just 24 hours from Tulsa where the US Open tees off on the 14th.

THE BRITISH OPEN

Much will depend upon the weather and indeed the tee times. Nevertheless I believe DARREN CLARKE will win the 2001 British Open. He was T11th at Royal Lytham when it was last the venue in 1996 and Darren is a born-and-bred links player who is even sponsored by a links course. He didn't take his chance at Royal Troon (T2nd in 1997) but he's an immensely better player now than then. A huge hitter with enormous natural talent, I think that he now may be about to emerge as a truly world-class player, especially as his confidence was boosted by his World Match Play win over Tiger this year.

40/1 was available this year and at that price he'd represent a sound each-way bet.

THE USPGA

In the fourteen years from 1985-1998 there were eleven winners in their thirties and eleven first-time winners, with Davis Love (40/1 1997) and Vijay Singh (50/1 1998) examples....then along came Tiger to win in both 1999 and 2000.

With wider fairways than in the US Open there are usually close finishes with three play-offs in the last six years and in 2001 I expect JESPER PARNEVIK to go very close. T20th in 1995, T5th in 1996 and T10th in 1999, he did not play this year. He'll be well over his hip problems next year and as a class act and a proven winner in his thirties looking for his first major he sure fits the bill.

2001 MAJOR SELECTIONS

		Est. odds
US Masters	David Duval	14/1
US Open	Tiger Woods	11/8
British Open	Darren Clarke	40/1
USPGA	Jesper Parnevik	40/1

Last year's major men in Part 2 were:-

Phil Mickelson my Augusta selection to 'go close' finished T7th.

Jim Furyk was selected at Pebble Beach to be 'thereabouts'. He wasn't (T60th).

Vijay Singh the USPGA selection won the US Masters!

Tiger Woods fulfilled all my expectations to land the British Open.

TO KEEP UP TO DATE IN 2001 JOIN MY SPORTSLINE SERVICE

Of course, giving selections in the pages of this book up to fifteen months in advance is highly speculative. If you would like to keep bang up to date with my up-to-the-minute selections based on all the latest news and up-to-date stats please do consider joining or ringing my Sportsline service.

If you want carefully researched analysis and information please join. You will see the adverts on pages xii, 44 and 240.

Pro-Golf 2001

Pro-Golf, the European Tour Media Guide respected throughout the golfing world as an essential work of reference, has been chronicling the achievements of the European Tour for 30 years and the 2001 edition is packed full of records and revealing statistics.

In an arena full of great champions find out how Thomas Björn, Michael Campbell, Darren Clarke, Ernie Els, and Lee Westwood, winner of no fewer than five European Tour titles, challenged Colin Montgomerie's seven-year reign as Europe's Number One. Pro-Golf tells the full story of the race for the Volvo Order of Merit title.

On the world stage Tiger Woods spent the millennium year re-writing the record books, but European Tour Members pushed him harder than anyone. Darren Clarke rose to the challenge by defeating Woods in the 36-hole final of the WGC - Andersen Consulting Match Play. Then after the excitement of Augusta, Pebble Beach and St Andrews, Bob May almost tamed the Tiger at Valhalla when he tied for the title after a thrilling duel before losing a sudden-death play-off. The figures and facts behind the winning of the major championships and all the events that make up the European Tour International Schedule can be found in Pro-Golf 2001.

Suberb biographies of the international stars who make the European Tour unique combined with more than 400 pages on the Tour history, tournament results, prize money and facts and figures make the illustrated Pro-Golf 2001, a must for all students of the game.

Ordering copy of Pro-Golf 2001 is simple: send a cheque for £15 UK and Europe (which includes postage and packaging) and £20 Overseas (which includes postage and packaging), made payable to the PGA European Tour to Emily Doughty, Communications Division, European Tour, Wentworth Drive, Virginia Water, Surrey GU25 4LX or call +44 1344 840442 with credit card details.

THE 2001 AMERICAN TOUR

January

3-7   **WGC Andersen Consulting Match Play Championship** Metropolitan G.C., Melbourne, Australia

11-14   **Mercedes Championships** Plantation Course at Kapalua, Hawaii

11-14   **Touchstone Energy Tucson Open** Omni Tucson, Arizona

18-21   **Sony Open** Waialae C.C., Honolulu, Hawaii

25-28   **Phoenix Open** TPC of Scottsdale, Arizona

February

1-4   **AT&T Pebble Beach National Pro-Am** Pebble Beach, California

8-11   **Buick Invitational** Torrey Pines, San Diego, California

15-18   **Bob Hope Chrysler Classic** Bermuda Dunes, California

22-25   **Nissan Open** Riviera C.C., Los Angeles, California

March

1-4   **Doral-Ryder Open** Miami, Florida

8-11   **Honda Classic** TPC at Heron Bay, Coral Springs, Florida

15-18   **Bay Hill Invitational** Bay Hill, Orlando, Florida

22-25   **The Players Championship** TPC at Sawgrass, Ponte Vedra Beach, Florida

29-1 Apr **Bell South Classic** TPC at Sugarloaf, Duluth, Georgia

April

5-8   **US Masters** Augusta National, Augusta, Georgia

12-15   **Worldcom Classic** Harbour Town Golf Links, Hilton Head, South Carolina

19-22   **Shell Houston Open** TPC at The Woodlands, Texas

26-29   **Greater Greensboro Classic** Forest Oaks C.C., Greensboro, North Carolina

May

3-6   **Compaq Classic** English Turn G. & C.C., New Orleans, Louisiana

10-13   **Verizon Byron Nelson Classic** TPC at Four Seasons, Irving, Texas

17-20   **MasterCard Colonial** Colonial C.C., Fort Worth, Texas

24-27   **Kemper Insurance Open** TPC at Avenel, Potomac, Maryland

31-3 Jun **Memorial Tournament** Muirfield Village G.C., Dublin, Ohio

June

7-10   **FedEx St Jude Classic** TPC at Southwind, Memphis, Tennessee

14-17   **US Open** Southern Hills C.C., Tulsa, Oklahoma

21-24   **Buick Classic** Westchester C.C., Harrison, New York

28-1 Jul **Canon Greater Hartford Open** TPC at River Highlands, Cromwell, Connecticut

July

5-8	**Advil Western Open** Cog Hill G. & C.C., Lemont, Illinois
12-15	**Greater Milwaukee Open** Brown Deer Park G.C., Milwaukee, Wisconsin
19-22	**130th British Open** Royal Lytham & St Annes, Lancs, England
19-22	**BC Open** En-Joie G.C., Endicott, New York
26-29	**John Deere Classic** TPC at Deere Run, Silvis, Illinois

August

2-5	**The International** Castle Pines G.C., Castle Rock, Colorado
9-12	**Buick Open** Warwick Hills, Grand Blanc, Michigan
16-19	**USPGA** Atlanta Athletic Club, Duluth, Georgia
23-26	**WGC NEC Invitational** Firestone C.C., Akron, Ohio
23-26	**Reno-Tahoe Open** Montreux G. & C.C., Reno, Nevada
30-2 Sep	**Air Canada Championship** Northview G. & C.C., Surrey, British Columbia

Sept

6-9	**Bell Canadian Open** Royal Montreal G.C., Quebec
13-16	**WGC American Express Championship** Bellerive C.C., St Louis, Missouri
20-23	**Marconi Pennsylvania Classic** Laurel Valley G.C., Ligonier, Pennsylvania
28-30	**The 34th Ryder Cup Matches** The De Vere Belfry, Wishaw, England
27-30	**Texas Open** LaCantera G.C., San Antonio, Texas

October

4-7	**Michelob Championship** Kingsmill G.C., Williamsburg, Virginia
11-14	**Invensys Classic At Las Vegas** TPC at Summerlin, Las Vegas, Nevada
18-21	**NCR Classic at Walt Disney** Lake Buena Vista, Florida
25-28	**Buick Challenge** Callaway Gardens, Pine Mountain, Georgia

November

1-4	**Tour Championship** Champions G.C., Houston, Texas
1-4	**Southern Farm Bureau Classic** Annandale, Madison, Mississippi
15-18	**WGC EMC World Cup** Taiheyo Club, Shizuoka, Japan

CHANGES COMPARED TO 2000

This year there are very few changes, and no new tournaments.

Four minor changes

> Tucson Open moves earlier from 24th February to 11th January

> Bob Hope Chrysler Classic moves back from 19th January to 15th February

> The Buick Challenge moves back from 28th September to 25th October

> In 2001 the St Jude Classic will be the final tournament before the US Open

2001 EUROPEAN TOUR

November

16-19   **Johnnie Walker Classic** Alpine G. & S. Club, Bangkok, Thailand

January

3-7   **WGC Andersen Consulting Match Play Championship** Metropolitan G.C., Melbourne, Australia

18-21   **Alfred Dunhill Championship** Houghton G.C., Johannesburg, South Africa

25-28   **Mercedes-Benz South African Open** East London G.C., South Africa

February

1-4   **Heineken Classic** The Vines Resort, Perth, Australia

8-11   **Greg Norman Holden International** The Lakes G.C., Sydney, Australia

15-18   **Carlsberg Malaysian Open** Saujana Island C.C., Malaysia

22-25   **Singapore Masters** Singapore Island C.C., Singapore

March

1-4   **Dubai Desert Classic** Emirates G.C., Dubai

8-11   **Qatar Masters** Doha G.C., Qatar

15-18   **Turespana Master** tbc (Spain)

22-25   **Madeira Island Open** Santo da Serra, Madeira

April

5-8   **US Masters Tournament**, Augusta National, Georgia, USA

12-15   **Moroccan Open** tbc (Morocco)

19-22   **Algarve Portuguese Open** Quinta do Lago, Algarve, Portugal

26-29   **Open de Espana** PGA Golf de Catalunya, Girona, Spain

May

3-6   **Novotel Perrier Open de France** Lyon G.C., Villette d'Anthon, France

10-13   **Benson and Hedges International Open** The De Vere Belfry, Wishaw, England

17-20   **Deutsche Bank - SAP Open TPC of Europe** St Leon Rot, Heidelberg, Germany

25-28   **Volvo PGA Championship** Wentworth Club, Surrey, England

June

31-3   **Victor Chandler British Masters**, Woburn, Milton Keynes, England

7-10   **The Compass Group English Open**, Marriott Forest of Arden Hotel, England

14-17   **US Open** Southern Hills C.C., Tulsa, Oklahoma, USA

21-24   **Compaq European Grand Prix**, De Vere Slaley Hall, Northumberland, England

28-1 Jul **Murphy's Irish Open** Fota Island, Cork, Ireland

July

5-8   **Smurfit European Open** The K Club, Dublin, Ireland

12-15   **Loch Lomond World Invitational** Loch Lomond, Glasgow, Scotland

19-22   **130th Open Championship** Royal Lytham & St Annes, Lancs, England

26-29   **TNT Dutch Open** Noordwijkse G.C., Noordwijk, The Netherlands

Aug

2-5   **Volvo Scandinavian Masters** Barseback G. & C.C., Sweden

9-12   **The Celtic Manor Resort Wales Open** The Celtic Manor Resort, Newport, Wales

16-19   **USPGA** Atlanta Athletic Club, Duluth, Georgia, USA

16-19   **West of Ireland Open** tbc (Ireland)

23-26   **WGC NEC Invitational** Firestone C.C., Akron, Ohio, USA

23-26   **Scottish PGA Championship** Gleneagles Hotel, Scotland

30-2 Sep **BMW International Open** Golfclub Munchen Nord-Eichenried, Munich

Sept

6-9   **Omega European Masters** Crans-sur-Sierre G.C., Switzerland

13-16   **WGC American Express Championship** Bellerive C.C., St Louis, Missouri, USA

22-23   **Trophee Lancome** Saint-Nom-la-Breteche G.C., Paris, France

28-30   **The 34th Ryder Cup Matches** The De Vere Belfry, Wishaw, England

Oct

4-7   **Linde German Masters** Gut Larchenhof, Cologne, Germany

11-14   **Belgacom Open**, Royal Zoute G.C., Knokke Heist, Belgium

18-21   **Alfred Dunhill Links Championship** St Andrews, Scotland

25-28   **BBVA Masters de Madrid** (tbc) Madrid, Spain

Nov

1-4   **Italian Open** Is Molas G.C., Sardinia, Italy

8-11   **Volvo Masters** Montecastillo G.C., Jerez, Spain

15-18   **WGC EMC World Cup*** Taiheyo Club, Shizuoka, Japan

Date to be   **Cisco World Matchplay Championship***, Wentworth Club,
confirmed   Surrey, England

* Denotes Approved Special Events

THE 2000/2001 ANZ (AUSTRALIA/NEW ZEALAND) TOUR

Nov

16-19   **Johnnie Walker Classic**** Alpine G. & S. Club, Bangkok, Thailand

23-26   **Holden Australian Open Classic** Kingston Heath G.C., Melbourne, VIC

30-Dec 3 **Australian PGA Championship** Royal Queensland G.C., Brisbane, QLD

Dec

7-10   **Ford Open Championship** Kooyonga G.C., Adelaide, SA

14-17   **Coolum Classic** Hyatt Coolum Resort, Coolum, QLD

Jan 2001

3-7   **WGC Andersen Consulting Match Play Championship** Metropolitan G.C., Melbourne, VIC

11-14   **Victorian Open Championship** Cranbourne G.C., Melbourne, VIC

18-21   **New Zealand Open Championship**, Grange G.C., Auckland, NZ

25-28   **Canon Challenge** Castle Hill C.C., Sydney, NSW

Feb

1-4   **Heineken Classic*** The Vines Resort, Perth, WA

8-11   **Greg Norman Holden International*** The Lakes G.C., Sydney, NSW

15-18   **Ericsson Masters** Huntingdale G.C., Melbourne, VIC

22-25   **ANZ Championship** Concord Golf Club, NSW

*   Co-sanctioned event with European Tour

** Tri-sanctioned event with European Tour and the Asian Tour.

EUROPEAN TOUR FORM 2000   PART 3

THE EUROPEAN ORDER OF MERIT

Date	from November 1999 in Taiwan to November 2000 in Spain
Courses	Various
Par	70-72
Yardage	Various
First Prize	Title of Europe's top player

The Order of Merit is simply the monetary league table of all the European Tour players based on their aggregate prize money winnings over the full season.

2000 ODDS

fav	6/4	Colin Montgomerie	50/1*	Thomas Bjorn
	9/2	Lee Westwood	50/1*	Ernie Els
	7/1*	Sergio Garcia	66/1*	Paul Lawrie
	14/1*	M A Jimenez	80/1	Robert Karlsson
	16/1	Retief Goosen	80/1*	Bernhard Langer
	20/1*	Darren Clarke	80/1	Jarmo Sandelin
	28/1	Padraig Harrington	125/1	BAR
	40/1	J M Olazabal		

Please note:– The above were the best prices available before the Johnnie Walker Classic in November 1999.

2000 RESULT

1	9/2	Lee Westwood
2	20/1*	Darren Clarke
3	50/1*	Ernie Els
4	125/1	Michael Campbell

PUNTERS' POINTS

● The favourite, or second favourite, has been successful throughout each of the last six years.

● However past results are not a perfect guide as those lumping on Monty this year have discovered.

1999 RESULT

1	4/1	Colin Montgomerie
2	fav 3/1	Lee Westwood
3	100/1	Sergio Garcia
4	50/1	M A Jimenez

1998 RESULT

1	fav 4/1	Colin Montgomerie
2	14/1	Darren Clarke
3	6/1	Lee Westwood
4	80/1	M A Jimenez

WINNERS IN THE LAST TEN YEARS

1991	Seve Ballesteros	1996	Colin Montgomerie
1992	Nick Faldo	1997	Colin Montgomerie
1993	Colin Montgomerie	1998	Colin Montgomerie
1994	Colin Montgomerie	1999	Colin Montgomerie
1995	Colin Montgomerie	2000	Lee Westwood

PUNTERS' GUIDE

● The 2001 European Order of Merit started in November 2000 with the Johnnie Walker Classic

● The players with the best recent records are:-

	2000	1999	1998	1997
Monty	-	W	W	W
Lee Westwood	W	2	3	3
M A Jimenez	-	4	4	-
Darren Clarke	2	-	2	4

● The player whose profile refers to this betting market is Lee Westwood.

All the tournaments. All the odds. All the ways to bet.

Open a telephone or online account and we'll match your bet
£ for £ up to a maximum of £10. Please quote ref: EGF10.

Get on course
for a
big win.
Have
a bet.

CALL FREE

0800 126 725

eurobet.co.uk

DELTA

4 TELETEXT pg **611/612/613**
YTEXT pg **358/366**

les apply. £5 minimum stake
r telephone bet. UK residents
years and over only

BET YOUR WAY WITH

TOP 5 FINISHES ON THE EUROPEAN TOUR

1	2	3	4	5

Johnnie Walker Classic (November 1999)

1	2	3	4	5
66/1* M Campbell	100/1* G Ogilvy	12/1 E Els	11/1 V Singh	80/1* P Senior

Alfred Dunhill Championship (54 holes)

1	2	3	4	5
100/1** A Wall	50/1 P Price	–	10/1f R Goosen	125/1 D Lynn
	50/1 G Orr		16/1 D Frost	40/1 P McGinley
				100/1 T Van der Walt
				50/1* T Dodds

Mercedes-Benz - Vodacom South African Open

1	2	3	4	5
66/1 M Gronberg	8/1f N Price	–	–	80/1 T Van der Walt
	100/1 R Gonzalez			125/1 J-F Remesy
	150/1 D Fichardt			100/1 A Roestoff
				12/1 R Goosen
				150/1 J Mellor

Heineken Classic

1	2	3	4	5
33/1* M Campbell	40/1* T Bjorn	150/1 A Forsyth	13/2f E Els	40/1 S Leaney

Greg Norman Holden International

1	2	3	4	5
100/1* L Parsons	66/1* P Senior	66/1 P-U Johansson	–	125/1 D Park
		66/1* A Coltart		

Benson and Hedges Malaysian Open

1	2	3	4	5
125/1 W-T Yeh	66/1 C Hainline	–	–	9/1f R Goosen
	100/1* D Terblanche			80/1* N Van Rensburg
	25/1 P Harrington			66/1* J M Singh
				80/1* L-W Zhang

Algarve Portuguese Open

1	2	3	4	5
22/1 G Orr	28/1 P Price	25/1 P McGinley	–	–
		66/1* T Johnstone		
		100/1* B Davis		

WGC Andersen Consulting World Match Play

1	2	3	4	5
80/1 D Clarke	11/2f T Woods	18/1 D Duval	20/1 D Love	–

Dubai Desert Classic

1	2	3	4	5
125/1 J Coceres	50/1 P McGinley	–	150/1* S Gallacher	–
	66/1 P Sjoland		40/1 P Lawrie	
			12/1 L Westwood	
			100/1 J Spence	

Qatar Masters

1	2	3	4	5
150/1 R Muntz	20/1 I Woosnam	50/1* E Romero	–	80/1* B Davis
		66/1* S Leaney		40/1 M A Martin

Madeira Island Open

66/1*	N Fasth	100/1*	R Drummond	–		–		12/1	J Bickerton
		150/1	M Davis					150/1	R Sjoberg
		80/1	R S Johnson						

Brazil Rio de Janeiro 500 Years Open

| 150/1 | R Chapman | 16/1 | P Harrington | 20/1 | J Coceres | 80/1 | J Haeggman | – |
| | | | | | | 80/1 | J Berendt | |

Brazil Sao Paolo 500 Years Open

12/1f	P Harrington	125/1**	G Norquist	40/1	G Owen	–	–
				25/1	E Romero		
				100/1	I Poulter		
				200/1	P R Martinez		
				50/1	Steve Webster		

US Masters

| 50/1 | V Singh | 25/1 | E Els | 125/1 | L Roberts | – | 5/2f | T Woods |
| | | | | 16/1 | D Duval | | | |

Moroccan Open

33/1*	J Spence	100/1**	I Poulter	–	–	40/1	D Terblanche
		200/1	S Delagrange				
		80/1*	T Levet				

Peugot Spanish Open

| 100/1* | B Davis | 150/1* | M Brier | 100/1* | P Baker | – | 15/2 | C Montgomerie |
| | | | | 50/1* | E Romero | | | |

Novotel Perrier Open de France

13/2f	C Montgomerie	150/1	J Lomas	150/1	R Davis	125/1	J Senden	–
						150/1	R Wessels	
						100/1	F Jacobson	

Benson and Hedges International

40/1	J M Olazabal	66/1	P Price	50/1	J Coceres	–	125/1	S Gallacher
				66/1	A Coltart		125/1	A Wall
							6/1f	C Montgomerie
							100/1	A Scott

Deutsche Bank Open

33/1	L Westwood	200/1*	E Canonica	5/2f	T Woods	–	–
				80/1	J Van de Velde		
				80/1	I Woosnam		

Volvo PGA

5/1f	C Montgomerie	16/1	D Clarke	–	–	125/1	R Green
		10/1	L Westwood			25/1	S Garcia
		66/1	A Coltart				

Compass Group English Open

| 9/1 | D Clarke | 33/1 | M Campbell | – | 9/1 | L Westwood | – |
| | | 125/1 | M James | | 150/1* | R Gonzalez | |

Wales Open

100/1*	S Tinning	50/1*	D Howell	125/1	F Jacobson	–		50/1*	M McNulty
				11/1f	I Woosnam			20/1	P Price
								40/1	N O'Hern

US Open

3/1f	T Woods	20/1	E Els	–		80/1	J Huston	125/1	P Harrington
		100/1	M A Jimenez					40/1	L Westwood

Compaq European Grand Prix

9/2f	L Westwood	100/1	F Jacobson	100/1*	E Canonica	–		125/1	A Oldcorn
				6/1	D Clarke				

Murphy's Irish Open

100/1*	P Sjoland	66/1	F Jacobson	125/1	R Muntz	–		125/1	P Lonard
				50/1	P McGinley				

Smurfit European Open

7/1	L Westwood	50/1	A Cabrera	100/1	P-U Johansson	100/1	M Gronberg	125/1	I Garrido
								80/1	J Sandelin

Standard Life Loch Lomond World Invitational

12/1	E Els	25/1	T Lehman	8/1f	C Montgomerie	40/1	N Begay	–	
						50/1*	R Goosen		
						125/1	S Allan		

129th British Open

5/2f	T Woods	100/1	T Bjorn	–		33/1	T Lehman	–	
		16/1	E Els			150/1	D Toms		

TNT Dutch Open

66/1*	S Leaney	28/1	B Langer	33/1	A Cabrera	–		–	
				66/1	M Gronberg				
				9/2f	L Westwood				

Scandinavian Masters

13/2	L Westwood	25/1	M Campbell	150/1*	R Russell	150/1	D Borrego	–	
						80/1	J Spence		

Victor Chandler British Masters

50/1	G Orr	33/1	P-U Johansson	7/2f	C Montgomerie	100/1*	M McNulty	33/1	B May
								50/1	A Coltart
								50/1*	P Lawrie

The USPGA

7/4f	T Woods	150/1	B May	125/1	T Bjorn	80/1	S Appleby	–	
						100/1	J M Olazabal		
						150/1	G Chalmers		

West of Ireland Classic

50/1	M Scarpa	150/1	M Lundberg	150/1	A Beal	66/1*	C Rodiles	–	
						150/1	G Houston		
						150/1	T Dier		

Scottish PGA

16/1	P Fulke	100/1*	H Nystrom	125/1	R Jacquelin	200/1	B Barham	66/1	O Karlsson

World Golf Championships NEC Invitational

11/8f	T Woods	250/1*	P Price	–		40/1	J Furyk	–
		66/1	J Leonard			11/1	P Mickelson	
						50/1*	H Sutton	

BMW International Open

16/1	T Bjorn	25/1	B Langer	125/1	C Suneson	125/1	I Garrido	125/1	M A Martin
								200/1	G Rojas
								11/2jf	E Els
								150/1	E Canonica
								100/1	G Owen
								150/1	D Lee

Canon European Masters

50/1	E Romero	10/1	T Bjorn	10/1	D Clarke	125/1	N Fasth	40/1	M Gronberg

Lancome Trophy

33/1	R Goosen	25/1	M Campbell	–		14/1	V Singh	–
		12/1	D Clarke			100/1	A Cejka	

Belgacom Open

7/1f	L Westwood	40/1	E Romero	33/1	P Harrington	–		80/1*	D Robertson
				125/1	T Gillis			100/1	A Forsyth

German Masters

28/1	M Campbell	80/1*	J Coceres	12/1	C Montgomerie	–		22/1	T Bjorn
				25/1	P Harrington				

Cisco World Matchplay

5/1	L Westwood	4/1	C Montgomerie	–		–		–

BBVA Open Turespana Masters

16/1	P Harrington	50/1	G Orr	33/1	P-U Johansson	10/1	D Clarke	40/1	P McGinley
								200/1	F Cea

Italian Open

125/1	I Poulter	150/1	G Brand Jr	125/1	R Green	–		66/1	P Baker
				100/1*	F Cea			125/1	V Phillips

Volvo Masters

50/1	P Fulke	12/1	D Clarke	20/1*	M Campbell	-		33/1	J M Olazabal
				7/1f	L Westwood			50/1	A Cabrera

WGC American Express Championship

66/1	M Weir	12/1	L Westwood	28/1	V Singh	-		40/1	P Harrington
				150/1	D Waldorf			33/1	S Garcia
								40/1	N Price
								11/8f	T Woods

THE JOHNNIE WALKER CLASSIC

Date	11th - 14th November 1999
Course	The Westin Resort, Ta Shee, Taiwan
Par	72
Yardage	7,150
First Prize	£133,330
Total Purse	£800,000

THE TOURNAMENT

This tournament is played in the Far East and amazingly it is the first in the 2000 European Order of Merit. The winners in the previous six years had all been major winners.

THE COURSE

This Robert Trent Jones course had four par 5s which were all reachable in two shots by the huge hitters such as Tiger Woods. This 'long' course played short because drives got a lot of run off the hard, fast fairways. The final hole is a 233-yard par 3 short hole. The wind played a significant part on this course.

2000 ODDS

fav	15/8	Tiger Woods	66/1*	Robert Allenby
	11/1	Vijay Singh	66/1*	Mark McNulty
	12/1	Ernie Els	66/1*	Nick Faldo
	16/1	Jim Furyk	80/1	Paul McGinley
	50/1	Eduardo Romero	80/1*	Peter Lonard
	50/1	Angel Cabrera	80/1*	Peter Senior
	66/1*	Michael Campbell	80/1	Marc Farry
	66/1	Peter O'Malley	80/1	Phillip Price
	66/1	Patrik Sjoland	80/1	Gary Evans

1999 RESULT

1	66/1*	Michael Campbell	66 71 69 70 276
2	100/1*	Geoff Ogilvy	70 71 68 68 277
3	12/1	Ernie Els	70 67 73 68 278
4	11/1	Vijay Singh	71 72 68 68 279
5	80/1*	Peter Senior	67 72 74 67 280

6	T Woods	68 72 70 71 281			W Smith	72 73 69 75 289
T7	F Nobilo	72 71 70 69 282			M Wheelhouse	72 69 72 76 289
	Phillip Price	68 72 75 67 282		T39	C Pena	73 73 75 69 290
T9	R Backwell	72 70 73 68 283			K Eriksson	71 73 74 72 290
	S Tinning	69 71 72 71 283			P Gow	74 72 72 72 290
	A Cabrera	70 71 69 73 283			E Romero	72 74 72 72 290
T12	P Marksaeng	71 70 73 70 284			J-F Remesy	73 73 70 74 290
	P O'Malley	72 70 70 72 284			D Park	74 72 70 74 290
	N Faldo	72 72 69 71 284			H Otto	73 71 71 75 290
T15	R Wessels	69 73 72 71 285		T46	D Mckenzie	73 72 76 70 291
	K Druce	75 70 70 70 285			R Byrd	70 76 71 74 291
T17	K Nogami	72 68 76 70 286			W Riley	73 73 71 74 291
	P Lonard	69 73 70 74 286			Terry Price	74 68 72 77 291
	L H Han	74 71 69 72 286		T50	D Chia	71 74 78 69 292
	F Casas	71 74 70 71 286			R Winchester	71 74 77 70 292
	J M Singh	71 74 71 70 286			J Guepy	71 74 76 71 292
	A Pitts	69 72 73 72 286			W-T Lu	75 71 74 72 292
	C Plaphol	74 72 70 70 286			J Kingston	73 72 74 73 292
T24	J Furyk	76 73 78 69 287		T55	A Johl	71 70 79 73 293
	B King	70 71 75 71 287			W Ter-Chang	74 71 75 73 293
	N O'Hern	67 71 77 72 287			P Nilbrink	70 74 73 76 293
T27	S Yates	72 74 73 69 288		T58	S Kjeldsen	75 71 76 73 295
	J Robinson	66 78 73 71 288			G Hanrahan	73 70 77 75 295
	R Allenby	70 72 76 70 288		60	J Skold	66 73 77 81 297
	M Olander	68 70 76 74 288		T61	M McNulty	74 71 76 77 298
	W-S Kang	73 72 72 71 288			T Elliott	74 72 75 77 298
T32	S Lyle	72 71 76 70 289		63	G Hutcheon	73 73 75 78 299
	L Parsons	73 71 75 70 289		64	M Lafeber	73 72 78 77 300
	A Stolz	70 76 70 73 289		T65	R Cuello	72 74 78 77 301
	S Tait	71 72 72 74 289			E Carlberg	70 72 77 82 301
	Soren Hansen	70 75 70 74 289		67	T Ichihara	73 72 73 84 302

ROUND BY ROUND LEADERBOARD

FIRST ROUND

M CAMPBELL	6 under
J Skold	6 under
J Robinson	6 under
N O'Hern	5 under
P Senior	5 under
J Furyk	5 under
T Woods	4 under

SECOND ROUND

M CAMPBELL	7 under
M Olander	6 under
N O'Hern	6 under
P Senior	5 under
P Price	4 under
T Woods	4 under
S Tinning	4 under

THIRD ROUND

M CAMPBELL	10 under
G Ogilvy	7 under
E Els	6 under
A Cabrera	6 under
T Woods	6 under
V Singh	5 under

FINAL ROUND

M CAMPBELL	12 under
G Ogilvy	11 under
E Els	10 under
V Singh	9 under
P Senior	8 under

RESULTS IN OTHER MARKETS

Multi-Sports created a market without Tiger Woods

1	33/1	M Campbell
2	80/1	G Ogilvy
3	8/1	E Els
4	fav 11/2	V Singh
5	80/1	P Senior

PUNTERS' POINTS

● "My baby son Thomas has inspired me to this victory," so the 'nappy factor' still rules, OK! Michael Campbell after his first European tour victory stressed that the realisation that, "I had to be supporter of my family, the provider," had been his driving force.

Having had the pressure of leading he kept his nerve so that, "finally I have got the monkey off my back".

● Tiger Woods's putter let him down so that he didn't make it five wins in a row, and proved to those who backed him at prices below 2/1 that he's only human!

● 50/1 Angel Cabrera was T3rd after R3 so his final (over par) round of 73 when in contention was very disappointing for 'El Pato', who finished T9th.

● Geoff Ogilvy is a star of the future. "Believe me, this guy can play," were the words that led his player profile last year, and here his 8 under for the last 36 holes was the joint tournament best as he revelled in the wind.

● The DYM system also rules OK! With three DYMs in the front 5, including 66/1 Michael Campbell, this proven system got off to a 'flier'. It has three great attractions—it's clear, it's simple and it works!

● In-form Steen Tinning dropped 3 shots in the last 6 holes in R4 so instead of finishing 5th he ended up T9th. It's a round to be filed under "learning experience".

1998 RESULT		
1	fav 5/1	Tiger Woods
won at the second play-off hole		
2	10/1	Ernie Els
3	40/1	Retief Goosen
T4	50/1	Andrew Coltart
T4	12/1	Lee Westwood
T4	80/1	Alex Cejka
T4	66/1	Peter O'Malley

1997 RESULT		
1	12/1	Ernie Els
T2	80/1	Michael Long
T2	66/1	Peter Lonard
T4	16/1	Nick Faldo
T4	14/1	Fred Couples
T4	66/1	Anthony Painter

WINNERS IN RECENT YEARS

1993	Nick Faldo	Singapore Island
1994	Greg Norman	Blue Canyon C.C., Phuket, Thailand
1995	Fred Couples	Manila, Philippines
1996	Ian Woosnam	Tanah Merah, Singapore
1997	Ernie Els	Hope Island, Queensland, Australia
1998	Tiger Woods	Blue Canyon C.C., Phuket, Thailand
1999	Michael Campbell	Ta Shee, Taiwan

PUNTERS' GUIDE

This tournament will be held in mid-late November 2000 before this book is published so guidelines here would be inappropriate.

THE ALFRED DUNHILL CHAMPIONSHIP

Date	13th - 16th January
Course	Houghton G.C., Johannesburg
Par	72
Yardage	7,309
First Prize	£78,000
Total Purse	£500,000

THE TOURNAMENT

This tournament, formerly the national PGA Championship, became the first European Tournament of the New Millennium and the second tournament on this season's Order of Merit after last November's Johnnie Walker Classic.

THE COURSE

Houghton is a well-established, suburban Johannesburg course. It demands accuracy especially from the tee, and at over 7,300 yards it is clearly long. However, played at altitude the ball travels further through the air so making club selection tricky for players unused to such conditions. The Kikuya rough is especially tough after wet weather.

2000 ODDS

fav	10/1	Retief Goosen	50/1	Gary Orr
	16/1	David Frost	50/1	Phillip Price
	16/1	Bernhard Langer	66/1**	Tony Johnstone
	22/1	Ian Woosnam	66/1*	Steve Webster
	25/1	Mark McNulty	66/1	Marco Gortana
	25/1	Jarmo Sandelin	66/1*	Sven Struver
	40/1*	Hennie Otto	66/1*	Paul Broadhurst
	40/1	Paul McGinley	66/1*	Mathias Gronberg
	40/1	Jean Van de Velde	66/1*	Andrew McLardy
	40/1	Peter Baker	66/1**	Geoff Ogilvy
	40/1	Ignacio Garrido	66/1*	Jeev Milkha Singh
	50/1	Peter Lonard	80/1	Roger Wessels
	50/1*	Trevor Dodds	80/1	Nico Van Rensburg
	50/1*	Nik Henning	80/1	K H Han
	50/1*	David Howell		

2000 RESULT

1	100/1**	Anthony Wall	69 67 68 204
T2	50/1	Phillip Price	72 67 67 206
T2	50/1	Gary Orr	69 67 70 206
4	fav 10/1	Retief Goosen	72 69 66 207
T5	125/1	David Lynn	71 71 66 208
T5	16/1	David Frost	71 68 69 208
T5	40/1	Paul McGinley	73 66 69 208
T5	100/1	Tjaart Van der Walt	72 68 68 208
T5	50/1*	Trevor Dodds	69 65 74 208

T10	Anders Hansen	71 72 66 209			M Gortana	69 74 72 215
	Brian Davis	68 74 67 209			P Eales	72 72 71 215
	N Henning	71 68 70 209			W Coetsee	71 73 71 215
	J M Singh	69 70 70 209			W Riley	70 72 73 215
T14	M McKenzie	72 71 67 210			D Lee	74 68 73 215
	M Gronberg	72 69 69 210			R Bilbo Jr	76 68 71 215
	B Langer	70 69 71 210			S Rowe	75 69 71 215
	P Baker	68 70 72 210		T53	I Garbutt	74 69 73 216
T18	F Tarnaud	72 71 68 211			P Golding	69 73 74 216
	D Terblanche	69 70 72 211			J Mashego	73 71 72 216
	R Gonzalez	70 68 73 211			J Kingston	71 73 72 216
21	P Broadhurst	68 70 74 212			P Nyman	72 72 72 216
T22	J Senden	70 73 70 213			C Whitelaw	70 75 71 216
	I Poulter	74 69 70 213		T59	D Fichardt	71 71 75 217
	Soren Hansen	71 71 71 213			J Mellor	70 72 75 217
	J Lomas	72 72 69 213			A Da Silva	72 72 73 217
	I Garrido	71 71 71 213			K Storgaard	73 71 73 217
	B Lincoln	71 71 71 213			J Rose	76 69 72 217
	R Jacquelin	74 68 71 213			B Davison	71 74 72 217
	P Fowler	72 70 71 213		T65	A Michell	75 68 75 218
	G Hutcheon	73 71 69 213			C Williams	73 69 76 218
	M Lafeber	71 70 72 213			R Sailer	72 72 74 218
	T Gillis	71 69 73 213			M Cayeux	70 71 77 218
	S Webster	70 69 74 213			B Dredge	75 69 74 218
	D Van Staden	73 72 68 213			T Gogele	74 70 74 218
	P Lonard	74 71 68 213			K Carissimi	71 74 73 218
T36	J Hobday	69 74 71 214			N Maart	73 72 73 218
	M Murless	75 68 71 214			B Hlophe	73 72 73 218
	D Botes	72 69 73 214			R Byrd	75 70 73 218
	M McNulty	74 71 69 214		T75	R McCann	69 74 76 219
	S Gallacher	71 74 69 214			G Levenson	75 70 74 219
	N Van Rensburg	70 75 69 214			D De Vooght	75 70 74 219
	A Cruse	71 74 69 214			A Forsyth	71 74 74 219
T43	B Pappas	73 70 72 215		79	W Bradley	71 74 75 220
	D Howell	72 71 72 215		T80	R Stewart	71 73 77 221
	N Fasth	72 71 72 215			A Bossert	72 73 76 221

NOTE: This season the top 70 (and ties) make the cut on the European tour compared to the top 65 (and ties) last year.

The main players to miss the cut (made at 1 over) were:-

I Woosnam (+2)	S Van Vuuren (+2)	J-F Remesy (+2)	P Affleck (+3)
I Pyman (+3)	G Ogilvy (+3)	J Sandelin (+4)	T Levet (+4)
C Hanell (+4)	T Johnstone (+5)	R Wessels (+5)	J Hugo (+5)
A McLardy (+7)	T Immelman (+7)	P Nyman (+7)	G Owen (+7)
J Van de Velde (+8)	S Struver (+8)	S Kjeldsen (+8)	A McLean (+9)

Hennie Otto (in R2) and Richard Kaplan (in R1) withdrew.

ROUND BY ROUND LEADERBOARD

FIRST ROUND

P Baker	4 under
P Broadhurst	4 under
B Davis	4 under
M Gortana	3 under
P Golding	3 under
G Orr	3 under
A WALL	3 under
T Dodds	3 under
D Terblanche	3 under
J M Singh	3 under
J Hobday	3 under
R McCann	3 under

SECOND ROUND

T Dodds	10 under
G Orr	8 under
A WALL	8 under
P McGinley	6 under
D Frost	6 under
B Langer	6 under
P Baker	6 under
P Broadhurst	6 under

THIRD AND FINAL ROUND

A WALL	12 under
P Price	10 under
G Orr	10 under
R Goosen	9 under
D Lynn	8 under
D Frost	8 under
P McGinley	8 under
T Van der Walt	8 under
T Dodds	8 under

This tournament was ruined by torrential rain which delayed the start on Thursday and subsequently caused regular interruptions so that only the first 2 rounds were completed by Saturday. The tournament was reduced to 54 holes with the final round started and completed on Sunday.

PUNTERS' POINTS

● 'Wonder Wall' was the headline after 24-year-old Anthony Wall achieved his breakthrough maiden win in the rain-reduced (and rain-ruined) Alfred Dunhill Championship.

It may only have been a 54-hole tournament yet all the players knew this when heading out for the third and final round on Sunday so R4 was a real test of nerve.

● 7th here in 1998, Wall was an improving player with a chance, one recognised by Don Stewart, Victor Chandler's odds compiler, who went just 33/1 about the Londoner when Heathorns quoted 100/1, making Wall a TYM success.

● Trevor Dodds played 4 holes on Thursday, 32 (!) on Friday and 18 on the final day. However after his brilliant 65 in R2 he slipped up over the final 4 holes on Sunday to finish T5th.

● It is interesting to note that the only occasions this tournament has been won by a European (1996 and 2000), have been the only two occasions that it has been reduced to a three-round event.

● The 'value' that can be obtained in tournaments such as these when compilers don't always know the field or the recent form was shown by two facts.

> In the overall Racing Post pricewise chart there were an amazing (all-comers record!) twelve TYMs, and of course one of them won!

> Of the seventeen players best priced from 50/1 to 80/1 (inclusive) nine were DYMs and two TYMs.

1999 RESULT

1	fav 5/1	Ernie Els
2	125/1	Richard Kaplan
T3	40/1	Stephen Leaney
T3	25/1	David Frost
T3	100/1	Steve Webster
T3	150/1	Jeev Milkha Singh

1998 RESULT

1	100/1	Tony Johnstone
2	fav 5/1	Ernie Els
T3	33/1	Retief Goosen
T3	8/1	Nick Price
5	100/1	Scott Dunlap

WINNERS IN THE LAST TEN YEARS

1991	Roger Wessels	1996	Sven Struver (3 rounds)
1992	Ernie Els	1997	Nick Price
1993	Mark McNulty	1998	Tony Johnstone
1994	David Frost	1999	Ernie Els
1995	Ernie Els	2000	Anthony Wall (3 rounds)

PUNTERS' GUIDE

● This course is made for Ernie Els (winner in 1992, 1995 and 1999) and if he plays in 2001 he'll clearly have a favourite's chance.

● The very best recent course form on this course-specialists' track, has been shown by :-

> Retief Goosen   4th 2000: DNP 1999: T3rd 1998: 4th 1997

> David Frost   T5th 2000: T3rd 1999: 2nd 1997

● Four other players to note are

> Nic Henning   T10th 2000: T14th 1999: T16th 1998

> Tjaart Van der Walt   T5th 2000: T19th 1999

> Peter Baker   T14th 2000: 9th 1999
> Jeev Milkha Singh   T10th 2000: T3rd 1999
> Mathias Gronberg   T14th 2000: T22nd 1999: 9th 1998

● Roger Wessels and Richard Kaplan (2nd 1999), the club pro, are both members at Houghton.

● The players whose profiles point to this tournament include Retief Goosen, David Frost, Mathias Gronberg, Peter Baker, Steve Webster, Phillip Price and Anders Hansen.

MERCEDES-BENZ-VODACOM SOUTH AFRICAN OPEN

Date	20th - 23rd January
Course	Randpark G.C., Johannesburg
Par	72
Yardage	7,500
First Prize	£100,000
Total Purse	£600,000

THE TOURNAMENT

The world's second oldest Open returned to the Randpark course in Johannesburg for the first time since 1995 when Retief Goosen was the winner.

THE COURSE

This is a very long course at 7,500 yards (not 6,806 as in the press) with a par 5 final hole reachable in two shots. The course is well bunkered and features a number of water hazards.

2000 ODDS

fav	8/1*	Nick Price	50/1	Ignacio Garrido
	10/1	Lee Westwood	50/1	Hennie Otto
	12/1	Retief Goosen	50/1*	Phillip Price
	20/1	David Frost (DC)	50/1	Peter Baker
	22/1	Thomas Bjorn	50/1	Jarmo Sandelin
	25/1	Bernhard Langer	66/1*	Peter Lonard
	40/1	Nic Henning	66/1	David Howell
	40/1	Mark McNulty	66/1*	Jeev Milkha Singh
	40/1	Ian Woosnam	66/1	Steve Webster
	40/1*	Trevor Dodds	66/1*	Paul Broadhurst
	40/1	Patrik Sjoland	66/1	Mathias Gronberg
	40/1	Anthony Wall (PWW)	80/1*	Geoff Ogilvy
	50/1	Gary Orr	80/1	Tjaart Van der Walt

2000 RESULT

1	66/1	Mathias Gronberg	70 70 67 67 274
T2	100/1	Ricardo Gonzalez	75 66 68 66 275
T2	fav 8/1	Nick Price	72 69 67 67 275
T2	150/1	Darren Fichardt	68 67 67 73 275
T5	80/1	Tjaart Van der Walt	71 70 69 66 276
T5	125/1	J-F Remesy	68 70 69 69 276
T5	100/1	Ashley Roestoff	69 69 69 69 276
T5	12/1	Retief Goosen	68 71 68 69 276
T5	150/1	John Mellor	72 72 63 69 276

T10	B Langer	74 69 68 66 277
	L Westwood	69 68 72 68 277
	G Owen	66 72 69 70 277
T13	S Tinning	71 73 69 65 278
	C Hanell	71 70 69 68 278
	P Eales	66 69 69 74 278
T16	Brian Davis	70 73 70 66 279
	G Orr	70 73 66 70 279
	T Levet	74 66 68 71 279
T19	R Green	68 73 73 66 280
	S Struver	74 68 70 68 280
	B Vaughan	71 73 66 70 280
	D Gammon	68 68 72 72 280
	D Terblanche	66 72 65 77 280
T24	M McNulty	72 69 71 69 281
	I Woosnam	70 66 74 71 281
T26	S Webster	68 75 72 67 282
	J Olver (am)	72 72 70 68 282
	P Lonard	69 75 70 68 282
	G Ogilvy	69 73 70 70 282
	S Yates	71 71 70 70 282
	M Brier	72 70 69 71 282
	S Gallacher	69 72 70 71 282
	W Coetsee	65 71 71 75 282
T34	A Wall	70 71 72 70 283
	H Otto	72 71 69 71 283
	J Hugo	70 73 68 72 283
T37	N Van Rensburg	68 72 73 71 284
	F Lindgren	73 70 70 71 284
	J Rose	72 72 69 71 284
	D Botes	72 70 70 72 284
	J M Singh	70 71 69 74 284
	T Johnstone	68 73 69 74 284

T43	M Lafeber	69 74 72 70 285
	B Vaughan	69 74 71 71 285
	P Broadhurst	71 71 71 72 285
	J Sandelin	71 72 70 72 285
	C Whitelaw	74 70 69 72 285
	J Lomas	69 71 72 73 285
T49	C Kamps	73 71 74 68 286
	N Vanhootegem	71 72 74 69 286
	A McKenna	73 71 73 69 286
	T Moore	69 72 75 70 286
	A Da Silva	71 72 73 70 286
	J Kingston	75 69 72 70 286
	C Williams	72 72 72 70 286
	A McLardy	72 70 72 72 286
	W Bradley	69 73 72 72 286
T58	G Hutcheon	72 71 74 70 287
	D Crawford	72 71 73 71 287
	Phillip Price	69 75 72 71 287
	K Horne	70 72 71 74 287
	S Van Vuuren	73 68 71 75 287
T63	R McCann	71 72 74 71 288
	T Immelman	68 74 73 73 288
	J Senden	69 73 70 76 288
T66	P Nyman	74 69 72 74 289
	E Canonica	75 69 71 74 289
68	D De Vooght	73 70 73 76 292
T69	D McGuigan	70 74 76 73 293
	D Howell	71 72 77 73 293
	D Pappas	71 72 75 75 293
T72	I Palmer	71 72 80 72 295
	B Liddle	72 71 77 75 296
74	J Loughnane	72 69 80 75 296
75	R Jacquelin	70 73 75 79 297

The main players to miss the cut (made at level) were:-

A Hansen (+1)	V Phillips (+2)	T Gillis (+2)	M Jonzon (+2)
N Henning (+2)	J Hobday (+2)	P Sjoland (+2)	R Wessels (+2)
T Bjorn (+3)	B Pappas (+3)	T Gogele (+3)	D Frost (+3)
S Kjeldsen (+4)	T Dodds (+4)	A Cruse (+5)	I Pyman (+7)
M Gortana (+10)	R Kaplan (+11)		

Paul Affleck (4 under after R3) and Ignacio Garrido were both disqualified.

ROUND BY ROUND LEADERBOARD

FIRST ROUND

W Coetsee	7 under
G Owen	6 under
D Terblanche	6 under
9 players at	4 under
M GRONBERG	2 under

SECOND ROUND

P Eales	9 under
D Fichardt	9 under
D Gammon	8 under
W Coetsee	8 under
I Woosnam	8 under
L Westwood	7 under
M GRONBERG	4 under

THIRD ROUND

D Fichardt	14 under
D Terblanche	13 under
P Eales	12 under
M GRONBERG	9 under
J Mellor	9 under
R Goosen	9 under
A Roestoff	9 under
G Owen	9 under
J-F Remesy	9 under
W Coetsee	9 under

FINAL ROUND

M GRONBERG	14 under
N Price	13 under
R Gonzalez	13 under
D Fichardt	13 under
R Goosen	12 under
T Van der Walt	12 under
A Roestoff	12 under
J-F Remesy	12 under
J Mellor	12 under

Rain interrupted the final round on Sunday. Tjaart Van der Walt was the leader at the time.

PUNTERS' POINTS

● 66/1 Mathias Gronberg won a four-way battle with a birdie at the par 5 last hole to become the sixth foreigner to win the South African Open. He did so in fast-fading light after a storm-induced delay of 2¾ hours.

● Promising young Argentinean Ricardo Gonzalez missed a 5-foot eagle putt on the last to miss a play-off.

● Feature of the betting was Ladbrokes' 4/1 Nick Price and 6/1 Lee Westwood at combined odds of under 2/1!! Although Price came close in a tournament he's yet to win, a rusty Westwood lost his chance in R3.

● An early opening-round tee time was again very helpful here as the rain-softened greens marked up by the time the afternoon players went out.

● What a disgrace! Only Sporting Index amongst the spread firms offered finishing positions—and then on only four players!

● Retief Goosen had a first-class chance on a course he knew so well and on which he won this title in 1995. Delighted with the success of recent laser eye surgery this in-form long hitter was well fancied. However despite a birdie-eagle finish his putting let him down.

1999 RESULT

1	18/1	David Frost
T2	80/1	Jeev Milkha Singh
T2	100/1	Scott Dunlap
4	50/1	Sven Struver
5	150/1	Hennie Otto

1998 RESULT

1	fav 9/2	Ernie Els
2	33/1	David Frost
3	50/1	Patrik Sjoland
T4	200/1	Nic Henning
T4	100/1	Marco Gortana
T4	12/1	Bernhard Langer

WINNERS IN THE LAST TEN YEARS

1991	Wayne Westner	1996	Ernie Els
1992	Ernie Els	1997	Vijay Singh
1993	Clinton Whitelaw	1998	Ernie Els
1994	Tony Johnstone	1999	David Frost
1995	Retief Goosen	2000	Mathias Gronberg

PUNTERS' GUIDE

● The only player to post successive top 15 finishes is South African Ashley Roestoff, from the Benoni Club. T15th in 1999, this year he was T5th and the only player to shoot four rounds in the 60s. He must be noted in 2001.

● Another four players have posted two top 20s in the last three years.

> Ernie (who els?)   DNP 2000: T6th 1999: Won 1998

> David Frost   MC 2000: Won 1999: 2nd 1998

> Bernhard Langer   T10th 2000: T4th 1998 (T27th 1999)

> Sven Struver   T19th 2000: 4th 1999 (T47th 1998)

● Tjaart Van der Walt, my 80/1 outsider this year when T5th, is a promising young player to remember. He was T5th last week in the Alfred Dunhill. Worth keeping on your side in the early South African events in 2001.

● It is clearly an advantage for a European player to have played last week. Acclimatised and having shaken 'off the rust', he'll be at an advantage compared to those whose season starts here.

● Players whose profiles point to this tournament include Sven Struver, Gary Orr, Steen Tinning, David Frost, Bernhard Langer and Retief Goosen.

THE HEINEKEN CLASSIC

Date	27th - 30th January
Course	The Vines, Perth, Australia
Par	72
Yardage	7,059
First Prize	£122,000
Total Purse	£656,000

THE TOURNAMENT

This prestigious tournament was a European tour event for the fifth successive year with The Vines the venue for the eleventh consecutive time.

THE COURSE

The Vines provides a demanding test, requiring accuracy rather than length. It has a number of tight dog-leg holes and has large, fast, undulating greens. Its closing hole is a reachable par 5. The wind (the Freemantle Doctor) can be severe. "The course makes the player think...you can use your driver, but you don't need it often."
— Wayne Smith, local player.

2000 ODDS

fav	13/2	Ernie Els	50/1	Jarmo Sandelin
	16/1	Greg Norman	50/1	Alex Cejka
	16/1	Retief Goosen	66/1*	Andrew Coltart
	25/1	Craig Parry	66/1*	Nick O'Hern
	28/1	Padraig Harrington	66/1	Gary Orr
	28/1	J M Olazabal	66/1	Patrik Sjoland
	33/1*	M Campbell (PWW-ANZ)	66/1	P-U Johansson
	33/1	Greg Turner	80/1*	Geoff Ogilvy
	40/1*	Thomas Bjorn	80/1*	Anthony Wall
	40/1	Peter Lonard	80/1*	Peter Senior
	40/1	Paul Lawrie	80/1	Steen Tinning
	40/1	Stephen Leaney	80/1*	Paul Gow
	50/1	Mathias Gronberg (PWW)	80/1*	Steve Webster
	50/1	Jarrod Moseley (DC)	80/1	David Howell
	50/1	Paul McGinley	80/1	Phillip Price

2000 RESULT

1	33/1*	Michael Campbell	68 69 65 66 268
2	40/1*	Thomas Bjorn	68 68 68 70 274
3	150/1	Alastair Forsyth	72 68 68 67 275
4	fav 13/2	Ernie Els	72 69 68 67 276
5	40/1	Stephen Leaney	70 69 69 71 279

6	G Turner	74 69 67 70 280	T38	R Pampling	69 75 72 72 288
T7	S Tait	72 71 68 70 281		Soren Hansen	72 73 71 72 288
	P Gow	71 69 70 71 281		G Simpson	75 67 73 73 288
	D Smail	70 70 69 72 281		T Elliott	71 74 73 70 288
	G Norman	73 71 69 68 281		K Storgaard	73 68 76 71 288
	J Skold	71 67 70 73 281		V Phillips	73 72 72 71 288
12	C Gray	67 74 71 70 282		B Rumford	71 74 69 74 288
T13	P Senior	71 72 69 71 283		J Lomas	71 71 69 77 288
	P Sjoland	69 71 71 72 283		J M Singh	70 72 71 75 288
	M Brier	72 67 71 73 283	T47	G Hutcheon	72 71 73 73 289
T16	N Kerry	74 69 72 69 284		P Moloney	74 71 71 73 289
	B Ogle	72 69 69 74 284		G Ogilvy	67 74 71 77 289
T18	M Clayton	69 70 76 70 285	T50	S Laycock	72 72 74 72 290
	S Gallacher	73 71 71 70 285		R Wessels	74 71 72 73 290
	A Cejka	72 66 70 77 285		R Chapman	70 72 74 74 290
	P O'Malley	68 71 69 77 285		K H Han	70 73 73 74 290
	P McGinley	71 70 70 74 285		G Coles	71 72 71 76 290
	J Bickerton	69 76 69 71 285	T55	B King	70 73 78 70 291
	C Parry	70 71 72 72 285		J Sandelin	72 72 71 76 291
T25	J Senden	70 75 71 70 286		T Mills	74 70 73 74 291
	R Jacquelin	71 72 72 71 286	T58	M Allen	71 72 74 75 292
	A Coltart	71 73 71 71 286		P Baker	72 72 73 75 292
	P Davenport	72 70 75 69 286		J Benepe	74 71 72 75 292
	Anders Hansen	71 70 75 70 286		P Lawrie	70 71 73 78 292
	S Struver	69 72 75 70 286		M Cain	73 69 71 79 292
	G Evans	73 70 70 73 286	63	E Walters	72 71 72 78 293
	C Hanell	74 69 70 73 286	T64	P Fowler	73 71 76 74 294
T33	S Kjeldsen	75 69 71 72 287		G Emerson	75 70 74 75 294
	Grant Dodd	73 70 74 70 287		C Gaunt	73 70 75 76 294
	S Tinning	70 74 73 70 287	67	J Moseley	72 73 74 76 295
	W Smith	67 73 74 73 287	68	A Wall	75 70 73 79 297
	W Riley	73 68 71 75 287	69	Terry Price	73 72 82 71 298

The main players to miss the cut (made at 1 over) were:-

P Price (+2)	R Goosen (+2)	I Garbutt (+2)	L Parsons (+2)
D Howell (+2)	A McLardy (+2)	N O'Hern (+3)	G Orr (+3)
H Otto (+3)	D Carter (+3)	J M Olazabal (+3)	P Nyman (+3)
C Hainline (+4)	T Gogele (+4)	M Farry (+5)	R Green (+5)
P Harrington (+5)	P Lonard (+5)	R Russell (+5)	K Druce (+6)
G Owen (+7)	P Broadhurst (+8)	R Claydon (+11)	J Rose (+11)

Steve Webster, 71 in R1, retired and Per-Ulrik Johansson withdrew after 75 in R1.

ROUND BY ROUND LEADERBOARD

FIRST ROUND

G Ogilvy	5 under
W Smith	5 under
C Gray	5 under
M CAMPBELL	4 under
T Bjorn	4 under
P O'Malley	4 under
R Goosen	4 under

SECOND ROUND

T Bjorn	8 under
M CAMPBELL	7 under
J Skold	6 under
A Cejka	6 under
P O'Malley	5 under
M Clayton	5 under
M Brier	5 under
S Leaney	5 under

THIRD ROUND

M CAMPBELL	14 under
T Bjorn	12 under
A Forsyth	8 under
P O'Malley	8 under
A Cejka	8 under
J Skold	8 under
S Leaney	8 under

FINAL ROUND

M CAMPBELL	20 under
T Bjorn	14 under
A Forsyth	13 under
E Els	12 under
S Leaney	9 under

In R2 the winds were strong and blustery.

In R3 the heat was extraordinary with temperatures reaching 47°C (115° Fahrenheit in 'old money').

In R4 rain caused a delay with Bjorn and Campbell (3 ahead) having 3 to play.

PUNTERS' POINTS

● What a performance! Michael Campbell followed up last week's victory in his home New Zealand Open with a superb performance here to win by 6 shots after shooting the day's lowest score on both Saturday and Sunday.

● After his second round Campbell said that he'd felt emotionally tired after last week's NZ Open win in front of over a hundred relatives. However the momentum of growing confidence overcame any mental let down (MLD).

● The Nappy Factor still rules OK! Campbell himself admits that he's a more relaxed and determined player since the birth of his son Thomas.

● He is proving to be another Duval. Massive talent yet unable to win....then after a breakthrough success he can't stop winning. It's a phenomenon that's worth looking for with very promising yet winless young players.

● Another triumph for the DYM system.

    > Here the top 2 were both DYMs

    > There have now been three DYM wins in the European tour's first four events.

1999 RESULT

1	250/1	Jarrod Moseley
T2	20/1	Bernhard Langer
T2	fav 11/2	Ernie Els
4	40/1	Peter Lonard
5	100/1	Bob May

1998 RESULT

1	33/1	Thomas Bjorn
2	22/1	Ian Woosnam
T3	16/1	J M Olazabal
T3	25/1	Padraig Harrington
T3	fav 7/1	Ernie Els
T3	66/1	Peter Baker

WINNERS IN THE LAST TEN YEARS

1991	Blaine McCallister	1996	Ian Woosnam
1992	Ian Baker Finch	1997	M A Martin
1993	Peter Senior	1998	Thomas Bjorn
1994	Mike Clayton	1999	Jarrod Moseley
1995	Robert Allenby	2000	Michael Campbell

PUNTERS' GUIDE

● Last year I said, "we must be very wary of European players who make their seasonal debut in this event." Course-record holder Padraig Harrington's 80 in R1 and Olazabal's missed cut proved the point this year. It is clearly wise to note the 'match-fit' players who have already played in South Africa as they have a clear advantage.

● Course experience here is important, both for club selection off the tee and in handling both the wind and the fast, undulating greens.

● Only two players have posted a top 20 finish here in each of the last three years.

> Ernie Els (easily the best record)   4th 2000: T2nd 1999: T3rd 1998

> Craig Parry   T18th 2000: 6th 1999: T20th 1998.

Both have played eleven of those twelve rounds at or under par.

● Other players with solid course form include

> Alex Cejka   T18th 2000 (R4 77): T13th 1999

> Peter O'Malley   T18th 2000 (R4 77): T19th 1999

> Jarmo Sandelin   MC 2000: T7th 1999: T8th 1998

> Andrew Coltart   T25th 2000: T13th 1999: T15th 1998

> and particularly Thomas Bjorn   2nd 2000: Won 1998

● The Heineken Classic from 2002-2005 inclusive will be staged at the Royal Melbourne Golf Club. As the 2001 World Match Play Championship will also take place at Royal Melbourne in 2001 there will be some course form for punters to use.

● Players whose profiles refer to this tournament include Ernie Els, Alex Cejka, Thomas Bjorn, John Senden, Craig Parry and Peter O'Malley.

THE GREG NORMAN HOLDEN INTERNATIONAL

Date	3rd - 6th February
Course	The Lakes G.C., Sydney
Par	73
Yardage	6,904
First Prize	£146,000
Total Purse	£773,000

THE TOURNAMENT

With a million dollars of Greg Norman's own 'hard earned' put into the kitty this is Australia's richest tournament. It is co-sanctioned by the Australasian and European tours.

THE COURSE

This is a tough par 73 course with plenty of water on the back nine. It demands accuracy off the tee. Scores can soar when the wind really blows, as they did last year on the final day. The 18th is a 195-yard par 3.

2000 ODDS

jt fav	12/1	Greg Norman	66/1*	Peter Senior
jt fav	12/1	Michael Campbell (PWW2)	66/1	Jarmo Sandelin
	14/1	Stuart Appleby	66/1	Paul McGinley
	20/1	Bernhard Langer	66/1*	Mathias Gronberg
	20/1	Thomas Bjorn	66/1	P-U Johansson
	22/1	Retief Goosen	80/1*	Jarrod Moseley
	25/1	Craig Parry	80/1*	Nick O'Hern
	28/1	Greg Turner	80/1*	Geoff Ogilvy
	33/1	Stephen Leaney	80/1*	Gary Orr
	40/1	Bob Estes	80/1*	Paul Gow
	40/1*	Aaron Baddeley	80/1*	Anthony Wall
	40/1	Padraig Harrington	80/1*	Alastair Forsyth
	40/1*	J M Olazabal	80/1*	John Daly
	50/1*	Peter O'Malley	80/1	Sven Struver
	50/1	Alex Cejka	80/1	Steen Tinning
	66/1*	Andrew Coltart	80/1	Brett Rumford
	66/1	Peter Lonard	80/1*	Phillip Price
	66/1	Patrik Sjoland		

2000 RESULT

1	100/1*	Lucas Parsons	70 66 70 67 273
2	66/1*	Peter Senior	67 70 71 69 277
T3	66/1	P-U Johansson	71 68 71 69 279
T3	66/1*	Andrew Coltart	67 68 73 71 279
5	125/1	David Park	68 65 73 74 280

T6	Anders Hansen	68 71 72 70 281		M Lane	73 71 73 72 289
	W Smith	74 67 67 73 281		T Gogele	76 68 72 73 289
T8	G Orr	78 65 72 67 282		K Druce	72 72 72 73 289
	Phillip Price	72 70 70 70 282		B Rumford	69 69 77 74 289
	S Gardiner (am)	75 69 68 70 282		R Willis	73 71 71 74 289
	I Garbutt	71 71 69 71 282		J Rose	76 69 70 74 289
	J M Olazabal	72 70 66 74 282	T50	D McKenzie	73 72 74 71 290
T13	R Wessels	72 70 71 70 283		P Burke	75 71 73 71 290
	C Hanell	71 66 75 71 283		T Gillis	73 73 72 72 290
	B Ogle	73 71 68 71 283		P Gow	72 74 70 74 290
	C Parry	71 72 66 74 283		V Phillips	71 73 71 75 290
T17	R Goosen	70 72 71 71 284		R Stephens	73 73 69 75 290
	C Hainline	71 70 71 72 284		A Cejka	73 68 73 76 290
	L-W Zhang	68 73 71 72 284		J Cooper	76 67 71 76 290
	G Evans	71 71 69 73 284	T58	R McFarlane	69 77 73 72 291
	P O'Malley	72 70 69 73 284		P Lonard	69 71 77 74 291
T22	S Appleby	73 69 75 68 285		M Ecob	74 72 71 74 291
	N Vanhootegem	75 68 73 69 285		S Kjeldsen	73 73 69 76 291
	A Baddeley (am)	71 73 72 69 285		C Gray	71 72 71 77 291
	A Bonhomme	72 74 68 71 285	T63	R Russell	75 71 74 72 292
	Soren Hansen	70 70 73 72 285		D Chopra	74 69 74 75 292
	A McLardy	71 66 75 73 285		S Bouvier	70 73 71 78 292
	Grant Dodd	69 71 71 74 285		S Allan	72 72 69 79 292
T29	B Langer	71 72 71 72 286		D Carter	70 71 70 81 292
	Rodger Davis	75 67 71 73 286	T68	P Golding	68 75 73 77 293
	N O'Hern	70 74 68 74 286		M Lafeber	66 74 74 79 293
	P McGinley	71 74 67 74 286	T70	G Coles	74 71 75 74 294
T33	S Laycock	78 68 70 71 287		M Roberts	72 73 74 75 294
	B Estes	71 74 70 72 287		A Forsyth	76 69 73 76 294
	P Broadhurst	72 74 69 72 287	T73	Terry Price	74 70 74 77 295
	W Riley	71 70 73 73 287		A Stolz	72 72 71 80 295
	J Moseley	69 71 73 74 287		P Baker	69 74 71 81 295
	S Tait	68 72 72 75 287	76	B Teilleria	74 70 74 78 296
T39	J Sandelin	73 71 73 71 288	T77	G Hutcheon	74 70 76 77 297
	M Scarpa	73 73 69 73 288		M Ferguson	71 75 73 78 297
	S Tinning	71 70 73 74 288	79	S Struver	73 68 76 81 298
	A Scott (am)	75 63 72 78 288	80	G Emerson	66 77 77 79 299
T43	J Daly	73 70 74 72 289			

The main players to miss the cut (made at level) were:-

S Webster (+1)	R Green (+1)	T Levet (+1)	D Smail (+1)
P Harrington (+2)	K Felton (+2)	S Leaney (+3)	G Turner (+3)
A Painter (+3)	J Bickerton (+3)	R Claydon (+4)	M Campbell (+4)
B Lane (+4)	D Howell (+4)	J M Singh (+4)	G Norman (+5)
A Wall (+5)	J Lomas (+5)	R Jacquelin (+6)	G Ogilvy (+6)
P Sjoland (+6)	J Senden (+7)	H Otto (+7)	R Pampling (+8)

Brett Partridge (76) retired after R1 and Markus Brier (74) was disqualified.

ROUND BY ROUND LEADERBOARD

FIRST ROUND

M Lafeber	7 under
G Emerson	7 under
A Coltart	6 under
P Senior	6 under
P Golding	5 under
A Hansen	5 under
S Tait	5 under
L-W Zhang	5 under
D Park	5 under
L PARSONS	2 under

SECOND ROUND

D Park	13 under
A Coltart	11 under
L PARSONS	10 under
P Senior	9 under
C Hanell	9 under
A McLardy	9 under

THIRD ROUND

L PARSONS	13 under
D Park	13 under
J M Olazabal	11 under
W Smith	11 under
P Senior	11 under
A Coltart	11 under
C Parry	10 under

FINAL ROUND

L PARSONS	19 under
P Senior	15 under
P-U Johansson	13 under
A Coltart	13 under
D Park	12 under

PUNTER'S POINTS

● 30-year-old 100/1 DYM Lucas Parsons' victory after a superb final round 67 highlighted three key punters' points

> He once more showed how important 'home' advantage is in pro golf. A Sydney resident ("this is a very special event to me") he was playing on his home-town course.

> This was the fifth European tournament of the season and the fourth won by a DYM player. Indeed it was the second successive week in which the top 2 were both DYMs.

> Parsons was a proven winner with three ANZ tour wins and two last year on the European Challenge tour. In fact he's now won a tournament every year (except 1996 when in the States) since 1993!

● Andrew Coltart's fine performance showed his resilience. 2 over after 10 holes, he then had the best run of his career to go 8 under for his last 8 holes in R1 with just 12 putts on the back nine as he went left hand below right when putting.

- MLD (eventually) rules OK! Michael Campbell's tremendous run of form stopped abruptly here as the mentally exhausted Kiwi missed the cut.

- Caddies count! Greg Norman had to play without his long-time caddie Tony Navarro. He had to do his own yardages, "for the first time in many years," and he too missed the cut in his event.

- How the early scores can deceive. R1 joint leaders Gary Emerson and Maarten Lafeber finished plumb last and T68th respectively!

1999 RESULT

(at The Lakes G.C., Sydney)

1	80/1	Michael Long
2	66/1	Michael Campbell
3	11/1	Bernhard Langer
T4	100/1	Rodney Pampling
T4	20/1	Peter O'Malley
T4	66/1	Anthony Painter

1998 RESULT

(at The Australian G.C., Sydney)

1	fav 6/1	Greg Norman
2	14/1	J M Olazabal
T3	16/1	Steve Elkington
T3	40/1	Stuart Appleby
T3	28/1	John Cook

WINNERS IN THE PAST

1993	Curtis Strange at The Lakes
1994	Anthony Gilligan at Royal Melbourne
1995	Craig Parry at The Lakes
1996	Peter Senior at Royal Melbourne
1997	Tournament not held
1998	Greg Norman at The Australian
1999	Michael Long at The Lakes
2000	Lucas Parsons at The Lakes

PUNTERS' GUIDE

- On the last three occasions that The Lakes course has been used for this tournament the top 2 have been Australasian players, pointing to the advantage the 'home' players have.

- The players with the best record in the last four stagings of this tournament (no event in 1997) are
  - > Peter Senior   2nd 2000: 7th 1999: T11th 1998: Won 1996
  - > Peter O'Malley   T17th 2000: T4th 1999: T11th 1998
  - > Lucas Parsons   Won 2000: T15th 1999: T19th 1996
  - > Craig Parry   T13th 2000: T12th 1999: T19th 1996
  - > Michael Campbell MC 2000 (MLD!): 2nd 1999: T16th 1996

- An early tee time is usually an advantage as the wind can get up in the afternoon.

- Sydney residents include Kenny Druce, Paul Gow, Neil Kerry, Peter Lonard, Brett Ogle, Peter O'Malley, Craig Parry, Robert Willis and Jeff Wagner.

- Players whose profiles refer to this tournament include Stuart Appleby, Craig Parry, Peter O'Malley, Gary Orr and Peter Senior.

THE BENSON AND HEDGES MALAYSIAN OPEN

Date	10th - 13th February
Course	Templer Park C.C., Kuala Lumpur, Malaysia
Par	72
Yardage	7,176
First Prize	£83,700
Total Purse	£518,000

THE TOURNAMENT

For the second successive year the Malaysian Open was co-sanctioned by the European and Asian tours.

THE COURSE

The Jumbo Ozaki-designed Templer Park course staged the Malaysian Open in 1995 and 1996. Since then it has changed a lot with water features coming into play on 11 holes.

2000 ODDS

fav	9/1	Retief Goosen	66/1	Craig Hainline
	12/1	Thomas Bjorn (did not start)	66/1*	K H Han
	14/1	Bernhard Langer	66/1*	J M Singh
	20/1	Andrew Coltart	66/1*	John Bickerton
	22/1	P-U Johansson	80/1	Soren Hansen
	25/1	Padraig Harrington	80/1	Wayne Riley
	28/1	Alex Cejka	80/1*	Prayad Marksaeng
	40/1	David Park	80/1*	Nico Van Rensburg
	40/1	Gary Evans	80/1*	Lian-Wei Zhang
	40/1	Mathias Gronberg	80/1*	Andrew McLardy
	40/1	Steen Tinning	80/1	Roger Wessels
	40/1	Patrik Sjoland	80/1	Gerry Norquist (DC)

2000 RESULT

1	125/1	**Wei-Tze Yeh**	**74 68 67 69 278**
T2	66/1	**Craig Hainline**	**71 72 69 67 279**
T2	25/1	**Padraig Harrington**	**68 69 72 70 279**
T2	100/1*	**Des Terblanche**	**71 71 69 68 279**
T5	fav 9/1	**Retief Goosen**	**68 74 67 71 280**
T5	80/1*	**Nico Van Rensburg**	**71 65 71 73 280**
T5	66/1*	**Jeev Milkha Singh**	**68 72 70 70 280**
T5	80/1*	**Lian-Wei Zhang**	**66 71 75 68 280**

T9	A Atwal	65 70 75 71 281			T Levet	70 71 73 73 287
	P-U Johansson	71 71 68 71 281			S Kjeldsen	72 72 72 71 287
T11	Soren Hansen	71 67 74 70 282			M Florioli	71 72 71 73 287
	J Payne	72 68 69 73 282			A McLardy	72 73 72 70 287
	W Riley	72 71 67 72 282		T43	J Skold	77 68 73 70 288
	T Purdy	67 72 76 67 282			S Tinning	67 70 71 80 288
	M Gronberg	73 72 67 70 282			P Gunasegaran	72 71 68 77 288
T16	Z Moe	75 68 71 69 283			A Kang	73 72 74 69 288
	G Norquist	71 68 72 72 283			S Taylor	69 73 71 75 288
	J Haeggman	70 69 75 69 283		T48	D Lynn	75 69 73 72 289
	B Langer	73 71 70 69 283			A Raitt	70 70 76 73 289
	S Daniels	72 71 70 70 283		T50	Per G Nyman	72 71 75 72 290
	D Park	70 72 72 69 283			T Ichihara	72 72 74 72 290
	T Sriroj	68 72 73 70 283			G Hamerton	73 72 70 75 290
T23	T Hussain	72 68 68 76 284			A Percey	71 74 69 76 290
	I Poulter	71 70 70 73 284		T54	S Dyson	70 70 76 75 291
	T-C Wang	72 71 72 69 284			A Pitts	71 70 75 75 291
	P Marksaeng	71 71 71 71 284			S Oide	71 71 73 76 291
	P Sjoland	70 71 68 75 284			H Buhrmann	70 72 76 73 291
	G Emerson	72 72 71 69 284		T58	T Yamanaka	72 69 75 76 292
T29	K H Han	75 68 74 68 285			A Johl	72 72 75 73 292
	G Hanrahan	74 70 68 73 285		T60	P Teravainen	73 71 75 74 293
	T Jaidee	67 71 68 79 285			M Scarpa	68 74 69 82 293
	J Randhawa	72 72 69 72 285			A Butterfield	68 75 72 78 293
	M Mouland	67 74 72 72 285		63	A Coltart	72 73 77 73 295
T34	A Cejka	74 66 74 72 286		T64	I Hutchings	69 72 76 79 296
	J Bickerton	72 71 73 70 286			B Ruangkit	68 74 80 74 296
T36	G Hutcheon	72 67 69 79 287		66	S Tajima	72 73 71 81 294
	R Coles	73 71 73 70 287		67	C Pena	72 73 74 79 298
	J Rutledge	73 71 73 70 287				

The main players to miss the cut (made at 1 over) were:-

J Rose (+2)	R Jacquelin (+2)	R Wessels (+2)	T Gillis (+3)
S Scahill (+3)	W S Kang (+4)	G Evans (+4)	C Chernock (+4)
K Druce (+5)	J Kingston (+6)	F Tarnaud (+7)	M Jonzon (+8)
C Plaphol (+9)	A Rizman (am) (+9)		

ROUND BY ROUND LEADERBOARD

FIRST ROUND		SECOND ROUND	
A Atwal	7 under	A Atwal	9 under
L-W Zhang	6 under	N Van Rensburg	8 under
T Jaidee	5 under	S Tinning	7 under
M Mouland	5 under	L-W Zhang	7 under
S Tinning	5 under	P Harrington	7 under
T Purdy	5 under	T Jaidee	6 under
W-T YEH	2 OVER!	S Hansen	6 under
		W-T YEH	2 under

THIRD ROUND		FINAL ROUND	
T Jaidee	10 under	W-T YEH	10 under
N Van Rensburg	9 under	C Hainline	9 under
T Hussein	8 under	P Harrington	9 under
S Tinning	8 under	D Terblanche	9 under
G Hutcheon	8 under	R Goosen	8 under
W-T YEH	7 under	N Van Rensburg	8 under
		J M Singh	8 under
		L-W Zhang	8 under

PUNTERS' POINTS

● Taiwan's 125/1 rank outsider Wei-Tze Yeh amazed bookies, punters and himself by gaining his first-ever professional win. It earned him a three-year exemption to the European tour.

● Padraig Harrington bogeyed the last 2 holes to finish runner up for the sixth time in four years! His hopes were dashed at the last when he was unlucky to be plugged in a greenside bunker.

● Nico Van Rensburg needed a birdie at the last to force a play-off. Instead he bogeyed and Yeh secured his victory. However do remember Nico V-R as he's won twice in Malaysia on the Asian PGA tour.

● Two European players were T3rd after R3 with a serious chance of winning their first tournament.

> Steen Tinning shot 80 (!) to finish T43rd!

> Greig Hutcheon shot 79 to finish T36th!

● Of the eight players to finish in the top 5 (or T5th) four were DYMs, and of the eight DYMs priced 66/1 to 80/1 three finished in the 'front 5'.

1999 RESULT

1	125/1	Gerry Norquist
T2	20/1	Alex Cejka
T2	40/1	Bob May
T4	20/1	Andrew Coltart
T4	40/1	Chawalit Plaphol
T4	125/1	Padraig Harrington
T4	125/1	Shaun Micheel

1998 RESULT

1	Ed Fryatt
won at second play-off hole	
2	Lee Westwood
T3	W-S Kang
T3	Christian Chernock
5	Paul McGinley

PUNTERS' GUIDE

● Five players have posted successive top 25 finishes in this tournament.

> Padraig Harrington   T2nd 2000: T4th 1999

> Craig Hainline   T2nd 2000: T11th 1999

> Prayad Marksaeng (Thailand) T23rd 2000: T9th 1999

> Gerry Norquist   T16th 2000: Won 1999

> Ter-Chang Wang   T23rd 2000: T11th 1999

Marksaeng is the only player to have scored par or better in those eight rounds!

● In making your selections proven ability to handle the high humidity and the grainy greens is very important.

● However with successive 125/1 winners in the last two years when this tournament has been on the European tour it should really carry a punter wealth warning attached!

● Players whose profiles point to this tournament include Craig Hainline, Padraig Harrington, Des Terblanche and Gerry Norquist.

THE ALGARVE PORTUGUESE OPEN

Date	17th - 20th February
Course	Le Meridien Penina Golf Club, Algarve, Portugal
Par	72
Yardage	6,875
First Prize	£166,600
Total Purse	£600,000

THE TOURNAMENT

This is a well-established tournament which returned to the Penina course for the third successive year.

THE COURSE

Set in its own 360-acre estate, woods and water come into play at almost every hole on this low-lying, tree-lined course. The greens are long and narrow. Precise shot making and accuracy off the tee are required. The par 3 13th and 16th (hardest) holes are both demanding at over 200 yards each. The final hole is a reachable 477-yard par 5. The wind can be an important factor.

2000 ODDS

fav	16/1	Ian Woosnam	50/1*	Peter Mitchell
	22/1	Gary Orr	50/1*	Peter Baker
	25/1	David Park	50/1*	Anders Hansen
	25/1	M A Martin	50/1	Stephen Gallacher
	25/1	Paul McGinley	50/1	Jamie Spence
	28/1	Ignacio Garrido	66/1*	Van Phillips (DC)
	28/1	Phillip Price	66/1	J-F Remesy
	33/1	Wayne Riley	66/1*	Alastair Forsyth
	33/1	John Bickerton	66/1*	Joakim Haeggman
	33/1	Costantino Rocca	66/1	Francisco Cea
	40/1*	Santiago Luna	66/1	Paul Eales
	40/1	Anthony Wall	66/1*	Tony Johnstone
	40/1	David Howell	66/1	Carl Suneson
	50/1*	Ian Garbutt	80/1	Jose Rivero
	50/1	Paul Broadhurst	80/1*	Emanuele Canonica

2000 RESULT

1	22/1	Gary Orr	69 67 70 69 275
2	28/1	Phillip Price	68 73 65 70 276
T3	25/1	Paul McGinley	70 72 67 70 279
T3	66/1*	Tony Johnstone	72 70 68 69 279
T3	100/1*	Brian Davis	73 68 73 65 279

T6	W Riley	70 70 71 69 280			E Darcy	73 73 72 71 289
	G Owen	72 71 68 69 280			R Chapman	73 73 77 66 289
	R S Johnson	73 70 69 68 280		T43	M Mouland	72 73 68 77 290
T9	E Canonica	73 69 70 69 281			S Kjeldsen	70 72 75 73 290
	I Woosnam	74 72 69 66 281			P Golding	74 73 70 73 290
T11	A Oldcorn	77 68 67 70 282			S Wakefield	75 71 74 70 290
	P Broadhurst	76 68 69 69 282		T47	N Ludwell	70 73 76 72 291
	J Haeggman	72 71 71 68 282			A Raitt	74 71 77 69 291
T14	N Fasth	72 70 70 71 283		T49	M A Martin	70 73 73 76 292
	C Suneson	74 69 70 70 283			G Brand Jr	75 70 73 74 292
	M Mackenzie	74 70 69 70 283			D Park	74 74 73 71 292
	A Wall	71 72 72 68 283			T Gogele	72 73 76 71 292
T18	J Bickerton	68 70 73 73 284		T53	K Carissimi	73 72 74 74 293
	O Edmond	71 72 70 71 284			D De Vooght	70 72 77 74 293
	P Mitchell	72 70 71 71 284			R Claydon	69 76 75 73 293
	I Poulter	71 74 70 69 284			M Lanner	77 71 74 71 293
	M Jonzon	76 69 71 68 284		T57	P Nyman	77 69 72 76 294
23	B Lane	72 70 72 71 285			R Winchester	73 74 71 76 294
T24	B Teilleria	71 73 69 73 286			I Pyman	76 69 73 76 294
	B Dredge	71 71 71 73 286			Rodolfo Gonzalez	71 73 75 75 294
	G Hamerton	72 72 70 72 286			D Lynn	70 75 76 73 294
	D Hospital	72 71 72 71 286		T62	S Field	70 75 76 74 295
	R Coles	73 72 73 68 286			M Blackey	72 74 76 73 295
T29	V Phillips	71 71 72 73 287			S Rowe	70 77 76 72 295
	A Forsbrand	72 74 69 72 287		T65	J Lomas	73 73 74 76 296
	F Lindgren	71 74 71 71 287			G Hutcheon	72 75 74 75 296
	Jamie Spence	72 68 77 70 287			G Murphy	73 75 74 74 296
	P Eales	72 74 71 70 287			O Eliasson	72 73 77 74 296
T34	Anders Hansen	71 72 71 74 288			P Affleck	72 74 77 73 296
	S Gallacher	73 72 70 73 288		T70	I Garrido	70 74 75 78 297
	A Forsyth	71 71 73 73 288			J Rose	72 71 77 77 297
	P Baker	72 71 73 72 288			G Emerson	74 73 74 76 297
	M Anglert	72 71 75 70 288		73	J Rivero	74 74 74 76 298
T39	F Cea	73 73 70 73 289		74	R McFarlane	75 73 77 76 301
	I Giner	71 70 75 73 289		75	E Boult	74 74 79 77 304

NOTE: The first 70 and ties made the cut.

The main players to miss the cut (made at 4 over) were:-

J-F Remesy (+5)	D Howell (+6)	J Skold (+6)	F Tarnaud (+6)
I Garbutt (+7)	H Nystrom (+7)	M Lafeber (+8)	C Rocca (+8)
D Smyth (+8)	M Florioli (+8)	P Linhart (+9)	

ROUND BY ROUND LEADERBOARD

FIRST ROUND

J Bickerton	4 under
P Price	4 under
G ORR	3 under
J Remesy	3 under
R Claydon	3 under

SECOND ROUND

G ORR	8 under
J Bickerton	6 under
W Riley	4 under
J Spence	4 under
P Price	3 under
I Giner	3 under
B Davis	3 under
N Fasth	3 under

THIRD ROUND

G ORR	10 under
P Price	10 under
P McGinley	7 under
T Johnstone	6 under
G Owen	5 under
N Fasth	5 under
J Bickerton	5 under
W Riley	5 under

FOURTH ROUND

G ORR	13 under
P Price	12 under
P McGinley	9 under
T Johnstone	9 under
B Davis	9 under

PUNTERS' POINTS

● 22/1 Gary Orr recorded his first tour success after shooting a brilliant eagle at the par 5 last hole to overtake Phillip Price who could only make a par.

● Five key points emerged:-

> The front 2 were both fully 'match fit' and confident having played really well in South Africa and Australia.

> Neither had played last week in the humidity of the Malaysian Open. It was noticeable that players like John Bickerton and Soren Kjeldsen, who had played in Malaysia, fell away when reaching the top places on the leaderboard, although Wayne Riley 'toughed' it out.

> 'Rusty' players making their seasonal debuts who have the game for Penina, such as Miguel Martin (T49th), Santiago Luna (MC) and Francisco Cea (T39th), were never in contention.

> Players with PMAs with Portugal regularly play well in the country, e.g. Price, Riley, Jonzon and Bickerton.

> The first 2, especially the winner, are accurate players, a major requirement on this tough track.

1999 RESULT

1	100/1	Van Phillips
won at the first play-off hole		
2	80/1*	John Bickerton
T3	33/1	Robert Karlsson
T3	16/1	Alex Cejka
T3	66/1	Santiago Luna

1998 RESULT

1	66/1	Peter Mitchell
T2	33/1	David Gilford
T2	80/1	Jarmo Sandelin
T4	33/1	Eduardo Romero
T4	66/1	Sam Torrance
T4	125/1	Jonathan Lomas

WINNERS IN THE LAST TEN YEARS

1991	Steven Richardson	Estela, Rio Alto
1992	Ronan Rafferty	Vila Sol, Vilamonra
1993	David Gilford	Vila Sol, Vilamonra
1994	Phillip Price	Penha Longa
1995	Adam Hunter	Penha Longa
1996	Wayne Riley	Aroeira, Lisbon
1997	Michael Jonzon	Aroeira, Lisbon
1998	Peter Mitchell	Le Meridien, Algarve
1999	Van Phillips	Le Meridien, Algarve
2000	Gary Orr	Le Meridien, Algarve

PUNTERS' GUIDE

● Best records over the three years at the Le Meridien course are held by :-

> Peter Mitchell   T18th 2000: T19th 1999: Won 1998

> John Bickerton   T18th 2000: 2nd 1999: T16th 1998

> Anthony Wall   T14th 2000: 6th 1999

> Wayne Riley   T6th 2000: T7th 1998

> Paul Broadhurst   T11th 2000: T9th 1999

> Tony Johnstone   T3rd 2000: T10th 1998

● It is worth noting that three of the last four winners have been first-time tour winners.

● This course places a premium on accuracy so do consult the driving accuracy and greens in regulation stats.

● Players whose profiles refer to this tournament include Ian Garbutt, Santiago Luna, Paul Broadhurst, Peter Mitchell, John Bickerton, Anthony Wall, Wayne Riley, Mark Davis, Niclas Fasth, Adam Scott and Paul McGinley.

THE DUBAI DESERT CLASSIC

Date	2nd - 5th March
Course	Dubai Creek Golf and Yacht Club, Dubai
Par	72
Yardage	6,853
First Prize	£141,660
Total Purse	£850,000

THE TOURNAMENT

This is the first tournament on the tour's 'Middle Eastern' swing. It was played at the Emirates golf club until last year, so the Dubai Creek course was being used for only the second time for this event.

THE COURSE

The Dubai Creek course is not long yet it demands accuracy off the tee with tough rough and water in play on 13 holes. Last year only thirty players beat par. The desert wind, the shemal, can be an important factor, as it was in R2 this year, but, despite the wind, the course played easier this year than in 1999 because the rough was not as severe.

2000 ODDS

fav	8/1	Colin Montgomerie	66/1	John Bickerton
	12/1	Lee Westwood	66/1*	Stephen Leaney
	14/1	Darren Clarke	66/1	Angel Cabrera
	20/1	Justin Leonard	66/1	Mathias Gronberg
	20/1	M A Jimenez	66/1	David Park
	25/1	Thomas Bjorn	66/1	Eduardo Romero
	40/1	Paul Lawrie	80/1	Patrik Sjoland
	40/1*	J M Olazabal	80/1	Anthony Wall
	40/1	Mark O'Meara	80/1	Jarmo Sandelin
	40/1	Gary Orr	80/1	David Howell (DC)
	40/1	Ian Woosnam	80/1	Ignacio Garrido
	40/1	P-U Johansson	80/1	Tony Johnstone
	50/1	Paul McGinley	80/1	M A Martin
	50/1	Alex Cejka	80/1	Costantino Rocca
	50/1	Andrew Coltart	80/1	J M Singh
	66/1*	Phillip Price	80/1	Peter Baker
	66/1*	Wayne Riley		

2000 RESULT

1	125/1	**Jose Coceres**	64 69 68 73	274
T2	50/1	**Paul McGinley**	67 72 70 67	276
T2	66/1	**Patrik Sjoland**	71 72 66 67	276
T4	150/1*	**Stephen Gallacher**	69 74 68 67	278
T4	40/1	**Paul Lawrie**	66 75 69 68	278
T4	12/1	**Lee Westwood**	64 75 68 71	278
T4	100/1	**Jamie Spence**	70 67 69 72	278

8	R Claydon	70 73 64 72 279		Soren Hansen	68 76 71 73 288
T9	A Forsyth	68 72 70 70 280		T Levet	74 69 71 74 288
	P Affleck	67 71 70 72 280		C Suneson	68 77 68 75 288
T11	R McFarlane	70 75 68 68 281		W Riley	68 76 68 76 288
	J Rivero	66 72 74 69 281	T46	P Lonard	69 78 74 68 289
T13	J Berendt	70 72 71 69 282		K H Han	75 72 73 69 289
	G Owen	68 70 74 70 282		R Muntz	69 76 73 71 289
	T Bjorn	67 71 72 72 282		M O'Meara	73 72 71 73 289
	V Phillips	71 70 69 72 282		C Montgomerie	71 75 70 73 289
T17	M A Martin	69 76 70 68 283		Brian Davis	76 71 68 74 289
	T Gogele	69 76 69 69 283		N Vanhootegem	74 72 69 74 289
	D Clarke	71 70 69 73 283		M A Jimenez	69 75 70 75 289
T20	P Mitchell	68 74 72 70 284	T54	L-W Zhang	71 73 75 71 290
	T Johnstone	72 74 68 70 284		P Baker	69 75 74 72 290
	J Bickerton	69 75 68 72 284	T56	J Lomas	70 77 73 71 291
	R Winchester	72 75 65 72 284		F Lindgren	70 76 72 73 291
T24	I Garbutt	66 76 74 69 285		Ricardo Gonzalez	71 75 71 74 291
	J-F Remesy	69 76 70 70 285		D Carter	69 77 69 76 291
	J M Olazabal	71 74 68 72 285	T60	Mark Davis	72 74 75 71 292
	D Park	71 71 69 74 285		D Lee	74 73 70 75 292
	J Sandelin	68 79 63 75 285		J Skold	70 73 72 77 292
T29	T Gillis	70 74 69 73 286	63	G Evans	69 70 77 77 293
	G Orr	68 75 70 73 286	T64	S Luna	70 74 75 75 294
	J Leonard	72 73 68 73 286		W-T Yeh	71 73 74 76 294
T32	B Dredge	70 77 70 70 287		D Howell	74 73 71 76 294
	R Chapman	67 78 71 71 287		J Payne	69 78 71 76 294
	S Webster	73 74 69 71 287	68	D Smyth	74 73 73 75 295
	E Romero	71 73 70 73 287	T69	A Bossert	74 72 74 76 296
	A Cejka	67 74 72 74 287		S Allan	71 76 70 79 296
T37	M Lanner	69 74 75 70 288	T71	G Murphy	68 79 75 75 297
	D Lynn	70 75 73 70 288		C Hanell	70 77 75 75 297
	J Randhawa	70 75 72 71 288	73	F Casas	71 76 73 78 298
	Phillip Price	73 74 70 71 288	74	P Downie	71 75 81 78 305
	A McLardy	74 72 70 72 288			

The main players to miss the cut (made at 3 over) were:-

I Woosnam (+4)	C Hainline (+4)	S Struver (+4)	H Otto (+4)
F Cea (+5)	A Cabrera (+5)	J Haeggman (+5)	J Rose (+5)
P Eales (+5)	A Hansen (+6)	M Gronberg (+6)	R Jacquelin (+7)
N Fasth (+7)	S Leaney (+7)	P Nyman (+7)	P-U Johansson (+8)
C Rocca (+9)	I Garrido (+9)	J M Singh (+9)	A Coltart (+10)
S Kjeldsen (+11)			

Paul Broadhurst withdrew in pain during R2 (would probably have missed the cut) with a damaged hand.

ROUND BY ROUND LEADERBOARD

FIRST ROUND		SECOND ROUND	
J COCERES	8 under	J COCERES	11 under
L Westwood	8 under	J Spence	7 under
I Garbutt	6 under	J Rivero	6 under
P Lawrie	6 under	T Bjorn	6 under
J Rivero	6 under	G Owen	6 under
		P Affleck	6 under

THIRD ROUND		FINAL ROUND	
J COCERES	15 under	J COCERES	14 under
J Spence	10 under	P McGinley	12 under
L Westwood	9 under	P Sjoland	12 under
R Claydon	9 under	S Gallacher	10 under
P Affleck	8 under	P Lawrie	10 under
P McGinley	7 under	L Westwood	10 under
P Sjoland	7 under		

In R2 the later players in particular faced the severe local wind (the shemal) at its worst. On average scores were 4 shots higher than in R1.

PUNTERS' POINTS

● He led from the start, played superbly in the wind in R2 and with his all-round game in first-class shape Jose Coceres deservedly won, to the delight of all those in Argentina who got up at 5 a.m. to watch him.

● The normal advice is to avoid players on their seasonal re-appearance because 'rustiness', especially in their short game, will prove too big a handicap. Coceres' 125/1 win on his seasonal debut showed that that is not always the case.

● There can be early value in golf tournaments, as the 66/1 quote about Paul McGinleys from Stan James proved. T3rd here last year and T3rd in his last tournament, he was 'real value' place only at 16½/1 as he posted another top 4 finish.

● Eight players proved themselves to be excellent wind players with good (below par) scores in R2. They were :-

>	Jose Coceres	69	>	Darren Clarke	70
>	Jamie Spence	67	>	David Park	71
>	Gary Evans	70	>	Paul Affleck	71
>	Van Phillips	70	>	Thomas Bjorn	71
>	Greg Owen	70	>	Brian Davis	71

● This year only eight players had four rounds at or under par. They were Paul McGinley, Patrik Sjoland, Jamie Spence, Alastair Forsyth, Paul Affleck, Jorge Berendt, Thomas Bjorn and Van Phillips.

1999 RESULT
(Dubai Creek G.C.)

1	66/1	David Howell
2	11/1	Lee Westwood
T3	50/1	Paul McGinley
T3	100/1	Mark James
T5	fav 8/1	Colin Montgomerie
T5	80/1	Ed Fryatt
T5	150/1*	Wayne Riley

1998 RESULT
(Emirates course)

1	16/1	J M Olazabal
2	200/1	Stephen Allan
T3	fav 8/1	Ernie Els
T3	100/1	Robert Karlsson
5	20/1	Ian Woosnam

WINNERS IN THE LAST TEN YEARS

1991	No tournament - Gulf War		1996	Colin Montgomerie
1992	Seve Ballesteros		1997	Richard Green
1993	Wayne Westner		1998	J M Olazabal
1994	Ernie Els		1999	David Howell
1995	Fred Couples		2000	Jose Coceres

PUNTERS' GUIDE

● We now have two years of course form at the 'Creek' and only four players have posted successive top 20 finishes.

> Lee Westwood   T4th 2000: 2nd 1999
> Paul McGinley   T2nd 2000: T3rd 1999
> Paul Affleck   T9th 2000: T15th 1999
> John Bickerton   T20th 2000: T15th 1999

● Thomas Bjorn lives in Dubai, met his wife there and represents Dubai golf at the Creek club so he does have local knowledge. This year he finished T13th with all rounds at or under par.

● Straight hitting and an ability to play in the wind are essential requirements for success on this course.

● The Emirates Golf Club, which was the tournament venue up to and including 1998, will once more host this event in 2001. In 1998 it was criticised as being too easy with wide fairways and large flat greens. It will doubtless be toughened up when it is used in 2001.

● Players whose profiles refer to this tournament include Jorge Berendt, Jamie Spence, Paul Affleck, Paul McGinley, Thomas Bjorn, Pierre Fulke, Jean-Francois Remesy and John Bickerton.

QATAR MASTERS

Date	9th - 12th March
Course	Doha Golf Club
Par	72
Yardage	7,268
First Prize	£83,330
Total Purse	£500,000

THE TOURNAMENT

This was the third Qatar Masters. The tournament is popular with the players because of the 'money no object' treatment they receive. The Doha Club is a private club owned by the State of Qatar.

THE COURSE

This is a long course that ironically does not necessarily favour the long hitters as the wins of Coltart, Lawrie and the second place (1998) of Sherborne show. The Bermuda greens are grainy and this year the rough was very tough. The winds can be very severe in the afternoons.

2000 ODDS

fav	16/1	Patrik Sjoland
	20/1	Paul McGinley
	20/1	Ian Woosnam
	28/1	Gary Orr
	28/1	Phillip Price
	33/1	P-U Johansson
	33/1	John Bickerton
	40/1	Andrew Coltart
	40/1	Jarmo Sandelin
	40/1	M A Martin
	40/1	David Park
	40/1	Alex Cejka
	40/1	Wayne Riley
	50/1	Stephen Gallacher
	50/1*	Eduardo Romero
	50/1	Angel Cabrera
	50/1	Jose Coceres (PWW)
	50/1	Jamie Spence
	50/1	Alistair Forsyth

50/1	Mathias Gronberg
50/1	Van Phillips
50/1	Tony Johnstone
66/1*	Stephen Leaney
66/1	Peter Lonard
66/1	Steen Tinning
66/1	Ignacio Garrido
66/1*	Peter Mitchell
66/1	Greg Owen
66/1	Peter Baker
80/1*	J M Singh
80/1	Gary Evans
80/1*	Brian Davis
80/1*	Costantino Rocca
80/1*	Ricardo Gonzalez
80/1*	Christopher Hanell
80/1*	Soren Kjeldsen
80/1*	Steve Webster

2000 RESULT

1	150/1	**Rolf Muntz**	**68 73 67 72 280**
2	20/1	**Ian Woosnam**	**71 75 71 68 285**
T3	50/1*	**Eduardo Romero**	**75 74 71 69 289**
T3	66/1*	**Stephen Leaney**	**70 74 70 75 289**
T5	80/1*	**Brian Davis**	**75 70 75 70 290**
T5	40/1	**M A Martin**	**73 73 71 73 290**

T7	J Coceres	74 73 71 73 291		S Luna	75 75 72 75 297
	P Fowler	72 72 73 74 291		Phillip Price	72 73 73 79 297
	P McGinley	72 70 74 75 291	T46	S Scahill	73 74 78 73 298
	S Kjeldsen	73 70 73 75 291		C Hanell	73 73 78 74 298
T11	S Webster	72 75 72 73 292		J Mellor	72 74 78 74 298
	A Butterfield	72 77 70 73 292		G Orr	70 74 79 75 298
	I Poulter	74 71 72 74 292		Jamie Spence	74 71 78 75 298
T14	A Cabrera	71 76 74 72 293		O Eliasson	75 75 73 75 298
	O Edmond	74 73 74 72 293		N Fasth	73 74 74 77 298
	M Brier	70 76 73 74 293		R Claydon	71 72 75 80 298
	D Carter	73 74 72 74 293	T54	P Lonard	67 78 78 76 299
	Soren Hansen	73 75 69 76 293		T Levet	72 73 76 78 299
T19	B Lane	71 79 74 70 294		R Byrd	78 71 72 78 299
	M Mackenzie	75 75 72 72 294		D Park	75 74 72 78 299
	P Baker	75 72 74 73 294		P-U Johansson	73 77 70 79 299
	P Sjoland	74 74 73 73 294	T59	G Evans	73 76 76 75 300
	W Riley	73 76 72 73 294		S Richardson	76 73 75 76 300
	P Nyman	77 72 71 74 294		M Farry	74 74 75 77 300
	C Suneson	74 73 72 75 294		M Anglert	72 72 77 79 300
	V Phillips	72 75 70 77 294		Ricardo Gonzalez	74 71 76 79 300
T27	R S Johnson	74 72 78 71 295		P Golding	72 75 74 79 300
	J Sandelin	74 74 75 72 295	T65	P Walton	73 77 78 73 301
	J Rivero	75 71 76 73 295		R McFarlane	74 75 77 75 301
	E Darcy	74 73 75 73 295		J M Carriles	74 76 74 77 301
	G Murphy	75 75 72 73 295		T Gogele	74 72 76 79 301
	D Lynn	68 76 77 74 295	T69	N Vanhootegem	73 75 80 74 302
	G Owen	71 78 72 74 295		F Cea	73 76 77 76 302
	M Gronberg	71 70 75 79 295		T Johnstone	76 73 75 78 302
T35	M Blackey	75 74 74 73 296		P Affleck	75 75 74 78 302
	J Bickerton	73 74 75 74 296		R Russell	74 75 74 79 302
	L-W Zhang	73 74 75 74 296	74	J Payne	73 76 73 81 303
	R Chapman	75 74 73 74 296	T75	S D Hurley	72 78 78 76 304
	C Hainline	73 76 72 75 296		A Bossert	76 74 78 76 304
T40	S Struver	72 76 77 72 297		S Field	75 75 76 78 304
	D Howell	78 72 75 72 297		J Skold	73 77 75 79 304
	A Cejka	72 77 75 73 297		B Dredge	74 76 71 83 304
	R Winchester	75 75 72 75 297			

The main players to miss the cut (made at 6 over) were:–

P Mitchell (+7)	S Tinning (+7)	M Lanner (+7)	D Borrego (+7)
M Davis (+7)	D Smyth (+8)	W-S Kang (+8)	A McLardy (+8)
R Wessels (+9)	I Garrido (+9)	E Boult (+9)	A Forsyth (+9)
R Jacquelin (+9)	S Gallacher (+10)	J Lomas (+11)	P Eales (+11)
J Rose (+12)	C Rocca (+15)	A Coltart (+15)	H Otto (+16)

Stephen Allan, Andrew Oldcorn, Joakim Haeggman, G Brand Jr, Massimo Scarpa and Seve Ballesteros all withdrew.

ROUND BY ROUND LEADERBOARD

FIRST ROUND

P Lonard	5 under
R MUNTZ	4 under
D Lynn	4 under
S Leaney	2 under
M Brier	2 under

SECOND ROUND

R MUNTZ	3 under
M Gronberg	3 under
P McGinley	2 under
R Claydon	1 under
S Kjeldsen	1 under

THIRD ROUND

R MUNTZ	8 under
S Leaney	2 under
S Kjeldsen	level
M Gronberg	level
P McGinley	level

FINAL ROUND

R MUNTZ	8 under
I Woosnam	3 under
E Romero	1 over
S Leaney	1 over
B Davis	2 over
M A Martin	2 over

Apart from the early hours on Thursday the gusting wind was really severe throughout the tournament.

PUNTERS' POINTS

● 5th here in the inaugural Qatar Masters in 1998, when he was the equal best player over the final 54 holes, Rolf Muntz had the proven course form here. He became the third successive winner who was recording his first tour victory.

● The tournament was dominated every day by the severe afternoon winds. A key pointer to note is the advantage of an early R1 tee time. Here five of the first 6 after R1 had morning tee times with Muntz's momentum created by an opening 68 shot from being in the third group out from the first tee.

● Ian Woosnam played particularly well, as he always does in the wind, to finish a very creditable 2nd. However his putting still does not match the quality of his iron play. In really windy conditions he can be followed with confidence as he proved with a truly memorable victory in the 1996 wind-ravaged Scottish Open.

● With two DYMs in the front 5 last year, and three in the frame again this year this is a tournament in which DYMs simply must be considered.

● The toughening of the course and the severity of the winds is shown by the number of players breaking par each year.

1998	67	1999	39	2000	2!!

1999 RESULT

1	125/1	Paul Lawrie
T2	150/1	Soren Kjeldsen
T2	66/1*	Phillip Price
4	125/1	John Bickerton
T5	125/1	Christopher Hanell
T5	66/1*	Raymond Russell
T5	80/1*	Jean Van de Velde

1998 RESULT

1	33/1	Andrew Coltart
T2	66/1	Patrik Sjoland
T2	200/1	Andrew Sherborne
4	200/1	Van Phillips
T5	40/1	Retief Goosen
T5	125/1	Rolf Munz
T5	80/1	David Carter

WINNERS OF THIS TOURNAMENT

1998	Andrew Coltart
1999	Paul Lawrie
2000	Rolf Muntz

PUNTERS' GUIDE

● With three Qatars now in the form book the players with a consistent record include:-

> Patrik Sjoland	T19th 2000: T11th 1999: T2nd 1998
> Paul McGinley	T7th 2000: T16th 1999: T21st 1998
> Ian Woosnam	2nd 2000: T8th 1999: T9th 1998
> Van Phillips	T19th 2000: 4th 1998
> Angel Cabrera	T14th 2000: T17th 1998
> Soren Kjeldsen	T7th 2000: T2nd 1999
> Retief Goosen	DNP 2000: T20th 1999: T5th 1998

● In making an outright selection go for a player with four key characteristics.

> An early R1 tee time

> Seeking his first tour win

> Proven ability in this tournament

> He is a big price

● This is not a course on which it is easy to play 'catch-up' so it will probably pay to continue to back the halfway leader each way.

> 1998 Andrew Sherborne finished T2nd

> 1999 Paul Lawrie won

> 2000 Rolf Muntz (joint halfway leader) won

As the above record shows it is a profitable policy.

● Players whose profiles refer to this tournament include Steve Webster, Soren Kjeldsen, Patrik Sjoland, Van Phillips, Angel Cabrera, Stephen Gallacher, Jose Coceres and Ian Woosnam.

THE MADEIRA ISLAND OPEN

Date	16th - 19th March
Course	Santo de Serra, Madeira
Par	72
Yardage	6,606
First Prize	£57,000
Total Purse	£343,000

THE TOURNAMENT

Invariably this tournament attracts the weakest field of the year so it gives a real opportunity to the lesser known players.

THE COURSE

The Santo de Serra track is on a cliff top exposed to the Atlantic winds. At just over 6,600 yards it is not long. However the ball travels further than usual in the thin air. The combination of that thin air and the winds make club selection difficult. Course experience is therefore an advantage.

2000 ODDS

fav	8/1	Paul McGinley	50/1	Diego Borrego
	12/1	John Bickerton	66/1*	Niclas Fasth
	16/1	Wayne Riley	66/1*	Marcus Brier
	20/1	Peter Mitchell	66/1	David Lynn
	25/1	Des Terblanche	66/1*	Eric Carlberg
	28/1	Steen Tinning	66/1	Bradley Dredge
	33/1	Christopher Hanell	80/1	Gary Emerson
	33/1	Andrew McLardy	80/1*	Thomas Gogele
	40/1	Ian Poulter	80/1	Richard S Johnson
	40/1	Nik Henning	80/1	Andrew Raitt
	50/1	Mats Lanner	80/1*	Alberto Binaghi
	50/1	Pedro Linhart (DC)	80/1*	Hennie Otto
	50/1*	Peter Fowler	80/1	Scott Rowe
	50/1	Jorge Berendt		

2000 RESULT

Pos	Odds	Player	Scores
1	66/1*	Niclas Fasth	66 72 68 73 279
T2	100/1*	Ross Drummond	72 69 73 67 281
T2	150/1	Mark Davis	73 69 72 67 281
T2	80/1	Richard S Johnson	70 75 67 69 281
T5	12/1	John Bickerton	70 70 73 69 282
T5	150/1	Raimo Sjoberg	71 69 70 72 282

Pos	Player	Scores		Pos	Player	Scores
T7	B Dredge	74 71 71 67 283			A McLardy	76 71 72 71 290
	D Lynn	74 72 69 68 283			E Carlberg	70 72 78 70 290
	M Brier	69 70 75 69 283			R J Derksen	74 70 70 76 290
	T Gogele	74 69 71 69 283		T46	J F Lucquin	75 70 73 73 291
T11	A Beal	70 70 75 69 284			P McGinley	70 77 69 75 291
	S Hurd	72 73 70 69 284			H Nystrom	73 71 72 75 291
13	F Cupillard	70 71 73 71 285			R Sailer	73 72 75 71 291
T14	F Valera	75 69 73 69 286			P Nilbrink	76 68 71 76 291
	C Hanell	69 73 73 71 286			E Boult	68 76 77 70 291
	Peter Lawrie	72 72 70 72 286		T52	L Kelly	71 74 75 72 292
	J Payne	71 69 68 78 286			M Pendaries	76 67 72 77 292
T18	S Cage	70 74 73 70 287			P Fowler	76 71 74 71 292
	J M Lara	71 69 77 70 287		T55	Stephen Dodd	72 72 72 77 293
	D Lee	72 71 71 73 287			M Lanner	70 75 75 73 293
	D Terblanche	71 74 69 73 287			L Claverie	71 76 73 73 293
	S Tinning	71 73 70 73 287			W Riley	74 74 74 71 293
	H Stenson	68 73 70 76 287			I Poulter	74 74 77 68 293
T24	A Binaghi	71 70 76 71 288		60	S Richardson	73 73 77 71 294
	J M Arruti	73 75 72 68 288		T61	C Pena	73 72 72 78 295
	D Borrego	72 67 74 75 288			C Rodiles	73 71 75 76 295
	M Lundberg	69 71 72 76 288			V Casado	73 74 73 75 295
	F Henge	71 71 70 76 288			I Hutchings	73 69 78 75 295
T29	M Blackey	77 67 73 72 289			P Linhart	75 73 73 74 295
	G Emerson	71 71 75 72 289			A Sobrinho	74 73 74 74 295
	P Mitchell	73 71 73 72 289			M Pilkington	71 76 75 73 295
	S Little	73 72 72 72 289			R Bland	70 78 76 71 295
	T J Munoz	74 72 72 71 289		T69	N Marin	68 74 78 76 296
	J Rose	74 72 71 72 289			J Rystrom	77 70 75 74 296
	J Berendt	72 73 72 72 289			L Stanford	73 75 73 75 296
	N Henning	70 72 74 73 289		T72	G Baruffaldi	72 75 76 74 297
	F Roca	71 73 74 71 289			G Houston	75 73 76 73 297
	S D Hurley	75 71 74 69 289		T74	J Dias	72 76 74 76 298
	S Rowe	73 70 71 75 289			P Hedblom	70 77 78 73 298
	J Robinson	72 74 78 65 289			J Umbelino (am)	69 74 81 74 298
T41	Peter Gustafsson	70 72 74 74 290		77	K Carissimi	79 69 76 76 300
	J Hepworth	72 74 73 71 290		78	F Widmark	75 71 75 80 301

The main players to miss the cut (made at 4 over) were:–

F Jacobson (+5)	D Smyth (+5)	A Butterfield (+5)	M Mouland (+5)
A Raitt (+6)	C Cevaer (+6)	M Florioli (+7)	S Henderson (+8)
S Ballesteros (+8)	S Field (+10)	A Sherborne (+10)	F Tarnaud (+11)
Shaun Webster (+11)	P Nyman (+13)	G Storm (am) (+13)	

ROUND BY ROUND LEADERBOARD

FIRST ROUND		SECOND ROUND	
N FASTH	6 under	N FASTH	6 under
E Boult	4 under	M Brier	5 under
N Marin	4 under	D Borrego	5 under
H Stenson	4 under	M Lundberg	4 under
M Lundberg	3 under	A Beal	4 under
M Brier	3 under	J Payne	4 under
C Hanell	3 under	J Bickerton	4 under
J Umbelino	3 under	R Sjoberg	4 under
		J M Lara	4 under

THIRD ROUND		FINAL ROUND	
N FASTH	10 under	N FASTH	9 under
J Payne	8 under	R Drummond	7 under
R Sjoberg	6 under	M Davis	7 under
H Stenson	5 under	R S Johnson	7 under
R S Johnson	4 under	J Bickerton	6 under
F Henge	4 under	R Sjoberg	6 under
M Lundberg	4 under		

PUNTERS' POINTS

● 2nd at Q School last November, Niclas Fasth used his course experience (T13th last year with all rounds at or under par) to lead from start to finish and record his first tour win.

● In life 'we move towards what we think about' (what do you think accident prone people think about?), and Fasth demonstrated this when after taking the R1 lead he said, "I want to be the next Swedish winner, I'm definitely going to be up there on Sunday, I just know it."

● The Racing Post was really scathing about this tournament describing it as a "farce" played "on a goat's track". I just do not agree with this elitist approach. It is obviously a tournament for the second, third, even fourth division players. So what? It still provides a real betting opportunity for members of the wide awake club. Indeed one of my selections, course-proven Ross Drummond, fresh from a good performance in a mini-tour event in Scotland, was T2nd at a tasty 100/1 to prove the point.

● DYMs came through to finish first and tied second. It was the FIFTH of the ten European tournaments so far to have had a DYM winner!

● Bookmakers don't always do their homework! Here we had an S Webster in the field. Of course if it was Steve he'd have an outstanding chance and so was given a 25/1 quote from Tote, Chandlers and 28/1 from Corals. However, it was actually Shaun Webster who was understandably priced from 100/1 - 150/1 elsewhere.

It's a good job bookies knew P Lawrie was Peter not Paul!

- Jim Payne, back after all sorts of medical problems, got into contention when 2nd after R3. 'Contention rust' then set in when he shot 78 in R4 to finish T14th.

1999 RESULT

1	125/1	Pedro Linhart
2	40/1	Mark James
3	18/1	David Howell
T4	25/1	John Bickerton
T4	28/1	Retief Goosen
T4	40/1	Padraig Harrington
T4	20/1	Andrew Coltart
T4	100/1	Diego Borrego
T4	125/1	Alberto Binaghi

1998 RESULT

1	80/1	Mats Lanner
2	80/1	Stephen Scahill
3	80/1	Andrew Beal
T4	25/1	Thomas Gogele
T4	66/1	Francesco Cea

WINNERS OF THIS TOURNAMENT

1993	Mark James	1997 Peter Mitchell (3 rounds)
1994	Mats Lanner (3 rounds)	1998 Mats Lanner
1995	Santiago Luna	1999 Pedro Linhart
1996	Jarmo Sandelin	2000 Niclas Fasth

PUNTERS' GUIDE

- Course experience on this quirky course, and in this thin air, really is vital. Best recent course records belong to:-

John Bickerton	T5th 2000: T4th 1999: T14th 1998: T13th 1997
Thomas Gogele	T7th 2000: T4th 1998: T7th 1997: T12th 1996
Ross Drummond	T2nd 2000: T10th 1999: T14th 1998
Fredrik Jacobson	T10th 1999: T10th 1998: 2nd 1997

- This year there were three Swedes in the top 6 with Fasth the fourth Swedish winner in the last eight years.... "Maybe it's because it's up a mountain and it can get cold, but Swedes do love to play here." So do consider Swedes in 2001.

- In its eight-year history Fasth at 27 was the youngest winner - 39, 37, 32, 32, 38, 36, 28 and 27 have been the winning ages for an average of 33.6.

- In the last six years of the thirty-seven players in the top 4 (or T4th)
  > 56.7% (i.e. twenty-one) started at or over 66/1
  > 35.1% (i.e. thirteen) started at or over 100/1

- Players whose profiles refer to this tournament include Diego Borrego, John Bickerton, Carl Suneson, Christopher Hanell, Fredrik Jacobson, Steen Tinning, Mark Davis, Iain Pyman, Richard S Johnson and David Lynn.

BRAZIL RIO DE JANEIRO 500 YEARS OPEN

Date	24th - 26th March
Course	Itanhanga G.C., Rio de Janeiro, Brazil
Par	72
Yardage	6,618
First Prize	£69,000
Total Purse	£416,000

THE TOURNAMENT

This was the first of two tournaments in 'the Brazilian Swing'.

THE COURSE

The course is short at just over 6,600 yards and provides real opportunities for the straight hitters and 'hot' putters to shoot low numbers.

2000 ODDS

fav	16/1	Padraig Harrington	50/1	Stephen Gallacher
	20/1	Eduardo Romero	66/1	R S Johnson
	20/1	Jose Coceres	66/1*	David Howell
	20/1	Angel Cabrera	66/1	Gary Evans
	25/1	M A Martin	66/1	Ignacio Garrido
	28/1	Jarmo Sandelin	66/1	Santiago Luna
	28/1	Robert Karlsson	80/1*	Joakim Haeggman
	33/1	Mathias Gronberg	80/1	Andrew McLardy
	33/1	David Park	80/1*	Nic Henning
	40/1	Steve Webster	80/1	Soren Kjeldsen
	50/1*	Brian Davis	80/1*	Thomas Gogele
	50/1	Des Terblanche	80/1*	Ricardo Gonzalez
	50/1	David Carter	80/1*	Anders Hansen
	50/1	Andy Forsyth	80/1	Jorge Berendt
	50/1	Peter Lonard	80/1*	Jose Rivero
	50/1	Greg Owen	80/1*	Costantino Rocca

2000 RESULT

1	150/1	**Roger Chapman**	70 64 71 65 270
		Chapman won at the second play-off hole	
2	fav 16/1	**Padraig Harrington**	67 62 71 70 270
3	20/1	**Jose Coceres**	66 70 69 66 271
T4	80/1*	**Joakim Haeggman**	69 67 69 68 273
T4	80/1	**Jorge Berendt**	67 67 69 70 273

T6	S Luna	70 70 65 70 275			M Florioli	71 70 74 68 283
	A Forsyth	65 62 75 73 275			F Jacobson	73 67 72 71 283
	M Gronberg	66 75 67 67 275			S Cage	71 67 71 74 283
	R Byrd	70 71 66 68 275		T44	G Norquist	70 68 74 72 284
	N Vanhootegem	71 71 70 63 275			P Nyman	70 71 74 69 284
T11	P Quirici	65 69 69 73 276			H Otto	67 70 75 72 284
	I Garrido	70 65 69 72 276			D A Vancsik	68 72 70 74 284
T13	G Owen	69 68 67 73 277			D Borrego	69 70 70 75 284
	P Eales	71 69 67 70 277			S Webster	76 67 69 72 284
	D Park	71 67 68 71 277			A Binaghi	69 72 74 69 284
	R Russell	68 66 70 73 277			T J Muyoz	73 70 71 70 284
T17	P Lonard	62 74 71 71 278		52	T Gillis	69 73 74 69 285
	R Coles	69 72 70 67 278		T53	K Carissimi	68 74 74 70 286
	J Rystrom	71 68 72 67 278			P Golding	65 73 75 73 286
	P R Martinez	73 68 67 70 278			M Anglert	76 66 69 75 286
T21	D Terblanche	72 67 69 71 279			I Pyman	70 67 73 76 286
	A Cabrera	68 71 70 70 279			I Giner	67 70 74 75 286
	F Cea	67 69 73 70 279			P Affleck	71 71 72 72 286
	P Fowler	73 65 70 71 279			O Eliasson	69 69 72 76 286
T25	G Hamerton	69 69 74 68 280		T60	A Raitt	72 71 74 70 287
	O Edmond	71 70 67 72 280			S Grappasonni	72 69 73 73 287
	M Mackenzie	68 75 69 68 280			J Mellor	72 68 74 73 287
	R Winchester	70 70 69 71 280			C Rocca	70 73 74 70 287
	J Sandelin	72 68 69 71 280			J Skold	71 72 74 70 287
T30	A Franco	74 67 66 74 281			S Richardson	69 74 70 74 287
	E Romero	68 70 72 71 281			A Butterfield	72 70 72 73 287
	R Karlsson	67 69 67 78 281		T67	R Jacquelin	68 75 76 69 288
	W A Miranda	70 70 70 71 281			S D Hurley	71 72 73 72 288
	D Lynn	69 72 69 71 281			J-F Remesy	70 73 74 71 288
	M Farry	67 73 67 74 281			J Rivero	69 74 76 69 288
T36	C Pena	73 68 71 70 282		71	G Rojas	71 72 74 73 290
	H Nystrom	72 69 70 71 282		T72	R Navarro	72 70 76 73 291
	J M Carriles	67 72 72 71 282			D De Vooght	70 72 77 72 291
	M A Martin	71 70 70 71 282			A Sherborne	69 73 76 73 291
T40	P Walton	69 72 76 66 283		75	D Cooper	72 69 76 79 296

The main player to miss the cut (made at 1 under) were:–

I Garbutt (E)	S Gallacher (E)	T Gogele (E)	A Hansen (E)
M Lafeber (E)	S Kjeldsen (E)	C Suneson (+1)	B Davis (+2)
A McLardy (+2)	R S Johnson (+3)	D Carter (+4)	M Jonzon (+4)
T Levet (+6)	Ric Gonzalez (+7)	P Nyman (+8)	N Henning (+8)

David Howell (76) and Gary Evans (72) both retired after R1.

ROUND BY ROUND LEADERBOARD

FIRST ROUND

P Lonard	10 under
A Forsyth	7 under
P Quirici	7 under
P Golding	7 under
J Coceres	6 under
M Gronberg	6 under
R CHAPMAN	2 under

SECOND ROUND

A Forsyth	17 under
P Harrington	15 under
R CHAPMAN	10 under
R Russell	10 under
P Quirici	10 under
J Berendt	10 under
I Garrido	9 under

THIRD ROUND

P Harrington	16 under
A Forsyth	14 under
P Quirici	13 under
J Berendt	13 under
R Karlsson	13 under
I Garrido	12 under
R Russell	12 under
G Owen	12 under
R CHAPMAN	11 under

FINAL ROUND

R CHAPMAN	18 under
P Harrington	18 under
J Coceres	17 under
J Haegmann	15 under
J Berendt	15 under

PUNTERS' POINTS

● Would you believe it? After 472 tournaments, twelve runner-up places worldwide and a return to Q School last November, Roger Chapman won his first tournament as a 150/1 no hoper.

● He had considered giving up last autumn, "Then Payne Stewart died. He wanted to play golf and couldn't, and I could play golf but wouldn't. I took a serious look at myself and went to Tour School and got my card back."

● Chapman won the play-off despite putting his ball in the water at the first extra hole as Harrington three putted for bogey!

● Padraig Harrington notched yet another 2nd-place finish. His seventh in eleven months, after 3 putting the first extra hole and finding the water at the second. So bogey-bogey in 'extra time' after a disappointing 71-70 finish will have left the jury out re. his 'bottle' when in serious contention.

● Alistair Forsyth, 2-shot leader at halfway, will also be concerned after a 4 over par final 36 holes.

● Joakim Haeggman was the only player to shoot four rounds in the sixties as his improved form this year continued.

PAST RESULTS AND RECENT WINNERS

This was the inaugural Rio de Janeiro 500 Years Open.

PUNTERS' GUIDE

● This tournament created little punter interest as it was played alongside the wall-to-wall TV coverage of the prestigious Players Championship and there was no course form to go on.

● The evidence of this year suggests that this short course favours the accurate straight hitters such as Chapman, Coceres and Berendt rather than the longer hitters.

● The driving distance stats for this tournament make interesting reading -

> Only two (Gronberg and Garrido) of the top 16 players were ranked in the top 10 for driving distance.

> None of the first 5 were in the top 15 for long hitting on this track.

● Perhaps not surprisingly the Argentinian players Jose Coceres (3rd) and Jorge Berendt (T4th) did well.

● This is clearly a course on which 'streakers can't keep it up' so do oppose them in the round after their low score.

> Alistair Forsyth   62 in R2 then 75 in R3
> Padraig Harrington   62 in R2 then 71 in R3
> Peter Lonard   62 in R1 then 74 in R2
> Roger Chapman   64 in R2 then 71 in R3

BRAZIL SAO PAULO 500 YEARS OPEN

Date	30th March - 2nd April
Course	Sao Paulo G.C., Sao Paulo, Brazil
Par	71
Yardage	6,646
First Prize	£78,667
Total Purse	£470,000

THE TOURNAMENT

This is the second tournament on 'the Brazilian Swing' in the week before the US Masters.

THE COURSE

This is an unusual course. It has five par 3s and four par 5s in a par of 71. The course is short and suits the accurate player as the rough is punishing. The greens are Bermuda and fast at 10 on the stimpmeter. The 'signature' hole is the 9th, a par 3 over water.

2000 ODDS

fav	12/1	Padraig Harrington	50/1	Jorge Berendt
	14/1	Jose Coceres	50/1	Santiago Luna
	20/1	Angel Cabrera	50/1	Steve Webster
	25/1	Mathias Gronberg	66/1*	Brian Davis
	25/1	Eduardo Romero	66/1*	Des Terblanche
	25/1	M A Martin	66/1	Raymond Russell
	28/1	David Park	80/1*	Olivier Edmond
	33/1*	Robert Karlsson	80/1*	David Lynn
	33/1	Alistair Forsyth	80/1*	Roger Chapman
	33/1	Jarmo Sandelin	80/1	Paul Eales
	40/1*	Joakim Haeggman	80/1	Francisco Cea
	40/1	Greg Owen	80/1*	Gary Evans
	40/1	Peter Lonard	80/1	Peter Fowler
	40/1	Ignacio Garrido	80/1	Richard S Johnson

2000 RESULT

1	fav 12/1	**Padraig Harrington**	69 68 65 68	270
2	125/1**	**Gerry Norquist**	69 71 64 68	272
T3	40/1	**Greg Owen**	68 70 71 65	274
T3	25/1	**Eduardo Romero**	68 69 69 68	274
T3	100/1	**Ian Poulter**	69 67 69 69	274
T3	200/1	**Pedro R Martinez**	69 68 68 69	274
T3	50/1	**Steve Webster**	71 66 68 69	274

T8	Anders Hansen	71 66 69 69 275		C Pena	70 68 73 71 282
	J-F Remesy	69 67 68 71 275		O Eliasson	72 70 69 71 282
	M A Martin	69 68 66 72 275		M Florioli	75 68 68 71 282
T11	R S Johnson	67 72 68 69 276		B Teilleria	70 72 67 73 282
	M Gronberg	73 68 65 70 276	T49	J Skold	68 72 75 68 283
T13	A McLardy	70 70 68 69 277		S D Hurley	74 69 70 70 283
	R Karlsson	70 69 68 70 277		R Winchester	74 68 70 71 283
	J Berendt	71 66 69 71 277		C Larrain	70 73 69 71 283
	M Blackey	70 63 71 73 277		D Terblanche	68 70 73 72 283
T17	P Affleck	66 72 72 68 278		F Roca	69 73 69 72 283
	J Rivero	71 66 71 70 278		A J Pedro	72 71 68 72 283
	G Rojas	70 73 65 70 278		N Vanhootegem	71 65 74 73 283
	A Sherborne	69 68 69 72 278		D Borrego	70 71 69 73 283
	D Park	67 67 68 76 278		F Jacobson	70 69 70 74 283
T22	T Levet	69 71 72 67 279	T59	P Edmond	72 71 70 71 284
	Brian Davis	73 67 70 69 279		T Gillis	72 68 72 72 284
	M Anglert	70 72 68 69 279		J Haeggman	70 71 71 72 284
	R Byrd	72 69 68 70 279		S Wakefield	70 72 70 72 284
	A Jose Da Silva	70 73 66 70 279		J Lomas	68 74 70 72 284
	K Storgaard	70 70 66 73 279		Ricardo Gonzalez	73 70 69 72 284
T28	A Cabrera	75 68 69 68 280		A Butterfield	72 69 70 73 284
	P Lonard	72 65 72 71 280		T J Munoz	67 68 75 74 284
	D De Vooght	73 68 68 71 280		A Franco	72 71 66 75 284
	C Suneson	69 72 68 71 280	T68	P Archer	70 72 74 69 285
	P Nyman	67 68 72 73 280		J Sandelin	71 70 72 72 285
	S Rowe	68 73 67 72 280	T70	A Binaghi	68 74 73 71 286
T34	P Fowler	69 73 71 68 281		S Watson	71 72 73 70 286
	A Beal	72 70 70 69 281	T72	Rodolfo Gonzalez	70 69 74 74 287
	P Quirici	71 71 69 70 281		R Felizardo	67 73 71 76 287
	J Coceres	69 73 67 72 281	74	J Hobday	75 68 72 73 288
	J M Kula	71 66 68 76 281	T75	R Russell	71 71 76 71 289
T39	R Chapman	73 70 71 68 282		I Garrido	70 69 72 78 289
	D Chopra	72 70 72 68 282		S Kjeldsen	72 68 70 79 289
	M Mouland	71 72 71 68 282	78	L Martins	69 72 79 73 293
	T Gogele	70 72 71 69 282	79	D A Vancsik	73 68 76 80 297
	D Lynn	72 70 71 69 282	80	P Nilbrink	73 70 77 78 298
	I Garbutt	72 69 71 70 282			

The main players to miss the cut (made at 1 over) were:–

S Luna (+2)	M Mackenzie (+2)	S Scahill (+2)	M Jonzon (+2)
A Forsyth (+2)	N Henning (+2)	F Tarnaud (+2)	O Edmond (+3)
G Evans (+3)	F Cea (+3)	M Farry (+3)	R Jacquelin (+4)
C Rocca (+4)	H Otto (+4)	Pl Eales (+4)	H Nystrom (+5)

ROUND BY ROUND LEADERBOARD

FIRST ROUND		SECOND ROUND	
P Affleck	5 under	M Blackey	9 under
T Munoz	4 under	D Park	8 under
D Park	4 under	T J Munoz	7 under
J Aderbal	4 under	P Nyman	7 under
R Felizardo	4 under	I Poulter	6 under
R S Johnson	4 under	J-F Remesy	6 under
P Nyman	4 under	N Vanhootegem	6 under
P HARRINGTON	2 under	P HARRINGTON	5 under

THIRD ROUND		FINAL ROUND	
P HARRINGTON	11 under	P HARRINGTON	14 under
D Park	11 under	G Norquist	12 under
M A Martin	10 under	G Owen	10 under
G Norquist	9 under	E Romero	10 under
J-F Remesy	9 under	P R Martinez	10 under
M Blackey	9 under	I Poulter	10 under
		S Webster	10 under

PUNTERS' POINTS

● A week after losing a play-off in Rio Padraig Harrington ended a run of seven (yes, seven) 2nd places in eleven months with a 2-shot victory in the Sao Paulo Open.

● Harrington had decided to play the two Brazil Opens after failing to make the World top 50 to get into the Players Championship. After his missed cut at Bay Hill he flew to Brazil.

● Miguel Martin (bogeys at the 8th & 9th), and David Park (double bogey at the 12th) went backwards as Gerry Norquist (birdied the last 3 holes) and Eduardo Romero (eagle at the last) surged forward.

● Matthew Blackey, after a brilliant 63 in R2 to take the halfway lead, found that streakers can't keep it up by shooting 71-73 to finish T13th.

● Angel Cabrera, a previous winner on the course, made a disastrous 4 over par start. Then finding his form he was 8 under for the last 54 holes.

● Fifty-eight players beat par to show how easy the course had played.

PAST RESULTS AND RECENT WINNERS

This was the first time this tournament has been part of the European tour.

PUNTERS' GUIDE

● Over the two weeks of the Brazilian Swing six players posted successive top 20 finishes:-

	This week	Last week
Padraig Harrington	W	2nd
Jorge Berendt	T13	T4
Mathias Gronberg	T11	T6
Greg Owen	T3	T13
Pedro Martinez	T3	T17
David Park	T17	T13

● One very interesting fact - Greg Owen was No. 1 for greens in regulation in both tournaments!

● The lowest individual rounds were by:-

	Brazil Sao Paulo	Rio de Janeiro
Gerry Norquist	64 (R3)	—
Greg Owen	65 (R4)	—
Gustavo Rojas	65 (R3)	—
Roger Chapman	—	64 (R2) 65 (R4)
Padraig Harrington	—	62 (R2)
Ignacio Garrido	—	65 (R2)
Paolo Quirici	—	65 (R1)
Alistair Forsyth	—	65 (R1) 62 (R2)
Santiago Luna	—	65 (R3)

● It is worth noting that 'local' players, fast-finishing Angel Cabrera, Pedro Martinez (T3rd) and course record (61) holder Eduardo Romero (T3rd), have fine form on this track.

THE 64TH US MASTERS

Date	6th - 9th April
Course	Augusta National, Augusta, Georgia
Par	72
Yardage	6,985
First Prize	$650,000
Total Purse	$3.5 million

PLEASE SEE PART 6.

THE EUROBET SEVE BALLESTEROS TROPHY

Date	14th - 16th April
Course	Sunningdale Old Course, Berkshire
Par	70
Yardage	6,601
First Prize	£92,000 per member of winning team
Runners Up	£55,000 per member of losing team

THE TOURNAMENT

The inaugural Eurobet Seve Ballesteros Trophy featured two teams of ten players. A total of 26 points was at stake through a series of foursomes, fourballs, greensomes and singles.

Each member of the winning team received £92,000 and each member of the losing side £55,000.

Great Britain & Ireland	Continental Europe
Colin Montgomerie (Capt)	Seve Ballesteros (Capt)
John Bickerton	Thomas Bjorn
Darren Clarke	Alex Cejka
Padraig Harrington	Sergio Garcia
David Howell	M A Jimenez
Paul Lawrie	Robert Karlsson
Gary Orr	Bernhard Langer
Phillip Price	J M Olazabal
Lee Westwood	Jarmo Sandelin
Ian Woosnam	Jean Van de Velde

THE COURSE

The Old course at Sunningdale is short at 6,601 yards and with only two par 5s has a par 70. It demands accuracy.

THE ODDS

	Highest Odds	Lowest Odds	
GB & Ireland	11/10	8/11	
Europe	11/8	10/11	
Tie	10/1	8/1	Europe won at 11/8

THE CORRECT SCORE

GB & Ireland		Continental Europe
9/1	13½ – 12½	10/1
10/1	14 – 12	11/1
11/1	14½ – 11½	14/1
14/1	15 – 11	16/1
16/1	15½ – 10½	20/1
20/1	16 – 10	25/1
25/1	16½ – 9½	40/1
40/1	17 – 9	66/1
50/1	17½ – 8½	100/1
80/1	18 – 8	150/1
125/1	18½ – 7½	250/1

WINNING RESULT

Europe won 13½ - 12½ at 10/1

TOP POINTS SCORER

GB & Ireland		Continental Europe	
11/4	C Montgomerie	4/1	S Garcia
9/2	D Clarke	5/1	B Langer
5/1	L Westwood	6/1	T Bjorn
8/1	P Harrington	6/1	J M Olazabal
10/1	P Lawrie	7/1	M A Jimenez
11/1	I Woosnam	2/1	J Van de Velde
20/1	G Orr	14/1	A Cejka
25/1	P Price	16/1	J Sandelin
25/1	J Bickerton	16/1	R Karlsson
50/1*	D Howell	50/1*	S Ballesteros

RESULT

1	5/1	Lee Westwood	4 pts	1	4/1	Sergio Garcia	3½ pts
T2	25/1	Phillip Price	2½ pts	T2	6/1	Thomas Bjorn	3 pts
T2	9/2	Darren Clarke	2½ pts	T2	5/1	Bernhard Langer	3 pts
T2	10/1	Paul Lawrie	2½ pts				
T2	8/1	Padraig Harrington	2½ pts				

THE INDIVIDUAL MATCHES

FIRST DAY'S PLAY

Morning foursomes (each team has one ball played alternately by each player)

C Montgomerie & I Woosnam beat J M Olazabal & M A Jimenez 2 and 1

D Clarke & L Westwood beat A Cejka & B Langer 4 and 3

P Harrington & P Price beat T Bjorn & R Karlsson 1 up

P Lawrie & G Orr lost to S Garcia and J Van de Velde 3 and 2

MORNING SCORE   GB & Ireland 3   Continental Europe 1

Afternoon fourballs (each player plays his own ball)

L Westwood & D Howell beat J M Olazabal & S Ballesteros 2 and 1

D Clarke & J Bickerton lost to M A Jimenez & T Bjorn 1 hole

I Woosnam & P Harrington lost to A Cejka & B Langer 2 and 1

C Montgomerie & P Lawrie lost to J Sandelin & S Garcia 3 and 2

AFTERNOON SCORE   GB & Ireland 1   Continental Europe 3

OVERALL SCORE   GB & Ireland 4   Continental Europe 4

SECOND DAY'S PLAY

Morning fourballs

These games were played in continuous rain on a saturated course.

I Woosnam & C Montgomerie lost to M A Jimenez & J M Olazabal 6 and 5

P Lawrie & G Orr beat J Sandelin & R Karlson 1 up

P Price & J Bickerton lost to T Bjorn & S Garcia 1 up

D Clarke & L Westwood beat A Cejka & J Van de Velde 3 and 1

SCORE   GB & Ireland 2   Continental Europe 2

OVERALL SCORE   GB & Ireland 6   Continental Europe 6

Afternoon greensomes (both players drive then select the better ball)

Because of Saturday's torrential rain these games were actually played on Sunday morning.

G Orr & P Lawrie halved with M A Jimenez & J M Olazabal

C Montgomerie & D Howell beat S Garcia & J Van de Velde 2 and 1

D Clarke & L Westwood lost to T Bjorn & B Langer 4 & 3

P Harrington & P Price halved with A Cejka & R Karlsson

GREENSOMES SCORE   GB & Ireland 2   Continental Europe 2

OVERALL SCORE   GB & Ireland 8   Continental Europe 8

FINAL DAY

Singles

Played on Sunday afternoon after the Greensomes were completed on Sunday morning

Colin Montgomerie lost to Seve Ballesteros 2 and 1

Darren Clarke halved with Sergio Garcia

John Bickerton lost to Jarmo Sandelin 2 and 1

Lee Westwood beat Thomas Bjorn 1 up

Phillip Price beat Alex Cejka 2 and 1

Ian Woosnam lost to Bernhard Langer 4 and 3

David Howell lost to Robert Karlsson 2 and 1

Gary Orr lost to J M Olazabal 2 and 1

Paul Lawrie beat Jean Van de Velde 5 and 4

Padraig Harrington beat M A Jimenez 1 up

SINGLES SCORE	GB & Ireland 4½	Continental Europe 5½
OVERALL FINAL SCORE	GB & Ireland 12½	Continental Europe 13½

THE SUMMARY

● It's easy to knock this tournament yet I do think it was a deserved success.

It provides valuable Ryder Cup-style experience as well as genuinely interesting TV viewing.

● It was refreshing, after the disgraceful scenes at Brookline last year in the Ryder Cup, to see a competitive serious match played in such fine spirit.

● Seve's singles victory over Monty on Sunday in the singles was probably the biggest surprise in this format ever. However a mentally-jaded Monty had played in all four games on Friday, Saturday and Sunday morning as well as pursuing his duties as captain. Seve got off to a 'flier' and held on for a memorable win.

PUNTERS' GUIDE

Outright Betting

1. Expect these matches to be very close indeed

   > In each of the last seven Ryder Cups there has never been more than 2 points between the sides.

   > In this inaugural Seve Ballesteros Trophy again there was only one point in it.

Match Betting

2. In the Ryder Cup it pays to oppose players in the singles who have played in all 4 rounds on the first two days so long as their opponent has already played.

> In 1997 there were five bets, and four wins at 15/8, 7/4, 11/8 and 5/4 with a 100% return on capital.

> In 1999 there were five bets and (like 1997) four wins for a 78% return on capital.

> In this inaugural Seve Ballesteros trophy in the singles there were the following bets (excluding those singles in which both players had played in all four matches).

*	Seve to beat Monty	WON 9/2
*	Phillip Price to beat Cejka	WON Evens
*	Padraig Harrington to beat M A Jimenez	WON Evens
*	Gary Orr to beat J M Olazabal	LOST 13/8
*	Thomas Bjorn to beat Lee Westwood	LOST 7/4
*	Jean Van de Velde to beat Paul Lawrie	LOST 11/8

So a much lower success rate than in the Ryder Cup (just 50%) probably because there is much less pressure in a more relaxed atmosphere here. Nevertheless there was a LSP of 3½ pts for a 6 pt stake and a 58.3% return on capital based on Eurobet (the sponsors) odds.

THE MOROCCAN OPEN

Date   20th - 23rd April
Course   Golf d'Amelkis Course, Morocco
Par   72
Yardage   7,280
First Prize   £68,000
Total Purse   £415,000

THE TOURNAMENT

This year the Moroccan Open celebrated its tenth anniversary, moving from its recent venue, the Golf Royal d'Agadir (fairway-grass problems) to the Golf d'Amelkis at Marrakech.

THE COURSE

At 7,280 yards Golf d'Amelkis is a long course with three of its par 3s measuring well over 200 yards. The final hole is a reachable par 5 with water on the right and provides a real challenge for a player striving to win. Without any real rough, reachable par 5s, large greens and calm weather, scoring was low before the final day when the wind got up and the greens were particularly fast.

2000 ODDS

fav	14/1	Patrik Sjoland	66/1		Thomas Gogele
	18/1	John Bickerton	66/1*		Marcus Brier
	22/1	Andrew Coltart	66/1*		Carl Suneson
	25/1	Wayne Riley	66/1		Nic Henning
	33/1	Peter Mitchell	66/1		Mark Davis
	33/1*	Jamie Spence	66/1		Ross Drummond
	33/1*	Van Phillips	80/1*		Soren Kjeldsen
	33/1*	Ignacio Garrido	80/1*		Thomas Levet
	33/1	Santiago Luna	80/1		Francisco Cea
	33/1	Joakim Haeggman	80/1		Roger Winchester
	40/1	Des Terblanche	80/1		Bradley Dredge
	50/1*	Chris Hanell	80/1*		Robin Byrd
	50/1	Roger Chapman			

2000 RESULT

1	33/1*	Jamie Spence	66 68 68 64 266
T2	100/1**	Ian Poulter	69 64 68 69 270
T2	200/1	Seb Delagrange	66 69 65 70 270
T2	80/1*	Thomas Levet	66 74 64 66 270
5	40/1	Des Terblanche	68 66 65 70 271

T6	P R Martinez	64 66 71 72 273		C Hanell	68 72 69 70 279
	A Scott (am)	66 66 69 72 273		J M Kula	73 67 67 72 279
T8	E Boult	67 70 69 68 274		M Pilkington	67 66 73 73 279
	B Dredge	67 68 68 71 274		D Smyth	68 70 71 70 279
	M Mackenzie	68 67 68 71 274		T Gogele	70 69 71 69 279
	I Garrido	68 64 67 75 274		F Henge	73 67 73 66 279
T12	M Olander	68 69 70 68 275	T 49	A Coltart	67 70 71 72 280
	Shaun Webster	69 65 70 71 275		R Coles	71 66 71 72 280
T14	R Byrd	71 68 69 68 276		R Jacquelin	67 72 70 71 280
	Ulrik Gustafsson	69 66 73 68 276		B Teilleria	70 70 70 70 280
	M Lundberg	66 72 69 69 276		J Bickerton	70 67 67 76 280
	S Rowe	68 68 70 70 276	T54	W Riley	73 67 70 71 281
	P Sjoland	71 65 70 70 276		V Phillips	66 69 75 71 281
	Mark Davis	69 70 71 66 276	T56	S Watson	70 70 68 74 282
	R Winchester	69 71 65 71 276		K Storgaard	70 69 68 75 282
	S Luna	68 67 69 72 276		K Carissimi	69 71 70 72 282
T22	R Chapman	69 67 71 70 277		S Hurd	71 69 70 72 282
	Stephen Dodd	70 66 72 69 277		Rodolfo Gonzalez	68 72 71 71 282
	O Eliasson	71 66 70 70 277	T61	F Cupillard	70 70 69 74 283
	J Haeggman	70 68 69 70 277		D Chopra	72 68 75 68 283
	S Grappasonni	70 70 67 70 277	T63	M Florioli	70 67 71 76 284
	N Henning	70 67 68 72 277		C Pottier	70 68 71 75 284
	T Gillis	71 68 66 72 277		F Roca	69 68 72 75 284
	S Kjeldsen	68 66 70 73 277		S D Hurley	73 66 72 73 284
	J M Lara	69 67 68 73 277		P Way	69 71 71 73 284
T31	F Andersson	70 68 70 70 278	T68	B Nelson	66 72 70 77 285
	P Sherman	70 66 71 71 278		F Lindgren	69 70 73 73 285
	D Higgins	68 70 69 71 278		T J Munoz	70 69 73 73 285
	A Raitt	71 69 69 69 278		I Pyman	68 69 76 72 285
	F Jacobson	65 71 70 72 278	T72	S Richardson	70 70 72 74 286
	P Mitchell	68 69 72 69 278		G Murphy	69 71 73 73 286
	M Eliasson	68 69 69 72 278	T74	N Cheetham	70 67 75 75 287
	K Eriksson	68 72 70 68 278		A Binaghi	70 70 74 73 287
	Peter Gustafsson	70 68 67 73 278	76	T Carolan	69 69 74 77 289
T40	A Butterfield	72 67 69 71 279	77	B Pettersson	68 72 74 76 291
	R Drummond	66 68 73 72 279	78	I Giner	67 72 74 80 293
	R J Derksen	69 67 72 71 279			

The main players to miss the cut (made at 4 under) were:–

S Henderson (-3)	E Canonica (-3)	J Rystrom (-3)	C Watts (-3)
J Wade (-2)	M Blackey (-2)	J Skold (-2)	G Emerson (-1)
P Hedblom (-1)	P Nyman (-1)	J Rose (E)	C Suneson (E)
E Carlberg (+2)	G Hutcheon (+2)	H Nystrom (+2)	P Walton (+3)
D Lee (+3)	S Cage (+4)	F Cea (+6)	

M Mouland (76) and Marc Pendaries (72) retired after R1.

ROUND BY ROUND LEADERBOARD

FIRST ROUND

P R Martinez	8 under
F Jacobson	7 under
S Delagrange	6 under
T Levet	6 under
J Dahlstrom	6 under
R Drummond	6 under
J SPENCE	6 under
V Phillips	6 under
M Lundberg	6 under
B Nelson	6 under
A Scott (am)	6 under

SECOND ROUND

P R Martinez	14 under
I Garrido	12 under
A Scott	12 under
M Pilkington	11 under
I Poulter	11 under
J SPENCE	10 under

THIRD ROUND

I Garrido	17 under
S Delagrange	16 under
D Terblanche	15 under
P Martinez	15 under
A Scott	15 under
I Poulter	15 under
J SPENCE	14 under

FINAL ROUND

J SPENCE	22 under
T Levet	18 under
I Poulter	18 under
S Delagrange	18 under
D Terblanche	17 under

PUNTERS' POINTS

● Jamie Spence thoroughly deserved this his second tour victory after a brilliant, faultless 64 on Sunday. Accuracy, superb putting and some fine work by Janet Squire his caddie were the highlights of superb Sky TV final-round coverage.

● Watch out for Ian Poulter. I had tipped him each way at 100/1 and he played really well to shoot just 31 over the final 9 holes to secure T2nd place after a birdie - eagle finish. He's a fine putter and a live candidate for Rookie of the Year.

● South African Des Terblanche obviously avoids dieticians, keep fit experts and weightwatchers, yet he can certainly putt as he proved to finish 5th.

● The big future star here was surely Aussie star amateur Adam Scott. An inspired 125/1 headline selection by Jeremy Chapman, he played well throughout, although his putting let him down on Sunday as he slipped to finish T6th to the delight of the bookies who had avoided an each-way payout.

● Pedro Martinez, fresh from his T3rd finish in San Paolo, is a 'feel' player who manipulates the ball and creates shots in his own idiosyncratic way. The former caddie from a family of twelve aims to secure his 2001 tour card.

● Given the bottle in last year's book after throwing away four winning chances in two years, Ignacio Garrido went into Sunday with a clear lead. However without his regular caddie, without his driver (damaged in R2) and without self belief, he shot 74 in R4 to finish T6th.

● With a DYM winner, a TYM T2nd and a further DYM T2nd this tournament again highlighted the value for punters in 'second division' tournaments.

1999 RESULT

Royal Agadir G.C.

1	40/1	M A Martin
won at the sixth play-off hole		
2	100/1	David Park
3	100/1	Klas Eriksson
T4	50/1*	Jorge Berendt
T4	125/1	Eric Carlberg

1998 RESULT

Royal Agadir G.C.

1	66/1	Stephen Leaney
2	fav 12/1	Robert Karlsson
3	100/1	Mathias Gronberg
T4	33/1	M A Martin
T4	150/1	Mark Davis

WINNERS IN PREVIOUS YEARS

1992	David Gilford	1997	Clinton Whitelaw
1993	David Gilford	1998	Stephen Leaney
1994	Anders Forsbrand	1999	M A Martin
1995	Mark James	2000	Jamie Spence
1996	Peter Hedblom		

PUNTERS' GUIDE

● This tournament over the last two years has provided real punter value

> 1999 75% of the players best priced from 33/1- 80/1 were DYMs

> 2000 42.8% of the players best priced from 33/1 - 80/1 were DYMs

So in 2001 be on the look out for improving, lesser-known players, like Poulter this year.

● In 2001 if the Golf Royal Agadir Club (the venue from 1992 to 1999, except 1996) is used again there will be a premium on accuracy.

However if the Golf d'Amelkis course is used once more then expect it to be toughened up. This year's form must then obviously be studied.

● Players whose profiles include references to this tournament include Tom Gillis, Mark Davis, Carl Suneson, Roger Chapman and Ian Poulter.

THE PEUGEOT SPANISH OPEN

Date	Friday, 28th April - Monday, 1st May
Course	Golf de Catalunya, Girona
Par	72
Yardage	7,204
First Prize	£105,000
Total Purse	£630,000

THE TOURNAMENT

This well established tournament has been won by only one Spanish player (Seve in 1982, 1985 and 1995) in the last two decades.

THE COURSE

After two years at El Prat the tournament this year moved to the Catalunya course which played host to the 1999 Sarazen World Open (p 191 of last year's book). The course, designed by Angel Gallardo and Neil Coles has reachable par 5s.

2000 ODDS

fav	13/2	Colin Montgomerie	66/1*	Peter O'Malley
	10/1	Sergio Garcia	66/1	Ian Poulter
	16/1	Thomas Bjorn	66/1*	Phillip Price
	20/1	M A Jimenez	66/1	Des Terblanche
	25/1	J M Olazabal	66/1	Steve Webster
	40/1	Jose Coceres	66/1	John Bickerton
	40/1*	Ian Woosnam	66/1	Alistair Forsyth
	50/1*	Eduardo Romero	80/1*	Greg Owen
	50/1	M A Martin	80/1*	Andrew Coltart
	50/1	Gary Orr	80/1*	Santiago Luna
	50/1*	Patrik Sjoland	80/1	Peter Mitchell
	50/1	Ignacio Garrido	80/1*	Thomas Levet
	50/1	P-U Johansson	80/1	Anthony Wall
	66/1*	Angel Cabrera	80/1	Van Phillips
	66/1*	Jarmo Sandelin (DC)	80/1*	Pedro Martinez
	66/1	Alex Cejka	80/1	Joakim Haeggman
	66/1*	David Park		

2000 RESULT

1	100/1*	Brian Davis	71 68 66 69 274
2	150/1*	Marcus Brier	69 70 67 71 277
T3	50/1*	Eduardo Romero	70 72 65 71 278
T3	100/1*	Peter Baker	70 73 71 64 278
5	fav 13/2	Colin Montgomerie	67 71 70 71 279

6	G Orr	68 73 68 71 280	T43	D Borrego	74 72 71 71 288
T7	G Evans	70 67 77 67 281		T Bjorn	68 76 73 71 288
	N Fasth	70 73 70 68 281		M Mackenzie	72 73 70 73 288
	C Rodiles	72 69 67 73 281		O Eliasson	71 76 68 73 288
T10	P Quirici	66 78 71 67 282		Soren Hansen	70 74 67 77 288
	V Phillips	73 70 70 69 282	T48	J Moseley	74 71 71 73 289
T12	M A Martin	73 74 68 68 283		D Howell	70 75 73 71 289
	D Robertson	65 76 73 69 283		P-U Johansson	69 78 72 70 289
	G Murphy	72 72 70 69 283		R S Johnson	71 76 67 75 289
	I Pyman	71 69 72 71 283	T52	P Sjoland	72 75 73 70 290
	S Garcia	70 74 66 73 283		E Boult	71 75 68 76 290
T17	G Owen	70 72 73 69 284	T54	T Levet	72 68 76 75 291
	J Quiros	66 70 77 71 284		J C Aguero	72 72 73 74 291
	A Coltart	70 69 73 72 284		D Hospital	72 73 74 72 291
	Phillip Price	70 73 69 72 284		Steve Webster	74 71 75 71 291
T21	M Florioli	73 74 69 69 285		H Otto	71 72 78 70 291
	A Cabrera	73 72 70 70 285		J Lomas	70 71 73 77 291
	Anders Hansen	71 73 70 71 285	T60	R Green	73 72 71 76 292
	S Rowe	70 71 70 74 285		D Lynn	73 70 74 75 292
	S Struver	68 74 69 74 285		R Coles	71 76 71 74 292
	T Gogele	72 70 67 76 285		G Brand Jnr	71 76 71 74 292
T27	O Edmond	72 73 72 69 286		T J Muyoz	72 72 74 74 292
	S Tinning	71 72 74 69 286		I Hutchings	72 74 73 73 292
	E Canonica	73 67 77 69 286		R Finch (am)	73 74 73 72 292
	R Chapman	74 71 70 71 286	T67	F Roca	72 73 72 76 293
	D De Vooght	72 70 72 72 286		A Forsyth	78 69 71 75 293
	C Suneson	71 70 70 75 286		J Sandelin	68 77 73 75 293
T33	J Bickerton	70 76 70 71 287		S Gallacher	71 74 76 72 293
	J M Olazabal	69 76 71 71 287		P Affleck	68 77 70 78 293
	D Carter	72 72 72 71 287	T72	B Lane	70 74 72 78 294
	J Coceres	73 70 73 71 287		J M Arruti	73 71 76 74 294
	N O'Hern	66 77 74 70 287		M Lanner	74 72 75 73 294
	I Woosnam	73 69 75 70 287		S Luna	75 68 78 73 294
	T Johnstone	71 70 74 72 287	76	D Gilford	73 72 76 74 295
	F Cea	69 76 70 72 287	77	E de la Riva (am)	71 73 76 76 296
	S Scahill	69 69 73 76 287	78	B Teilleria	72 73 74 78 297
	J Senden	71 69 71 76 287			

The main players to miss the cut (made at 3 over) were:–

R Wessels (+4)	G Emerson (+4)	J Berendt (+4)	P Mitchell (+4)
B Dredge (+4)	R Gonzalez (+4)	T Gillis (+4)	I Garrido (+4)
J Rivero (+4)	N Vanhootegem (+4)	S Kjeldsen (+4)	S Delagrange (+4)
I Garbutt (+4)	F Lindgren (+4)	J M Lara (+5)	R Claydon (+5)
P Martinez (+5)	A Forsbrand (+5)	J Haeggman (+5)	D Terblanche (+6)
S Ballesteros (+6)	M James (+6)	M Lafeber (+6)	A Cejka (+7)
D Park (+7)	M Farry (+7)	M A Jimenez (+7)	W Riley (+7)
J-F Remesy (+8)	A McLardy (+9)	I Poulter (+9)	P O'Malley (+10)
R Russell (+10)	P Linhart (+10)	R Jacquelin (+10)	A Sherborne (+11)
R Byrd (+12)	J Rose (+12)	R McFarlane (+12)	M Jonzon (+15)

Anthony Wall withdrew after R2 at 3 over par having just made the cut.

ROUND BY ROUND LEADERBOARD

FIRST ROUND		SECOND ROUND	
D Robertson	7 under	J Quiros	8 under
J Quiros	6 under	G Evans	7 under
P Quirici	6 under	C Montgomerie	6 under
N O'Hern	6 under	S Scahill	6 under
C Montgomerie	5 under	B DAVIS	5 under
G Hamerton	5 under	A Coltart	5 under
B DAVIS	1 under	M Brier	5 under

THIRD ROUND		FINAL ROUND	
B DAVIS	11 under	B DAVIS	14 under
M Brier	10 under	M Brier	11 under
E Romero	9 under	E Romero	11 under
C Rodiles	8 under	P Baker	10 under
C Montgomerie	8 under	C Montgomerie	9 under
G Orr	7 under		
T Gogele	7 under		

PUNTERS' POINTS

● R1 leader in the Alfred Dunhill in South Africa (finished T10th), T3rd in the Portuguese Open, and T5th in the Qatar Masters, Brian Davis here built on that superb form to post his first European tour win as a 100/1 DYM.

● Congratulations to Nick King who put him in at just 50/1 when 100/1 was the quote from Stan James and Ladrokes. It was Nick's last golf odds compilation for Sunderlands before he moves to join Stanley's internet service in Malta.

● 150/1 Marcus Brier was another DYM. Here he showed consistent form to finish in a career-best 2nd.

● T3rd 50/1 DYM Eduardo Romero has a fine record in this tournament and he maintained it thanks in part to the new (and illegal in USA) Callaway ERC driver which has given the Argentinian vital extra distance. However his putting is still solid rather than inspired.

● Peter Baker was T18th on this course in the Sarazen last year when he was T4th for greens in regulation, so he clearly had a chance if he could putt....and he did in a brilliant course record 64 in R4 to finish T3rd as another 100/1 DYM.

● The value of the DYM system was clearly illustrated here:-

> The first 4 were all DYMs.

> Davis' victory completed a transatlantic double as the first two home in America in the Shell Houston Open were also both 100/1 DYMs!!

1999 RESULT
(El Prat, Barcelona)

1	66/1*	Jarmo Sandelin
T2	20/1	M A Jimenez
T2	40/1	Ignacio Garrido
T2	50/1	Paul McGinley
T5	125/1	Jamie Spence
T5	150/1	Juan Carlos Aguero

1998 RESULT
(El Prat, Barcelona)

1	40/1	Thomas Bjorn
T2	80/1	Greg Chalmers
T2	fav 8/1	J M Olazabal
T4	33/1	Eduardo Romero
T4	66/1	Mark James

WINNERS IN THE LAST TEN YEARS

1991	Eduardo Romero	1996	Padraig Harrington
1992	Andrew Sherborne	1997	Mark James
1993	Joakim Haeggman	1998	Thomas Bjorn
1994	Colin Montgomerie	1999	Jarmo Sandelin
1995	Seve Ballesteros	2000	Brian Davis

PUNTERS' GUIDE

● With regular changes in venue there appears to be little pattern to recent results. However four facts do emerge:-

> Apart from Seve there has been no other Spanish winner in the last two decades.

> Outsiders have done well in recent years with eight (exactly 50%) of the sixteen players in the top 5 (or T5th) in the last three years starting at or over 66/1.

> The best tournament record is held by Eduardo Romero. Winner in 1991 he has finished in the top 6 in five of the last six years!

> The last two winners, Sandelin at 66/1 and Davis at 100/1, were both DYMs.

● Players whose player profiles refer to this tournament include Eduardo Romero, Miguel Angel Martin, Niclas Fasth, Adam Scott, Gary Evans, Miguel Angel Jimenez and Sergio Garcia.

THE NOVOTEL PERRIER FRENCH OPEN

Date	4th - 7th May
Course	Le Golf National, Paris
Par	72
Yardage	7,098
First Prize	£116,600
Total Purse	£700,000

THE TOURNAMENT

This year the 94th French Open returned to the National course in Paris, the regular venue in the previous eight years, before last year's move to Golf du Medoc in Bordeaux.

THE COURSE

This course has been toughened up in the last couple of years so that it now provides a severe examination. This Albatross course, opened in 1990, was designed by Hubert Chesneau and would probably be the Ryder Cup venue if that event ever came to France. The final hole is a 514-yard, reachable par 5 which can make for an exciting climax. This year some of the greens were in sub-optimal condition following a very wet spell early in the year.

2000 ODDS

fav	13/2	Colin Montgomerie	66/1*	Jamie Spence
	14/1	Retief Goosen (DC)	66/1	Peter Baker
	20/1	Michael Campbell	66/1	Andrew Coltart
	33/1*	Eduardo Romero	66/1	Ignacio Garrido
	40/1	Jose Coceres	66/1*	Greg Owen
	40/1	Robert Karlsson	66/1	Marcus Brier
	40/1	Greg Turner	66/1	Alex Cejka
	40/1	Jean Van de Velde	66/1*	Brian Davis (PWW)
	50/1*	Stephen Leaney	66/1	Peter O'Malley
	50/1*	Gary Orr (non runner)	66/1	Angel Cabrera
	50/1*	Paul McGinley	80/1*	Santiago Luna
	50/1	Jarmo Sandelin	80/1	Ian Poulter
	66/1*	M A Martin	80/1	David Park
	66/1*	Mathias Gronberg	80/1*	Dean Robertson
	66/1*	P-U Johansson	80/1	David Howell

2000 RESULT

1	fav 13/2	Colin Montgomerie	71 68 65 68 272
2	150/1	Jonathan Lomas	72 64 69 69 274
3	150/1	Rodger Davis	69 68 70 70 277
T4	125/1	John Senden	73 67 70 68 278
T4	150/1	Roger Wessels	69 70 72 67 278
T4	125/1	Fredrik Jacobson	71 70 69 68 278

T7	P O'Malley	68 75 68 68 279
	D Gilford	73 69 68 69 279
	R Coles	74 68 71 66 279
	J Van de Velde	68 74 68 69 279
	Soren Hansen	68 74 68 69 279
	C Rodiles	70 70 68 71 279
	A Coltart	69 68 70 72 279
	M Campbell	70 66 69 74 279
T15	N Vanhootegem	70 74 70 66 280
	S Luna	72 70 67 71 280
	J Coceres	70 71 71 68 280
	N O'Hern	69 70 71 70 280
	Anders Hansen	70 65 74 71 280
T20	R Byrd	69 71 71 70 281
	M A Martin	69 70 71 71 281
T22	D Smyth	70 73 72 67 282
	S Leaney	71 72 68 71 282
	Ricardo Gonzalez	74 70 69 69 282
	V Phillips	76 69 69 68 282
	S Rowe	70 72 68 72 282
	N Joakimides	73 69 71 69 282
	A Cejka	70 70 69 73 282
	D Park	71 69 69 73 282
	F Roca	67 68 72 75 282
T31	R Karlsson	71 72 68 72 283
	R Green	73 71 67 72 283
	S Kjeldsen	70 69 72 72 283
	A Binaghi	66 73 71 73 283
	J Haeggman	69 68 73 73 283
T36	R Goosen	73 70 73 68 284
	G Murphy	76 69 68 71 284
	I Garrido	72 73 72 67 284
	Jamie Spence	73 69 73 69 284
	S Tinning	69 70 74 71 284
T41	A Wall	71 72 73 69 285
	G Owen	70 72 70 73 285
	E Romero	73 67 73 72 285

T44	G Hamerton	71 72 73 70 286
	A Forsyth	73 71 72 70 286
	O Edmond	70 74 70 72 286
T47	M Gronberg	71 72 75 69 287
	J Rivero	70 75 75 67 287
	J-F Remesy	70 70 74 73 287
T50	S Gallacher	72 70 71 75 288
	G Rojas	70 73 71 74 288
	T Levet	75 70 71 72 288
	B Dredge	71 71 73 73 288
	R Winchester	69 71 75 73 288
	S Struver	73 67 71 77 288
T56	S Ballesteros	72 71 72 74 289
	B Teilleria	72 72 72 73 289
	P Lonard	70 70 76 73 289
T59	O Eliasson	72 70 75 73 290
	P Baker	74 69 76 71 290
	R Jacquelin	75 69 75 71 290
	Brian Davis	71 73 71 75 290
	D Lynn	73 72 72 73 290
	F Tarnaud	74 71 74 71 290
	M Mackenzie	73 68 72 77 290
T66	C Hainline	72 71 72 76 291
	S Allan	68 77 70 76 291
T68	S Delagrange	73 70 73 76 292
	P McGinley	70 74 74 74 292
	P-U Johansson	72 73 77 70 292
T71	L Alexandre	71 74 76 72 293
	B Lecuona (am)	70 73 76 74 293
T73	R Claydon	72 71 76 75 294
	I Poulter	77 68 71 78 294
75	P Golding	73 70 75 77 295
76	G Ogilvy	74 70 75 77 296
77	M Jonzon	71 74 72 81 298
78	M Cain	74 70 80 83 307
	J Sandelin	68 67 78 Disq.

The main players to miss the cut (made at 1 over) were:–

J Moseley (+2)	R Muntz (+2)	D Borrego (+2)	P Quirici (+2)
J Berendt (+2)	F Cea (+2)	B Lane (+2)	H Otto (+2)
I Garbutt (+2)	P Mitchell (+2)	T Gillis (+2)	I Pyman (+3)
J Skold (+3)	P Linhart (+3)	M Florioli (+3)	M Lanner (+3)
A Sherborne (+3)	A McLardy (+3)	J Rose (+4)	G Brand Jr (+4)
G Evans (+4)	M Farry (+4)	E Canonica (+4)	C Hanell (+4)
A Cabrera (+4)	M Davis (+5)	C Rocca (+5)	G Emerson (+5)
D Hospital (+5)	L Parsons (+6)	P Walton (+7)	M Brier (+8)
W Riley (+8)	E Darcy (+8)	D Robertson (+9)	M Scarpa (+9)
P Nyman (+9)	P Eales (+10)	A Bossert (+10)	C Cevaer (+10)
A Forsbrand (+13)	P Fowler (+15)		

I Hutchings (78), N Ludwell (80), D de Vooght (73), M Lafeber (78), R McFarlane (78), D Howell (80), S Scahill (79), Greg Turner (74) and G Hutcheon (76) all retired.
David Carter (75) withdrew.

ROUND BY ROUND LEADERBOARD

FIRST ROUND		SECOND ROUND	
A Binaghi	6 under	F Roca	9 under
F Cea	5 under	J Sandelin	9 under
F Roca	5 under	Anders Hansen	9 under
J Sandelin	4 under	J Lomas	8 under
Soren Hansen	4 under	M Campbell	8 under
J Van de Velde	4 under	A Coltart	7 under
S Allan	4 under	R Davis	7 under
P O'Malley	4 under	C MONTGOMERIE	5 under
C MONTGOMERIE	1 under		

THIRD ROUND		FINAL ROUND	
C MONTGOMERIE	12 under	C MONTGOMERIE	16 under
J Lomas	11 under	J Lomas	14 under
M Campbell	11 under	R Davis	11 under
A Coltart	9 under	J Senden	10 under
R Davis	9 under	R Wessels	10 under
C Rodiles	8 under	F Jacobson	10 under
F Roca	8 under		

On Friday play was incomplete with sixty-two players still to finish when lightning prevented further play.

Play was suspended during R3 on Saturday when Miguel Martin refused to carry on when he heard thunder. A backlog of players waiting to play developed so play was suspended. Nevertheless, the round was completed on Saturday.

PUNTERS' POINTS

● Colin Montgomerie came into this tournament worried about his putting and started an uneasy, unfancied and untipped favourite. However once more he left as the clear winner having taking the lead late on Saturday when he shot 65 in R3.

- "I began the third round very relaxed and that was because my wife came in yesterday afternoon and it does relax me when I can go out for dinner with her instead of looking at the four walls of my room." So now we have the 'her indoors' factor to add to MLD, PMAs and IBC!

- Brilliant eagles on the 14th and the last holes in R4 gave Monty his twenty-third (!!) European tour victory.

- After his sparkling early season form it was sad to see Kiwi star Michael Campbell return to his old ways on Sunday as his patience fell as his score increased. T2nd after R3, he finished T7th to mirror his collapse here two years ago (T1st after R3, he finished T11th).

- As usual a Bank Holiday Monday created time pressure on compilers to the punters' benefit.

  > of the twenty-six players best priced from 33/1 to 80/1 inclusive half (thirteen) were DYMs.

  > of the eighteen players at 100/1 ten were DYMs

  > so of the forty-four players best priced from 33/1 to 100/1 inclusive twenty-three (52.3%) were DYMs.

- Extrovert Swede Jarmo Sandelin had an extraordinary tournament.

  > In R1 he was 100% both for driving accuracy and greens in regulation.

  > At halfway at 9 under he was the joint leader

  > He shot a poor 6 over par 78 in R3

  > In R4 exasperated by his poor putting he bent his putter over his knee and proceeded to putt with it. He was, therefore, disqualified for using a club whose characteristics he had changed!

1999 RESULT

(Golf du Medoc, Bordeaux)

1	20/1	Retief Goosen

won at the second play-off hole

2	33/1*	Greg Turner
T3	33/1	Santiago Luna
T3	150/1*	Jose Coceres
T5	150/1	Eamonn Darcy
T5	20/1	Ian Woosnam
T5	150/1	Jorge Berendt

1998 RESULT

(Le Golf, National, Paris)

1	80/1	Sam Torrance
T2	125/1	Massimo Florioli
T2	150/1	Olivier Edmond
T2	14/1	Bernhard Langer
T2	66/1	Mathew Goggin

WINNERS IN THE LAST TEN YEARS

1991	Eduardo Romero	1996	Robert Allenby
1992	M A Martin	1997	Retief Goosen
1993	Costantino Rocca	1998	Sam Torrance
1994	Mark Roe	1999	Retief Goosen
1995	Paul Broadhurst	2000	Colin Montgomerie

PUNTERS' GUIDE

● When held at the Golf National course this has become a tournament for outsiders. In the last five French Opens held on this track of the twenty-eight players who finished in the top 5 (or T5th).

> eighteen (64.28%) started at or over 66/1

> fourteen (50%) started at or over 80/1

> twelve (42.85%) started at or over 100/1

● Best records on this course in 1997, 1998 and 2000 are held by

> Alex Cejka	T22nd 2000: T11th 1998
> Michael Campbell	T7th 2000: T11th 1998
> Jean Van de Velde	T7th 2000: T16th 1998
> Jarmo Sandelin	Disq 2000: T11th 1998: 14th 1997
> Retief Goosen	T16th 1998: Won 1997
> Robert Coles	T7th 2000: Disq 1998: T8th 1997
> Van Phillips	T22nd 2000: T29th 1998: T3rd 1997
> Andrew Coltart	T7th 2000: MC 1998: T3rd 1997
> Jose Coceres	T15th 2000: MC 1998: T5th 1997

● In 2001 the venue moves to the Lyon G.C. Villette d'Anthon.

● Players whose profiles refer to this tournament include Robert Coles, Van Phillips, Santiago Luna, Jarmo Sandelin, Retief Goosen, Jean Van de Velde and Peter O'Malley.

THE BENSON AND HEDGES INTERNATIONAL OPEN

Date	11th - 14th May
Course	Brabazon course, the Belfry, Sutton Coldfield
Par	72
Yardage	7,118
First Prize	£166,660
Total Purse	£1 million

THE TOURNAMENT

This well-established tournament moved to its third venue having been held previously at St Mellion (1990-95) and the Oxfordshire (1996-99).

THE COURSE

The Brabazon course at the Belfry was being used on the tour for the first time since the 1992 English Open. Remodelled since, with over 120 key changes to its layout, the course will be used for the 2001 Ryder Cup.

2000 ODDS

fav	6/1	Colin Montgomerie (PWW)	66/1*	Robert Karlsson
	14/1	Lee Westwood	66/1	Paul McGinley
	16/1	Darren Clarke	66/1	M A Martin
	25/1	Michael Campbell	66/1	Peter O'Malley
	25/1	Retief Goosen	66/1	Phillip Price
	33/1	Thomas Bjorn	66/1	Greg Turner
	33/1	Padraig Harrington	80/1*	Jamie Spence
	33/1	M A Jimenez	80/1	Mathias Gronberg
	33/1	Bernhard Langer	80/1	Angel Cabrera
	40/1	J M Olazabal	80/1	David Park
	40/1	Paul Lawrie	80/1	Brian Davis
	50/1	Eduardo Romero	80/1	Ignacio Garrido
	50/1	Ian Woosnam	80/1	P-U Johansson
	50/1	J Van de Velde	80/1	Santiago Luna
	50/1	Jose Coceres	80/1	Des Terblanche
	50/1	Stephen Leaney	80/1	Peter Baker
	66/1	Andrew Coltart	80/1	John Bickerton

2000 RESULT

1	40/1	J M Olazabal	75 68 66 66 275
2	66/1	Phillip Price	69 72 68 69 278
T3	50/1	Jose Coceres	74 74 68 67 283
T3	66/1	Andrew Coltart	75 71 71 66 283
T5	125/1	Stephen Gallacher	76 71 69 71 287
T5	125/1	Anthony Wall	75 69 73 70 287
T5	fav 6/1	Colin Montgomerie	76 69 73 69 287
T5	100/1	Adam Scott (am)	71 75 67 74 287

T9	J Lomas	71 71 73 73 288		D Terblanche	76 74 73 71 294
	P O'Malley	73 75 69 71 288		R Jacquelin	77 73 75 69 294
	J-F Remesy	73 76 70 69 288	T44	I Woosnam	77 73 68 77 295
	M A Jimenez	76 72 71 69 288		G Owen	76 69 75 75 295
	A Cabrera	72 72 77 67 288		Ricardo Gonzalez	78 72 71 74 295
T14	J Van de Velde	70 75 70 74 289		C Suneson	73 78 73 71 295
	J Senden	73 73 69 74 289		D Robertson	72 78 76 69 295
	G Ogilvy	73 75 68 73 289	T49	D Park	75 72 73 76 296
	Anders Hansen	76 73 72 68 289		S Luna	78 72 73 73 296
T18	P McGinley	73 71 72 74 290		S Tinning	75 74 75 72 296
	B Langer	76 70 73 71 290	T52	M Campbell	78 73 72 74 297
	R Green	78 69 72 71 290		P Lonard	77 72 75 73 297
	M Florioli	76 75 68 71 290	T54	R Byrd	71 76 73 78 298
T22	P Mitchell	76 74 67 74 291		M Blackey	75 75 72 76 298
	P Quirici	73 73 72 73 291		P Affleck	76 73 75 74 298
	I Poulter	73 74 72 72 291		B Dredge	77 73 76 72 298
	N Fasth	75 75 70 71 291		L Westwood	77 74 76 71 298
	T Gillis	77 74 70 70 291	T59	D Gilford	75 75 70 79 299
	D Clarke	78 72 72 69 291		O Eliasson	74 77 75 73 299
T28	R Karlsson	76 70 70 76 292	T61	M A Martin	75 76 69 80 300
	D Carter	79 70 68 75 292		D Hospital	76 69 78 77 300
	C Rocca	74 70 74 74 292	T63	S Kjeldsen	79 71 71 80 301
	Brian Davis	76 73 71 72 292		J Berendt	74 76 78 73 301
	N O'Hern	75 74 71 72 292	65	A Sherborne	75 73 76 78 302
	Soren Hansen	75 76 70 71 292	T66	J Bickerton	73 76 73 81 303
T34	M Lafeber	77 72 68 76 293		J Payne	75 74 77 77 303
	I Garbutt	76 71 72 74 293		F Cea	76 75 75 77 303
	E Romero	75 73 74 71 293	T69	E Boult	76 75 73 80 304
	C Rodiles	74 77 72 70 293		P Senior	76 75 76 77 304
T38	S Struver	76 71 70 77 294		S Torrance	77 72 79 76 304
	G Brand Jr	71 80 70 73 294	72	M Scarpa	77 72 75 81 305
	K Storgaard	81 69 71 73 294	73	B Lane	77 74 83 78 312
	D Lynn	77 72 73 72 294	74	P Harrington	71 69 64 Disq

The main players to miss the cut (made at 7 over) were:–

G Rojas (+8)	M Farry (+8)	J Haeggman (+8)	P Lawrie (+8)
S Webster (+8)	N Vanhootegem (+8)	P Eales (+8)	E Darcy (+8)
F Jacobson (+8)	R Coles (+9)	P-U Johansson (+9)	M Davis (+9)
G Turner (+9)	T Bjorn (+9)	O Karlsson (+9)	G Emerson (+9)
D Cooper (+9)	H Otto (+9)	J Moseley (+10)	S Allan (+10)
J Robinson (+10)	T Gogele (+10)	S Leaney (+10)	C Hanell (+10)
R Goosen (+10)	A Forsyth (+10)	D Howell (+10)	V Phillips (+10)
P Walton (+10)	J Skold (+10)	R Russell (+11)	M Lanner (+11)
L Parsons (+11)	R S Johnson (+11)	M McNulty (+11)	D Borrego (+11)
M Mackenzie (+11)	I Pyman (+12)	P Baker (+12)	R Chapman (+12)
J Rivero (+12)	G Hutcheon (+13)	T Johnstone (+13)	J Spence (+13)
M Brier (+13)	A Forsbrand (+13)	E Canonica (+13)	S Scahill (+14)
R McFarlane (+14)	M Gronberg (+14)	M James (+14)	R Claydon (+15)
R Winchester (+16)	W Bennett (+16)	W Riley (+16)	F Lindgren (+16)
R Wessels (+16)	C Hainline (+17)	A McLardy (+18)	S Ballesteros (+25!)

Des Smyth, Philip Golding, Gary Evans and Padraig Harrington were all disqualified.

ROUND BY ROUND LEADERBOARD

FIRST ROUND

P Price	3 under
J Van de Velde	2 under
T Gogele	2 under
A Scott (am)	1 under
J Lomas	1 under
G Brand Jr	1 under
R Byrd	1 under
P Harrington	1 under
J M OLAZABAL	3 over!

SECOND ROUND

P Harrington	4 under
P Price	3 under
J Lomas	2 under
J M OLAZABAL	1 under
P McGinley	level
C Rocca	level
A Cabrera	level
A Wall	level

THIRD ROUND

P Harrington	12 under (then disq.)
J M OLAZABAL	7 under
P Price	7 under
A Scott	3 under
J Van de Velde	1 under
J Lomas	1 under
J Senden	1 under

FINAL ROUND

J M OLAZABAL	13 under
P Price	10 under
J Coceres	5 under
A Coltart	5 under
A Wall	1 under
A Scott	1 under
C Montgomerie	1 under
S Gallacher	1 under

Thursday	On a cold and very blustery day the Belfry provided a severe test with only eight players beating par.
Friday	Conditions were easier although the course was still the winner.
Saturday	Warm and sunny with only a slight breeze.
Sunday	Calm and warm again after a delayed start because of early fog.

PUNTERS' POINTS

● Padraig Harrington's sensational disqualification on Sunday morning when the 5-shot (7/1 on) leader (fully discussed in Part 1) put a completely new complexion on the final round.

● After hearing the news Olazabal said, "I just couldn't believe it.....my approach to the day became completely different because now it's Phillip and I leading." Olly went on to his first win since the 1999 US Masters and his first on the European tour since the 1998 Dubai Desert Classic — and that after an opening 75!

● 66/1 Phillip Price had to settle for his third runners-up spot of a very consistent season and here he was the only player NOT to shoot an over par round.

● Jonathan Lomas, 2nd last week, was also consistent, being one of only three players to have all his rounds at or under 73, to finish T9th.

● Adam Scott, so impressive when 6th in the Moroccan Open, once more took the eye here to finish T5th. He's one helluva player with one helluva future!

● With only eight players beating par the Belfry was the clear winner and will provide a severe test for the Ryder Cup players in 2001.

1999 RESULT
(The Oxfordshire)

1	fav 12/1	Colin Montgomerie
T2	125/1	Angel Cabrera
T2	50/1*	P-U Johansson
T4	28/1	M A Jimenez
T4	125/1	Diego Borrego

1998 RESULT
(The Oxfordshire)

1		33/1	Darren Clarke
2		100/1	Santiago Luna
T3		150/1	Massimo Florioli
T3		20/1	Thomas Bjorn
T5	jt fav	10/1	Colin Montgomerie
T5		33/1	Retief Goosen

WINNERS OVER THE LAST TEN YEARS

1991	Bernhard Langer	1996	Stephen Ames
1992	Peter Senior	1997	Bernhard Langer
1993	Paul Broadhurst	1998	Darren Clarke
1994	Seve Ballesteros	1999	Colin Montgomerie
1995	Peter O'Malley	2000	J M Olazabal

1990-95 St Mellion
1996-99 The Oxfordshire
2000   The Belfry

PUNTERS' GUIDE

● In last year's players profile I suggested that Padraig Harrington would be, "worth a bet to be a 'shock' 40/1 winner in May at the Belfry in the Benson and Hedges International." Well we got the 40/1 (available Tuesday morning) and we got the 'shock'.... on Sunday with his disqualification. Perhaps in 2001 we'll get the winner when Padraig must once more have an outstanding chance.

● Clearly in 2001 this year's course form must be consulted. However the form figures of the top 8 players in their last tournament shows the crucial importance of recent form.

Olazabal	33	Gallacher	67 - 50	Harrington	Won
Price	17	Wall	Wd - 41	Coceres	33 - 15
Monty	5 - Won	Coltart	17 - 7	Scott	6

So (including Harrington) of the top players

> all made the cut in their last tournament

> two were playing after a victory, another two after a top 10, and another two after a top 20.

OK....it's only one year....nevertheless it seems fair to conclude that the Belfry is not the place to 'find your game'—so remember in 2001 to look for in-form players.

● Players whose profiles that refer to this tournament include Padraig Harrington, Niclas Fasth, Paolo Quirici, Anthony Wall, Richard Green and Miguel Angel Jimenez.

THE DEUTSCHE BANK OPEN

Date	18th - 21st May
Course	Gut Kaden, Hamburg, Germany
Par	72
Yardage	7,085
First Prize	£266,660
Total Purse	£1.6 million

THE TOURNAMENT

This very valuable tournament invariably attracts a very strong field, and this year it had the biggest-ever European purse. The full 1999 European Ryder Cup team plus Tiger Woods and Nick Price were in the field. The winner receives a five-year European tour exemption.

THE COURSE

Gut Kaden is a flat, dull, tree-lined course on which the wind can play a decisive part. Indeed being near the sea it has links characteristics. In calm weather it can be a birdie-eagle paradise for the aggressive player.

2000 ODDS

fav	5/2	Tiger Woods (DC)	80/1*	Jose Coceres
	10/1	Colin Montgomerie	80/1	Andrew Coltart
	16/1	Jesper Parnevik	80/1	Gary Orr
	20/1	Darren Clarke	80/1	Jean Van de Velde
	25/1	Sergio Garcia	80/1	Eduardo Romero
	33/1	Nick Price	80/1	Robert Karlsson
	33/1	J M Olazabal (PWW)	80/1	Phillip Price
	33/1	Padraig Harrington	80/1	Ian Woosnam
	33/1	Lee Westwood	80/1	M A Martin
	40/1	Bernhard Langer	80/1	Paul McGinley
	50/1	Michael Campbell	80/1	Peter O'Malley
	50/1	M A Jimenez	80/1	Angel Cabrera
	66/1*	Thomas Bjorn	80/1	Paul Lawrie
	66/1*	Retief Goosen		

2000 RESULT

1	33/1	Lee Westwood	71 69 69 64 273
2	200/1*	Emanuele Canonica	69 69 71 67 276
T3	fav 5/2	Tiger Woods	70 70 67 70 277
T3	80/1	Jean Van de Velde	69 71 70 67 277
T3	80/1	Ian Woosnam	71 71 69 66 277

T6	G Ogilvy	72 71 66 69 278			G Turner	73 72 70 71 286
	M A Jimenez	67 69 73 69 278			R Rafferty	72 71 69 74 286
	C Montgomerie	73 70 68 67 278		T45	M Brier	72 73 69 73 287
T9	S Kjeldsen	77 67 66 69 279			R S Johnson	72 69 73 73 287
	D Howell	71 69 72 67 279			P Golding	72 73 69 73 287
	G Orr	73 66 72 68 279			S Struver	72 71 74 70 287
	P McGinley	73 65 72 69 279			Phillip Price	72 69 71 75 287
T13	R Goosen	68 71 71 70 280			G Murphy	74 69 73 71 287
	Brian Davis	72 68 72 68 280			B May	71 68 74 74 287
T15	P Lawrie	68 73 70 70 281		T52	P Eales	75 68 74 71 288
	D Clarke	72 69 68 72 281			N Vanhootegem	70 74 73 71 288
T17	P Mitchell	71 72 67 72 282			M McNulty	70 74 70 74 288
	I Poulter	71 70 72 69 282			Jamie Spence	73 72 71 72 288
	P Harrington	73 70 69 70 282			V Phillips	73 70 71 74 288
	M A Martin	69 71 71 71 282			E Darcy	71 72 74 71 288
	P Baker	71 69 71 71 282			J Skold	72 73 73 70 288
	Nick Price	72 71 70 69 282			A Cejka	73 69 78 68 288
T23	J Parnevik	70 73 68 72 283		T60	Rodger Davis	72 71 73 73 289
	A Cabrera	75 69 67 72 283			J Berendt	72 73 72 72 289
	S Webster	72 67 73 71 283			J Robinson	74 71 78 66 289
T26	J Haeggman	69 71 73 71 284			S Allan	69 74 73 73 289
	M James	74 70 70 70 284			N O'Hern	72 70 75 72 289
	M Campbell	74 66 71 73 284		T65	I Garrido	72 73 72 73 290
	B Teilleria	70 75 70 69 284			J Sandelin	74 71 70 75 290
	R Jacquelin	71 72 68 73 284		T67	L Parsons	71 72 67 81 291
T31	P O'Malley	72 72 70 71 285			M Farry	71 73 72 75 291
	S Garcia	72 70 71 72 285			C Hainline	73 72 71 75 291
	P Quirici	70 73 71 71 285		T70	Ricardo Gonzalez	72 73 72 75 292
	D Hospital	69 74 69 73 285			C Rocca	71 73 74 74 292
T35	J Bickerton	72 73 70 71 286		T72	D Robertson	71 72 74 76 293
	T Bjorn	75 70 73 68 286			M Jonzon	72 73 74 74 293
	M Gronberg	71 74 70 71 286			K Storgaard	71 72 75 75 293
	D Carter	72 73 71 70 286		T75	T Johnstone	71 74 72 78 295
	R Chapman	68 74 72 72 286			C Suneson	74 70 76 75 295
	J M Olazabal	75 65 74 72 286		77	Anders Hansen	75 70 77 74 296
	S Leaney	70 70 74 72 286		78	S McGregor	72 73 77 81 303
	D Lynn	74 68 74 70 286				

The main players to miss the cut (made at 1 over) were:–

J Coceres (+2)	R Karlsson (+2)	G Emerson (+2)	F Jacobson (+2)
S Tinning (+2)	P-U Johansson (+2)	P Affleck (+2)	A Wall (+2)
N Fasth (+2)	P Fowler (+2)	P Lonard (+2)	I Garbutt (+3)
A Forsyth (+3)	R Wessels (+3)	M Davis (+3)	R Green (+3)
D Gilford (+3)	A McLardy (+3)	E Romero (+3)	C Hanell (+4)
B Langer (+4)	J Rivero (+4)	B Dredge (+4)	M Lafeber (+4)
G Evans (+5)	F Lindgren (+5)	R McFarlane (+5)	W Riley (+5)
A Bossert (+5)	P Senior (+5)	S Hansen (+6)	M Mackenzie (+6)
M Lanner (+6)	A Coltart (+6)	W Bennett (+6)	R Muntz (+6)
R Coles (+6)	J Lomas (+7)	S Gallacher (+7)	D Borrego (+7)
D Terblanche (+7)	F Cea (+8)	R Winchester (+8)	I Pyman (+8)
J Senden (+9)	T Levet (+9)	T Gogele (+9)	D Park (+10)
S Luna (+11)	G Owen (+11)	H Otto (+11)	J Moseley (+11)
R Russell (+12)	M Scarpa (+13)	S Scahill (+14)	

Russell Clayden (77), Per Nyman (78), John Mellor (82) and J-F Remesy (80) all retired.

ROUND BY ROUND LEADERBOARD

FIRST ROUND

M A Jimenez	5 under
P Lawrie	4 under
R Chapman	4 under
R Goosen	4 under
J Van de Velde	3 under
S Allan	3 under
D Hospital	3 under
E Canonica	3 under
M A Martin	3 under
J Haeggman	3 under
L WESTWOOD	1 under

SECOND ROUND

M A Jimenez	8 under
E Canonica	6 under
P McGinley	6 under
G Orr	5 under
R Goosen	5 under
B May	5 under
S Webster	5 under
L WESTWOOD	4 under

THIRD ROUND

T Woods	9 under
G Ogilvy	7 under
L WESTWOOD	7 under
E Canonica	7 under
M A Jimenez	7 under
D Clarke	7 under

FINAL ROUND

L WESTWOOD	15 under
E Canonica	12 under
T Woods	11 under
J Van de Velde	11 under
I Woosnam	11 under

Thursday and Friday	Occasional showers, cold and windy
Saturday	Overcast and calm
Sunday	Delayed start because of fog then mainly sunny.

PUNTERS' POINTS

● 'A week is a long time in golf.' Dejected, demotivated and decidedly sad, Lee Westwood cut a forlorn figure last weekend after finishing T54th at the Belfry. Here he was back on the course where he won this title in 1998 and he deservedly won again after storming past Tiger Woods and the rest of the field with a superb 64 in R4.

● Westwood fans prepared to forget his 'form' last weekend and to remember his course record 61 here two years ago were rewarded with a juicy "S.P." of 33/1......and that won't be repeated in future!

● Tiger 'blew it' at the 11th in R4 with a double bogey, so his customary victory once in the lead on a Sunday didn't materialise.

● Emanuele Canonica shot a fine 67 on Sunday to climb from 119th to 12th on the Order of Merit.

● After successive 7th-place finishes in this event Miguel Angel Jimenez finished T6th to reward his followers on the spreads and in match bets against Langer, Coltart, Campbell and Coceres.

● Course specialist Darren Clarke played steadily enough to finish T15th yet could never really get in a blow

● After the events of last weekend it was pleasing to see Padraig (I'll always sign in future) Harrington finish in the top 20 here.

● Bernhard Langer, ten times a European tour winner in his native Germany, missed the cut here by 3 shots to suggest he may be in decline.

1999 RESULT
(St Leon-Rot G.C.,Heidelberg)

1	fav 10/1	Tiger Woods
2	40/1	Retief Goosen
3	20/1	Nick Price
4	100/1	Peter Baker
T5	14/1	Ernie Els
T5	200/1	Brian Davis

1998 RESULT
(Gut Kaden, Hamburg)

1	22/1	Lee Westwood
2	20/1	Darren Clarke
3	25/1	Mark O'Meara
T4	200/1	Phillip Walton
T4	16/1	Bernhard Langer
T4	100/1	Peter Senior

WINNERS IN THE LAST NINE YEARS

1992	Bernhard Langer	1997	Ross McFarlane
1993	Sam Torrance	1998	Lee Westwood
1994	Robert Allenby	1999	Tiger Woods
1995	Bernhard Langer	2000	Lee Westwood
1996	Frank Nobilo		

PUNTERS' GUIDE

● Best recent Gut Kaden form is held by

Lee Westwood	Won 2000, Won 1998 (including a course record 61)
Miguel Jimenez	T6th 2000, T7th 1998
Darren Clarke	T15th 2000, 2nd 1998, 4th 1997
Paul McGinley	T9th 2000: T22nd 1998: T5th 1997

● Sound recent form in this mega-rich tournament over the last couple of years has been shown by five players with successive top 20 finishes

	2000 Gut Kaden	1999 Heidelberg
Tiger Woods	T3rd	Won
M A Jiminez	T6th	T7th
Retief Goosen	T13th	2nd
Brian Davis	T13th	T5th
Gary Orr	T9th	16th
Peter Baker	T17th	4th
Nick Price	T17th	3rd
Jean Van de Velde	T3rd	T17th

● In 2001 the tournament returns to St Leon-Rot course at Heidelberg.

● Players whose profiles refer to this tournament include Darren Clarke, Gary Orr, Brian Davis, Miguel Angel Jimenez, Retief Goosen, Nick Price, Peter Baker and Soren Kjeldsen.

THE VOLVO PGA CHAMPIONSHIP

Date	Friday 26th May - Monday 29th May
Course	West Course, Wentworth
Par	72
Yardage	7,047
First Prize	£250,000
Total Purse	£1.5 million

THE TOURNAMENT

This event always starts on the Friday of the late-May Bank Holiday weekend ending on the Bank Holiday Monday. It is one of the biggest tournaments on the European tour calendar.

THE COURSE

This is very much a course-specialists' track with accuracy off the tee absolutely vital. This year the wet course played its full length.

2000 ODDS

fav	5/1	Colin Montgomerie	50/1	Paul McGinley
	10/1	Lee Westwood	66/1*	Stephen Leaney
	16/1	Darren Clarke	66/1	M A Martin
	25/1	Padraig Harrington	66/1	Andrew Coltart
	25/1	Sergio Garcia	66/1	Eduardo Romero
	28/1	J M Olazabal	66/1	Geoff Ogilvy
	33/1	Ian Woosnam	66/1	Phillip Price
	33/1	M A Jimenez	80/1	Paul Lawrie
	33/1	Bernhard Langer	80/1	Peter O'Malley
	40/1	Retief Goosen	80/1	Angel Cabrera
	40/1	Jean Van de Velde	80/1	Jose Coceres
	40/1	Thomas Bjorn	80/1*	Brian Davis
	40/1	Michael Campbell	80/1	Robert Karlsson
	40/1	Gary Orr	80/1	Jarmo Sandelin

2000 RESULT

1	fav 5/1	Colin Montgomerie	67 65 70 69 271
T2	16/1	Darren Clarke	68 68 72 66 274
T2	10/1	Lee Westwood	71 70 65 68 274
T2	66/1	Andrew Coltart	67 69 69 69 274
T5	125/1	Richard Green	67 67 73 70 277
T5	25/1	Sergio Garcia	68 71 68 70 277

T7	R Goosen	74 70 68 67 279			M Lanner	73 70 75 70 288
	O Edmond	68 74 69 68 279			T Johnstone	72 73 74 69 288
	I Woosnam	72 71 68 68 279			O Karlsson	72 74 74 68 288
	P O'Malley	68 73 69 69 279			L-W Zhang	75 71 70 72 288
T11	M Campbell	73 68 71 68 280			S Torrance	69 72 73 74 288
	N O'Hern	65 74 71 70 280			G Rojas	68 75 71 74 288
T13	R Jacquelin	70 75 71 65 281	T51		A Cabrera	71 73 73 72 289
	R Chapman	71 72 70 68 281			C Suneson	71 72 74 72 289
	B May	68 75 68 70 281			B Teilleria	72 73 73 71 289
	R Karlsson	67 69 74 71 281			M A Martin	72 73 73 71 289
T17	P Harrington	72 74 69 67 282			J Rivero	70 72 76 71 289
	G Emerson	69 69 73 71 282	T56		C Hanell	73 72 72 73 290
	B Langer	69 71 71 71 282			S Luna	72 71 75 72 290
T20	T Gogele	71 73 74 65 283			A McLardy	74 71 74 71 290
	R Winchester	71 75 68 69 283			J M Olazabal	71 75 70 74 290
	M A Jimenez	69 75 70 69 283			E Romero	72 73 71 74 290
	P McGinley	70 70 72 71 283			G Ogilvy	68 76 72 74 290
	Anders Hansen	70 73 69 71 283	T62		E Canonica	72 73 73 73 291
	Phillip Price	72 67 69 75 283			C Rocca	69 77 73 72 291
T26	D Smyth	77 69 70 68 284			T Bjorn	70 75 75 71 291
	G Orr	72 71 72 69 284			I Garrido	73 73 74 71 291
	P Mitchell	71 73 71 69 284			M Scarpa	72 71 78 70 291
	Ricardo Gonzalez	73 68 70 73 284			P Baker	70 76 70 75 291
T30	J Bickerton	69 74 73 69 285			D Howell	69 76 70 76 291
	D Robertson	73 71 73 68 285	T69		V Phillips	72 71 76 73 292
	S Little	68 75 74 68 285			J Sandelin	72 70 78 72 292
	W Riley	72 70 70 73 285	T71		M James	73 73 73 74 293
T34	M McNulty	71 71 72 72 286			D Terblanche	73 73 75 72 293
	A Cejka	71 71 72 72 286			A Bossert	70 76 77 70 293
	I Pyman	72 71 70 73 286			M Lafeber	69 71 75 78 293
	J-F Remesy	69 74 70 73 286	75		S Webster	71 72 74 77 294
T38	J Van de Velde	68 75 73 71 287	76		P Way	72 72 77 74 295
	B Lane	73 71 73 70 287	T77		J Mellor	72 72 77 75 296
	A Forsyth	72 71 74 70 287			P Senior	70 75 77 74 296
	S Kjeldsen	68 73 76 70 287			J Senden	70 74 78 72 296
	D Carter	76 70 73 68 287	80		P R Simpson	70 74 78 77 299
T43	S Leaney	71 71 74 72 288	81		S Ballesteros	70 74 79 80 303
	Jamie Spence	75 70 73 70 288				

The main players to miss the cut (made at 2 over) were:–

J M Singh (+3)	D Gilford (+3)	S Struver (+3)	A Wall (+3)
H Otto (+3)	S Tinning (+3)	J Moseley (+3)	P-U Johansson (+3)
P Quirici (+3)	D Borrego (+3)	R Muntz (+3)	P Lonard (+3)
D Park (+3)	P Sjoland (+3)	N Fasth (+3)	M Farry (+4)
C Hainline (+4)	R Wessels (+4)	F Cea (+4)	R McFarlane (+5)
D Hospital (+5)	P Eales (+5)	G Owen (+4)	J Berendt (+5)
M Gronberg (+6)	J Coceres (+6)	S Allan (+6)	M Brier (+6)
E Darcy (+6)	W Bennett (+7)	M Davis (+7)	G Turner (+7)
I Garbutt (+7)	J Lomas (+7)	G Evans (+8)	A Forsbrand (+8)
S Lyle (+9)	B Davis (+9)	L Parsons (+9)	S Scahill (+10)
T Levet (+11)	S Gallacher (+11)	P Nyman (+12)	B Dredge (+12)
A Oldcorn (+14)	I Poulter (+14)	P Affleck (+14)	

Paul Lawrie (69), Raymond Russell (77) and Russell Claydon (83) all withdrew.

ROUND BY ROUND LEADERBOARD

FIRST ROUND
N O'Hern	7 under
R Green	5 under
R Karlsson	5 under
C MONTGOMERIE	5 under
A Coltart	5 under

SECOND ROUND
C MONTGOMERIE	12 under
R Green	10 under
D Clarke	8 under
A Coltart	8 under
R Karlsson	8 under

THIRD ROUND
C MONTGOMERIE	14 under
A Coltart	11 under
L Westwood	10 under
R Green	9 under
S Garcia	9 under
D Clarke	8 under
P Price	8 under

FINAL ROUND
C MONTGOMERIE	17 under
D Clarke	14 under
L Westwood	14 under
A Coltart	14 under
R Green	11 under
S Garcia	11 under

Heavy rain effectively spoilt the flow and continuity of this tournament.

R1 had to be completed on the second day, R2 on the third day and so on.

POINTERS' POINTS

● A three-peat for Monty. The big Scot's third consecutive win in the Volvo PGA came in a rain-ravaged tournament which tested Monty's character and patience.

"I don't need the money any more.....my only motivation for playing now is the competition." Here he fought off pretenders to his crown to record a deserved victory.

● Darren Clarke with a superb 66 in R4 could never really mount a sustained challenge. His huge lead in the Order of Merit is being reduced weekly by Monty at present.

● The only player to shoot four sub-70 rounds was the in-form 66/1 Andrew Coltart who was tipped for this event in his player profile last year. He celebrated his 30th birthday two weeks ago and now the experienced Scot in his 'nappy factor' year could be about to 'breakthrough big time'.

● T7th Olivier Edmond, rookie of the year in 1998, is a player to note. Having defeated testicular cancer Trevor Dodds won in the States last year, and the Frenchman could well do the same having made a similar recovery.

1999 RESULT

1	jt fav 9/1	Colin Montgomerie
2	150/1	Mark James
3	150/1	Paul Eales
T4	jt fav 9/1	Ernie Els
T4	33/1	Retief Goosen
T4	80/1	Stephen Leaney

1998 RESULT

1	10/1	Colin Montgomerie
T2	fav 9/1	Ernie Els
T2	40/1	Patrik Sjoland
T2	150/1	Gary Orr
T5	50/1	Andrew Coltart
T5	150/1	Peter Lonard
T5	20/1	Thomas Bjorn
T5	250/1	Mats Hallberg
T5	200/1	Dean Robertson

WINNERS IN THE LAST TEN YEARS

1991	Seve Ballesteros	1996	Costantino Rocca
1992	Tony Johnstone	1997	Ian Woosnam
1993	Bernhard Langer	1998	Colin Montgomerie
1994	J M Olazabal	1999	Colin Montgomerie
1995	Bernhard Langer	2000	Colin Montgomerie

PUNTERS' GUIDE

● Players with the most consistent records in the Volvo PGA include

> Colin Montgomerie Winner last 3 years

> Ian Woosnam Won 1997: T7th 2000

> Gary Orr T7th 1996: T2nd 1998: Top 30 last two years

> Darren Clarke T2nd in both 1997 and 2000

> Retief Goosen T7th 2000: T4th 1999

> Andrew Coltart T2nd 2000: T5th 1998

● This is very much a course-specialists' track which suits players whose forte is accuracy off the tee.

In 2001 Monty will be going for an amazing fourth consecutive win and will obviously start a very short-priced favourite.

● Players whose profiles refer to this tournament include Colin Montgomerie, Andrew Coltart, Stephen Leaney, Ian Woosnam, Gary Orr, Retief Goosen and Padraig Harrington.

THE COMPASS GROUP ENGLISH OPEN

Date   1st - 4th June
Course   Marriott Forest of Arden Meriden Hotel
Par   72
Yardage   7,102
First Prize £125,000
Total Purse £750,000

THE TOURNAMENT

This like the French, Spanish and Italian Open is a national Open usually with a fairly strong field.

THE COURSE

After three years at the Hanbury Manor course the English Open returned to the Forest of Arden which was the venue from 1993 to 1996 inclusive. The 1997 and 1998 British Masters were also held on this course. The course has recently been revamped and improved with the greens being altered to increase their difficulty. The final two holes are interesting—the 17th is a reachable (over water) 511-yard par 5, and the last a long, tough, 200-yards+ par 3.

2000 ODDS

fav				
	7/2	Colin Montgomerie (PWW)	100/1*	Patrik Sjoland
	9/1	Darren Clarke (DC)	100/1*	Peter Baker
	9/1	Lee Westwood	100/1*	John Bickerton
	22/1	Retief Goosen	100/1*	Brian Davis
	33/1	Andrew Coltart	100/1*	Simon Dyson
	33/1	Michael Campbell	100/1*	Brett Rumford
	40/1	Thomas Bjorn	100/1*	Greg Turner
	50/1	Gary Orr	100/1	Mark McNulty
	50/1	Stephen Leaney	100/1	P-U Johansson
	66/1*	Paul McGinley (non runner)	100/1*	David Park
	66/1*	Peter O'Malley	100/1	Richard Green
	80/1	M A Martin	100/1*	Mathias Gronberg
	80/1*	Nick O'Hern	100/1	Peter Lonard
	80/1	David Howell	100/1	Joakim Haeggman
	100/1	David Carter	100/1	Dean Robertson

2000 RESULT

1	9/1	**Darren Clarke**	**70 72 68 65 275**
T2	33/1	**Michael Campbell**	**63 69 72 72 276**
T2	125/1	**Mark James**	**73 69 65 69 276**
T4	150/1*	**Ricardo Gonzalez**	**71 69 69 69 278**
T4	9/1	**Lee Westwood**	**69 70 67 72 278**

T6	G Orr	69 72 71 67 279		R Goosen	74 71 71 73 289
	Brian Davis	74 67 70 68 279		P Baker	75 70 68 76 289
8	C Montgomerie	71 68 69 72 280		Mark Davis	76 70 72 71 289
9	D Lynn	70 73 68 70 281		F Lindgren	74 71 70 74 289
T10	P O'Malley	72 65 71 74 282		I Pyman	74 69 73 73 289
	I Garbutt	72 69 74 67 282	T47	R Chapman	74 72 70 74 290
T12	N O'Hern	73 69 70 71 283		M Eliasson	75 71 73 71 290
	M Farry	75 69 71 68 283		S Luna	74 72 71 73 290
	M Gronberg	73 67 71 72 283		S Field	71 75 70 74 290
	G Turner	73 71 67 72 283		S Leaney	73 70 72 75 290
	M Lafeber	76 67 68 72 283		J Haeggman	72 74 72 72 290
T17	G Evans	70 73 70 71 284		H Otto	71 71 74 74 290
	M McNulty	69 75 70 70 284	T54	J Mellor	75 69 73 74 291
	T Johnstone	72 70 73 69 284		Per Nyman	73 70 74 74 291
	A Wall	72 74 69 69 284		S Torrance	70 75 74 72 291
	T Bjorn	73 71 68 72 284		C Rocca	72 74 69 76 291
	W Riley	73 72 71 68 284		B Rumford	70 73 80 68 291
T23	S Webster	70 69 71 75 285	T59	J Robinson	75 71 74 72 292
	J Bickerton	73 73 69 70 285		R Russell	71 74 75 72 292
	D Howell	72 69 74 70 285		A Oldcorn	72 74 72 74 292
T26	C Hanell	76 68 69 73 286		I Hutchings	74 69 75 74 292
	D Carter	73 70 70 73 286	T63	D Lee	72 74 73 74 293
	G Rojas	73 72 68 73 286		S Lyle	74 71 75 73 293
	R Winchester	75 70 73 68 286	T65	S Gallacher	75 69 73 77 294
	T Gillis	74 72 70 70 286		D Borrego	73 73 74 74 294
	Soren Hansen	74 71 69 72 286		M Florioli	71 75 76 72 294
T32	G Murphy	73 73 71 70 287		C Hainline	74 71 77 72 294
	M A Martin	73 72 71 71 287		D Park	74 71 76 73 294
	J M Carriles	72 69 72 74 287		P Quirici	75 71 77 71 294
	G Brand Jr	74 70 70 73 287	T71	C Hall	70 75 76 74 295
T36	P Mitchell	69 74 75 70 288		I Giner	72 72 76 75 295
	B Teilleria	69 74 74 71 288		G Hutcheon	73 71 73 78 295
	N Vanhootegem	73 69 71 75 288		F Cea	74 72 74 75 295
	O Edmond	73 72 72 71 288	75	P Fowler	72 72 76 79 299
	N Ludwell	72 71 73 72 288	76	J Skold	73 71 76 80 300
T41	F Jacobson	74 72 71 72 289			

The main players to miss the cut (made at 2 over) were:–

P Eales (+3)	R Muntz (+3)	P Affleck (+3)	A Forsyth (+3)
D Robertson (+3)	S Rowe (+3)	R Davis (+3)	J Berendt (+3)
V Phillips (+3)	S Allan (+4)	A Raitt (+4)	P Sjoland (+4)
C Suneson (+4)	S Scahill (+4)	D Smyth (+5)	M Mackenzie (+5)
R Jacquelin (+5)	A Coltart (+5)	E Darcy (+5)	W Bennett (+5)
P Lonard (+5)	J Rivero (+5)	S Dyson (+6)	J Lomas (+6)
G Owen (+6)	L Parsons (+6)	R Wessels (+6)	J Moseley (+6)
B Lane (+6)	P Walton (+6)	W-T Yeh (+7)	D Gilford (+7)
J M Singh (+7)	R McFarlane (+7)	P G Nyman (+8)	R Gonzalez (+8)
M Scarpa (+8)	J Rose (+9)	F Tarnaud (+9)	R Green (+10)
R Claydon (+11)	T Levet (+11)	S Ballesteros (+11)	J-F Remesey (+12)
D Hospital (+12)			

Per-Ulrik Johansson (74), Thomas Gogele (80), and Ian Poulter (79) all withdrew.

ROUND BY ROUND LEADERBOARD

FIRST ROUND

M Campbell	9 (!) under
P Mitchell	3 under
G Orr	3 under
M McNulty	3 under
L Westwood	3 under
B Teilleria	3 under
D CLARKE	2 under

SECOND ROUND

M Campbell	12 under
P O'Malley	7 under
C Montgomerie	5 under
L Westwood	5 under
S Webster	5 under
D CLARKE	2 under

THIRD ROUND

M Campbell	12 under
L Westwood	10 under
M James	9 under
C Montgomerie	8 under
P O'Malley	8 under
R Gonzalez	7 under
D CLARKE	6 under

FINAL ROUND

D CLARKE	13 under
M Campbell	12 under
M James	12 under
R Gonzalez	10 under
L Westwood	10 under

PUNTERS' POINTS

● Brilliant iron play by the mercurial Darren Clarke swept the Irishman past all-the-way leader Michael Campbell to retain his English Open title after a ten-birdie R4 of 65! His final-round sparkle was reminiscent of his dazzling form against Tiger Woods in the World Match Play.

● Michael Campbell had set the pace after an astonishing 63 in R1. However he was caught by Clarke on the back nine on Sunday and despite a brilliant birdie (nearly eagle) - par (almost birdie!) finish Campbell could not force a play-off.

● Mark James found himself in the headlines following the serialisation of his autobiography so his performance here was right 'out of the blue'. However he may have shown 'contention rust' at the 16th and 17th in R4 when missing very makeable putts.

● 7/2 heavily-backed favourite Colin Montgomerie was never at ease on the greens, so despite his amazing course record (two wins and two 2nds) he was never really in serious contention, finishing 8th.

● T10th Peter O'Malley, clear 2nd at halfway, showed both his brilliance (65 in R2) and his achilles heel (a tendency to hook under pressure). He really should be winning with his talent.

● T6th Brian Davis' superb R4 hit the buffers with a double bogey at the 13th. Nevertheless his T6th finish confirms the progress the 25-year-old cockney is still making following his maiden win in the Spanish Open. It was his fourth top 6 finish this year!

1999 RESULT

(Hanbury Manor, Ware)

1	16/1	Darren Clarke
2	125/1*	John Bickerton
T3	66/1*	David Carter
T3	33/1	Stephen Leaney
T5	fav 11/2	Colin Montgomerie
T5	50/1	Andrew Coltart

1998 RESULT

(Hanbury Manor, Ware)

1	10/1	Lee Westwood
T2	200/1	Olle Karlsson
T2	80/1	Greg Chalmers
4	fav 7/1	Colin Montgomerie
5	40/1	Patrik Sjoland

WINNERS IN THE LAST TEN YEARS

1991	David Gilford	1996	Robert Allenby
1992	Vicente Fernandez	1997	P-U Johansson
1993	Ian Woosnam	1998	Lee Westwood
1994	Colin Montgomerie	1999	Darren Clarke
1995	Phillip Walton	2000	Darren Clarke

1991 and 1992 The Belfry   1997 - 1999 Hanbury Manor
1993 - 1996 Forest of Arden   2000 Forest of Arden

PUNTERS' GUIDE

● Winner in the last two years on different courses Darren Clarke will be going for a three-peat in 2001

● This year at the Forest of Arden thirty-five players beat par compared to sixty-one in 1999 at the Hanbury Manor. The Forest of Arden requires good quality iron play and a sure touch on the greens which were of variable pace this year.

● The best recent records in this tournament are held by the following players. However do remember that from 1997-99 inclusive the Hanbury Manor course was the venue.

	2000	1999	1998	1997
Ian Garbutt	T10th	T25th	T25th	T12th
Colin Montgomerie	8th	T5th	4th	T12th

Gary Orr	T6th	T7th	T32nd	T10th
Darren Clarke	Won	Won	T49th	T12th
Stephen Leaney	T47th	T3rd	T10th	—

- Current form has proved very important in this tournament over the past three years
  > 2000 The form figures of the first 5 were (latest on the right):-

Darren Clarke	22-15-2
Michael Campbell	7-52-26-11
Mark James	MC-26-71
Ricardo Gonzalez	22-44-70-26
Lee Westwood	54-W-2

All five had made the cut in their last two events, and three (Campbell, Clarke and Westwood) had already won earlier in the season
  > 1999 four of the top 6 players had posted a top 10 finish in one of their last two starts.
  > 1998 three of the top 5 players had a win or 2nd place in one of their last two starts.
- Players whose profiles refer to this tournament include David Carter, Peter O'Malley, Greg Turner, Gary Orr, Ian Garbutt, Darren Clarke, Anthony Wall, Nick O'Hern and Brian Davis.

THE WALES OPEN

Date	8th - 11th June
Course	Celtic Manor G.C., Newport, South Wales
Par	72
Yardage	7,403
First Prize	£125,000
Total Purse	£750,000

THE TOURNAMENT

This is a new tournament and the first time the European tour had visited Wales since 1991.

THE COURSE

This new course that winds its way along and round the River Usk has been developed as a possible future (2009) Ryder Cup venue. The Robert Trent Jones-designed Wentwood Hills course is long at 7,403 yards with genuine par 5s (two at over 610 yards) reachable normally in three shots. It emphasises quality iron play and being a long, undulating course it is physically very demanding.

2000 ODDS

fav	11/1	Ian Woosnam	50/1*	David Howell
	18/1	Andrew Coltart	50/1*	Mark McNulty
	20/1*	Gary Orr	50/1	David Carter
	20/1	Phillip Price	66/1	Olivier Edmond
	20/1	Peter O'Malley	66/1*	Peter Mitchell
	22/1	Brian Davis	66/1	Anthony Wall
	25/1	Paul McGinley	66/1	Steve Webster
	33/1	Stephen Leaney	66/1	David Park
	40/1	Nick O'Hern	80/1	Gary Evans
	40/1	Greg Turner	80/1*	Jamie Spence
	40/1	Brett Rumford	80/1*	Wayne Riley
	40/1	Mark James	80/1*	Peter Baker
	40/1	John Bickerton	80/1	Dean Robertson

2000 RESULT

1	100/1*	Steen Tinning	70 68 66 69 273
2	50/1*	David Howell	72 67 67 68 274
T3	125/1	Fredrik Jacobson	71 68 70 67 276
T3	fav 11/1	Ian Woosnam	68 69 66 73 276
T5	50/1*	Mark McNulty	70 67 72 69 278
T5	20/1	Phillip Price	71 70 72 65 278
T5	40/1	Nick O'Hern	71 68 69 70 278

T8	R Coles	64 79 67 69 279			P Affleck	74 70 71 72 287
	I Garbutt	68 71 67 73 279			I Pyman	67 75 74 71 287
	M James	67 72 69 71 279		T46	D Hospital	73 72 69 74 288
	G Brand Jr	72 70 68 69 279			S Leaney	72 74 65 77 288
T12	D Lynn	71 73 69 68 281			V Phillips	74 69 75 70 288
	H Nystrom	71 71 64 75 281			D Robertson	71 75 67 75 288
T14	B Rumford	70 71 71 70 282			T Gogele	73 71 74 70 288
	J Senden	69 75 70 68 282			N Vanhootegem	70 71 76 71 288
	A Coltart	72 74 65 71 282			P Nyman	72 69 75 72 288
T17	Jamie Spence	71 70 70 72 283			I Giner	67 77 70 74 288
	R Green	74 71 69 69 283			D Lee	74 70 72 72 288
	A Oldcorn	70 74 68 71 283		T55	A Wall	70 72 76 71 289
	M Lafeber	73 69 71 70 283			P Eales	72 71 71 75 289
T21	J Robinson	70 73 71 70 284			J Haeggman	71 71 74 73 289
	D Park	69 71 73 71 284			S Dyson	72 72 70 75 289
	C Suneson	70 71 67 76 284		T59	S Richardson	73 69 74 74 290
	S Kjeldsen	72 71 72 69 284			P Golding	70 76 74 70 290
	R J Derksen	72 70 68 74 284			W-T Yeh	72 72 73 73 290
	R Wessels	70 76 69 69 284			S Torrance	73 71 71 75 290
T27	R Chapman	69 73 73 70 285		T63	R Drummond	70 74 70 77 291
	S Allan	74 69 72 70 285			R McFarlane	70 68 78 75 291
T29	P Fulke	71 75 69 71 286			M Anglert	72 68 78 73 291
	P Baker	70 76 68 72 286			E Boult	71 75 75 70 291
	B Lane	69 73 67 77 286		T67	P O'Malley	75 71 76 70 292
	Anders Hansen	68 73 70 75 286			M Plummer	72 74 72 74 292
	M Farry	73 72 72 69 286		T69	A Beal	74 69 74 76 293
	T Levet	69 73 71 73 286			S Wakefield	70 75 74 74 293
	G Orr	71 74 71 70 286			P McGinley	77 67 68 81 293
	G Evans	72 74 71 69 286		T72	L Parsons	72 74 73 75 294
	D Carter	76 68 71 71 286			Soren Hansen	72 73 75 74 294
	F Lindgren	74 72 67 73 286			R Russell	70 69 80 75 294
T39	M Mouland	74 71 73 69 287		T75	M Litton	70 76 73 76 295
	J Moseley	72 72 70 73 287			R Dinsdale	73 70 73 79 295
	R Winchester	70 71 74 72 287			P Walton	72 70 80 73 295
	A Forsyth	73 72 69 73 287		78	M Jonzon	74 70 79 74 297
	M Cain	73 71 70 73 287				

The main players to miss the cut (made at 2 over) were:-

G Emerson (+3)	J M Singh (+3)	B Davis (+3)	M Brier (+3)
M MacKenzie (+3)	R Gonzalez (+3)	F Tarnaud (+3)	S Lyle (+3)
W Riley (+3)	S Gallacher (+3)	M Scarpa (+3)	J Payne (+4)
F Roca (+4)	R Byrd (+4)	D Cooper (+4)	D Smyth (+4)
R S Johnson (+4)	S Rowe (+4)	P Way (+4)	J Bickerton (+5)
O Edmond (+5)	T Carolan (+5)	C Rocca (+5)	M Davis (+5)
D Borrego (+5)	A Raitt (+6)	G Murphy (+6)	D Chopra (+6)
M Lanner (+6)	R Jacquelin (+6)	B Teilleria (+6)	S Delagrange (+7)
O Karlsson (+7)	P Mitchell (+7)	T Johnstone (+7)	E Darcy (+7)
C Hainline (+7)	R Muntz (+7)	F Cea (+8)	T Gillis (+8)
G Hutcheon (+8)	W Bennett (+9)	P Fowler (+9)	A Sherborne (+10)
S Cage (+10)	H Otto (+11)	J Rose (+13)	

ROUND BY ROUND LEADERBOARD

FIRST ROUND

R Coles	8 under
M James	5 under
I Pyman	5 under
I Woosnam	4 under
I Garbutt	4 under
A Hansen	4 under
S TINNING	2 under

SECOND ROUND

I Woosnam	7 under
M McNulty	7 under
R McFarlane	6 under
S TINNING	6 under
N O'Hern	5 under
M James	5 under
R Russell	5 under
D Howell	5 under
F Jacobson	5 under
I Garbutt	5 under

THIRD ROUND

I Woosnam	13 under
S TINNING	12 under
H Nystrom	10 under
I Garbutt	10 under
D Howell	10 under
N O'Hern	8 under
C Suneson	8 under
M James	8 under

FINAL ROUND

S TINNING	15 under
D Howell	14 under
F Jacobson	12 under
I Woosnam	12 under
M McNulty	10 under
P Price	10 under
N O'Hern	10 under

PUNTERS' POINTS

● 100/1 DYM Steen Tinning ended a fourteen-year wait with his first Euro tour win. The key to his success has been the improvement in his mental skills learned from his fellow Dane Arne Neillson, a world champion canoeist.

● However on Sunday the big story was the poor performance of Ian Woosnam. Starting best priced 4/6 with a clear lead Woosy, without a win for three years, went over par to finish T3rd. "I felt the pressure," said the diminutive Welshman.

● David Howell was a superb 14 under par for the last 54 holes. However a missed tiddler putt on the 17th in R4 was his downfall. He'll be a major contender here in 2001.

● Phillip Price's superb 65 in R4 came a bit late, yet it showed that the local guy will, like Howell, be a major contender here in future years.

● Only four players posted four sub-par rounds—Steen Tinning, Fredrik Jacobson, Nick O'Hern, and interestingly T14th young Aussie Brett Rumford.

● This inaugural tournament was a real triumph for DYM followers with 100/1 Steen Tinning, 2nd-placed 50/1 David Howell and T5th 50/1 Mark McNulty all DYMs.

PAST RESULTS AND RECENT WINNERS

This was the inaugural Wales Open.

PUNTERS' GUIDE

● Forty-five players broke par in this year's first Wales Open, suggesting that this long undulating course maybe tough physically yet low scoring is clearly possible, even if 'clean and place' rules this year meant that low scores did not qualify as a course record.

● This year it was noticeable that the current form of the seven players in the top 5 was very solid indeed.

> five had at least a top 25 in their last tournament

> five had at least a top 12 finish in one of their last three starts

> four had posted a top 10 in at least one of their three tournaments

● With so many top proven winners not playing it was perhaps not surprising to find that five of the top 11 finishers this year were looking for a first win.

● Overall the evidence from just one year suggests that in 2001 we consider:-

> Any DYM

> Current form

> Players looking for their first tour success

> Any player in this year's top 20

● Players whose profiles refer to this tournament include Phillip Price, David Howell, Robert Coles, Nick O'Hern, Stephen Leaney, Richard Green, Andrew Coltart, John Senden, Mark James, David Park and Carl Suneson.

THE 100TH US OPEN

Date	15th - 18th June
Course	Pebble Beach, Monterey Peninsula, California
Par	71
Yardage	6,846
First Prize	$900,000
Total Purse	$4.5 million

PLEASE SEE PART 6.

THE COMPAQ EUROPEAN GRAND PRIX

Date	22nd - 25th June
Course	Slaley Hall G.C., Hexham, Northumberland
Par	72
Yardage	7,073
First Prize	£100,000
Total Purse	£600,000

THE TOURNAMENT

This tournament started in 1996 so this was its fifth year, although with the 1998 abandonment there have only been four winners so far. The drainage has been much improved over the last two years so there is little likelihood now of another void tournament.

THE COURSE

This course has huge bunkers and raised greens, typical of a Dave Thomas-designed course. It is set among rolling moorland, imposing pines and water with 'the sleeping giant', the tough long par 4 9th, its signature hole. The raised greens are first class and the course suits the longer hitter. This year the players reported that the rough was thicker than in the past.

2000 ODDS

fav	9/2	Lee Westwood	66/1	Geoff Ogilvy
	6/1	Darren Clarke	66/1	Steve Webster
	25/1	Andrew Coltart	66/1	Peter Baker
	33/1	David Howell	66/1*	David Carter
	33/1	Paul Lawrie	66/1	Gary Evans
	40/1	Nick O'Hern	80/1*	Richard Green
	40/1	Jamie Spence	80/1	John Bickerton
	40/1	Mark James	80/1	Dean Robertson
	40/1*	Adam Scott	80/1	David Lynn
	50/1	Brett Rumford	80/1	Peter Mitchell
	50/1*	Brian Davis	80/1	Santiago Luna
	50/1*	David Park (DC)	80/1	John Senden
	66/1	Ian Garbutt		

2000 RESULT

1	fav 9/2	Lee Westwood	68 68 70 70 276
2	100/1*	Fredrik Jacobson	69 70 70 70 279
T3	100/1*	Emanuele Canonica	69 73 71 68 281
T3	6/1	Darren Clarke	69 75 68 69 281
5	125/1	Andrew Oldcorn	71 73 66 72 282

T6	Jamie Spence	69 74 72 69 284		D Hospital	74 76 75 69 294
	S Allan	71 73 71 69 284		P Eales	75 76 71 72 294
8	N Vanhootegem	70 71 72 72 285		S Rowe	75 75 72 72 294
T9	G Turner	71 76 70 69 286		N Cheetham	72 78 71 73 294
	E Boult	69 76 71 70 286		D Lynn	77 75 68 74 294
11	P Fowler	70 80 69 68 287	T45	S Luna	73 78 73 71 295
T12	G Emerson	71 74 70 73 288		J-F Remesy	75 75 72 73 295
	M Scarpa	70 75 73 70 288		G Hutcheon	76 74 71 74 295
T14	S Torrance	66 79 71 73 289		Shaun Webster	70 80 70 75 295
	I Poulter	69 78 70 72 289		J Lomas	73 79 75 68 295
	O Karlsson	70 79 70 70 289		B Dredge	71 79 70 75 295
	H Nystrom	72 76 67 74 289		J Payne	73 76 76 70 295
T18	R Green	73 78 70 69 290	T52	D Cooper	73 79 72 72 296
	S D Hurley	70 75 72 73 290		T Gillis	74 77 75 70 296
	F Cea	67 77 74 72 290		E Little	77 74 72 73 296
	A Coltart	68 81 72 69 290		M Archer	71 81 73 71 296
T22	G Brand Jr	70 75 77 69 291		J Robinson	74 75 73 74 296
	C Suneson	75 73 71 72 291		S Field	71 79 72 74 296
	S Richardson	75 74 69 73 291		G Evans	73 77 73 73 296
	I Pyman	73 79 66 73 291		T J Munoz	73 76 73 74 296
	D Robertson	72 75 72 72 291		R Russell	70 81 68 77 296
	D Lee	73 75 71 72 291	T61	J Bickerton	71 79 72 75 297
	D Carter	72 75 71 73 291		A Scott	72 79 69 77 297
	G Storm	72 76 72 71 291	T63	M Cain	75 76 76 71 298
T30	N O'Hern	73 79 72 68 292		R Wragg	75 77 77 69 298
	A Binaghi	70 75 75 72 292		W-T Yeh	73 76 76 73 298
T32	Brian Davis	76 76 73 68 293	T66	R Byrd	78 73 76 72 299
	P Mitchell	71 79 73 70 293		S Delagrange	71 74 77 77 299
	D Borrego	72 74 75 72 293		D Chopra	73 78 74 74 299
	P Lawrie	77 75 69 72 293	69	J M Carriles	72 80 74 74 300
T36	M Mouland	74 77 70 73 294	70	I Hutchings	73 74 74 81 302
	Anders Hansen	70 78 73 73 294	71	S Scahill	73 79 78 73 303
	K Ferrie	74 77 72 71 294	72	N Ludwell	75 77 78 75 305
	P Baker	73 76 73 72 294	73	T Carolan	76 76 74 80 306

The main players to miss the cut (made at 8(!) over) were:–

F Tarnaud (+9)	J M Singh (+9)	D Howell (+9)	G Ogilvy (+9)
I Garbutt (+9)	M Jones (+9)	J Robson (+9)	P Lonard (+9)
D Shacklady (+9)	J Wade (+10)	C Pena (+10)	J Rose (+10)
N Henning (+10)	G Hamerton (+10)	J M Kula (+10)	R Wessels (+10)
D De Vooght (+10)	P Affleck (+10)	A Raitt (+10)	R Coles (+10)
J Senden (+10)	G Owen (+10)	M Blackey (+10)	A McLardy (+11)
A Sherborne (+11)	G Rankin (+11)	R J Derksen (+11)	A Clapp (+11)
J Moseley (+11)	P Archer (+11)	I Giner (+12)	D Ray (+12)
G Murphy (+12)	P Sherman (+12)	M Mackenzie (+12)	D Gilford (+12)
M Eliasson (+12)	J Hepworth (+12)	M Tunnicliff (+12)	Z Scotland (am) (+12)
S Dyson (+13)	C Hanell (+13)	D Park (+13)	S Struver (+13)
M Florioli (+13)	R Gonzalez (+13)	P Golding (+13)	S Wakefield (+14)
S Watson (+14)	O Eliasson (+14)	B Rumford (+14)	D Clark (+14)
R Drummond (+14)	L Parsons (+14)	M James (+16)	M Anglert (+17)
P Rowe (am) (+17)	A Butterfield (+18)	A Forsyth (+18)	K Vainola (+18)
S Cage (+20)	C Hislop (+20)	P Nilbrink (+20)	R McFarlane (+21)
G Dodd (+21)	R Claydon (+23)		

Paul Way (81), Andrew Beal (74), and Philip Walton (76) all withdrew.
Warren Bennett (73 - 76) having made the cut withdrew.

ROUND BY ROUND LEADERBOARD

FIRST ROUND

S Torrance	6 under
F Cea	5 under
L WESTWOOD	4 under
A Coltart	4 under
E Boult	3 under
E Canonica	3 under
D Clarke	3 under
I Poulter	3 under
J Spence	3 under
F Jacobson	3 under

SECOND ROUND

L WESTWOOD	7 under
F Jacobson	5 under
N Vanhootegem	3 under
E Canonica	2 under
J Spence	1 under

THIRD ROUND

L WESTWOOD	10 under
F Jacobson	7 under
A Oldcorn	6 under
D Clarke	4 under
N Vanhootegem	3 under
E Canonica	3 under

FINAL ROUND

L WESTWOOD	12 under
F Jacobson	9 under
E Canonica	7 under
D Clarke	7 under
A Oldcorn	6 under

The wind really blew on Friday to make R2 scoring very difficult with forty-six players failing to break 80, so only five were under par at halfway.

PUNTERS' POINTS

● "When I started out it felt like midnight. I felt lethargic," so said a jet-lagged Lee Westwood after coming straight from Pebble Beach to shoot an opening round 68. As the jet lag got out of his system he went from strength to strength to win comfortably. At the top of his game, on a course ideal for his long, straight hitting he proved both his skill and his resilience. He even overcame a back muscle problem (having on-course physio!) during R3.

● Rarely do you find a player quoted at 100/1 after a top 3 finish. Yet Fredrik Jacobson, T3rd in the Wales Open, was given that quote and maintained his form to post a second successive top 3.

● Three players coming back from early season injury did well here

> Andrew Oldcorn, had an early season virus and wrist injury, was 4th here in 1996, so his 5th this year was his second top 5 in four years.

> Stephen Allan had an intercostal muscle injury (sand boarding) early this year. However, a good finish in the Wales Open and a fine T6th here make him a player to note, especially in the wind.

> Greg Turner had injured left wrist tendons early in season. T12th in the English Open and T9th here shows he is back to form.

● It will be worth remembering the players who made good scores in the tough conditions in R3. They included (apart from Lee Westwood)

> Frederik Jacobson (70)

> Nicolas Vanhootegem (71)

> Stephen Allan and Carl Suneson (73)

1999 RESULT

1	100/1	David Park
T2	25/1	David Carter
T2	12/1	Retief Goosen
4	66/1*	Peter O'Malley
5	16/1	Lee Westwood

1998 RESULT

The tournament was abandoned. At the time of abondonment only 43 players had completed R2. (please see p 101 of Elliott's Golf Form 1999 for full details).

WINNERS OF THIS TOURNAMENT

1996	Retief Goosen	1999	David Park
1997	Colin Montgomerie	2000	Lee Westwood
1998	Tournament Void		

PUNTERS' GUIDE

● The best course records are held by

> Lee Westwood   W 2000: 5th 1999: 3rd 1997

> Retief Goosen   T2nd 1999: 2nd 1997: W 1996 - stroke average of 68.92!!

> Jamie Spence   T6th 2000: T11th 1996: T6th 1997: T9th 1996

> Andrew Coltart   T18th 2000: T16th 1999: T17th 1996

> David Carter   T22nd 2000: T2nd 1999: T6th 1997

- In 2001 much will depend on the positioning of this tournament in the calendar. If it's once more straight after the US Open it will attract few of the top Euros. If it isn't then Goosen and Monty, who have fine track records, might participate.

- It is an interesting fact that the four winners of this event were all leading (or T1st) after R3 so front-runners have 100% record here on the final day.

- Players whose profiles refer to this tournament include Lee Westwood, Emanuele Canonica, David Carter, Stephen Allan, Nicolas Vanhootegem, Dean Robertson, Andrew Oldcorn, Jamie Spence, Ian Poulter, Massimo Scarpa and Greg Turner.

THE MURPHY'S IRISH OPEN

Date	29th June - 2nd July
Course	Ballybunion, County Kerry, Eire
Par	71
Yardage	6,620
First Prize	£157,000
Total Purse	£943,000

THE TOURNAMENT

The Irish Open used four courses in the nineties. This year for the first time it moved with much anticipation to the Ballybunion course situated on the far west coast in County Kerry.

THE COURSE

Ballybunion is a rugged links course featuring many large sand dunes. Not surprisingly it gets buffeted by the wind from the Atlantic. It has an unusual par 71 including five par 3s and four par 5s so there are only nine par 4s. It is a very highly rated course (world top 10) with small greens which were measured no higher than ten on the stimpmeter.

2000 ODDS

fav	15/2	Darren Clarke	66/1	Mark McNulty
	14/1	Sergio Garcia (DC)	66/1*	Angel Cabrera
	16/1	Padraig Harrington	66/1	Stephen Leaney
	16/1	M A Jimenez	66/1	Greg Turner
	22/1	J M Olazabal	66/1	Peter O'Malley
	28/1	Ian Woosnam	66/1	Eduardo Romero
	28/1	Retief Goosen	66/1	Fredrik Jacobson
	40/1	Bernhard Langer	80/1*	M A Martin
	50/1*	Thomas Bjorn	80/1	Emanuele Canonica
	50/1	Phillip Price	80/1	David Carter
	50/1	Paul McGinley	80/1*	Jose Coceres
	50/1	Adam Scott	80/1	Mathias Gronberg
	50/1	Nick O'Hern	80/1	David Howell
	66/1	Robert Karlsson	80/1*	Mark James

2000 RESULT

1	100/1*	Patrik Sjoland	64 65 71 70 270
2	66/1	Fredrik Jacobson	69 63 69 71 272
T3	125/1	Rolf Muntz	66 64 68 76 274
T3	50/1	Paul McGinley	67 70 66 71 274
5	125/1	Peter Lonard	69 68 72 66 275

T6	E Romero	68 66 70 72 276		T45	A Oldcorn	69 71 71 73 284
	D Smyth	65 70 70 71 276			J Moseley	67 75 71 71 284
	N O'Hern	69 68 70 69 276			A Bossert	69 69 74 72 284
	B Dredge	70 68 73 65 276			T Bjorn	68 69 70 77 284
T10	B Langer	73 66 70 68 277			G Owen	70 68 74 72 284
	P Walton	67 67 71 72 277			S Allan	73 68 73 70 284
	S Garcia	64 70 66 77 277			D Robertson	71 68 73 72 284
	Mark Davis	73 66 69 69 277			P Gribben	69 67 70 78 284
	J M Olazabal	73 67 66 71 277		T53	T Johnstone	73 69 73 70 285
	A Cabrera	69 69 72 67 277			M Mackenzie	73 69 73 70 285
	R Wessels	68 68 71 70 277			S Webster	73 66 74 72 285
	J Sandelin	71 71 66 69 277			T Gogele	72 68 70 75 285
	D Carter	67 70 72 68 277			I Garbutt	65 71 73 76 285
	A Scott	73 68 67 69 277			V Phillips	72 70 71 72 285
20	T Levet	69 68 72 69 278		T59	S Hamill	72 65 74 75 286
T21	P Mitchell	69 70 69 71 279			M Scarpa	73 63 75 75 286
	R Goosen	69 68 74 28 279			D Lynn	70 70 78 68 286
T23	Rodger Davis	72 67 73 68 280			N Fasth	72 67 71 76 286
	A McLardy	73 66 71 70 280		T63	I Woosnam	71 68 73 75 287
	Robert Karlsson	71 70 68 71 280			D Hospital	76 66 72 73 287
	S Gallacher	70 66 74 70 280			R S Johnson	73 68 72 74 287
	A Forsyth	72 66 70 72 280			B Teilleria	72 67 74 74 287
T28	P Harrington	67 71 72 71 281			L Parsons	65 73 76 73 287
	S Tinning	69 71 70 71 281		T68	Soren Hansen	71 67 73 77 288
	J Robinson	70 70 69 72 281			J Skold	65 74 79 70 288
	Ricardo Gonzalez	74 68 70 69 281		T70	B Lane	70 72 74 73 289
T32	R Chapman	73 66 72 71 282			R Coughlan	71 70 75 73 289
	M Farry	72 67 70 73 282			G Rojas	74 67 68 80 289
	S Struver	71 71 73 67 282		T73	P O'Malley	69 70 72 79 290
	S Leaney	70 70 71 71 282			E Canonica	71 71 75 73 290
	H Otto	70 69 74 69 282			G Hamerton	70 72 74 74 290
	D Clarke	72 70 68 72 282		76	J Haeggman	73 69 74 75 291
	J Coceres	70 67 77 68 282		T77	M Lanner	70 71 75 76 292
	S Dyson	67 69 68 78 282			P Fowler	71 71 75 75 292
T40	A Forsbrand	70 68 72 73 283			M Murphy	70 70 79 73 292
	G Emerson	71 69 67 76 283		80	G Turner	75 67 73 78 293
	A Butterfield	71 68 71 73 283		T81	D McGrane	73 69 74 78 294
	R Russell	67 69 72 75 283			S Quinlivan	72 70 69 83 294
	C Hanell	69 73 68 73 283		83	M Lafeber	71 70 75 79 295

The main players to miss the cut (made at level) were:-

W Riley (+1)	S Torrance (+1)	G Murphy (+1)	R Jacquelin (+1)
J Rose (+1)	P Eales (+1)	M Kuchar (+1)	R Winchester (+1)
P Price (+1)	R Coles (+1)	W-T Yeh (+1)	S Lyle (+2)
M A Martin (+2)	A Wall (+2)	E Boult (+2)	I Poulter (+2)
R Byrd (+2)	P Nyman (+2)	J Berendt (+2)	S Scahill (+2)
I Pyman (+2)	J Bickerton (+2)	D Higgins (+2)	G Spring (+3)
G Hutcheon (+3)	P Baker (+3)	M James (+4)	C Rocca (+4)
K Storgaard (+4)	P Quirici (+4)	M Florioli (+4)	M Blackey (+4)
E Darcy (+5)	J Rivero (+5)	P Lawrie (+5)	C Hainline (+5)
I Garrido (+5)	M Brier (+5)	M Jonzon (+5)	J Dwyer (+5)
M McNulty (+6)	T Gillis (+6)	P Golding (+6)	G Ogilvy (+6)
S Rowe (+6)	J Lomas (+6)	G Evans (+6)	N Vanhootegem (+6)
D De Vooght (+6)	J G Kelly (+6)	S Ballesteros (+7)	B McGovern (+7)
D Borrego (+7)	S Kjeldsen (+8)	J Senden (+8)	F Lindgren (+8)
M Gronberg (+8)	E Brady (+8)	F Cea (+9)	D Park (+9)
D Howell (+10)	R McFarlane (+10)	R Green (+10)	P Fulke (+10)
O Eliasson (+10)	C Suneson (+13)		

J M Singh (76) and Ronan Rafferty (69) retired.
M A Jimenez withdrew at the 5th in R1 suffering from flu.

ROUND BY ROUND LEADERBOARD

FIRST ROUND

P SJOLAND	7 under
S Garcia	7 under
L Parsons	6 under
I Garbutt	6 under
J Skold	6 under
D Smyth	6 under

SECOND ROUND

P SJOLAND	13 under
R Muntz	12 under
F Jacobson	10 under
S Garcia	8 under
E Romero	8 under
P Walton	8 under

THIRD ROUND

R Muntz	15 under
P SJOLAND	13 under
S Garcia	13 under
F Jacobson	12 under
P McGinley	10 under
E Romero	9 under
S Dyson	9 under

FINAL ROUND

P SJOLAND	14 under
F Jacobson	12 under
R Muntz	10 under
P McGinley	10 under
P Lonard	9 under

Conditions were perfect on Thursday morning, giving the early starters an advantage. The breeze got up in the afternoon to penalise the afternoon players.

PUNTERS' POINTS

● 'The Nappy Factor rules again (and so does the DYM system!)'. Seven weeks after the birth of his first child, a son Patrik (call him Paddy now), Sjoland kept his nerve to post a sub-par final round to record his first 72-hole European tour win.

With Don Stewart, Victor Chandler's shrewd compiler, pricing him up at just 50/1 Sjoland was a DYM with 100/1 on offer from Ladbrokes.

- The feature of the final round was the nervy play of the main contenders.
  - Sergio Garcia showed his brittle links temperament with a 77.
  - Rolf Muntz went 4 over par on the back nine in a 76.
  - Fredrik Jacobson had looked the steadiest player of all. Then, standing 1 up with 2 holes to play, his nerves took over his swing and course management deserted him as he finished bogey-bogey.
- Paul McGinley, having missed the cut in three of the last five years in his national championship, finished strongly (eagle at 17th) to claim a share of 3rd place.
- However, the key player to note here was surely Aussie Adam Scott, playing in only his second tournament as a professional. He finished T10th, although his final three rounds (all in the 60s) were truly brilliant. A certain future star? You'd better ADAM and eve it; great SCOTT what more evidence do we need?
- The advantage of an early tee time in R1 was well illustrated here as Sjoland gained vital momentum with a 6 under par 65 to go into a tie for the lead.
- Isn't it a shame there was no market this year on the top Irish player? The result would have been 1. P McGinley, 2. D Smyth, 3. P Walton with D Clarke (5th) and P Harrington (4th) both unplaced.

1999 RESULT

1	33/1	Sergio Garcia
2	100/1	Angel Cabrera
3	150/1	Jarrod Moseley
T4	150/1*	Eamonn Darcy
T4	66/1*	Thomas Bjorn
T4	80/1*	M A Martin

1998 RESULT

1	125/1	David Carter
won play-off at first play-off hole		
2	fav 8/1	Colin Montgomerie
T3	80/1	Peter Baker
T3	250/1	John McHenry
5	250/1	Craig Hainline

WINNERS IN THE LAST TEN YEARS

1991 Nick Faldo, Killarney
1992 Nick Faldo, Killarney
1993 Nick Faldo, Mt Juliet
1994 Bernhard Langer, Mt Juliet
1995 Sam Torrance, Mt Juliet

1996 Colin Montgomerie, Druids Glen
1997 Colin Montgomerie, Druids Glen
1998 David Carter, Druids Glen
1999 Sergio Garcia, Druids Glen
2000 Patrik Sjoland, Ballybunion

PUNTERS' GUIDE

- In the last three years this tournament has favoured the big-priced outsiders. Of the sixteen players who have finished in the front 5 (or T5th).
  - nine (56.25%) have been priced at or over 100/1
  - eleven (68.75%) have been priced at or over 80/1
  - thirteen (81.25%) have been priced at or over 66/1
  - Only two players have been placed who were priced at or under 33/1.

● In 2001 the tournament moves once more to a new venue east of Cork. However some players clearly enjoy this tournament whatever its venue.

The best recent records belong to

	2000	1999	1998	1997
Jose Maria Olazabal	10	–	9	6
David Carter	10	21	Won	15
Peter Lonard	5	57	8	–
Angel Cabrera	10	2	70	MC

● Players whose profiles refer to this tournament include David Carter, Peter Lonard, Andrew McLardy, Stephen Leaney, Angel Cabrera, Jose Maria Olazabal, Padraig Harrington, Nick O'Hern, Des Smyth and Ricardo Gonzalez

THE SMURFIT EUROPEAN OPEN

Date	6th - 9th July
Course	K Club, Dublin
Par	72
Yardage	7,179
First Prize	£250,000
Total Purse	£1.5 million

THE TOURNAMENT

This is one of the most valuable non-majors on the European tour and attracts a very strong field. This year the tournament was brought forward by three weeks so that it preceded the British Open.

THE COURSE

This is a long par 72 course tightened up considerably since Johansson's 1997 win and especially since Darren Clarke's 60 in R2 last year. As the venue for the 2005 Ryder Cup it now provides a severe test with only the par 5 4th and 18th holes providing real birdie/eagle chances. Length off the tee is an advantage here.

2000 ODDS

fav	6/1	Colin Montgomerie	66/1*	Andrew Coltart
	7/1	Lee Westwood (DC)	66/1*	Adam Scott
	12/1	Darren Clarke	66/1	Nick O'Hern
	22/1	Padraig Harrington	66/1	Phillip Price
	28/1	Michael Campbell	66/1	Fredrik Jacobson
	28/1	J M Olazabal	66/1	Robert Karlsson
	33/1	Retief Goosen	66/1	Eduardo Romero
	40/1	Paul McGinley	80/1*	Paul Lawrie
	40/1	Ian Woosnam	80/1	Jarmo Sandelin
	50/1	Bernhard Langer	80/1	Jose Coceres
	50/1	Thomas Bjorn	80/1	David Carter
	50/1	Angel Cabrera	80/1	Stephen Leaney
	50/1	Gary Orr	80/1	Peter O'Malley
	50/1	Jean Van de Velde	80/1	Jamie Spence
	50/1	Patrik Sjoland (PWW)	80/1	Greg Turner

2000 RESULT

1	7/1 Lee Westwood	71 68 71 66 276
2	50/1 Angel Cabrera	67 72 70 68 277
3	100/1 P-U Johansson	70 71 70 67 278
4	100/1 Mathias Gronberg	73 69 70 67 279
T5	125/1 Ignacio Garrido	70 70 71 69 280
T5	80/1 Jarmo Sandelin	70 71 69 70 280

7	D Clarke	72 67 72 71 282		N Fasth	72 74 72 74 292
T8	C Montgomerie	67 73 73 72 285		P Harrington	73 71 71 77 292
	P Lawrie	74 73 68 70 285		T Gillis	75 66 78 73 292
	T Bjorn	70 74 69 72 285		S Torrance	71 73 76 72 292
	G Evans	69 70 76 70 285		S Gallacher	72 73 74 73 292
12	D Lynn	75 70 69 72 286		R Chapman	73 73 76 70 292
T13	D Robertson	75 67 73 72 287	T46	S Leaney	72 74 77 70 293
	Phillip Price	70 69 73 75 287		P Fulke	68 72 77 76 293
	Mark Davis	72 71 70 74 287		J-F Remesy	69 75 75 74 293
	C Hanell	69 72 76 70 287		Ricardo Gonzalez	69 71 73 80 293
	P McGinley	69 72 70 76 287		S Lyle	71 73 78 71 293
	S Webster	74 73 71 69 287		J Rose	76 70 72 75 293
	R Wessels	75 71 69 72 287	T52	J M Olazabal	74 72 74 74 294
	J Coceres	75 67 70 75 287		D Borrego	70 74 74 76 294
T21	G Owen	69 77 73 69 288		T Levet	73 73 72 76 294
	D Gilford	70 71 72 75 288	T55	E Canonica	75 72 74 74 295
	P O'Malley	70 72 76 70 288		B Langer	72 73 78 72 295
	S Allan	72 68 75 73 288		N Vanhootegem	70 75 73 77 295
T25	S Kjeldsen	71 75 71 72 289		N O'Hern	71 71 75 78 295
	Jamie Spence	72 75 71 71 289		B Lane	73 73 72 77 295
	E Romero	72 72 73 72 289	T60	D Smyth	72 75 76 73 296
T28	A Oldcorn	70 73 72 75 290		Brian Davis	70 76 77 73 296
	M Scarpa	67 77 75 71 290	T62	P Walton	69 73 78 77 297
	S Tinning	72 72 72 74 290		M Lafeber	72 75 76 74 297
	R Goosen	74 73 69 74 290	T64	J Moseley	73 73 77 75 298
	S Struver	71 73 70 76 290		R Karlsson	72 71 79 76 298
	M Farry	73 70 77 70 290		M Mackenzie	75 71 77 75 298
T34	L Parsons	70 74 72 75 291		P Eales	77 68 75 78 298
	G Orr	72 74 71 74 291	68	O Eliasson	72 73 75 79 299
	M Campbell	77 69 73 72 291	T69	P Nyman	75 72 78 75 300
	A McLardy	74 72 72 73 291		G Emerson	70 69 85 76 300
	D Carter	69 77 74 71 291	T71	J Van de Velde	71 75 79 77 302
T39	M Blackey	74 71 74 73 292		J Skold	74 72 78 81 305

The main players to miss the cut (made at 3 over) were:–

A Forsbrand (+4)	P Mitchell (+4)	B Rumford (+4)	D McGrane (+4)
M McNulty (+3)	O Edmond (+4)	R Winchester (+4)	G Murphy (+4)
V Phillips (+4)	G Brand Jr (+4)	J Berendt (+4)	R Green (+4)
A Cejka (+4)	G Rojas (+4)	J Senden (+4)	R Davis (+4)
I Garbutt (+4)	S Luna (+4)	M Lanner (+5)	S Rowe (+5)
A Hansen (+5)	S Hansen (+5)	A Coltart (+5)	P Senior (+5)
D Hospital (+5)	D Howell (+5)	A Butterfield (+5)	C Hainline (+5)
J Dwyer (+6)	R S Johnson (+6)	C Suneson (+6)	H Otto (+6)
R McFarlane (+6)	K Storgaard (+6)	B Dredge (+6)	E Boult (+6)
G Ogilvy (+7)	J Robinson (+7)	B Teilleria (+7)	P Sjoland (+7)
P Fowler (+7)	I Poulter (+7)	F Jacobson (+7)	I Woosnam (+7)
D Park (+7)	R Claydon (+7)	P Golding (+7)	J Bickerton (+7)
A Bossert (+7)	W-T Yeh (+7)	P Lawrie (+7)	W Riley (+8)

A Scott (+8)	R Byrd (+8)	M A Martin (+8)	E Darcy (+8)
J Rivero (+9)	M Jonzon (+9)	P Quirici (+9)	R Jacquelin (+9)
M Brier (+10)	F Cea (+10)	A Wall (+10)	J Haeggman (+10)
R Rafferty (+10)	P Way (+10)	I Pyman (+11)	C Rocca (+11)
S Scahill (+11)	P Lonard (+11)	G Hamerton (+11)	F Lindgren (+12)
M Florioli (+12)	R Russell (+12)	J Lomas (+12)	R Coles (+12)
G Turner (+13)	D De Vooght (+14)	S Ballesteros (+14)	S Hamill (+14)
P Baker (+15)	G Hutcheon (+15)	T Gogele (+15)	

ROUND BY ROUND LEADERBOARD

FIRST ROUND

C Montgomerie	5 under
M Scarpa	5 under
A Cabrera	5 under
P Fulke	4 under
P Mitchell	4 under
all above were morning starters	
L WESTWOOD	1 under

SECOND ROUND

A Cabrera	5 under
D Clarke	5 under
G Emerson	5 under
L WESTWOOD	5 under
P Price	5 under
G Evans	5 under

THIRD ROUND

A Cabrera	7 under
J Sandelin	6 under
L WESTWOOD	6 under
P-U Johansson	5 under
P McGinley	5 under
D Clarke	5 under
I Garrido	5 under

FINAL ROUND

L WESTWOOD	12 under
A Cabrera	11 under
P-U Johansson	10 under
M Gronberg	9 under
I Garrido	8 under
J Sandelin	8 under

Scoring was difficult on Saturday when as Lee Westwood said, "the bad weather sorted out the men from the boys."

The conditions were blustery, raining and cold on the final day when some of the scores were extremely low in difficult circumstances.

RESULTS IN OTHER MARKETS

Well done to Surrey for creating a specialist TOP SCANDINAVIAN market. The result with three Swedes finishing in the top 6 in the tournament was :-

1	16/1	P-U Johansson
2	14/1	Mathias Gronberg
3	8/1	Jarmo Sandelin

PUNTERS' POINTS

● 7/1 Lee Westwood had never successfully defended a title before...that is until he came to the K Club this week. His final round 66 in difficult, windy wet weather was a mini masterpiece and his second successive win.

● Per-Ulrik Johansson has had hip and lower back problems this season. However he has PMA's with the K Club after his double triumph in 1996 and 1997 and played really well especially in R4. He'd been on offer at a massive 40/1 at the halfway stage.

● 50/1 Angel Cabrera loves July and has a fine K Club record. Helped by an early Thursday tee time he got up the leaderboard and stayed there. However, his driving in R4 was occasionally wayward. Nevertheless he's clearly a 'winner waiting to haρpen'.

● Let's keep an eye on young David Lynn - making his seventeenth consecutive cut he was posting his fifth top 12 finish in a very solid, promising season.

● This tough course can create havoc

> Gary Emerson tied 1st at halfway shot 85-76 to finish T69th

> Peter Baker shot 84 in R2 including a 9 (13th) and a 12 (!!) at the tough 17th to miss the cut by a mile.

> Only twenty players beat par over the four rounds.

1999 RESULT			**1998 RESULT**		
1	10/1	Lee Westwood	1	125/1	Mathias Gronberg
T2	14/1	Darren Clarke	T2	66/1	M A Jimenez
T2	66/1	Peter O'Malley	T2	125/1	Phillip Price
T4	66/1	Costantino Rocca	4	18/1	Darren Clarke
T4	100/1*	Robert Karlsson	T5	125/1	Angel Cabrera
			T5	100/1	Craig Hainline

WINNERS IN THE LAST TEN YEARS

1991	Mike Harwood	1996	P-U Johansson
1992	Nick Faldo	1997	P-U Johansson
1993	Gordon Brand Jr	1998	Mathias Gronberg
1994	David Gilford	1999	Lee Westwood
1995	Bernhard Langer	2000	Lee Westwood

From 1995 onwards the K Club has been the venue.

PUNTERS' GUIDE

● With the considerable tightening up of the course recently the form at the K Club from 1995-97 is of dubious value, although players who did well then (eg Johansson) will still have PMA's with the K Club on the current remodelled course.

● Over these last two years only seven players have posted successive top 20 finishes.

Their 1998 results are also shown.

	2000	1999	1998
Lee Westwood	W	W	–
Angel Cabrera	2	6	5
Per-Ulrik Johansson	3	10	MC
Jose Coceres	13	6	20
Paul Lawrie	8	15	10
Darren Clarke	7	2	4
Colin Montgomerie	8	15	MC

● It is worth noting that a European tournament in Ireland has not been won by an Irishman since 1982(!), so if you're thinking of backing Clarke, McGinley or Harrington (combined odds of just over 5/1 in 2000) beware. Whether it's the expectations, the back-slapping hospitality or the Guinness—or all three—it's an interesting stat.

● Early starters in R1 have a clear advantage, getting the best of the conditions and having a real chance to early momentum. The front 5 after R1 this year were all out early

● Players whose profiles refer to this tournament include Per-Ulrik Johansson, Jose Coceres, Paul Lawrie, Angel Cabrera, Colin Montgomerie, Darren Clarke, Lee Westwood, Steve Webster, Jarmo Sandelin and Mathias Gronberg.

THE STANDARD LIFE LOCH LOMOND WORLD INVITATIONAL

Date	Wednesday 12th July - Saturday, 15th July
Course	Loch Lomond G.C., near Glasgow
Par	71
Yardage	7,050
First Prize	£183,330
Total Purse	£1.1 million

THE TOURNAMENT

This tournament was being held for the fifth successive year, all on this course. It was the fourth consecutive year in which it has been played in the week before the British Open.

THE COURSE

Set in beautiful surroundings, this Tom Weiskopf-designed course has an American feel to it. A solid all-round game is needed, although the longer hitters are favoured. The wind can make this track a very severe examination.

2000ODDS

fav	8/1	Colin Montgomerie (DC)	50/1	Phillip Price
	12/1	Ernie Els	50/1	Jarmo Sandelin
	18/1	Jesper Parnevik	80/1*	Ian Woosnam
	20/1*	David Duval	80/1	Andrew Coltart
	20/1*	Phil Mickelson	80/1*	Glen Day
	25/1	Tom Lehman	80/1	Eduardo Romero
	25/1	Michael Campbell	80/1	Jose Coceres
	40/1	Notah Begay	80/1*	P-U Johansson
	40/1	Thomas Bjorn	80/1	Stephen Leaney
	40/1*	M A Jimenez	80/1*	Bob May
	40/1	J M Olazabal	80/1	Nick O'Hern
	50/1*	Retief Goosen	80/1	Gary Orr
	50/1	Angel Cabrera	80/1	Robert Karlsson
	50/1	Paul Lawrie	80/1	Peter O'Malley
	50/1	Paul McGinley		

2000 RESULT

1	12/1	Ernie Els	69 67 69 68 273
2	25/1	Tom Lehman	66 71 68 69 274
3	fav 8/1	Colin Montgomerie	70 68 68 69 275
T4	40/1	Notah Begay	65 72 68 72 276
T4	50/1*	Retief Goosen	65 72 69 71 276
T4	125/1	Stephen Allan	66 72 72 67 276

T7	J Sandelin	67 69 73 69 278		T41	D Howell	69 74 76 70 289
	P Mickelson	68 72 73 65 278			G Ogilvy	68 74 74 73 289
T9	N Faldo	67 69 70 73 279			P Quirici	68 74 74 73 289
	J M Olazabal	70 71 72 66 279			D Park	70 74 73 72 289
	M Campbell	70 67 70 72 279			C Hanell	69 68 75 77 289
12	A Scott	66 70 71 73 280			O Edmond	72 70 74 73 289
T13	G Orr	69 73 71 68 281			T Levet	69 72 77 71 289
	R Russell	69 71 69 72 281		T48	A Forsyth	69 69 80 72 290
T15	P-U Johansson	67 73 71 71 282			D Duval	70 73 76 71 290
	D Waldorf	71 69 74 68 282			Anders Hansen	72 72 76 70 290
	B May	69 71 72 70 282		T51	R Wessels	73 70 74 74 291
	D Gossett (am)	70 71 72 69 282			I Garrido	69 74 74 74 291
T19	P Lawrie	67 72 74 70 283			M Mackenzie	74 71 72 74 291
	Phillip Price	67 72 70 74 283			P Eales	71 74 76 70 291
	T Bjorn	74 69 73 67 283		T55	A Cejka	73 70 74 75 292
T22	J Coceres	70 74 71 69 284			T Gogele	72 71 78 71 292
	S Leaney	67 77 69 71 284			J Berendt	71 73 76 72 292
	R Green	69 67 72 76 284		T58	R S Johnson	74 71 77 71 293
	J Moseley	69 71 72 72 284			M Farry	72 71 76 74 293
	M Kuchar (am)	69 73 73 69 284		T60	J Senden	68 75 76 75 294
T27	I Pyman	71 72 69 73 285			R Coles	69 75 74 76 294
	J Carter	70 72 74 69 285			D Gilford	73 71 74 76 294
T29	A Cabrera	72 72 73 69 286		T63	S Gallacher	70 73 77 75 295
	D Carter	73 70 71 72 286			R Claydon	68 74 74 79 295
	N Fasth	69 74 72 71 286		T65	B Teilleria	68 75 77 76 296
T32	A Coltart	71 71 73 72 287			A Wall	72 73 76 75 296
	J Rivero	75 69 71 72 287			G Nicklaus	73 72 76 75 296
	B Lane	71 72 73 71 287			C Hainline	72 73 77 74 296
	N O'Hern	69 73 73 72 287		T69	P Sjoland	72 73 76 76 297
	E Romero	72 71 72 72 287			M Gronberg	70 75 80 72 297
	D Robertson	72 67 76 72 287			A McLardy	73 72 76 76 297
T38	J Lomas	72 71 72 73 288		T72	R Gonzalez	75 70 76 77 298
	I Woosnam	70 73 73 72 288			P Lonard	72 71 76 79 298
	M Lafeber	69 72 76 71 288		74	H Otto	71 73 85 78 307

The main players to miss the cut (made at 3 over) were:–

F Lindgren (+4)	G Day (+4)	J Bickerton (+4)	R Muntz (+4)
D De Vooght (+4)	I Poulter (+4)	D Hospital (+4)	J Spence (+4)
P Mitchell (+4)	M Lanner (+4)	P Nyman (+4)	P Baker (+5)
D Lynn (+5)	S Kjeldsen (+5)	S Hansen (+5)	J Parnevik (+5)
W Riley (+5)	S Webster (+5)	D Smyth (+5)	I Garbutt (+5)
S Luna (+5)	S Scahill (+5)	R Jacquelin (+5)	S Struver (+5)
P Fulke (+6)	M A Jimenez (+6)	M James (+6)	G Hutcheon (+6)
C Suneson (+6)	R Karlsson (+6)	D Frost (+7)	M McNulty (+7)
E Canonica (+7)	V Phillips (+7)	B Rumford (+7)	P Affleck (+7)
B Dredge (+8)	M Jonzon (+8)	S Torrance (+8)	P O'Malley (+8)
L Parsons (+8)	G Owen (+8)	R Winchester (+8)	S Lyle (+9)
R McFarlane (+9)	M Brier (+9)	G Turner (+9)	M Scarpa (+9)
D Borrego (+10)	G Evans (+10)	E Darcy (+10)	A Oldcorn (+10)
P Senior (+11)	W-T Yeh (+11)	G Emerson (+11)	J Robinson (+11)
C Rocca (+12)	D Cooper (+12)	R Byrd (+13)	G Brand Jr (+13)
J-F Remesy (+15)	R Davis (+17)	J Skold (+19)	

Mark Davis (79) and Roger Chapman (69) were disqualified. Brian Davis (72) withdrew.

ROUND BY ROUND LEADERBOARD

FIRST ROUND		**SECOND ROUND**	
R Goosen	6 under	N Faldo	6 under
N Begay	6 under	A Scott	6 under
S Allan	5 under	R Green	6 under
T Lehman	5 under	E ELS	6 under
A Scott	5 under	J Sandelin	6 under
6 players at	4 under	5 players at	5 under
E ELS	2 under		

THIRD ROUND		**FINAL ROUND**	
T Lehman	8 under	E ELS	11 under
N Begay	8 under	T Lehman	10 under
E ELS	8 under	C Montgomerie	9 under
R Goosen	7 under	N Begay	8 under
N Faldo	7 under	R Goosen	8 under
C Montgomerie	7 under	S Allan	8 under

Conditions were benign on the first day with the early starters (including the top 5 on the leaderboard) having their customary advantage.

On the second day the 'stagger unwound' as the afternoon players (Thursday's early starters) faced windy difficult conditions.

Round 3 saw high scoring in unpredictable winds.

Round 4 conditions were easier, although the pin positions were tough.

RESULTS IN OTHER MARKETS

TOP AMERICAN

Corals (C), Hills (H), Multi-Sports (MS) and Surrey (S) created odds in this fourteen-runner field with 1/4 odds 1, 2, 3 except for Multi-Sports' poor 1/5 odds 1,2,3. The result was:-

1	9/2 (H,S,MS)	Tom Lehman
2	9/1 (C)	Notah Begay
3	7/2 (S)	Phil Mickelson

TOP AUSTRALASIAN

Corals (C), Surrey (S) and Multi-Sports (MS) created odds in this eighteen-runner field with 1/4 odds 1,2,3,4. Again it was just 1/5 1,2,3 at Multi-Sports. The result was :-

1	20/1 (MS)	Stephen Allan
2	10/1 (C)	Adam Scott
T3	9/1 (S)	Stephen Leaney
T3	25/1 (MS)	Richard Green
T3	25/1 (S)	Jarrod Moseley

TOP SCANDINAVIAN

Only Multi-Sports opened up this specialist market with 1/5 odds 1,2,3,4 in a sixteen-runner field. The result was :-

1	7/1	Jarmo Sandelin
2	7/1	P-U Johansson
3	20/1	Niclas Fasth

TOP SCOT

Once more only Multi-Sports quoted in this market, again with 1/5 odds 1,2,3 in a fourteen-runner field.

1	Evens	Colin Montgomerie
T2	11/2	Gary Orr
T2	20/1	Raymond Russell

PUNTERS' POINTS

- "Els well that ends well," ran the headlines after Big Ernie's first win for seventeen months.
- However the back nine in R4 showed the raw nerves among the challengers.
  > Goosen: twice led in R4 then had three bogeys in the last 5 holes.
  > Lehman: needing par at the last for a play-off drove into the water.
  > Monty: poor drive at the last.
  > Begay: some wild driving over last 6 holes.
  > Scott: four bogeys in the last 4 holes.
- 'Contention rust' set in for Nick Faldo in R4. He drove poorly, shooting the poorest final round score of all the leading contenders.
- Ignore Jesper Parnevik's form here (missed cut at 5 over par) as he's still troubled by his left hip.
- T69th Mathias Gronberg aced the par 3 17th hole in R4 to win a cool £100,000 whereas in R3 Jarmo Sandelin's hole in one on that green got only prolonged applause. The big prize applied only to R4.

● With five American tour players in the top 10 it can be seen that this US-style course is well suited to those who are full time 'across the pond'.

1999 RESULT			1998 RESULT		
1	fav 8/1	Colin Montgomerie	1	16/1	Lee Westwood
T2	125/1	Michael Jonzon	T2	25/1	Ian Woosnam
T2	20/1	Sergio Garcia	T2	50/1	Eduardo Romero
T2	200/1	Mats Lanner	T2	66/1	Robert Allenby
T5	25/1	Jesper Parnevik	T2	66/1	David Howell
T5	16/1	Lee Westwood	T2	200/1	Dennis Edlund

LOCH LOMOND WINNERS TO DATE

1996	Thomas Bjorn	1999	Colin Montgomerie
1997	Tom Lehman	2000	Ernie Els
1998	Lee Westwood		

PUNTERS' GUIDE

● In each of its five years this tournament has 'thrown up' at least one unconsidered outsider in the top 5 - Van de Velde 125/1 (1996), Pierre Fulke 80/1 (1997), Denis Edlund 200/1 (1998), Mats Lanner 200/1 and Michael Jonzen 125/1 in 1999, and Stephen Allan 125/1 this year.

Who could it be in 2001? Two players starting at 80/1 this year with solid chances next year can be found in the player profiles.

● The momentum gained from a fast start off an early tee time is very important here. The front 5 after R1 were always high on the leaderboard throughout the tournament.

● The course at Loch Lomond is not a good preparation for the following week's British Open played on a links course. However a good Loch Lomond gives a player a much-needed injection of confidence at just the right time.

● Players with the best records here include.

> Ernie Els   Won 2000: 2nd 1997 in only two starts

> Colin Montgomerie From 1996 his form figures are 4-10-7-W-3!

> Retief Goosen   T4 2000: 10th 1999: DNP 1998: 3rd 1997

> Thomas Bjorn   From 1996 W-13-33-20-19

> Michael Campbell   T7th 1999: T9th 2000 for successive top 10s

> Tom Lehman   2nd 2000: T9th 1998: W 1997

● European players whose profiles refer to this tournament include Retief Goosen, Thomas Bjorn, Michael Campbell, Stephen Leaney, Colin Montgomerie and Gary Orr.

USA tour players include Ernie Els, Tom Lehman, Bob May, Robert Allenby and Duffy Waldorf.

THE FOUR FINAL QUALIFYING STAGES FOR THE BRITISH OPEN

Lundin

T1	33/1	Raymond Russell
T1	100/1	Jim Carriles
T1	33/1	Pierre Fulke
4	28/1	David Sutherland

Scotscraig

1	20/1*	Jamie Spence
2	33/1*	Simon Dyson
3	66/1	Paul Eales
T4	33/1*	Sam Torrance
T4	100/1	J Randhawa

Leven Links

1	20/1	Mark McNulty
2	25/1	Roger Chapman
T3	40/1	Luke Donald
T3	11/1	Eduardo Romero
T3	25/1	Greg Owen

Ladybank

1	100/1	Paul Affleck
2	50/1*	Andrew Oldcorn
T3	100/1	Sam Little
T3	100/1	Scott Watson
T3	100/1	Gary Emerson
T3	66/1	J-F Remesey

Congratulations to Corals, Hills, Surrey and Multi-Sports who all opened up markets on these four courses with 1/4 1,2,3,4 the place odds.

PUNTERS' GUIDE

● In normal outright betting there is always a winner even if it takes a play-off. These particular markets are different as it is possible to have a dead heat, as at the Lundin course.

● There clearly is pressure on the players, although it cannot be compared to the 'heat' of the back nine in R4 on Sunday in a normal tournament.

● The 'value' that can be thrown up here was well illustrated by Raymond Russell's 33/1 (dh) success at Lundin.

> 4th in the Open itself two years ago

> a fine T13th in the Loch Lomond the day before the pre-qualifying

> a recognised links player

> a Scot with local knowledge and he was 33/1!

So even in these unusual markets there are sound bets to be had if you dig deeply enough!

THE 129TH BRITISH OPEN

Date	20th - 23rd July
Course	St Andrews
Par	72
Yardage	7,115
First Prize	£500,000
Total Purse	£2.75 million

PLEASE SEE PART 6.

THE TNT DUTCH OPEN

Date	27th - 30th July
Course	Noordwijkse, near Amsterdam
Par	72
Yardage	6,879
First Prize	£133,300
Total Purse	£800,000

THE TOURNAMENT

This is a well-established tournament first played in 1919 and it is now regularly scheduled as the first tournament after the British Open.

THE COURSE

This year the Dutch Open moved from Hilversum to the Noordwijske course which is hilly and is a links course near the coast subject to winds from the North Sea. It was last used for this tournament from 1991-1993 inclusive.

2000 ODDS

fav	9/2	Lee Westwood (DC)	50/1	Eduardo Romero
	13/2	Darren Clarke	50/1	Mark McNulty
	16/1	Thomas Bjorn (non runner)	66/1*	Stephen Leaney
	16/1	Padraig Harrington	66/1	Mathias Gronberg
	20/1	John Huston	80/1*	Stephen Allan
	28/1	Bernhard Langer	80/1	Fredrik Jacobson
	33/1	Angel Cabrera	80/1*	Peter O'Malley
	33/1	Jose Coceres	80/1	Steen Tinning
	40/1*	Gary Orr	80/1	Greg Turner
	40/1	Paul McGinley	80/1	Richard Green
	40/1	Andrew Coltart		

2000 RESULT

1	66/1*	**Stephen Leaney**	**66 70 65 68 269**
2	28/1	**Bernhard Langer**	**69 68 68 68 273**
T3	33/1	**Angel Cabrera**	**68 69 69 68 274**
T3	66/1	**Mathias Gronberg**	**68 68 69 69 274**
T3	fav 9/2	**Lee Westwood**	**67 72 66 69 274**

6	R Wessels	73 69 68 65 275		T44	A Forsyth	71 71 75 67 284
T7	S Allan	68 67 69 72 276			T Emerson	70 73 72 69 284
	S Luna	68 69 71 68 276			G Hamerton	68 76 68 72 284
	J Rivero	70 68 69 69 276			G Evans	75 68 70 71 284
	G Owen	68 73 69 66 276		T48	E Darcy	71 73 69 72 285
T11	E Romero	69 67 72 69 277			S Richardson	68 71 69 77 285
	P Quirici	70 73 68 66 277			Olle Karlsson	69 73 73 70 285
	M Mouland	67 70 72 68 277		T51	G Turner	69 73 74 70 286
T14	G Brand Jr	72 71 72 63 278			A Forsbrand	72 69 72 73 286
	J Moseley	70 67 72 69 278			S Field	73 71 71 71 286
	P O'Malley	70 69 71 68 278			H Bensdorp	69 73 72 72 286
T17	S Kjeldsen	69 73 65 72 279			O Edmond	73 71 70 72 286
	M Tunnicliff	70 67 70 72 279		T56	D Park	69 71 74 73 287
	J Haeggman	72 68 72 67 279			Anders Hansen	67 74 75 71 287
	D Clarke	72 69 67 71 279		T58	A Oldcorn	70 73 72 73 288
	S Tinning	72 71 68 68 279			I Pyman	72 72 75 69 288
	F Jacobson	73 66 70 70 279			D Howell	71 73 73 71 288
	R Winchester	67 71 71 70 279			F Tarnaud	75 69 74 70 288
	J Bickerton	69 70 71 69 279			J Robinson	73 71 71 73 288
	E Little	69 72 72 66 279			J-F Remesy	70 73 73 72 288
T26	R Claydon	71 72 69 68 280			M Mackenzie	70 69 72 77 288
	S Struver	71 69 71 69 280		T65	P Affleck	71 70 72 76 289
T28	J Rose	68 72 69 72 281			H Nystrom	73 71 75 70 289
	P Harrington	69 70 73 69 281			M Anglert	74 70 72 73 289
	D Lee	72 71 68 70 281		T68	B Jones	70 74 73 73 290
	I Poulter	73 70 69 69 281			S Wakefield	73 71 71 75 290
	R S Johnson	66 70 74 71 281			J M Carriles	69 75 73 73 290
T33	C Suneson	74 70 70 68 282			I Giner	70 74 75 71 290
	S Dyson	71 68 72 71 282		T72	K Storgaard	69 74 71 77 291
	Soren Hansen	70 71 72 69 282			A Raitt	74 69 73 75 291
	J Huston	74 67 70 71 282			A Sherborne	72 72 73 74 291
	M Florioli	71 68 71 72 282		75	Brian Davis	74 68 78 72 292
	Ricardo Gonzalez	68 70 71 73 282		T76	R Miller	67 72 80 74 293
	A McLardy	70 70 73 69 282			R Russell	70 71 79 73 293
	V Phillips	71 71 70 70 282		78	G Hutcheon	71 72 75 76 294
T41	J Berendt	71 71 72 69 283		T79	O Eliasson	69 75 74 77 295
	I Garbutt	70 72 71 70 283			T J Munoz	71 71 77 76 295
	I Hutchings	70 69 72 72 283		81	K Carissimi	69 74 78 78 299

The main players to miss the cut (made at level) were:-

D Smyth (+1)	R Davis (+1)	A Coltart (+1)	M McNulty (+1)
N Vanhootegem (+1)	T Gogele (+1)	J Coceres (+1)	K Tomori (+1)
R Coles (+1)	R Green (+1)	M Lanner (+2)	R Jacquelin (+2)
P Fowler (+3)	F Cea (+3)	M Lafeber (+3)	P Lonard (+3)
P McGinley (+3)	R J Derksen (+3)	B Teilleria (+3)	D Gilford (+4)
T Gillis (+4)	D Hospital (+4)	J Senden (+4)	C Rocca (+4)
R McFarlane (+4)	A Beal (+4)	G Rojas (+5)	M Scarpa (+5)
C Hanell (+6)	E Boult (+6)	P Walton (+6)	P Mitchell (+6)
P G Nyman (+6)	P Way (+6)	P Nyman (+6)	M Jonzon (+6)
F Roca (+7)	M Davis (+7)	S McAllister (+7)	D Lynn (+8)
D Borrego (+10)	W Riley (+13)		

Jonathan Lomas (74), Marc Farry (81) and Jim Payne (76) all withdrew.
Gary Orr withdrew at the first hole (!) with a bad back.
Anthony Wall withdrew when 3 over after 15 holes in R1 due to glandular fever.

ROUND BY ROUND LEADERBOARD

FIRST ROUND		SECOND ROUND	
S LEANEY	6 under	S Allan	9 under
R S Johnson	6 under	R S Johnson	8 under
L Westwood	5 under	M Gronberg	8 under
R Miller	5 under	S LEANEY	8 under
M Mouland	5 under	E Romero	8 under
R Winchester	5 under	6 players at	7 under
A Hansen	5 under		

THIRD ROUND		FINAL ROUND	
S LEANEY	15 under	S LEANEY	19 under
S Allan	12 under	B Langer	15 under
L Westwood	11 under	A Cabrera	14 under
B Langer	11 under	L Westwood	14 under
M Gronberg	11 under	M Gronberg	14 under
A Cabrera	10 under		

Without too many long holes, and with a light breeze rather than windy conditions, there were plenty of birdie chances.

PUNTERS' POINTS

● Stephen Leaney's win was very, very impressive. Making only one bogey all week, he proved here once more that he is a fine front runner, mentally strong, a superb ball striker and he loves this tournament which he won two years ago on a different course.

● It was another triumph for the DYM system as Leaney, 66/1 at Hills, was just 33/1 at Corals and the second-shortest DYM in the field.

● 28/1 Bernhard Langer finished well in the British Open and was proven here as the winner in 1992. He played well to finish 2nd.

● Stephen Allan is a fine links player, in good form and was over-priced at Stan James's 80/1. However the pressure told in R4 as he slipped back to finish T7th.

● Gordon Brand Jr, who lost in a play-off here in 1992, showed once more his liking for this course with a 63 in R4 to finish T14th.

● T10th in the Irish Open, very unlucky not to prequalify for the British Open (lost in a play-off) and a fast finishing 6th here, Roger Wessels proved once more that he's a fine links player.

1999 RESULT

1	jt fav 12/1	Lee Westwood
2	80/1*	Gary Orr
T3	40/1	Eduardo Romero
T3	100/1	Jarrod Moseley
T5	125/1	Craig Spence
T5	150/1	Martin Lafeber
T5	jt fav 12/1	Darren Clarke

1998 RESULT

1	125/1	Stephen Leaney
2	22/1	Darren Clarke
T3	14/1	Nick Price
T3	fav 10/1	Lee Westwood
5	40/1	Costantino Rocca

WINNERS IN THE LAST TEN YEARS

1991	Payne Stewart	1996	Mark McNulty
1992	Bernhard Langer	1997	Sven Struver
1993	Colin Montgomerie	1998	Stephen Leaney
1994	M A Jimenez	1999	Lee Westwood
1995	Scott Hoch	2000	Stephen Leaney

Noordwijkse from 1991–93 and in 2000
Hilversum from 1994–1999

PUNTERS' GUIDE

● Seven players who had posted a top 20 here between 1992-94 again had a top 20 finish this year. They were:-

> Bernhard Langer	W 1992: 2nd 2000
> Roger Winchester	T10th 1992: T17th 2000
> Eduardo Romero	T10th 1994: T11th 2000
> Steen Tinning	T6th 1993: T17th 2000
> Peter O'Malley	T20th 1992: T14th 2000
> Gordon Brand Jr	2nd 1992: T14th 2000 (63 in R4)
> Mark Mouland	T7th 1992: T11th 2000

● Players with a good record in Holland on both the Hilversum (H) course and the Noordwijkse (N) course include:-

> Lee Westwood   T3rd 2000 (N): W 1999 (H): T3rd 1998 (H)

> Jarrod Moseley   T14th 2000 (N): T3rd 1999 (H)

> Angel Cabrera   T3rd 2000 (N): T8th 1999 (H): T3rd 1997 (H)

> Eduard Romero   T11th 2000 (N): T3rd 1999 (H)

> Stephen Leaney   W 2000 (N): T15th 1999 (H): W 1998 (H)

● Players coming here having been in serious contention in the British Open the previous week rarely do well. This year Darren Clarke (T4th after R3 in the British Open) suffered MLD, never 'got going' and came home a tired T17th. Jose Coceres (7 under after R3 last week) missed the cut here and Thomas Bjorn was so jaded he withdrew late on.

● The stats for this tournament were:-

Driving Accuracy		Greens In Reg		Putts per GIR	
T1	P Harrington	1	J Bickerton	1	M Gronberg
T1	I Hutchings	2	P O'Malley	2	R Claydon
T3	P Quirici	T3	G Owen	3	A Cabrera
T3	E Darcy	T3	I Garbutt	4	J-F Remesy

● In 2001 the tournament will stay at the Noordwijkse course used this year.

● Players whose profiles refer to this tournament include Gordon Brand Jr, Roger Winchester, Steen Tinning, Lee Westwood, Angel Cabrera, Jarrod Moseley, Stephen Allan, Roger Wessels, Fredrik Jacobson, Bernhard Langer, Stephen Leaney and Jose Coceres.

THE SCANDINAVIAN MASTERS

Date   3rd - 6th August
Course   Kungsangen G.C., Stockholm
Par   72
Yardage   6,724
First Prize   £160,000
Total Purse   £960,000

THE TOURNAMENT

This tournament started in 1991 and has yet to be played on the same course in consecutive years.

THE COURSE

Designed by Anders Forsbrand and opened in 1994, the Kungsangen course was used for this tournament in 1998. It is a parkland course built in and around pine forests. It is one of the flagship courses of the PGA European Tour Courses plc. Accuracy off the tee is particularly important.

2000 ODDS

fav	11/2	Colin Montgomerie	66/1	Andrew Coltart
	13/2	Lee Westwood	66/1	Ian Woosnam
	10/1	Jesper Parnevik	66/1*	Phillip Price
	12/1	Darren Clarke	66/1	Patrik Sjoland
	22/1	Thomas Bjorn	80/1	Steen Tinning
	25/1	Michael Campbell	80/1	David Carter
	33/1	Mathias Gronberg	80/1*	Fredrik Jacobson
	40/1	P-U Johansson	80/1*	Jarrod Moseley
	50/1	Nick O'Hern	80/1	Jamie Spence
	50/1	Stephen Allan	80/1	Greg Turner
	66/1	Gary Orr	80/1	Roger Wessels

2000 RESULTS

1	13/2	Lee Westwood	63 67 69 71	270
2	25/1	Michael Campbell	69 71 66 67	273
3	150/1*	Raymond Russell	69 69 69 67	274
T4	150/1	Diego Borrego	66 70 71 68	275
T4	80/1	Jamie Spence	70 69 70 66	275

T6	K Tomori	65 73 68 70	276
	M Lafeber	67 66 72 71	276
	T Gillis	70 69 67 70	276
	S Tinning	71 68 67 70	276
10	J Senden	70 64 74 69	277
T11	B Lane	69 63 76 70	278
	J Parnevik	71 69 69 69	278
	G Turner	71 70 71 66	278
	H Stenson	69 71 70 68	278
	Ricardo Gonzalez	71 68 70 69	278
	C Hanell	68 73 68 69	278
T17	I Woosnam	72 71 68 68	279
	S Webster	72 64 73 70	279
	C Montgomerie	68 71 70 70	279
	P-U Johansson	69 72 67 71	279
	P Fulke	75 67 67 70	279
	F Tarnaud	72 65 69 73	279
T23	D Gilford	67 74 69 70	280
	A McLardy	70 69 68 73	280
	P Quirici	73 68 73 66	280
	D Clarke	69 66 74 71	280
	T Bjorn	71 72 68 69	280
	A Coltart	70 73 67 70	280
T29	D Lee	71 68 70 72	281
	S Gallacher	71 70 72 68	281
T31	G Brand Jr	68 70 75 69	282
	T Levet	69 71 68 74	282
	O Karlsson	66 69 76 71	282
	M Gronberg	71 70 69 72	282
	P Sjoland	72 70 71 69	282
T36	S Struver	69 71 70 73	283
	A Forsyth	72 70 69 72	283
T38	K Storgaard	73 67 72 72	284
	J Rose	69 72 71 72	284
	F Lindgren	68 68 74 74	284
	P Nyman	71 69 72 72	284

	I Hutchings	67 70 74 73	284
	G Orr	73 69 71 71	284
	D Lynn	69 71 71 73	284
T45	Anders Hansen	72 70 71 72	285
	J Moseley	73 66 74 72	285
	T Gogele	71 71 71 72	285
	J Bickerton	70 72 70 73	285
	S Dyson	71 68 75 71	285
T50	T Johnstone	72 68 75 71	286
	A Butterfield	71 71 71 73	286
T52	D Smyth	73 70 69 75	287
	I Poulter	69 74 70 74	287
	P Golding	73 70 74 70	287
	J Haeggman	71 72 73 71	287
	R Sjoberg	74 69 73 71	287
	G Norquist	71 71 74 71	287
T58	K Eriksson	71 71 72 74	288
	R McFarlane	72 71 73 72	288
	M Florioli	73 69 73 73	288
	M Anglert	71 72 72 73	288
T62	R Chapman	72 70 74 73	289
	D Carter	73 69 71 76	289
T64	G Murphy	72 68 75 75	290
	S Field	70 73 73 74	290
	Phillip Price	72 69 70 79	290
	G Hamerton	73 70 75 72	290
T68	P Eales	71 71 73 76	291
	L Parsons	72 71 74 74	291
T70	D Edlund	70 73 75 74	292
	M Scarpa	72 71 73 76	292
	M Brier	71 72 75 74	292
73	L Petterson (am)	69 74 75 76	294
74	S D Hurley	71 69 81 74	295
	J Robinson	71 72 74 78	295
76	S Richardson	70 73 76 77	296

The main players to miss the cut (made at 1 over) were:-

I Pyman (+2)	P Affleck (+2)	J Rystrom (+2)	M Farry (+2)
J Rask (+2)	H Nystrom (+2)	P Fowler (+2)	S Allan (+2)
V Phillips (+2)	D Robertson (+2)	H Otto (+2)	C Hainline (+2)
W Riley (+2)	N O'Hern (+2)	R Coles (+2)	I Giner (+2)
C Suneson (+2)	S Kjeldsen (+2)	P Lonard (+3)	R Wessels (+3)
M A Martin (+3)	M Lanner (+3)	G Evans (+3)	G Emerson (+3)
N Vanhootegem (+3)	M Mackenzie (+3)	R Winchester (+3)	N Fasth (+3)
S Hansen (+3)	F Jacobson (+3)	D Howell (+3)	S Luna (+3)
D Park (+5)	R Green (+5)	R Karlsson (+5)	A Forsbrand (+5)
J Berendt (+5)	J Rivero (+5)	I Garrido (+6)	S Rowe (+6)
R Davis (+7)	P Baker (+7)	C Rocca (+7)	M Hallberg (+7)
R Claydon (+8)	R S Johnson (+10)	R Jacquelin (+11)	S Scahill (+11)
D De Vooght (+12)	F Cea (+15)	F Roca (+15)	M Jonzon (+15)

Andrew Oldcorn (73), Nick Ludwell (80), Bradley Dredge (76) and Elliot Boult (77) all retired.

ROUND BY ROUND LEADERBOARD

FIRST ROUND

L WESTWOOD	8 under
K Tomori	6 under
O Karlsson	5 under
D Borrego	5 under
M Lafeber	4 under
D Gilford	4 under
I Hutchings	4 under

SECOND ROUND

L WESTWOOD	12 under
B Lane	10 under
M Lafeber	9 under
J Senden	8 under
D Clarke	7 under
O Karlsson	7 under

THIRD ROUND

L WESTWOOD	14 under
M Lafeber	8 under
M Campbell	7 under
T Gillis	7 under
S Tinning	7 under
K Tomori	7 under
F Tarnaud	7 under

FINAL ROUND

L WESTWOOD	14 under
M Campbell	11 under
R Russell	10 under
D Borrego	9 under
J Spence	9 under
T Gillis	9 under

RESULTS IN OTHER MARKETS

TOP SCANDINAVIAN PLAYER

Well done to Surrey (S) and Corals (C) who opened up this market.

1	16/1 (S)	Steen Tinning
T2	66/1 (S,C)	Henrik Stenson
T2 fav	3/1 (S,C)	Jesper Parnevik
T2	33/1 (S)	Chris Hanell

1/4 odds 1 - 4

The results in recent years were

1999 (no market opened)		1998 (Corals & Sunderlands)		
1	Jesper Parnevik	1	fav 4/1	Jesper Parnevik
2	Robert Karlsson	2	33/1	Michael Jonzon
3	Steen Tinning	T3	25/1	Mats Lanner
T4	Mathias Gronberg	T3	33/1	Mathias Gronberg
T4	Per Nyman	T3	20/1	P-U Johansson

PUNTERS' POINTS

● 13/2 Lee Westwood recorded his fourth win of the year and went top of the Order of Merit after winning from wire to wire. It was in this tournament that he recorded his first tour win back in 1996 (he's now had thirteen wins) so Lee had real PMAs with the Scandinavian Masters.

● The form here of defending champion Jesper Parnevik can again be forgotten. His confidence and form has clearly been set back by his hip injury. Expect him to mount a real challenge in 2001.

● Monty's form here (T17th) can also be forgotten. Suffering from migraines he never ever got even near to being in contention.

● Tom Gillis' bogey-bogey finish will have disappointed the 32-year-old American who recorded his equal best-ever tour finish.

● 'The Law of the Streaker' applied here again to Barry Lane who followed his 63 in R3 with a 76!

1999 RESULT

1	fav 7/1	Colin Montgomerie
2	12/1	Jesper Parnevik
T3	100/1*	Bob May
T3	100/1*	Geoff Ogilvy
T5	50/1	Robert Karlsson
T5	80/1*	Katsuyoshi Tomori
T5	150/1	Francisco Cea
T5	150/1	Andrew McLardy

1998 RESULT

1	14/1	Jesper Parnevik
2	16/1	Darren Clarke
3	200/1	Stephen Field
T4	100/1	Jean Van de Velde
T4	125/1	Michael Jonzon

WINNERS IN THE '90s

1991	Colin Montgomerie, Drottningholm
1992	Nick Faldo, Barseback
1993	Peter Baker, Forsgardens
1994	Vijay Singh, Drottningholm
1995	Jesper Parnevik, Barseback
1996	Lee Westwood, Forsgardens
1997	Joakim Haeggman, Barseback
1998	Jesper Parnevik, Kungsangen
1999	Colin Montgomerie, Barseback
2000	Lee Westwood, Kungsangen

PUNTERS' GUIDE

● The key to winner finding here is without question really good current form. The winners in the last nine years have all been in good form with at least a top 25 finish in one of their last two starts, and all made the cut last time out.

● However outsiders have shone in the last four years

> Of the twenty-three players in the top 5 (or T5th) sixteen, i.e. 69.6%, have started at or over 80/1; and twelve, i.e. 52.2%, have started at or over 100/1.

● Players with the best record in this tournament irrespective of venue are:-

	2000	1999	1998
Katsuyoshi Tomori	6	5	11
Jesper Parnevik	11	2	W
Greg Turner	11	9	16
Michael Campbell	2	14	64
Steen Tinning	6	14	RTD
Mathias Gronberg	31	18	7
Colin Montgomerie	17	W	16
Darren Clarke	23	-	2
Paolo Quirici	23	21	7

● The AXA stats showed the following:-

Driving Accuracy		Greens In Reg		Putts per GIR	
1	Anders Hansen	1	Lee Westwood	1	Jamie Spence
2	John Senden	2	Anders Hansen	2	Katsuyoshi Tomori
T3	Steve Webster	3	Steen Tinning	3	Joakim Haeggman
T3	Ross McFarlane	T4	John Senden	4	Gerry Norquist
T3	Paolo Quirici	T4	David Gilford		
T3	Per Nyman	T4	John Bickerton		

● In 2001 the tournament returns to the Barseback course used in 1992, 1995, 1997 and 1999.

● Players whose profiles refer to this tournament include Steen Tinning, Jesper Parnevik, Greg Turner, Michael Campbell, Andrew McLardy, Henrik Stenson, David Carter, Brian Davis and Paolo Quirici.

THE VICTOR CHANDLER BRITISH MASTERS

Date	10th - 13th August
Course	Dukes Course, Woburn, Milton Keynes
Par	72
Yardage	6,883
First Prize	£133,280
Total Purse	£800,000

THE TOURNAMENT

This was the second year of Victor Chandler's sponsorship of the British Masters. They are the official bookmakers to the European tour. It was played at Woburn from 1981 - 1994 and returned there last year.

THE COURSE

The Dukes course used last year for the first time since 1994 was again the venue this year. It is a traditional parklands track with fast, true greens. Unusually it has an outward par of 34 and an inward par of 38 (three par 5s and one par 3). The back nine is the easier half.

2000 ODDS

fav	7/2	Colin Montgomerie	50/1	Andrew Coltart
	18/1	Bernhard Langer	66/1	Stephen Allan
	18/1	Retief Goosen	66/1*	Peter O'Malley
	20/1	Thomas Bjorn	66/1	Phillip Price (non runner)
	33/1	Stephen Leaney	66/1	Greg Turner
	33/1	Bob May (DC)	66/1	Nick O'Hern
	33/1	P-U Johansson	66/1	Patrik Sjoland
	40/1	Adam Scott	66/1*	Raymond Russell
	40/1	Ian Woosnam	66/1	Chris Hanell
	40/1	Jarmo Sandelin	66/1	Jarrod Moseley
	40/1	Mathias Gronberg	80/1*	Jamie Spence
	50/1	Paul McGinley	80/1*	Steve Webster
	50/1	Steen Tinning	80/1	Pierre Fulke
	50/1*	Paul Lawrie	80/1	Greg Owen
	50/1	Gary Orr		

2000 RESULT

1	50/1	Gary Orr	67 62 68 70 267
2	33/1	P-U Johansson	68 65 69 67 269
3	fav 7/2	Colin Montgomerie	64 69 66 71 270
4	100/1*	Mark McNulty	65 65 71 70 271
T5	33/1	Bob May	69 68 67 68 272
T5	50/1	Andrew Coltart	70 65 68 69 272
T5	50/1*	Paul Lawrie	68 70 64 70 272

T8	J Sandelin	69 72 67 65 273		R Claydon	69 69 75 69 282
	P Sjoland	68 68 68 69 273		S Field	69 70 71 72 282
10	R Russell	67 71 69 67 274		C Hanell	69 72 71 70 282
T11	R S Johnson	68 70 71 66 275		S Wakefield	73 69 70 70 282
	J Moseley	70 66 66 73 275		S Struver	71 70 70 71 282
	P Fulke	69 72 68 66 275		T Levet	74 68 69 71 282
	I Woosnam	71 69 67 68 275	T50	P Eales	71 71 69 72 283
	S Allan	70 69 70 66 275		T Bjorn	69 71 70 73 283
T16	P Quirici	69 67 72 68 276		S Torrance	68 69 76 70 283
	I Garbutt	69 65 68 74 276		L Parsons	76 66 71 70 283
T18	M Gronberg	67 70 74 66 277		N Vanhootegem	71 70 70 72 283
	J Skold	70 71 72 64 277	T55	M Lanner	72 70 73 69 284
T20	P O'Malley	70 68 68 72 278		A McLardy	69 71 70 74 284
	G Owen	69 67 69 73 278		J Bickerton	68 73 73 70 284
	N Fasth	71 69 69 69 278		P Mitchell	70 68 74 72 284
T23	A Forsyth	74 68 72 65 279		D Park	71 71 75 67 284
	M Farry	71 67 71 70 279		A Sherborne	70 72 65 77 284
	R Chapman	71 71 72 65 279		D Gilford	70 72 70 72 284
	S Tinning	69 70 70 70 279	T62	T Gillis	69 69 75 72 285
	Steve Webster	72 69 70 68 279		R Coughlan	75 66 73 71 285
	D Borrego	70 71 69 69 279		J-F Remesy	69 72 71 73 285
T29	T Gogele	68 70 71 71 280		D Carter	71 69 75 70 285
	B Lane	71 69 71 69 280		J Berendt	70 72 73 70 285
	K Tomori	71 70 68 71 280		F Tarnaud	70 72 70 73 285
	D Smyth	71 70 70 69 280		A Forsbrand	73 69 73 70 285
	G Rojas	71 68 73 68 280	T69	K H Han	72 68 75 71 286
	Anders Hansen	69 73 69 69 280		S Kjeldsen	70 69 75 72 286
	Per Nyman	69 70 73 68 280		T J Munoz	68 73 67 78 286
T36	M Lafeber	71 69 73 68 281		H Otto	72 70 71 73 286
	N O'Hern	68 73 72 68 281	T73	I Giner	68 72 74 73 287
	V Phillips	68 71 71 71 281		F Jacobson	72 70 75 70 287
	M Mouland	70 72 66 73 281		S Leaney	73 68 73 73 287
	P Affleck	72 67 70 72 281		G Emerson	72 70 71 74 287
	P Walton	70 69 72 70 281	77	P Baker	72 67 73 76 288
	M Scarpa	70 71 70 70 281	78	I Garrido	71 67 74 78 290
T43	M Anglert	70 66 73 73 282			

The main players to miss the cut (made at 2 under) were:-

G Norquist (-1)	E Darcy (-1)	R Goosen (-1)	K Storgaard (-1)
S Luna (-1)	J Mellor (-1)	S Hansen (-1)	E Boult (E)
R Coles (E)	I Poulter (E)	S Lyle (E)	M A Martin (E)
B Davis (E)	B Langer (E)	D Howell (E)	J Lomas (E)
C Suneson (E)	F Lindgren (E)	R Green (+1)	J Rose (+1)
M Mackenzie (+1)	C Rocca (+1)	T Johnstone (+1)	G Turner (+1)
A Scott (+1)	R Karlsson (+1)	R McFarlane (+1)	M Florioli (+1)
P Archer (+1)	J Spence (+1)	D De Vooght (+2)	J M Carriles (+2)

P McGinley (+2)	R Wessels (+2)	G Murphy (+2)	R Winchester (+2)
I Hutchings (+2)	R Jacquelin (+2)	R Byrd (+2)	B Dredge (+2)
S Gallacher (+3)	H Nystrom (+3)	G Evans (+3)	A Raitt (+3)
S Rowe (+3)	M Brier (+3)	M Davis (+3)	M Blackey (+3)
P Golding (+4)	C Hainline (+4)	S Scahill (+4)	P Fowler (+4)
M Gates (+5)	F Cea (+5)	G Hutcheon (+5)	D Lynn (+5)
I Pyman (+5)	J Senden (+6)	W Riley (+6)	R Davis (+6)
D Chopra (+6)			

Gordon Brand Jr (77) and Dean Robertson (69) retired.

ROUND BY ROUND LEADERBOARD

FIRST ROUND

C Montgomerie	8 under
M McNulty	7 under
M Gronberg	5 under
R Russell	5 under
G ORR	5 under

SECOND ROUND

G ORR	15 under
M McNulty	14 under
P-U Johansson	11 under
C Montgomerie	11 under
I Garbutt	10 under
A Coltart	9 under

THIRD ROUND

G ORR	19 under
C Montgomerie	17 under
M McNulty	15 under
J Moseley	14 under
P Lawrie	14 under
P-U Johansson	14 under
I Garbutt	14 under

FINAL ROUND

G ORR	21 under
P-U Johansson	19 under
C Montgomerie	18 under
M McNulty	17 under
B May	16 under
A Coltart	16 under
P Lawrie	16 under

PRICES IN OTHER MARKETS

Victor Chandler created three specialist markets all with place odds of 1/4 1,2,3. The results were:-

TOP EUROPEAN
1	10/1	P-U Johansson
2	14/1	Jarmo Sandelin
3	20/1	Patrik Sjoland

TOP BRIT
1	22/1	Gary Orr
2	fav 11/8	Colin Montgomerie
T3	22/1	Andrew Coltart
T3	14/1	Paul Lawrie

TOP REST OF THE WORLD
1	12/1	Mark McNulty
2	10/1	Bob May
T3	25/1	Jarrod Moseley
T3	18/1	Stephen Allan

TWO HOLES IN ONE IN THE SAME 2-BALL

In R4 both Roger Chapman and Alastair Forsyth holed in one on different holes during matching rounds of 65. Don Stewart, Victor Chandler's ace golf compiler, reckoned it was a 5,000/1 chance!

PUNTERS' POINTS

● 50/1 Gary Orr recorded his second victory of the year when he held off the challenges first of Montgomerie and then of Johansson on the final day.

● On this track an early tee time from the 10th tee is an advantage as the player faces the easier half of the course (three par 5s) straight away. After a solid 5 under in R1 in the afternoon Gary Orr took full advantage off the 10th early on in R2....shooting 62.

● Slimline Colin Montgomerie was disappointing as he dropped shots in R4 to fall back after catching Orr early on. His confidence going to the USPGA will not be high.

● Per-Ulrik Johansson continued his vastly improved recent form to finish a really creditable 2nd at 33/1.

● The success of Bob May last year, Gary Orr this year and Monty's high finishes are testament to the crucial importance of accuracy off the tee on this course.

● Only three players shot all four rounds in the 60s - T8th Patrik Sjoland, T5th Bob May and 2nd Per-Ulrik Johansson.

1999 RESULT
(Woburn)

1	66/1	Bob May
2	fav 11/2	Colin Montgomerie
3	150/1	Christopher Hanell
T4	150/1	Greg Owen
T4	7/1	Lee Westwood

1998 RESULT
(Forest of Arden)

1	fav 10/1	Colin Montgomerie
T2	125/1	Pierre Fulke
T2	40/1	Eduardo Romero
T4	200/1	Andrew Oldcorn
T4	66/1	Ignacio Garrido
T4	125/1	Paolo Quirici

WINNERS IN THE LAST TEN YEARS

1991	Seve Ballesteros, Woburn
1992	Christie O'Connor Jr, Woburn
1993	Peter Baker, Woburn
1994	Ian Woosnam, Woburn
1995	Sam Torrance, Collingtree
1996	Robert Allenby, Collingtree
1997	Greg Turner, Forest of Arden
1998	Colin Montgomerie, Forest of Arden
1998	Colin Montgomerie, Forest of Arden
1999	Bob May, Woburn
2000	Gary Orr, Woburn

PUNTERS' GUIDE

- This year there was little advantage from early tee times although starting on the first morning from the 10th tee had some advantage as they faced the easier half of course early on.

- In benign conditions with three easily reachable par 5s the Dukes' course at Woburn had, in effect, a par 69 this year.

- Next year however the tournament moves to the Marquess course which it is believed will be one of the finest inland British courses. As a result there will be no course form to study so in 2001 the sensible strategy, given the absence of any course form, will be to go for a player with three characteristics -

  > Solid current form

  > Accuracy off the tee

  > Although it had little effect this year an early start in R1 will probably be an advantage.

- This year the AXA stats showed the top 4 players in each category to be :-

Driving Accuracy		Greens In Reg		Putts per GIR	
1	Paolo Quirici	1	Gary Orr	1	Colin Montgomerie
2	Ian Garbutt	2	Ian Garbutt	2	Patrik Sjoland
3	Greg Owen	T3	Andrew Coltart	3	Russell Claydon
4	Simon Wakefield	T3	Paul Affleck	4	Paolo Quirici

- Players with good recent records in this tournament on two different courses include:-

  > Colin Montgomerie   3rd 2000: 2nd 1999: Won 1998: 2nd 1997

  > Mark McNulty   4th 2000: T18th 1999

  > Patrik Sjoland   T8th 2000: T26th 1999: DNP 1998: T8th 1997

  > Raymond Russell   T10th 2000: T10th 1999: MC 1998: T4th 1997

  > Pierre Fulke   T11th 2000: T38th 1999: T2nd 1998

- Players whose profiles refer to this tournament include Pierre Fulke, Patrik Sjoland, Colin Montgomerie, Raymond Russell, Greg Owen, Andrew Coltart, Stephen Leaney, Anders Hansen, Mark McNulty and Per-Ulrik Johansson.

NORTH WEST OF IRELAND GOLF CLASSIC

Date	17th - 20th August
Course	Slieve Russell Hotel G. & C.C., County Cavan, Ireland
Par	72
Yardage	7,053
First Prize	£35,000
Total Purse	£210,000

THE TOURNAMENT

This was the second year for this tournament which gives a big chance to the tour's third division players as well as those on the Challenge tour.

THE COURSE

This is a new course on the tour with a conventional par 72 (36 out: 36 back). It is situated a couple of hours from Dublin, 15 miles north of Cavan Town.

2000 ODDS

jt fav	20/1	Peter Baker	50/1*	Gary Emerson
jt fav	20/1	Katsuyoshi Tomori	50/1	Nic Henning
jt fav	20/1	Diego Borrego	50/1*	Ian Hutchings
	25/1	Philip Walton	50/1	Daren Lee
	25/1	Des Terblanche	50/1	Christian Cevaer
	33/1*	Brendan Jones	66/1*	Ross Drummond
	33/1	Mark Mouland	66/1*	Carlos Rodiles
	40/1	Olle Karlsson	66/1	Eamonn Darcy
	40/1	Olivier Edmond	66/1*	Massimo Florioli
	40/1	Costantino Rocco (DC)	66/1	Wayne Westner
	40/1*	Des Smyth	66/1*	Hennie Otto
	40/1*	Henrik Stenson	66/1*	Justin Rose
	50/1	Eric Carlberg	66/1*	Trevor Immelman
	50/1	Massimo Scarpa	80/1*	Fredrik Lindgren

2000 RESULT

1	50/1	**Massimo Scarpa**	**67 70 68 70 275**
2	150/1	**Mikael Lundberg**	**70 69 67 70 276**
3	150/1	**Andrew Beal**	**67 69 71 70 277**
T4	66/1*	**Carlos Rodiles**	**70 71 70 67 278**
T4	150/1	**Gary Houston**	**67 69 73 69 278**
T4	150/1	**Tobias Dier**	**71 71 65 71 278**

T7	G Emerson	67 75 70 67 279			G Rankin	71 73 75 67 286
	L Claverie	66 72 70 71 279			M Backhausen	73 70 75 68 286
	G Murphy	70 66 70 73 279			F Andersson	70 70 75 71 286
	R Drummond	72 66 69 72 279			E Simsek	69 71 74 72 286
T11	R Coles	72 70 71 67 280			M Bernardini	77 67 70 72 286
	O Karlsson	72 66 68 74 280			D Smyth	67 73 73 73 286
	H Stenson	72 71 65 72 280			M Piltz	72 69 71 74 286
14	K Tomori	71 70 68 72 281			D Westermark	70 71 70 75 286
T15	T Immelman	75 69 71 67 282		T51	D Lee	72 72 72 71 287
	M Mouland	69 72 73 68 282			B Pettersson	74 67 74 72 287
	M MacKenzie	71 71 69 71 282			N Cheetham	75 67 71 74 287
	P Archer	70 73 67 72 282			M Erlandsson	75 69 69 74 287
T19	J Rose	74 70 70 69 283			R J Derksen	74 69 69 75 287
	P Sherman	70 71 71 71 283			F Guermani	72 69 70 76 287
	J Rask	73 68 71 71 283		T57	P Gottfridson	74 70 75 69 288
	S Field	71 72 69 71 283			J Rystrom	70 73 72 73 288
	J M Lara	66 75 70 72 283			R Bland	71 73 71 73 288
	D Terblanche	69 68 72 74 283			N Rorbaek	68 72 74 74 288
	M Pilkington	73 69 67 74 283			C Challen	69 71 72 76 288
T26	M Pendaries	72 71 73 68 284		T62	A Sherborne	72 70 73 74 289
	D Edlund	72 70 70 72 284			F Widmark	71 72 72 74 289
	H Nystrom	70 73 68 73 284			A Raitt	70 70 74 75 289
	G Storm	67 73 70 74 284			D Chopra	74 67 72 76 289
T30	M Eliasson	69 74 73 69 285		T66	R Sjoberg	72 72 74 72 290
	J M Arruti	74 68 73 70 285			M Anglert	71 71 75 73 290
	S Wakefield	71 73 71 70 285			C Pottier	69 72 75 74 290
	Grant Dodd	69 74 71 71 285			G Clark	71 73 72 74 290
	Stephen Dodd	71 73 70 71 285		70	C Rocca	71 71 74 75 291
	A Mednick	73 68 72 72 285		T71	D Nouailhac	74 70 77 71 292
	S Richardson	71 70 72 72 285			M Olander	72 72 77 71 292
	E Little	70 72 70 73 285		73	Tim Spence	70 73 79 71 293
	F Henge	72 71 69 73 285		T74	Per G Nyman	72 71 71 80 294
	K Vainola	71 69 71 74 285			J Hepworth	73 69 69 83 294
	I Giner	74 69 68 74 285		76	R Guillard	73 71 74 78 296
	B Nelson	70 71 69 75 285		77	D Mills	74 68 76 79 297
T42	S Delagrange	71 73 75 67 286				

The main players to miss the cut (made at level) were:–

D Borrego (+1)	D Higgins (+1)	F Lindgren (+1)	K Eriksson (+1)
S Webster (+1)	P Baker (+2)	I Hutchings (+2)	C Cevaer (+2)
W Westner (+3)	E Carlberg (+3)	P Walton (+3)	S Henderson (+4)
M Florioli (+4)	D Cooper (+6)	B Jones (+6)	H Otto (+8)
N Henning (+11)			

E Darcy (76) withdrew.

ROUND BY ROUND LEADERBOARD

FIRST ROUND		SECOND ROUND	
L Claverie	5 under	A Beal	8 under
J M Lara	6 under	G Murphy	8 under
M SCARPA	5 under	G Houston	8 under
G Storm	5 under	M SCARPA	7 under
D Smyth	5 under	D Terblanche	7 under
G Emerson	5 under		
G Houston	5 under		
A Beal	5 under		

THIRD ROUND		FINAL ROUND	
M SCARPA	11 under	M SCARPA	13 under
M Lundberg	10 under	M Lundberg	12 under
O Karlsson	10 under	A Beal	11 under
G Murphy	10 under	C Rodiles	10 under
A Beal	9 under	G Houston	10 under
R Drummond	9 under	T Dier	10 under
T Dier	9 under		

PUNTERS' POINTS

● 50/1 Massimo Scarpa was playing the 17th in the last group out when lightning stopped play. On the resumption he made a bogey. However so did his playing partner Lundberg. So with a 1-shot lead he parred the last for his first European tour win.

● It earned the 30-year-old Italian a one-year exemption on the PGA European tour. He had showed his liking for playing in Ireland having shot a 63 in R2 of this year's Irish Open.

● Scarpa is a unique player, playing mainly right handed, he switches to left-handed shots from 60 yards in, so he carries four wedges, two left-handed and two right.

● Runner-up 26-year-old Swede Mikael Lundberg, currently 22nd on the Challenge tour Order of Merit, has one victory and three 2nd places on that tour to his credit.

● Des Terblanche, who is no stranger to the sweet trolley, was T4th at halfway then played poorly (72 - 74) to finish T19th.

1999 RESULT

1	12/1	Costantino Rocca
2	fav 10/1	Padraig Harrington
T3	28/1*	Paul Broadhurst
T3	33/1*	Gary Evans
T3	66/1*	Des Smyth

This was the first time this tournament had been held.

PUNTERS' GUIDE

- My 'magnificient seven among the 'lesser lights' for you to note in this tournament in 2001 are:-
  - > Malcolm MacKenzie: Off scratch at 15. 7th in Irish Open 1999, and four sub-par rounds when T15th in this tournament this year.
  - > Trevor Immelman: 20-year-old 'class act' from South Africa who was the best finisher this year (9 under last three rounds).
  - > Robert Coles: T11th this year and with solid tour form compared to most in this field.
  - > Gary Murphy: Irishman who was T35th last year and T7th this time (without a practice round) having backed himself at 80/1.
  - > Gary Emerson: T6th 1999 and T7th 2000, is the only player with successive top 20s finishes in this event.
  - > Carlos Rodiles: top 7 finishes in 2000 Spanish and French Opens, and T4th here this year.
  - > Henrik Stenson: went into this year's tournament clear top of the Challenge Tour Order of Merit, T11th here.
- Players whose profiles refer to this tournament include Stephen Gallacher and Des Smyth.

THE WORLD GOLF CHAMPIONSHIPS NEC INVITATIONAL

Date	24th - 27th August
Course	South Course, Firestone G.C., Akron, Ohio
Par	70
Yardage	7,189
First Prize	$1 million
Total Purse	$5 million

PLEASE SEE PART 5.

SCOTTISH PGA CHAMPIONSHIP

Date	24th - 27th August
Course	Gleneagles, Perthshire, Scotland
Par	72
Yardage	7,053
First Prize	£66,660
Total Purse	£400,000

THE TOURNAMENT

This tournament was introduced to the European tour schedule in 1999 so this was its second year.

THE COURSE

The Jack Nicklaus-designed Monarch's course used last year was again the venue. It is a testing links course with a par 72 (36 out: 36 back).

2000 ODDS

fav	10/1	Paul Lawrie	66/1	Ross Drummond
	16/1	Raymond Russell	66/1	Joakim Haeggman
	16/1	Pierre Fulke	66/1	Olle Karlsson
	16/1	Jamie Spence	66/1*	Mark Mouland
	25/1*	Dean Robertson	66/1*	Andrew Oldcorn
	33/1*	Mark James	66/1*	Henrik Stenson
	40/1	Ignacio Garrido	66/1*	David Gilford
	40/1	Alistair Forsyth	66/1*	Per Nyman
	40/1	Sam Torrance	66/1**	Andrew McLardy
	50/1*	Roger Chapman	66/1*	Van Phillips
	50/1*	Rolf Muntz	80/1*	Jonathan Lomas
	50/1	Peter Mitchell	80/1*	Klas Eriksson
	50/1	Anders Hansen	80/1*	Stephen Gallacher
	50/1*	Gary Evans	80/1	Russell Claydon
	66/1*	Gary Emerson	80/1*	Roger Winchester
	66/1*	John Senden		

2000 RESULT

1	16/1	Pierre Fulke	70 63 68 70 271
2	100/1*	Henrik Nystrom	70 66 68 69 273
3	125/1	Raphael Jacquelin	64 71 73 69 277
4	200/1	Benn Barham	65 74 70 69 278
5	66/1	Olle Karlsson	71 73 69 66 279

6	H Otto	71 71 69 69 280			P Sherman	76 68 74 72 290
T7	G Hamerton	72 70 70 69 281			J Rose	74 71 72 73 290
	A Forsyth	70 65 71 75 281			A Beal	74 71 73 72 290
T9	J Robinson	73 69 68 72 282			I Garrido	72 69 73 76 290
	N Ludwell	71 70 71 70 282			M Blackey	72 72 76 70 290
T11	A Oldcorn	74 69 70 70 283		T50	David J Russell	77 68 69 77 291
	J Senden	73 71 68 71 283			G Emerson	72 74 72 73 291
	H Stenson	77 67 72 67 283			C Gillies	76 71 71 72 291
	R Bland	70 71 68 74 283			S Branger	75 71 75 70 291
	J Skold	71 71 75 66 283			Tim Spence	71 76 73 71 291
T16	S Torrance	70 71 73 70 284			G Pietrobono	72 72 69 78 291
	S Field	73 68 70 73 284			I Giner	71 74 76 70 291
	J Lomas	71 74 72 67 284		57	R Coles	73 72 72 75 292
	P Lawrie	67 74 75 68 284		T58	M Mouland	71 76 75 71 293
T20	R Drummond	71 68 72 74 285			Mark Davis	72 75 69 77 293
	A McLardy	75 71 70 69 285			P Archer	74 73 76 70 293
	R Muntz	71 69 73 72 285			E Little	72 72 76 73 293
	C Challen	73 70 71 71 285			G Hutcheon	75 71 76 71 293
T24	R Chapman	76 70 69 71 286			I Hutchings	76 70 74 73 293
	M James	72 70 72 72 286			F Tarnaud	74 70 75 74 293
	Grant Dodd	71 70 74 71 286			T J Munoz	73 73 74 73 293
	R Winchester	71 74 69 72 286			V Phillips	73 74 73 73 293
T28	B Longmuir	71 73 73 70 287			Raymond Russell	75 70 76 72 293
	K Eriksson	70 67 74 76 287			F Cupillard	75 72 72 74 293
	M Tunnicliff	77 69 70 71 287			F Widmark	75 71 73 74 293
	A Mednick	74 70 72 71 287		T70	T Carolan	74 73 72 75 294
	J Hepworth	72 72 72 71 287			B Nelson	75 72 74 73 294
T33	P Mitchell	76 69 71 72 288		T72	D Gilford	75 71 75 74 295
	J Chillas	71 72 72 73 288			P Affleck	72 75 73 75 295
	L Claverie	75 70 73 70 288			A Barnett	72 70 76 77 295
T36	M Mackenzie	74 72 71 72 289			S Henderson	74 72 75 74 295
	G Murphy	75 71 71 72 289			T Norret	74 70 76 75 295
	J M Carriles	75 67 74 73 289		T77	A Butterfield	73 71 79 73 296
	S D Hurley	74 69 75 71 289			L Stanford	74 70 78 74 296
	S Little	73 69 75 72 289		79	D Lee	73 74 76 75 298
	B Dredge	75 68 75 71 289		80	D McKay	72 74 81 75 302
	F Cea	71 73 75 70 289		81	S McAllister	73 74 81 75 303
	I Pyman	73 74 74 68 289		82	P Malmgren	70 73 79 85 307
T44	W Riley	71 75 71 73 290				

The main players to miss the cut (made at 3 over) were:–

S Scahill (+4)	D Cooper (+4)	P Fowler (+4)	R McFarlane (+4)
M Florioli (+5)	E Boult (+5)	S Rowe (+5)	S Delagrange (+5)
G Sherry (+6)	J Haeggman (+6)	P Nyman (+6)	J Payne (+6)
G Evans (+7)	D Robertson (+7)	S Gallacher (+7)	R Claydon (+9)
P Walton (+10)			

N Henning (76) retired

ROUND BY ROUND LEADERBOARD

FIRST ROUND		SECOND ROUND	
R Jacquelin	8 under	P FULKE	11 under
P Lawrie	5 under	R Jacquelin	9 under
S Rowe	3 under	A Forsyth	9 under
P Fowler	3 under	H Nystrom	8 under
P FULKE	2 under	K Eriksson	7 under
A Forsyth	2 under	R Drummond	5 under
K Eriksson	2 under	B Barham	5 under
S Torrance	2 under		
R Bland	2 under		
H Nystrom	2 under		

THIRD ROUND		FINAL ROUND	
P FULKE	15 under	P FULKE	17 under
H Nystrom	12 under	H Nystrom	15 under
A Forsyth	10 under	R Jacquelin	11 under
R Jacquelin	8 under	B Barham	10 under
R Bland	7 under	O Karlsson	9 under
B Barham	7 under		

PUNTERS' POINTS

● 16/1 Pierre Fulke won his second European tour event after leading from halfway. Henrik Nystrom took the lead at the turn in R4 only to double bogey the 13th. In the end the more experienced Swede won.

● Fulke was very much on the 'comeback trail' having missed seven months because of a wrist injury sustained in last autumn's Belgacom Open. In superb recent form, including 7th in the British Open, his accurate play here was the basis for his success.

● 40/1 local hope Alistair Forsyth, T2nd at halfway, slumped with a poor 75 in R4 to finish T7th.

● Raphael Jacquelin after eight (!) successive missed cuts found his form with an early R1 tee time to shoot 64 in R1 and 'hung on' to finish 3rd.

1999 RESULT

1	66/1*	Warren Bennett

won at the first extra hole

2	100/1*	Rolf Muntz
T3	80/1*	Roger Winchester
T3	80/1*	Klas Eriksson
5	125/1	Per Nyman

This was the first time this tournament had been a European tour event.

PUNTERS' GUIDE

● Once more tremendous value for punters in this tournament:

> Of the seventeen players priced 66/1 to 80/1 inclusive fourteen (82.4%) were at least DYMs

> Of the twenty-nine players priced 66/1 to 100/1 inclusive twenty-one (72.4%) were at least DYMs

> Last year 63% of players priced 28/1 to 100/1 inclusive were at least DYMs with the first four all DYMs.

● The five players with the best records in this event so far are:-

	2000	1999	Both yrs combined to par
Grant Hamerton	T7	T11	-5
Andrew McLardy	T20	T6	-4
Roger Winchester	T24	T3	-7
Ross Drummond	T20	T22	+1
Klas Eriksson	T28	T3	-6

● Players whose profiles refer to this tournament include John Senden, Andrew Oldcorn, Olle Karlsson, Hennie Otto, Alistair Forsyth, Henrik Stenson, Rolf Muntz, Jonathan Lomas, Andrew McLardy, Frederik Jacobson, Stephen Gallacher and Roger Winchester.

THE BMW INTERNATIONAL OPEN

Date	31st August - 3rd September
Course	Golf Club Munchen Nord-Eichenried, Munich, Germany
Par	72
Yardage	7,053
First Prize	£153,000
Total Purse	1,520,142 Euros?!

THE TOURNAMENT

For the fourth successive year this tournament was held at the Golf Club Munchen course which was also its venue from 1989-93.

THE COURSE

This is a wide-fairway, flat (flattest on the tour) course that becomes a birdie feast with large, top-quality, easy-to-read greens. Accuracy to the pin and a very hot putter are required. This year the rough was more severe than in previous years to penalise the wayward

2000 ODDS

jt fav	11/2	Colin Montgomerie	50/1	Jarrod Moseley
jt fav	11/2	Ernie Els	66/1	Patrik Sjoland
	16/1	Thomas Bjorn	66/1	Nick O'Hern
	22/1	Greg Norman	66/1	Jamie Spence
	25/1	Padraig Harrington	66/1	Steen Tinning
	25/1	Bernhard Langer	66/1	Peter O'Malley
	25/1	P-U Johansson	80/1	Stephen Allan
	33/1	Jarmo Sandelin	80/1*	Robert Karlsson
	50/1*	Mathias Gronberg	80/1	Raymond Russell
	50/1*	Pierre Fulke	80/1	Greg Turner
	50/1	Mark McNulty		

2000 RESULT

1	16/1	Thomas Bjorn	69 63 69 67 268
2	25/1	Bernhard Langer	69 69 66 67 271
3	125/1	Carl Suneson	67 67 67 71 272
4	125/1	Ignacio Garrido	67 69 71 68 275
T5	200/1	Gustavo Rojas	68 71 66 71 276
T5	jt fav 11/2	Ernie Els	70 71 69 66 276
T5	150/1	Emanuele Canonica	70 67 68 71 276
T5	125/1	M A Martin	67 66 73 70 276
T5	150/1	Daren Lee	66 70 66 74 276
T5	100/1	Greg Owen	72 68 68 68 276

T11	J Rose	68 69 70 70 277		T46	A McLardy	71 68 70 75 284
	B Lane	67 69 71 70 277			T Levet	67 67 73 77 284
T13	T Gogele	69 69 67 73 278			J Haeggman	69 70 73 72 284
	I Garbutt	68 71 71 68 278		T49	F Lindgren	69 70 72 74 285
	J Sandelin	68 68 69 73 278			B Dredge	72 68 71 74 285
T16	C Hanell	67 70 72 70 279			M Gronberg	68 72 70 75 285
	K Storgaard	66 73 71 69 279			M James	70 70 71 74 285
	A Wall	70 68 68 73 279			N Vanhootegem	68 69 71 77 285
	S Luna	67 72 70 70 279			V Phillips	71 67 76 71 285
T20	H Nystrom	67 71 70 72 280		T55	T Johnstone	71 69 73 73 286
	R Winchester	67 70 68 75 280			S Gallacher	71 69 70 76 286
	P Harrington	67 66 74 73 280			S Torrance	71 70 69 76 286
	D Howell	68 68 72 72 280			P Baker	71 69 72 74 286
	G Turner	65 72 74 69 280			R Wessels	67 69 74 76 286
T25	A Oldcorn	69 69 72 71 281			D Gilford	64 73 78 71 286
	A Cejka	72 68 69 72 281		T61	D Park	68 70 72 77 287
	Brian Davis	71 69 71 70 281			J Moseley	68 73 72 74 287
	N Fasth	70 69 71 71 281			M Anglert	70 70 72 75 287
	G Brand Jr	71 68 70 72 281		T64	P Eales	68 72 76 72 288
	Soren Hansen	67 68 73 73 281			J Senden	70 65 73 80 288
	W Riley	65 71 72 73 281			B Teilleria	70 67 75 76 288
T32	D Lynn	68 68 73 73 282			P O'Malley	70 71 72 75 288
	P-U Johansson	64 74 74 70 282			J Bickerton	67 71 75 75 288
	G Norman	67 70 74 71 282			T Dier	72 69 69 78 288
	S Kjeldsen	69 71 68 74 282		T70	D Robertson	70 69 75 75 289
	A Forsbrand	67 70 74 71 282			S D Hurley	68 69 74 78 289
	R Russell	67 68 76 71 282		72	S Wakefield	70 70 76 74 290
T38	G Ogilvy	67 70 71 75 283		T73	J Skold	71 69 71 80 291
	J Berendt	72 69 73 69 283			F Tarnaud	69 70 70 82 291
	S Rowe	68 73 70 72 283			J Lomas	71 70 77 73 291
	W Huget	68 71 68 76 283			O Edmond	71 70 77 73 291
	R Karlsson	70 68 73 72 283		77	R Claydon	70 71 73 78 292
	A Forsyth	71 69 72 71 283		78	P Fowler	69 72 72 80 293
	I Poulter	70 69 72 72 283		79	G Murphy	68 73 73 83 297
	H Otto	70 70 67 76 283				

The main players to miss the cut (made at 3 under) were:–

M Florioli (-2)	M McNulty (-2)	R Jacquelin (-2)	M Lafeber (-2)
S Webster (-2)	N O'Hern (-2)	A Binaghi (-2)	P Fulke (-2)
R Gonzalez (-2)	S Richardson (-2)	N Ludwell (-2)	M Brier (-2)
P Sjoland (-2)	R McFarlane (-1)	B Barham (-1)	R Chapman (-1)
R Davis (-1)	S Struver (-1)	J Spence (-1)	I Hutchings (-1)
F Roca (E)	M Lanner (E)	M Farry (E)	S Tinning (E)
P Mitchell (E)	R Byrd (E)	O Karlsson (E)	I Pyman (E)
D Carter (E)	J Mellor (E)	S Ballesteros (+1)	M Mackenzie (+1)
R Johnson (+1)	P Affleck (+1)	L Parsons (+1)	F Jacobson (+2)
C Montgomerie (+2)!!	T Munoz (+2)	G Hamerton (+2)	I Giner (+2)
D Hospital (+3)	J-F Remesy (+3)	P Golding (+3)	P Quirici (+3)
M Scarpa (+3)	J Carriles (+4)	P Nyman (+4)	F Cea (+4)
T Gillis (+5)	E Boult (+5)	D Borrego (+6)	R Rafferty (+7)
S Scahill (+8)	S Allan (+9)	G Hutcheon (+10)	S Field (+10)
M Jonzon (+11)			

G Evans (74), E Darcy (78), G Emerson (71), J Robinson (76) and M Davis all withdrew.

ROUND BY ROUND LEADERBOARD

FIRST ROUND

P-U Johansson	8 under
D Gilford	8 under
W Riley	7 under
G Turner	7 under
K Storgaard	6 under
D Lee	6 under
T BJORN	3 under

SECOND ROUND

T BJORN	12 under
P Harrington	11 under
M A Martin	11 under
T Levet	10 under
C Suneson	10 under

THIRD ROUND

T BJORN	15 under
C Suneson	15 under
D Lee	14 under
B Langer	12 under
E Canonica	11 under
J Sandelin	11 under
R Winchester	11 under
T Gogele	11 under
G Rojas	11 under

FINAL ROUND

T BJORN	20 under
B Langer	17 under
C Suneson	16 under
I Garrido	13 under
G Rojas	12 under
E Els	12 under
E Canonica	12 under
M A Martin	12 under
D Lee	12 under
G Owen	12 under

PUNTERS' POINTS

● 2nd in the British Open and 3rd in the USPGA, Thomas Bjorn won his first title of the year and stated that he felt he'd lifted his game to 'a higher level'.

● Bernhard Langer has five German Opens, three German Masters, a Deutsche Bank Open and a Honda Open all in his native Germany.....however he still needs the BMW for the full set after finishing a very creditable 2nd here.

● The tournament started sensationally when defending champion Monty, getting his tee time wrong, arrived 50 seconds late on the first tee and was penalised 2 shots. Starting with a double bogey in a state of shock he never recovered and missed the cut.

● A number of players would be disappointed with their finishes here.

> Padraig Harrington   2nd after R2. He shot 74-73 to finish T20th!!

> Thomas Levet   T4th after R2. He shot 73-77 to finish T46th

> Per Ulrik Johansson   T1st after R1, he finished T32nd.

> David Gilford   T1st after R1. He then shot 73-78-71 to finish T55th.

> Roger Winchester   T5th after R3 he then shot 75 to finish T20th

> Jarmo Sandelin   T5th after R3 he then shot 73 to finish T13th

> Thomas Gogele   T5th after R3 he then shot 73 to finish T13th

> Daren Lee   3rd after R3 he then shot 74 to finish T5th

> John Senden   9 under and in contention at halfway, then 73-80 to finish T64

1999 RESULT

1	fav 6/1	Colin Montgomerie
2	33/1	Padraig Harrington
3	66/1	Jarrod Moseley
4	100/1*	John Bickerton
T5	80/1	David Howell
T5	40/1	Andrew Coltart
T5	66/1	Gary Orr
T5	66/1	Mark James

1998 RESULT

1	125/1	Russell Claydon
2	125/1	Jamie Spence
3	125/1	Thomas Gogele
T4	80/1	Angel Cabrera
T4	12/1	Bernhard Langer

WINNERS IN THE LAST TEN YEARS

1991	Sandy Lyle	1996	Marc Farry (36 holes)*
1992	Paul Azinger	1997	Robert Karlsson
1993	Peter Fowler	1998	Russell Claydon
1994	Mark McNulty*	1999	Colin Montgomerie
1995	Frank Nobilo*	2000	Thomas Bjorn

* Venue was the St Eurach Laud-Und G.C.

PUNTERS' GUIDE

● If ever there is an outsiders tournament this is it. Of the twenty-eight players who were in the top 5 (or T5) in the last four years

> sixteen (57%) have started at or over 80/1

> thirteen (46.4%) have started at or over 100/1

Nevertheless the last two winners have started at 16/1 and 6/1 favourite.

● The AXA stats showed the following players in the top four in the key categories.

Driving Accuracy		Greens In Reg		Putts per GIR		Putts per round	
1	B Lane	1	I Garbutt	1	R Russell	T1	J Haeggman
T2	A Oldcorn	2	G Owen	2	G Turner	T1	R Russell
T2	D Lee	T3	T Bjorn	3	G Rojas	3	T Gogele
T2	J Bickerton	T3	A Wall	4	P Harrington	T4	T Bjorn
						T4	G Rojas

● The best recent course records belong to

> Padraig Harrington 20th 2000: 2nd 1999; 9th 1997; 3rd 1996

> Ernie Els T5th 2000: T26th 1997 in two starts

> Bernhard Langer 2-15-4-12-16 in last five years

> Thomas Bjorn W-34-6-5 in last four years

> Colin Montgomerie Won 1999: 3rd 1997 and two missed cuts in last four years

● Players whose profiles refer to this tournament include Thomas Gogele, Bernhard Langer, David Howell, Greg Turner, Greg Owen, Wayne Riley and Jarmo Sandelin.

THE CANON EUROPEAN MASTERS

Date   7th - 10th September
Course   Crans-Sur-Sierre G.C., Switzerland
Par   71
Yardage   6,848
First Prize   £150,000
Total Purse   £900,000

THE TOURNAMENT

As usual this is the first tournament to count for points for the next (2001) Ryder Cup side. As a result Nick Faldo was playing. This was the last year of Canon's sponsorship which started in 1991. From 2001 this will become the Omega European Masters for five years .

THE COURSE

Set in the 'Sound of Music' country high on an Alpine plateau it has been an easy course with a course record of 60. However it has been toughened up by Seve Ballesteros recently and now provides a sound test. Narrower fairways, tougher rough and, in particular, reshaped greens (some up-turned-saucer style) make course form up to and including 1998 essentially redundant. In 1999 the cut was made 8 shots greater than in 1998!! According to stablemates Darren Clarke and Lee Westwood the course is 'no longer any fun'.

2000 ODDS

fav	9/2	Lee Westwood (DC)	50/1	Eduardo Romero
	10/1	Darren Clarke	66/1*	Stephen Leaney
	10/1	Thomas Bjorn (PWW)	66/1	Ignacio Garrido
	25/1	Padraig Harrington	66/1*	Patrik Sjoland
	25/1	Michael Campbell	66/1	Jose Coceres
	28/1	Jarmo Sandelin	66/1	M A Martin
	33/1*	M A Jimenez	66/1	Mark McNulty
	33/1	P-U Johansson	66/1	Jarrod Moseley
	40/1	Angel Cabrera	80/1	Greg Owen
	40/1	Mathias Gronberg	80/1*	Alex Cejka
	50/1	Nick Faldo	80/1	Robert Karlsson
	50/1	Phillip Price	80/1	Stephen Allan
	50/1	Paul Lawrie	80/1	Emanuele Canonica

2000 RESULT

1	50/1	**Eduardo Romero**	**64 68 62 67 261**
2	10/1	**Thomas Bjorn**	**72 64 69 66 271**
3	10/1	**Darren Clarke**	**68 67 67 70 272**
4	125/1	**Niclas Fasth**	**74 66 69 64 273**
5	40/1	**Mathias Gronberg**	**72 66 67 69 274**

T6	N Faldo	69 73 66 67 275		D Howell	72 70 73 69 284
	Phillip Price	69 68 67 71 275		F Valera	72 72 71 69 284
T8	M Blackey	71 69 69 67 276		I Poulter	73 68 74 69 284
	J Moseley	68 67 71 70 276		Brian Davis	73 68 69 74 284
T10	A Cabrera	69 72 69 67 277		Ricardo Gonzalez	74 71 72 67 284
	M Campbell	65 74 70 68 277	T49	S Gallacher	74 70 69 72 285
	D Robertson	71 73 63 70 277		S Luna	72 72 69 72 285
T13	T Gogele	73 69 69 67 278		J M Carriles	72 72 69 72 285
	V Phillips	71 69 69 69 278		G Owen	73 69 71 72 285
	M Brier	70 70 68 70 278		E Darcy	69 70 73 73 285
	P Quirici	67 71 66 74 278		D Lee	70 71 71 73 285
T17	F Jacobson	73 72 67 67 279		G Brand Jr	70 75 71 69 285
	I Garbutt	71 70 69 69 279		G Murphy	74 71 71 69 285
	M Mouland	70 69 70 70 279		N O'Hern	75 69 72 69 285
	A Forsbrand	71 69 67 72 279		S Torrance	75 69 74 67 285
T21	L Westwood	69 66 74 71 280	T59	P Sjoland	73 71 69 73 286
	M A Jimenez	69 71 69 71 280		D Carter	72 73 68 73 286
T23	S Leaney	75 67 70 69 281		M A Martin	73 72 71 70 286
	Soren Hansen	69 73 69 70 281		H Otto	66 69 75 76 286
	J Coceres	71 71 68 71 281	T63	D Gilford	71 73 70 73 287
	R Chapman	68 73 68 72 281		M Jonzon	74 71 71 71 287
	C Hanell	72 67 69 73 281		I Hutchings	71 72 73 71 287
T28	F Lindgren	74 69 70 69 282	T66	S Ballesteros	74 71 70 73 288
	P Senior	72 68 73 69 282		S D Huxley	75 69 72 72 288
	M Florioli	72 70 72 68 282		D Borrego	73 70 74 71 288
	R Jacquelin	70 75 68 69 282		M Mackenzie	72 72 74 70 288
	A Bossert	74 67 70 71 282	T70	H Nystrom	71 71 73 74 289
	N Vanhootegem	71 70 69 72 282		S Allan	69 75 72 73 289
T34	A Forsyth	72 71 70 70 283		J Robinson	73 72 72 72 289
	Jamie Spence	71 72 70 70 283	T73	O Karlsson	70 74 72 74 290
	M Lafeber	72 73 68 70 283		W Riley	72 72 74 72 290
	M McNulty	69 72 72 70 283	75	J Mellor	75 68 73 76 292
	G Emerson	69 70 74 70 283	T76	D Bieri	74 70 75 74 293
	B Rumford	67 72 73 71 283		S Rowe	71 73 74 75 293
	P Lawrie	74 67 73 69 283	T78	I Pyman	70 75 74 75 294
	A McLardy	76 68 73 66 283		S Field	69 74 76 75 294
T42	B Lane	71 71 70 72 284	T80	S Rey	71 73 76 77 297
	L Parsons	71 74 70 69 284		J Skold	74 71 78 74 297

The main players to miss the cut (made at 3 over) were:–

K Storgaard (+4)	C Rocca (+4)	P Walton (+4)	P Fowler (+4)
P Harrington (+4)	J Remesy (+4)	A Hansen (+4)	J Senden (+4)
J Rose (+4)	I Garrido (+4)	D De Vooght (+4)	S Richardson (+4)
G Rojas (+4)	D Lynn (+4)	D Park (+4)	B Teilleria (+4)
I Giner (+5)	J Bickerton (+5)	R Rafferty (+5)	P Nyman (+5)
A Cejka (+5)	R Byrd (+6)	S Kjeldsen (+6)	T Gillis (+6)
P Eales (+6)	P Affleck (+6)	J Haeggman (+6)	J Lomas (+6)
E Canonica (+6)	S Scahill (+6)	F Cea (+6)	J Sandelin (+6)
O Eliasson (+6)	R Coles (+7)	M Lanner (+7)	D Smyth (+7)
G Ogilvy (+7)	R Karlsson (+7)	R Wessels (+7)	A Raitt (+7)
B Dredge (+7)	F Tarnaud (+8)	M Pinero (+8)	S Grappasonni (+8)
S Struver (+8)	C Suneson (+8)	J Berendt (+8)	M Anglert (+8)
G Hamerton (+9)	J Rivero (+9)	P Golding (+9)	R Clayton (+9)
M Scarpa (+9)	G Hutcheon (+11)	T Levet (+12)	

Richard S Johnson (75) and Andrew Oldcorn (77) withdrew.
Craig Hainline (76) was disqualified.

ROUND BY ROUND LEADERBOARD

FIRST ROUND		**SECOND ROUND**	
E ROMERO	7 under	E ROMERO	10 under
M Campbell	6 under	J Moseley	7 under
H Otto	5 under	H Otto	7 under
P Quirici	4 under	D Clarke	7 under
B Rumford	4 under	L Westwood	7 under
T Bjorn	6 under		
P Price	5 under		

THIRD ROUND		**FINAL ROUND**	
E ROMERO	19 under	E ROMERO	23 under
D Clarke	11 under	T Bjorn	13 under
P Price	9 under	D Clarke	12 under
P Quirici	9 under	N Fasth	11 under
T Bjorn	8 under	M Gronberg	10 under
M Gronberg	8 under		

PUNTERS' POINTS

● 50/1 Eduardo Romero, tipped for this tournament in last year's player profile, took the lead on Thursday then built on it, especially with a superb new course record 62 in R3, to finish the runaway winner by 10 shots. At 46 he was the oldest winner on the tour for eight years. It was his first win for six years, he last won .....here at Crans!

● Romero lives at altitude in Argentina so he felt at home here at Crans.

● Thomas Bjorn continued his superb form to finish a very creditable, if very distant, runner-up.

● Darren Clarke played well from tee to green yet he found the Seve Ballesteros re-designed greens difficult to read, missing countless putts.

- Early Ryder Cup points were scored by 4th placed Niclas Fasth (7/1 to make the team) and by Nick Faldo (Corals went 8/1 for Nicholas Alexander to make the team).

- The disappointing player was the 9/2 favourite and defending champion Lee Westwood who started well before closing 74-71 to finish T21st. He suggested his concentration was affected by his recent removals as he moved house.

1999 RESULT

1	fav 9/1	Lee Westwood
2	33/1	Thomas Bjorn
3	66/1*	Alex Cejka
T4	125/1*	Sam Torrance
T4	125/1	Marc Farry

1998 RESULT

1	80/1	Sven Struver
won at the first play-off hole		
2	40/1	Patrik Sjoland
3	14/1	Darren Clarke
4	22/1	Costantino Rocca
T5	80/1	Alex Cejka
T5	100/1	Gordon Brand Jr

WINNERS IN THE LAST TEN YEARS

1991	Jeff Hawkes	1996	Colin Montgomerie
1992	Jamie Spence	1997	Costantino Rocca
1993	Barry Lane	1998	Sven Struver
1994	Eduardo Romero	1999	Lee Westwood
1995	Mathias Gronberg	2000	Eduardo Romero

PUNTERS' GUIDE

- The course has been redesigned by Seve Ballesteros so that only the course form of the last two years is really worthwhile. The players with the best recent records are :-

	2000	1999	1998
Eduardo Romero	Won	T9	T20
Mathias Gronberg	5	T50	T7
Thomas Bjorn	2	2	T30
Lee Westwood	T21	Won	T12
Dean Robertson	T10	T15	DNP
Michael Campbell	T10	T15	DNP
M A Jimenez	T21	T6	T7
Darren Clarke	3	T28	3
Patrik Sjoland	T59	T9	2
Sven Struver	MC	T6	Won
Alex Cejka	MC	3	T5

● The AXA stats showed:-

Driving Accuracy	Greens In Reg	Putts per GIR
1 Paolo Quirici	1 Gary Emerson	T1 Lucas Parsons
T2 M A Jimenez	T2 Ian Garbutt	T1 Gordon Brand Jr
T2 Stephen Field	T2 Greg Owen	T3 Niclas Fasth
4 Alistair Forsyth	T4 Matthew Blackey	T3 Mathias Gronberg
5 Jose Coceres	T4 Eduardo Romero	5 Michael Campbell
	T4 Gary Murphy	

● Players whose profiles refer to this tournament include Eduardo Romero, Michael Campbell, Mathias Gronberg, Dean Robertson, Thomas Bjorn, Niclas Fasth, Angel Cabrera, Darren Clarke, Ian Garbutt and Alex Cejka.

THE LANCOME TROPHY

Date	14th - 17th September
Course	St Nom-la-Breteche, Paris
Par	71
Yardage	6,903
First Prize	£133,300
Total Purse	£800,000

THE TOURNAMENT

This is a very well-established tournament being played for the thirty-second time and they have all been on the same St Nom-la-Breteche course at Versailles.

THE COURSE

This track places a premium on accuracy with water in play particularly on the 5th and 9th. The final hole is a very demanding par 3 with water in play on the right. The par 4 14th is the toughest hole. When the wind gets up the back nine in particular are very testing.

2000 ODDS

fav	8/1	Colin Montgomerie	50/1	Mathias Gronberg
	10/1	Lee Westwood	50/1	Jean Van de Velde
	12/1	Darren Clarke	66/1*	Nick Faldo
	14/1	Vijay Singh	66/1	Pierre Fulke (DC)
	16/1	Thomas Bjorn	66/1	Paul Lawrie
	25/1	Michael Campbell	66/1	Stephen Leaney
	33/1*	M A Jimenez	66/1	Andrew Coltart
	33/1	Jarmo Sandelin	66/1	Jarrod Moseley
	33/1	Retief Goosen	66/1	Ian Woosnam
	40/1**	J M Olazabal	80/1	Mark McNulty
	40/1	Eduardo Romero (PWW)	80/1	Jose Coceres
	50/1	Gary Orr	80/1	Patrik Sjoland
	50/1*	Angel Cabrera	80/1	Peter O'Malley
	50/1	Phillip Price		

2000 RESULT

1	33/1	**Retief Goosen**	**69 71 64 67 271**
T2	25/1	**Michael Campbell**	**72 68 65 67 272**
T2	12/1	**Darren Clarke**	**67 70 67 68 272**
T4	14/1	**Vijay Singh**	**67 72 68 66 273**
T4	100/1	**Alex Cejka**	**67 69 66 71 273**

6	Phillip Price	70 72 69 63 274		R Karlsson	73 70 70 69 282
T7	M A Martin	64 72 73 66 275		D Park	70 71 72 69 282
	N O'Hern	64 69 72 70 275		A Coltart	66 72 77 67 282
	D Robertson	69 65 70 71 275	T46	Brian Davis	74 66 73 70 283
	L Westwood	68 68 71 68 275		A McLardy	75 68 72 68 283
	B Rumford	68 66 74 67 275		C Montgomerie	69 72 68 74 283
T12	N Faldo	70 67 74 66 277		F Lindgren	67 74 70 72 283
	T Johnstone	70 68 68 71 277		C Suneson	71 69 72 71 283
	Anders Hansen	70 65 71 71 277		D Borrego	71 68 74 70 283
	P Lawrie	67 68 75 67 277		G Orr	72 68 74 69 283
T16	S Torrance	68 71 70 69 278	T53	G Evans	69 73 69 73 284
	M Farry	67 72 69 70 278		N Joakimides	71 72 72 69 284
	P McGinley	71 71 71 65 278		J Bickerton	72 71 70 71 284
	J Coceres	69 66 72 71 278		L Parsons	72 70 75 67 284
	T Bjorn	66 75 73 64 278		A Forsyth	67 71 77 69 284
	A Cabrera	71 70 67 70 278	T58	M Lanner	68 74 72 71 285
T22	E Romero	69 71 69 70 279		S Luna	65 74 71 75 285
	S Gallacher	68 69 67 75 279		J Lomas	70 68 76 71 285
T24	I Woosnam	68 70 77 65 280		P O'Malley	72 71 71 71 285
	R Jacquelin	74 67 71 68 280		M Blackey	68 70 75 72 285
	M Lafeber	66 76 66 72 280	T63	A Wall	69 72 71 74 286
	J Senden	69 69 73 69 280		T Levet	70 72 74 70 286
	M A Jimenez	69 72 70 69 280		J Robinson	73 70 73 70 286
	I Garbutt	71 72 71 66 280		V Phillips	72 69 74 71 286
T30	D Gilford	67 72 71 71 281		S Allan	70 69 75 72 286
	S Kjeldsen	69 71 72 69 281	68	M Brier	67 74 74 72 287
	G Emerson	69 71 72 69 281	69	Rodger Davis	71 71 77 69 288
	P Mitchell	70 71 73 67 281	T70	J Rivero	71 69 77 72 289
	P Eales	68 73 70 70 281		P Fowler	69 73 75 72 289
	I Garrido	73 65 72 71 281		D Howell	73 68 77 71 289
	B Dredge	71 68 73 69 281		R Claydon	71 71 75 72 289
	F Jacobson	68 69 77 67 281	T74	J Van de Velde	71 72 73 75 291
T38	D Smyth	70 72 70 70 282		S Little	71 72 72 76 291
	M McNulty	70 71 71 70 282	76	E Canonica	70 73 74 75 292
	J M Olazabal	65 72 75 70 282	77	M Gronberg	69 74 76 74 293
	S Leaney	67 72 74 69 282	78	P Nyman	72 70 78 74 294
	G Havret	68 72 69 73 282	79	P Fulke	71 72 76 79 298

The main players to miss the cut (made at 1 over) were:–

G Brand Jr (+2)	R Chapman (+2)	P Affleck (+2)	R Winchester (+2)
M James (+2)	S Tinning (+2)	P Sjoland (+2)	G Turner (+2)
K Storgaard (+2)	S Delagrange (+2)	P Golding (+2)	R Wessels (+2)
C Rocca (+2)	W Riley (+3)	R McFarlane (+3)	P Baker (+3)
J Berendt (+3)	C Hainline (+3)	I Poulter (+3)	C Hanell (+3)
E Darcy (+3)	I Pyman (+3)	B Lane (+4)	G Owen (+4)
A Forsbrand (+4)	S Scahill (+4)	H Otto (+4)	C Cevaer (+4)
R Green (+4)	R Gonzalez (+4)	P Senior (+5)	S Struver (+5)
J Skold (+5)	J-F Remesy (+5)	R Russell (+5)	B Teilleria (+5)
I Giner (+6)	S Richardson (+6)	P Quirici (+6)	G Rojas (+6)
F Cea (+6)	T Gogele (+7)	M Jonzon (+7)	J Mellor (+8)
G Ogilvy (+8)	N Fasth (+9)	O Edmond (+10)	S Ballesteros (+10)
D De Vooght (+13)	J Sandelin (+13)	F Tarnaud (+14)	

Andrew Oldcorn (71), David Carter (75) and Jarrod Moseley (75) all withdrew.

ROUND BY ROUND LEADERBOARD

FIRST ROUND

R Wessels	8 under
N O'Hern	7 under
M A Martin	7 under
J M Olazabal	6 under
S Luna	6 under
R GOOSEN	2 under

SECOND ROUND

N O'Hern	9 under
D Robertson	8 under
B Rumford	8 under
P Lawrie	7 under
J Coceres	7 under
A Hansen	7 under
R GOOSEN	2 under

THIRD ROUND

A Cejka	11 under
D Clarke	9 under
R GOOSEN	9 under
S Gallacher	9 under
D Robertson	9 under
N O'Hern	8 under
M Campbell	8 under

FINAL ROUND

R GOOSEN	13 under
M Campbell	12 under
D Clarke	12 under
V Singh	11 under
A Cejka	11 under

PUNTERS' POINTS

● 33/1 Retief Goosen won his fourth European tournament and it was his third on French soil. The best player on this course over the last three rounds last year, he again finished fast (11 under in the last two rounds) to win well.

● This year the fastest finisher was 25/1 Michael Campbell, so will he follow Retief's example in 2001?

● Alex Cejka, leader by 2 after R3, clearly suffered from 'contention rust' in R4 as he started with a double bogey.

● Stephen Gallacher (74 in R4) will be very disappointed with his final round when in serious contention. He 'lost his way' on the back nine.

● Current form always takes precedence over course form?

Yes.....Course specialist Jarmo Sandelin (2-2-6 last three years) missed the cut last week and with his swing fault uncorrected missed again here.....at 13 (!) over par.

Not necessarily.....last week Alex Cejka, on a track where he's played well, missed the cut yet this week he finished T4th.

● As we discussed in Part 1 in the 'law of the streaker', players find it difficult to follow up a low round. Here Roger Wessels became the first Tour player to miss the cut (63-81) after being the R1 leader, since Aussie Rod Pampling in last year's British Open

1999 RESULT			1998 RESULT		
1	150/1	Pierre Fulke	1	50/1	M A Jimenez
2	100/1	Ignacio Garrido	T2	14/1	David Duval
T3	100/1	Santiago Luna	T2	16/1	Mark O'Meara
T3	125/1	Greg Owen	T2	150/1	Jarmo Sandelin
T3	fav 5/1	Colin Montgomerie	T2	66/1	Greg Turner

WINNERS IN THE LAST TEN YEARS

1991	Frank Nobilo	1996	Jesper Parnevik
1992	Mark Roe	1997	Mark O'Meara
1993	Ian Woosnam	1998	M A Jimenez
1994	Vijay Singh	1999	Pierre Fulke
1995	Colin Montgomerie	2000	Retief Goosen

PUNTERS' GUIDE

● Best recent form (most recent on the left) has been shown by :-

> Alex Cejka	T4-T10-T11 last three years
> M A Jimenez	T24-T10-Won-T27-T10 last five years
> Jarmo Sandelin	MC-T6-T2-T2 last four years
> Paul McGinley	T16-T24-T27 last three years
> Retief Goosen	Won: T15: DNP: T13 last four years
> Thomas Bjorn	T16-T24-T18 last three years
> Angel Cabrera	T16: T10 last two years
> Michael Campbell	T2: T18 last two years
> Lee Westwood	T7: DNP T73: T8 last four years
> Vijay Singh	Won (1994): T4 (2000) in his two starts
> Paul Lawrie	T12: T18 : T57: T8 last four years

● Current form is important here. In the last two years of the ten players in the top 5
  > nine had made their last cut
  > seven had posted a top 15 in their last tournament
  > six had posted a top 10 in their last tournament.
● What a contrast a year makes
  > In 1999 (Ryder Cup year) four of the first five were priced 100/1+
  > In 2000 (non Ryder Cup year) four of the first five were priced at or under 33/1
  In recent years this tournament cannot easily be clarified as either a favourites' or an outsiders' tournament.
● It may well be that in Ryder Cup years the top European players have their full concentration on the forthcoming American clash. If so in 2001 it could well be an outsiders' year again as it was in 1999 with non Ryders doing particularly well.
● The AXA European stats showed the following

Driving Accuracy	Greens In Reg	Putts per GIR
1 Gary Orr	1 Maarten Lafeber	1 Marc Farry
2 Jose Coceres	2 Retief Goosen	2 Nick O'Hern
3 Brett Rumford	T3 Jose Coceres	3 Paul Lawrie
4 Alex Cejka	T3 Angel Cabrera	4 Fredrik Lindgren

● Players whose profiles refer to this tournament include Jose Coceres, Miguel Angel Jimenez, Jarmo Sandelin, Michael Campbell, Alex Cejka, Nick O'Hern and Paul Lawrie.

THE BELGACOM OPEN

Date	21st - 24th September
Course	Royal Zoute G.C., Knokke, Belgium
Par	71
Yardage	6,907
First Prize	£116,600
Total Purse	£700,000

THE TOURNAMENT

Started in 1998 this year the tournament was being played four weeks earlier than last year.

THE COURSE

The Royal Zoute course has been the venue from the tournament's inception in 1998. It had earlier been the venue for the Alfred Dunhill Open in 1993 and 1994, and the Belgian Open in 1992. It is essentially a links course, with the wind from the sea very significant, but there are a huge number of trees.

2000 ODDS

fav	7/1	Lee Westwood	66/1	M A Martin
	9/1	Darren Clarke	66/1	Andrew Coltart
	9/1	Colin Montgomerie	66/1*	Robert Karlsson (DC)
	14/1	Thomas Bjorn	66/1	Nick O'Hern
	25/1	Bernhard Langer	80/1*	Dean Robertson
	28/1	J M Olazabal	80/1	Jarrod Moseley
	33/1	Padraig Harrington	80/1	Jamie Spence
	40/1*	Angel Cabrera	80/1	Paul McGinley
	40/1	Eduardo Romero	80/1*	Greg Turner
	50/1*	Stephen Leaney	80/1	Ian Garbutt
	50/1	Gary Orr	80/1	Peter O'Malley
	50/1	Jose Coceres	80/1	Steen Tinning

2000 RESULT

1	fav 7/1	Lee Westwood	65 69 67 65 266
2	40/1	Eduardo Romero	69 67 68 66 270
T3	33/1	Padraig Harrington	65 67 68 71 271
T3	125/1	Tom Gillis	67 64 71 69 271
T5	80/1*	Dean Robertson	69 67 68 68 272
T5	100/1	Alistair Forsyth	69 69 67 67 272

T7	Soren Hansen	67 71 63 72 273
	D Park	68 68 68 69 273
	M Farry	65 69 71 68 273
	P McGinley	68 68 71 66 273
	J-F Remesy	66 69 72 66 273
T12	P Quirici	70 65 70 70 275
	P Fulke	67 72 67 69 275
	O Karlsson	65 71 73 66 275
	A Scott	69 70 66 70 275
	G Emerson	68 69 66 72 275
	A Raitt	66 69 70 70 275
T18	P Baker	70 70 63 73 276
	G Ogilvy	70 69 72 65 276
	R Winchester	69 69 70 68 276
	P Archer	69 66 70 71 276
T22	J Wade	74 65 68 70 277
	E Darcy	71 68 68 70 277
	H Otto	64 72 67 74 277
	R Wessels	70 64 72 71 277
T26	J Coceres	68 67 74 69 278
	C Montgomerie	69 69 70 70 278
	G Evans	66 68 74 70 278
	J Rose	69 72 70 67 278
T30	W Riley	67 74 67 71 279
	D Gilford	70 72 68 69 279
	J Lomas	70 67 72 70 279
	N O'Hern	69 68 73 69 279
	D Lee	70 70 67 72 279
	J Berendt	69 68 69 73 279
	M Lafeber	71 69 69 70 279
	S Scahill	65 73 71 70 279
T38	P Fowler	72 68 68 72 280
	Anders Hansen	71 70 71 68 280
	M A Martin	69 72 71 68 280
	B Langer	69 72 67 72 280
	G Orr	71 68 70 71 280
	R Russell	68 71 75 66 280
	R Coles	69 70 72 69 280
	A Wall	68 69 74 69 280

	S Luna	69 70 70 71 280
T47	S Gallacher	68 68 72 73 281
	I Hutchings	69 73 70 69 281
	B Rumford	68 72 69 72 281
	I Giner	69 69 69 74 281
	S Field	71 67 71 72 281
	T Levet	69 68 73 71 281
	S Kjeldsen	72 68 71 70 281
	A Oldcorn	69 73 68 71 281
	M Florioli	70 70 71 70 281
T56	M Mouland	71 70 69 72 282
	A Forsbrand	68 72 71 71 282
	G Murphy	70 72 68 72 282
	J Robinson	71 69 70 72 282
T60	R S Johnson	70 71 72 70 283
	P Affleck	66 72 75 70 283
	S Struver	68 73 71 71 283
	S Allan	70 69 67 77 283
	R Karlsson	69 73 69 72 283
	G Turner	70 72 71 70 283
	D Smyth	68 74 71 70 283
	J Moseley	75 67 67 74 283
	P Eales	70 72 69 72 283
69	J Rivero	70 69 72 73 284
T70	Rodger Davis	70 65 76 74 285
	B Dredge	72 69 71 73 285
	R Green	71 70 72 72 285
T73	O Edmond	73 68 74 71 286
	R McFarlane	70 69 74 73 286
75	S D Hurley	71 71 75 70 287
T76	J Mellor	69 73 71 75 288
	J M Carriles	70 71 72 75 288
	M Blackey	72 70 71 75 288
	C Rocca	70 71 71 76 288
	J M Olazabal	70 72 72 74 288
T81	N Vanhootegem	72 68 77 72 289
	G Rojas	72 70 72 75 289
83	I Poulter	71 67 79 77 294

The main players to miss the cut (made at level) were:–

F Tarnaud (+1)	P Mitchell (+1)	P O'Malley (+1)	C Hanell (+1)
T Johnstone (+1)	F Jacobson (+1)	C Hainline (+1)	R Gonzalez (+1)
F Cea (+2)	S Rowe (+2)	S Leaney (+2)	M James (+2)
I Garbutt (+2)	A Cabrera (+2)	G Brand Jnr (+2)	C Suneson (+2)
D Borrego (+2)	J Senden (+2)	C Cavaer (+2)	V Phillips (+3)
D Lynn (+3)	O Sellberg (+4)	A Sherborne (+4)	D Clarke (+4)
M Brier (+4)	B Davis (+5)	F Lindgren (+5)	T Gogele (+5)

H Nystrom (+5)	J Skold (+6)	S Tinning (+6)	A Coltart (+6)
M Johzon (+6)	S Richardson (+7)	P Nyman (+7)	D De Vooght (+7)
R Claydon (+7)	G Hamerton (+8)	R Byrd (+8)	M Mackenzie (+9)
G J Brand (+9)	M Lanner (+12)		

Thomas Bjorn (after 3 holes), John Bickerton (70), Patrik Sjoland (73) and Jamie Spence (76) all withdrew. Iain Pyman (75) was disqualified.

ROUND BY ROUND LEADERBOARD

FIRST ROUND

H Otto	7 under
L WESTWOOD	6 under
P Harrington	6 under
M Farry	6 under
O Karlsson	6 under
S Scahill	6 under

SECOND ROUND

T Gillis	11 under
P Harrington	10 under
L WESTWOOD	8 under
M Farry	8 under
G Evans	8 under
R Wessels	8 under

THIRD ROUND

P Harrington	13 under
L WESTWOOD	12 under
Soren Hansen	12 under
T Gillis	11 under
P Baker	10 under
G Emerson	10 under
H Otto	10 under

FINAL ROUND

L WESTWOOD	18 under
E Romero	14 under
P Harrington	13 under
T Gillis	13 under
D Robertson	12 under
A Forsyth	12 under

PUNTERS' POINTS

● 7/1 Lee Westwood won his fifth title of the season to go the top of the European Order of Merit. He'd won the inaugural Belgacom Open here two years ago.

● 40/1 Eduardo Romero's fine form on links courses this year continued here with his putting much improved - "every time I look at the cup it looks as big as a football."

● Disappointing final rounds were posted by:-

> Hennie Otto   T5th after R3, 74 in R4 to finish T22nd!

> Peter Baker   T5th after R3, 73 in R4 to finish T18th

> Soren Hanson   T2nd after R3, 72 in R4 to finish T7th

> Gary Emerson   T5th after R3, 72 in R4 to finish T12th

> Padraig Harrington   leader after R3, 71 in R4 to finish T3rd.

● Thomas Bjorn played 3 holes in R1 before withdrawing with an inflamed left foot. All bets on him therefore lost including one of £400 ew!

● Slimline Monty finished T26th to give him for figs of MC-46-26!! Only Spreadex quoted his finishing position (16-19) to give punters a chance to oppose the calorie-controlled Scot!

1999 RESULT

1	40/1	Robert Karlsson
T2	100/1	Jamie Spence
T2	20/1	Retief Goosen
T4	50/1*	Greg Turner
T4	50/1*	P-U Johansson

1998 RESULT

1	fav 8/1	Lee Westwood

won at the first play-off hole

2	150/1	Fredrik Jacobson
T3	33/1	Robert Karlsson
T3	33/1	Greg Turner
T5	66/1	Peter Mitchell
T5	33/1	Jarmo Sandelin

WINNERS IN THE '90s on this course

1992	Belgian Open	M A Jimenez
1993	Alfred Dunhill Open	Darren Clarke
1994	Alfred Dunhill Open	Nick Faldo
1998	The Belgacom Open	Lee Westwood
1999	The Belgacom Open	Robert Karlsson
2000	The Belgacom Open	Lee Westwood

PUNTERS' GUIDE

● The most consistent players over the last three years have been

	2000	1999	1998
> Lee Westwood	W	14	W
> Dean Robertson	5	30	17
> Peter Baker	18	22	34
> Anthony Wall	38	13	10
> Gary Evans	26	55	21

● However two players whose game is well suited here must be remembered in future. They were both well below their best form this year.

> Greg Turner   T60th 2000: T4th 1999: T3rd 1998

> Robert Karlsson   T60th 2000: Won 1999: T3rd 1998

● The AXA stats show the following

Driving Accuracy	Greens In Reg	Putts per GIR
1 Adam Scott	1 Colin Montgomerie	1 Jarrod Moseley
2 Lee Westwood	T2 Alistair Forsyth	2 Olle Karlsson
3 Santiago Luna	T2 Gary Orr	3 Jonathan Lomas
4 Soren Hansen	4 Jose Rivero	4 Roger Winchester

● Players whose profile refers to this tournament include Robert Karlsson, Greg Turner, Dean Robertson, Peter Baker, Bernhard Langer, Stephen Gallacher, Nick O'Hern and Adam Scott.

GERMAN MASTERS

Date	28th September - 1st October
Course	Gut Larchenhof G.C., Cologne, Germany
Par	72
Yardage	7,289
First Prize	£270,000
Total Purse	£1.62 million

THE TOURNAMENT

This is a well-established tournament co-sponsored by Bernhard Langer's marketing company. The veteran German himself has won the tournament three times.

THE COURSE

This Jack Nicklaus-designed course was being used for the third successive year. Last year the course was lengthened (by 300 yards) and the fairways narrowed following Monty's 22 (!) under par victory in 1998. Accuracy off the tee is now particularly significant, with length also important especially on the par 5s.

2000 ODDS

fav	6/1	Lee Westwood (PWW)	66/1*	Angel Cabrera
	12/1	Sergio Garcia (DC)	66/1	Paul McGinley
	12/1	Colin Montgomerie	66/1*	Adam Scott
	14/1	Vijay Singh	66/1	Paul Lawrie
	22/1	Thomas Bjorn	66/1	Dean Robertson
	25/1	Retief Goosen	80/1*	Jean Van de Velde
	25/1	Padraig Harrington	80/1	Pierre Fulke
	28/1	Michael Campbell	80/1	Stephen Leaney
	33/1	Carlos Franco	80/1	Jose Coceres
	33/1	Bernhard Langer	80/1	Mathias Gronberg
	40/1	M A Jimenez	80/1*	Gary Orr
	40/1	Eduardo Romero	80/1	Ian Woosnam
	40/1	J M Olazabal	80/1	Mark McNulty
	50/1	Nick Faldo	80/1	Jarrod Moseley
	50/1	P-U Johansson	80/1	Alex Cejka
	66/1*	Phillip Price	80/1	Andrew Coltart
	66/1	Jarmo Sandelin		

2000 RESULTS

1	28/1	Michael Campbell	68 64 65 197
2	80/1*	Jose Coceres	66 67 65 198
T3	12/1	Colin Montgomerie	67 68 66 201
T3	25/1	Padraig Harrington	66 66 69 201
5	22/1	Thomas Bjorn	68 66 68 202

T6	B Langer	67 67 69 203		T41	S Luna	69 71 69 209
	M A Jimenez	68 70 65 203			S Tinning	71 67 71 209
	A Scott	70 65 68 203			D Robertson	69 70 70 209
	S Torrance	70 67 66 203			V Singh	69 70 70 209
	I Garrido	69 67 67 203			S Struver	73 69 67 209
T11	J Van de Velde	71 64 69 204			Brian Davis	69 73 67 209
	L Westwood	70 66 68 204			C Hanell	70 69 70 209
	A Cabrera	66 69 69 204			T Dier	72 68 69 209
T14	R Chapman	70 67 68 205		T49	G Owen	70 70 70 210
	P McGinley	71 70 64 205			G Orr	67 72 71 210
	P Fulke	71 67 67 205		T51	K Vainola	73 66 72 211
T17	G Turner	71 65 70 206			R Wessels	71 70 70 211
	P Lawrie	72 66 68 206			A Wall	69 70 72 211
	P Sjoland	66 71 69 206			E Darcy	73 67 71 211
	S Garcia	72 65 69 206			R Muntz	72 69 70 211
	M McNulty	71 68 67 206		T56	C Rocca	74 68 70 212
T22	R Winchester	67 71 69 207			E Romero	69 70 73 212
	J Moseley	70 67 70 207			S Leaney	71 70 71 212
	D Howell	70 68 69 207			D Park	72 69 71 212
	P Mitchell	68 70 69 207			K Ekjord	73 69 70 212
	Phillip Price	70 72 65 207			M Florioli	68 72 72 212
	A Cejka	69 67 71 207			P Quirici	70 70 72 212
	P-U Johansson	68 71 68 207		T63	N Fasth	70 71 72 213
	J Bickerton	68 69 70 207			M Lanner	70 72 71 213
T30	A McLardy	68 70 70 208			G Evans	71 67 75 213
	M Farry	71 71 66 208		T66	P Baker	73 68 73 214
	I Garbutt	70 68 70 208			R Goosen	70 71 73 214
	J Senden	68 70 70 208			M Gronberg	69 72 73 214
	E Canonica	67 70 71 208			D Borrego	73 69 72 214
	N Faldo	70 68 70 208		T70	W Huget	68 74 73 215
	E Simsek	72 68 68 208			F Lubenau	73 69 73 215
	A Coltart	68 70 70 208		72	F Cea	72 70 74 216
	R Claydon	68 70 70 208		73	S Webster	71 71 77 219
	D Carter	67 74 67 208		74	M Jonzon	71 71 80 222
	P Eales	72 67 69 208				

The main players to miss the cut (made at 2 under) were:–

S Kjeldsen (-1)	J Spence (-1)	J M Olazabal (-1)	G Ogilvy (-1)
M Scarpa (E)	A Forsbrand (E)	J Sandelin (E)	I Woosnam (E)
J Rivero (E)	T Gogele (+1)	P O'Malley (+1)	T Johnstone (+2)
A Bossert (+2)	R Gonzalez (+2)	M A Martin (+3)	S Hansen (+3)
V Phillips (+3)	R McFarlane (+4)	R Rafferty (+4)	T Levet (+4)
T Gillis (+4)	L Parsons (+4)	A Forsyth (+5)	S Richardson (+5)
S Ballesteros (+9)	M James (+11)	S Allan (+12)	

ROUND BY ROUND LEADERBOARD

FIRST ROUND

P Sjoland	6 under
P Harrington	6 under
A Cabrera	6 under
J Coceres	6 under
6 players at	5 under
M CAMPBELL	4 under

SECOND ROUND

M CAMPBELL	12 under
P Harrington	12 under
J Coceres	11 under
B Langer	10 under
T Bjorn	10 under

THIRD & FINAL ROUND

M CAMPBELL	19 under
J Coceres	18 under
C Montgomerie	15 under
P Harrington	15 under
T Bjorn	14 under

PUNTERS' POINTS

● With the final round washed out the scores after R3 became the final result so we will never know whether Michael Campbell would have held his nerve to go on to win.

● 28/1 Campbell was winning for the first time ever on European soil. It was his FIFTH win within twelve months and gave him recent European tour form figures of W-2-10-2!!

● Jose Coceres reckoned he was striking the ball every bit as well as when he won the Dubai Desert Classic earlier this season. He sure was a 'value' price as a DYM 80/1 here.

● 25/1 Padraig Harrington's T3rd place gives him form on this course over the last three years of T3-T2-T8 for a three-year stroke average of 68.18.

● Fast-finishing T6th Adam Scott's long hitting was well suited here. He could go very close again next year.

1999 RESULT			1998 RESULT		
1	18/1	Sergio Garcia	1	fav 10/1	Colin Montgomerie
won at the first play-off hole			T2	16/1	Vijay Singh
T2	50/1	Padraig Harrington	T2	80/1	Robert Karlsson
T2	50/1	Ian Woosnam	4	150/1	Steve Webster
T4	100/1	Peter Baker	5	33/1	P-U Johansson
T4	200/1	Jose Rivero			

WINNERS IN THE LAST TEN YEARS

1991	Bernhard Langer	Monsheim, Stuttgart
1992	Barry Lane	Monsheim, Stuttgart
1993	Steven Richardson	Monsheim, Stuttgart
1994	Seve Ballesteros	MotzenerSee, Berlin
1995	Anders Forsbrand	MotzenerSee, Berlin
1996	Darren Clarke	MotzenerSee, Berlin
1997	Bernhard Langer	MotzenerSee, Berlin
1998	Colin Montgomerie	Gut Larchenhof, Cologne
1999	Sergio Garcia	Gut Larchenhof, Cologne
2000	Michael Campbell	Gut larchenhof, Cologne

PUNTERS' GUIDE

● In 2001 this tournament is the VERY FIRST after the Ryder Cup and with the inevitable let down there will surely be a big opportunity for a non-Ryder player to win.

● The best form over the last four years belongs to :-

	2000	1999	1998	1997
Colin Montgomerie	3	9	W	2
Bernhard Langer	6	9	15	W
Vijay Singh	41	12	2	-
Padraig Harrington	3	2	8	27
Sergio Garcia	17	W	-	-
Greg Turner	17	17	21	-
Thomas Bjorn	5	16	WD	3

However the last two years on the revamped course are the most important.

● The AXA stats showed the following:-

Driving Accuracy	Greens In Reg	Putts per GIR
1 Jose Coceres	1 Jose Coceres	1 Jean Van de Velde
T2 Adam Scott	T2 M A Jimenez	2 Michael Campbell
T2 Pierre Fulke	T2 John Bickerton	3 Paul McGinley
4 Santiago Luna	T4 Sam Torrance	4 Mathias Gronberg
T5 John Bickerton	T4 Adam Scott	5 Sergio Garcia
T5 Costantino Rocca	T4 Greg Owen	
	T4 Alex Cejka	

● Players whose profiles refer to this tournament include Adam Scott, Jose Coceres, Paul McGinley, Paul Lawrie, Alex Cejka, Angel Cabrera and Retief Goosen.

CISCO WORLD MATCHPLAY CHAMPIONSHIP

Date	5th - 8th October
Course	West Course, Wentworth
Par	71
Yardage	7,047
Winner	£250,000: Runner Up £120,000: Semi Finalists £85,000 (x2)

Quarter Finalists £65,000 (x4): R1 losers (x4) £50,000

THE TOURNAMENT

This well-established tournament has twelve competitors. Eight unseeded players play on the first day for the right to join the four seeds in the quarter-finals. All the matches are over 36 holes.

THE COURSE

The famous West course at Wentworth is the venue for this traditional event. Earlier in the season it hosts the Volvo PGA. It is a par 72 (35-37). The course was wet after recent heavy rain and played long. The last 2 holes are both reachable par 5s.

2000 ODDS

fav	7/2	Ernie Els +	18/1	Thomas Bjorn
	4/1	Colin Montgomerie +	20/1	Padraig Harrington
	5/1	Lee Westwood +	33/1	Retief Goosen
	13/2	Vijay Singh +	40/1	Bob May
	12/1	Darren Clarke	40/1	Nick Faldo
	12/1	Sergio Garcia	50/1*	Adam Scott

+ Seeded players.
1/2 odds 1,2
1/3 odds 1,2 (V Chandler, Corals, Heathorns, Stan James)

2000 RESULT

FIRST ROUND

4/6 Padraig Harrington beat 6/4 Bob May 6 and 5
4/7 Sergio Garcia beat 7/4 Adam Scott 2 and 1
4/7 Darren Clarke beat 13/8 Nick Faldo at the 40th (!) hole with an eagle!!
(this match was finished on Friday morning)
5/4 Retief Goosen beat 8/11 Thomas Bjorn 5 and 4

QUARTER FINALS

4/7 Colin Montgomerie beat 6/4 Padraig Harrington 5 and 3
4/6 Lee Westwood beat 6/5 Sergio Garcia 2 and 1
5/6 Vijay Singh beat 5/6 Darren Clarke 5 and 4
8/15 Ernie Els beat 13/8 Retief Goosen 2 and 1
N.B. All four seeds won

SEMI FINALS

4/6 Colin Montgomerie beat 6/4 Vijay Singh 5 and 4
6/5 Lee Westwood beat 5/6 Ernie Els 1 up
N.B. Both matches were finished on Sunday, having not started at 3.45 p.m. on
Saturday because of really heavy rain.

FINAL

Lee Westwood beat Colin Montgomerie at the 38th hole
N.B. The final 18 holes were completed on Monday.

RESULTS IN OTHER MARKETS

Sadly only one firm (Ladbrokes) quoted odds for naming the two finalists. They
went 6/1 for a Monty-Westwood shoot-out. Let's hope more firms offer quotes in
2001.

PUNTERS' POINTS

● Europe's finest battled it out and it was always going to be a close photo-finish,
with Westwood emerging the narrow winner. Overall I felt Monty was unlucky as
he'd played superbly throughout the tournament on his favourite course and Els
had 'given' his S-F to Westwood after missing a tiddler on the last.

Nevertheless perhaps it was fitting that Europe's new No. 1 player should beat
our long-term top player! The baton had been passed down a generation.

1999 RESULT

Final   C Montgomerie beat M O'Meara 3 and 2

SF   M O'Meara beat N Price 1 hole
SF   C Montgomerie beat P Harrington 7 and 6

1998 RESULT

Final M O'Meara beat T Woods 1 hole

SF   M O'Meara beat V Singh 11 and 10
SF   T Woods beat L Westwood 5 and 4

WINNERS IN THE LAST TEN YEARS

1991 Ballesteros beat Price 3 and 2
1992 Faldo beat Sluman 8 and 7
1993 Pavin beat Faldo 1 hole
1994 Els beat Montgomerie 4 and 2
1995 Els beat Elkington 3 and 1
1996 Els beat Singh 3 and 2
1997 Singh beat Els 1 hole
1998 O'Meara beat Woods 1 hole
1999 Montgomerie beat O'Meara 3 and 2
2000 Westwood beat Montgomerie at the 38th hole

PUNTERS' GUIDE

● In the last sixteen years thirteen seeds (81.12% strike rate) have won, and this year the unseeded players were all blown away in the quarter-finals.

The unseeded players have a massive handicap to overcome given that they must play an extra 36 holes in R1.

> EXPECT A SEED TO WIN AGAIN IN 2001

● However the outsiders in R1 who had a 75% strike rate over the previous three years fared less well this year, winning only one of the four matches. However, had 13/8 Nick Faldo won the 'system' of backing the first-day outsiders would have shown another healthy profit.

As it is over the last four years the record is sixteen bets tenwins LSP 6.57. 41% return

> ALWAYS CLOSELY EXAMINE THE OUTSIDERS IN THE FIRST ROUND

AND FINALLY

● Sadly this tournament is covered by the BBC with its regular interruptions for local and national news. However this year they excelled themselves as with sole coverage they didn't show a single minute of the exciting final 18 holes on Monday live. The usual daytime drivel stayed in place. It really did show everyone what the Beeb thinks of golf in particular, and sport in general.

THE ALFRED DUNHILL CUP

Date	12th - 15th October	
Course	Old Course, St Andrews, Scotland	
Par	72	
Yardage	7,115	
Prize Money	£1 million	
Winners	£300,000	£100,000 per player
Runners Up	£150,000	£50,000 per player
Semi-Finalists	£95,000	£31,666 per player

THE TOURNAMENT

This is a magnificent team event with a very unusual stroke-play match format that means every match must go to the last green, or further. Sixteen three-man teams are drawn into four groups and play in a 'round robin' over the first three days with the winners of each group advancing to the semi-finals on Sunday morning.

THE COURSE

The famous Old Course, 'the Old Lady', that was the scene for Tiger Woods's British Open win in July this year was again the venue. The infamous 17th, the road hole, can see a 2- or 3-shot swing in any match.

2000 ODDS Before the Draw

4/1	South Africa
7/1	Argentina
7/1	Scotland
8/1	Spain
8/1	New Zealand (11/1)
12/1	Sweden
14/1	Zimbabwe (16/1)
16/1	Ireland (20/1)
16/1	USA
16/1	Australia
25/1	Wales
33/1	Germany (40/1)
40/1	England (80/1*)
50/1	France (125/1*)
125/1*	Japan (150/1*)
200/1*	China

Please Note: changes in odds made after Wednesday morning's draw are given in brackets.

ALL QUOTED 1/2 odds 1,2

Stan James and Multi-Sports went just 1/3 odds 1,2

GROUP 1

11/10	Scotland
3/1	WALES
13/2	Germany
10/1	England

DAY ONE

8/13 Wales beat 15/8 England 3-0

4/5 I Woosnam (72) beat 15/8 R Chapman (73)

4/5 P Price (70) beat 7/4 B Davis (73)

6/5 D Park (67) beat 11/10 J Spence (73)

5/2 Germany beat 2/5 Scotland 2-1

11/10 B Langer (68) beat 11/8 G Orr (70)

15/8 T Gogele (71) lost to 8/11 A Coltart (70)

10/3 S Struver (66) beat 4/9 C Montgomerie (70)

DAY TWO

4/11 Scotland beat 3/1 England 2-1

1/2 C Montgomerie (69) beat 7/2 B Davis (70)

4/5 A Coltart (68) beat 2/1 J Spence (73)

8/11 Gary Orr (69) lost to 2/1 R Chapman (69) at the 19th hole

5/6 Wales beat 6/4 Germany 2-1

6/4 I Woosnam (70) beat 5/6 B Langer (72)

6/5 D Park (71) lost to 6/5 S Struver (71) at the 19th hole

8/11 P Price (69) beat 13/8 T Gogele (70)

DAY THREE

9/4 Wales beat 4/6 Scotland 3-0

9/4 I Woosnam (73) beat 8/13 C Montgomerie (73) at the 19th hole

11/10 P Price (69) beat 11/10 G Orr (72)

13/8 D Park (69) beat 5/6 A Coltart (72)

4/6 Germany beat 9/4 England 3-0

8/13 B Langer (71) beat 9/4 J Spence (76)

11/10 T Gogele (69) beat 11/8 R Chapman (72)

1/1 S Struver (72) beat 6/4 B Davis (74)

FINAL TABLE	PL	W	Games Won
WALES	3	3	8
Germany	3	2	6
Scotland	3	1	3
England	3	0	1

GROUP 2

1/1	SOUTH AFRICA
13/5	New Zealand
9/2	Ireland
33/1*	France

DAY ONE

1/5 South Africa beat 6/1 France 2-1

10/11 D Frost (68) beat 9/4 J-F Remesy (74)

4/7 R Goosen (72) lost to 10/3 R Jacquelin (70)

4/11 E Els (68) beat 4/1 T Levet (74)

6/4 Ireland beat 4/6 New Zealand 2-1

7/4 D Smyth (69) lost to 8/11 G Turner (69) at the 19th hole

10/11 P Harrington (68) beat 11/8 G Waite (71)

2/1 P McGinley (67) beat 5/6 M Campbell (69)

DAY TWO

2/5 New Zealand beat 10/3 France 3-0

8/11 G Turner (73) beat 11/5 J-F Remesy (74)

8/11 G Waite (70) beat 15/8 R Jacquelin (72)

4/7 M Campbell (69) beat 11/4 T Levet (70)

1/2 South Africa beat 15/8 Ireland 3-0

5/6 D Frost (66) beat 13/8 D Smyth (68)

10/11 R Goosen (71) beat 11/8 P McGinley (71) at the 19th hole

8/11 E Els (67) beat 7/4 P Harrington (69)

DAY THREE

1/2 South Africa beat 7/4 New Zealand 2-1

4/5 R Goosen (71) beat 13/8 G Turner (71) at the 19th hole

1/1 D Frost (75) lost to 5/4 G Waite (71)

4/6 E Els (68) beat 15/8 M Campbell (69)

1/3 Ireland beat 3/1 France 3-0

8/11 P McGinley (67) beat 15/8 R Jacquelin (69)

10/11 D Smyth (70) beat 7/4 J-F Remesy (76)

8/15 P Harrington (69) beat 9/4 T Levet (74)

FINAL TABLE	PL	W	Games Won
SOUTH AFRICA	3	3	7
Ireland	3	2	5
New Zealand	3	1	5
France	3	0	1

GROUP 3

6/4	SPAIN
11/5	Sweden
7/2	Zimbabwe
100/1*	China

DAY ONE

1/10 Spain beat 9/1 China 3-0

2/7 M A Jimenez (66) beat 5/1 Wu Xiang-Bin (79)

8/11 M A Martin (70) beat 7/2 Zhang Lian-Wei (71)

2/7 J M Olazabal (66) beat 5/1 Liang Wen-Chong (71)

5/6 Sweden beat 6/5 Zimbabwe 2-1

6/5 P Sjoland (72) lost to 11/10 M McNulty (67)

4/6 P-U Johansson (69) beat 15/8 T Johnstone (75)

7/4 M Gronberg (69) beat 8/11 N Price (73)

DAY TWO

1/9 Sweden beat 8/1 China 3-0

1/2 P Sjoland (67) beat 11/4 Liang Wen-Chong (72)

4/11 P-U Johansson (72) beat 11/2 Wu Xiang-Bin (80)

4/7 M Gronberg (71) beat 9/4 Zhang Lian-Wei (72)

4/7 Spain beat 5/2 Zimbabwe 2-1

4/5 M A Martin (73) lost to 7/4 T Johnstone (72)

1/1 M A Jimenez (67) beat 6/5 N Price (68)

5/6 J M Olazabal (67) beat 13/8 M McNulty (71)

DAY THREE

8/11 Spain beat 6/4 Sweden 2-1

4/5 M A Jimenez (72) lost to 6/4 P-U Johansson (71)

13/8 M A Martin (69) beat 10/11 P Sjoland (70)

8/11 J M Olazabal (72) beat 15/8 M Gronberg (74)

1/5 Zimbabwe beat 9/1 China 2-1

4/9 T Johnstone (69) beat 11/2 Wu Xiang-Bin (76)

8/15 M McNulty (71) beat 7/2 Liang Wen-Chong (74)

8/15 N Price (71) lost to 4/1 Zhang Lian-Wei (68)

FINAL TABLE	PL	W	Games Won
SPAIN	3	3	7
Sweden	3	2	6
Zimbabwe	3	1	4
China	3	0	1

GROUP 4

5/4	ARGENTINA
3/1	USA
7/2	Australia
33/1*	Japan

DAY ONE

1/6 Argentina beat 13/2 Japan 3-0

2/5 E Romero (70) beat 4/1 T Nishikawa (72)

4/9 A Cabrera (70) beat 9/2 I Aoki (71)

4/7 J Coceres (66) beat 3/1 T Watanabe (71)

1/1 Australia beat 11/10 USA 2-1

11/10 S Leaney (67) beat 6/5 J Daly (70)

1/1 N O'Hern (65) (!) beat 6/4 L Mize (71)

2/1 P O'Malley (73) lost to 4/6 T Lehman (68)

DAY TWO

8/13 Argentina beat 2/1 USA 3-0

4/6 E Romero (70) beat 9/4 L Mize (72)

10/11 J Coceres (73) beat 6/4 J Daly (75)

6/4 A Cabrera (68) beat 1/1 T Lehman (71)

1/4 Australia beat 11/2 Japan 3-0

4/9 N O'Hern (70) beat 9/2 I Aoki (71)

4/7 S Leaney (73) beat 5/2 T Watanabe (74)

10/11 P O'Malley (69) beat 2/1 T Nishikawa (70)

DAY THREE

4/6 Argentina beat 7/4 Australia 2-1

5/6 E Romero (72) lost to 11/8 N O'Hern (69)

10/11 A Cabrera (70) beat 6/4 S Leaney (75)

10/11 J Coceres (74) beat 11/8 P O'Malley (76)

4/11 USA beat 5/1 Japan 2-1

1/1 J Daly (73) lost to 15/8 I Aoki (73) at the 21st hole

4/9 T Lehman (74) beat 3/1 T Nishikawa (75)

4/5 L Mize (70) beat 9/4 T Watanabe (76)

FINAL TABLE	PL	W	Games Won
ARGENTINA	3	3	8
Australia	3	2	6
USA	3	1	3
Japan	3	0	1

SEMI-FINALS

2/5 South Africa beat 7/4 Wales 2½ - ½

R Goosen (68) tied with P Price (68)

E Els (69) beat D Park (77)

D Frost (70) beat I Woosnam (76)

8/11 Spain beat 1/1 Argentina 2-1

M A Jimenez (71) lost to E Romero (69)

J M Olazabal (69) beat A Cabrera (71)

M A Martin (71) beat J Coceres (72)

FINAL

5/4 Spain beat 4/6 South Africa 2-1

M A Martin (74) beat D Frost (74) at the 19th

M A Jimenez (70) beat R Goosen (72)

J M Olazabal (70) lost to E Els (68)

TOURNAMENT WINNERS IN THE LAST TEN YEARS

1991	Sweden beat South Africa 2-1
1992	England beat Scotland 3-0
1993	USA beat England 2-1
1994	Canada beat USA 2-1
1995	Scotland beat Zimbabwe 2-1
1996	USA beat New Zealand 2-1
1997	South Africa beat Sweden 2-1
1998	South Africa beat Spain 3-0
1999	Spain beat Australia 2-1
2000	Spain beat South Africa 2-1

NOTE:

● Spain reached the final for the third successive year.

● South Africa reached the final for the third time in the last four years.

● The Spain - South Africa final was a repeat of the 1998 final. This time however Spain triumphed and retained the title they won in 1999.

● In the crucial match Miguel Martin's outrageous fluky 50-foot putt at the last forced a play-off which he then won at the 19th.

TOP INDIVIDUAL POINTS SCORERS

8/1	Ernie Els	40/1	Stephen Leaney
10/1	Colin Montgomerie	40/1	M A Martin
14/1	Retief Goosen	50/1*	Andrew Coltart
18/1	Michael Campbell	50/1	Mathias Gronberg
18/1	J M Olazabal	50/1	Bernhard Langer
20/1	M A Jimenez	50/1	Patrik Sjoland
22/1	Eduardo Romero	50/1	Mark McNulty
25/1	Tom Lehman	50/1	Nick O'Hern
25/1	Padraig Harrington	50/1	Phillip Price
28/1	Nick Price	66/1*	Ian Woosnam
28/1	Angel Cabrera	66/1*	Greg Turner
28/1	Jose Coceres	66/1*	John Daly
33/1	David Frost	66/1	Peter O'Malley
33/1	Grant Waite	80/1	Larry Mize
33/1	Gary Orr	80/1*	Paul McGinley
33/1	P-U Johansson		

2000 RESULT

1	fav 8/1	Ernie Els	5 points
T2	33/1	M A Martin	4 points
T2	18/1	J M Olazabal	4 points
4	50/1	Phillip Price	3½ points

Els's rounds were 68,67,68,69 and 68 for a stroke average of 68!

1999 RESULT

T1	33/1	Craig Parry	4 pts
T1	12/1	Ernie Els	4 pts
T1	22/1	J M Olazabal	4 pts
T4	66/1*	Carlos Franco	3 pts
T4	11/1	Sergio Garcia	3 pts
T4	20/1	M A Jimenez	3 pts
T4	50/1*	Stephen Leaney	3 pts
T4	40/1	Jarmo Sandelin	3 pts
T4	40/1	David Frost	3 pts

1998 RESULT

1	40/1	Retief Goosen	5 pts
2	33/1	John Daly	4 pts
T3	40/1	M A Jimenez	3 pts
T3	33/1	Greg Turner	3 pts
T3	20/1	Darren Clarke	3 pts
T3	16/1	Steve Elkington	3 pts
T3	22/1	Nick Price	3 pts
T3	40/1	Craig Parry	3 pts
T3	6/1	Tiger Woods	3 pts
T3	66/1*	David Frost	3 pts

PUNTERS' GUIDE

● This year was the final time that the Dunhill Cup team tournament, with its brilliant unique format, will be played. I feel that is very sad as the format has provided us with many years of exciting golf and many nice betting opportunities.

● In 2001 there will be a replacement tournament which will be played as a celebration of links golf using a trio of links courses (Carnoustie, St Andrews and the new Kingsbarns course) and following a celebrity pro-am format on the lines used in the AT&T event in America. The new tournament WILL count towards the European Order of Merit.

So expect to see pro-am teams like Ian Botham and Ian Woosnam lining up.

BBVA OPEN TURESPANA MASTERS

Date	19th - 22nd October
Course	Club de Campo, Madrid
Par	71
Yardage	6,939
First Prize	£100,000
Total Purse	£600,000

THE TOURNAMENT

The Turespana Masters returned to the European tour nineteen months after it was last played in Malaga in March 1999. Spanish players had won the previous four stagings of this event from 1996.

THE COURSE

The Club de Campo course was last used four years ago for the Spanish Open when Padraig Harrington was the winner at 16 under par and the cut was made at even par. Since 1996 Manuel Pinero has toughened the course with more undulations on the greens. The par (72 in 1996) is now 71 following the long 12th becoming a par 4. The course is 2,500 feet about sea level and the ball therefore travels further than normal.

2000 ODDS

fav	8/1	Sergio Garcia	50/1	Gary Orr
	10/1	Darren Clarke	50/1	Ian Woosnam
	14/1	M A Jimenez (DC)	66/1*	Pierre Fulke
	16/1	Padraig Harrington	66/1	Andrew Coltart
	25/1	Bernhard Langer	66/1	Dean Robertson
	25/1	Eduardo Romero	66/1*	Jarmo Sandelin
	33/1*	Phillip Price	66/1*	Mathias Gronberg
	33/1	Angel Cabrera	66/1*	Alex Cejka
	33/1	P-U Johansson	66/1	Patrik Sjoland
	40/1	Paul McGinley	80/1*	Ignacio Garrido
	50/1	Paul Lawrie	80/1	Jarrod Moseley
	50/1	M A Martin	80/1	David Park

2000 RESULT

1	16/1	**Padraig Harrington**	67 64 66 70 267
2	50/1	**Gary Orr**	67 68 68 66 269
3	33/1	**P-U Johansson**	72 63 67 68 270
4	10/1	**Darren Clarke**	66 70 70 65 271
T5	40/1	**Paul McGinley**	67 69 68 68 272
T5	200/1	**Francisco Cea**	68 67 70 67 272

T7	E Romero	72 66 67 68 273		R Green	68 73 71 68 280
	M A Jimenez	66 66 69 72 273		I Garbutt	70 68 70 72 280
T9	E Darcy	69 67 67 71 274		R Chapman	70 70 68 72 280
	R Wessels	68 65 69 72 274	T43	J Skold	73 68 68 72 281
	S Luna	65 70 66 73 274		C Suneson	71 68 71 71 281
T12	R Jacquelin	72 65 72 66 275		P Lonard	67 72 71 71 281
	A Cabrera	72 66 69 68 275		Rodger Davis	70 65 73 73 281
	F Lindgren	70 69 68 68 275		Phillip Price	69 67 72 73 281
T15	G Owen	70 70 69 67 276		D Gilford	67 70 71 73 281
	R Russell	69 70 66 71 276		N Fasth	71 69 66 75 281
	D Howell	70 67 67 72 276	T50	I Garrido	74 65 70 73 282
	P Baker	68 71 65 72 276		J Moseley	70 66 74 72 282
T19	G Evans	74 65 70 68 277		M Gronberg	69 71 71 71 282
	A Wall	67 69 73 68 277		P Sjoland	71 68 70 73 282
	S Tinning	69 70 72 66 277	T54	S Scahill	69 72 69 73 283
	M Siem	68 67 73 69 277		S Torrance	69 71 72 71 283
	P Fulke	68 68 71 70 277		B Langer	72 69 71 71 283
	S Gallacher	67 69 68 73 277		S Kjeldsen	69 71 73 70 283
T25	P Mitchell	72 69 68 69 278		S Webster	71 68 70 74 283
	M Brier	64 72 72 70 278	59	J M Lara	70 70 75 69 284
	S Garcia	68 69 71 70 278	T60	J C Aguero	73 67 69 76 285
	D Smyth	70 69 69 70 278		M Farry	71 70 73 71 285
	G Emerson	67 70 70 71 278		R Muntz	71 70 73 71 285
T30	A Coltart	71 70 70 68 279		V Phillips	68 71 76 70 285
	J Quiros	67 72 70 70 279		P Golding	69 71 75 70 285
	M A Martin	70 68 69 72 279		I Pyman	72 66 77 70 285
	Soren Hansen	72 68 67 72 279		K Storgaard	72 69 75 69 285
	T Johnstone	66 70 70 73 279	T67	J Mellor	67 70 72 77 286
T35	J Rivero	67 69 73 71 280		P Affleck	71 70 72 73 286
	C Hanell	71 68 71 70 280		Anders Hansen	69 71 75 71 286
	M Jonzon	71 70 69 70 280	70	P Nyman	70 68 76 73 287
	G Rojas	71 67 72 70 280	71	M Lafeber	70 70 74 74 288
	C Rodiles	68 69 73 70 280			

The main players to miss the cut (made at 1 under) were:–

B Teilleria (E)	G Murphy (E)	J Berendt (E)	D Hospital (E)
M Lanner (E)	C Hainline (E)	P Quirici (E)	B Lane (+1)
D Park (+1)	P Linhart (+1)	D Lee (+1)	A Bossert (+1)
M Moreno (+1)	J Bickerton (+1)	P Lawrie (+1)	G Brand Jr (+1)
D De Vooght (+1)	A Cejka (+2)	R Karlsson (+2)	D Cooper (+2)
R Winchester (+2)	W Riley (+2)	J Lomas (+2)	R Gonzalez (+2)
D Borrego (+2)	J Robinson (+2)	F Jacobson (+3)	S Ballesteros (+3)
R Claydon (+3)	D Robertson (+3)	S Struver (+3)	A Oldcorn (+3)
R Ballesteros (am) (+3)	T Levet (+4)	O Edmond (+4)	J Sandelin (+5)
D Carter (+5)	H Otto (+5)	M Pinero (+6)	G Hutcheon (+6)
P Eales (+7)	B Dredge (+7)	A Sherborne (+7)	R Rafferty (+11)

ROUND BY ROUND LEADERBOARD

FIRST ROUND

M Brier	7 under
S Luna	6 under
D Clarke	5 under
M A Jimenez	5 under
T Johnstone	5 under
P HARRINGTON	4 under

SECOND ROUND

P HARRINGTON	11 under
M A Jimenez	10 under
R Wessels	9 under
P-U Johansson	7 under
S Luna	7 under
F Cea	7 under
G Orr	7 under
M Brier	7 under
R Davis	7 under
M Siem	7 under

THIRD ROUND

P HARRINGTON	16 under
M A Jimenez	12 under
S Luna	12 under
P-U Johansson	11 under
R Wessels	11 under
G Orr	10 under
E Darcy	10 under

FINAL ROUND

P HARRINGTON	17 under
G Orr	15 under
P-U Johansson	14 under
D Clarke	13 under
P McGinley	12 under
F Cea	12 under

PUNTERS' POINTS

● "Coming here was an inspired decision." A late entry by 16/1 Padraig Harrington to play on the course where he first won on the European tour certainly paid off. However the truth was that he played unimpressively over the back nine in R4, especially with a double bogey on the 13th. Nevertheless it was compensation for the genial Irishman for his early season disqualification at the Belfry.

● Gary Orr made three successive bogeys round the turn in R4 yet nevertheless secured 2nd place and shot up to 6th place in the Ryder Cup table.

● Per-Ulrik Johansson showed signs of 'contention rust' over the final holes, yet he secured his second successive top 5 finish in an event he obviously enjoys.

● Going for a third successive win in this event, Miguel Angel Jimenez made a poor start to R4 and never really got back into contention.

1999 RESULT

Parador, Malaga

1	20/1	M A Jimenez
2	50/1	Steve Webster
3	125/1	Raphael Jacquelin
4	150/1	Marc Farry
T5	125/1	Fredrik Lindgren
T5	33/1	P-U Johansson
T5	16/1	Alex Cejka

1998 RESULT

Santa Ponsa, Mallorca

1	22/1	M A Jimenez
2	16/1	M A Martin
T3	80/1	Katsuyoshi Tomori
T3		Paul McGinley
5	125/1	Van Phillips

McGinley was a late entrant, unquoted in the bookies' lists and regarded as a non-runner.

PAST WINNERS OF THIS TOURNAMENT

1992	Vijay Singh	Parador, Malaga de Golf
1993	Andrew Oldcorn	Novo Sancti Petri, Chicarva, Cadiz
1994	Carl Mason	Montecastillo Jerez
1995	Alex Cejka	Istantilla, Huelva
1996	Diego Borrego	El Saler, Valencia
1997	J M Olazabal	Maspalomas, Gran Canaria
1998	M A Jimenez	Santa Ponsa 1, Mallorca
1999	M A Jimenez	Parador, Malaga del Golf
2000	Padraig Harrington	Club de Campo, Madrid

PUNTERS' GUIDE

● The tournament returns to a mid-March slot in 2001.

● Players with at least two top 20 finishes in this tournament in the last three years include:-

	2000	1999	1998
P-U Johansson	3	5	-
G Orr	2	8	-
M A Jimenez	7	W	W
R Jacquelin	12	3	27
P McGinley	5	-	3
J Bickerton	MC	10	19
A Wall	19	20	23
F Cea	5	40	19
G Owen	15	20	35
D Howell	15	MC	15
A Cabrera	12	30	8

● In 2001 do keep your eye on the young German Marcel Siem who made his professional tour debut here and shot three sub-70 rounds in posting an impressive top 20 finish.

● Players whose profiles refer to this tournament include Carlos Rodiles, Per-Ulrik Johansson, Gary Orr, Miguel Angel Jimenez, Paul McGinley, Raphael Jacquelin, Francisco Cea and Greg Owen.

THE ITALIAN OPEN

Date	26th - 29th October
Course	Is Molas, Sardinia
Par	72
Yardage	7,080
First Prize	£100,000
Total Purse	£600,000

THE TOURNAMENT

After visiting different venues each year the Italian Open has found a new home on the Is Molas course (on the island of Sardinia). It will host the tournament until the end of 2006. It is intended to act as a great boost to Italian tourism.

THE COURSE

The course was last used for this event in 1982 when Mark James was the winner. However in recent years it has been the venue for the Is Molas Challenge on the Challenge tour. After a par 5 opening hole the next par 5 is on the 12th so there are three reachable par 5s in the last 7 holes. The par is 35 out - 37 back. Widish fairways do not penalise the inaccurate drivers. The toughest hole is the par 4 8th.

2000 ODDS

fav	5/2	Lee Westwood	66/1	Ian Garbutt
	7/1	Thomas Bjorn	66/1*	David Howell
	25/1	Pierre Fulke	66/1	Raphael Jacquelin
	40/1	Dean Robertson (DC)	66/1	David Park
	40/1	Ian Woosnam	66/1	Sam Torrance
	50/1	Ray Russell	66/1	Roger Wessels
	66/1*	Steen Tinning	80/1	Anders Hansen
	66/1	Peter Baker	80/1	Soren Hansen
	66/1*	Emanuele Canonica	80/1	Gary Evans
	66/1	Santiago Luna	80/1*	Alistair Forsyth
	66/1*	Jarmo Sandelin	80/1	Steve Webster
	66/1*	Jarrod Moseley	80/1	John Bickerton
	66/1	Stephen Gallacher	80/1*	Robert Karlsson

2000 RESULT

1	125/1	Ian Poulter	66 67 65 69 267
2	150/1	Gordon Brand Jr	67 69 66 66 268
T3	125/1	Richard Green	67 65 70 68 270
T3	100/1*	Francesco Cea	70 63 68 69 270
T5	66/1	Peter Baker	68 65 70 68 271
T5	125/1	Van Phillips	65 68 68 70 271

T7	A Oldborn	67 68 68 69 272		K Storgaard	74 68 72 65 279
	C Suneson	67 69 71 65 272		M Florioli	69 71 71 68 279
	P Fulke	66 74 70 62 272		M Scarpa	69 72 70 68 279
	R Wessels	67 66 68 71 272		N Vanhootegem	70 71 71 67 279
	J Bickerton	67 70 67 68 272		G Rojas	68 73 70 68 279
T12	E Boult	66 66 70 71 273		B Dredge	73 69 67 70 279
	P Eales	69 69 69 66 273		I Pyman	69 71 70 69 279
	T Gogele	69 69 65 70 273		S Gallacher	67 70 71 71 279
	Ricardo Gonzalez	66 67 68 72 273	T53	E Canonica	66 69 72 73 280
	L Westwood	67 70 70 66 273		D Park	70 67 73 70 280
T17	E Darcy	65 68 70 71 274		R Russell	70 72 67 71 280
	J Robinson	66 69 70 69 274		D Robertson	68 70 73 69 280
	M Jonzon	69 72 68 65 274	T57	I Woosnam	69 70 73 69 281
	M Blackey	72 68 67 67 274		Soren Hansen	70 70 72 69 281
T21	S Luna	69 71 66 69 275	T59	C Rocca	70 69 70 73 282
	D Howell	70 65 69 71 275		G Murphy	73 69 72 68 282
	J Rose	70 69 69 67 275		S Kjeldsen	69 72 71 70 282
	S Tinning	66 70 67 72 275		D Borrego	72 70 69 71 282
	G Evans	70 68 66 71 275		D Lee	70 72 70 70 282
T26	R Jacquelin	67 69 69 71 276	T64	M Lanner	69 73 68 73 283
	R Winchester	68 70 73 65 276		P Golding	71 70 75 67 283
	P Lonard	70 69 69 68 276		J Berendt	68 74 68 73 283
	S Scahill	69 65 71 71 276		M Brier	71 71 71 70 283
	J Skold	70 67 70 69 276		M Bernardini	71 70 71 71 283
T31	S Torrance	65 70 70 72 277	T69	S Grappasonni	72 69 74 69 284
	A Napoleoni	71 68 70 68 277		P Mitchell	69 71 72 72 284
	Anders Hansen	70 71 67 69 277		D De Vooght	73 68 70 73 284
	G Hutcheon	71 67 71 68 277		G Hamerton	74 68 68 74 284
	F Lindgren	67 68 72 70 277		E Molinari (am)	72 70 75 67 284
	R Claydon	72 68 66 71 277	T74	O Edmond	73 69 73 70 285
	J Lomas	68 69 71 69 277		F Guermani	70 68 74 73 285
	R Coles	71 67 71 68 277	T76	M Harwood	69 73 69 75 286
T39	R Boxall	70 69 69 70 278		C Hainline	72 70 70 74 286
	R Rafferty	70 69 70 69 278	T78	M Santi	69 70 74 74 287
	J Rivero	69 72 68 69 278		D Lynn	72 70 76 69 287
	M Lafeber	71 70 67 70 278		F Bisazza	70 72 71 74 287
	I Garbutt	67 72 74 65 278		B Teilleria	65 75 72 75 287
T24	Steve Webster	73 66 70 70 279	82	J Moseley	71 70 72 75 288

The main players to miss the cut (made at 2 under) were:–

T Levet (-1)	P Quirici (-1)	P Affleck (-1)	R Davis (-1)
M Mackenzie (-1)	I Hutchings (-1)	J Payne (E)	D Smyth (E)
T Bjorn (E)	A McLardy (E)	P Fowler (E)	R Karlsson (+1)
J Sandelin (+1)	A Bossert (+2)	H Otto (+2)	D Gilford (+2)
R Byrd (+3)	P Nyman (+4)	A Forsyth (+4)	J Mellor (+4)
A Binaghi (+5)	M Anglert (+5)		

ROUND BY ROUND LEADERBOARD

FIRST ROUND

V Phillips	7 under
S Torrance	7 under
E Darcy	7 under
B Teilleria	7 under
I POULTER	6 under
6 others at	6 under

SECOND ROUND

R Green	12 under
E Boult	12 under
F Cea	11 under
E Darcy	11 under
V Phillips	11 under
P Baker	11 under
R Wessels	11 under
I POULTER	11 under
Ricardo Gonzalez	11 under

THIRD ROUND

I POULTER	18 under
F Cea	15 under
V Phillips	15 under
Ricardo Gonzalez	15 under
R Wessels	15 under

FINAL ROUND

I POULTER	21 under
G Brand Jr	20 under
R Green	18 under
F Cea	18 under
P Baker	17 under
V Phillips	17 under

PUNTERS' POINTS

● With three birdies in the last 6 holes 125/1 rookie Ian Poulter secured his first tour win. His length is well suited to this course which he knew from his Challenge tour days.

● 150/1 Gordon Brand Jr had missed his last three cuts yet played well until the pressure told and he bogeyed the last hole.

● 100/1* Francisco Cea, after a superb T5th last week, played really well again here under massive pressure to save his card. An accurate player reverting to his traditional fade he'll do well in 2001.

● Beware of 'star' players using an 'ordinary' tournament as a warm up

> Unplaced 5/2 favourite Lee Westwood admitted he was rusty 'after a two-week break'

> 7/1 Thomas Bjorn didn't have to admit it. He missed the cut!

● 'Name' players maybe out of form or rusty, yet they do create value. In the R1 3-ball betting Thomas Bjorn (using the event as a warm up) and Woosnam (dodgy back and putting poorly) were against Emanuele Canonica (knows the course, which suits him). Canonica was 3/1 with Hills with Bjorn 5/6 and Woosy 9/4.

Result: Canonica 66, Woosy 69, and Bjorn 72!!

1999 RESULT

Circolo G.C., Turin

1	150/1	Dean Robertson
2	80/1*	Padraig Harrington
T3	40/1	Phillip Price
T3	150/1	Russell Claydon
T3	100/1*	Gary Evans

1998 RESULT

Castel Conturbia, Milan (3 rounds)

1	66/1	Patrik Sjoland
T2	8/1	J M Olazabal
T2	80/1	Joakim Haeggman
4	20/1	Thomas Bjorn
5	66/1	Peter Baker

WINNERS IN THE LAST TEN YEARS

1991	Craig Parry	1996	Jim Payne
1992	Sandy Lyle	1997	Bernhard Langer
1993	Greg Turner	1998	Patrik Sjoland (3 rounds)
1994	Eduardo Romero	1999	Dean Robertson
1995	Sam Torrance	2000	Ian Poulter

PUNTERS' GUIDE

● With this course being the settled venue till the end of 2006 punters can build up a bank of course form.

● This tournament really does provide a first-class opportunity for the talented younger players to register their first tour win. Indeed in the last five years there have been four first-time winners.

● In the last five years there have been twenty-six players in the top 5 positions.

> twelve of the 26 (46.1%) have started at or over 100/1

> eighteen of the 26 (69.2%) have started at or over 66/1

So in 2001 consider players at big odds, especially if they are seeking their first win.

● The reachable par 5s and the wide fairways make this an easy test especially in the benign weather found this year. Remember a course record 62 was shot by Pierre Fulke in R4.

● Players with a good tournament record over the last four years include.

> Francisco Cea   T6th last year and T3rd in 2000 in two starts

> Ricardo Gonzalez   T6th last year and T12th in 2000 in two starts

> Dean Robertson   T6th in 1997: Winner 1999 and made cut 1998 & 2000

> Gary Evans   T3rd in 1999 and T21st 2000

> Peter Baker   5th 1998: T23rd 1999: T5th 2000

● Players whose profiles refer to this tournament include Van Phillips, Emanuele Canonica, John Bickerton, Carl Suneson, Francisco Cea, Thomas Gogele, Steve Webster, Ricardo Gonzalez and Peter Baker.

THE VOLVO MASTERS

Date	2nd - 5th November
Course	Montecastillo, Jerez, Spain
Par	72
Yardage	7,060
First Prize	£333,000
Total Purse	£2 million

THE TOURNAMENT

Before the advent of the World Championships the Volvo Masters was traditionally the final tournament on the tour. There is a 66 man field with no halfway cut, so every player is guaranteed a cheque. The top 55 on the Order of Merit all play.

THE COURSE

This Jack Nicklaus course has generous fairways, large greens, and tends to play fairly easily. The wind can be a factor here. The 14th (par 4) is the toughest hole with the reachable par 5 16th a key hole.

2000 ODDS

fav	7/1	Lee Westwood	50/1	Gary Orr
	10/1	Colin Montgomerie	66/1*	Nick Faldo
	12/1	Darren Clarke	66/1	Paul Lawrie
	16/1	Padraig Harrington	66/1*	Phillip Price
	18/1	Sergio Garcia	66/1*	Jose Coceres
	20/1*	Michael Campbell	66/1	Paul McGinley
	20/1	M A Jimenez	80/1*	Andrew Coltart
	25/1	Thomas Bjorn	80/1	Stephen Leaney
	33/1	J M Olazabal	80/1	M A Martin
	33/1	Bernhard Langer	80/1	Peter O'Malley
	40/1	Eduardo Romero	80/1*	Jean Van de Velde
	40/1*	Retief Goosen	80/1	Ian Woosnam
	50/1	P-U Johansson	80/1	Ian Poulter
	50/1	Angel Cabrera	80/1	Roger Wessels
	50/1	Pierre Fulke		

2000 RESULT

1	50/1	**Pierre Fulke**	**67 68 70 67 272**
2	12/1	**Darren Clarke**	**68 69 68 68 273**
T3	20/1*	**Michael Campbell**	**73 67 72 63 275**
T3	fav 7/1	**Lee Westwood**	**76 69 65 65 275**
T5	33/1	**J M Olazabal**	**67 69 72 68 276**
T5	50/1	**Angel Cabrera**	**69 70 69 68 276**

T7	R Wessels	71 68 72 66 277			D Howell	72 71 68 75 286
	Ricardo Gonzalez	71 68 69 69 277		T38	A Cejka	72 70 74 71 287
9	C Montgomerie	69 69 75 65 278			P Baker	71 72 70 74 287
T10	P Senior	71 71 69 68 279		T40	Anders Hansen	76 69 72 71 288
	A Coltart	73 69 68 69 279			R Green	74 69 71 74 288
	F Jacobson	72 65 71 71 279		42	M A Jimenez	73 71 73 72 289
13	S Garcia	73 71 70 66 280		43	I Garbutt	74 74 70 72 290
T14	G Brand Jr	69 70 73 69 281		T44	L-W Zhang	73 75 76 67 291
	P Harrington	72 69 69 71 281			J Sandelin	74 72 76 69 291
	B Langer	70 72 68 71 281			C Rocca	73 74 72 72 291
T17	R Chapman	71 72 69 70 282			N O'Hern	71 72 75 73 291
	P Sjoland	71 72 69 70 282			S Tinning	73 76 69 73 291
	G Owen	68 71 72 71 282			P-U Johansson	76 70 71 74 291
	J Van de Velde	74 68 68 72 282		T50	L Parsons	75 71 72 74 292
	P Lawrie	72 70 68 72 282			G Ogilvy	80 67 70 75 292
22	R Goosen	71 72 69 71 283		52	M Gronberg	75 70 74 74 293
T23	T Johnstone	72 72 71 69 284		53	A Forsyth	75 76 72 71 294
	A Wall	75 71 68 70 284		T54	J Coceres	74 73 74 74 295
	I Poulter	74 67 70 73 284			S Gallacher	75 75 72 73 295
	Phillip Price	71 70 69 74 284			N Fasth	73 72 74 76 295
	S Leaney	71 66 69 78 284		T57	I Garrido	78 76 72 70 296
T28	E Romero	70 72 75 68 285			Brian Davis	77 74 72 73 296
	T Bjorn	78 71 68 68 285		T59	G Orr	74 76 73 74 297
	N Faldo	74 68 73 70 285			R Rafferty	73 74 73 77 297
	D Robertson	68 74 73 70 285		T61	S Ballesteros	80 72 74 74 300
	M A Martin	72 70 70 73 285			I Woosnam	75 77 73 75 300
	E Canonica	72 68 70 75 285		63	R Muntz	74 76 75 76 301
T34	P O'Malley	72 73 70 71 286		64	M Harwood	79 73 76 74 302
	P McGinley	73 70 70 73 286		65	J Lomas	77 74 78 79 308
	M McNulty	71 75 67 73 286		66	Jamie Spence	76 76 76 WD

ROUND BY ROUND LEADERBOARD

FIRST ROUND		SECOND ROUND	
P FULKE	5 under	P FULKE	9 under
J M Olazabal	5 under	J M Olazabal	8 under
D Robertson	4 under	F Jacobson	7 under
G Owen	4 under	S Leaney	7 under
D Clarke	4 under	D Clarke	7 under
		C Montgomerie	6 under

THIRD ROUND		FINAL ROUND	
P FULKE	11 under	P FULKE	16 under
D Clarke	11 under	D Clarke	15 under
S Leaney	10 under	M Campbell	13 under
F Jacobson	9 under	L Westwood	13 under
Ricardo Gonzalez	9 under	J M Olazabal	12 under
A Cabrera	9 under	A Cabrera	12 under
J M Olazabal	9 under		

RESULTS IN OTHER MARKETS

Top British & Irish Player
1	11/2	Darren Clarke
2	fav 3/1	Lee Westwood
3	7/2	Colin Montgomerie

Top European Player
1	14/1	Pierre Fulke
2	9/1	J M Olazabal
3	40/1	F Jacobson

Top Rest of The World
1	fav 7/2	Michael Campbell
2	8/1	Angel Cabrera
T3	33/1	Ricardo Gonzalez
T3	20/1	Roger Wessels

PUNTERS' POINTS

● 50/1 Pierre Fulke could be fancied here for five reasons.

> He was the No. 1 putter last week in the Italian Open.

> His recent form was really impressive. Form figs were 12-14-19-7 with a 62 in R4 last Sunday.

> Unlike so many rivals he was not 'rusty'. Indeed having started his season 'late' he was fresh.

> He had a brilliant R1 early tee time.

> Last year when playing with a damaged wrist he still shot 66 in R4.

- Over the final 9 holes he outplayed Darren Clarke who hooked his drive at the 17th after Fulke had eagled the previous hole. The Swede was mighty impressive!

- Compared to last year (when many players had played the Belgacom Open the week before) we had a number of players 'rusty' early on.

- On Thursday the top players all had afternoon tee times for the TV cameras and got very much the worst of the conditions.

- Lee Westwood's final 36 holes were easily (by 6 shots) the best in the tournament.

1999 RESULT			**1998 RESULT**		
1	28/1	M A Jimenez	1	22/1	Darren Clarke
T2	25/1	Padraig Harrington	2	66/1	Andrew Coltart
T2	40/1	Bernhard Langer	3	fav 9/1	Colin Montgomerie
T5	20/1	Darren Clarke	T4	50/1	Peter O'Malley
T5	10/1	Sergio Garcia			

WINNERS IN THE LAST TEN YEAR

1991	Rodger Davis		1996	Mark McNulty
1992	Sandy Lyle		1997	Lee Westwood (3 rounds)
1993	Colin Montgomerie		1998	Darren Clarke
1994	Bernhard Langer		1999	M A Jimenez
1995	Alex Cejka		2000	Pierre Fulke

PUNTERS' GUIDE

- This course with reachable par 5s and forgiving fairways favours longer hitters who are not necessarily always accurate off the tee.

- Over the last four years the following players have posted at least two top 10s

  > Michael Campbell: T7 1999: T3 2000 incl 63

  > Darren Clarke: T15 1997: Won 1998: T5 1999: 2 2000

  > Peter O'Malley: T5 1997: T4 1998: T10 1999

  > Bernhard Langer: T15 1997: 6 1998: T2 1999: T14 2000

  > Colin Montgomerie: 8 1997: 3 1998: T16 1999: 9 2000

  > Lee Westwood: Won 1997: T12 1998: T29 1999: T3 2000

  > J M Olazabal: 3 1997: 7 1998: T5 2000

  > Padraig Harrington: 2 1997: T16 1998: T2 1999: T14 2000

  > Andrew Coltart: 2 1998: T10 2000

  > Ian Woosnam: T9 1997: T10 1999

● The AXA stats showed

Driving Accuracy		Greens in Reg		Putts per GIR	
1	Richard Green (89.3%)	T1	Gordon Brand Jr (81.9%)	1	Lee Westwood
2	Michael Campbell	T1	Jose Coceres (81.9%)	2	Darren Clarke
3	Alistair Forsyth	3	Roger Wessels	3	Dean Robertson
4	Mark McNulty	T4	Roger Chapman	4	Thomas Bjorn
5	Jose Coceres	T4	Angel Cabrera	5	David Howell

N.B. Angel Cabrera at 309.9 yards was (by over 9 yards) the longest driver.

● Players whose profiles refer to this tournament include Lee Westwood, Jose Maria Olazabal, Darren Clarke, Michael Campbell, Andrew Coltart, Gordon Brand Jr and Padraig Harrington.

AMERICAN TOUR FORM 2000 — PART 4

THE AMERICAN MONEY LIST

Date	6th January - 5th November 2000
Courses	Various
Par	70 - 73
Yardage	Various
First Prize	The US Tour's Number 1

2000 ODDS

fav	8/15	Tiger Woods	50/1	Nick Price
	5/1	David Duval	66/1	Chris Perry
	25/1	Davis Love	80/1*	Tom Lehman
	25/1	Vijay Singh	80/1	Carlos Franco
	33/1	Ernie Els	80/1	Jesper Parnevik
	33/1	Phil Mickelson	100/1*	Fred Couples
	33/1	Hal Sutton	100/1**	Steve Elkington
	50/1*	Sergio Garcia	100/1*	Greg Norman
	50/1	Justin Leonard	150/1	BAR
	50/1	Jim Furyk		

1/4 odds 1,2,3,4. Note The Tote sadly went just 1/4 1,2,3.

2000 RESULT

1	fav 8/15	Tiger Woods
2	33/1	Phil Mickelson
3	33/1	Ernie Els
4	33/1	Hal Sutton

PUNTERS' POINTS

● Clearly in future there is going to be little life in this market as Tiger looks an annual 'cert'.

1999 RESULT

1	fav 7/2	Tiger Woods
2	5/1	David Duval
3	20/1	Davis Love
4	14/1	Vijay Singh

1998 RESULT

1	16/1	David Duval
2	40/1	Vijay Singh
3	25/1	Jim Furyk
4	fav 11/4	Tiger Woods

WINNERS OVER THE LAST TEN YEARS

1991	Corey Pavin	1996	Tom Lehman
1992	Fred Couples	1997	Tiger Woods
1993	Nick Price	1998	David Duval
1994	Nick Price	1999	Tiger Woods
1995	Greg Norman	2000	Tiger Woods

THE AMERICAN MONEY LIST (Betting without Tiger Woods and David Duval)

Corals and Sunderlands showed real enterprise by breathing life into the Money list betting by pricing up all the players except the two 'certainties' Tiger Woods and David Duval.

2000 ODDS (w/o Woods and Duval)

fav	9/2	Vijay Singh	33/1	John Huston
	5/1	Davis Love	33/1	Jesper Parnevik
	10/1	Ernie Els	40/1	Fred Couples
	12/1	Phil Mickelson	40/1	Mark O'Meara
	13/1	Jim Furyk	40/1	Fred Funk
	14/1	Hal Sutton	50/1	Steve Pate
	16/1	Tom Lehman	50/1	Jeff Sluman
	16/1	Justin Leonard	50/1	Stuart Appleby
	20/1	Sergio Garcia	50/1	Lee Janzen
	25/1	Chris Perry	50/1	Greg Norman
	28/1	Carlos Franco	50/1	Bob Estes
	33/1	Nick Price	50/1	Steve Stricker
	33/1	Jeff Maggert	50/1	Mike Weir
	33/1	Steve Elkington	66/1	BAR

2000 RESULT

1	12/1	Phil Mickelson
2	10/1	Ernie Els
3	14/1	Hal Sutton
4	fav 9/2	Vijay Singh

PUNTERS' GUIDE

Recent Results (w/o Woods and Duval)

2000 Result	1999 Result	1998 Result	1997 Result
1 P Mickelson	1 D Love	1 V Singh	1 D Love
2 E Els	2 V Singh	2 J Furyk	2 J Furyk
3 H Sutton	3 C Perry	3 H Sutton	3 J Leonard
4 V Singh	4 H Sutton	4 P Mickelson	4 S Hoch

Recent results W/O Woods, including Duval

2000	1999	1998	1997
1 P Mickelson	1 D Duval	1 D Duval	1 D Duval
2 E Els	2 D Love	2 V Singh	2 D Love
3 H Sutton	3 V Singh	3 J Furyk	3 J Furyk
4 V Singh	4 C Perry	4 H Sutton	4 J Leonard

● In 2001 the bookmakers will open up a w/o Woods market and the best recent records are held by

> David Duval   Won 1997, Won 1998, Won 1999
> Vijay Singh   2nd 1998, 3rd 1999 and 4th 2000
> Jim Furyk   3rd 1997, 3rd 1998

● Players whose profiles refer to this betting market include Phil Mickelson, Robert Allenby and David Duval.

TOP 5 FINISHES ON THE USPGA TOUR

1		2		3		4		5	

Mercedes Championship

| 10/3f | T Woods | 14/1 | E Els | 5/1 | D Duval | 50/1 | M Weir | - | |
| | | | | | | 16/1 | J Furyk | | |

Sony Open in Hawaii

| 80/1* | P Azinger | 40/1 | S Appleby | 20/1 | J Huston | - | | 9/1f | E Els |
| | | | | 25/1 | J Parnevik | | | | |

Bob Hope Chrysler Classic

| 25/1 | J Parnevik | 150/1 | R Sabbatini | 125/1 | J L Lewis | - | | 7/1f | D Duval |
| | | | | 66/1* | D Toms | | | 33/1 | H Sutton |

Phoenix Open

28/1	T Lehman	66/1	R Mediate	-		125/1	B Jobe	-	
		100/1	R Allenby			125/1	K Triplett		
						28/1	H Sutton		

AT&T Pebble Beach National Pro-Am

7/2f	T Woods	125/1	M Gogel	-		125/1	J Kelly	-	
		33/1	V Singh			200/1	J Green		
						125/1	N Begay		

Buick Invitational

20/1	P Mickelson	7/4f	T Woods	-		20/1	D Love	80/1*	K Sutherland
		125/1	S Maruyama					100/1	K Triplett
								40/1	F Couples

Nissan Open

100/1*	K Triplett	33/1	J Parnevik	250/1	R Freeman	150/1	R Cochran	100/1*	S Flesch
								66/1	S Cink
								125/1	B Hughes
								25/1	F Couples
								150/1	T Armour

WGC Andersen Consulting World Match Play

| 80/1 | D Clarke | 11/2f | T Woods | 18/1 | D Duval | 20/1 | D Love | - | |

Touchstone Energy Tucson Open

80/1	J Carter	80/1	C DiMarco	-		-		125/1	R Fehr
		100/1	J Van de Velde					66/1*	S Jones
		100/1*	T Scherrer						

Doral Ryder Open

| 33/1 | J Furyk | 150/1 | F Langham | 25/1 | N Price | 8/1f | D Duval | - | |
| | | | | | | 66/1 | S Maruyama | | |

Honda Classic

| 50/1 | D Hart | 150/1 | K Wentworth | - | | 14/1 | J Furyk | - | |
| | | 80/1 | J P Hayes | | | 150/1 | B Gay | | |

Bay Hill Invitational

9/2f T Woods	18/1 D Love	125/1 S Kendall	150/1 N Lancaster	-	
			80/1 L Roberts		

Players Championship

40/1 H Sutton	7/2f T Woods	200/1* R Damron	-	-
		200/1* S Dunlap		
		100/1 J Maggert		
		33/1 C Montgomerie		
		33/1 N Price		

Bell South Classic (54 holes)

22/1 P Mickelson	150/1 G Nicklaus	80/1* K Perry	-	100/1* J D Blake	
		125/1 H Frazar		150/1 T Pernice Jr	
				80/1 S Jones	
				150/1 J Sindelar	
				33/1 J Huston	

US Masters

50/1 V Singh	25/1 E Els	125/1 L Roberts	-	5/2f T Woods
		16/1 D Duval		

MCI Classic

40/1 S Cink	18/1 T Lehman	16/1 V Singh	-	-
		150/1 E Fryatt		
		150/1 D Forsman		
		125/1 L Mize		
		12/1jf D Love		
		12/1jf E Els		

Greater Greensboro Chrysler Classic

16/1 H Sutton	100/1 A Magee	66/1* M Calcavecchia	-	150/1 D Dunakey	
		33/1 D Hart		40/1 C Perry	
				80/1 J Kaye	

Shell Houston Open

100/1* R Allenby	100/1* C Stadler	40/1 L Roberts	-	80/1* M Brooks
		150/1 J Edwards		125/1 B Fabel

Compaq Classic

25/1 C Franco	125/1 B McCallister	80/1* H Frazar	80/1 S Stricker	-
			100/1 S Ames	

GTE Byron Nelson Classic

33/1 J Parnevik	22/1 P Mickelson	-	50/1 J Huston	-
	25/1 D Love		4/1f T Woods	

MasterCard Colonial

14/1 P Mickelson	40/1 S Cink	-	50/1 D Toms	-
	14/1 D Love		100/1 R Mediate	

Memorial Tournament

7/2f	T Woods	20/1 80/1	E Els J Leonard	-	66/1	M Weir	80/1 50/1 125/1	P Azinger S Flesch S Lowery

Kemper Open

125/1	T Scherrer	150/1 20/1 150/1 80/1* 125/1	K Hosokawa J Leonard G Chalmers S Lowery F Langham	-		-		-

Buick Classic

100/1	D Paulson	12/1jf	D Duval	33/1	S Garcia	66/1	G Norman	22/1 125/1 125/1 12/1jf 50/1	J Parnevik J Sindelar J Cook E Els C Perry

100th US Open

3/1f	T Woods	20/1 100/1	E Els M A Jimenez	–	80/1	J Huston	125/1 40/1	P Harrington L Westwood

Fedex St Jude Classic

80/1	N Begay	150/1* 100/1	C DiMarco B May	-	125/1 100/1 150/1	P Jordan R Cochran J Ogilvie	-

Greater Hartford Open

40/1	N Begay	40/1*	M Calcavecchia	50/1	K Triplett	22/1	J Furyk	80/1 33/1 125/1 125/1	C DiMarco S Flesch D Barron E Fryatt

Advil Western Open

100/1	R Allenby	33/1	N Price	125/1 80/1 25/1	G Kraft S Maruyama J Furyk	-	-

Greater Milwaukee Open

16/1	L Roberts	50/1	F Langham	33/1 40/1 150/1 66/1	S Pate K Perry M Goggin J P Hayes	-	-

129th British Open

5/2f	T Woods	100/1 16/1	T Bjorn E Els	–	33/1 150/1	T Lehman D Toms	–

BC Open

25/1*	B Faxon	125/1	E Toledo	16/1f 125/1	B Glasson G Hnatiuk	-	100/1 125/1** 50/1 80/1*	B Quigley R Zokol J Kelly D Stockton Jr

John Deere Classic

200/1*	M Clark	28/1	K Triplett	200/1***	C Howell	150/1**	C Riley
						33/1	S Lowery
						150/1	S Micheel

International

10/1jf	E Els	10/1jf	P Mickelson	50/1	S Appleby	100/1*	G Norman	150/1	C A Spence

Buick Open

100/1	R Mediate	66/1	C Perry	40/1	H Sutton	200/1	W Austin	-
						14/1	P Mickelson

The USPGA

7/4f	T Woods	150/1	B May	125/1	T Bjorn	80/1	S Appleby	-
						100/1	J M Olazabal
						150/1	G Chalmers

World Golf Championships NEC Invitational

11/8f	T Woods	250/1*	P Price	-		40/1	J Furyk	-
		66/1	J Leonard			11/1	P Mickelson
						50/1*	H Sutton

Reno-Tahoe Open

66/1	S Verplank	100/1	J Van de Velde	33/1	B May	125/1	S McCarron	-
						150/1	D Dunakey
						100/1	B Henninger

Air Canada Championship

100/1	R Sabbatini	100/1	G Waite	22/1	M Calcavecchia	125/1	D Barron	-
						50/1	M Clark
						14/1f	S Garcia
						80/1	C Riley

Bell Canadian Open

5/4f	T Woods	100/1	G Waite	20/1	S Garcia	66/1	G Chalmers	-
						150/1	C Perks

SEI Pennsylvania Classic

100/1*	C DiMarco	28/1	M Calcavecchia	-		-		-
		125/1	B Elder				
		40/1	S Hoch				
		125/1*	J Kaye				
		28/1	C Perry				

Westin Texas Open

16/1	J Leonard	150/1	M Wiebe	100/1	B McCallister	-		80/1	F Lickliter
				200/1*	J Gallagher Jr			

Buick Challenge

11/1f	D Duval	50/1	J Maggert	-		125/1	C Paulson	125/1	J Edwards
		33/1	N Price					100/1	B Geiberger
								40/1	S Hoch

Michelob Championship

50/1	D Toms	50/1	M Weir	66/1	F Lickliter	80/1	T Scherrer	80/1	S Ames
								150/1	B Hughes
								150/1	S Murphy
								150/1	M Reid

Invensys Classic in Las Vegas

150/1	B Andrade	10/1f	P Mickelson	33/1	S Cink	-		80/1	J Cook
				80/1*	J Kaye			80/1	C DiMarco
								100/1	S McCarron
								150/1	S Micheel

Tampa Bay Classic

66/1*	J Huston	100/1*	C Paulson	50/1*	F Lickliter	-		80/1*	J Durant
				100/1*	L Mattiace				

NCR Golf Classic at Walt Disney

100/1	D Waldorf	40/1	S Flesch	5/4f	T Woods	100/1	F Funk	-
						50/1	S Verplank	

Southern Farm Bureau Classic

25/1*	S Lowery	40/1	S Kendall	40/1	K Perry	25/1	B Faxon	-
						200/1*	P Jordan	

Tour Championship

14/1	P Mickelson	5/4f	T Woods	16/1	E Els	-	-
				50/1	N Price		
				33/1*	V Singh		

WGC American Express Championship

66/1	M Weir	12/1	L Westwood	28/1	V Singh	-		40/1	P Harrington
				150/1	D Waldorf			33/1	S Garcia
								40/1	N Price
								11/8f	T Woods

THE MERCEDES CHAMPIONSHIP

Date	6th - 9th January
Course	Plantation Course, Kapalua, Maui, Hawaii
Par	73
Yardage	7,263
First Prize	$468,000
Total Purse	$2.9 million

THE TOURNAMENT

This is the traditional season opening tournament that is open to all the winners on the previous year's USPGA tour. J M Olazabal did not play so there was a thirty-man field. There is no halfway cut

THE COURSE

The Plantation Course can be very demanding for three key reasons. Firstly the grain on its Bermuda grass greens makes putting very tricky, secondly the course is long and physically very demanding, and thirdly when the trade winds blow (up to 40-50 mph) conditions become really testing.

2000 ODDS

fav	10/3	Tiger Woods	50/1	Notah Begay
	5/1	David Duval (DC)	50/1	Glen Day
	14/1	Ernie Els	50/1	Loren Roberts
	14/1	Vijay Singh	50/1	Brent Geiberger
	16/1	Jim Furyk	50/1	Ted Tryba
	20/1	Hal Sutton	50/1	Brad Faxon
	33/1	Steve Elkington	66/1*	Paul Lawrie
	33/1*	Jesper Parnevik	66/1	Duffy Waldorf
	33/1	Carlos Franco	66/1	Rocco Mediate
	40/1	Jeff Maggert	80/1*	Olin Browne
	40/1	David Toms	80/1*	Brian Henninger
	40/1	Stuart Appleby	100/1	Gabriel Hjerstedt
	40/1	Jeff Sluman	100/1	J L Lewis
	40/1	Tim Herron	100/1	Tom Pernice Jr
	50/1	Mike Weir	125/1	Rich Beem

ALL QUOTED

2000 RESULT

1	fav 10/3	Tiger Woods	71 66 71 68	276

Woods won at the second play-off hole

2	14/1	Ernie Els	71 70 67 68	276
3	5/1	David Duval	72 73 67 68	280
T4	50/1	Mike Weir	76 73 69 67	285
T4	16/1	Jim Furyk	72 73 71 69	285

T6	C Franco	78 73 70 66 287		T19	D Toms	75 75 74 71 295
	J Parnevik	69 74 73 71 287			D Waldorf	70 76 72 77 295
T8	G Day	74 75 69 71 289		T21	O Browne	77 75 74 70 296
	V Singh	73 77 67 72 289			H Sutton	77 73 74 72 296
	P Lawrie	76 73 68 72 289		T23	T Tryba	80 70 73 74 297
	T Pernice Jr	75 76 65 73 289			T Herron	74 71 75 77 297
	B Faxon	72 76 68 73 289		25	N Begay	73 79 73 73 298
	B Geiberger	73 73 67 76 289		26	G Hjertstedt	78 74 73 76 301
14	J Sluman	72 72 74 72 290		T27	B Henninger	77 78 75 73 303
15	S Appleby	73 76 70 72 291			J L Lewis	78 81 70 74 303
T16	R Mediate	79 73 73 68 293		29	L Roberts	76 80 73 75 304
	J Maggert	80 72 69 72 293		30	R Beem	84 77 76 70 307
18	S Elkington	76 74 71 73 294				

ROUND BY ROUND LEADERBOARD

FIRST ROUND

J Parnevik	4 under
D Waldorf	3 under
E Els	2 under
T WOODS	2 under
T Herron	1 under
D Duval	1 under
J Furyk	1 under

SECOND ROUND

T WOODS	9 under
E Els	5 under
J Parnevik	3 under
J Sluman	2 under

THIRD ROUND

T WOODS	11 under
E Els	11 under
D Duval	7 under
B Geiberger	6 under
T Pernice Jr	3 under
B Faxon	3 under
J Furyk	3 under
J Parnevik	3 under

FINAL ROUND

T WOODS	16 under
E Els	16 under
D Duval	12 under
M Weir	7 under
J Furyk	7 under

PUNTERS' POINTS

● Tiger Woods' domination of World golf continued as he secured his fifth consecutive PGA tour victory, the best since Ben Hogan won five in a row in 1948.

● It was a brilliant finish as Woods and Els exchanged eagles on the final hole to force a play-off. The Tiger was to win with a 40-foot (!) putt on the second extra hole.

- Ernie Els, fresh from his first-ever victory in the Sun City Challenge, pushed Tiger all the way with a brilliant display. Clearly back to his best, 'The Big Easy' is set for a very big year!

- Three other players put up noteworthy performances:-

  > Carlos Franco   T4th over the final 54 holes.

  > Mike Weir   A superb T4th finish.

  > Tom Pernice Jr   A tournament best round of 65 (R3).

- When analysing this tournament do remember that the NE trade winds created havoc in R1 and (to a lesser extent) in R2 as shown by the following:-

	R1	R2	R3	R4
Players to beat or equal par	11	14	23	23

- Guess which player drove the 11th green (373 yards) as Jim Furyk lined up a putt?

1999 RESULT

(at Kapalua)

1	9/1	David Duval
2	18/1	Mark O'Meara
T2	40/1	Billy Mayfair
4	16/1	Vijay Singh
T5	22/1	Justin Leonard
T5	fav 6/1	Tiger Woods
T5	40/1	Fred Funk

1998 RESULT

(at Carlsbad, California)

1	14/1	Phil Mickelson
T2	fav 11/2	Tiger Woods
T2	25/1	Mark O'Meara
T4	33/1	John Cook
T4	16/1	Nick Price

WINNERS IN THE LAST TEN YEARS

1991	Tom Kite	1996	Mark O'Meara
1992	Steve Elkington	1997	Tiger Woods
1993	Davis Love	1998	Phil Mickelson
1994	Phil Mickelson	1999	David Duval
1995	Steve Elkington	2000	Tiger Woods

PUNTERS' GUIDE

- At his best when fresh, Tiger Woods has a superb record in this event (Won 10/3 2000: T5th 6/1 1999: T2nd 11/2 1998: Won 12/1 1997) in his five starts. He'll be a clear favourite in 2001 to win it again.

- However let's remember that David Duval shot seven of his eight rounds here in the last two years under par, won last year by 9 shots and was joint best (11 under) this year over the last 36 holes when the conditions were calm.

- The weather will once more be crucial, so do check the forecast. It was relatively calm in 1999 whereas in 2000 the NE trade winds were up to 40-50 mph during the first two rounds.

● The following players will be invited to play in 2001.

Robert Allenby	David Duval	Steve Lowery	Hal Sutton
Billy Andrade	Ernie Els	Rocco Mediate	David Toms
Paul Azinger	Brad Faxon	Phil Mickelson	Kirk Triplett
Notah Begay	Carlos Franco	Jesper Parnevik	Scott Verplank
Jim Carter	Jim Furyk	Dennis Paulson	Duffy Waldorf
Stewart Cink	Dudley Hart	Loren Roberts	Mike Weir
Michael Clark	John Huston	Rory Sabbatini	Tiger Woods
Darren Clarke	Tom Lehman	Tom Scherrer	
Chris DiMarco	Justin Leonard	Vijay Singh	

● The players whose profiles point to this tournament include David Duval, Jesper Parnevik, Ernie Els and Tiger Woods.

THE SONY OPEN IN HAWAII

Date	13th - 16th January
Course	Waialae C.C., Honolulu, Hawaii
Par	70
Yardage	7,060
First Prize	$522,000
Total Purse	$2.9 million

THE TOURNAMENT

This is a very well-established tournament that is always held at the Waialae country club. Previously known as the Hawaiian Open, with new sponsors it became the Sony Open in Hawaii for the first time in 1999.

THE COURSE

This oceanside course was toughened up last year in reaction to John Huston's runaway (28 under par) success in 1998. With narrower fairways and a reduced par of 70 it now suits the players noted for their accuracy rather than their length who can keep the ball low. The greens are Bermuda.

2000 ODDS

fav	9/1	Ernie Els	66/1*	Brad Faxon
	12/1	Jim Furyk	66/1*	Loren Roberts
	16/1	Vijay Singh	66/1*	Tim Herron
	16/1	Tom Lehman	66/1	Notah Begay
	20/1	John Huston	66/1	Paul Lawrie
	25/1	Jesper Parnevik	66/1	Duffy Waldorf
	33/1	Carlos Franco	66/1	Ted Tryba
	33/1	Jeff Sluman (DC)	80/1*	Paul Azinger
	40/1	Jeff Maggert	80/1*	Steve Jones
	40/1	Stuart Appleby	80/1	Skip Kendall
	40/1	Fred Funk	80/1*	John Cook
	40/1	Steve Stricker	80/1	Paul Goydos
	40/1	Lee Janzen	80/1*	Corey Pavin
	50/1	Glen Day	80/1	Olin Browne

2000 RESULT

1	80/1*	Paul Azinger	63 65 68 65 261
2	40/1	Stuart Appleby	66 67 68 67 268
T3	20/1	John Huston	66 67 70 67 270
T3	25/1	Jesper Parnevik	70 65 66 69 270
5	fav 9/1	Ernie Els	67 68 69 67 271

T6	S Murphy	68 67 70 67 272		R Fehr	70 70 71 70 281
	S Dunlap	68 67 67 70 272		T Herron	69 71 71 70 281
	T Lehman	68 69 65 70 272		T Tryba	71 65 74 71 281
T9	C Franco	68 68 72 67 275		B Henninger	71 67 72 71 281
	S Maruyama	67 69 70 69 275		M Sposa	71 69 70 71 281
	B Burns	70 69 67 69 275		Bart Bryant	72 67 71 71 281
	J Maggert	69 67 68 71 275		J Furyk	66 67 73 75 281
	J Kelly	67 67 69 72 275	T48	C Barlow	71 68 74 69 282
T14	J Sluman	67 67 73 69 276		B May	68 71 73 70 282
	L Mize	72 63 72 69 276		G Hnatiuk	67 70 73 72 282
	S Stricker	70 68 69 69 276		F Allem	70 69 71 72 282
	E Toledo	67 69 70 70 276		O Uresti	69 70 70 73 282
	Jerry Smith	68 68 70 70 276	T53	J Buha	69 70 74 70 283
T19	V Singh	66 68 75 68 277		P Jacobsen	68 71 72 72 283
	C Pavin	70 70 68 69 277		P Jordan	71 68 71 73 283
	Joel Edwards	67 71 69 70 277		C Raulerson	71 68 71 73 283
T22	B Cheesman	70 70 72 66 278		Tom Byrum	71 69 70 73 283
	C DiMarco	68 66 75 69 278	T58	J L Lewis	69 71 76 68 284
	J Cook	66 70 71 71 278		F Funk	66 71 76 71 284
	S Jones	68 69 69 72 278		D Peoples	70 69 74 71 284
T26	B Friend	70 68 74 67 279		S Lowery	69 71 72 72 284
	J Carter	68 70 74 67 279		C Stadler	70 68 72 74 284
	P Goydos	72 67 71 69 279		J D Blake	72 68 70 74 284
	N Begay	70 70 69 70 279	T64	A Bengoechea	70 70 74 71 285
	N Lancaster	68 67 72 72 279		D Barron	72 68 74 71 285
	C Riley	67 68 72 72 279		S Ames	69 71 73 72 285
	J Williamson	69 70 68 72 279	T67	Jeff Gallagher	68 72 75 71 286
	K Yokoo	69 69 68 73 279		F Lickliter	69 71 73 73 286
T34	D Waldorf	68 69 74 69 280	69	M Springer	70 67 76 74 287
	J Green	69 70 72 69 280	T70	C A Spence	71 68 76 73 288
	G Kraft	69 70 72 69 280		B Bates	66 71 73 78 288
	O Browne	72 66 71 71 280	T72	D Mast	70 70 78 72 290
	M Reid	71 68 70 71 280		G Nicklaus	69 70 72 79 290
T39	R Allenby	70 68 75 68 281	74	D Ishii	68 72 71 81 292
	B Quigley	68 68 76 69 281			

The main players to miss the cut (made at level par) were:–

J Durant (+1)	S Gump (+1)	L Janzen (+1)	E Fryatt (+1)
B Faxon (+1)	R Sabbatini (+1)	B Andrade (+2)	J Maginnes (+2)
D Ogrin (+3)	S Kendall (+3)	M Gogel (+3)	J Kaye (+3)
C Paulson (+4)	S Micheel (+4)	S Lyle (+4)	Larry Rinker (+5)
L Roberts (+6)	G Waite (+7)	L Mattiace (+8)	G Chalmers (+8)
D Pride (+8)	W Austin (+9)	M Hulbert (+10)	P Lawrie (+10)
D Dunakey (+11)			

Mathew Goggin (70) withdrew.

ROUND BY ROUND LEADERBOARD

FIRST ROUND		SECOND ROUND	
P AZINGER	7 under	P AZINGER	12 under
J Furyk	4 under	J Huston	7 under
J Cook	4 under	J Furyk	7 under
S Appleby	4 under	S Appleby	7 under
B Bates	4 under	J Kelly	6 under
F Funk	4 under	V Singh	6 under
V Singh	4 under	C DiMarco	6 under
J Huston	4 under	J Sluman	6 under

THIRD ROUND		FINAL ROUND	
P AZINGER	14 under	P AZINGER	19 under
S Appleby	9 under	S Appleby	12 under
J Parnevik	9 under	J Huston	10 under
S Dunlap	8 under	J Parnevik	10 under
T Lehman	8 under	E Els	9 under
J Huston	7 under		
J Kelly	7 under		

PUNTERS' POINTS

● Paul Azinger here landed his first victory for seven years in a tournament he loves as his low ball flight is so well suited to the winds on this course. Never headed, he was a comfortable 80/1 DYM success.

● Déjà vu rules OK! In 1998 John Huston had an early tee time, shot 63 in R1, and was never headed as he went on to a runaway 7-shot victory. This year the 'Zinger followed the exact same pattern — early tee time, 63 in R1, and a 7-shot win. The point emphasised so heavily in Part 1 last year re tee times really has applied here.

● Last year of the front six players only one, Len Mattiace, had solid course form. However this year the course specialists really thrived. Indeed the first three home were all well written up for this tournament in last year's book on the basis of their course form.

● Make a note of Scott Dunlap. Fresh from winning the Argentinean Open and a proven early-season player, he was my 100/1 outsider and played really well on a course suited to his game. Sadly, like all good each-way bets he was T6th! Keep him in mind here in 2001.

● Stuart Appleby having shed 'the rust' last week, had an early tee time in R1, shot 66, and went on to finish 2nd, in the top 20 for the third successive year. He's a superb wind player.

● Do remember Larry Mize especially in 3 balls (63 in R1 this year) and match bets. He loves this track which suits his accurate game. He's never missed the cut in thirteen starts, has a long-term stroke average of under 70, and has had three successive top 15 finishes.

1999 RESULT

1	50/1	Jeff Sluman
T2	80/1	Chris Perry
T2	125/1	Len Mattiace
T2	50/1	Jeff Maggert
T2	125/1	Tommy Tolles
T2	jt fav 12/1	Davis Love

1998 RESULT

1	50/1	John Huston
2	22/1	Tom Watson
3	125/1	Trevor Dodds
T4	150/1	Mike Reid
T4	200/1	Brett Quigley
T4	150/1	Greg Kraft

WINNERS IN THE LAST TEN YEARS

1991	Lanny Wadkins	1996	Jim Furyk
1992	John Cook	1997	Paul Stankowski
1993	Howard Twitty	1998	John Huston
1994	Brett Ogle	1999	Jeff Sluman
1995	John Morse	2000	Paul Azinger

PUNTERS' GUIDE

● Go for a player with three key characteristics

> An early R1 tee time

> A proven ability in the wind

> A straight hitter off the tee — particularly important since the course redesign after Huston's 1998 victory.

● Players who clearly enjoy this course include

> Paul Azinger   This year's winner now has four top 4s here!

> Tom Lehman   T6th 2000: 6th 1997: T4th 1996: T2nd 1995

> Jeff Sluman   Loves Hawaii. Winner in 1999: T14th 2000. Course changes ideal for him

> Jeff Maggert   T9th and T2nd last two years

● Players whose profiles point to this tournament include Scott Dunlap, Jeff Sluman, Jeff Maggert, Stuart Appleby, Tom Lehman, Paul Azinger, Jim Furyk, Steve Stricker, Chris Riley, John Huston, Bob Burns, Shigeki Maruyama, Chris DiMarco and Esteban Toledo.

THE BOB HOPE CHRYSLER CLASSIC

Date	19th - 23rd January			
Course	Bermuda Dunes	Indian Wells	La Quinta	PGA West
Par	71	72	72	72
Yardage	6829	6478	7060	6950
First Prize	$540,000			
Total Purse	$3 million			

THE TOURNAMENT

This is a five-round event with the first four rounds played as a pro-am format on the four courses in rotation before the cut is made after R4. The final round this year was at Bermuda Dunes.

THE COURSES

The courses all have wide fairways to suit the amateurs and in calm weather scores are always low. The greens are bentgrass. The easiest and shortest course is Indian Wells. Bermuda Dunes, inaccurately given a par 72 in the Press, had a par of 71.

2000 ODDS

fav	7/1	David Duval (DC)	66/1*	David Toms
	16/1	Davis Love	66/1*	Steve Jones
	25/1	Phil Mickelson	66/1	Bob Tway
	25/1	Jesper Parnevik	66/1*	Mark Calcavecchia
	25/1	Justin Leonard	66/1	Glen Day
	28/1*	John Huston	66/1*	Bob Estes
	33/1*	Fred Couples	80/1	Bill Glasson
	33/1	Chris Perry	80/1	Skip Kendall
	33/1	Hal Sutton	80/1*	Brent Geiberger
	40/1	Steve Stricker	80/1	Paul Goydos
	40/1*	Fred Funk	80/1	Ted Tryba
	50/1	Scott Hoch	80/1	Scott Verplank
	50/1	Steve Pate	80/1*	Andrew Magee
	50/1*	Jeff Sluman	80/1	Corey Pavin
	50/1	Mike Weir	80/1	Kenny Perry
	50/1*	Stewart Cink	80/1	Kirk Triplett
	66/1**	John Cook		

2000 RESULT

1	25/1	Jesper Parnevik	69 67 66 64 65 331
2	150/1	Rory Sabbatini	67 67 66 64 68 332
T3	125/1	J L Lewis	65 66 70 66 66 333
T3	66/1*	David Toms	63 68 66 70 66 333
T5	fav 7/1	David Duval	68 67 63 68 69 335
T5	33/1	Hal Sutton	68 66 66 69 66 335

T7	F Funk	68 68 74 63 63 336		Chris Perry	69 67 69 65 72 342
	J Huston	69 65 68 67 67 336		J Leonard	68 70 68 68 68 342
	M Gogel	66 67 64 68 71 336		B Glasson	66 69 69 70 68 342
T10	K Triplett	69 64 69 65 70 337		E Fryatt	67 69 70 69 67 342
	A Magee	66 65 69 68 69 337		Dennis Paulson	68 68 72 67 67 342
T12	R Allenby	68 70 66 68 66 338		P Stankowski	70 66 69 70 67 342
	B Hughes	66 74 65 66 67 338		B Elder	70 70 64 71 67 342
	B Geiberger	70 61 71 67 69 338	T46	J P Hayes	68 69 70 65 71 343
	R Beem	67 63 65 71 72 338		M Goggin	67 68 67 71 70 343
T16	G Day	65 68 69 69 68 339		J Kelly	66 68 71 68 70 343
	P Mickelson	67 72 64 68 68 339		D Peoples	67 70 69 68 69 343
	O Browne	65 67 69 69 69 339		F Couples	68 68 67 73 67 343
	R Mediate	66 68 67 69 69 339	T51	E Toledo	65 71 66 71 71 344
	J Maginnes	67 67 68 67 70 339		B Lietzke	70 65 69 69 71 344
	P Jacobsen	69 64 66 70 70 339		S McCarron	67 67 71 68 71 344
	R Gamez	70 64 67 68 70 339		J Kaye	70 66 67 68 73 344
T23	S Stricker	70 66 68 69 67 340		Jerry Smith	68 69 67 70 70 344
	Kevin Sutherland	71 64 68 68 69 340		S Gump	68 70 69 67 70 344
	J Sluman	67 70 64 67 72 340		S Kendall	71 67 67 70 69 344
	N Lancaster	64 68 71 65 72 340		R Freeman	67 69 71 68 69 344
	B Cheesman	69 62 72 65 72 340	T59	M Calcavecchia	67 69 66 70 73 345
T28	G Kraft	65 65 69 73 69 341		J D Blake	70 67 70 69 69 345
	S Flesch	68 70 69 65 69 341	T61	B Tway	64 67 72 72 71 346
	G Chalmers	69 70 65 69 68 341		C Strange	69 69 67 71 70 346
	D Love	66 70 67 70 68 341		Jeff Freeman	72 67 68 69 70 346
	R Damron	64 70 68 67 72 341		T Kite	73 68 67 68 70 346
	T Pernice Jr	67 67 72 68 67 341	65	Kenny Perry	71 66 69 70 71 347
	F Lickliter	69 69 67 62 74 341	T66	B Chamblee	69 68 69 68 74 348
	G Hnatiuk	68 70 71 67 65 341		N Henke	71 66 68 71 72 348
T36	B Heintz	67 68 71 67 69 342	T68	P Goydos	64 69 69 72 75 349
	C Barlow	70 64 64 73 71 342		T Armour III	71 70 66 69 73 349
	M Brooks	68 67 72 64 71 342			

The main players to miss the cut (made at 11 under) were:−

S Pate (-10)	B Jobe (-10)	B Estes (-10)	C A Spence (-10)
T Tryba (-9)	S Cink (-9)	C Pavin (-9)	B Andrade (-9)
S Verplank (-9)	J Durant (-8)	H Frazar (-7)	S Micheel (-7)
C Stadler (-7)	F Langham (-6)	S Hoch (-6)	C DiMarco (-6)
J Cook (-5)	J Haas (-5)	B Mayfair (-4)	T Tolles (-2)
J Daly (-2)	F Nobilo (-1)	L Mattiace (+3)	S Jones (+7)

Sandy Lyle was disqualified after R4.
Stephen Ames, T3rd after R4, withdrew with a shoulder-muscle injury.

ROUND BY ROUND LEADERBOARD

FIRST ROUND		SECOND ROUND	
D Toms	9 under	G Kraft	14 under
R Damron	8 under	R Beem	13 under
B Tway	8 under	A Magee	13 under
P Goydos	8 under	B Geiberger	13 under
N Lancaster	7 under	D Toms	12 under
J PARNEVIK	3 under	B Tway	12 under
		J L Lewis	12 under
		B Cheesman	12 under
		J PARNEVIK	8 under

THIRD ROUND		FOURTH ROUND	
R Beem	20 under	R Sabbatini	23 under
M Gogel	19 under	M Gogel	22 under
D Duval	18 under	S Ames	21 under
D Toms	18 under	R Beem	21 under
C Barlow	17 under	J PARNEVIK	21 under
P Jacobsen	17 under	D Duval	21 under
G Kraft	16 under		
J PARNEVIK	14 under		

FINAL ROUND	
J PARNEVIK	27 under
R Sabbatini	26 under
J L Lewis	25 under
D Toms	25 under
H Sutton	23 under
D Duval	23 under

PUNTERS' POINTS

● In-form Jesper Parnevik, son of a comedian, won the comedians' tournament in an event in which the 'giggle golf' razzmatazz of the first four days suits him so well. "When I have fun on the golf course, that's when I play my best golf."

● R4 leader Rory Sabbatini made final-round, back-to-back bogeys after an argument with a marshall at the 10th. He could only par the last when needing a birdie 4 for a play-off.

● The lowest scores on the various courses will help with 3-ball betting in 2001. They were :-

Bermuda Dunes	Indian Wells	La Quinta	PGA West
63 F Funk	61 B Geiberger	64 P Jacobsen	64 R Damron
64 N Lancaster	62 F Lickliter	64 P Mickelson	64 C Barlow
64 S Ames	63 S Ames	65 R Beem	65 C Perry
64&65 J Parnevik	63 D Duval	65 G Kraft	65 S Flesch
64 C Barlow	63 D Toms	65 J P Hayes	
	63 F Funk		

Please note: Indian Wells is far and away the shortest and easiest course on which seventeen players shot a round of 7 under or better this year.

● Stephen Ames, T3rd after R4, had to withdraw with a shoulder injury. He was 9th in 1999 in the other 90-hole tournament, the Las Vegas International, so he clearly enjoys the desert and pro-ams. Remember him in 2001.

1999 RESULT			1998 RESULT		
1	fav 6/1	David Duval	1	22/1	Fred Couples
2	100/1	Steve Pate	*won at the first play-off hole*		
3	22/1	John Huston	2	200/1	Bruce Lietzke
T4	66/1	Bob Estes	3	50/1	Andrew Magee
T4	40/1	Fred Funk	T4	14/1	David Duval
			T4	28/1	Steve Jones

WINNERS IN THE LAST TEN YEARS

1991	Corey Pavin	1996	Mark Brooks
1992	John Cook	1997	John Cook
1993	Tom Kite	1998	Fred Couples
1994	Scott Hoch	1999	David Duval
1995	Kenny Perry	2000	Jesper Parnevik

PUNTERS' GUIDE

● Only two players have posted three successive top 10s

> David Duval   T5th 2000: Won 1999: T4th 1998

> John Huston   T7th 2000: 3rd 1999: T10th 1998

One player has posted three successive top 20s

> Kirk Triplett   T10th 2000: T18th 1999: T10th 1998

Three others have posted two consecutive top 20s

> Fred Funk   T7th 2000: T4th 1999

> John Maginnes   T16th 2000: T13th 1999

> Robert Allenby   T12th 2000: T11th 1999

● The usual identikit picture of the 'Hope' winner is clear, and worked again this year.

> A proven winner

> A player in his thirties or very early forties. (Ten of the last eleven fit this age group)

> A pro-am track record where slow play, giggling and patience are all needed. The other 90-hole tournament is the Las Vegas International.

● Players whose profiles refer to this tournament include David Duval, John Huston, Peter Jacobsen, Fred Funk, Andrew Magee, Mark O'Meara, Rory Sabbatini, Russ Cochran, Stephen Ames, Steve Jones, Tom Pernice Jr and Kirk Triplett.

THE PHOENIX OPEN

Date	27th - 30th January
Course	TPC at Scottsdale, Arizona
Par	71
Yardage	7,059
First Prize	$576,000
Total Purse	$3.2 million

THE TOURNAMENT

'The Phoenix' has been held on this TPC (Tournament Players' Course) since 1987. The crowd, pushing half a million, creates a raucous atmosphere and this can get to one or two non-local players, as David Duval found out this year.

THE COURSE

The fairways, narrowed for last year's tournament, are a fair width, although the rough can be severe. The final 3 holes are a tough and very nasty par 3, a reachable off the tee par 4, and a 438-yard par 4 at the last that demands real accuracy. The pin positions on the fast greens made scoring much more difficult over the final two rounds.

2000 ODDS

fav	7/1	David Duval	66/1*	Steve Stricker
	16/1	Jesper Parnevik (PWW)	66/1	Mark Calcavecchia
	20/1	Davis Love	66/1	Stewart Cink
	20/1	Phil Mickelson	66/1	Brent Geiberger
	20/1	Sergio Garcia	66/1*	Dudley Hart
	25/1	Vijay Singh	66/1	Rocco Mediate (DC)
	25/1	Justin Leonard	66/1	Bill Glasson
	28/1	Tom Lehman	66/1	Steve Pate
	28/1	Hal Sutton	80/1*	Steve Jones
	33/1	Jim Furyk	80/1	Mike Weir
	33/1	John Huston	80/1	Andrew Magee
	40/1	David Toms	80/1	Tim Herron
	50/1	Chris Perry	80/1	Scott Hoch
	50/1	Lee Janzen	80/1	Olin Browne
	50/1	Paul Azinger	80/1	Duffy Waldorf
	50/1	Fred Funk	80/1	Notah Begay
	66/1*	Jeff Maggert		

2000 RESULT

1	28/1	Tom Lehman	63 67 73 67 270
T2	66/1	Rocco Mediate	67 70 67 67 271
T2	100/1	Robert Allenby	67 67 68 69 271
T4	125/1	Brandt Jobe	67 68 72 65 272
T4	125/1	Kirk Triplett	70 69 66 67 272
T4	28/1	Hal Sutton	67 67 69 69 272

T7	E Fryatt	73 67 68 65 273	
	M Calcavecchia	71 68 66 68 273	
	S Flesch	70 65 68 70 273	
T10	D Waldorf	71 68 69 66 274	
	S Cink	67 68 72 67 274	
	Kevin Sutherland	67 69 70 68 274	
	M Weir	71 66 68 69 274	
	B Mayfair	67 71 67 69 274	
	P Stankowski	67 69 67 71 274	
	F Lickliter	67 64 69 74 274	
	P Mickelson	63 73 65 73 274	
T18	L Janzen	69 67 72 68 276	
	D Love	68 73 65 70 276	
	G Hjertstedt	69 70 67 70 276	
	B Chamblee	67 70 69 70 276	
	D Toms	69 69 66 72 276	
T23	Chris Perry	70 72 67 68 277	
	J Maggert	72 69 69 67 277	
	J Leonard	69 70 68 70 277	
	T Pernice Jr	68 68 70 71 277	
	Kenny Perry	67 69 70 71 277	
T28	Dennis Paulson	66 72 70 70 278	
	Tom Byrum	67 72 66 73 278	
T30	A Magee	67 75 67 70 279	
	D Peoples	68 71 71 69 279	
	D Duval	66 71 73 69 279	
	B Cheesman	72 69 70 68 279	
	Joel Edwards	69 69 69 72 279	
	P Goydos	71 66 70 72 279	
	B Hughes	68 66 71 74 279	
T37	J Furyk	71 71 67 71 280	
	M Brisky	71 67 70 72 280	
	J Parnevik	68 70 72 70 280	
	J Huston	71 69 68 72 280	
T41	N Lancaster	72 70 67 72 281	
	B Geiberger	70 70 69 72 281	
	Dudley Hart	67 73 70 71 281	

	T Tryba	69 69 70 73 281	
	T Herron	71 71 68 71 281	
	D Forsman	69 70 72 70 281	
	R Gamez	69 70 67 75 281	
	V Singh	69 69 67 76 281	
	S Gump	69 68 67 77 281	
T50	B McCallister	72 69 69 72 282	
	J Delsing	71 71 69 71 282	
	B Andrade	69 73 75 65 282	
T53	C Beck	71 71 67 74 283	
	C Raulerson	66 74 69 74 283	
	M Brooks	68 73 70 72 283	
	F Nobilo	70 71 70 72 283	
	E Fiori	72 69 70 72 283	
T58	M Dawson	72 67 70 75 284	
	R Sabbatini	68 73 68 75 284	
	E Booker	71 71 73 69 284	
T61	S Maruyama	70 71 70 74 285	
	S Jones	69 70 74 72 285	
	C DiMarco	71 71 72 71 285	
	B Tway	72 70 73 70 285	
T65	M Wiebe	67 74 70 75 286	
	T Armour III	69 73 69 75 286	
	F Funk	74 68 71 73 286	
	L Mattiace	69 72 73 72 286	
T69	C Martin	68 73 71 75 287	
	Jerry Smith	70 72 72 73 287	
	David Sutherland	69 73 73 72 287	
T72	J Carter	74 68 70 76 288	
	J Daly	70 67 76 75 288	
	J D Blake	69 73 74 72 288	
T75	G Hnatiuk	72 69 73 75 289	
	S Verplank	74 68 73 74 289	
77	S Hoch	70 72 70 79 291	
78	E Toledo	66 75 77 74 292	
79	J Williamson	68 74 75 78 295	

The main players to miss the cut (made at level) were:–

J Kaye (+1)	J P Hayes (+1)	G Chalmers (+1)	S McCarron (+1)
S Ames (+1)	N Begay (+1)	S Pate (+1)	O Browne (+1)
J Van de Velde (+1)	M Gogel (+1)	F Langham (+2)	S Stricker (+2)
M Goggin (+2)	C Paulson (+3)	S Dunlap (+3)	H Frazar (+3)
R Beem (+4)	S Lowery (+4)	C Barlow (+4)	P Azinger (+4)
S Garcia (+4)	R Damron (+5)	J L Lewis (+6)	J Durant (+6)
S Kendall (+6)	G Kraft (+6)	K Wentworth (+8)	J Maginnes (+8)

Omar Uresti (72) withdrew.

ROUND BY ROUND LEADERBOARD

FIRST ROUND
T LEHMAN	8 under
P Mickelson	8 under
D Duval	5 under
C Raulerson	5 under
D Paulson	5 under
E Toledo	5 under

SECOND ROUND
T LEHMAN	12 under
F Lickliter	11 under
H Sutton	8 under
R Allenby	8 under
B Hughes	8 under
S Flesch	7 under
S Cink	7 under
B Jobe	7 under

THIRD ROUND
F Lickliter	13 under
P Mickelson	12 under
R Allenby	11 under
H Sutton	10 under
P Stankowski	10 under
S Flesch	10 under
T LEHMAN	10 under

FINAL ROUND
T LEHMAN	14 under
R Mediate	13 under
R Allenby	13 under
B Jobe	12 under
K Triplett	12 under
H Sutton	12 under

On Friday frost delayed the start for 30 minutes and darkness prevented twenty-one golfers from completing R2.

PUNTERS' POINTS

● A tremendous televised finish to a superbly exciting tournament, as players at the top of the leaderboard slipped backwards.

> Phil Mickelson dropped 4 shots over the last 8 holes.

> Hal Sutton dropped 3 shots (including a double bogey at the par 3 16th) over the last 3 holes.

> David Toms, early R4 leader, finished T18th.

> Frank Lickliter, leader entering R4, dropped 4 shots over the first 3 holes!

● However halfway leader and 'home' player Tom Lehman recovered from a poor R3 to putt well in R4 and keep his nerve for a fine victory, finishing with a brilliant par at the last after he'd driven into a dreadful lie in the rough.

● Robert Allenby made par-saving putts on the back nine until he made bogey at the last to miss a play-off. In his previous seventy US starts he'd had just two top 10s.

● Lehman's win was proof positive of two points strongly emphasised in Part 1 of last year's volume.

> 'Home' advantage: Lehman a Scottsdale resident, had also won the unofficial Williams Challenge early in the New Year at the Greyhawk Club, also in Scottsdale.

> The comeback trail (CT): Lehman was of four players highlighted on the CT in 2000.

1999 RESULT				1998 RESULT		
1	100/1	Rocco Mediate		1	33/1	Jesper Parnevik
2	25/1	Justin Leonard		T2	150/1	Tommy Armour III
3	7/1	Tiger Woods		T2	200/1	Steve Pate
4	66/1	Hal Sutton		T2	125/1	Brent Geiberger
5	66/1	Bill Glasson		T2	66/1	Tom Watson

WINNERS IN THE LAST TEN YEARS

1991	Nolan Henke	1996	Phil Mickelson
1992	Mark Calcavecchia	1997	Steve Jones
1993	Lee Janzen	1998	Jesper Parnevik
1994	Bill Glasson	1999	Rocco Mediate
1995	Vijay Singh	2000	Tom Lehman

PUNTERS' GUIDE

● It may well be that the tightening of the fairways and toughening of the rough introduced before the 1999 event make the form since then the most significant, and in that time only six players have posted successive top 25s.

> Rocco Mediate   2nd 2000: Won 1999

> Hal Sutton   T4th 2000: 4th 1999

> Stewart Cink   T10th 2000: T10th 1999

> Mike Weir   T10th 2000: T22nd 1999

> Lee Janzen   T18th 2000: T10th 1999

> Justin Leonard   T23rd 2000: 2nd 1999

● Scottsdale Arizona residents who have 'home advantage' here include Tom Lehman, Phil Mickelson, Billy Mayfair and Kirk Triplett.

● The Phoenix now has a unique record because it's been won in both 1999 (100/1) and 2000 (28/1) by a comeback-trail player, i.e. one whose profile included the rare CT symbol. Will 2001 see a hat-trick?

● The players whose profiles point to this tournament include Phil Mickelson, Billy Mayfair, Kirk Triplett, Rocco Mediate, David Duval, Vijay Singh, Mark Calcavecchia, Jeff Maggert, Harrison Frazar, Lee Janzen, Kenny Perry and Stewart Cink.

[handwritten notes] LUE JORZON 2·003
VONDAE YOKOO ʹʹ ʹʹ

AT&T PEBBLE BEACH NATIONAL PRO-AM

Date	3rd - 6th February		
Course	Pebble Beach	Spyglass Hill	Poppy Hills
Par	72	72	72
Yardage	6,816	6,855	6,833
First Prize	$720,000		
Total Purse	$4 million		

THE TOURNAMENT

A unique tournament held annually in California on three courses. There is a pro-am format for all four days. The cut is made after R3. The top 60 (and ties) plus the leading amateurs then play the final round at Pebble Beach. This year, with Pebble Beach the venue for the US Open later in the season, there was the strongest possible field.

THE COURSES

Pebble Beach (played twice) is the host course. It is exposed to the winds, and demands accuracy with the irons to its small greens. The hardest course is Spyglass, while Poppy Hills, with very large greens, is the easiest of the three. They all have bentgrass greens.

2000 ODDS

fav	7/2	Tiger Woods	40/1	David Toms
	12/1	David Duval	50/1	Stewart Cink
	20/1	Tom Lehman (PWW)	66/1	Frank Lickliter
	25/1	Davis Love	66/1	Chris Perry
	25/1	Phil Mickelson	66/1	Lee Janzen
	33/1	Hal Sutton	66/1*	Jeff Maggert
	33/1	Jim Furyk	66/1	Jeff Sluman
	33/1	Vijay Singh	66/1	Mike Weir
	33/1	Sergio Garcia	80/1	Mark Calcavecchia
	40/1	Justin Leonard	80/1	Tim Herron
	40/1	Fred Couples	80/1	Steve Flesch
	40/1	Steve Elkington	80/1	Dudley Hart
	40/1	Mark O'Meara	80/1	Andrew Magee
	40/1	Paul Azinger	80/1	Brad Faxon

2000 RESULT

1	fav 7/2	**Tiger Woods**	**68 73 68 64 273**
T2	125/1	**Matt Gogel**	**69 68 67 71 275**
T2	33/1	**Vijay Singh**	**66 67 72 70 275**
T4	125/1	**Jerry Kelly**	**71 70 68 67 276**
T4	200/1	**Jimmy Green**	**72 68 68 68 276**
T4	125/1	**Notah Begay**	**66 68 72 70 276**

T7	M Brooks	71 67 66 74 278		C A Spence	72 74 70 69 285
	T Lehman	69 70 72 67 278	T35	Bobby Cochran	73 71 69 73 286
	A Magee	69 75 67 67 278		S Flesch	72 68 72 74 286
	M Weir	72 71 69 66 278		P Stankowski	71 73 70 72 286
T11	J D Blake	72 70 67 70 279		David Edwards	75 71 70 70 286
	R Sabbatini	72 69 68 70 279		S Garcia	71 75 70 70 286
	J Williamson	69 70 69 71 279		L Janzen	68 74 71 73 286
14	G Waite	68 71 71 70 280		J Kaye	76 67 69 74 286
T15	N Lancaster	74 71 68 68 281	T42	J Carter	69 74 73 71 287
	J Leonard	73 70 68 70 281		G Hjertstedt	76 72 67 72 287
	C Stadler	70 73 71 67 281		J Sluman	70 73 71 73 287
T18	C DiMarco	69 70 69 74 282		Jerry Smith	75 69 71 72 287
	J Furyk	76 69 64 73 282	T46	S Elkington	77 69 69 73 288
T20	M Calcavecchia	70 73 69 71 283		S Gotsche	72 72 72 72 288
	G Day	72 69 69 73 283		G Nicklaus	72 73 71 72 288
	B Elder	74 70 67 72 283	T49	B Gilder	72 72 70 75 289
	B Faxon	73 70 68 72 283		B May	70 73 72 74 289
	Dudley Hart	69 72 73 69 283	T51	S Dunlap	74 70 72 74 290
	D Love	72 72 72 67 283		Joel Edwards	72 73 71 74 290
	J Ogilvie	77 68 69 69 283		B Jobe	73 73 68 76 290
	Kenny Perry	73 70 69 71 283		G Kraft	71 73 71 75 290
T28	F Couples	71 73 68 72 284		D Pride	73 72 69 76 290
	Chris Perry	78 70 68 68 284	T56	D Forsman	77 70 69 75 291
	T Scherrer	70 72 72 70 284		David Sutherland	71 69 73 78 291
T31	S Kendall	72 74 66 73 285		W Wood	73 71 72 75 291
	R Mediate	69 69 72 75 285	59	B Bates	76 72 68 78 294
	M Reid	72 74 69 70 285	60	B Watts	73 75 68 79 295

The main players to miss the cut (made at level) were:–

P Azinger (+1)	J Van de Velde (+1)	S Cink (+1)	D Duval (+1)
T Herron (+1)	P Mickelson (+1)	H Frazar (+1)	S McCarron (+2)
S Micheel (+2)	R Fehr (+2)	M O'Meara (+2)	M Dawson (+2)
D Toms (+2)	J Haas (+2)	P Jacobsen (+2)	B Andrade (+3)
F Lickliter (+3)	K Sutherland (+3)	J Maggert (+4)	C Riley (+4)
C Pavin (+4)	J Cook (+5)	B Hughes (+5)	T Tolles (+5)
D A Weibring (+5)	J L Lewis (+6)	K Triplett (+6)	J Sindelar (+6)
J Maginnes (+6)	M Bradley (+7)	R Damron (+8)	T Pernice Jr (+10)
D Paulson (+11)	F Nobilo (+11)	M Goggin (+13)	E Fryatt (+18)

Barry Cheesman (82-74) and Phil Tataurangi (74-83) both withdrew.

ROUND BY ROUND LEADERBOARD

FIRST ROUND		SECOND ROUND	
D Duval	6 under	V Singh	11 under
V Singh	6 under	N Begay	10 under
N Begay	6 under	M Gogel	7 under
T WOODS	4 under	M Brooks	6 under
L Janzen	4 under	R Mediate	6 under
G Waite	4 under	G Waite	5 under
S Scott	4 under	C DiMarco	5 under
		J Williamson	5 under
		T Lehman	5 under
		T WOODS	3 under

THIRD ROUND		FINAL ROUND	
M Brooks	12 under	T WOODS	15 under
M Gogel	12 under	M Gogel	13 under
V Singh	11 under	V Singh	13 under
N Begay	10 under	J Kelly	12 under
C DiMarco	8 under	J Green	12 under
J Green	8 under	N Begay	12 under
J Williamson	8 under		
T WOODS	7 under		

R1 was stopped on Thursday because of heavy rain and high winds with the early players at Pebble Beach particularly disadvantaged. The round was completed on Friday.

As a result R2 was on Saturday, R3 on Sunday, and the final round at Pebble Beach on Monday.

PUNTERS' POINTS

● Watching Tiger Woods live on the Monday evening over the back nine was truly awesome. An eagle-birdie-par-birdie finish enabled him to overtake Matt Gogel and land his sixth successive USPGA tour victory.

● After this astonishing performance the best 'Tiger' odds in the village were

> To equal Byron Nelson's record of 11 straight wins   200/1 Ladbrokes

> To pass Byron Nelson's record of 11 straight wins   500/1 Ladbrokes

> To win the Grand Slam   125/1 Surrey

> To win the US Money List   6/1 on Sunderlands

● 28-year-old tour rookie Matt Gogel, after a superb start in R4 (three straight birdies), shot 40 on the back nine. He was so shaken by the Tiger that he missed a tiddler for par at the last, so only tying for 2nd place.

● The players playing Pebble Beach in R1 on Thursday had an insurmountable hurdle to overcome as they really struggled in the high winds. They included Hal Sutton, Paul Azinger and Jeff Maggert, who all missed the cut.

- Mark Brooks (T7th), Jerry Kelly (T4th), Mike Weir (T7th) and Justin Leonard (T15th) all played Pebble in the worst weather on Thursday, so their final positions were especially praiseworthy.

- To help with 3-ball betting in future the best scores on the individual courses were:-

Pebble Beach	Poppy Hills	Spyglass Hill
T Woods 64 (R4) 68	V Singh 66	J Kaye 67
M Weir 66 (R4)	M Brooks 66	M Brooks 67
V Singh 67	N Begay 66	B Jobe 68
M Gogel 67	J D Blake 67	N Lancaster 68
J Kelly 67 (R4)	M Gogel 68	
A Magee 67 (R4)	B Faxon 68	
T Lehman 67 (R4)	J Kelly 68	
C Stadler 67 (R4)	S Flesch 68	
N Begay 68	J Green 68	
R Sabbatini 68		
J Green 68 (twice)		
C Perry 68 (R4)		
N Lancaster 68 (R4)		

1999 RESULT

1	50/1	Payne Stewart
2	125/1	Frank Lickliter
3	100/1*	Craig Stadler
T4	28/1	Fred Couples
T4	200/1	Ronnie Black
T4	20/1	Justin Leonard
T4	200/1	Jay Williamson

1998 RESULT

1	22/1	Phil Mickelson
2	250/1	Tom Pernice Jr
T3	40/1	Jim Furyk
T3	125/1	Paul Azinger
T3	250/1	J P Hayes

WINNERS IN THE LAST TEN YEARS

1991	Paul Azinger	1996	VOID (only 2 rounds played)
1992	Mark O'Meara	1997	Mark O'Meara
1993	Brett Ogle	1998	Phil Mickelson (3 rounds only)
1994	Johnny Miller	1999	Payne Stewart (3 rounds only)
1995	Peter Jacobsen	2000	Tiger Woods

PUNTERS' GUIDE

- Weather warning.

  Three times in the last five years (and nearly again this year) this tournament has been reduced to three rounds or declared void (1996). Positioned on the

Monterrey Peninsula, this is always a real danger when the tournament is held early in the year. As a result:-

> Always check both the weather forecast and the tee times schedule. This year the early Thursday Pebble Beach players (Azinger, Sutton and Maggert) were simply 'blown away'.

> Had the event been stopped this year after three rounds we'd have had two 125/1 chances as joint winners heading for a play-off, with 7/2 favourite Tiger Woods T8th. So despite Woods's ultimate win it's probably wisest to back long-priced players.

● The pro-am format.

This unique tournament can be played very slowly (up to six hours per round) and the best amateurs still play in R4, so players with a proven record in celebrity events are worth noting.

● In the last three years eight players have posted two top 20s.

>	Justin Leonard	T15th 2000: T4th 1999
>	Craig Stadler	T15th 2000: 3rd 1999
>	Jay Williamson	T11th 2000: T4th 1999
>	Neal Lancaster	T15th 2000: T8th 1999
>	Vijay Singh	T2nd 2000: T10th 1999
>	Tom Lehman	T7th 2000: T9th 1998
>	Paul Azinger	T10th 1999: T3rd 1998
>	Tim Herron	T10th 1999: T19th 1998

● Players whose profiles point to this event include Paul Azinger, Tom Lehman, Jim Furyk, Justin Leonard, Tim Herron, Neal Lancaster, Jay Williamson, Jimmy Green, Craig Stadler and Vijay Singh.

THE BUICK INVITATIONAL

Date	10th - 13th February
Course	Torrey Pines, California

Par	North Course	South Course
	72	72
Yardage	6,854	7,033
First Prize	$540,000	
Total Purse	$3 million	

THE TOURNAMENT

This well-established tournament has been held at Torrey Pines since 1968.

THE COURSES

Players use the North and South courses alternately over the first couple of days when the cut is made. Then the South course is used for the final two rounds. The par 5s are reachable on both courses, especially for the big hitters. The greens are bent grass.

2000 ODDS

fav	7/4	Tiger Woods	66/1*	Steve Pate
	20/1	Davis Love	66/1*	Loren Roberts
	20/1	Phil Mickelson	66/1	Craig Stadler
	40/1	Fred Couples	66/1	Steve Flesch
	40/1	Steve Elkington	66/1	Brad Faxon
	40/1	David Toms	80/1*	Bill Glasson
	40/1	Chris Perry	80/1	Frank Lickliter
	50/1*	Jeff Sluman	80/1*	Dudley Hart
	50/1	Brent Geiberger	80/1	Duffy Waldorf
	50/1	Stewart Cink	80/1*	Matt Gogel
	66/1*	Mark O'Meara	80/1	Billy Mayfair
	66/1*	Notah Begay	80/1*	Kevin Sutherland
	66/1*	Steve Stricker	80/1	Rory Sabbatini
	66/1	Andrew Magee		

2000 RESULT

1	20/1	**Phil Mickelson**	**66 67 67 70 270**
T2	fav 7/4	**Tiger Woods**	**71 68 67 68 274**
T2	125/1	**Shigeki Maruyama**	**69 64 69 72 274**
4	20/1	**Davis Love**	**65 71 69 70 275**
T5	80/1*	**Kevin Sutherland**	**73 66 69 68 276**
T5	100/1	**Kirk Triplett**	**69 64 73 70 276**
T5	40/1	**Fred Couples**	**68 71 67 70 276**

T8	B Hughes	68 67 73 69 277		R Freeman	72 69 68 75 284
	S Sear	72 67 69 69 277	T41	N Begay	70 67 75 73 285
T10	B Geiberger	69 72 70 68 279		M O'Meara	72 69 73 71 285
	J P Hayes	67 71 72 69 279		S Ames	74 67 73 71 285
	S Lyle	68 66 74 71 279		C Raulerson	71 68 70 76 285
	S Flesch	69 68 69 73 279		J Van de Velde	68 74 73 70 285
T14	B Tway	71 67 74 68 280		A Bengoechea	68 71 77 69 285
	C Stadler	70 67 73 70 280		S Micheel	68 68 70 79 285
	J D Blake	71 67 72 70 280	T48	T Armour III	72 70 72 72 286
	David Sutherland	71 71 71 67 280		J Gove	73 69 72 72 286
	D Toms	69 70 70 71 280		D Berganio	72 68 75 71 286
	S Pate	71 70 68 71 280		F Lickliter	75 67 73 71 286
	Joe Ozaki	74 66 69 71 280	T52	M Dawson	71 69 73 74 287
T21	T Dodds	70 69 73 69 281		A Magee	70 70 74 73 287
	N Lancaster	71 68 74 68 281		B McCallister	71 70 73 73 287
	Dennis Paulson	73 67 70 71 281		B Chamblee	71 69 75 72 287
	L Roberts	70 70 70 71 281		S Lowery	68 70 70 79 287
	F Allem	69 69 71 72 281		Carl Paulson	73 68 76 70 287
	C Beck	70 69 69 73 281	T58	P Curry	69 68 75 76 288
	J Sluman	70 70 66 75 281		B Cheesman	71 71 70 76 288
T28	S Kendall	71 66 73 72 282		D Morland IV	73 69 73 73 288
	B Elder	70 70 70 72 282		S Gotsche	72 70 75 71 288
	S Stricker	70 67 72 73 282		B Burns	75 67 76 70 288
	S Cink	74 65 70 73 282	T63	E Booker	72 70 73 74 289
	J Kaye	70 70 69 73 282		S Elkington	70 72 75 72 289
T33	R Howison	69 71 72 71 283		L Mattiace	70 72 76 71 289
	B Fabel	73 68 71 71 283	T66	J Kelly	70 71 73 76 290
	C Bowden	71 70 72 70 283		Tom Byrum	71 71 75 73 290
	D Waldorf	69 69 75 70 283	T68	J Williamson	73 67 75 76 291
	B May	68 73 74 68 283		B Gay	71 70 75 75 291
T38	J L Lewis	67 71 73 73 284	70	K Nolan	70 72 77 74 293
	S Verplank	67 71 72 74 284	71	B Bates	73 69 76 78 296

The main players to miss the cut (made at 2 under) were:–

B Jobe (-1)	O Uresti (-1)	D Stockton Jr (-1)	B Faxon (-1)
C Perry (-1)	M Gogel (-1)	M Bradley (E)	S McCarron (E)
P Goydos (E)	R Beem (E)	D Frost (E)	T Tryba (E)
R Sabbatini (E)	J Cook (+1)	B Andrade (+1)	T Pernice Jr (+2)
G Chalmers (+2)	B Glasson (+2)	M Goggin (+3)	J Sindelar (+3)
B Mayfair (+3)	C Pavin (+3)	J Maginnes (+3)	S Jones (+3)
S Gump (+4)			

Mike Springer (78), Brian Watts (78) and Grant Waite (81) all withdrew after R1.

ROUND BY ROUND LEADERBOARD

FIRST ROUND

D Love	7 under
P MICKELSON	6 under
J L Lewis	5 under
S Verplank	5 under
J P Hayes	5 under

SECOND ROUND

P MICKELSON	11 under
K Triplett	11 under
S Maruyama	11 under
S Lyle	10 under
B Hughes	9 under
D Love	8 under
S Micheel	8 under

THIRD ROUND

P MICKELSON	16 under
S Maruyama	14 under
D Love	11 under
F Couples	10 under
S Micheel	10 under
J Sluman	10 under
K Triplett	10 under
T Woods	10 under
S Flesch	10 under

FOURTH ROUND

P MICKELSON	18 under
T Woods	14 under
S Maruyama	14 under
D Love	13 under
K Sutherland	12 under
K Triplett	12 under
F Couples	12 under

RESULTS IN OTHER MARKETS

With 'Tigermania' at its height Multi-Sports created a 'without Woods' market. The result was :-

1	12/1	Phil Mickelson
2	80/1	Shigeki Maruyama
3	fav 10/1	Davis Love
T4	33/1	Kevin Sutherland
T4	50/1	Kirk Triplett
T5	20/1	Fred Couples

1/4 odds 1-5

PUNTERS' POINTS

● Mickelson's win highlighted three key punter points.

> The importance of following players on 'the comeback trail'. Two weeks ago it was Lehman now Mickelson — both proven winners who have had a winless year or two and now are more determined than ever to get back to 'the winner's enclosure'.

> 'Home' advantage really counts in golf and Mickelson won here seven years ago for his first pro victory and also played the front nine three times a week in high school because he was born in San Diego.

> That Tiger Woods is human! Backed at prices from 2/1 downwards Woods admitted he was tired after last week's extra day and without his regular caddie he was not at his best in R4 as his long game deserted him.

- At one point after birdieing the par 5 13th Woods had come from 7 back to tie Mickelson who then showed real skill and resilience to make three birdies in the last 6 holes to win comfortably.
- Tiger Woods was well below his best yet still finished T2nd so he rewarded any spread punters who sold his finishing position (as low as 7 - 10 with IG). The Tiger has yet to defend a title successfully!
- Davis Love, having made changes to his swing, has reverted to steel shafts (from graphite) in his irons to stop him overhitting.

1999 RESULT

1	fav 7/1	Tiger Woods
2	200/1	Billy Ray Brown
3	66/1*	Bill Glasson
T4	66/1	Chris Perry
T4	150/1	Omar Uresti
T4	80/1	Kevin Sutherland

1998 RESULT

1	150/1	Scott Simpson
won at the first play-off hole		
2	100/1	Skip Kendall
T3	fav 13/2	Tiger Woods
T3	14/1	Davis Love
T3	150/1	Kevin Sutherland

WINNERS IN THE LAST TEN YEARS

1991	Jay Don Blake	1996	Davis Love
1992	Steve Pate (3 rounds)	1997	Mark O'Meara
1993	Phil Mickelson	1998	Scott Simpson (3 rounds only)
1994	Craig Stadler	1999	Tiger Woods
1995	Peter Jacobsen	2000	Phil Mickelson

PUNTERS' GUIDE

- Over the last three years only three players have posted consecutive top 25 finishes.
  - > Tiger Woods — T2nd 2000: Won 1999: T3rd 1998
  - > Kevin Sutherland — T5th 2000(best player over the last 54 holes): T4th 1999: T3rd 1998
  - > Jeff Sluman — T21st 2000: T18th 1999: T16th 1998
- 'Local' players have now won in seven of the last nine years. (Please remember Californian-based and Californian-born players are discussed in Part 1).
- Good weather blessed the tournament again this year. However it has been weather reduced in 1986, 1992 and 1998, so keep the barometer in mind when assessing this event.
- The North course is easier than the South course (by between one and a half and two shots) so any player with an early Thursday tee time on that course has a marginal advantage.
- Players whose profiles refer to this tournament include Davis Love, Jay Don Blake, Loren Roberts, Bob Tway, Jeff Sluman, Craig Stadler, Brent Geiberger, Steve Pate, Spike McRoy and Phil Mickelson.

THE NISSAN OPEN

Date	17th - 20th February
Course	Riviera C.C., Pacific Palisades, California
Par	71
Yardage	6,987
First Prize	$558,000
Total Purse	$ 3.1 million

THE TOURNAMENT

Since 1973 the Nissan Open has been played every year (apart from 1998) at the superb Riviera Country Club. The course has also been host to two USPGAs (most recent 1995) and a US Open.

THE COURSE

Unusually Riviera has Kikuyu grass fairways which tend to stop the ball. The Kikuyu grass rough is severe. This is a tight course with small (once bent, now Bermuda) greens. It favours shot makers and 'faders' of the ball. Riviera has only three par 5s.

2000 ODDS

fav	7/2	Tiger Woods	66/1	Stewart Cink
	14/1	Ernie Els (DC)	80/1*	Carlos Franco
	14/1	David Duval	80/1	Jeff Maggert
	25/1	Fred Couples	80/1	Mike Weir
	28/1	Vijay Singh	80/1	Mark Calcavecchia
	28/1	Tom Lehman	80/1*	Craig Stadler
	28/1	Lee Westwood	80/1	Fred Funk
	33/1	Jesper Parnevik	80/1*	Mark O'Meara
	40/1	Nick Price	80/1*	Darren Clarke
	40/1	Jim Furyk	80/1*	Scott Hoch
	40/1	Hal Sutton	80/1	Shigeki Maruyama
	50/1	Justin Leonard	80/1	Robert Allenby
	66/1	Stuart Appleby	80/1	Rocco Mediate
	66/1	Brent Geiberger	80/1	Steve Pate
	66/1	Jeff Sluman	80/1	Notah Begay
	66/1	Lee Janzen	80/1	Andrew Magee
	66/1	Bob Estes	80/1	Tim Herron

2000 RESULT

1	100/1*	Kirk Triplett	67 70 68 67 272
2	33/1	Jesper Parnevik	71 67 67 68 273
3	250/1	Robin Freeman	65 72 69 68 274
4	150/1	Russ Cochran	69 71 66 69 275
T5	100/1*	Steve Flesch	69 69 70 68 276
T5	66/1	Stewart Cink	67 70 70 69 276
T5	125/1	Bradley Hughes	69 66 71 70 276
T5	25/1	Fred Couples	72 66 68 70 276
T5	150/1	Tommy Armour III	68 68 69 71 276

T10	J P Hayes	64 70 72 71 277		K Yokoo	70 69 68 75 282
	B Chamblee	71 65 69 72 277		S Verplank	69 69 74 70 282
T12	R Sabbatini	67 73 69 69 278	T43	C Pavin	73 65 71 74 283
	C A Spence	67 69 70 72 278		D Frost	69 70 70 74 283
	L Janzen	70 67 69 72 278		Nick Price	67 72 69 75 283
	J Haas	70 67 69 72 278		C Raulerson	68 71 72 72 283
	S Dunlap	71 67 68 72 278		L Mattiace	72 66 73 72 283
	David Sutherland	67 69 68 74 278		Joe Ozaki	70 70 71 72 283
T18	V Singh	68 70 72 69 279		H Sutton	69 67 75 72 283
	G Chalmers	67 66 74 72 279		R Allenby	69 70 67 77 283
	S Appleby	70 68 72 69 279		J Kaye	69 72 71 71 283
	Dennis Paulson	72 68 67 72 279	T52	F Nobilo	71 68 70 75 284
	T Woods	68 70 69 72 279		E Fryatt	68 70 72 74 284
	R Mediate	71 70 64 74 279		M Brooks	66 72 70 76 284
	L Roberts	71 69 73 66 279		M Reid	68 70 73 73 284
T25	Kevin Sutherland	71 66 71 72 280		T Pernice Jr	67 69 75 73 284
	B Mayfair	72 67 71 70 280		C Barlow	71 68 73 72 284
	E Toledo	70 67 70 73 280		F Funk	69 68 79 68 284
	D Waldorf	70 71 69 70 280	T59	C Stadler	72 69 68 76 285
	S Hoch	67 70 69 74 280		A Magee	68 69 74 74 285
	B Tway	66 67 72 75 280	T61	S Ames	70 68 70 78 286
T31	C DiMarco	71 68 71 71 281		M Dawson	70 70 70 76 286
	Kenny Perry	69 71 70 71 281		C Martin	71 68 73 74 286
	L Mize	71 68 68 74 281		S Pate	71 70 72 73 286
	D Duval	70 68 69 74 281	65	B Elder	70 67 76 74 287
	T Scherrer	67 68 71 75 281	T66	Carl Paulson	73 67 71 77 288
	F Langham	70 71 70 70 281		S McCarron	72 68 72 76 288
T37	B McCallister	75 66 68 73 282		E Els	69 71 72 76 288
	Jeff Freeman	66 68 73 75 282	T69	T Dodds	70 71 71 77 289
	J Furyk	68 72 70 72 282		S Gump	69 70 75 75 289
	M Wiebe	68 71 68 75 282		N Begay	71 67 79 72 289

The main players to miss the cut (made at 1 under) were:–

F Lickliter (E)	M Goggin (E)	P Jacobsen (E)	J Cook (E)
M Weir (E)	B Henninger (E)	J Sluman (E)	O Browne (E)
J Daly (E)	B Faxon (E)	B Estes (E)	T Lehman (+1)
J Van de Velde (+1)	N Henke (+2)	P Stankowski (+2)	M O'Meara (+2)
S Maruyama (+2)	N Faldo (+2)	B Jobe (+2)	J Leonard (+2)
R Damron (+3)	J Don Blake (+3)	N Lancaster (+3)	B Andrade (+3)
O Uresti (+3)	C Franco (+3)	B May (+3)	J Maggert (+3)
G Hjerstedt (+4)	T Herron (+4)	J Kelly (+4)	R Beem (+5)
D Clarke (+5)	T Tryba (+6)		

Lee Westwood (72) and Sandy Lyle (79) both withdrew after R1.

ROUND BY ROUND LEADERBOARD

FIRST ROUND

J P Hayes	7 under
R Freeman	6 under
N Lancaster	5 under
M Brooks	5 under
B Tway	5 under
J Freeman	5 under
K TRIPLETT	4 under

SECOND ROUND

B Tway	9 under
G Chalmers	9 under
J Freeman	8 under
J P Hayes	8 under
T Scherrer	7 under
B Hughes	7 under
K TRIPLETT	5 under

THIRD ROUND

D Sutherland	9 under
T Armour III	8 under
B Chamblee	8 under
R Mediate	8 under
J Parnevik	8 under
K TRIPLETT	8 under
B Tway	8 under

FINAL ROUND

K TRIPLETT	12 under
J Parnevik	11 under
R Freeman	10 under
R Cochran	9 under
S Flesch	8 under
S Cink	8 under
B Hughes	8 under
F Couples	8 under
T Armour III	8 under

RESULTS IN OTHER MARKETS

Sunderlands introduced two special markets:–

Top Rest of The World player

1	16/1	Bradley Hughes
T2	33/1	Craig Spence
T2	25/1	Rory Sabbatini
T4	33/1	Greg Chalmers
T4	11/2	Vijay Singh
T4	14/1	Stuart Appleby

1/4 odds 1-4

Top European player

1	2/1	Jesper Parnevik
2	16/1	Ed Fryatt
T3	16/1	Jean Van de Velde
T3	10/1	Paul Lawrie

9 'ran' ; 1/5 odds 1-3

PUNTERS' POINTS

- He'd had thirty-nine top 10s in 266 starts yet this was the first win for Kirk Triplett on a course so suited to his fade and his accurate approach play.
- Jesper Parnevik in bright pink trousers showed that golf is still the moral game when he said, "I'm very happy for him" and meant it!
- Tiger Woods's performance is summarised in one stat - he took 118 putts in all including a truly amazing 4-putt from 6 feet in R3!! So those 'buying money' by selling his finishing position of 10-13 were on a loser when he finished T18th.
- Four punter points are worth noting:-
  > In-form Kirk Triplett was a 100/1 triumph for the DYM system on a course suited to his game where he had exposed form.

> Tiger Woods is not at his best when in continuous play, and on a course with only three par 5s.

> 'Streakers don't keep it up'. The lowest tournament round by Rocco Mediate (64) in R3 was followed by a 10-shot worse 74 on Sunday.

> Ernie Els (like Mickelson and Couples) showed here the same tendency to lose concentration in R4 when well out of contention. The defending champion shot a very poor 76!

● And finally a question for a pub quiz - simply ask for the christian name of the golfer whose twins are actually triplets??

1999 RESULT			1998 RESULT		
(at Riviera)			(at Valencia C.C.)		
1	18/1	Ernie Els	1	100/1	Billy Mayfair
T2	100/1	Ted Tryba	won at the first extra hole		
T2	fav 15/2	Tiger Woods	2	fav 5/1	Tiger Woods
T2	22/1	Davis Love	3	125/1	Stephen Ames
T5	33/1	Nick Price	T4	50/1	Payne Stewart
T5	9/1	David Duval	T4	66/1	John Daly

WINNERS IN THE LAST TEN YEARS

1991	Ted Schulz		1996	Craig Stadler
1992	Fred Couples		1997	Nick Faldo
1993	Tom Kite (3 rounds)		1998	Billy Mayfair
1994	Corey Pavin		1999	Ernie Els
1995	Corey Pavin		2000	Kirk Triplett

PUNTERS' GUIDE

● The Riviera course suits players who fade the ball, with its small greens demanding accurate approach play off the tee and fairway.

● In the last three Riviera Nissans (2000,1999 and 1997) the best records are held by:-

> Tiger Woods   T18th 2000: T2nd 1999: T20th 1997

> Bradley Hughes   T5th 2000: T15th 1999

> Brandel Chamblee   T10th 2000: T15th 1999

> Rocco Mediate   T18th 2000: T15th 1999

> Robin Freeman   3rd 2000: 6th 1997

> Fred Couples   T5th 2000: T9th 1997

> Scott Hoch   7th 1999: 3rd 1997

> Ted Tryba   2nd 1999: T9th 1997

● Players whose profiles refer to this tournament include Bradley Hughes, Brandel Chamblee, Steve Flesch, Robin Freeman, Fred Couples, Tom Lehman, David Sutherland, Ernie Els, Jay Haas and Tommy Armour III.

THE TOUCHSTONE ENERGY TUCSON OPEN

Date	24th - 27th February
Course	Omni Tucson National Golf Resort, Arizona
Par	72
Yardage	7,109
First Prize	$540,000
Total Purse	$3 million

THE TOURNAMENT

The Tucson Open is the ninth oldest tournament on the tour and for the second successive year it was being played alongside the first World Golf Championship event, giving an opportunity to players outside the top 65 in the world rankings. Before 1997 it used a two-course format. Since then it has been held solely at the Tucson National course. The total purse was $1.5 million greater than it was just two years ago.

THE COURSE

The course does not provide a stiff test (sixty-seven of this year's seventy-two finishers beat par) as the rough is not penal. However accuracy to the small bentgrass greens is essential.

2000 ODDS

jt fav	25/1	Kirk Triplett (PWW)	66/1	Scott Dunlap
jt fav	25/1	Steve Flesch	66/1	Jay Don Blake
	28/1	Robert Allenby	66/1	John Daly
	33/1	Kevin Sutherland	66/1	Greg Chalmers
	33/1*	Craig Stadler	66/1	Paul Goydos
	33/1*	Mark Brooks	66/1*	Mike Reid
	33/1	Brad Faxon	66/1*	Scott Verplank
	40/1	Bill Glasson	66/1*	David Sutherland
	40/1*	Kenny Perry	80/1*	Trevor Dodds
	40/1	Rory Sabbatini	80/1*	Steve Lowery
	40/1	Tommy Armour III	80/1*	Larry Mize
	50/1	Paul Stankowski	80/1	Chris DiMarco
	50/1	Jerry Kelly	80/1	Dan Forsman
	50/1*	Skip Kendall	80/1*	Robert Karlsson
	50/1	Gabriel Hjerstedt (DC)	80/1	Stephen Ames
	66/1*	Steve Jones	80/1	Tom Byrum
	66/1*	Corey Pavin	80/1	Jim Carter
	66/1*	Brandel Chamblee	80/1*	Robin Freeman
	66/1*	Craig Spence	80/1	Scott Gump
	66/1	Russ Cochran	80/1	Bob May
	66/1*	John Cook		

2000 RESULT

1	80/1	Jim Carter	66 68 69 66 269
T2	80/1	Chris DiMarco	68 69 68 66 271
T2	100/1	Jean Van de Velde	68 69 65 69 271
T2	100/1*	Tom Scherrer	65 66 68 72 271
T5	125/1	Rick Fehr	69 71 66 66 272
T5	66/1*	Steve Jones	66 70 67 69 272

T7	S Lowery	64 72 71 66 273		T40	David Sutherland	64 77 67 72 280
	K Triplett	67 70 69 67 273			G Nicklaus	72 65 70 73 280
	W Austin	70 68 67 68 273			P Stankowski	72 68 69 71 280
	S Flesch	66 69 68 70 273			B McCallister	66 74 69 71 280
T11	Kevin Sutherland	69 66 70 69 274			F Nobilo	69 70 70 71 280
	T Purdy	68 66 66 74 274			S Micheel	69 72 69 70 280
T13	Jerry Smith	68 72 67 68 275			G Kraft	69 66 70 75 280
	Kenny Perry	69 67 70 69 275			P Goydos	74 66 71 69 280
	Tom Byrum	68 65 72 70 275			T Purtzer	68 73 72 67 280
	B Gay	71 65 69 70 275			L Mattiace	68 67 68 77 280
T17	S Verplank	69 69 70 68 276		T50	K Gibson	70 66 71 74 281
	C Martin	67 70 68 71 276			E Fryatt	70 71 67 73 281
	R Black	69 66 69 72 276			S McCarron	70 71 70 70 281
	B Faxon	71 67 67 71 276			P Moss	73 68 73 67 281
	M Wiebe	69 69 66 72 276		T54	B Friend	71 66 71 74 282
	B Kontak	66 71 67 72 276			D Stockton	69 67 69 77 282
	J Kaye	68 68 65 75 276		T56	Bart Bryant	71 70 66 76 283
	S Ames	68 68 64 76 276			D Forsman	70 72 70 71 283
T25	P Jordan	70 66 71 70 277			M Sposa	70 69 73 71 283
	R Gamez	69 69 70 69 277			M Reid	73 67 73 70 283
	S Dunlap	71 67 70 69 277		60	R Sabbatini	69 72 71 72 284
	J Ogilvie	72 70 67 68 277		T61	J Gove	71 70 72 72 285
	G Chalmers	73 68 70 66 277			S Gotsche	72 68 74 71 285
	B Elder	69 68 67 73 277		63	J Green	74 68 70 74 286
T31	K Wentworth	65 71 71 71 278		T64	R Allenby	70 72 71 74 287
	M Dawson	71 66 70 71 278			T Dodds	69 71 73 74 287
	M Springer	67 66 73 72 278			G Hnatiuk	73 69 74 71 287
	Bobby Cochran	68 69 71 70 278			F Langham	70 71 75 71 287
	C Riley	70 69 70 69 278		68	C Raulerson	71 68 72 77 288
T36	B Chamblee	70 69 68 72 279		T69	D Peoples	72 68 71 78 289
	C Tidland	69 67 70 73 279			J Caron	67 72 74 76 289
	Russ Cochran	72 67 70 70 279			K J Choi	73 69 74 73 289
	L Mize	73 74 69 73 279		72	J Williams	72 70 75 74 291

The main players to miss the cut (made at 2 under) were:–

B Cheesman (-1)	B May (-1)	G Waite (E)	E Toledo (E)
J D Blake (E)	M Bradley (E)	J Cook (E)	J Kelly (E)
C Stadler (E)	C A Spence (+1)	M Goggin (+2)	S Kendall (+2)
G Hjerstedt (+2)	R Karlsson (+3)	C Pavin (+4)	M Brooks (+4)
T Armour III (+6)	B Glasson (+6)	R Damron (+11)	

ROUND BY ROUND LEADERBOARD

FIRST ROUND

S Lowery	8 under
D Sutherland	8 under
K Wentworth	7 under
T Scherrer	7 under
J CARTER	6 under
S Flesch	6 under
S Jones	6 under
B Kontak	6 under
B McCallister	6 under

SECOND ROUND

T Scherrer	13 under
T Byrum	11 under
M Springer	11 under
J CARTER	10 under
T Purdy	10 under

THIRD ROUND

T Scherrer	17 under
S Ames	16 under
T Purdy	16 under
J Kaye	15 under
J Van de Velde	14 under
J CARTER	13 under

FINAL ROUND

J CARTER	19 under
C DiMarco	17 under
J Van de Velde	17 under
T Scherrer	17 under
R Fehr	16 under
S Jones	16 under

PUNTERS' POINTS

● Home advantage rules again, OK? Jim Carter's first win in his 292nd event was a triumph for Carter's use of positive thinking. He had won two college tournaments in Arizona in 1984 including one on this course. "I was talking to myself saying, 'You know that you won tournaments on this course before' so I was trying to put good positive thoughts in my head."

● The key punters' point to come from the two Arizona desert tournaments is that both have been won by local residents – Tom Lehman in the Phoenix, and now Jim Carter in the Tucson.

● Three players in with a real chance after R3 noticeably disappointed on Sunday to throw away a big opportunity.

> Local resident Ted Purdy, T2nd after R3, shot 74 to finish T11th.

> Jonathan Kaye, T4th after R3, shot 75 (!) to finish T17th.

> Stephen Ames, T2nd after R3, shot 76 (!) to finish T17th.

● The importance of an early tee time was well illustrated this year when the best draw (first out on 1st tee in R1, and 1st out from 10th tee in R2 in the afternoon) favoured Jim Carter (winner), Steve Flesch and Stephen Ames. Between them they shot six sub-70 rounds in R1 and R2, averaging 67.5!

● For the second successive year only one spread firm bothered to give golf punters the opportunity to bet. So well done to IG for once more creating a ten-runner index which went to form with Steve Flesch and Kirk Triplett dead-heating for top place.

1999 RESULT

1	125/1	Gabriel Hjerstedt
won at the first play-off hole		
2	100/1	Tommy Armour III
T3	66/1	Mike Reid
T3	66/1*	Kirk Triplett
T5	66/1*	Brent Geiberger
T5	125/1	Barry Cheesman

1998 RESULT

1	20/1	David Duval
T2	33/1	Justin Leonard
T2	125/1	David Toms
T4	100/1	Tim Herron
T4	150/1	Steve Lowery

WINNERS IN THE LAST TEN YEARS

1991	Phil Mickelson	1996	Phil Mickelson
1992	Lee Janzen	1997	Jeff Sluman
1993	Larry Mize	1998	David Duval
1994	Andrew Magee	1999	Gabriel Hjerstedt
1995	Phil Mickelson	2000	Jim Carter

PUNTERS' GUIDE

● Since the tournament was held solely on the Tucson National course in 1997 the best form figures are held by

> Steve Lowery   T7th 2000: T20th 1999: T4th 1998

> Kenny Perry   T13th 2000: T13th 1999: T31st 1998

> Kirk Triplett   T7th 2000: T3rd 1999: T13th 1997

● In those four years this has become a tournament for outsiders. Of the seventeen players finishing in the top 4 (or T4th)

> thirteen have started at or over 66/1

> eight have started at or over 100/1

> The four winners have been priced at 100/1, 20/1, 125/1* and 80/1.

● The players whose profiles refer to this tournament include Greg Chalmers, Steve Flesch, Steve Jones, Steve Lowery, Kirk Triplett, Kenny Perry, Jonathan Kaye, Andrew Magee and Tom Scherrer.

THE DORAL RYDER OPEN

Date	2nd - 5th March
Course	Doral Resort & Country Club, Miami, Florida
Par	72
Yardage	7,125
First Prize	$540,000
Total Purse	$ 3 million

THE TOURNAMENT

The Doral marks the start of the 'Florida Swing' as the tour moves across country from the West coast to the East. It has lost some of its prestige as it follows the week after the World Match Play.

THE COURSE

The 'Blue Monster' was redesigned with thirty-four new very steep-faced bunkers to toughen it up in 1997. So the last three years' form is the only course form that is worthwhile on a track where accuracy is essential. The wind is a factor, as it can get up in the afternoon, and experience of the grainy Bermuda greens is vital. The par 4 final hole over the water is very demanding and one of the toughest on the whole tour.

2000 ODDS

fav	8/1	David Duval	66/1	Retief Goosen
	14/1	Ernie Els	66/1	Bernhard Langer
	16/1	Jesper Parnevik	66/1	Shigeki Maruyama
	20/1	Phil Mickelson	66/1	Steve Stricker
	25/1	Vijay Singh	66/1	Dudley Hart
	25/1	Nick Price	66/1	Robert Allenby
	33/1	Jim Furyk	66/1	Billy Mayfair
	33/1	Steve Elkington (DC)	80/1*	Glen Day
	33/1	John Huston	80/1	Fred Funk
	40/1	David Toms	80/1	Scott Dunlap
	40/1	Bob Tway	80/1	Brad Faxon
	50/1*	Scott Hoch	80/1	Tom Scherrer
	50/1	Greg Norman	80/1	Craig Stadler
	50/1	Chris Perry	80/1	Jean Van de Velde
	50/1	Jeff Sluman	80/1	Jay Haas
	66/1*	Mark Calcavecchia		

2000 RESULT

1	33/1	**Jim Furyk**	**65 67 68 65 265**
2	150/1	**Franklin Langham**	**66 63 68 70 267**
3	25/1	**Nick Price**	**66 71 66 67 270**
T4	fav 8/1	**David Duval**	**71 64 70 66 271**
T4	66/1	**Shigeki Maruyama**	**67 65 70 69 271**

T6	Russ Cochran	69 67 69 67 272			E Toledo	68 68 73 71 280
	S Verplank	67 69 68 68 272			M Brooks	69 70 69 72 280
8	S Ames	71 61 69 72 273			Joel Edwards	69 72 67 72 280
T9	J D Blake	69 70 71 64 274			B Langer	66 69 72 73 280
	E Fryatt	75 62 71 66 274			V Singh	65 67 73 75 280
	B Lietzke	65 70 69 70 274	T45		S Gump	71 70 74 66 281
T12	G Norman	68 70 68 69 275			D Toms	70 70 71 70 281
	R Allenby	69 67 68 71 275			G Chalmers	69 72 70 70 281
	R Damron	72 67 65 71 275			B Gay	70 71 69 71 281
T15	Chris Perry	67 70 73 66 276			J Green	70 71 69 71 281
	J Carter	71 65 71 69 276			B May	68 66 74 73 281
	E Els	67 68 71 70 276	T51		Kenny Perry	70 70 73 69 282
	B Tway	66 68 71 71 276			T Tolles	67 72 73 70 282
	J L Lewis	70 65 70 71 276			R Black	68 73 71 70 282
	H Frazar	65 69 70 72 276			J Van de Velde	69 71 71 71 282
T21	K J Choi	74 66 71 66 277			T Dodds	71 70 70 71 282
	N Faldo	69 72 70 66 277			S Murphy	71 70 69 72 282
	P Mickelson	66 73 68 70 277			O Browne	69 68 71 74 282
	J Sluman	67 69 71 70 277			David Edwards	70 69 69 74 282
	R Friend	68 71 68 70 277			D Mast	68 66 73 75 282
	J Haas	71 67 68 71 277	T60		S Young	72 69 74 68 283
	D Peoples	70 66 69 72 277			B Heintz	68 70 74 71 283
	T Tryba	68 70 67 72 277			F Funk	70 71 70 72 283
	F Nobilo	73 63 69 72 277			R Fehr	69 72 69 73 283
T30	P Jordan	69 67 74 68 278			J Restino	71 67 71 74 283
	W Austin	68 71 70 69 278	T65		J Caron	71 69 74 70 284
	S Hoch	67 66 74 71 278			F Allem	72 68 74 70 284
T33	L Mattiace	72 68 70 69 279			B Gage	69 71 72 72 284
	Jerry Smith	67 68 72 72 279			B Faxon	66 68 71 79 284
	R Goosen	67 67 72 73 279	T69		J Maginnes	73 68 71 73 285
T36	M Springer	71 70 70 69 280			C DiMarco	72 69 70 74 285
	B Andrade	70 69 71 70 280	71		D Pride	70 71 75 70 286
	B Elder	71 69 70 70 280	72		E Compton	72 69 78 71 290
	J Huston	68 67 74 71 280	73		M Calcavecchia	70 71 71 79 291

The main players to miss the cut (made at 3 under) were:–

PLEASE NOTE: At 3 under par the cut was the lowest ever in this tournament because of the calm, wind-free conditions.

O Uresti (-2)	M Dawson (-2)	M Bradley (-2)	J Sindelar (-2)
D Frost (-2)	G Day (-2)	B Mayfair (-2)	G Kraft (-2)
D Stockton (-1)	S Lowery (-1)	T Armour III (-1)	D Hart (E)
B Glasson (E)	S Kendall (E)	C A Spence (E)	T Scherrer (E)
S Elkington (+1)	K Gibson (+1)	C Stadler (+1)	C Paulson (+1)
B Hughes (+3)	J Cook (+3)	S Dunlap (+3)	S Stricker (+4)
M Goggin (+5)	J Daly (+7)		

N Lancaster (73) withdrew after R1.
J Parnevik (food poisoning) withdrew during R1.

ROUND BY ROUND LEADERBOARD

FIRST ROUND

J FURYK	7 under
H Frazar	7 under
V Singh	7 under
B Lietzke	7 under
N Price	6 under
F Langham	6 under
B Tway	6 under
B Langer	6 under
P Mickelson	6 under
B Faxon	6 under

SECOND ROUND

F Langham	15 under
J FURYK	12 under
S Ames	12 under
S Maruyama	12 under
V Singh	12 under
S Hoch	11 under

THIRD ROUND

F Langham	19 under
J FURYK	16 under
S Ames	15 under
S Maruyama	14 under
N Price	13 under
R Damron	12 under
S Verplank	12 under
R Allenby	12 under
B Lietzke	12 under
H Frazar	12 under

FINAL ROUND

J FURYK	23 under
F Langham	21 under
N Price	18 under
D Duval	17 under
S Maruyama	17 under

Still, warm air without any breeze created conditions for extremely low scoring in the first two rounds.

The wind got up during R3. "It was a little tougher," according to Jim Furyk.

RESULTS IN OTHER MARKETS

Sunderland's created a Top Non-American market.

1	9/1	Nick Price
2	20/1	Shigeki Maruyama
3	20/1	Stephen Ames
4	66/1	Ed Fryatt (from Rochdale!)

PUNTERS' POINTS

● Jim Furyk was a generous 33/1 with Hills given that he is Florida-based, was 8th in the driving accuracy stats, had shot a course-record 62 here in 1998, on his last visit, when his final three rounds were the best in the tournament.

● Here Franklin Langham, 6 ahead with 7 holes to play, lost his swing and his nerve and slowly but surely Furyk caught him up to take the lead at the 17th before he clinched his fifth victory with a brilliant final-hole birdie.

● Nick Price, however, would surely have won had his putting even half-matched his brilliant approach play.

● David Duval cancelled a holiday to play here and after he'd talked up his chances he was heavily backed. A poor R1 put paid to his chance.

● Apart from Furyk only two players shot all four rounds in the 60s — T6th Russ Cochran and T6th Scott Verplank.

● Once again Stephen Ames let a strong Sunday position slip. 3rd after R3, a disappointing 72 in R4 moved him down to 8th place.

1999 RESULT

1	33/1	Steve Elkington
2	125/1	Greg Kraft
T3	66/1	David Toms
T3	100/1	Tommy Armour III
T3	125/1	Jay Haas
T3	fav 11/1	Ernie Els
T3	125/1	Scott Dunlap

1998 RESULT

1	80/1	Michael Bradley
T2	66/1	Billy Mayfair
T2	66/1	John Huston
T4	33/1	Vijay Singh
T4	150/1	Mike Brisky
T4	50/1	Stewart Cink

WINNERS IN THE LAST TEN YEARS

1991	Rocco Mediate	1996	Greg Norman
1992	Raymond Floyd	1997	Steve Elkington
1993	Greg Norman	1998	Michael Bradley
1994	John Huston	1999	Steve Elkington
1995	Nick Faldo	2000	Jim Furyk

PUNTERS' GUIDE

● Since the course re-design the best records are held by

	2000	1999	1998	1997
Nick Price	3	10	36	2
Jim Furyk	W	DNP	9	45
Jay Haas	21	3	36	13
Jesper Parnevik	W/D R1	15	30	28
Bob Tway	15	15	9	9
Ernie Els	15	3	DNP	MC

● Florida-based Jim Furyk continued the pattern of Doral winners being Florida residents. Franklin Langham (Georgia-born and -based) however showed that non-Florida players can play well, too. However the general rule remains — always back Florida-based players.

● Your outright selection should have

> Proven course form

> Be a Florida-based player (please see Part 1 and Player Profiles)

> Solid early-season stats for accuracy

● Player profiles which refer to this tournament include Steve Elkington, Bob Tway, Nick Price, John Huston, Robert Allenby, Greg Chalmers, Vijay Singh and Ernie Els.

THE HONDA CLASSIC

Date	9th - 12th March
Course	TPC at Heron Bay, Coral Springs, Florida
Par	72
Yardage	7,268
First Prize	$522,000
Total Purse	$2.9 million

THE TOURNAMENT

Started in 1972 this event moved to Heron Bay in 1997, so this was the fourth successive year that the course was being used. Only six of the world's top 30 players played this year.

THE COURSE

The course is flat, long and dull, with over a hundred very large, unlipped bunkers. It has large Bermuda greens. It has five par 5s with only two usually reachable in two shots. The winds can blow so this track can play tough and demand patience. The par 3 (222 yards) 15th and the par 4 final hole are both very demanding.

2000 ODDS

fav	11/1	Davis Love	66/1	Aaron Baddeley
	12/1	Vijay Singh (DC)	66/1	Mark Brooks
	14/1	Jim Furyk (PWW)	66/1	Kenny Perry
	20/1	Stuart Appleby	66/1	Chris diMarco
	25/1	Hal Sutton	66/1	Rory Sabbatini
	33/1	Steve Flesch	66/1	Ted Tryba
	33/1	Mark Calcavecchia	80/1*	Glen Day
	40/1	Mike Weir	80/1*	Fred Funk
	50/1*	Carlos Franco	80/1	Tom Byrum
	50/1*	Bernhard Langer	80/1*	Jim Carter
	50/1	Tim Herron	80/1*	David Sutherland
	50/1	Craig Parry	80/1	Bradley Hughes
	50/1	Steve Pate	80/1	Ed Fryatt
	50/1	Stephen Ames	80/1	J P Hayes
	50/1	Dudley Hart		

2000 RESULT

1	50/1	**Dudley Hart**	**65 69 70 65 269**
T2	150/1	**Kevin Wentworth**	**67 67 71 65 270**
T2	80/1	**J P Hayes**	**65 67 68 70 270**
T4	14/1	**Jim Furyk**	**68 71 65 67 271**
T4	150/1	**Brian Gay**	**65 70 67 69 271**

6	J Kaye	69 66 67 70 272			G Kraft	69 68 72 70 279
T7	R Damron	70 68 69 66 273			S Gotsche	70 67 72 70 279
	H Sutton	67 66 72 68 273			L Mattiace	67 69 73 70 279
	M Calcavecchia	66 71 69 67 273			G Hnatiuk	69 71 70 69 279
	R Fehr	66 68 71 68 273			J Cook	68 72 70 69 279
	C Franco	65 69 71 68 273			S Dunlap	68 70 72 69 279
T12	M Brisky	65 72 71 66 274			B Jobe	67 70 73 69 279
	B Henninger	65 73 70 66 274			C DiMarco	68 71 72 68 279
	S Appleby	68 69 68 69 274		T50	O Uresti	70 69 70 71 280
	R Gamez	67 70 67 70 274			V Singh	70 69 69 72 280
T16	B Elder	70 67 71 67 275			K Gibson	70 69 69 72 280
	R Sabbatini	68 68 70 69 275			C Barlow	67 69 71 73 280
	J Daly	69 70 67 69 275			Joel Edwards	68 70 72 70 280
T19	J Caron	69 70 70 67 276			E Booker	68 71 72 69 280
	S Kendall	65 69 73 69 276			C Perks	70 68 73 69 280
	P Jordan	66 74 68 68 276		T57	D Peoples	67 72 71 71 281
	M Weir	67 69 70 70 276			A Baddeley (am)	69 68 73 71 281
	S Flesch	69 68 69 70 276			G Chalmers	69 66 71 75 281
	M Hulbert	68 68 70 70 276			B Fabel	72 68 71 70 281
	David Sutherland	67 66 72 71 276		T61	J Ogilvie	69 67 71 75 282
	S Ames	69 66 70 71 276			J L Lewis	68 72 70 72 282
	D Love	69 68 75 64 276			J Buha	67 69 74 72 282
T28	H Frazar	67 70 71 69 277			B Heintz	68 68 74 72 282
	C Riley	66 71 71 69 277			J Durant	67 71 73 71 282
	M Gogel	65 71 73 68 277		T66	C Martin	66 72 70 75 283
	Kenny Perry	66 70 71 70 277			Tom Byrum	66 71 73 73 283
	B Langer	70 69 68 70 277			S Murphy	67 70 76 70 283
	G Nicklaus	72 67 68 70 277			B McCallister	68 72 74 69 283
	Carl Paulson	69 71 67 70 277		70	M Clark II	68 72 72 72 284
	T Herron	67 70 73 67 277		T71	J Benedetti	69 70 75 71 285
T36	S Pate	68 72 69 69 278			M Dawson	67 69 78 71 285
	J Williamson	69 70 70 69 278		T73	T Tolles	68 71 71 76 286
	M Brooks	67 70 72 69 278			G Waite	69 70 72 75 286
	P Goydos	66 72 70 70 278			E Aubrey	70 70 74 72 286
	Jerry Smith	70 70 70 68 278		76	R Howison	72 67 72 76 287
T41	T Tryba	68 71 70 70 279				

The main players to miss the cut (made at 4 under) were:–

F Langham (-3)	C Parry (-3)	T Pernice Jr (-3)	G Day (-3)
J Carter (-3)	F Nobilo (-3)	N Lancaster (-3)	B May (-3)
F Funk (-2)	D Frost (-2)	R Freeman (-2)	M Bradley (-2)
E Toledo (-2)	J Kelly (-1)	B Hughes (-1)	O Browne (-1)
E Fryatt (-1)	M Goggin (E)	R Karlsson (+2)	D Dunakey (+2)

ROUND BY ROUND LEADERBOARD

FIRST ROUND		SECOND ROUND	
D HART	7 under	J P Hayes	12 under
S Kendall	7 under	D Sutherland	11 under
M Gogel	7 under	H Sutton	11 under
C Franco	7 under	D HART	10 under
J P Hayes	7 under	C Franco	10 under
B Henninger	7 under	K Wentworth	10 under
M Brisky	7 under	R Fehr	10 under
B Gay	7 under	S Kendall	10 under

THIRD ROUND		FINAL ROUND	
J P Hayes	16 under	D HART	19 under
J Kaye	14 under	K Wentworth	18 under
B Gay	14 under	J P Hayes	18 under
J Furyk	12 under	B Gay	17 under
R Gamez	12 under	J Furyk	17 under
D HART	12 under		

The weather was so benign over the first two rounds that only seventeen of the 144-man field were over par. The cut was made at 4 under, the lowest this year on the tour.

RESULTS IN OTHER MARKETS

Corals and Sunderland opened a Top Non-American market

Corals			Sunderlands		
1	13/2	Carlos Franco	1	9/1	Carlos Franco
2	5/1	Stuart Appleby	2	9/2	Stuart Appleby
T3	10/1	Mike Weir	3	20/1	Rory Sabbatini
T3	16/1	Stephen Ames	T4	9/1	Mike Weir
			T4	9/1	Stephen Ames

Please note: South African-born Rory Sabbatini is treated as a non-American by Sunderlands but not by Corals.

PUNTERS' POINTS

● Another thrilling Sunday night on Sky TV as Dudley Hart birdied the last 4 holes to win in a photo-finish. Living just 20 minutes from the course he proved once more just how important home advantage is in pro-golf.

● Spare a thought for Brian Gay whose only dropped shot in the final two rounds came at the last hole. However after that finish he was shown a video of the previous green where he had waited 15 seconds for his ball to fall in the hole and so he had to add a shot. That penalty cost him more than he won in 1999!

● Jonathan Kaye in the final group for the fourth time couldn't find the quality to post a top 5 finish. His turn will come.

- Dudley Hart, a 270-yard driver ranked T62nd for driving distance, proved that although length off the tee can be important (as it was for Vijay Singh last year) it is by no means essential here.
- Nevertheless, John Daly, No. 1 for driving distance at 302 yards, has a solid record here — 4th 1998, 27th 1999, and T16th this year.
- The only player to shoot all four rounds in the 60s was Stuart Appleby, the course specialist, who nevertheless could only finish T12th.

1999 RESULT			1998 RESULT		
1	25/1	Vijay Singh	1	40/1	Mark Calcavecchia
2	40/1	Payne Stewart	2	25/1	Vijay Singh
T3	150/1	Doug Dunakey	3	20/1	Colin Montgomerie
T3	100/1	Carlos Franco	T4	50/1	John Daly
T3	20/1	Mark O'Meara	T4	80/1	Jeff Maggert
T3	200/1	Eric Booker	T4	66/1	Stuart Appleby

WINNERS IN THE LAST TEN YEARS

1991	Steve Pate		1996	Tim Herron
1992	Corey Pavin		1997	Stuart Appleby
1993	Fred Couples		1998	Mark Calcavecchia
1994	Nick Price		1999	Vijay Singh
1995	Mark O'Meara		2000	Dudley Hart

PUNTERS' GUIDE

- After four years we can now say with some confidence that course form is important.

Course form

- > 2000 winner Dudley Hart — T9th 1999: T30th 1998
- > 1999 winner Vijay Singh — 2nd 1998: T30th 1997
- > 1998 winner Mark Calcavecchia — T37th 1997

- Players with a consistent record at Heron Bay include:-
  - > Dudley Hart — Won 2000: T9th 1999: T30th 1998
  - > Mark Calcavecchia — T7th 2000: Won 1998
  - > Stuart Appleby — T12th 2000: T9th 1999: 4th 1998: Won 1997
  - > Vijay Singh — Won 1999: 2nd 1998
  - > Jim Furyk — T4th 2000: T12th 1998 (only 2 starts)
  - > Steve Flesch — T19th 2000: T15th 1998 (only 2 starts)
  - > Carlos Franco — T7th 2000: T3rd 1999 (only 2 starts)

- Go for a player with three key characteristics:-
  - > Proven course form

> An ability to play longer-distance shots from sand
> A solid ball striker

● However please remember that in the last couple of years six of the eleven players finishing in the top 5 (or T5th) have started at or over 80/1.

● Players whose profiles refer to this tournament include Mark Calcavecchia, Stuart Appleby, Carlos Franco, Jim Furyk, Steve Flesch, Hal Sutton, Chris Riley, Doug Barron, Rory Sabbatini and Dudley Hart.

THE BAY HILL INVITATIONAL

Date	16th - 19th March
Course	Bay Hill, Orlando, Florida
Par	72
Yardage	7,208
First Prize	$504,000
Total Purse	$2.8 million

THE TOURNAMENT

Arnold Palmer's Bay Hill course has been the home of this tournament since 1979. It attracts a strong field as players prepare for next week's 'fifth major', the Players Championship.

THE COURSE

This is a long narrowish tough course which can be exceptionally severe, particularly in the afternoons, when the winds blow. The Bermuda greens are large and undulating. The recent lengthening of the course has obviously favoured the longer hitters. Players can run up some big numbers at the par 5 6th e.g. Daly 18 (1998), Mickelson 10 (2000).

2000 ODDS

fav	9/2	Tiger Woods	66/1	John Huston
	18/1	Davis Love	66/1	Shigeki Maruyama
	20/1	Ernie Els	66/1	David Toms
	25/1	Phil Mickelson	66/1	Mike Weir
	28/1	Colin Montgomerie	66/1	Chris Perry
	33/1	Tom Lehman	66/1	Stewart Cink
	33/1	Vijay Singh	66/1	Scott Hoch
	33/1	Sergio Garcia	80/1*	Steve Flesch
	33/1	Hal Sutton	80/1	Jeff Sluman
	40/1	Lee Westwood	80/1*	Kirk Triplett
	40/1	Carlos Franco	80/1	Brent Geiberger
	50/1	Darren Clarke	80/1	Lee Janzen
	50/1*	Stuart Appleby	80/1	Bernhard Langer
	66/1*	Robert Damron	80/1	Steve Pate
	66/1	Dudley Hart (PWW)	80/1	Loren Roberts

2000 RESULT

1	fav 9/2	**Tiger Woods**	**69 64 67 70 270**
2	18/1	**Davis Love**	**72 67 63 72 274**
3	125/1	**Skip Kendall**	**70 67 71 67 275**
T4	150/1	**Neal Lancaster**	**70 68 69 70 277**
T4	80/1	**Loren Roberts**	**71 69 70 67 277**

6	S Cink	71 67 70 70 278			S Dunlap	76 68 69 74 287
T7	M Weir	70 64 72 73 279			Robin Freeman	74 70 69 74 287
	J Williamson	72 70 69 68 279			S Garcia	75 68 70 74 287
9	W Austin	71 67 71 71 280		T46	M Calcavecchia	73 69 69 77 288
T10	B Chamblee	76 68 68 69 281			E Fryatt	72 72 73 71 288
	P Goydos	69 69 72 71 281			J Huston	72 64 75 77 288
	T Herron	72 71 67 71 281			L Janzen	72 69 72 75 288
	B Mayfair	71 69 69 72 281			P Mickelson	70 67 73 78 288
T14	E Els	72 68 74 68 282			C Pavin	72 70 71 75 288
	S Hoch	72 71 67 72 282		T52	G Day	75 69 72 73 289
	J Kaye	69 69 72 72 282			F Lickliter	73 71 73 72 289
	T Purtzer	75 67 69 71 282			M Nicolette	69 75 74 71 289
T18	S Flesch	70 65 74 74 283			Joe Ozaki	70 74 71 74 289
	B Langer	75 69 71 68 283			T Scherrer	71 73 69 76 289
	S Maruyama	72 70 71 70 283		T57	Joel Edwards	76 67 76 71 290
	D Toms	69 69 72 73 283			S Jones	72 68 77 73 290
T22	B Andrade	73 68 69 74 284			L Mattiace	72 70 72 76 290
	T Lehman	72 71 68 73 284		T60	C Parry	71 73 74 73 291
	S Lowery	70 70 69 75 284			D Pride	73 71 75 72 291
	M O'Meara	70 72 73 69 284			T Tryba	72 70 68 81 291
	T Pernice Jr	71 68 73 72 284			J Van de Velde	72 67 71 81 291
	K Triplett	74 69 72 69 284		T64	S Appleby	70 72 76 74 292
	L Westwood	72 68 71 73 284			B Elder	74 69 74 75 292
T29	R Allenby	71 71 70 73 285			S Pate	70 74 72 76 292
	O Browne	74 67 68 76 285			D A Weibring	72 70 74 76 292
	Dudley Hart	69 71 71 74 285		T68	M Gogel	70 72 70 81 293
	J L Lewis	72 69 71 73 285			David Sutherland	72 70 76 75 293
	C Montgomerie	72 71 69 73 285		T70	B Glasson	73 70 72 79 294
	Dennis Paulson	73 71 68 73 285			J P Hayes	70 73 73 78 294
	V Singh	68 73 73 71 285			B Jobe	73 70 75 76 294
	H Sutton	71 71 71 72 285		73	B Geiberger	69 69 74 83 295
	D Waldorf	68 72 72 73 285		T74	B Cheesman	71 70 78 78 297
T38	S Ames	73 66 71 76 286			B Watts	73 71 74 79 297
	W Grady	72 65 73 76 286		T76	R Gamez	71 73 79 75 298
	R Mediate	70 68 73 75 286			M Hulbert	71 71 74 82 298
	Chris Perry	71 73 69 73 286		78	J Daly	72 72 75 87 306
T42	D Clarke	72 68 72 75 287				

The main players to miss the cut (made at level) were:–

F Nobilo (+1)	J Sindelar (+1)	F Allem (+1)	N Faldo (+2)
J Sluman (+2)	P Harrington (+2)	C Franco (+2)	K Sutherland (+2)
P Jacobsen (+3)	S McCarron (+3)	J Carter (+3)	R Beem (+3)
S Gump (+4)	J Haas (+4)	R Damron (+4)	C DiMarco (+4)
N Begay (+4)	G Kraft (+4)	T Bjorn (+4)	R Goosen (+4)
A Baddeley (am) (+5)			

Fuzzy Zoeller withdrew after 74 in R1.

Rory Sabbatini (74) was disqualified after R1.

ROUND BY ROUND LEADERBOARD

FIRST ROUND		SECOND ROUND	
V Singh	4 under	T WOODS	11 under
D Waldorf	4 under	M Weir	10 under
P Goydos	3 under	S Flesch	9 under
T WOODS	3 under	J Huston	8 under
B Geiberger	3 under	W Grady	7 under
D Hart	3 under	S Kendall	7 under
D Toms	3 under	P Mickelson	7 under
J Kaye	3 under		
M Nicolette	3 under		

THIRD ROUND		FINAL ROUND	
T WOODS	16 under	T WOODS	18 under
D Love	14 under	D Love	14 under
M Weir	10 under	S Kendall	13 under
N Lancaster	9 under	L Roberts	11 under
S Cink	8 under	N Lancaster	11 under
S Kendall	8 under		

RESULTS IN OTHER MARKETS

Top European Player (Corals, Hills, Sunderlands)

1	10/1	Bernhard Langer	
2	7/2	Lee Westwood	
3	7/2	Colin Montgomerie	1/4 odds 1-3

Top Australasian Player (Corals)

1	jt fav 7/2	Robert Allenby	
2	20/1	Wayne Grady	
3	jt fav 7/2	Craig Parry	1/5 odds 1-3

Top Non-American Player (Corals)

1	fav 6/1	Ernie Els	
2	16/1	Bernhard Langer	
3	16/1	Shigeki Maruyama	
4	9/1	Lee Westwood	1/4 odds 1-4

PUNTERS' POINTS

● Woods's victory was quite remarkable.

> He has now completed a full year with 18th his worst finish in a stroke-play event.

> This win was his tenth in his last sixteen tournaments.

> It was the thirteenth consecutive time on tour that Tiger has had at least a share of a 54-hole lead and gone on to win.

● Davis Love now has an 0-5 record against Woods since late 1996 when Woods notched his first pro victory.

● The tendency for Phil Mickelson and John Daly to lose concentration in R4 when not in contention was well illustrated here as Daly shot 87 (!) and 'Lefty' shot 78 including a 10 at the par 5 6th after hitting three balls into the water!!

● The criteria for Woods to have his very best chances for a victory were all met here, viz:

> Fresh from a break

> Par 72 including four par 5s (he was 12 under on the par 5s this week)

> His dad is fairly fit

So despite the fact he had poor course form last year, and was 77th (yes, 77th) on the putting stats, his chance was clear.

1999 RESULT				**1998 RESULT**		
1	80/1	Tim Herron		1	20/1	Ernie Els
won at the second play-off hole				T2	66/1	Jeff Maggert
2	80/1*	Tom Lehman		T2	100/1	Bob Estes
3	18/1	Davis Love		T4	40/1	Bernhard Langer
4	125/1	Robert Damron		T4	40/1	Mark Calcavecchia
T5	100/1	Craig Parry				
T5	50/1*	Scott Hoch				
T5	150/1	Dicky Pride				
T5	33/1	Phil Mickelson				
T5	66/1*	Bob Estes				
T5	100/1	Brandel Chamblee				

WINNERS IN THE LAST TEN YEARS

1991	Andrew Magee (54 holes)	1996	Paul Goydos
1992	Fred Couples	1997	Phil Mickelson
1993	Ben Crenshaw	1998	Ernie Els
1994	Loren Roberts	1999	Tim Herron
1995	Loren Roberts	2000	Tiger Woods

PUNTERS' GUIDE

● Last year I suggested that Bay Hill course form may not be a critical factor. Tiger's victory here seems to emphasise the point:-

Year	Winner	Bay Hill form (latest on right)
> 2000	Tiger Woods	9/13/56
> 1999	Tim Herron	MC/6/MC
≥ 1998	Ernie Els	MC/42/42/MC
> 1997	Phil Mickelson	-/MC/MC

● The lengthening of the course has undoubtedly given the longer hitters an advantage over the last couple of years. In 1999 Tim Herron was 9th in driving distance and this year Davis Love (6th) and Tiger Woods (10th) were both in the top 10.

● Last year's advice stands. It was to go for a player

> with a proven record on the Bermuda greens

> who is in the top 25 for driving distance

> in sound form

● Players whose profiles refer to this tournament include Brandel Chamblee, Davis Love, Tiger Woods, Robert Damron, Bernhard Langer, Robert Allenby, Bob Estes, Craig Parry and Tim Herron.

THE PLAYERS CHAMPIONSHIP

Date	23rd - 26th March
Course	TPC at Sawgrass, Ponte Vedre Beach, Florida
Par	72
Yardage	6,950
First Prize	$1.08 million
Total Purse	$6 million

THE TOURNAMENT

This is the 'fifth' major which has been held at Sawgrass since 1982. This year, as usual, it had a very strong field with only the ever-absent Jumbo Ozaki missing from the world's top 50 players. It is the final tournament on 'the Florida Swing'. The venue is also the home of the USPGA tour offices. There is wall-to-wall TV coverage on Sky.

THE COURSE

Sawgrass above all demands accuracy off the tee and the fairway as the rough is very severe and water is a factor throughout. The Bermuda greens are small (three quarters of the tour's average size), undulating and lightning fast. The signature hole is par 3 17th which is on an island green surrounded by water.

2000 ODDS

fav	7/2	Tiger Woods (PWW)	66/1	Stuart Appleby
	12/1	David Duval (DC)	66/1	Darren Clarke
	20/1	Davis Love	66/1	Scott Hoch
	25/1	Ernie Els	66/1	Dudley Hart
	28/1	Jim Furyk	80/1	Stewart Cink
	33/1	Phil Mickelson	80/1	Steve Flesch
	33/1	Lee Westwood	80/1	John Huston
	33/1	Colin Montgomerie	80/1	Mark Calcavecchia
	33/1	Nick Price	80/1	Steve Elkington (did not start)
	33/1	Jesper Parnevik	80/1	Carlos Franco
	40/1	Tom Lehman	80/1	David Toms
	40/1	Hal Sutton	80/1	Lee Janzen
	40/1	Fred Couples	80/1	J M Olazabal
	40/1	Vijay Singh	80/1	Greg Norman
	50/1	Sergio Garcia	80/1*	Kirk Triplett
	50/1	Justin Leonard	80/1	Skip Kendall
	66/1	Mike Weir		

2000 RESULT

1	40/1	Hal Sutton	69 69 69 71 278
2	fav 7/2	Tiger Woods	71 71 66 71 279
T3	200/1*	Robert Damron	78 70 66 70 284
T3	200/1*	Scott Dunlap	73 70 71 70 284
T3	100/1	Jeff Maggert	77 68 71 68 284
T3	33/1	Colin Montgomerie	75 69 70 70 284
T3	33/1	Nick Price	73 71 73 67 284

8	T Lehman	71 68 72 74 285	
T9	G Chalmers	71 75 69 71 286	
	L Janzen	70 73 70 73 286	
	L Mattiace	70 72 73 71 286	
	M O'Meara	75 74 70 67 286	
T13	J Carter	73 71 72 71 287	
	D Duval	75 73 70 69 287	
	F Funk	74 73 68 72 287	
	S Hoch	73 75 68 71 287	
T17	P Azinger	75 69 70 74 288	
	B Mayfair	70 74 73 71 288	
	J Sluman	75 71 66 76 288	
T20	E Els	73 69 72 75 289	
	S Verplank	75 74 68 72 289	
T22	S Appleby	72 77 71 70 290	
	T Bjorn	76 73 72 69 290	
	G Kraft	77 72 70 71 290	
	J Leonard	71 76 69 74 290	
	C Parry	70 74 69 77 290	
T27	C Franco	73 73 73 72 291	
	S Jones	80 70 72 69 291	
	Joe Ozaki	70 77 73 71 291	
	S Pate	76 74 68 73 291	
	Kenny Perry	70 77 70 74 291	
	E Toledo	75 74 72 70 291	
T33	S Cink	75 73 69 75 292	
	F Couples	77 73 73 69 292	
	H Frazar	77 70 72 73 292	
	Chris Perry	76 70 71 75 292	
	V Singh	75 73 74 70 292	
T38	B Fabel	70 74 75 74 293	
	S Flesch	79 71 72 71 293	
	D Toms	77 72 72 72 293	
	O Uresti	71 68 80 74 293	
T42	S Ames	72 72 75 75 294	
	S Gump	72 75 73 74 294	
	J P Hayes	73 76 71 74 294	
	J Kelly	79 70 73 72 294	
	B Langer	70 76 75 73 294	
	K Triplett	75 72 74 73 294	
T48	J Daly	77 73 74 71 295	
	F Lickliter	75 74 71 75 295	
	D Love	73 75 72 75 295	
	C Riley	73 77 75 70 295	
	L Westwood	77 73 72 73 295	
T53	R Allenby	73 71 77 75 296	
	N Faldo	73 76 76 71 296	
	G Norman	75 71 73 77 296	
	David Sutherland	75 74 71 76 296	
T57	C Barlow	71 76 75 75 297	
	M Brooks	72 75 71 79 297	
	D Frost	78 69 78 72 297	
	B Glasson	74 72 80 71 297	
T61	W Austin	77 72 71 78 298	
	Russ Cochran	77 73 71 77 298	
	J Furyk	72 72 75 79 298	
	C Pavin	72 73 74 79 298	
	K Wentworth	74 72 75 77 298	
T66	F Allem	75 65 82 77 299	
	D Barron	72 74 76 77 299	
	B Chamblee	74 74 73 78 299	
	T Kite	75 72 77 75 299	
	S Lowery	76 74 71 78 299	
	S McCarron	78 67 77 77 299	
	I Woosnam	76 74 70 79 299	
T73	D Forsman	77 73 75 75 300	
	P Lawrie	76 74 71 79 300	
	T Tryba	75 71 80 74 300	
	B Watts	77 71 74 78 300	
T77	R Black	74 76 70 81 301	
	O Browne	77 73 71 80 301	
	B Faxon	79 71 76 75 301	
	N Henke	78 70 76 77 301	

The cut was made at 6 over par and the players to miss the cut were:–

7 over	S Kendall	N Begay	J Parnevik	K Sutherland
	C DiMarco	D Clarke	J L Lewis	J Cook
	B Tway			
8 over	T Scherrer	R Goosen	M Wiebe	C Raulerson
9 over	M A Jimenez	B Geiberger	T Pernice Jr	T Purtzer
	L Mize	J Sindelar		

10 over	J Kaye	P Mickelson	J M Olazabal	B Andrade
	L Roberts	T Byrum	J Van de Velde	S Garcia
	J Delsing	G Day	R Mediate	S Stricker
	J D Blake			
11 over	T Herron	G Hjerstedt	M Calcavecchia	D Pride
	P Goydos	M Reid		
12 over	B Cheesman	E Booker	M Gogel	J Huston
	R Beem			
13 over	B Hughes	J Haas	T Dodds	R Sabbatini
	A Magee			
14 over	B Crenshaw	T Armour III	B Henninger	D Waldorf
15 over	W Grady	P Stankowski	D Paulson	B Estes
16 over	M Weir	T Tolles	J Maginnes	
17 over	C Stadler			
18 over	F Langham			
26 over	M Brisky			

Dudley Hart (79) and Shigeki Maruyama (81) withdrew after R1.

ROUND BY ROUND LEADERBOARD

FIRST ROUND

H SUTTON	3 under
Joe Ozaki	2 under
K Perry	2 under
L Mattiace	2 under
B Mayfair	2 under
L Janzen	2 under
B Langer	2 under
B Fabel	2 under
C Parry	2 under

SECOND ROUND

H SUTTON	6 under
T Lehman	5 under
O Uresti	5 under
F Allem	4 under
E Els	2 under
T Woods	2 under
L Mattiace	2 under

THIRD ROUND

H SUTTON	9 under
T Woods	8 under
T Lehman	5 under
J Sluman	4 under
C Parry	3 under
L Janzen	3 under

WHEN PLAY SUSPENDED SUNDAY EVENING

H SUTTON	10 under thru 11
T Woods	7 under thru 11
N Price	4 under finished
J Maggert	4 under thru 17
C Montgomerie	4 under thru 14
L Janzen	4 under thru 13
T Lehman	4 under thru 12

FINAL ROUND

H SUTTON	10 under
T Woods	9 under
R Damron	4 under
S Dunlap	4 under
J Maggert	4 under
C Montgomerie	4 under
N Price	4 under

Conditions were the worst ever for an opening round at Sawgrass on Thursday because of a gusty swirling wind and rock-hard, lightning-fast greens. Twenty-one players had still to complete their first round at close of play. The average score was 76.2, and the worst eclectic (not gas!) score 120!

On Sunday play was suspended due to lightning with twenty players still on the course.

The tournament was completed on Monday.

RESULTS IN OTHER MARKETS

Top European Player

1	5/1	Colin Montgomerie	
2	33/1*	Thomas Bjorn	
3	14/1	Bernhard Langer	1/4 odds 1-3

Top Rest of the World Player (i.e. excl. US and European players)

1	6/1	Nick Price	
2	50/1	Greg Chalmers	
3	fav 9/4	Ernie Els	Surrey 1/5 odds 1-4
T4	14/1	Stuart Appleby	Stanley 1/4 odds 1-4
T4	25/1	Craig Parry	Generally 1/4 odds 1-3

European players

T3	Colin Montgomerie
T22	Thomas Bjorn
T42	Bernhard Langer
T48	Lee Westwood
T66	Ian Woosnam
T73	Paul Lawrie

Missed the cut

J Parnevik	D Clarke	R Goosen	M A Jimenez
J M Olazabal	S Garcia	J Van de Velde	

PUNTERS' POINTS

● Hal Sutton showed the vital importance of mental skills in top-class competitive golf. Before the tournament had started he had stressed –

> that in the Nissan Open's first two rounds this year he had played alongside Tiger and 'beaten' him.

> So if it ever came to a Sunday head to head he could do so again.

He meant it and completely focussed he won, leading from start to finish just as he had done when he won the 1983 USPGA.

● Head to head with Tiger he never flinched and despite Woods's late charge he held his nerve to finish par-par on the dangerous final two holes....and Sutton was to receive a superb sporting thumbs up from Woods after his brilliant approach to the last.

So 'the next Jack Nicklaus' had been beaten by the 'last next Jack Nicklaus'!

● Players who 'finished fast' this year may be worth noting in future. They included :-

	Final Position	Last 3 Rounds
Steve Jones	T27th	5 under
Robert Damron	T3rd	10 (!) under (late tee time round one)
Colin Montgomerie	T3rd	7 under (9 under last 63 holes after a late round one tee time)
Jeff Maggert	T3rd	9 under

● Greg Chalmers, on his Players' debut, played superbly to finish T9th. He came to Sawgrass 28th in the All Round stats, and 30th in Greens In Regulation. Well written up in last year's book (p537) he's surely got a big future!

● Outside the front two only five players showed real consistency with every round no worse than 1 over par. They were :-

> Scott Dunlap	T3rd
> Lee Janzen	T9th
> Len Mattiace	T9th
> Jim Carter	T13th
> (and unnoticed) Carlos Franco	T27th

1999 RESULT

1	fav 10/1	David Duval
2	125/1	Scott Gump
3	33/1	Nick Price
T4	66/1	Hal Sutton
T4	33/1	Fred Couples

1998 RESULT

1	50/1	Justin Leonard
T2	33/1	Tom Lehman
T2	200/1	Glen Day
4	40/1	Mark Calcavecchia
T5	50/1	Lee Westwood
T5	40/1	Scott Hoch
T5	200/1	Len Mattiace

WINNERS IN THE LAST TEN YEARS

1991	Steve Elkington	1996	Fred Couples
1992	Davis Love	1997	Steve Elkington
1993	Nick Price	1998	Justin Leonard
1994	Greg Norman	1999	David Duval
1995	Lee Janzen	2000	Hal Sutton

PUNTERS' GUIDE

● This is undoubtedly a tournament for proven successful players

> Every winner in the nineties, and now in 2000, was a previous winner.

> Sutton was the tenth straight champion who had been a member of either a Presidents Cup or Ryder Cup team in the nineties.

> The last seven winners had all won a major and had at least two tour wins.

● Sawgrass demands above all else accuracy off the tee and especially with the irons into the smallest greens on the regular tour (except for Pebble Beach). So it is not surprising to find that accuracy rather than putting brilliance is the key.

	Driving Accuracy	GIR	Putting
Hal Sutton	4th at 81%	8th at 74%	159th
Tiger Woods	12th at 76%	T9th at 73.6%	T39th

> None of the top 20 players in the putting stats finished in the top 30! However of the top 20 players in the driving accuracy stats five (Sutton, Funk, Woods, Verplank and Hoch) finished in the top 20.

● The Sawgrass guidelines given in recent volumes stand the test of time. So in making a pre-tournament outright selection go for a player with five key characteristics:-

> A proven winner

> Patience

> Made the cut at Sawgrass the previous year

> Has a high driving accuracy ranking

> Made the cut in his last tournament

● Sawgrass, being a tough, demanding, accuracy-based test, is a very difficult track, on which to play 'catch up'. So one key pointer

> In ten of the last eleven years the ultimate winner was in the first 3 (or T3rd) after the opening round. By applying the above guidelines and favouring any top 3 player after R1 who had an opening afternoon tee time you can probably chisel out a very solid bet.

● The best recent course records are held by the following players (with the latest result on the right).

> Hal Sutton   4 - Won

> Tiger Woods   10 - 2

> Tom Lehman   6-2-MC-8

> Scott Hoch   2-5-6-13

> Ernie Els   10-11-17-20

> Lee Westwood 5-6-48

> Nick Price   8-3-3

> David Duval   18-Won-13

● Players whose profiles refer to this tournament include Scott Hoch, Tom Lehman, Greg Chalmers, Lee Westwood, Colin Montgomerie, Len Mattiace, Joe Ozaki, Mark O'Meara, Nick Price and David Duval.

THE BELL SOUTH CLASSIC

Date	1st - 4th April
Course	TPC at Sugarloaf, Duluth, Georgia
Par	72
Yardage	7,259
First Prize	£504,000
Total Purse	$2.8 million

THE TOURNAMENT

This is a well-established tournament that was played at the Atlanta Country Club from 1967 to 1996. It moved to the Sugarloaf course in 1997, so this was the fourth year that it played host to the Bell South.

THE COURSE

The Greg Norman-designed Sugarloaf course favours the big hitters as the fairways are very wide on this long course. The greens are bentgrass. Water comes into play on ten holes. The course is very tiring as it is set in rolling undulating hills with huge distances between greens and tees e.g. from the 7th green to the 8th tee is 225 yards.

2000 ODDS

fav	11/2	David Duval (DC)	66/1*	Steve Elkington
	16/1	Nick Price	66/1	Scott Dunlap
	22/1	Phil Mickelson	66/1	Robert Allenby
	28/1	Justin Leonard	66/1	J M Olazabal
	28/1	Stewart Cink	66/1	Paul Azinger
	33/1	Fred Couples	80/1	Steve Stricker
	33/1	Lee Janzen	80/1	Brent Geiberger
	33/1	John Huston	80/1*	Kenny Perry
	40/1	Steve Flesch	80/1*	Bob Tway
	50/1	Mark Calcavecchia	80/1*	Billy Mayfair
	50/1	Greg Norman	80/1	Scott McCarron
	50/1	David Toms	80/1	Steve Jones
	50/1	Kirk Triplett	80/1	Retief Goosen
	50/1	Chris Perry	80/1	Jonathan Kaye
	66/1	Scott Verplank		

2000 RESULT

1	22/1	**Phil Mickelson**	**67 69 69 205**
		Mickelson won at the first play-off hole	
2	150/1	**Gary Nicklaus**	**68 69 68 205**
T3	80/1*	**Kenny Perry**	**67 70 70 207**
T3	125/1	**Harrison Frazar**	**69 68 70 207**
T5	100/1*	**Jay Don Blake**	**67 72 69 208**
T5	150/1	**Tom Pernice Jr**	**73 66 69 208**
T5	80/1	**Steve Jones**	**67 71 70 208**
T5	150/1	**Joey Sindelar**	**68 66 74 208**
T5	33/1	**John Huston**	**68 67 73 208**

T10	S Cink	71 71 67 209			J M Olazabal	71 72 70 213
	D Pride	73 68 68 209			B Bates	72 71 70 213
	Chris Perry	71 69 69 209			J Green	72 71 70 213
	S Flesch	73 67 69 209			B Glasson	70 69 74 213
	B McCallister	67 70 72 209		T49	D Forsman	69 72 73 214
T15	F Langham	74 67 69 210			B Tway	73 68 73 214
	T Dodds	73 68 69 210			L Mize	68 74 72 214
	D Toms	71 69 70 210			P Azinger	69 75 70 214
	D Peoples	68 73 69 210		T53	Jim Gallagher	74 68 73 215
	G Hjertstedt	68 71 71 210			C Pavin	72 69 74 215
	B Henninger	68 70 72 210			D Frost	71 71 73 215
	P Stankowski	66 70 74 210			O Uresti	71 71 73 215
T22	S Gump	70 72 69 211			Jerry Smith	72 71 72 215
	B Cheesman	70 70 71 211			J Buha	72 71 72 215
	J Delsing	71 69 71 211			S McCarron	74 70 71 215
	B Watts	71 72 68 211			J Durant	73 71 71 215
	Robin Freeman	75 68 68 211		T61	C Barlow	71 70 75 216
	B Jobe	69 70 72 211			E Booker	67 72 77 216
	T Scherrer	68 71 72 211		T63	S Murphy	71 72 74 217
	J Van de Velde	67 70 74 211			C DiMarco	73 70 74 217
T30	B Heintz	72 69 71 212			Carl Paulson	68 76 73 217
	J Kelly	72 71 69 212			S Elkington	73 71 73 217
	M Wiebe	71 68 73 212			J Leonard	72 72 73 217
	G Norman	71 73 68 212			J Maxon	70 74 73 217
	D Stockton	68 69 75 212		T69	F Lickliter	75 65 78 218
	B Burns	70 74 68 212			K J Choi	74 70 74 218
	B Gay	73 71 68 212			R Beem	71 73 74 218
T37	David Sutherland	69 72 72 213			B Faxon	71 73 74 218
	M Springer	70 71 72 213		T73	J Kaye	70 71 78 219
	M A Jimenez	71 71 71 213			D Duval	73 69 77 219
	B Geiberger	71 70 72 213			M Reid	69 74 76 219
	C Raulerson	70 73 70 213			P Blackmar	73 71 75 219
	N Faldo	72 71 70 213		T77	W Austin	71 71 79 221
	Kevin Sutherland	70 70 73 213			S Verplank	70 74 77 221
	L Mattiace	69 71 73 213				

The main players to miss the cut (made at level) were:–

S Dunlap (+1)	N Price (+1)	B Andrade (+1)	N Lancaster (+1)
R Allenby (+1)	A Magee (+2)	K Triplett (+2)	B Mayfair (+2)
D Paulson (+2)	S Lowery (+2)	B Chamblee (+2)	E Fryatt (+3)
B May (+3)	R Goosen (+3)	S Stricker (+3)	L Janzen (+4)
S Micheel (+4)	M Calcavecchia (+4)	B Fabel (+4)	J Williamson (+4)
E Toledo (+6)	C A Spence (+6)	R Sabbatini (+7)	K Wentworth (+7)
M Dawson (+7)	T Tolles (+9)	N Henke (+11)	

David Edwards withdrew after 73 in R1 and Rick Fehr was disqualified after 69 in R1.

ROUND BY ROUND LEADERBOARD

FIRST ROUND

P Stankowski	6 under
P MICKELSON	5 under
N Price	5 under
B McAllister	5 under
S Jones	5 under
J D Blake	5 under
E Booker	5 under
J Van de Velde	5 under

SECOND ROUND

J Sindelar	10 under
J Huston	9 under
P MICKELSON	8 under
P Stankowski	8 under
H Frazar	7 under
B McCallister	7 under
K Perry	7 under
D Stockton	7 under
J Van de Velde	7 under
G Nicklaus	7 under

THIRD AND FINAL ROUND

G Nicklaus	11 under
P MICKELSON	11 under
H Frazar	9 under
K Perry	9 under
S Jones	8 under
J Sindelar	8 under
J Huston	8 under
J D Blake	8 under
T Pernice Jr	8 under

There was a two-hour lightning delay on Thursday morning as a result of which thirty-one players had to complete R1 on Friday morning.

Rain forced the abandonment of R4 on Sunday and with the US Masters coming up, as well as a poor weather forecast, it was decided that the final round could not be played. As a result Mickelson and Nicklaus played off at the par 3 16th and Mickelson easily won with a birdie.

PUNTERS' POINTS

● With Sunday washed out and the organisers unwilling to play on the Monday of US Masters week Phil Mickelson and Gary Nicklaus started their play-off on the par 3 16th which had been 'dried out' by the green staff.

- Mickelson landed 18 feet from the pin, Nicklaus in the bunker from which he took two to get out. So Lefty had 2 putts to win and needed just one as he rolled in a birdie. Mickelson has now won all his three play-offs!
- It was his fifteenth tour title – and he's not yet 30 – and his second of this year.
- The consolation for Nicklaus was that he secured his tour card for next year so can now play relaxed golf.
- Joey Sindelar's form here illustrated two key points:-
    > An out of form player (he'd missed all six cuts this season) can suddenly "catch fire".
    > His 66 in R2 was followed by a 74 in R3 because "streakers can't keep it up".
- Steve Jones's eye-catching finish at Sawgrass was continued here with a fine performance to finish T5th.

1999 RESULT

1	fav 5/1	David Duval
2	40/1	Stewart Cink
T3	250/1	Rory Sabbatini
T3	25/1	John Huston
T5	125/1	Franklin Langham
T5	150/1	Mike Weir

1998 RESULT

1	fav 15/2	Tiger Woods
2	200/1	Jay Don Blake
T3	200/1	Esteban Toledo
T3	80/1	Steve Flesch
T5	150/1	Scott Verplank
T5	125/1	Bill Glasson
T5	80/1	Bob Tway
T5	50/1	John Huston
T5	50/1	Stewart Cink

WINNERS IN THE LAST TEN YEARS

1991	Corey Pavin	1996	Paul Stankowski
1992	Tom Kite	1997	Scott McCarron
1993	Nolan Henke	1998	Tiger Woods
1994	John Daly	1999	David Duval
1995	Mark Calcavecchia	2000	Phil Mickelson

Before 1997 Atlanta G.C., Marietta was the venue.

PUNTERS' GUIDE

- There have now been four years of Sugarloaf form, and all four winners have had three key characteristics.
    > They have been long hitters, in the top 10 for driving distance
    > They were all young men (31 the oldest) who could "handle" this most physically demanding of courses.
    > They all had morning tee times (indeed all were no later than in the sixth group out on the Thursday morning) to give them early momentum.

● Over the four Sugarloaf years the best records are held by:-

	2000	1999	1998	1997
John Huston	5	3	5	–
David Duval	73 (!)	W	14	2
Phil Mickelson	W	7	–	–
Jay Don Blake	5	16	2	28
Kenny Perry	3	36	36	19
David Toms	15	10	MC	5
Stewart Cink	10	2	5	MC
Steve Flesch	10	36	3	–

● This course provides a sound preparation for Augusta. This is shown by :-

> The similar course confirmations of generous fairways and undulating bentgrass greens.

> The fact that the four winners and the player with best stroke average have all good US Masters' records

1997 winner Scott McCarron US Masters form (from 1996-99) 10-30-16-18

1998 winner Tiger Woods US Masters form (from 1997-99) 1-8-18

1999 winner David Duval US Masters form (from 1998-99) 2-6

2000 winner Phil Mickelson US Masters form (from 1996-99) 3-MC-12-6

> The best Sugarloaf stroke average (68.72) belongs to John Huston who from 1990-99 inclusive played in ten US Masters, making every cut and posting three top 20s plus a T3rd.

● The following player profiles refer to this tournament Stewart Cink, Steve Flesch, John Huston, David Duval, Jay Don Blake, Robin Freeman, David Toms, Brian Henninger, Harrison Frazar and Scott Dunlap.

THE 64TH US MASTERS

Date	6th - 9th April
Course	Augusta National, Augusta, Georgia
Par	72
Yardage	6,985
First Prize	$650,000
Total Purse	$3.5 million

PLEASE SEE PART 6.

THE MCI CLASSIC

Date	13th - 16th April
Course	Harbour Town Golf Links, Hilton Head, South Carolina
Par	71
Yardage	6,916
First Prize	$504,000
Total Course	$2.8 million

THE TOURNAMENT

Started in 1969 this tournament has always been held at the Harbour Town course. It is well established as the first event after the US Masters. In 2001 the tournament will be renamed the Worldcom Classic.

THE COURSE

A highly respected course which is a genuine seaside links track with only three par 5s and the smallest greens on the whole tour. The four par 3s are very tough and the front nine is much easier than the back nine. The winner must be accurate off the tee, find the greens in regulation and be at ease on the Bermuda greens. When the wind blows, as on the first day this year, it provides a severe test.

2000 ODDS

jt fav	12/1	Davis Love	50/1	Scott Hoch
jt fav	12/1	Ernie Els	50/1	Mark O'Meara
	16/1	Nick Price	66/1*	Glen Day (DC)
	16/1	Vijay Singh (PWW)	66/1	Dudley Hart
	18/1	Tom Lehman	66/1	Kenny Perry
	25/1	Jesper Parnevik	66/1	Bob Estes
	33/1	John Huston	66/1	Shigeki Maruyama
	40/1	Carlos Franco	80/1	Paul Azinger
	40/1	Chris Perry	80/1*	Fred Funk
	40/1	Greg Norman	80/1*	Rocco Mediate
	40/1	Jeff Sluman	80/1*	Steve Pate
	40/1	Stewart Cink	80/1*	Bob Tway
	40/1	Steve Flesch	80/1	Robert Allenby
	50/1	Lee Janzen	80/1	Retief Goosen
	50/1	Loren Roberts		

2000 RESULT

1	40/1	Stewart Cink	71 68 66 65 270
2	18/1	Tom Lehman	70 70 67 65 272
T3	16/1	Vijay Singh	70 70 71 64 275
T3	150/1	Ed Fryatt	67 74 65 69 275
T3	150/1	Dan Forsman	66 71 68 70 275
T3	125/1	Larry Mize	73 67 65 70 275
T3	jt fav 12/1	Davis Love	68 66 70 71 275
T3	jt fav 12/1	Ernie Els	68 67 66 74 275

T9	J Huston	71 68 69 68 276		R Goosen	71 73 66 71 281
	J Parnevik	70 69 67 70 276		Jerry Smith	72 69 68 72 281
T11	J Kaye	73 67 71 66 277		J Sluman	72 68 68 73 281
	S Verplank	70 71 69 67 277		B Fabel	71 67 69 74 281
	B Elder	70 71 68 68 277		T Herron	68 71 67 75 281
	S Lowery	73 64 66 74 277	T47	S Murphy	67 73 74 68 282
T15	S Pate	74 70 68 66 278		B Mayfair	73 71 66 72 282
	C Franco	73 70 68 67 278		F Nobilo	69 69 71 73 282
	C Stadler	76 65 69 68 278	T50	F Langham	71 72 73 67 283
	S Dunlap	72 70 68 68 278		C Riley	71 72 71 69 283
	M Wiebe	71 70 68 69 278		C A Spence	76 67 70 70 283
	Chris Perry	73 71 65 69 278		C Barlow	72 69 71 71 283
	J Kelly	70 71 66 71 278		Robin Freeman	72 72 67 72 283
	C Strange	73 69 65 71 278		B Faxon	72 69 69 73 283
	N Begay	71 66 68 73 278	56	G Nicklaus	73 71 65 75 284
	S Hoch	73 68 64 73 278	T57	J Durant	74 69 72 70 285
T25	Dudley Hart	72 72 70 65 279		E Toledo	75 69 71 70 285
	F Lickliter	72 71 70 66 279		Carl Paulson	74 69 71 71 285
	T Scherrer	73 71 68 67 279		J Carter	71 71 70 73 285
	P Azinger	70 70 70 69 279	T61	M Brisky	74 67 74 71 286
	T Tolles	74 67 69 69 279		G Day	74 69 72 71 286
	G Chalmers	72 70 68 69 279		R Black	71 72 71 72 286
	M O'Meara	73 68 68 70 279		T Pernice Jr	72 72 70 72 286
	F Funk	71 69 68 71 279		J Green	71 69 72 74 286
	B McCallister	74 67 67 71 279	T66	M McCumber	71 73 71 72 287
T34	B Tway	71 72 72 65 280		B Henninger	74 68 72 73 287
	R Damron	71 71 71 67 280		G Norman	71 71 70 75 287
	C Raulerson	79 65 67 69 280	69	O Uresti	71 72 71 74 288
	B Friend	71 69 69 71 280	70	S Kendall	72 71 73 73 289
	L Janzen	72 71 66 71 280	71	D Pride	73 71 72 74 290
T39	J D Blake	73 67 73 68 281	72	J Maginnes	72 72 75 72 291
	Nick Price	75 67 69 70 281	73	D Stockton	76 68 73 75 292
	C Pavin	72 71 67 71 281			

The main players to miss the cut (made at 2 over) were:–

S Gump (+3)	R Mediate (+3)	L Roberts (+3)	J Sindelar (+3)
J Cook (+3)	N Faldo (+3)	B Estes (+3)	H Frazar (+3)
D Frost (+3)	L Mattiace (+4)	S Maruyama (+4)	S Flesch (+4)
D Edwards (+4)	S Ames (+5)	B Cheesman (+5)	K Perry (+5)
M Bradley (+5)	B Hughes (+6)	O Browne (+6)	J Delsing (+6)
P Jacobsen (+6)	B Jobe (+7)	M Gogel (+7)	T Dodds (+8)
J Haas (+8)	P Stankowski (+8)	N Henke (+8)	W Austin (+10)
S McCarron (+12)	S Lyle (+12)		

J L Lewis (77) and Gabriel Hjerstedt (80) both withdrew after R1. Russ Cochran (71) was disqualified. Rich Beem 69-75-74 then withdrew when hit by a golf cart during R4 .... honest!

ROUND BY ROUND LEADERBOARD

FIRST ROUND

D Forsman	5 under
E Fryatt	4 under
S Murphy	4 under
T Herron	3 under
E Els	3 under
D Love	3 under
S CINK	level

SECOND ROUND

D Love	8 under
E Els	7 under
D Forsman	5 under
S Lowery	5 under
N Begay	5 under
F Nobilo	4 under
B Fabel	4 under
S CINK	3 under

THIRD ROUND

E Els	12 under
S Lowery	10 under
D Love	9 under
D Forsman	8 under
N Begay	8 under
L Mize	8 under
S CINK	8 under
S Hoch	8 under

FINAL ROUND

S CINK	14 under
T Lehman	12 under
V Singh	9 under
E Fryatt	9 under
D Forsman	9 under
L Mize	9 under
D Love	9 under
E Els	9 under

Thursday: It became very windy and cold in the afternoon giving the early starters the best of the conditions. The average score was 73.25 whereas by Saturday in benign conditions the average was 69.16!

PUNTERS' POINTS

● "I played terrible. I don't know what to say." Well Ernie Els's collapse was scarcely a surprise as he'd been awarded the 'bottle' in last year's book after a series of poor R4 finishes.

● Stewart Cink's 40/1 win could be anticipated on the basis of consistent form (four top 10s) and solid stats (nine cuts in a row, top 35 for GIR & putting), yet this was his debut on a specialist's track. In the event he held his nerve really well to finish with three birdies on the last 4 holes to beat clubhouse leader Tom Lehman.

● Only three players posted four sub-par rounds
   > Runner up Tom Lehman
   > T9th   Jesper Parnevik
   > T25th (!)   Paul Azinger

● Disappointing final rounds were posted by
   > Ernie Els and Steve Lowery (last pair out) both 3 over par 74s
   > Notah Begay and Scott Hoch both 2 over par 73s.

● Normally the third-fastest finisher over the final three rounds is at least in the top 10...here Charles Raulerson, 12 under for his last 54 holes, finished T34th!!

1999 RESULT

1	80/1*	Glen Day
won at the first play-off hole		
T2	80/1	Jeff Sluman
T2	40/1	Payne Stewart
4	100/1	Chris Perry
T5	150/1	Corey Pavin
T5	150/1*	Nolan Henke
T5	40/1*	John Huston

1998 RESULT

1	20/1	Davis Love
2	80/1	Glen Day
T3	66/1	Payne Stewart
T3	20/1	Phil Mickelson
5	200/1	Fulton Allem

WINNERS IN THE LAST TEN YEARS

1991	Davis Love	1996	Loren Roberts
1992	Davis Love	1997	Nick Price
1993	David Edwards	1998	Davis Love
1994	Hale Irwin	1999	Glen Day
1995	Bob Tway	2000	Stewart Cink

PUNTERS' GUIDE

● The victory of a 26-year-old MCI debutant and the top 3 finishes of four players who had been in the top 10 in the US Masters 'broke the mould' of results at Hilton Head over the last ten years.

Usually the winner was an experienced guy in his mid-to-late 30s who had solid course form and had not been in contention at Augusta.

● Although Stewart Cink was making his debut here it is still true that Hilton Head is a course specialist's track. In the six years from 1994-1999 inclusive five of the six winners had finished in the top 20 in the previous year. Indeed in five years in the nineties the winner had been in the previous year's top 10.

● The Law of Hilton Head is fully discussed in Part 1.

● The best recent MCI form has been shown by

> John Huston	T9th 2000: T5th 1999: T10th 1998
> Jesper Parnevik	T9th 2000: T18th 1998: 2nd 1997
> Tom Lehman	2nd 2000: T36th 1999: T14th 1998: 4th 1997: 13th 1996
> Davis Love (4-time winner)	T3rd 2000: Won 1998: 9th 1997: 4th 1996
> Craig Stadler	T15th 2000: 12th 1999: 9th 1997
> Glen Day	T61st 2000: Won 1999: 2nd 1998

● At Hilton Head it is probably still wise to select players

> who were not in serious US Masters contention

> who have proven course form

> who have greens in regulation stats pointing to their accuracy

> preferably have a morning R1 tee time.

● The players whose profiles refer to this tournament include Chris Perry, Brad Elder, Scott Dunlap, Craig Stadler, Glen Day, Jesper Parnevik, Davis Love, John Huston, Rocco Mediate, Nick Price and Ed Fryatt.

THE GREATER GREENSBORO CHRYSLER CLASSIC

Date	20th - 23rd April
Course	Forest Hills G.C., Greensboro, North Carolina
Par	72
Yardage	7,062
First Prize	$542,000
Total Purse	$3 million

THE TOURNAMENT

This is one of the tour's oldest tournaments. Established in 1938 the first victor was the legendary Sam Snead. Forest Oaks has been the venue since 1977.

THE COURSE

The course is not long by current standards. It has three main features - huge Bentgrass greens with two, occasionally three tiers, very large fairway and greenside bunkers and five inch rough. The profile of past winners, together with a priori reasoning, suggest that accuracy off the greens, skilled bunker play and first class long putting are required here.

2000 ODDS

jt fav	12/1	Davis Love	66/1*	Steve Pate
jt fav	12/1	Tom Lehman	66/1	Bob Estes
	16/1	Jim Furyk	66/1	Tim Herron
	16/1	Jesper Parnevik (DC)	66/1	Scott Dunlap
	16/1	Hal Sutton	66/1	Scott Verplank
	33/1	Justin Leonard	80/1*	Kenny Perry
	33/1	Dudley Hart	80/1	Notah Begay
	40/1	Chris Perry	80/1*	Robert Damron
	40/1	Jeff Maggert	80/1	Jonathan Kaye
	40/1	Jeff Sluman	80/1	Skip Kendall
	40/1	Fred Funk	80/1	Shigeki Maruyama
	50/1	Steve Elkington	80/1*	Rocco Mediate
	66/1*	Steve Jones	80/1*	Paul Stankowski
	66/1*	Mark Calcavecchia	80/1	Stephen Ames

2000 RESULT

1	16/1	Hal Sutton	67 64 72 71 274
2	100/1	Andrew Magee	70 68 68 71 277
T3	66/1*	Mark Calcavecchia	72 70 71 65 278
T3	33/1	Dudley Hart	72 67 69 70 278
T5	150/1	Doug Dunakey	67 71 72 71 281
T5	40/1	Chris Perry	71 71 69 70 281
T5	80/1	Jonathan Kaye	71 67 71 72 281

T8	J Parnevik	69 69 74 70 282		S Pate	70 71 74 74 289
	Kenny Perry	73 70 69 70 282		J Furyk	70 74 71 74 289
	S Verplank	66 74 70 72 282	T46	T Herron	71 70 76 73 290
	S Maruyama	71 69 70 72 282		David Sutherland	72 71 74 73 290
	O Uresti	67 72 69 74 282		G Kraft	69 73 73 75 290
T13	C A Spence	73 66 75 69 283		M Gogel	70 72 73 75 290
	B Estes	68 72 73 70 283		K Wentworth	73 71 71 75 290
	B Cheesman	70 66 73 74 283		W Wood	70 72 72 76 290
T16	T Lehman	73 70 71 70 284		F Nobilo	70 72 72 76 290
	J Green	69 72 71 72 284	T53	Bart Bryant	72 72 72 75 291
	J Leonard	69 70 73 72 284		C DiMarco	70 70 75 76 291
	T Scherrer	71 72 69 72 284		J Restino	69 71 71 80 291
	S Dunlap	71 67 73 73 284	T56	E Booker	72 70 76 74 292
T21	B Mayfair	69 73 74 69 285		S Jones	71 71 76 74 292
	B Elder	70 68 74 73 285		G Waite	71 72 74 75 292
	S McCarron	72 70 70 73 285		J Rollins	72 72 73 75 292
	D Love	72 69 68 76 285		O Browne	71 68 77 76 292
	B Henninger	66 72 71 76 285		D Mast	72 72 72 76 292
T26	S Kendall	69 73 73 71 286	T62	B Andrade	70 72 77 74 293
	R Mediate	71 72 71 72 286		Dennis Paulson	75 68 75 75 293
T28	Kevin Sutherland	70 71 78 68 287		Robin Freeman	70 72 75 76 293
	G Hnatiuk	71 72 75 69 287		P Stankowski	70 70 75 78 293
	B Geiberger	71 71 75 70 287	T66	C Raulerson	70 73 79 72 294
	Joel Edwards	72 68 76 71 287		J Ogilvie	72 72 79 71 294
	Jeff Gallagher	71 69 73 74 287		R Gamez	70 72 78 74 294
	S Murphy	67 72 73 75 287		B Bates	73 70 75 76 294
T34	N Lancaster	73 70 76 69 288		J Daly	70 73 73 78 294
	D Peoples	70 69 78 71 288	T71	M Clark II	74 69 80 72 295
	J Carter	69 70 77 72 288		R Howison	71 70 79 75 295
	B May	72 67 77 72 288		P Jordan	72 72 77 74 295
	M Springer	71 70 75 72 288		R Fehr	68 76 76 75 295
	Ken Green	69 71 74 74 288	T75	J Maginnes	69 74 75 78 296
	B McCallister	72 71 71 74 288		Steve Hart	73 71 74 78 296
	J Kelly	71 70 70 77 288	77	B Hughes	72 72 76 77 297
T42	Carl Paulson	72 72 73 72 289	78	Jerry Smith	75 69 80 75 299
	P Blackmar	74 67 75 73 289	79	A Bengoechea	74 68 84 76 302

The main players to miss the cut (made at level) were:–

W Austin (+1)	T Tryba (+1)	E Fryatt (+1)	B Fabel (+1)
B Chamblee (+1)	RDamron (+1)	M Dawson (+1)	E Toledo (+2)
J Durant (+2)	F Lickliter (+2)	L Rinker (+2)	D Forsman (+2)
B Glasson (+3)	M Bradley (+3)	G Chalmers (+3)	F Funk (+3)
N Begay (+4)	S Ames (+4)	T Byrum (+4)	J Maggert (+5)
J Sindelar (+5)	J P Hayes (+5)	T Dodds (+5)	M Goggin (+5)
S Elkington (+7)	S Lyle (+7)	K Gibson (+8)	B Friend (+9)
D Stockton (+11)			

Mark Wiebe (75), Jeff Sluman (78) and Phil Tataurangi (92 - honest!) all withdrew after R1.

ROUND BY ROUND LEADERBOARD

FIRST ROUND

B Henninger	6 under
S Verplank	6 under
H SUTTON	5 under
O Uresti	5 under
S Murphy	5 under
D Dunakey	5 under

SECOND ROUND

H SUTTON	13 under
B Cheesman	8 under
B Henninger	6 under
B Elder	6 under
J Parnevik	6 under
S Dunlap	6 under
D Dunakey	6 under
A Magee	6 under
J Kaye	6 under

THIRD ROUND

H SUTTON	13 under
A Magee	10 under
O Uresti	8 under
D Hart	8 under
D Love	7 under
B Henninger	7 under
J Kaye	7 under
B Cheesman	7 under

FINAL ROUND

H SUTTON	14 under
A Magee	11 under
D Hart	10 under
M Calcavecchia	10 under
D Dunakey	7 under
C Perry	7 under
J Kaye	7 under

In R1 rain had softened the course and the scores were low (especially in the morning) despite 25 mph windy conditions.

R4 scoring on Sunday was high with only six sub-70 rounds.

PUNTERS' POINTS

● 16/1 Hal Sutton had the course form (17th - 8th last two years) and the current form (beat Tiger to win the Players Championship) so his second win of the season was not a good result for the layers.

His victory was based on his first two rounds (13 under) which gave him a lead he then defended over the last 36 holes (just 1 under).

● Andrew Magee, recovering from right elbow tendonitis and playing on the back of two missed cuts with no course form, suddenly hit top gear as he'd done last year in the World Match Play. He's now had seven 2nd places since his last win in 1994.

● Dudley Hart was clearly the best tee-to-green player, yet he couldn't buy a putt, especially in R4. Sadly as his performances here have improved his best odds have contracted, from 80/1 (1998) and 50/1 (1999) to just 33/1 this year.

● Apart from runner-up Magee only one other player, Chris Perry, shot four sub-par rounds. Expect him to do well in 2001 — he's a native of North Carolina and his accuracy is well suited to here.

● Disappointing final rounds were made by

> Omar Uresti   T3rd after R3 shot 74 to finish T8th
> Jerry Kelly   three sub-par rounds then 77!
> Barry Cheesman   T5th after R3 shot 74 to finish T13th
> Brian Henninger   T5th after R3 shot 76 to finish T21st
> Davis Love   T5th after R3 shot 76 to finish T21st

1999 RESULT

1	28/1	Jesper Parnevik
2	20/1	Jim Furyk
3	33/1	Jeff Maggert
4	50/1	Dudley Hart
5	22/1	Tom Lehman

1998 RESULT

1	125/1	Trevor Dodds
won at the first play-off hole		
2	125/1	Scott Verplank
3	28/1	Bob Estes
4	150/1	Neal Lancaster
5	50/1	Frank Nobilo

WINNERS IN THE LAST TEN YEARS

1991	Mark Brooks	1996	Mark O'Meara
1992	Davis Love	1997	Frank Nobilo
1993	Rocco Mediate	1998	Trevor Dodds
1994	Mike Springer	1999	Jesper Parnevik
1995	Jim Gallagher	2000	Hal Sutton

PUNTERS' GUIDE

● In the last seven years twenty-nine players have finished in the top 4 (or T4th)

> nineteen (65.5%) have been priced at or over 50/1
> twelve (41.38%) have been priced at or over 80/1
> nine (31%) have been priced at or over 100/1

So outsiders do have a solid record here.

● A morning start in R1 is definitely advantageous here.

> Make sure any outright selection has an early tee time
> If 'betting in running', do note any afternoon R1 starters who make a low opening score.

● Players with good recent records here include

   > Dudley Hart   T3rd 2000: 4th 1999: T11th 1998: T29th 1997

   > Hal Sutton   Won 2000: T17th 1999: 8th 1998

   > Jesper Parnevik   T8th 2000: Won 1999

   > Jim Furyk   T42nd 2000: 2nd 1999: T11th 1998: T14th 1997

   > Scott Verplank   T8th 2000: T48th 1999: 2nd 1998: T14th 1997

   > Bob Estes   T13th 2000: DNP 1999: 3rd 1998

   > Chris Perry   T5th 2000: T25th 1999: T38th 1998

   > Tom Lehman   T16th 2000: 5th 1999: T13th 1996 (last three starts)

● See if you can find a bookie who will give you a match bet of Lee Janzen against Bob Tway ... and then back it to be a tie at 16/1... No, I've not been drinking. It's just that in every one of the LAST FIVE YEARS they have finished level – T34th (2000), T8th (1999), T18th (1998), T30th (1997) and T15th (1996) ... so 16/1 looks a good bet, eh?

● Players whose profiles point to this tournament include Bob Estes, Craig Spence, Scott Verplank, Dudley Hart, Chris Perry, Neal Lancaster, Jim Furyk, Jerry Kelly, Jesper Parnevik, Tim Clark and Tom Lehman.

THE SHELL HOUSTON OPEN

Date	27th - 30th April
Course	TPC at the Woodlands, Houston, Texas
Par	72
Yardage	7,045
First Prize	$504,000
Total Purse	$2.8 million

THE TOURNAMENT

This well-established tournament started in 1946. Always held in Texas, it moved to the Woodlands course in 1975 and to the TPC in 1985, so this year was its fifteenth Houston Open.

THE COURSE

This is a tough course with water in play on half the holes. It is very much a 'fairways and greens' course, demanding accuracy as well as an ability to play in the wind and to be comfortable on the tricky Bermuda greens. The 17th and 18th holes are a severe test, especially on Sunday.

2000 ODDS

fav	7/1	Hal Sutton (PWW)	50/1	Steve Elkington
	20/1	Justin Leonard	50/1	Steve Jones
	25/1	Fred Couples	50/1	Jonathan Kaye
	25/1	Dudley Hart	66/1*	Andrew Magee
	25/1	Carlos Franco	66/1*	Steve Stricker
	25/1	Scott Hoch	66/1*	Billy Mayfair
	33/1	Stuart Appleby (DC)	80/1	Skip Kendall
	33/1	Jeff Maggert	80/1	Larry Mize
	40/1	Loren Roberts	80/1	Mark Brooks
	40/1	Mike Weir	80/1*	Kevin Sutherland
	50/1*	David Toms	80/1	J P Hayes
	50/1*	Fred Funk	80/1	Stephen Ames
	50/1	Scott Dunlap	80/1	Brad Faxon

2000 RESULT

1	100/1*	**Robert Allenby**	**68 67 68 72 275**	
		Allenby won at the fourth play-off hole		
2	100/1*	**Craig Stadler**	**66 69 69 71 275**	
T3	40/1	**Loren Roberts**	**68 67 72 69 276**	
T3	150/1	**Joel Edwards**	**68 71 67 70 276**	
T5	80/1*	**Mark Brooks**	**69 67 72 69 277**	
T5	125/1	**Brad Fabel**	**70 67 69 71 277**	

T7	S Lowery	73 67 70 68 278		J Maginnes	69 69 71 74 283
	David Sutherland	72 70 67 69 278		D Barron	67 71 71 74 283
	M Sposa	69 68 71 70 278	T45	J P Hayes	71 70 73 70 284
	S Hoch	71 65 69 73 278		O Uresti	74 68 72 70 284
T11	P Stankowski	67 69 78 65 279		C DiMarco	71 71 70 72 284
	P Jordan	69 72 71 67 279		B Hughes	68 74 70 72 284
	C Raulerson	68 69 74 68 279		D Stockton	67 70 72 75 284
	M Gogel	68 68 72 71 279		W Austin	68 71 70 75 284
	C Franco	65 71 72 71 279		B Gay	66 73 69 76 284
	J Kaye	72 66 68 73 279		C Martin	70 67 70 77 284
T17	E Toledo	70 70 73 67 280	T53	N Lancaster	71 69 74 71 285
	Carl Paulson	69 72 71 68 280		B Bates	72 69 71 73 285
	B Lietzke	69 71 70 70 280		M Reid	71 70 71 73 285
	J Maggert	70 71 69 70 280		F Couples	75 67 69 74 285
	J Gullion	74 68 68 70 280		Jerry Smith	66 75 70 74 285
	Kevin Sutherland	66 72 70 72 280		J McGovern	71 67 72 75 285
	D Forsman	70 68 70 72 280		S Micheel	68 70 69 78 285
	T Dodds	69 72 67 72 280	T60	M Brisky	74 68 76 68 286
	S Ames	68 71 68 73 280		J Haas	69 70 75 72 286
	F Funk	67 69 69 75 280		R Black	74 68 71 73 286
T27	D Toms	70 72 70 69 281		J Durant	69 72 71 74 286
	J Kelly	71 71 68 71 281		R Fehr	68 71 72 75 286
T29	T Pernice Jr	72 68 74 68 282	T65	D Peoples	68 72 76 71 287
	R Howison	70 70 74 68 282		S Dunlap	73 69 73 72 287
	S Kendall	68 72 73 69 282	T67	F Nobilo	69 73 73 73 288
	H Sutton	71 69 72 70 282		B Friend	71 70 75 72 288
	J Green	70 72 70 70 282		H Kuehne	65 74 74 75 288
	L Mize	72 65 72 73 282		T Thelen	72 69 72 75 288
	H Frazar	70 69 69 74 282		D Morland	70 70 73 75 288
	F Allem	68 71 68 75 282	T72	P Blackmar	73 69 72 75 289
	B May	72 66 69 75 282		T Armour III	70 71 72 76 289
T38	B Glasson	74 66 73 70 283		R Sabbatini	71 71 71 76 289
	C A Spence	74 68 71 70 283	75	S Gump	71 70 73 76 290
	B Mayfair	71 68 72 72 283	76	B Faxon	69 73 77 72 291
	David Edwards	70 72 69 72 283	77	W Levi	72 70 71 79 292
	F Lickliter	71 66 72 74 283			

The main players to miss the cut (made at 2 under) were:–

D Hart (-1)	G Nicklaus (-1)	A Magee (-1)	G Hjerstedt (-1)
D Frost (-1)	J Sindelar (-1)	D A Weibring (-1)	P Goydos (-1)
S Appleby (-1)	J Leonard (-1)	F Langham (-1)	B Jobe (E)
K Wentworth (E)	G Chalmers (E)	S Stricker (E)	S Jones (+1)
B Watts (+1)	L Mattiace (+1)	M Goggin (+1)	G Kraft (+2)
T Byrum (+2)	B Elder (+2)	N Henke (+3)	M Dawson (+4)
K Gibson (+4)	J Daly (+5)	D Dunakey (+5)	S McCarron (+6)
T Tryba (+6)	T Scherrer (+7)	R Beem (+8)	B Chamblee (+10)

⌐UND LEADERBOARD

FIRST ROUND		SECOND ROUND	
C Franco	7 under	R ALLENBY	9 under
H Kuene	7 under	L Roberts	9 under
B Gay	6 under	C Stadler	9 under
C Stadler	6 under	P Stankowski	8 under
J Smith	6 under	S Hoch	8 under
K Sutherland	6 under	F Funk	8 under
R ALLENBY	4 under	M Gogel	8 under
		M Brooks	8 under
		C Franco	8 under

THIRD ROUND		FINAL ROUND	
R ALLENBY	13 under	R ALLENBY	13 under
C Stadler	12 under	C Stadler	13 under
S Hoch	11 under	L Roberts	12 under
F Funk	11 under	J Edwards	12 under
J Edwards	10 under	M Brooks	11 under
J Kaye	10 under	B Fabel	11 under
B Fabel	10 under		

PUNTERS' POINTS

- What a TV nail-biter, as two 100/1 DYMs fought out an exciting play-off. Stadler had a putt to win on the 18th in R4 after Allenby found the water, and then had very makeable putts to win on each of the first 3 extra holes before Allenby won with a par at the fourth.

- Allenby deservedly won overall as he'd been the most consistent ball striker over the final 9 holes. His victory was based on two keys.
  > A new cross-handed putting grip
  > He was 12 under for the tournament on the par 5s!

- Allenby had missed his last two cuts, yet he'd played solid here last year (T33rd), was 5th in total driving and in the all-round stats. Sadly I had him down for next week, the Compaq Classic, for which he was tipped in his player profile last year.

- His win continued the fine form of Australian players here in recent years. A tough, firm course played in windy conditions clearly suits 'the wizards of Oz'.

- Two players had similar tournaments. Paul Stankowski and Charles Raulerson both finished T11th and both had three sub-70 rounds either side of a poor R3. They will be worth noting here in 2001.

- The tendency for Steve Lowery to shoot low in R4 was noted in his player profile last year. Once more he played well on Sunday, shooting 68.

- Disappointing final rounds were played by Fred Funk (75), Bob May (75), Harrison Frazar (74), Casey Martin (77) and Shaun Micheel (78).

1999 RESULT

1	80/1*	Stuart Appleby
T2	66/1*	John Cook
T2	33/1	Hal Sutton
4	150/1	Mark Wiebe
T5	150/1*	Clark Dennis
T5	150/1*	Jonathan Kaye
T5	20/1	Vijay Singh
T5	150/1	J P Hayes
T5	80/1*	Loren Roberts

1998 RESULT

1	fav 11/1	David Duval
2	20/1	Jeff Maggert
3	14/1	Fred Couples
T4	28/1	Lee Janzen
T4	66/1	Dudley Hart

WINNERS IN THE LAST TEN YEARS

1991	Fulton Allem	1996	Mark Brooks
1992	Fred Funk	1997	Phil Blackmar
1993	Jim McGovern	1998	David Duval
1994	Mike Heinen	1999	Stuart Appleby
1995	Payne Stewart	2000	Robert Allenby

PUNTERS' GUIDE

● Of the fifteen players in the last two years who finished in the top 5 (or T5th)

> eight were DYMs, including the last two winners

> eleven (73%) started at or over 80/1, eight at or over 100/1 and five started at 150/1

So outsiders and DYMs have a brilliant recent record.

● Texans playing 'at home' had a good record here until the last two years so Harrison Frazar, Fred Couples, Brad Elder, Mark Brooks, Omar Uresti, Jeff Maggert, J P Hayes, Tom Byrum, Justin Leonard and, if fit, Steve Elkington must enter into calculations.

● This tournament has a reputation for throwing up first-time winners. It produced five in the nineties and now Allenby this year.

● In R1 3-ball betting keep an eye on Texan veteran Bruce Lietzke. He has shot successive sub-70s here in R1 in the last three years – 69 (2000), 69 (1999), 67 (1998).

● Best records in the last four years are held by

Loren Roberts	T3rd 2000: T5th 1999
Hal Sutton	MLD? T29th 2000: 2nd 1999: 6th 1998: T4th 1997
Scott Hoch	T7th 2000: 10th 1999: 12th 1998: T4th 1997
Jonathan Kaye	T11th 2000: T5th 1999

● Players whose profiles refer to this tournament include Hal Sutton, David Sutherland, Jerry Kelly, Jeff Maggert, Jonathan Kaye, Stephen Ames, Scott Hoch, Mark Brooks, Loren Roberts, Joel Edwards, Harrison Frazar and J P Hayes.

THE COMPAQ CLASSIC

Date	4th - 7th May
Course	English Turn, New Orleans, Louisiana
Par	72
Yardage	7,106
First Prize	$540,000
Total Purse	$3 million

THE TOURNAMENT

Started in 1938, the tournament has always been held in New Orleans with the English Turn course the venue since 1989. Formerly titled the Freeport McDermott Classic it became the Compaq Classic in 1999.

THE COURSE

This Jack Nicklaus-designed course has seen some very low scoring, with Dennis Paulson's 62 in 1994 the course record. It tends to suit long hitters, although some shorter drivers (Faxon, Frost, Beck and Crenshaw) have been successful. The greens are Bermuda. The signature hole is the par 5 island-green 15th. The final holes – the par 3 17th, and the par 4 18th, the course's hardest hole (only two birdies in R4 this year), provide a very severe late examination.

2000 ODDS

jt fav	14/1	Vijay Singh	66/1	Steve Elkington
jt fav	14/1	Ernie Els	66/1	Craig Parry
	16/1	Phil Mickelson	66/1	Kirk Triplett
	16/1	Hal Sutton	66/1	Steve Pate
	20/1	Nick Price	80/1*	Craig Stadler
	25/1	Carlos Franco (DC)	80/1	Paul Stankowski
	33/1	Steve Flesch	80/1	Steve Stricker
	33/1	Scott Hoch	80/1	Scott Dunlap
	40/1	Chris Perry	80/1*	Harrison Frazar
	40/1*	Fred Couples	80/1*	Steve Lowery
	50/1	Jeff Sluman	80/1*	Scott Verplank
	50/1	Jonathan Kaye	80/1*	Mark Brooks
	50/1	David Toms	80/1	Andrew Magee
	50/1	Lee Janzen	80/1*	Glen Day
	66/1*	Stuart Appleby	80/1	Aaron Baddeley
	66/1*	Mark Calcavecchia	80/1	Robert Damron
	66/1*	Jeff Maggert	80/1	Kevin Sutherland

2000 RESULT

1	25/1	**Carlos Franco**	**67 67 68 68 270**

Franco won at the second play-off hole

2	125/1	**Blaine McCallister**	**69 65 68 68 270**
3	80/1*	**Harrison Frazar**	**71 68 64 68 271**
T4	80/1	**Steve Stricker**	**70 71 67 64 272**
T4	100/1	**Stephen Ames**	**69 67 68 68 272**

T6	K Triplett	72 69 67 65 273		T43	M Bradley	70 71 74 67 282
	S Flesch	69 68 67 69 273			C DiMarco	70 72 73 67 282
	B Burns	67 73 64 69 273			K Wentworth	68 75 70 69 282
T9	S Hoch	71 68 69 66 274			W Austin	70 68 75 69 282
	J Durant	71 68 68 67 274			J Sindelar	69 69 72 72 282
T11	F Langham	74 69 68 64 275			J Haas	69 69 71 73 282
	S Appleby	69 66 69 71 275			S Dunlap	71 67 70 74 282
T13	G Day	67 69 72 68 276		T50	B May	69 73 70 71 283
	M Clark II	70 70 69 67 276			J Green	69 72 69 73 283
	Steve Hart	67 72 66 71 276			E Els	67 74 69 73 283
16	P Stankowski	66 70 69 72 277			E Booker	72 66 69 76 283
T17	Nick Price	69 72 69 68 278		T54	J D Blake	72 69 75 68 284
	S McCarron	67 70 71 70 278			C Riley	69 74 71 70 284
	M Brooks	71 69 68 70 278			C Parry	72 68 74 70 284
	R Damron	70 70 68 70 278			B Friend	69 73 72 70 284
	P Mickelson	71 67 69 71 278			T Pernice Jr	76 67 70 71 284
	D Peoples	69 70 68 71 278			R Sabbatini	71 72 69 72 284
	Joel Edwards	69 66 69 74 278			B Bates	70 70 72 72 284
T24	M Standly	72 69 71 67 279			J Cook	73 69 69 73 284
	B Schwarzrock	70 71 70 68 279			H Sutton	72 70 68 74 284
	B Tway	71 71 67 70 279		T63	B Elder	72 71 73 69 285
	Tom Byrum	73 66 69 71 279			F Allem	70 71 71 73 285
	B Glasson	68 69 69 73 279			B Wetterich	73 68 71 73 285
	V Singh	68 71 68 72 279			J Restino	74 65 72 74 285
T30	Carl Paulson	72 71 73 64 280		T67	C Raulerson	70 69 78 69 286
	D Morland IV	72 70 71 67 280			C Bowden	71 72 71 72 286
	J Ogilvie	73 69 69 69 280			J Rollins	72 70 71 73 286
	S Verplank	70 73 67 70 280			T Tryba	68 73 70 75 286
	F Lickliter	69 72 68 71 280		T71	P Jordan	76 67 72 72 287
	L Janzen	68 70 70 72 280			B Watts	69 73 72 73 287
	Kevin Sutherland	71 69 68 72 280			T Tolles	72 71 70 74 287
T37	D Toms	72 69 73 67 281		T74	E Toledo	71 72 75 70 288
	E Aubrey	70 71 71 69 281			K J Choi	67 73 75 73 288
	S Micheel	70 70 72 69 281			J Sluman	74 69 70 75 288
	D Forsman	68 75 68 70 281		77	J Williamson	68 68 81 72 289
	Jeff Gallagher	69 70 71 71 281		78	K Gibson	72 71 73 74 290
	P Curry	71 69 70 71 281				

The main players to miss the cut (made at 1 under) were:–

O Uresti (E)	T Scherrer (E)	B Chamblee (E)	A Magee (E)
T Dodds (E)	B Fabel (E)	M Dawson (E)	J Smith (E)
D Waldorf (E)	C Perry (E)	S Pate (E)	C Beck (E)
R Black (+1)	P Goydos (+1)	B Hughes (+1)	F Couples (+1)
D Paulson (+1)	B Cheesman (+1)	J Carter (+1)	G Hjerstedt (+1)
R Freeman (+1)	D Dunakey (+1)	M Wiebe (+1)	M Sposa (+1)
M Calcavecchia (+2)	A Baddeley (+2)	S Murphy (+2)	S Gump (+2)
J Kaye (+4)	M Hulbert (+4)	D Edwards (+4)	R Cochran (+4)
D Pride (+4)	B Faxon (+4)	B Andrade (+4)	G Waite (+4)
E Fryatt (+4)	N Henke (+4)	B Gay (+4)	D Sutherland (+5)
S Lowery (+5)	D Frost (+6)	J Maggert (+8)	M Goggin (+8)

Mike Springer (75) and Neal Lancaster (78) both withdrew after R1.

ROUND BY ROUND LEADERBOARD

FIRST ROUND		SECOND ROUND	
P Stankowski	6 under	C FRANCO	10 under
S McCarron	5 under	B McCallister	10 under
C FRANCO	5 under	J Edwards	9 under
E Els	5 under	S Appleby	9 under
B Burns	5 under	G Day	8 under
K J Choi	5 under	S Ames	8 under
G Day	5 under	P Stankowski	8 under
S Hart	5 under	J Williamson	8 under

THIRD ROUND		FINAL ROUND	
C FRANCO	14 under	C FRANCO	18 under
B McCallister	14 under	B McCallister	18 under
H Frazar	13 under	H Frazar	17 under
B Burns	12 under	S Ames	16 under
S Ames	12 under	S Stricker	16 under
S Flesch	12 under		
J Edwards	12 under		
S Appleby	12 under		

On the first two days there were 25 mph gusty winds. On Saturday with just a 10 mph breeze scores fell as sixty-five of the seventy-eight players played at par or better.

PUNTERS' POINTS

- Once again a rivetting Sunday golf night on Sky, as Carlos Franco, playing well below his best, scrambled well to stay in contention, and then accepted the tournament when first Harrison Frazar and then Blaine McCallister handed it to him.

- McCallister bogeyed the 72nd hole and was forced into a play-off when Franco saved par from 5 feet. Back to the 18th for the first play-off hole and McCallister three putted to let Franco get away with a poorly-played bogey. Then at the second extra hole McCallister went to pieces as Franco made par.

- Harrison Frazar was the leader standing on the 17th tee. He then shot a double bogey to lose his chance.
- Stephen Ames had poor Sunday showings when in contention three times last season, and again in the Tucson and Doral this season. This time the kept his nerve in R4 to finish T4th.
- Steve Stricker finished really well shooting 13 under over the last 36 holes. Four of his last eight rounds here have been 67 or lower!

1999 RESULT			1998 RESULT		
1	100/1	Carlos Franco	1	20/1	Lee Westwood
T2	150/1*	Harrison Frazar	2	200/1	Steve Flesch
T2	80/1	Steve Flesch	T3	150/1	Jim Carter
T4	200/1	Craig Barlow	T3	150/1	Mark Wiebe
T4	125/1	Dennis Paulson	T3	50/1	Glen Day
T4	150/1	Eric Booker	T3	80/1	Steve Lowery

WINNERS IN THE LAST TEN YEARS

1991	Ian Woosnam	1996	Scott McCarron
1992	Chip Beck	1997	Brad Faxon
1993	Mike Standly	1998	Lee Westwood
1994	Ben Crenshaw	1999	Carlos Franco
1995	Davis Love	2000	Carlos Franco

PUNTERS' GUIDE

- This is clearly becoming a course specialists' track :-
  - > The top 3 in 1999 finished first, third and T6th this year.
  - > Seven of this year's top 10 players had finished in the top 20 last year.
- On this track it is possible to shoot very low numbers (especially on the front nine). Nevertheless in six of the last seven years the winner has been the leader (or tied leader) after R3.
- In the last three years seventeen players have finished in the first 5 (or T5th).
  - > fourteen (82.3%) have been priced at or over 80/1
  - > nineteen (58.8%) have been priced at or over 100/1

  So it is absolutely clear that outsiders have a very, very strong recent record here.
- This tournament has been won five times in the nineties (Woosnam, Standly, McCarron, Westwood and Franco) by first-time winners.
- The players with good recent records include
  - > Carlos Franco   Won 2000 & 1999
  - > Harrison Frazar   3rd 2000: T2nd 1999
  - > Steve Flesch   T6th 2000: T2nd 1999: 2nd 1998

> Steve Stricker   T4th 2000: T20th 1999
> Scott Hoch   T9th 2000: T12th 1999: T12th 1998: T11th 1997
> Glen Day   T13th 2000: T7th 1999: T3rd 1998
> Kirk Triplett   T6th 2000: T12th 1999: T4th 1997

● Players whose profiles refer to this tournament include Steve Flesch, Harrison Frazar, Steve Stricker, Dennis Paulson, Franklin Langham, Kirk Triplett, Robert Allenby, Glen Day, Steve Lowery, Bill Glasson, Joel Edwards and Scott Hoch.

THE GTE BYRON NELSON CLASSIC

Date	11th - 14th May	
Venue	Irving, Texas	
Courses	TPC Las Colinas (Host course)	Cottonwood Valley
Par	70	70
Yardage	6,924	6,846
First Prize	$720,000	
Total Purse	$4 million	

THE TOURNAMENT

Started in 1944, this event moved to its current two-venue format in 1994. The TPC at Las Colinas and Cottonwood are played alternately on the first two days. The host course at Las Colinas is then used for the final two rounds.

THE COURSE

Both these courses are narrow and short, with accuracy rather power being the key requirement. There are just two par 5s on each track, with the above-average sized Bentgrass greens yielding plenty of birdie opportunities. Cottonwood usually plays almost a shot easier than Las Colinas.

2000 ODDS

fav	4/1	Tiger Woods	50/1	Chris Perry
	14/1	David Duval	50/1	Justin Leonard
	22/1	Phil Mickelson	66/1	Lee Janzen
	25/1	Davis Love	66/1	Steve Striker
	28/1	Vijay Singh	66/1	Mike Weir
	28/1	Hal Sutton	80/1	Robert Allenby
	33/1*	Jesper Parnevik	80/1	David Toms
	33/1	Jim Furyk	80/1	Kirk Triplett
	33/1	Nick Price	80/1	Mark Calcavecchia
	40/1	Sergio Garcia	80/1	Steve Pate
	50/1	Loren Roberts (DC)	80/1	Jeff Sluman
	50/1	John Huston	80/1	Jeff Maggert
	50/1	Stewart Cink	80/1	Bob Estes
	50/1	Steve Flesch	80/1	Stephen Ames

2000 RESULT

1	33/1	**Jesper Parnevik**	**70 65 68 66**	**269**

Parnevik won at the third play-off hole

T2	22/1	**Phil Mickelson**	**73 63 68 65**	**269**
T2	25/1	**Davis Love**	**66 63 71 69**	**269**
T4	50/1	**John Huston**	**68 65 67 70**	**270**
T4	fav 4/1	**Tiger Woods**	**73 67 67 63**	**270**

6	B Estes	69 68 68 66 271		D Peoples	71 69 72 69 281
T7	M Brooks	69 66 70 67 272		V Singh	69 69 73 70 281
	B Chamblee	72 65 71 64 272		K J Choi	74 68 69 70 281
9	Jerry Smith	68 68 70 67 273	T49	B Cheesman	72 67 73 70 282
T10	T Armour III	70 66 72 66 274		C DiMarco	73 70 72 67 282
	S Dunlap	73 65 70 66 274		G Kraft	72 68 72 70 282
	P Stankowski	72 67 66 69 274		David Sutherland	73 68 71 70 282
T13	H Kuehne	71 72 64 68 275		B Tway	72 70 73 67 282
	G Day	69 66 72 68 275		B Watts	73 68 71 70 282
T15	A Magee	71 71 66 68 276		K Wentworth	71 71 72 68 282
	B McCallister	66 69 71 70 276	T56	M Brisky	71 71 70 71 283
	Nick Price	70 68 70 68 276		B May	70 73 72 68 283
	B Bates	71 69 69 67 276		H Sutton	72 69 73 69 283
	S Garcia	`68 70 68 70 276		D A Weibring	72 70 71 70 283
T20	D Duval	70 69 68 70 277		C Riley	71 67 74 71 283
	J Furyk	73 66 73 65 277		E Booker	71 72 71 69 283
	F Langham	71 70 68 68 277	T62	S Ames	70 66 77 71 284
	S Maruyama	69 68 69 71 277		J Carter	73 70 74 67 284
	D Toms	70 71 67 69 277		L Janzen	68 70 75 71 284
T25	B Andrade	68 68 74 68 278		S Jones	70 68 73 73 284
	Tom Byrum	69 69 74 66 278		M Springer	75 68 75 66 284
	L Roberts	70 70 68 70 278	T67	Robin Freeman	73 70 70 72 285
	Kevin Sutherland	68 67 74 69 278		N Henke	72 70 75 68 285
	S Verplank	70 68 70 70 278		L Mattiace	74 69 68 74 285
T30	C Parry	72 67 71 69 279		T Purtzer	73 68 75 69 285
	T Tolles	73 70 67 69 279		H Frazar	71 66 76 72 285
	B Gay	75 67 69 68 279	T72	F Allem	72 68 77 69 286
T33	R Damron	75 67 67 71 280		S Gump	71 67 76 72 286
	D Forsman	71 66 73 70 280		B Lietzke	74 69 73 70 286
	S Lowery	77 66 70 67 280		E Fryatt	72 70 74 70 286
	T Scherrer	71 70 71 68 280	76	J Ogilvie	71 71 73 72 287
	M Wiebe	70 69 74 67 280	T77	B Crenshaw	73 70 71 74 288
	J Williamson	71 67 69 73 280		S Pate	76 67 74 71 288
	G Chalmers	71 72 72 65 280	T79	D Barron	71 71 74 73 289
	S Flesch	72 66 73 69 280		Bruce Smith	75 68 72 74 289
T41	N Faldo	70 70 73 68 281	T81	B Burns	70 73 77 70 290
	G Hjertstedt	69 70 74 68 281		B Mayfair	69 73 72 76 290
	S Kendall	70 70 73 68 281	T83	R Fehr	72 70 75 75 292
	N Lancaster	69 66 75 71 281		T Tryba	71 71 76 74 292
	J L Lewis	71 71 72 67 281			

The main players to miss the cut (made at 3 over) were:-

S Cink (+4)	B Henninger (+4)	J Sluman (+4)	M Weir (+4)
C A Spence (+4)	B Geiberger (+4)	B Fabel (+5)	R Allenby (+5)
C Perry (+5)	T Herron (+5)	B Elder (+5)	A Baddely (+5)
D Frost (+5)	W Austin (+5)	T Pernice Jr (+5)	J Cook (+5)
K Triplett (+5)	T Dodds (+5)	J Durant (+5)	E Toledo (+6)
J Edwards (+6)	O Browne (+6)	D Waldorf (+6)	B Jobe (+6)
C Pavin (+6)	N Begay (+6)	J Maggert (+7)	M Gogel (+7)
C Paulson (+7)	S McCarron (+7)	B Hughes (+8)	G Nicklaus (+8)
E Aubrey (+8)	D Stockton (+9)	J Leonard (+9)	J D Blake (+11)
J P Hayes (+11)	S Stricker (+11)	M Calcavecchia (+12)	C Raulerson (+13)
C Martin (+14)			

Paul Goydos (73), Rory Sabbatini (75) and Michael Bradley (77) all withdrew.

ROUND BY ROUND LEADERBOARD

FIRST ROUND
D Love	4 under
B McCallister	4 under
B Andrade	2 under
J Huston	2 under
S Garcia	2 under
J Smith	2 under
K Sutherland	2 under
L Janzen	2 under
J PARNEVIK	level

SECOND ROUND
D Love	11 under
J Huston	7 under
K Sutherland	5 under
M Brooks	5 under
G Day	5 under
J PARNEVIK	5 under
N Lancaster	5 under
B McCallister	5 under

THIRD ROUND
D Love	10 under
J Huston	10 under
J PARNEVIK	7 under
P Mickelson	6 under
M Brooks	5 under
P Stankowski	5 under
B Estes	5 under

FINAL ROUND
J PARNEVIK	11 under
P Mickelson	11 under
D Love	11 under
J Huston	10 under
T Woods	10 under

Thursday Last year 103 players beat par in R1. This year in winds gusting up to 38 mph only seventeen players were under the card.

Friday With reduced wind, scoring was restored to its normal low level.

PUNTERS' POINTS

● Jesper Parnevik missed a 1-foot tiddler putt on the 12th hole in R4, yet recovered to force a play-off which he won at the third extra hole, beating Davis Love after Phil Mickelson had been eliminated at the previous extra hole.

This was Parnevik's fourth USPGA Tour victory and moved him into the world top 10....and achieved wearing 'hot pink' pants!

- Tiger Woods very nearly pulled off one of the biggest-ever R4 comebacks, shooting 63 to come up just a shot short. It was the sixteenth time in the last nineteen tour events that Woods has posted a top 5 finish.

- 6th-placed Bob Estes was the only player to shoot four sub-par rounds.

- Phil Mickelson's profile last year pointed to his liking for this event and here he played really well after a poor start. However he only needed to par the last to win and he made bogey. Nevertheless, he's having a fine season, and with I.G. quoting 25-28 for his finishing position spread sellers had a nice touch.

- Paul Stankowski's return to form continued here with a solid 8 under par for the final 54 holes for him to finish T10th. His form figures now read 11-16-10....Stanko's back!

1999 RESULT

1	66/1	Loren Roberts
won at the first extra hole		
2	66/1	Steve Pate
T3	150/1	Chris DiMarco
T3	50/1	Lee Janzen
T3	100/1	Brian Watts
T3	100/1	Sergio Garcia

1998 RESULT

1	66/1	John Cook
T2	50/1	Hal Sutton
T2	22/1	Fred Couples
T2	150/1	Harrison Frazar
5	80/1	Steve Stricker

WINNERS IN THE LAST TEN YEARS

1991	Nick Price	1996	Phil Mickelson
1992	Billy Ray Brown	1997	Tiger Woods
1993	Scott Simpson	1998	John Cook
1994	Neil Lancaster	1999	Loren Roberts
1995	Ernie Els	2000	Jesper Parnevik

PUNTERS' GUIDE

- This year with the front 5 all starting at or under 50/1 the shorter-priced players came to the fore. This reversed the trend over the previous six years when 69% of those finishing in the top 4 (or T4th) had started at or over 66/1.

  'Normal service', with outsiders high up the leaderboard, may well be resumed in 2001.

- Best recent course form belongs to

Tiger Woods	Won 1997: 12th 1998: 7th 1999: T4th 2000
Phil Mickelson	Won 1996: T12th 1997: T6th 1998: MC 1999: T2nd 2000
Sergio Garcia	T3rd 1999: T15th 2000
Andrew Magee	T5th 1997: 12th 1999: T15th 2000

- Players whose profiles refer to this tournament include Tiger Woods, Sergio Garcia, Phil Mickelson, Andrew Magee, Paul Stankowski, Loren Roberts and Harrison Frazar.

THE MASTERCARD COLONIAL

Date	18th - 21st May
Course	Colonial Country Club, Fort Worth, Texas
Par	70
Yardage	7,010
First Prize	$594,000
Total Purse	$3.3 million

THE TOURNAMENT

This very prestigious event has always been held at the Colonial Club since its inception in 1946.

THE COURSE

With just two par 5s, tight fairways and small greens, this course suits accurate shot makers. It favours the straight-hitting, 'fairways and greens' player rather than the young, 300-yards-off-the-tee guys. The greens are bent grass. Recently the fairways have been slightly narrowed and the greens reduced in size. Holes 3 to 5 are known as 'the horseshoe' because of their collective shape. The 5th is the most difficult on the course, and on the whole tour, with the par 3 4th also very tricky.

2000 ODDS

fav	10/1	David Duval	66/1*	Mark O'Meara
	14/1	Phil Mickelson	66/1*	Fred Funk
	14/1	Davis Love	66/1*	Glen Day
	20/1	Vijay Singh	66/1	Mark Brooks
	22/1	Carlos Franco	66/1	Kenny Perry
	22/1	Jim Furyk	66/1	Craig Parry
	25/1	John Huston	66/1	Robert Allenby
	33/1	Scott Hoch	66/1	Mark Calcavecchia
	40/1	Stuart Appleby	80/1*	Mike Weir
	40/1	Steve Flesch	80/1	Harrison Frazar
	40/1	Loren Roberts	80/1	Stephen Ames
	40/1	Stewart Cink	80/1	Steve Elkington
	50/1	Fred Couples	80/1	Shigeki Maruyama
	50/1	Bob Estes	80/1	Kirk Triplett
	50/1	Dudley Hart (non runner)	80/1*	Billy Mayfair
	50/1	Lee Janzen	80/1	Scott Verplank
	50/1	Justin Leonard	80/1	Tim Herron
	50/1	Jeff Sluman	80/1	Jonathan Kaye
	50/1	David Toms	80/1	Scott Dunlap

2000 RESULT

1	14/1	Phil Mickelson	67 68 70 63 268
T2	40/1	Stewart Cink	70 64 65 71 270
T2	14/1	Davis Love	67 66 69 68 270
T4	50/1	David Toms	67 66 72 67 272
T4	100/1	Rocco Mediate	68 67 69 68 272

T6	B Estes	69 72 66 66 273		S Appleby	71 71 69 69 280
	G Kraft	67 68 71 67 273		S Dunlap	68 68 67 77 280
T8	J Furyk	69 66 72 67 274	T41	B Gay	70 70 70 71 281
	J Cook	66 70 70 68 274		Kenny Perry	70 71 70 70 281
	M Calcavecchia	72 67 67 68 274		J Haas	69 70 70 72 281
	L Mattiace	67 72 67 68 274		V Singh	73 67 72 69 281
	M Weir	67 68 69 70 274		M O'Meara	73 66 68 74 281
T13	K Triplett	72 66 71 66 275	T46	S Pate	70 69 71 72 282
	S Maruyama	69 70 70 66 275		K Clearwater	67 71 73 71 282
	F Funk	70 67 69 69 275		B Watts	69 68 69 76 282
	S Kendall	69 67 70 69 275		L Roberts	77 66 71 68 282
	Joel Edwards	68 72 65 70 275	T50	R Damron	71 72 69 71 283
	T Herron	70 66 69 70 275		J Kelly	75 68 70 70 283
	J Sluman	69 68 67 71 275		J Green	69 71 74 69 283
T20	J Huston	70 71 68 67 276		T Kite	69 72 73 69 283
	J D Blake	71 72 67 66 276		Tom Byrum	71 71 72 69 283
	S Verplank	69 72 67 68 276	T55	T Pernice Jr	72 70 70 72 284
	Kevin Sutherland	71 68 68 69 276		J P Hayes	70 70 67 77 284
T24	B Glasson	70 67 72 68 277		K Yokoo	72 69 72 71 284
	Russ Cochran	75 66 68 68 277		G Day	70 70 75 69 284
	B Geiberger	75 66 68 68 277	59	D Waldorf	73 69 70 73 285
	M Reid	75 66 70 66 277	60	P Goydos	74 68 69 75 286
	B Andrade	70 66 75 66 277	61	J Leonard	73 70 74 70 287
	Carl Paulson	69 73 71 64 277	T62	S Elkington	71 70 73 74 288
	F Couples	70 66 68 73 277		C Martin	74 69 71 74 288
T31	C Raulerson	70 70 71 67 278		R Allenby	71 68 77 72 288
	S Flesch	71 67 70 70 278		B Jobe	73 69 75 71 288
T33	J L Lewis	73 68 69 69 279		K Hosokawa	72 71 74 71 288
	D Frost	67 69 69 74 279	67	N Lancaster	72 70 71 76 289
T35	P Jacobsen	73 69 68 70 280	T68	N Faldo	71 70 75 74 290
	G Chalmers	73 69 68 70 280		J Carter	72 70 77 71 290
	F Nobilo	68 70 73 69 280	70	R Sabbatini	68 70 79 74 291
	Robin Freeman	70 69 69 72 280			

The main players to miss the cut (made at 3 over) were:–

O Browne (+4)	S Gump (+4)	F Langham (+4)	B Mayfair (+4)
C DiMarco (+5)	B Henninger (+5)	C Parry (+5)	D Paulson (+5)
N Begay (+5)	E Toledo (+5)	M Brooks (+6)	L Janzen (+6)
T Purtzer (+6)	J Sindelar (+6)	H Frazar (+6)	T Armour III (+7)
M Hulbert (+7)	J Ozaki (+7)	C Franco (+7)	G Nicklaus (+7)
S Hoch (+8)	B Lietzke (+8)	B Tway (+8)	E Fryatt (+8)
C Pavin (+9)	O Uresti (+9)	H Haas (am) (+9)	M Gogel (+10)
R Beem (+10)	B Crenshaw (+10)	S Ames (+11)	R Gamez (+11)
B Hughes (+11)	B McCallister (+11)	B Elder (+12)	

Ted Tryba (74), Jonathan Kaye (75) and Fulton Allem (77) all withdrew.

ROUND BY ROUND LEADERBOARD

FIRST ROUND

J Cook	4 under
P MICKELSON	3 under
K Clearwater	3 under
D Toms	3 under
L Mattiace	3 under
D Frost	3 under
D Love	3 under
M Weir	3 under
G Kraft	3 under

SECOND ROUND

D Love	7 under
D Toms	7 under
S Cink	6 under
J Furyk	5 under
G Kraft	5 under
R Mediate	5 under
M Weir	5 under
P MICKELSON	5 under

THIRD ROUND

S Cink	11 under
D Love	8 under
S Dunlap	7 under
M Weir	6 under
F Couples	6 under
R Mediate	6 under
J Sluman	6 under
P MICKELSON	5 under

FINAL ROUND

P MICKELSON	12 under
S Cink	10 under
D Love	10 under
D Toms	8 under
R Mediate	8 under

PUNTERS' POINTS

● Phil Mickelson shot 10 under for the last 27 holes to put pressure on Cink who clearly 'bottled' it. Three bogeys in the last 4 holes saw his lead evaporate to give 'lefty' his sixteenth tour win.

● 40/1 Cink, who was tipped for this tournament in his player profile last year, has a game well suited here. However he showed how tough it is to be a front runner rather than a chaser. After all, last week Mickelson lost a lead late on, whereas this week he charged home from 'off the pace' with a 63 while front-runner Cink collapsed.

● Disappointing final rounds must also be noted from

> Scott Dunlap, 3rd after R3, shoots 7 (!) over par in R4 to finish T35th.

> Course specialist Jeff Sluman, T4th after R3, shoots 1 over par in R4 to finish T13th.

> Fred Couples, T4th after R3, shoots 3 over par in R4 to finish T24th.

● Brent Geiberger has course form of 33-41-39 and was T24th this year. However his 8 under par for the final 54 holes this year was eye catching. Over those four years his eclectic (69.65.67.68) score is 11 under par. He could be a rank outsider with a squeak in 2001.

1999 RESULT

1	150/1	Olin Browne
T2	80/1	Paul Goydos
T2	33/1	Jeff Sluman
T2	80/1	Tim Herron
T2	80/1*	Fred Funk
T2	100/1	Greg Kraft

1998 RESULT

1	66/1	Tom Watson
2	25/1	Jim Furyk
3	66/1	Jeff Sluman
4	100/1	Harrison Frazar
5	33/1	John Cook

WINNERS IN THE LAST TEN YEARS

1991	Tom Purtzer		1996	Corey Pavin
1992	Bruce Lietzke		1997	David Frost
1993	Fulton Allem		1998	Tom Watson
1994	Nick Price		1999	Olin Browne
1995	Tom Lehman		2000	Phil Mickelson

PUNTERS' GUIDE

● The importance of course form was shown

> last year when six of the top 10 had posted a top 20 finish in one of the previous two years.

> this year five of the top 7 had finished in the top 21 in 1999.

● In the nineties three facts were noted

> Every winner was in his thirties or forties

> The youngest winner was 35

> The average winning age was 38.6

This year the ages of the the front 5 were Mickelson (30), Cink (27 on tournament Sunday), Love (36), Toms (33) and Mediate (37).

● The best Colonial records recently belong to

	2000	1999	1998	1997	1996
Jeff Sluman	13	2	3	13	2
John Cook	8	11	5	-	-
Jim Furyk	8	55	2	8	38
John Huston	20	7	18	9	46
Davis Love	2	11	-	70	5
Kirk Triplett	13	21	18	15	69
Bob Estes	6	7	MC	41	MC

● Of the top 6 players in last week's Byron Nelson four played this week.

	Nelson	Colonial
Phil Mickelson	T2nd	Won
Davis Love	T2nd	T2nd

Bob Estes	6th	T6th
John Huston	T4th	T20th

Their performances at Fort Worth show that the form from the Byron Nelson can be taken across Texas to the Colonial as both are played on short, tight, par 70 courses with bentgrass greens.

● Players whose profiles refer to this tournament include Jim Furyk, Davis Love, John Cook, Jeff Sluman, Stewart Cink, Bob Estes, Stuart Appleby, Len Mattiace, Harrison Frazar and Brent Geiberger.

THE MEMORIAL TOURNAMENT

Date	25th - 28th May
Course	Muirfield Village, Dublin, Ohio
Par	72
Yardage	7,185
First Prize	$558,000
Total Purse	$3.1 million

THE TOURNAMENT

Started in 1976, The Memorial has always been held at the Jack Nicklaus designed course at Muirfield Village. It has a reduced field of just 105 players compared to the usual 156.

THE COURSE

Despite Tiger's performance this year, this is not an easy course. It is long, the fairways have been narrowed, and the relatively small, undulating, bentgrass greens are not an easy target. The course suits the experienced, solid ball striker who can plot his way round. Length, especially in the usual wet conditions, is a clear advantage.

2000 ODDS

fav	7/2	Tiger Woods (DC)	66/1	Stuart Appleby
	10/1	David Duval	66/1	Bob Estes
	20/1	Ernie Els	66/1	Scott Hoch
	22/1	Vijay Singh	80/1	Mark Calcavecchia
	25/1	Tom Lehman	80/1	Justin Leonard
	33/1	Jim Furyk	80/1	Greg Norman
	33/1	Hal Sutton	80/1	Glen Day
	40/1	Carlos Franco	80/1	Scott Dunlap
	40/1	John Huston	80/1	Fred Funk
	50/1	Stewart Cink	80/1	Mark O'Meara
	50/1	Steve Flesch	80/1	Jeff Sluman
	50/1	Fred Couples	80/1	Shigeki Maruyama
	66/1	Chris Perry	80/1	Robert Allenby
	66/1	Mike Weir	80/1	Paul Azinger

2000 RESULT

1	fav 7/2	**Tiger Woods**	**71 63 65 70 269**
T2	20/1	**Ernie Els**	**73 64 72 65 274**
T2	80/1	**Justin Leonard**	**70 70 66 68 274**
4	66/1	**Mike Weir**	**74 65 68 69 276**
T5	80/1	**Paul Azinger**	**72 71 69 66 278**
T5	50/1	**Steve Flesch**	**76 68 64 70 278**
T5	125/1	**Steve Lowery**	**73 66 66 73 278**

T8	F Couples	74 69 69 67 279	T45	T Herron	74 71 75 69 289
	H Sutton	71 71 67 70 279		G Chalmers	71 75 72 71 289
T10	J P Hayes	74 66 71 69 280		F Nobilo	74 71 73 71 289
	S Maruyama	73 69 68 70 280		S Cink	76 72 69 72 289
12	B Elder	71 68 69 73 281		P Jacobsen	74 68 74 73 289
T13	S Hoch	74 67 71 70 282		N Begay	72 74 68 75 289
	R Mediate	73 71 68 70 282	T51	L Donald (am)	74 71 73 72 290
	O Browne	71 68 72 71 282		Joe Ozaki	72 71 74 73 290
	G Kraft	70 73 68 71 282		D Waldorf	74 68 75 73 290
T17	Chris Perry	74 70 71 68 283		B Geiberger	72 72 73 73 290
	S Appleby	76 69 69 69 283		T Scherrer	69 71 75 75 290
	J Haas	75 70 69 69 283		R Beem	71 69 75 75 290
T20	A Magee	76 71 71 66 284		M O'Meara	73 69 73 75 290
	S Verplank	71 72 73 68 284	T58	N Faldo	79 69 71 72 291
	C Franco	73 71 70 70 284		David Edwards	71 72 77 71 291
	H Frazar	66 69 78 71 284		S Dunlap	76 72 71 72 291
	B Glasson	72 68 73 71 284		J Huston	71 72 72 76 291
T25	Gary Nicklaus	72 68 74 71 285		F Funk	73 70 71 77 291
	R Damron	74 69 71 71 285	63	B Tway	74 69 70 79 292
	J Sluman	73 71 70 71 285	T64	Dennis Paulson	79 69 73 72 293
	J Kaye	72 69 72 72 285		Jack Nicklaus	75 73 72 73 293
	J Kelly	72 71 70 72 285		T Pernice Jr	77 71 72 73 293
	L Mize	74 71 67 73 285	67	T Tryba	72 74 72 76 294
	J Furyk	73 70 69 73 285	T68	C Pavin	77 71 76 71 295
	D Duval	73 69 68 75 285		S Jones	74 73 77 71 295
T33	J L Lewis	74 74 70 68 286		K Fergus	73 75 73 74 295
	B Faxon	74 73 68 71 286		J Cook	76 72 72 75 295
	P Goydos	72 72 70 72 286		Joel Edwards	73 74 73 75 295
	M Brooks	72 69 72 73 286		S Stricker	74 72 73 76 295
	G Hjertstedt	70 70 72 74 286		N Lancaster	74 71 74 76 295
	V Singh	72 69 68 77 286		S Kendall	73 72 73 77 295
T39	F Lickliter	76 71 69 71 287	T76	D Pooley	76 72 77 71 296
	Kenny Perry	69 72 70 76 287		B Mayfair	75 72 74 75 296
T41	E Fryatt	78 70 70 70 288		B Estes	71 71 75 79 296
	M Calcavecchia	71 72 73 72 288	79	J D Blake	76 72 76 73 297
	T Lehman	72 71 72 73 288		G Norman	70 71 76 WD
	G Day	72 73 68 75 288			

The main players to miss the cut (made at 4 over) were:–

K Sutherland (+5)	B Watts (+5)	J Carter (+5)	F Langham (+5)
F Zoeller (+6)	B Henninger (+6)	C A Spence (+6)	C DiMarco (+6)
J Daly (+6)	B Andrade (+6)	J Sindelar (+7)	J Maggert (+7)
R Allenby (+7)	M Gogel (+7)	K Wentworth (+8)	S Gump (+8)
J Smith (+8)	G Storm (am) (+9)	R Sabbatini (+12)	A Baddeley (am) (+13)
D Sutherland (+15)	K Hosokawa (+15)	H Haas (am) (+16)	

Greg Norman and Craig Stadler withdrew.

ROUND BY ROUND LEADERBOARD

FIRST ROUND		SECOND ROUND	
H Frazar	6 under	T WOODS	10 under
T Scherrer	3 under	H Frazar	9 under
K Perry	3 under	E Els	7 under
G Kraft	2 under	B Elder	5 under
G Hjerstedt	2 under	S Lowery	5 under
G Norman	2 under	O Browne	5 under
J Leonard	2 under	M Weir	5 under
T WOODS	1 under		

THIRD ROUND		FINAL ROUND	
T WOODS	17 under	T WOODS	19 under
S Lowery	11 under	E Els	14 under
J Leonard	10 under	J Leonard	14 under
M Weir	9 under	M Weir	12 under
S Flesch	8 under	P Azinger	10 under
B Elder	8 under	S Flesch	10 under
		S Lowery	10 under

Thursday	Sunny skies above and 20 mph winds below
Friday	Warm, windless day made for low scoring
Saturday	As a storm was expected players went out in threes on a soft, soggy Muirfield Village course
Sunday	Play could not be completed so the tournament went into a Monday for the third time in its history.

PUNTERS' POINTS

● "Man, he's just awesome," said Ernie Els, and probably many others, as Tiger became the first successful defending champion in the Memorial's 25-year history.

● Woods's domination of world golf is shown by the fact that he won for the eleventh time in his last twenty tournaments and has finished out of the top 10 just five times in his last thirty-four tournaments worldwide.

"In his own mind he can get better," said Els, "in everyone else's mind, he's as good as we want him to play."

"He's just making mincemeat out of golf courses" said Jack Nicklaus.

● Justin Leonard, in the worst slump of his career, started at 80/1. However he won the 1992 Amateur title here, likes the course, and tied for first 'in the other tournament' alongside Ernie Els.

● Mike Weir's impressive finish (14 under last 54 holes) took him to 4th spot, and gives him a real chance of making the US Presidents Cup team.

● Left-hander Steve Flesch also finished well (also 14 under last three rounds) as he keeps 'knocking the door' looking for his first victory.

● Harrison Frazar, not for the first time, showed real nerves. 2nd at halfway, playing alongside Tiger in R3 he shot a 78!! The young Texan is learning the hard way just how tough it can be when at or near the top of the leaderboard.

1999 RESULT			1998 RESULT		
1	11/1	Tiger Woods	1	25/1	Fred Couples
2	25/1	Vijay Singh	2	125/1	Andrew Magee
T3	fav 9/1	David Duval	3	14/1	David Duval
T3	100/1	Olin Browne	4	22/1	Jim Furyk
T3	80/1	Carlos Franco	T5	20/1	Davis Love
			T5	150/1	Brandel Chamblee

WINNERS IN THE LAST TEN YEARS

		Age			Age
1991	Kenny Perry	30	1996	Tom Watson	46
1992	David Edwards	36	1997	Vijay Singh	34
1993	Paul Azinger	33	1998	Fred Couples	38
1994	Tom Lehman	35	1999	Tiger Woods	23 (!)
1995	Greg Norman	40	2000	Tiger Woods	24 (!)

PUNTERS' GUIDE

● This tournament, founded by Jack Nicklaus in 1976, has now had twenty-three out of one hundred rounds either delayed, suspended or cancelled because of rain. An ability to handle damp conditions and interruptions is certainly needed at Muirfield Village.

● In making an outright selection go for a player who has
> preferably an early tee time to beat the potentially dodgy weather
> accuracy off tee and fairways
> course experience
> R4 'bottle' as experienced players (and Tiger) tend to win here.

● Remember that the first-round leader has yet to win the Memorial.

● Best recent records are held by
> Tiger Woods   Winner in both 2000 and 1999
> David Duval   Three top 3 finishes in the last five years
> Ernie Els   Four top 7 finishes in the last five years
> Jim Furyk   Two top 4 finishes in the last four years
> Vijay Singh   Victory (1997) and a 2nd in the last four years
> Justin Leonard   Form figs 16-7-2 last three years

● The players whose profiles refer to this tournament include Tiger Woods, Mike Weir, David Duval, Ernie Els, Justin Leonard, Vijay Singh, Paul Azinger and Chris Perry.

THE KEMPER OPEN

Date	1st - 4th June
Course	TPC at Avenel, Potomac, Maryland
Par	71
Yardage	7,005
First Prize	$540,000
Total Purse	$3 million

THE TOURNAMENT

Started in 1968 the Kemper moved to the TPC at Avenel in 1987. So this was the fourteenth Kemper to be staged here. It has a reputation for producing first-time winners with eight first-timers victorious in the last seventeen years, including 500/1 Rich Beem in 1999.

THE COURSE

The Avenel TPC was specifically built to provide maximum viewing for the galleries. It is a very tough, long, par 71 course. It has severe rough and large bentgrass greens. It has become a course-specialists' track.

2000 ODDS

fav	9/1	Ernie Els	50/1	Fred Funk
	16/1	Tom Lehman	50/1	Jeff Sluman
	20/1	Justin Leonard	50/1	Steve Stricker
	25/1	Carlos Franco	66/1	Tim Herron
	25/1	Stewart Cink	66/1	Bill Glasson
	28/1	Stuart Appleby	66/1	Kirk Triplett
	33/1*	Scott Hoch	66/1	Paul Stankowski
	33/1	David Toms	66/1	Jonathan Kaye
	40/1	Bob Estes	66/1	Andrew Magee
	40/1	Lee Janzen	80/1*	Steve Elkington
	40/1*	Loren Roberts	80/1*	Steve Lowery
	40/1	Dudley Hart	80/1	Robert Allenby
	50/1	Mark O'Meara	80/1	Steve Jones

2000 RESULT

1	125/1	Tom Scherrer	67 68 69 67 271
T2	150/1	Kazuhiko Hosokawa	73 68 66 66 273
T2	20/1	Justin Leonard	65 68 71 69 273
T2	150/1	Greg Chalmers	65 71 69 68 273
T2	80/1*	Steve Lowery	64 68 70 71 273
T2	125/1	Franklin Langham	70 67 66 70 273

T7	S Appleby	70 73 64 68 275
	T Herron	66 69 71 69 275
	D Peoples	71 68 67 69 275
T10	D Hammond	67 66 74 69 276
	B Glasson	68 68 70 70 276
	K Triplett	68 70 68 70 276
T13	T Lehman	68 72 70 67 277
	J D Blake	70 71 68 68 277
	P Stankowski	67 68 68 74 277
T16	B Faxon	69 74 69 66 278
	L Janzen	68 74 68 68 278
	J Gove	71 68 68 71 278
	G Waite	71 67 68 72 278
T20	M Clark II	68 73 75 63 279
	B Gay	72 69 74 64 279
	Dudley Hart	69 71 74 65 279
	C Barlow	65 75 72 67 279
	B Burns	71 70 69 69 279
	J Williamson	64 74 70 71 279
	Joe Ozaki	70 71 67 71 279
	S Cink	69 69 68 73 279
T28	E Toledo	70 71 71 68 280
	J Kaye	69 68 74 69 280
	J Green	68 73 69 70 280
	C DiMarco	67 66 76 71 280
T32	C A Spence	74 68 70 69 281
	B Elder	70 71 69 71 281
T34	S Hoch	69 74 72 67 282
	E Els	72 70 72 68 282
	C Riley	73 70 70 69 282
	B Quigley	65 75 72 70 282
	S Jones	73 68 71 70 282
	B McCallister	70 69 71 72 282
	O Browne	74 67 69 72 282
	S Micheel	73 69 68 72 282
	J Daly	72 71 67 72 282
	F Nobilo	68 70 71 73 282

T44	J Ogilvie	71 71 71 70 283
	L Roberts	71 67 74 71 283
	B Friend	67 73 71 72 283
T47	Larry Rinker	72 69 72 71 284
	S Gotsche	72 71 70 71 284
	P Jordan	68 72 72 72 284
	B Andrade	67 75 70 72 284
	Tom Byrum	68 70 73 73 284
	R Allenby	71 72 68 73 284
	B Chamblee	69 71 70 74 284
	J Durant	71 69 69 75 284
	C Martin	68 71 67 78 284
T56	S Elkington	75 68 73 69 285
	M Bradley	72 70 73 70 285
	F Lickliter	68 73 73 71 285
	S Stricker	72 68 71 74 285
T60	J Restino	74 68 74 70 286
	B Estes	70 72 73 71 286
	G Hnatiuk	72 71 72 71 286
	J Buha	73 70 70 73 286
	S McCarron	70 70 71 75 286
T65	M Carnevale	74 67 77 70 288
	J Delsing	72 70 74 72 288
	C Beck	69 74 72 73 288
	A Magee	71 69 73 75 288
T69	B Gilder	73 70 75 71 289
	David Sutherland	68 74 76 71 289
	E Fryatt	69 72 73 75 289
	R Black	67 75 72 75 289
	C Perks	71 72 71 75 289
T74	Willie Wood	70 71 77 72 290
	Brad Bryant	70 72 75 73 290
T76	N Lancaster	72 71 79 70 292
	E Booker	77 66 73 76 292
	M Wiebe	72 68 72 80 292
79	S Gangluff	70 73 78 73 294
80	C Franco	70 73 75 79 297

The main players to miss the cut (made at 1 over) were:–

R Gamez (+2)	B Hughes (+2)	O Uresti (+2)	W Austin (+2)
B Fabel (+2)	M Sposa (+2)	D Dunakey (+2)	J Gallagher (+2)
F Funk (+2)	R Beem (+2)	E Aubrey (+2)	M Springer (+3)
R Freeman (+3)	C Paulson (+3)	D Barron (+3)	J Maginnes (+3)
J Sluman (+3)	N Henke (+3)	M Hulbert (+3)	S Gump (+4)
D Forsman (+4)	D Toms (4)	M Brisky (+4)	D Pride (+4)
H Kuehne (+4)	B Bates (+5)	P H Horgan (+5)	M Reid (+5)
D Stockton (+5)	K Wentworth (+5)	D Frost (+5)	G Kraft (+6)
M O'Meara (+6)	T Armour III (+6)	C Beckman (+7)	J Sindelar (+8)
D Ogrin (+8)	P Blackmar (+8)	J Kelly (+9)	K Gibson (+10)
S Ames (+10)	T Dodds (+14)	M Goggin (+16)	

David Edwards (77) withdrew.

ROUND BY ROUND LEADERBOARD

FIRST ROUND

S Lowery	7 under
J Williamson	7 under
G Chalmers	6 under
B Quigley	6 under
J Leonard	6 under
C Barlow	6 under
T Herron	5 under
T SCHERRER	4 under

SECOND ROUND

S Lowery	10 under
D Hammond	9 under
J Leonard	9 under
C DiMarco	9 under
P Stankowski	7 under
T SCHERRER	7 under
T Herron	7 under

THIRD ROUND

S Lowery	11 under
F Langham	10 under
P Stankowski	10 under
T SCHERRER	9 under
J Leonard	9 under
G Chalmers	8 under

FINAL ROUND

T SCHERRER	13 under
K Hosokawa	11 under
J Leonard	11 under
G Chalmers	11 under
S Lowery	11 under
F Langham	11 under

PUNTERS' POINTS

● Tom Scherrer thoroughly deserved his first tour win. Although he made a poor drive at the 16th in R4 he was otherwise very composed over the back nine. Twice a winner on the Buy.com tour and T2nd earlier this season in the Tucson Open, he has clearly been inspired by 'the nappy factor' since the birth of his son Thomas last year. He has the fitness and the game to go on to further success.

● Steve Lowery led into R4 and was in contention when he found water at the 17th. He's in fine form now he's resettled in Alabama after his Florida home was burned down last year.

● Greg Chalmers, my 150/1 outsider, nearly gave Timeform Sportsline its biggest-ever win. However the left-handed Aussie, who led with 10 holes left, bogeyed the 9th, and double bogeyed the 12th, so ultimately had to be content with T2nd. A superb putter, he looks a future winner.

- Justin Leonard, who beat Tom Scherrer to win the 1992 US Amateur title, has a fine Kemper record, and he continued his recent improved form, although his double bogey at the 12th in R4 ruined his winning chance.
- Kazuhiko Hosokawa missed the cut by 11 shots last week at the Memorial yet here he played brilliantly (a tournament-best 13 under for the last 54 holes) to finish T2nd to the cheers of the bookies.
- Let's remember that, the winner apart, only three players posted four sub-par rounds
  > T2nd Franklin Langham
  > T10th Bill Glasson
  > T10th Kirk Triplett

1999 RESULT			1998 RESULT		
1	500/1	(now very) Rich Beem	1	100/1	Stuart Appleby
T2	150/1	Bradley Hughes	2	18/1	Scott Hoch
T2	50/1*	Bill Glasson	T3	20/1	Mark O'Meara
T4	28/1	Hal Sutton	T3	125/1	Brad Fabel
T4	150/1*	David Toms	T3	80/1	Clark Dennis
			T3	150/1	Tommy Tolles
			T3	100/1	Fred Funk

WINNERS IN THE LAST TEN YEARS

1991	Billy Andrade	1996	Steve Stricker
1992	Bill Glasson	1997	Justin Leonard
1993	Grant Waite	1998	Stuart Appleby
1994	Mark Brooks	1999	Rich Beem
1995	Lee Janzen	2000	Tom Scherrer

PUNTERS' GUIDE

- This tournament has built a reputation for producing first-time winners. Indeed it has produced nine in the last eighteen years including Rich Beem (500/1) and Tom Scherrer (125/1) in the last two.
- The outstanding recent record of outsiders is shown by key facts. In the last four years of the twenty-four players finishing in the top 5 (or T5th)
  > thirteen (54%) have been best priced at 100/1+
  > nine (37.5%) have been best priced at 150/1 (!!)+
- Throughout the nineties a clear age pattern of the winner emerged, with only one player over 33 winning. The average winning age was 30.3, and from 1991-1999 inclusive it was 28.8.

So Tom Scherrer at 29 years 11 months fell into the 'right' age category.

● So the identikit of the winner has often been
  > A first-time winner
  > Aged 27 to 31 years of age
  > At a big price
● The best course form in recent years has been recorded by

> Stuart Appleby	7-6-W-14-18, with fifteen of his twenty rounds under par
> Steve Stricker	Won 1996: 8th 1998: 10th 1999. M/cut 1997 and T56th 2000
> Bill Glasson	10th 2000: T2nd 1999 and won tournament twice, including in 1992 on this course
> David Toms	Last four starts - two missed cuts plus 4th 1999 and 6th 1996
> Justin Leonard	2-22-25-W-13 in last five years

● No R3 leader has been successful in the nineties and Steve Lowery maintained that sequence this year.
● Players whose profiles refer to this tournament include Stuart Appleby, Bill Glasson, Greg Chalmers, David Toms, Carlos Franco, Steve Stricker, Franklin Langham, Jonathan Kaye and Jay Williamson.

THE BUICK CLASSIC

Date	8th - 11th June
Course	Westchester, Harrison, New York
Par	71
Yardage	6,722
First Prize	$540,000
Total Purse	$3 million

THE TOURNAMENT

The Buick Classic this year was restored to its normal place as the tournament before the US Open. In the past this event has proved a very reliable guide to the second American major as the Westchester set up is so similar to that used in the US Open (please see p 28 of last year's volume).

THE COURSE

The Westchester course is set up in many ways as a mirror image of the US Open course to be faced next week. It is short but tight, with narrow fairways and very fast tiny bentgrass greens. There is a premium on accuracy off the tee and quality iron play. The final hole is a reachable par 5.

2000 ODDS

jt fav	12/1	David Duval	66/1	Steve Lowery
jt fav	12/1	Phil Mickelson	66/1	Shigeki Maruyama
jt fav	12/1	Ernie Els	66/1	Greg Norman
	14/1	Davis Love	66/1	J M Olazabal
	20/1	Tom Lehman	66/1	Fred Funk
	20/1	Vijay Singh	66/1	Paul Stankowski
	22/1	Jesper Parnevik	80/1*	Jeff Maggert
	25/1	Jim Furyk	80/1	Tom Scherrer (PWW)
	33/1	Sergio Garcia	80/1	Greg Chalmers
	40/1	Steve Flesch	80/1	M A Jimenez
	40/1	Fred Couples	80/1	Scott Dunlap
	50/1	Mike Weir	80/1	Rocco Mediate
	50/1	Chris Perry	80/1	Steve Pate
	66/1	Bill Glasson		

2000 RESULT

1	100/1	Dennis Paulson	65 68 75 68 276
2	jt fav 12/1	David Duval	70 67 70 69 276
3	33/1	Sergio Garcia	74 70 65 68 277
4	66/1	Greg Norman	71 72 68 67 278
T5	22/1	Jesper Parnevik	71 70 70 68 279
T5	125/1	Joey Sindelar	68 68 71 72 279
T5	125/1	John Cook	68 71 68 72 279
T5	jt fav 12/1	Ernie Els	70 69 68 72 279
T5	50/1	Chris Perry	69 70 68 72 279

10	S Lowery	70 69 69 72 280			S Kendall	67 68 72 80 287
T11	S Pate	71 72 69 69 281		T42	C Barlow	68 76 72 72 288
	J Carter	69 72 67 73 281			J Durant	72 72 72 72 288
T13	J Green	68 73 73 68 282			T Scherrer	74 70 72 72 288
	D Waldorf	66 72 68 76 282			P Jordan	73 68 75 72 288
	P Mickelson	69 70 68 75 282			W Austin	69 74 72 73 288
T16	F Couples	69 71 75 68 283			P Blackmar	72 69 74 73 288
	B Quigley	70 70 72 71 283			S Gump	75 64 75 74 288
	P Goydos	71 68 72 72 283			S Flesch	70 71 73 74 288
T19	Kevin Sutherland	72 71 73 68 284			Bobby Cochran	74 69 69 76 288
	J P Hayes	69 72 72 71 284		T51	Robin Freeman	68 70 78 73 289
	M Weir	68 70 73 73 284			J Furyk	70 70 76 73 289
	J Maginnes	67 71 72 74 284			S Micheel	68 73 73 75 289
	M A Jimenez	66 74 70 74 284		T54	B Bates	71 73 72 74 290
T24	V Singh	70 71 74 70 285			M Reid	71 72 70 77 290
	B Friend	72 71 71 71 285			Jerry Smith	69 72 72 77 290
	O Uresti	69 73 71 72 285		T57	R Fehr	75 69 75 72 291
	Russ Cochran	71 67 73 74 285			C Beckman	70 74 74 73 291
	D Briggs	70 71 70 74 285			A Bengoechea	72 71 74 74 291
T29	D Berganio	73 71 74 68 286			F Funk	73 70 73 75 291
	P H Horgan	68 72 72 74 286			M Wiebe	69 73 74 75 291
	L Mize	69 70 72 75 286			C Stadler	71 69 74 77 291
	S Maruyama	70 73 67 76 286			F Allem	73 68 72 78 291
T33	B Jobe	71 71 74 71 287		T64	B Burns	72 72 75 73 292
	R Beem	75 69 71 72 287			K J Choi	73 69 75 75 292
	M Goggin	70 73 72 72 287			Tom Byrum	73 70 73 76 292
	G Waite	70 73 71 73 287			D Stockton	74 68 74 76 292
	D Love	66 74 74 73 287		T68	B Faxon	71 73 77 72 293
	E Fryatt	72 72 69 74 287			G Kraft	68 76 75 74 293
	G Hjertstedt	67 72 73 75 287			Bart Bryant	70 73 77 73 293
	S Dunlap	71 67 73 76 287		71	C Riley	70 71 76 78 295

The main players to miss the cut (made at 2 over) were:–

L Mattiace (+3)	C Parry (+3)	T Pernice Jr (+3)	T Lehman (+3)
B Hughes (+3)	D Peoples (+3)	M Clark (+3)	S Ames (+3)
J M Olazabal (+3)	M Bradley (+3)	J Van de Velde (+3)	G Chalmers (+3)
D Barron (+4)	J Ozaki (+4)	G Hnatiuk (+4)	P Stankowski (+4)
E Booker (+4)	B Henninger (+4)	B McCallister (+5)	B Andrade (+5)
T Dodds (+5)	B Tway (+5)	D Dunakey (+5)	S Murphy (+5)
T Tryba (+5)	T Purtzer (+5)	O Browne (+5)	D Frost (+5)
B Fabel (+6)	B Gay (+6)	D Sutherland (+7)	M Gogel (+7)
E Toledo (+7)	G Nicklaus (+7)	M Hulbert (+7)	D Pride (+7)
J Haas (+8)	C A Spence (+8)	C Raulerson (+8)	S McCarron (+8)
M Brisky (+8)	E Aubrey (+9)	F Lickliter (+9)	J Delsing (+9)
J Williamson (+10)	N Henke (+10)	J Maggert (+10)(!)	J Gove (+11)
B Cheesman (+15)	K Gibson (+17)		

Mike Sposa (74), Rocco Mediate (75), Mike Springer (76) and Michael Christie (79) all withdrew.

ROUND BY ROUND LEADERBOARD

FIRST ROUND

D PAULSON	6 under
M A Jimenez	5 under
D Love	5 under
D Waldorf	5 under
J Maginnes	4 under
G Hjerstedt	4 under
S Kendall	4 under

SECOND ROUND

D PAULSON	9 under
S Kendall	7 under
J Sindelar	6 under
D Duval	5 under
M Weir	4 under
R Cochran	4 under
J Maginnes	4 under
D Waldorf	4 under
S Dunlap	4 under
R Freeman	4 under

THIRD ROUND

D Waldorf	7 under
E Els	6 under
C Perry	6 under
P Mickelson	6 under
D Duval	6 under
J Cook	6 under
S Kendall	6 under
J Sindelar	6 under
D PAULSON	4 under

FINAL ROUND

D PAULSON	8 under
D Duval	8 under
S Garcia	7 under
G Norman	6 under
J Parnevik	5 under
J Sindelar	5 under
J Cook	5 under
E Els	5 under

The course was drenched by 3 inches of rain on Tuesday before the tournament.

In R2 the later players were at a disadvantage because of the wind and the crusting, sun-dried greens.

PUNTERS' POINTS

● Dennis Paulson won his first tournament in his second straight play-off in the Buick Classic, beating World No. 2 David Duval with a 4-foot putt on the 4th extra hole.

● Duval, winless since early last season, had a chance to win in regulation after a 45-minute lightning delay, but missed a 25-foot birdie putt on the par 5 18th. He seems to be back to his best.

● Paulson, beaten in a play-off here last year, showed genuine resilience to comeback after a poor 75 in R3. He was 20/1 coming into R4.

● Sergio Garcia had the lead (10 under with 8 to go) only to lose it after an ill-judged, high-risk recovery shot at the 11th. He also complained of spectator trouble causing him to lose concentration.

● The Shark is back! A brilliant 7 under finish over the final 36 holes took Greg Norman into 4th place.

● Only two players posted four par or sub-par rounds – David Duval (all rounds under par) and T5th Jesper Parnevik.

● There were noteworthy disappointing final rounds from:-

> Skip Kendall   T2nd after R3, then 80 (!) to finish T33rd

> Scott Dunlap   2 under after R3, then 76 to finish T33rd

> Duffy Waldorf   leader after R3, then 76 to finish T13th

> Phil Mickelson   T2nd after R3, then 75 to finish T13th

● T13th Jimmy Green may be a name to note. The 30-year-old lives in Alabama, was 19th at Q School and finished T4th in the AT&T (including 68 twice at Pebble Beach). He's showed very solid current form.

1999 RESULT

1	125/1	Duffy Waldorf

won the first play-off hole

2	125/1	Dennis Paulson
3	66/1	Chris Perry
4	40/1	Scott Hoch
T5	200/1	Doug Barron
T5	12/1	Vijay Singh
T5	50/1	Loren Roberts
T5	150/1	Gabriel Hjerstedt
T5	100/1*	Jim Carter

1998 RESULT

1	250/1	J P Hayes

won at the first play-off hole

2	20/1	Jim Furyk
3	28/1	Tom Lehman
4	200/1	Bruce Fleisher
T5	200/1	Tom Byrum
T5	25/1	Jeff Maggert

(3-round tournament)

WINNERS IN THE LAST TEN YEARS

1991	Billy Andrade	1996	Ernie Els (by 8 shots!)
1992	David Frost	1997	Ernie Els
1993	Vijay Singh	1998	J P Hayes (54 holes)
1994	Lee Janzen	1999	Duffy Waldorf
1995	Vijay Singh	2000	Dennis Paulson

PUNTERS' GUIDE

● The value of course experience here is shown by the fact that

> The top 3 in 1999 were all well placed this year, viz. Waldorf (R3 leader and T13th), Paulson (winner) and Chris Perry (T5th).

> Five of the players in the top 10 (or T10th) in 1999 finished in the top 11 (or T11th) this year.

● There have been nine play-offs in the last sixteen years and this year's was the third in a row. On a really tough course its always likely to be close as no player will 'break away'. Another play-off in 2001?

● Early tee times in R1 are often an advantage. Here the two halfway leaders had 'identical' tee times

> Dennis Paulson   12 pm (R1 10th tee)   7 am (R2 1st tee)

> Skip Kendall   12 pm (R1 1st tee)   7 am (R2 10th tee)

● The tournament is held in Harrison, New York. Players born in 'the Big Apple' include Len Mattiace, Jeff Sluman, Tom Scherrer and, noteworthy in particularly, Joey Sindelar (T5th this year) who still lives in New York.

● Best recent Buick Classic records are held by

Dennis Paulson	W 2000: 2nd 1999
Jesper Parnevik	T10th 1998: T5th 2000 last two appearances
Chris Perry	T24-T17-T10-3-T5 are his progressive form figures
Jim Carter	T13th 2000: T5th 1999: 5th 1997 last three starts
Duffy Waldorf	T13th 2000: W 1999

● Players whose profiles refer to this tournament include Jim Carter, Jesper Parnevik, Ernie Els, Vijay Singh, Chris Perry, Kevin Sutherland, Duffy Waldorf, Dennis Paulson, David Duval, Joey Sindelar, Bob Estes, Tom Byrum and J P Hayes.

THE 100TH US OPEN

Date	15th - 18th June
Course	Pebble Beach, Monterey Peninsula, California
Par	71
Yardage	6,846
First Prize	$900,000
Total Purse	$4.5 million

PLEASE SEE PART 6.

THE FEDEX ST JUDE CLASSIC

Date	22nd - 25th June
Course	Southwind TPC, Memphis, Tennessee
Par	71
Yardage	7,030
First Prize	$540,000
Total Purse	$3 million

THE TOURNAMENT

Last year the St Jude was played the week before the US Open, this year the week after. So the question for punters was whether the Pebble Beach experience had made the US Open later-round players weak the week after. There is guaranteed hot, humid weather, with thunderstorms always possible.

THE COURSE

This TPC course has Zoysia-grass (Z-grass) fairways which are much stronger and thicker than the usual Bermuda. As the ball tends to sit up it can be 'swept' rather than played taking a divot. The bentgrass greens are tricky, undulating and relatively small. The toughest hole is the 231-yard par 3 14th, with the final two par 4 holes, especially the 18th, providing a very tough examination.

2000 ODDS

fav	12/1	Hal Sutton (non runner)	50/1	Bill Glasson
	20/1*	Nick Price	50/1	Jonathan Kaye
	20/1	Stewart Cink	66/1	Steve Pate
	20/1	John Huston	66/1	John Cook
	33/1	Dudley Hart	66/1*	Glen Day
	33/1	Scott Hoch	66/1	Robert Damron
	33/1	Loren Roberts	66/1	Tom Scherrer
	33/1*	Steve Flesch	66/1	Craig Parry
	33/1	Tim Herron	80/1*	Kevin Sutherland
	33/1*	Paul Azinger	80/1	Notah Begay
	40/1	David Toms	80/1*	Steve Elkington
	40/1	Kirk Triplett	80/1*	Mark Brooks
	40/1	Bob Estes	80/1	Ted Tryba (DC)
	50/1	Paul Stankowski	80/1	Jay Haas

2000 RESULT

1	80/1	**Notah Begay**	**66 69 67 69 271**
T2	150/1*	**Chris DiMarco**	**66 68 69 69 272**
T2	100/1	**Bob May**	**66 66 69 71 272**
T4	125/1	**Pete Jordan**	**71 67 69 66 273**
T4	100/1	**Russ Cochran**	**67 66 71 69 273**
T4	150/1	**Joe Ogilvie**	**65 68 70 70 273**

T7	T Scherrer	69 71 68 66 274			B Mayfair	69 73 70 69 281
	R Damron	71 64 71 68 274			G Hjertstedt	71 69 71 70 281
	L Roberts	67 70 69 68 274			T Tryba	70 71 70 70 281
	C Parry	70 65 69 70 274			F Nobilo	68 70 72 71 281
T11	D Peoples	65 70 75 65 275			B Estes	72 69 68 72 281
	J Durant	67 73 68 67 275			D Howser	72 70 66 73 281
	G Hnatiuk	68 72 65 70 275			Robin Freeman	69 66 72 74 281
	S Pate	67 65 70 73 275	T54		A Bean	70 69 72 71 282
T15	D Toms	65 69 75 67 276			M Bradley	71 70 68 73 282
	K Triplett	72 70 67 67 276			R Beem	68 69 71 74 282
	J Haas	70 69 67 70 276			B Friend	70 67 70 75 282
	B Glasson	69 71 65 71 276	T58		B Gilder	71 67 74 71 283
	Joel Edwards	70 69 67 70 276			C Barlow	74 68 70 71 283
T20	D Dunakey	70 65 75 67 277			Bobby Cochran	68 72 71 72 283
	B Gay	72 68 68 69 277			J Caron	69 73 69 72 283
	S Flesch	73 67 68 69 277			S Elkington	72 70 67 74 283
	P Azinger	71 71 65 70 277	T63		P H Hogan	68 70 78 68 284
	S Hoch	66 71 69 71 277			S Micheel	72 69 72 71 284
T25	Nick Price	71 66 74 67 278	T65		P Nanney Jr	74 67 73 71 285
	D A Weibring	70 69 72 67 278			J Williamson	74 68 71 72 285
	B Cheesman	69 73 69 67 278			P Goydos	71 71 71 72 285
	D Barron	70 68 72 68 278			M Standly	69 70 73 73 285
	D Hammond	71 68 70 69 278			C Riley	70 69 72 74 285
	R Fehr	71 69 68 70 278			J Kaye	73 68 69 75 285
	L Mattiace	68 72 67 71 278			M Clark II	69 68 72 76 285
	G Day	71 70 66 71 278			J Huston	71 70 68 76 285
T33	J Cook	72 70 70 67 279	T73		D Morland IV	69 68 77 72 286
	P Moss	73 69 70 67 279			Larry Rinker	72 69 71 74 286
	S Cink	71 67 71 70 279	T75		T Herron	70 71 75 71 287
	R Sabbatini	72 69 67 71 279			B Winston	72 70 73 72 287
	Tom Byrum	68 69 70 72 279			Steve Hart	71 71 73 72 287
T38	C Martin	69 71 72 68 280			Carl Paulson	67 71 74 75 287
	J Buha	69 73 70 68 280			C Raulerson	71 68 72 76 287
	J Van de Velde	71 70 69 70 280	80		J Kelly	71 68 75 74 288
	M Sposa	73 68 70 69 280	81		Kevin Sutherland	71 70 72 78 291
	Bart Bryant	71 66 72 71 280	82		C Strange	71 71 79 71 292
	J Delsing	74 67 68 71 280	83		C Perks	71 69 75 77 292
	B Bates	71 66 70 73 280	84		C Beckman	70 72 76 75 293
T45	P Stankowski	72 70 74 65 281	85		M Wiebe	73 68 75 78 294
	D Stockton	70 72 73 66 281				

The main players to miss the cut (made at level) were:–

J D Blake (+1)	M Hulbert (+1)	M Brooks (+1)	D Forsman (+1)
J McGovern (+1)	G Waite (+1)	B Quigley (+1)	D Hart (+1)
D Pride (+1)	M Donald (+1)	J Gove (+1)	P Curry (+1)
C Beck (+2)	M Springer (+2)	T Dodds (+2)	J Maginnes (+2)
G Hallberg (+2)	K J Choi (+2)	O Uresti (+2)	K Gibson (+2)
D Edwards (+2)	J Daly (+2)	E Toledo (+2)	S McCarron (+2)
K Wentworth (+2)	B Heintz (+2)	E Aubrey (+3)	J Smith (+3)
P Blackmar (+3)	S Murphy (+3)	G Sauers (+4)	B Watts (+4)
D Briggs (+4)	R Floyd (+4)	T Barranger (+4)	D Frost (+4)
W Austin (+4)	M Carnevale (+4)	R Gamez (+5)	N Lancaster (+5)
K Nolan (+5)	J Rollins (+5)	S Gotsche (+5)	M Christie (+5)
B Wadkins (+6)	N Henke (+6)	J Gallagher (+6)	C Bowden (+6)
R Howison (+6)	E Booker (+6)	W Grady (+6)	W Wood (+6)
B Schwarzrock (+7)	K Fergus (+8)	D Mast (+9)	B Fabel (+9)
B Burns (+9)	S Utley (+9)	F Zoeller (+10)	M Goggin (+15)

Keith Clearwater (76) and Ted Schulz (78) both withdrew.

ROUND BY ROUND LEADERBOARD

FIRST ROUND

D Toms	6 under
D Peoples	6 under
J Ogilvie	6 under
C DiMarco	5 under
N BEGAY	5 under
S Hoch	5 under
B May	5 under

SECOND ROUND

B May	10 under
S Pate	10 under
R Cochran	9 under
J Ogilvie	9 under
C DiMarco	8 under
D Toms	8 under
N BEGAY	7 under

THIRD ROUND

B May	12 under
N BEGAY	11 under
S Pate	11 under
C DiMarco	10 under
J Ogilvie	10 under
C Parry	9 under
R Cochran	9 under

FINAL ROUND

N BEGAY	13 under
C DiMarco	12 under
B May	12 under
P Jordan	11 under
R Cochran	11 under
J Ogilvie	11 under

Pre-tournament rain made the greens receptive, although the course played long, especially on Thursday. In R1 fifty-four players broke par, with the morning players having a definite advantage.

PUNTERS' POINTS

● 80/1 Notah Begay notched his third tour win in less than a year, and his first since he spent seven days in jail in March for a (second) drink driving offence.

● His win was founded on a magnificent lob wedge from off the green at the par 5 16th to give him a birdie putt. Begay's chip was "world class" according to his playing partner Bob May.

● Begay, a team mate of Tiger Woods at Stanford University, became the fifteenth winner on tour this year to come from behind on the final day.

● Bob May, a winner on the European tour, couldn't quite make his first USPGA tour win after an ordinary par 71 in R4.

● Chris DiMarco nearly made birdie at the last, and with the winner shared the distinction of being the only player in the field to shoot four rounds in the '60s.

● A fun question for your friends. In which tournament did the winner also finish 20th. This one....check it and you'll find B gay won with B gay also 20th!

1999 RESULT			1998 RESULT		
1	125/1	Ted Tryba	1	fav 16/1	Nick Price
T2	25/1	Tom Lehman	2	66/1	Jeff Sluman
T2	50/1	Tim Herron	3	66/1	Glen Day
T4	33/1	J M Olazabal	4	66/1	Bob Estes
T4	150/1	Kevin Wentworth	5	500/1	Tim Conley

WINNERS IN THE LAST TEN YEARS

1991	Fred Couples	1996	John Cook
1992	Jay Haas	1997	Greg Norman
1993	Nick Price	1998	Nick Price
1994	Dicky Pride	1999	Ted Tryba
1995	Jim Gallagher Jr	2000	Notah Begay

PUNTERS' GUIDE

● This sure is a tournament for outsiders. In the last six years there have been thirty-eight players in the top 5 (or T5th) of which

> twenty-six (or 68.4%) have started at or over 66/1

> twenty-one (or 55.3%) have started at or over 80/1

> seventeen (or 44.7%) have started at or over 100/1

● In the last five years the tournament has either been won by the R3 leader (three times) or a player within a couple of shots of the R3 lead. So although low R4 scores can be posted you should look to the top of the leaderboard for the winner on Sunday morning.

● At 27 Notah Begay broke the mould of older players winning. In the previous eight years the average age of the winner had been 35.75. However Begay had experience of the course last year when T36th after being 10 under after R3.

● With low scoring the order of the day an early tee time on the first day gives a player a significant advantage.

● Best recent tournament records (last year) are held by

> Kirk Triplett   two top 10s and two top 20s in the last five years

> Tim Herron   T13th: T12th: T2nd before this year's T75th!

> Michael Bradley   T7th: T5th: T12th then MC and T54th this year

> Paul Azinger   T7th 1998: T6th 1999: T20th 2000

> Robert Damron   T3rd 1997: T7th 1998: MC 1999: T7th 2000

The above five are the only players with three top 20s here in the last five years.

● Players whose profiles refer to this tournament include Paul Azinger, Brian Gay, Robert Damron, Kirk Triplett, Pete Jordan, Chris DiMarco, Tim Herron, Tom Scherrer, David Toms, Jay Don Blake, Joel Edwards and Joe Durant.

THE GREATER HARTFORD OPEN

Date	29th June - 2nd July
Course	TPC at River Highlands, Cromwell, Connecticut
Par	70
Yardage	6,860
First Prize	$504,000
Total Purse	$2.8 million

THE TOURNAMENT

This was the tenth successive year that the GHO has been played at the River Highlands course. The tournament rarely attracts the really big names, so providing a big opportunity for the lesser-known players.

THE COURSE

The course has just two par 5s in a total par of 70. Built on hilly, undulating land, the track has over one hundred and twenty bunkers. The bentgrass greens are small and fast. The emphasis here is very much on accuracy rather than length.

2000 ODDS

fav	14/1	Davis Love	50/1	Tom Scherrer
	16/1	Stewart Cink	66/1*	Steve Lowery
	18/1	Hal Sutton	66/1	Fred Funk
	22/1	Justin Leonard	66/1	Craig Parry
	22/1	Jim Furyk	66/1	Bob May
	25/1	John Huston	66/1	John Cook
	33/1	Scott Hoch	80/1	Harrison Frazar
	33/1	Steve Flesch	80/1*	Skip Kendal
	40/1*	Mark Calcavecchia	80/1*	Steve Elkington
	40/1*	Mike Weir	80/1*	Robert Allenby
	40/1	Notah Begay (PWW)	80/1*	Jeff Sluman
	40/1	Stuart Appleby	80/1	Scott Dunlap
	50/1	Kirk Triplett	80/1	Brent Geiberger (DC)
	50/1	Tim Herron	80/1	Chris DiMarco

2000 RESULT

1	40/1	Notah Begay	64 65 67 64 260
2	40/1*	Mark Calcavecchia	65 64 64 68 261
3	50/1	Kirk Triplett	64 72 61 67 264
4	22/1	Jim Furyk	66 66 67 67 266
T5	80/1	Chris DiMarco	69 66 67 66 268
T5	33/1	Steve Flesch	67 67 67 67 268
T5	125/1	Doug Barron	65 69 67 67 268
T5	125/1	Ed Fryatt	67 64 66 71 268

T9	Kevin Sutherland	68 70 66 65 269		J L Lewis	65 72 69 69 275
	J Huston	67 70 66 66 269		S Elkington	71 67 64 73 275
	S Dunlap	68 68 66 67 269	T48	B Burns	68 70 70 68 276
T12	D Stockton	66 66 70 68 270		F Nobilo	69 68 69 70 276
	B Tway	68 70 64 68 270		B Henninger	68 70 67 71 276
T14	R Gamez	64 70 70 67 271		J Caron	65 69 70 72 276
	S Cink	68 69 66 68 271		M Brooks	65 70 68 73 276
	G Hjertstedt	68 69 66 68 271	T53	B Friend	68 71 73 65 277
	R Allenby	69 64 69 69 271		J Williamson	71 68 70 68 277
T18	J D Blake	66 71 71 64 272		J Sindelar	69 70 69 69 277
	J Buha	69 67 68 68 272		J Van de Velde	69 68 69 71 277
	C Riley	69 66 69 68 272		H Sutton	67 65 72 73 277
	J Kaye	72 66 66 68 272	T58	Bart Bryant	65 70 75 68 278
	T Herron	67 69 67 69 272		P Jordan	71 67 72 68 278
	B Geiberger	67 66 69 70 272		F Funk	68 71 71 68 278
	J Durant	67 67 68 70 272		G Chalmers	67 70 72 69 278
T25	M Springer	69 69 70 65 273		W Grady	68 69 72 69 278
	D Forsman	64 71 71 67 273		Joel Edwards	71 67 70 70 278
	J Ogilvie	67 69 70 67 273		Gary Nicklaus	69 70 69 70 278
	D A Weibring	67 68 71 67 273		C Parry	69 69 69 71 278
	T Armour III	66 69 68 70 273	T66	B May	70 69 75 65 279
	P H Horgan	67 66 69 71 273		E Toledo	70 69 71 69 279
	J Sluman	70 67 65 71 273		D Briggs	68 71 71 69 279
T32	M Reid	66 73 69 66 274		B Fabel	67 70 71 71 279
	D Peoples	69 70 68 67 274		F Lickliter	67 68 72 72 279
	L Mattiace	70 69 68 67 274		N Henke	67 72 68 72 279
	C Howell	71 67 68 68 274		G Waite	68 70 67 74 279
	S Gump	67 68 70 69 274	T73	C Beckman	70 69 70 71 280
	P Gow	69 70 67 68 274		S Gotsche	67 72 69 72 280
	B Faxon	65 68 71 70 274		Bobby Cochran	65 72 70 73 280
	O Browne	71 67 66 70 274	T76	B Quigley	71 68 72 70 281
	S Kendall	67 70 67 70 274		K J Choi	69 70 71 71 281
	S Appleby	67 68 68 71 274		O Uresti	69 70 70 72 281
	S Lowery	65 69 69 71 274	79	B Bates	66 67 76 73 282
	P Goydos	66 67 68 73 274	80	T Dodds	71 66 77 69 283
T44	G Kraft	66 70 71 68 275	T81	W Levi	68 71 75 70 284
	J Cook	68 71 68 68 275		B Hughes	67 69 76 72 284

Billy Mayfair 70-68-70 then withdrew.

The main players to miss the cut (made at 1 under) were:–

S Ames (E)	B Andrade (E)	T Byrum (E)	S Hoch (E)
J Leonard (E)	D Love (E)	A Magee (E)	S Micheel (E)
D Pride (E)	M Standly (E)	W Wood (E	B Heintz (E)
K Nolan (E)	M Gogel (E)	H Mahan (E)	J Delsing (+1)
R Freeman (+1)	K Gibson (+1)	J Gullion (+1)	S Hart (+1)
K Wentworth (+1)	M Sposa (+1)	G Hnatiuk (+1)	C Beck (+2)
M Brisky (+2)	B Cheesman (+2)	D Sutherland (+2)	B Jobe (+2)
B Schwarzrock (+2)	M Goggin (+2)	B Gage (+2)	P Blackmar (+3)
C Bowden (+3)	P Moss (+3)	B Watts (+3)	C A Spence (+3)
C Martin (+3)	R Black (+4)	J Daly (+4)	J Haas (+4)
M Hulbert (+4)	C Paulson (+4)	T Pernice Jr (+4)	C Raulerson (+4)
D Dunakey (+4)	B Elder (+4)	M Clark (+4)	J Rollins (+4)
E Aubrey (+5)	T Barranger (+5)	N Lancaster (+5)	T Scherrer (+5)
D Edwards (+6)	J Maginnes (+6)	D Morland IV (+6)	J Gove (+6)
R Howison (+7)	F Zoeller (+7)	H Frazar (+7)	A Bengoechea (+7)
D Frost (+8)	M McCumber (+8)	T Tryba (+8)	C Barlow (+8)
C Perks (+10)	T Kelley (+10)	M Christie (+11)	P Curry (+11)
B Mackedon (+11)	B R Brown (+21)		

ROUND BY ROUND LEADERBOARD

FIRST ROUND

R Gamez	6 under
K Triplett	6 under
N BEGAY	6 under
D Forsman	6 under
9 players at	5 under

SECOND ROUND

M Calcavecchia	11 under
N BEGAY	11 under
E Fryatt	9 under
J Furyk	8 under
D Stockton	8 under
H Sutton	8 under

THIRD ROUND

M Calcavecchia	17 under
N BEGAY	14 under
K Triplett	13 under
E Fryatt	13 under
J Furyk	11 under
D Barron	9 under
S Flesch	9 under
P Goydos	9 under

FINAL ROUND

N BEGAY	20 under
M Calcavecchia	19 under
K Triplett	16 under
J Furyk	14 under
C DiMarco	12 under
S Flesch	12 under
D Barron	12 under
E Fryatt	12 under

PUNTERS' POINTS

● 40/1 Notah Begay recorded his second win in a week and his fourth in the last twelve months after overtaking Calcavecchia's 3-stroke Sunday lead. A 25-foot final hole birdie clinched it. He had finished 14th here on his debut last year.

● Course specialist Mark Calcavecchia was given a DYM quote of 40/1 from Heathorns and he so nearly won on the track which he knows so well. He may be winless since the 1998 Honda Classic yet Calc has now posted at least one top 3 finish on tour every year since 1986!

● Kirk Triplett also enjoys this course. 2nd in 1995, and with nine cuts in ten starts, he broke the course record with a 61 in R3. His 3rd place here was his fourth top 5 this season.

● Catching Jim Furyk right ain't easy for punters. With no course form and form figures of 25-51-60 he nevertheless posted a fine 14 under par to finish 4th, his best performance since early March in Florida.

● 80/1 Chris DiMarco posted a solid T5th place here on the back of his fine 2nd last week. He must now be firmly placed in the 'winner over the next twelve months' category.

● Starting R4 T3rd Rochdale-born, straight-hitter Ed Fryatt had a real chance. However a nervy 1 over par 71 saw him slip to finish T5th.

1999 RESULT

1	100/1*	Brent Geiberger
2	100/1	Skip Kendall
T3	40/1	Mark Calcavecchia
T3	20/1	Justin Leonard
T3	125/1	Ted Tryba

1998 RESULT

1	200/1	Olin Browne
won at first play-off hole		
T2	200/1	Larry Mize
T2	20/1	Stewart Cink
T4	100/1	Duffy Waldorf
T4	50/1	Fred Funk
T4	150/1	Doug Tewell

WINNERS IN THE LAST TEN YEARS

1991	Billy Ray Brown	1996	D A Weibring
1992	Lanny Wadkins	1997	Stewart Cink
1993	Nick Price	1998	Olin Browne
1994	David Frost	1999	Brent Geiberger
1995	Greg Norman	2000	Notah Begay

PUNTERS' GUIDE

● With three of the last five winners starting at 100/1 plus, and with nine of nineteen players in the top 5 (or T5th) in the last three years also over 100/1, this is a tournament in which outsiders do well.

● Four of the last ten winners have been first timers, so take heart if you fancy a promising player who has been 'knocking on the door'.

● The best recent course records are held by

	2000	1999	1998	1997	1996
Stewart Cink	T14	T8	T2	W	–
Mark Calcavecchia	2	T3	T16	5	T3
Chris DiMarco	T5	T20	T25	–	–
Joe Durant	T18	T34	T16	T17	–
Kevin Sutherland	T9	T17	T25	T13	T9
Mike Springer	T25	T8	T14	MC	MC
Tim Herron	T18	T8	T36	T40	–

● Although there are no Connecticut players – Brad Faxon and PH Horgan live nearby in Rhode Island, Billy Andrade locally in Massachusetts and Jeff Sluman in New York.

● Players whose profiles refer to this tournament include Dave Stockton Jr, Kevin Sutherland, Joe Durant, Stewart Cink, Mark Calcavecchia, Kirk Triplett, Mark Brooks, Skip Kendall, Chris DiMarco and Jonathan Kaye.

THE ADVIL WESTERN OPEN

Date	6th - 9th July
Course	Cog Hill G. & C.C., Lemont, Illinois
Par	72
Yardage	7,073
First Prize	$540,000
Total Purse	$3 million

THE TOURNAMENT

This is a very old tournament first held in 1899. It moved to Cog Hill in 1991 so this was the tenth successive year that it has been held on this track.

THE COURSE

The Cog Hill course is noted for its many bunkers and undulating bentgrass greens that have recently been enlarged. The key holes are in 'death valley' from the 12th to the 14th inclusive. With four par 5s it favours the long hitters.

2000 ODDS

fav	15/8	Tiger Woods (DC)	50/1	David Toms
	20/1	Phil Mickelson	66/1	Steve Pate
	20/1	Vijay Singh	66/1	Lee Janzen
	25/1	Jim Furyk	80/1	Steve Lowery
	33/1	Tom Lehman	80/1*	Jeff Sluman
	33/1	Nick Price	80/1*	Steve Stricker
	40/1	Steve Flesch	80/1*	Bill Glasson
	40/1	Fred Couples	80/1	Shigeki Maruyama
	50/1*	Mike Weir	80/1	Scott Dunlap
	50/1*	Stuart Appleby	80/1	Glen Day
	50/1	Chris Perry	80/1	Brent Geiberger
	50/1	Scott Hoch	80/1	Joe Durant

2000 RESULT

1	100/1	Robert Allenby	69 69 68 68 274

Allenby won at the first play-off hole

2	33/1	Nick Price	63 72 70 69 274
T3	125/1	Greg Kraft	69 69 70 68 276
T3	80/1	Shigeki Maruyama	72 68 66 70 276
T3	25/1	Jim Furyk	66 70 69 71 276

T6	J Maggert	70 71 68 68 277			J Kelly	70 72 71 71 284
	F Langham	69 65 74 69 277			J Williamson	69 74 70 71 284
	B Henninger	70 63 70 74 277			R Damron	75 68 69 72 284
T9	F Lickliter	74 67 70 67 278			M Gogel	70 70 71 73 284
	S Hoch	72 68 69 69 278			B Geiberger	71 69 71 73 284
	F Couples	67 68 73 70 278			Chris Perry	72 69 69 74 284
	Carl Paulson	67 70 70 71 278			Dennis Paulson	68 71 71 74 284
	D Toms	72 67 68 71 278		T51	M Weir	69 72 73 71 285
	S Flesch	69 66 68 75 278			J Carter	71 72 71 71 285
T15	B Elder	69 69 70 71 279			J Durant	68 70 73 74 285
	S Ames	72 63 72 72 279			D Morland IV	70 66 75 74 285
	B Glasson	68 70 69 72 279		T55	David Sutherland	71 72 73 70 286
	L Janzen	71 67 66 75 279			G Hjertstedt	68 75 73 70 286
	Kenny Perry	68 69 68 74 279			S Kendall	72 67 76 71 286
T20	F Funk	71 68 69 72 280			D Stockton	70 70 73 73 286
	S Appleby	67 68 72 73 280			T Lehman	73 70 69 74 286
	S Lowery	72 69 66 73 280			Robin Freeman	68 71 72 75 286
T23	J P Hayes	73 68 71 69 281		T61	N Lancaster	75 68 72 72 287
	T Woods	70 69 70 72 281			W Austin	72 69 72 74 287
	O Browne	68 71 70 72 281		T63	S McCarron	72 71 74 71 288
	T Armour III	69 72 67 73 281			F Nobilo	73 69 72 74 288
	M Wiebe	68 72 67 74 281			P Jordan	72 70 72 74 288
28	B Cheesman	70 70 69 73 282			B Estes	73 70 71 74 288
T29	R Fehr	71 70 74 68 283			K J Choi	72 67 74 75 288
	J D Blake	69 73 72 69 283			J Maginnes	71 70 72 75 288
	M Reid	72 68 73 70 283		T69	C Beckman	72 71 74 72 289
	P Jacobsen	71 72 70 70 283			D Dunakey	72 71 72 74 289
	H Frazar	69 71 72 71 283		T71	L Mattiace	72 71 75 72 290
	B Faxon	72 69 71 71 283			G Day	69 71 75 75 290
	J Ogilvie	74 67 71 71 283			R Howison	74 68 72 76 290
	M Goggin	72 71 69 71 283			J Sindelar	70 73 71 76 290
	J L Lewis	69 72 69 73 283		75	B Burns	76 67 76 72 291
	J Sluman	71 70 69 73 283		76	M Brooks	75 67 76 74 292
	S Stricker	67 74 68 74 283		77	B McCallister	73 70 74 76 293
	M Brisky	70 69 68 76 283		78	T Tryba	71 71 78 74 294
T41	D A Weibring	68 74 74 68 284		79	C Perks	71 72 74 78 295
	E Fryatt	72 69 74 69 284		80	J Green	72 69 82 73 296
	Kevin Sutherland	71 71 71 71 284				

The main players to miss the cut (made at 1 under) were:−

E Aubrey (E)	S Murphy (E)	M Springer (E)	J Smith (E)
G Hnatiuk (E)	G Chalmers (E)	J Buha (E)	M Clark II (E)
S Verplank (E)	B Mayfair (E)	P Mickelson (E)	D Hart (E)
R Beem (E)	P Curry (E)	R Cochran (+1)	B Andrade (+1)
V Singh (+1)	S Gump (+1)	B Heintz (+1)	L Donald (am)(+1)
J Gullion (+1)	M Sposa (+1)	B Tway (+1)	J Delsing (+1)
L Mize (+1)	T Dodds (+1)	C A Spence (+1)	J Gove (+1)
E Toledo (+2)	R Black (+2)	W Grady (+2)	S Pate (+2)
T Purtzer (+2)	C Stadler (+2)	T Pernice Jr (+2)	S Hart (+2)
A Bengoechea (+2)	R Floyd (+2)	B Hughes (+2)	J Rollins (+2)
B Friend (+3)	C Raulerson (+3)	S Micheel (+3)	D Forsman (+3)
D Peoples (+3)	B Bates (+3)	S Dunlap (+3)	S Gotsche (+3)
M McCumber (+4)	N Henke (+4)	B Jobe (+4)	P H Horgan (+4)
B Gay (+4)	C Beck (+4)	M Christie (+5)	B Fabel (+5)
C Martin (+5)	A Magee (+5)	D Pride (+5)	E Booker (+5)
J Edwards (+5)	K Holmes (+5)	O Uresti (+6)	B Cochran (+8)
K Gibson (+9)			

ROUND BY ROUND LEADERBOARD

FIRST ROUND

N Price	9 under
J Furyk	6 under
C Paulson	5 under
S Stricker	5 under
F Couples	5 under
S Appleby	5 under
R ALLENBY	3 under

SECOND ROUND

B Henninger	11 under
F Langham	10 under
F Couples	9 under
S Ames	9 under
S Appleby	9 under
S Flesch	9 under
N Price	9 under
R ALLENBY	6 under

THIRD ROUND

S Flesch	13 under
B Henninger	13 under
L Janzen	12 under
K Perry	11 under
J Furyk	11 under
N Price	11 under
R ALLENBY	10 under

FINAL ROUND

R ALLENBY	14 under
N Price	14 under
G Kraft	12 under
S Maruyama	12 under
J Furyk	12 under

PUNTERS' POINTS

● 100/1 Robert Allenby had a superb set of relevant stats coming into this event – 2nd for par 5 birdies, 3rd in total driving and 8th in the all-round stats so his game was clearly very well suited to Cog Hill. However, a late tee time and a missed cut last year on his only previous visit were potentially negative factors.

● In the event the tall Aussie beat Nick Price at the first play-off hole with a par. It gave Allenby a career record of six wins in six play-offs!!

● And it was another triumph for the 'nappy factor' as Robert Allenby became a first-time dad of a son last September and this year he's now won twice.

- Players who shot poor final rounds when high on the leaderboard included.
    - > Steve Flesch   T1st after R3, shot 75 to finish T9th
    - > Brian Henninger   T1st after R3, shot 74 to finish T6th
    - > Kenny Perry   T4th after R3, shot 74 to finish T15th
    - > Lee Janzen   3rd after R3, shot 75 to finish T15th

    All four clearly suffered 'contention rust'.
- Course specialist Vijay Singh never recovered after a late tee time to miss his first weekend after 26 consecutive cuts.
- The absurdity of lumping on Tiger Woods at 15/8 (or selling his finishing position at 7-10) was well shown here. The guy is human and MLD after his Pebble Beach effort was always very probable. T23rd was his worst finish since his 37th in the Sprint International last year. (Please see Law of the Tiger in Part 1.)

1999 RESULT

1	fav 6/1	Tiger Woods
2	125/1	Mike Weir
3	100/1	Brent Geiberger
4	10/1	Vijay Singh
5	200/1	Dicky Pride

1998 RESULT

1	125/1	Joe Durant
2	50/1	Vijay Singh
T3	100/1	Dudley Hart
T3	33/1	Lee Janzen
T5	33/1	Steve Stricker
T5	125/1	Greg Kraft

WINNERS IN THE LAST TEN YEARS

1991	Russ Cochran	1996	Steve Stricker
1992	Ben Crenshaw	1997	Tiger Woods
1993	Nick Price	1998	Joe Durant
1994	Nick Price	1999	Tiger Woods
1995	Billy Mayfair	2000	Robert Allenby

PUNTERS' GUIDE

- This has certainly been a tournament for outsiders in recent years.
    - > In the last five years over half (fourteen from twenty-seven) of the players that have been placed in the top 5 (or T5th) have started at or over 100/1!
    - > The winners' prices from 1996 have been 66/1, 8/1 (Tiger), 125/1, 6/1 (Tiger) and 100/1.
- Seven players have posted at least three top 20s here in the last five years.
    - > Tiger Woods   Won 1997: 9th 1998: Won 1999: MLD 2000
    - > Vijay Singh   8th 1996: 2nd 1998: 4th 1999
    - > Stuart Appleby   7th 1997: 9th 1998: 13th 1999: 20th 2000
    - > Scott Hoch   13th 1997: 7th 1998: 9th 2000
    - > Jim Furyk   6th 1997: 7th 1998: 3rd 2000

> Frank Lickliter   17th 1998: 17th 1999: 9th 2000
> Justin Leonard   8th 1996: 3rd 1997: 9th 1998: 20th 1999

● Is Cog Hill course form important? Yes and no!

> Yes, experience can only be of value — 2nd-placed Nick Price had won here twice (1993 and 1994) before — T3rd Furyk had form figures here of 34-7-6

> No, as the course form of the other top finishers showed

     – T3rd Maruyama had no experience at all

     – Winner Allenby missed the 1999 cut on his only appearance

     – T3rd Greg Kraft had missed the cut in two of his last three starts at Cog Hill

Overall if a player has the credentials for Cog Hill do not be put off if he lacks course experience.

● Players whose profiles refer to this tournament include Stuart Appleby, Tommy Armour III, Brad Elder, Franklin Langham, Frank Lickliter, Shigeki Maruyama, Vijay Singh, Steve Stricker, Tiger Woods, Carl Paulson, Mark Hensby and Greg Kraft.

THE GREATER MILWAUKEE OPEN

Date	13th - 16th July
Course	Brown Deer Park, Milwaukee
Par	71
Yardage	6,739
First Prize	$450,000
Total Purse	$2.5 million

THE TOURNAMENT

As in 1999 the GMO was positioned as the final tournament before the British Open. The Brown Deer Park course was being used for the seventh successive year. This was the first tournament Tiger Woods played as a pro back in 1996.

THE COURSE

Brown Deer Park is a public course and has been an easy track in recent years. This year the fairways have been slightly narrowed and the rough extended. Unusually it has five par 3s and only nine par 4s in its 6,793 yards, so it favours accuracy rather than length. After a lot of rain in recent weeks the bentgrass greens were in 'perfect' condition.

2000 ODDS

fav	14/1	Carlos Franco (DC)	66/1*	Harrison Frazar
	16/1	Loren Roberts	66/1	Olin Browne
	16/1	Mark Calcavecchia	66/1	Frank Lickliter
	16/1	Scott Hoch	66/1	Brad Elder
	16/1	Chris Perry	66/1	J P Hayes
	20/1	Steve Stricker	66/1*	Greg Kraft
	20/1	Bill Glasson	66/1	Jay Haas
	33/1	Steve Pate	80/1*	Andrew Magee
	40/1	Kenny Perry	80/1	Larry Mize
	40/1*	Fred Funk	80/1	J L Lewis
	40/1	Skip Kendall	80/1	Carl Paulson
	50/1	Jerry Kelly	80/1	John Maginnes
	50/1	Franklin Langham	80/1	Blaine McCallister
	50/1*	Robert Damron	80/1*	Russ Cochran
	66/1*	Joe Durant		

2000 RESULT

1	16/1	Loren Roberts	65 66 63 66 260
2	50/1	Franklin Langham	66 66 64 72 268
T3	33/1	Steve Pate	70 64 70 65 269
T3	40/1	Kenny Perry	64 70 67 68 269
T3	150/1	Mathew Goggin	68 68 65 68 269
T3	66/1	J P Hayes	66 66 68 69 269

T7	J Durant	66 70 69 65 270		B Friend	68 72 71 67 278
	Russ Cochran	70 65 70 65 270		R Howison	70 70 72 66 278
T9	J Rollins	68 68 72 63 271	T47	Larry Rinker	73 66 69 71 279
	O Browne	68 69 70 64 271		J Kelly	65 71 72 71 279
	S Kendall	69 68 66 68 271		P Jordan	68 70 69 72 279
	Chris Perry	66 67 68 70 271		W Grady	71 69 69 70 279
	F Lickliter	65 66 67 73 271		K J Choi	69 69 72 69 279
T14	G Waite	69 67 70 66 272		D Stockton	70 67 73 69 279
	J Ogilvie	70 67 67 68 272		S McCarron	71 68 71 69 279
	B Gay	69 65 66 72 272		B Bates	69 70 66 74 279
	J Gullion	71 67 63 71 272		M Sullivan	70 70 71 68 279
T18	J Sindelar	69 67 70 68 274	T56	D Mast	69 69 70 72 280
	R Black	67 68 70 69 274		G Sauers	71 68 70 71 280
	D Barron	68 68 68 70 274		A Bean	70 65 74 71 280
	C Pavin	65 68 69 72 274		M Wiebe	68 72 70 70 280
T22	W Austin	70 70 68 67 275		T Purtzer	68 70 73 69 280
	C Beckman	65 68 75 67 275		B Elder	67 72 72 69 280
	S Hoch	67 68 72 68 275		C Martin	68 71 73 68 280
	M Springer	68 72 67 68 275	T63	G Kraft	72 66 70 73 281
	D Ogrin	68 71 68 68 275		B Schwarzrock	72 66 71 72 281
	D Morland IV	71 68 72 64 275		B Watts	71 68 70 72 281
	P Curry	69 68 68 70 275		D Barr	71 68 71 71 281
	M Brisky	71 66 67 71 275		P Jacobsen	71 69 72 69 281
T30	L Mize	70 67 71 68 276		S Stricker	69 70 74 68 281
	B Glasson	67 68 70 71 276		K Gibson	70 70 74 67 281
	B McCallister	69 69 68 70 276	T70	C Franco	66 70 73 73 282
	J Williamson	64 69 71 72 276		B Andrade	72 68 70 72 282
	Jim Gallagher	68 68 68 72 276		J Haas	73 67 77 65 282
T35	B Chamblee	68 71 69 69 277	T73	B Gilder	71 66 73 73 283
	R Zokol	71 68 69 69 277		G Hallberg	66 72 73 72 283
	Tom Byrum	69 68 72 68 277		D Briggs	69 71 72 71 283
	B Cheesman	71 69 66 71 277		C Strange	71 69 72 71 283
	B Claar	67 71 68 71 277	T77	O Uresti	71 69 70 74 284
	T Pernice Jr	67 70 68 72 277		D Forsman	72 68 72 72 284
	R Damron	71 68 66 72 277	79	F Zoeller	73 67 73 73 286
	C Perks	69 70 72 66 277	80	C Stadler	69 68 75 76 288
T43	M Wilson	70 69 69 70 278	81	B Fabel	67 73 74 75 289
	T Barranger	68 69 71 70 278			

The main players to miss the cut (made at 2 under) were:–

B Quigley (-1)	M Sposa (-1)	J Green (-1)	M Standly (-1)
D Peoples (-1)	E Toledo (-1)	B Cochran (-1)	B Hughes (E)
S Gump (E)	J Gove (E)	M Clark II (E)	C Riley (E)
R Fehr (E)	D Pride (E)	R Freeman (E)	S Gotsche (E)
H Frazar (+1)	C Rose (+1)	M Hulbert (+1)	K Fergus (+1)
M Calcavecchia (+1)	D Pooley (+1)	N Henke (+1)	J Maginnes (+1)
B Jobe (+1)	R Gamez (+1)	K Clearwater (+1)	C Raulerson (+1)
K Hosokawa (+1)	J Delsing (+1)	J L Lewis (+1)	A Magee (+1)
M Gogel (+1)	S Murphy (+1)	F Funk (+2)	E Aubrey (+2)
P Moss (+2)	F Nobilo (+2)	C Paulson (+2)	N Lancaster (+2)
C A Spence (+2)	E Booker (+3)	P H Horgan (+3)	B Bryant (+3)
B Burns (+4)	D Dunakey (+4)	M Bradley (+5)	T Armour III (+5)
K Wentworth (+6)			

D A Weibring (77) withdrew.

ROUND BY ROUND LEADERBOARD

FIRST ROUND

J Williamson	7 under
K Perry	7 under
L ROBERTS	6 under
F Lickliter	6 under
J Kelly	6 under
C Pavin	6 under
C Beckman	6 under

SECOND ROUND

L ROBERTS	11 under
F Lickliter	11 under
F Langham	10 under
J P Hayes	10 under
C Perry	9 under
C Pavin	9 under
J Williamson	9 under
C Beckman	9 under

THIRD ROUND

L ROBERTS	19 under
F Langham	17 under
F Lickliter	15 under
B Gay	13 under
J P Hayes	13 under

FINAL ROUND

L ROBERTS	24 under
F Langham	16 under
S Pate	15 under
M Goggin	15 under
K Perry	15 under
J P Hayes	15 under

PUNTERS' POINTS

● In-form Loren Roberts, on a course tailor made for his straight driving (No. 1 in Driving Accuracy at 79%) and 'Boss of the Moss' smooth putting, turned the GMO into a procession, setting a 72-hole tournament record.

"This was a huge victory for me, at 45 years old, playing against guys in their 20's and 30's."

● 50/1 Franklin ("he never gave me a chance") Langham posted his third runners-up spot of the season after a disapointing over par 72 in R4.

● Players with disappointing final rounds included Franklin Langham (72), Frank Lickliter (73), Brian Gay (72), Corey Pavin (72) and Chris Perry (70).

● Defending champion Carlos Franco was never in contention after a poor second round. He finished T70th.

1999 RESULT

1	40/1	Carlos Franco
2	16/1	Tom Lehman
3	80/1	Jerry Kelly
T4	80/1	Steve Lowery
T4	80/1	Dan Forsman

1998 RESULT

1	33/1	Jeff Sluman
2	16/1	Steve Stricker
T3	33/1	Mark Calcavecchia
T3	100/1	Nolan Henke
T3	80/1	Chris Perry

PREVIOUS WINNERS ON THIS COURSE

1994	Mike Springer	1998	Jeff Sluman
1995	Scott Hoch	1999	Carlos Franco
1996	Loren Roberts	2000	Loren Roberts
1997	Scott Hoch		

PUNTERS' GUIDE

● At 6,739 yards, with five par 3s, Brown Deer Park requires straight (but not long) hitting and smooth putting. A putting contest in fact takes place after 'target golf'.

● It pays to consult the par 3 birdie stats to find the players with a good record on the short holes in the season to date. This year Franklin Langham, Joe Durant and Kenny Perry were among the top short-hole players at the GMO.

Players high on those stats must all come into calculations for 2- and 3-ball betting, in the outrights and on the spreads.

● Beware the opening round leader in the GMO. He has not won since Greg Norman obliged in 1989.

● The best recent records in this event are held by

> Loren Roberts — Won 2000, Won 1996, 2nd 1997. Won almost $1 million in 18 starts!

> Mark Calcavecchia — Plays every year. Nine top 10s. Sixteen of last eighteen rounds in the 60s.

> Jerry Kelly — 3rd 1999: T8th 1997: 2nd 1996

> Chris Perry — T9th 2000: T6th 1999: T3rd 1998

> Skip Kendall — T9th 2000: T6th 1999: 23rd 1998: T12th 1997

> Steve Stricker — T10th 1999: 2nd 1998: T12th 1997: T3rd 1996

● The USPGA tour has four players born in Wisconsin — Skip Kendall, Steve Stricker and Jerry Kelly (all in the above chart) and J P Hayes 18th in 1998 and T3rd this year. All four merit consideration each year, however a Wisconsin-born player has yet to win the GMO.

● Players whose profiles refer to this tournament include Joey Sindelar, Doug Barron, Kenny Perry, Joe Durant, J P Hayes, Skip Kendall, Steve Stricker, Jerry Kelly, Mark Calcavecchia, Loren Roberts and Billy Andrade.

THE BC OPEN

Date	20th - 23rd July
Course	En Joie, New York
Par	72
Yardage	6,994
First Prize	$360,000
Total Purse	$2 million

THE TOURNAMENT

This year the BC Open was brought forward (from mid-September) to be played 'opposite' the British Open. As a result all the big names were missing although defending champion Brad Faxon returned to play in New York having failed to prequalify for the British Open.

THE COURSE

The course was subject to major changes in 1997 with half the greens raised, enlarged and given greater undulations. The par was then increased to 72. Consequently pre-1997 form is of limited value. The En Joie course has fairly wide fairways, fairly small bentgrass greens and is one of the shortest on tour.

2000 ODDS

fav	16/1	Bill Glasson	50/1	Mike Brisky
	25/1	Jonathan Kaye	66/1*	Carl Paulson
	25/1	Joe Durant	66/1*	Paul Goydos
	25/1	Brad Faxon (DC)	66/1	Joey Sindelar
	33/1	Doug Barron	66/1*	Grant Waite
	33/1	Joe Ogilvie	66/1	Brian Watts
	40/1	Pete Jordan	66/1*	Peter Jacobsen
	40/1	Blaine McCallister	80/1**	Brian Gay
	40/1	Mathew Goggin	80/1*	John Maginnes
	50/1	Jerry Kelly	80/1*	Scott McCarron
	50/1*	Brad Elder	80/1*	Dave Stockton
	50/1*	Craig Stadler	80/1*	Jay Williamson
	50/1	Rory Sabbatini	80/1	Jimmy Green
	50/1	Ed Fryatt		

2000 RESULT

1	25/1*	Brad Faxon	68 66 68 68 270
2	125/1	Esteban Toledo	64 67 71 69 271
T3	fav 16/1	Bill Glasson	68 69 70 67 274
T3	125/1	Glen Hnatiuk	67 67 71 69 274
T5	100/1	Brett Quigley	69 69 69 68 275
T5	125/1**	Richard Zokol	70 67 70 68 275
T5	50/1	Jerry Kelly	74 63 67 71 275
T5	80/1*	Dave Stockton	75 67 65 68 275

9	M Goggin	71 68 71 66 276			D Briggs	68 73 68 72 281
T10	A Bean	69 69 72 67 277		T42	M Brisky	72 71 71 68 282
	B Heintz	71 65 73 68 277			S Randolph	75 68 67 72 282
	P Goydos	72 68 69 68 277			C Barlow	72 71 66 73 282
	J Ogilvie	69 70 67 71 277			M Clark	71 69 68 74 282
	G Waite	69 67 70 71 277		T46	B Gilder	75 68 71 69 283
T15	Jerry Smith	73 70 68 67 278			O Uresti	73 68 72 70 283
	C Riley	69 71 69 69 278			D Pohl	72 69 70 72 283
	Larry Rinker	71 69 67 71 278		T49	M Springer	75 68 71 70 284
T18	J Kaye	69 74 71 65 279			S Gotsche	71 70 72 71 284
	G Sauers	73 70 70 66 279			M Allen	68 70 73 73 284
	R Gamez	74 68 69 68 279			C Howell	72 70 69 73 284
	D Dunakey	71 68 72 68 279			S Utley	71 67 72 74 284
	J Gove	68 69 73 69 279		T54	J Williamson	72 68 77 68 285
	D Mast	71 64 74 70 279			J Delsing	73 70 71 71 285
	B Gay	67 68 74 70 279			C Wollmann	72 70 71 72 285
	E Loar	73 69 67 70 279			C A Spence	68 74 71 72 285
	T Barranger	71 69 68 71 279			B McCallister	71 69 72 73 285
T27	P Blackmar	69 73 70 68 280			G Twiggs	72 68 71 74 285
	P Moss	68 74 70 68 280		T60	J McGovern	72 71 72 71 286
	B Claar	74 69 68 69 280			T Dodds	74 69 70 73 286
	P Jordan	69 69 73 69 280			D Morland	73 70 70 73 286
	B Bates	68 72 71 69 280		T63	M Sullivan	74 69 74 70 287
	J Maginnes	72 67 71 70 280			N Lancaster	71 71 74 71 287
	J Sindelar	71 67 71 71 280			R W Eaks	74 69 70 74 287
	B Elder	70 69 69 72 280			K Gibson	73 70 70 74 287
	D Ogrin	72 69 67 72 280			Curt Byrum	73 69 71 74 287
	S McCarron	68 66 73 73 280			E Booker	71 70 71 75 287
T37	C Stadler	71 68 74 68 281		69	E Fiori	70 72 73 73 288
	Bart Bryant	71 68 73 69 281		T70	K Nolan	69 74 74 72 289
	M Standly	69 71 72 69 281			W Levi	75 67 75 72 289
	Carl Paulson	69 68 73 71 281		72	M Donald	71 71 77 77 296

The main players to miss the cut (made at 1 under) were:–

D Pride (E)	M Carnevale (E)	E Fryatt (E)	C Rose (E)
T Schulz (E)	S Micheel (E)	B Schwarzrock (E)	P H Horgan (E)
J Durant (E)	M Bradley (E)	M Hulbert (E)	P Curry (E)
J Rollins (E)	R Howison (E)	H Haas (E)	G Boros (+1)
D Barron (+1)	S Murphy (+1)	B Hughes (+1)	D Barr (+1)
K J Choi (+1)	M Heinen (+1)	B Watts (+1)	G Nicklaus (+2)
B Lohr (+2)	K Wentworth (+2)	D Pooley (+3)	D Hammond (+3)
B Cochran (+3)	N Henke (+3)	K Fergus (+3)	J Gallagher (+4)
P Jacobsen (+4)	S Scott (+4)	C Dennis (+5)	C Beck (+5)
W Wood (+5)	C Rymer (+6)	C Raulerson (+7)	C Perks (+7)

ROUND BY ROUND LEADERBOARD

FIRST ROUND		SECOND ROUND	
E Toledo	8 under	E Toledo	13 under
G Hnatiuk	5 under	S McCarron	10 under
B Gay	5 under	B FAXON	10 under
B FAXON	4 under	G Hnatiuk	9 under
8 others at	4 under	D Mast	9 under
		B Gay	9 under
		B Heintz	8 under
		G Waite	8 under

THIRD ROUND		FINAL ROUND	
B FAXON	14 under	B FAXON	18 under
E Toledo	14 under	E Toledo	17 under
J Kelly	12 under	B Glasson	14 under
G Hnatiuk	11 under	G Hnatiuk	14 under
B Gay	10 under	R Zokol	13 under
G Waite	10 under	B Quigley	13 under
J Ogilvie	10 under	J Kelly	13 under
		D Stockton	13 under

There were perfect conditions on the first day. Toledo's round came from an afternoon (4th out) tee time.

Due to rain delays thirty golfers were unable to finish R2 on Friday which was completed on Saturday.

PUNTERS' POINTS

● 25/1 DYM Brad Faxon became the first-ever successful defending champion at the BC Open. His putting (25 putts in R4) compensated for some loose driving with many lucky breaks off the trees lining the fairways also being crucial.

● "The whole week I made every single putt I had to make," said Brad Faxon, while Toledo said of the winner, "he was lucky"....and he sure was!

● 125/1 Esteban Toledo missed a birdie putt on the last, so he's still looking for his first win.

● Jerry Kelly, 3rd after R3, again had a disappointing final round to finish T5th.

● Fast finishing players included

> Paul Goydos   11 under last 54 holes

> Dave Stockton   16 under last 54 holes

> Jerry Smith   11 under last 54 holes

> Robert Gamez   11 under last 54 holes

> Brian Claar   10 under last 54 holes

1999 RESULT

1	50/1	Brad Faxon

won at the second play-off hole

2	20/1	Fred Funk
3	150/1*	Rory Sabbatini
T4	125/1*	Stephen Ames
T4	150/1	Craig Spence
T4	125/1	Jonathan Kaye
T4	150/1	Ronnie Black
T4	150/1	Mark Carnevale

1998 RESULT

1	25/1	Chris Perry
2	80/1	Peter Jacobsen
3	50/1	Nolan Henke
T4	150/1	Curt Byrum
T4	40/1	Robert Allenby
T4	100/1	Ted Tryba

WINNERS IN THE LAST TEN YEARS

1991	Fred Couples	1996	Fred Funk
1992	John Daly	1997	Gabriel Hjerestedt
1993	Blaine McCallister	1998	Chris Perry
1994	Mike Sullivan	1999	Brad Faxon
1995	Hal Sutton	2000	Brad Faxon

PUNTERS' GUIDE

● This has become very much an outsiders tournament!! In the last five years there have been thirty-three players in the top 5 (or T5th)

> thirteen (39.39%) have started at or over 125/1

> eighteen (54.54%) have started at or over 100/1

> twenty-two (66.66%) have started at or over 80/1

● This year of the twenty-one players quoted from 66/1 - 100/1 inclusive in the Racing Post no fewer than seventeen (81%) were at least DYMs.

So it is clear that in this outsider's tournament there is genuine value to be had.

● The switch to July from September has improved the probable weather conditions for this tournament.

● With tree-lined fairways accuracy off the tee is important here, unless like Faxon you get regular bounces off the tree trunks onto the fairways!!

● With the course changes in 1997 the form before then is not really very valuable. The players with the best recent records include

> Brad Faxon   Won 2000: Won 1999: DNP 1998 & 1997

> Doug Barron   MC 2000: T18th 1999: T7th 1998: T23rd 1997

> Jonathan Kaye   T18th 2000: T4th 1999: T51st 1998: T23rd 1997

> Joe Ogilvie   T10th 2000: T36th 1999

> Grant Waite   T10th 2000: T39th 1999: T40th 1998: T8th 1997

● Players whose profiles refer to this tournament include Dave Stockton Jr, Mathew Goggin, Joe Ogilvie, Grant Waite, Paul Goydos, Brad Elder, Bill Glasson, Glen Hnatiuk, Brian Gay, Chris Smith and Jonathan Kaye.

THE JOHN DEERE CLASSIC

Date	27th - 30th July
Course	TPC Deere Run, Silvis, Illinois
Par	71
Yardage	7,183
First Prize	$468,000
Total Purse	$2.6 million

THE TOURNAMENT

Started in 1972 it had been held at the Oakwood since 1975 before its move this year. Known as the Quad Cities Classic (1975-1985, and 1995-1998) and the Hardee's Golf Classic (1986 - 1994) it became the John Deere Classic in 1999.

It moved to July from September in 1997. In 1997 and 1998 it coincided with the Loch Lomond Invitational in Scotland. In 1999 and again this year it was the first tournament after the British Open.

THE COURSE

Although staying in the state of Illinois the tournament moved from Oakwood, Coal Valley to the D A Weibring-designed TPC Deere Run at Silvis which is a long par 71 with the three par 5s all over 540 yards. The large greens are bentgrass.

2000 ODDS

fav	14/1	David Toms	66/1*	Olin Browne
	16/1	Bill Glasson	66/1*	Robert Damron
	25/1	Steve Jones	66/1*	Brad Elder
	28/1	Kirk Triplett	66/1	Pete Jordan
	33/1*	Jeff Sluman	66/1	John Cook
	33/1*	Steve Lowery	66/1*	Kevin Sutherland
	33/1*	Joe Ogilvie	80/1*	Brian Gay
	40/1	Craig Parry	80/1*	Grant Waite
	40/1	Tim Herron	80/1	Harrison Frazar
	50/1	Jerry Kelly	80/1*	Stephen Ames
	50/1*	Fred Funk	80/1	Greg Chalmers
	50/1	Frank Lickliter	80/1	Brian Henninger
	50/1*	Scott Verplank	80/1*	Greg Kraft
	66/1*	Glen Day	80/1	Blaine McCallister
	66/1*	Mathew Goggin	80/1	Scott McCarron
	66/1*	Skip Kendal	80/1*	Bob Tway

2000 RESULT

1	200/1*	Michael Clark	70 65 63 67 265

Clark won at the fourth play-off hole

2	28/1	Kirk Triplett	67 66 62 70 265
3	200/1***	Charles Howell	69 64 67 66 266
4	150/1**	Chris Riley	68 67 65 67 267
T5	33/1	Steve Lowery	67 70 68 63 268
T5	150/1	Shaun Micheel	68 66 69 65 268

7	T Herron	65 65 70 69 269			Larry Rinker	68 70 69 69 276
T8	N Lancaster	69 68 67 66 270			D Pride	69 68 68 71 276
	D Frost	65 62 70 73 270			J Ogilvie	66 69 67 74 276
T10	J McGovern	69 68 66 68 271		T44	P H Horgan	66 70 73 68 277
	L Mattiace	70 68 65 68 271			Curt Byrum	67 66 75 69 277
T12	R Zokol	68 71 69 64 272			J Gullion	67 72 69 69 277
	J Cook	68 67 71 66 272			O Browne	68 67 72 70 277
	R Black	69 68 67 68 272			K Nolan	70 67 70 70 277
	S Verplank	67 68 68 69 272			B Claar	70 69 68 70 277
	S Jones	68 70 65 69 272		T50	B McCallister	71 64 75 68 278
	J Williamson	70 68 65 69 272			F Funk	68 69 70 71 278
	J Kelly	67 66 69 70 272			B Heintz	72 66 68 72 278
	S Gotsche	69 65 68 70 272			D Briggs	67 72 66 73 278
	B Quigley	70 65 67 70 272			J L Lewis	70 68 67 73 278
	P Curry	63 69 69 71 272		T55	B Watts	69 70 73 67 279
	B Glasson	66 66 68 72 272			J Gove	65 71 72 71 279
T23	S Ames	69 70 67 67 273			T Tryba	73 65 70 71 279
	J Sluman	68 69 68 68 273			J Durant	69 69 70 71 279
	M Sposa	66 70 69 68 273			G Kraft	68 67 69 75 279
	Kevin Sutherland	71 67 67 68 273		T60	B Bates	68 71 73 68 280
	K Hosokawa	68 70 66 69 273			W Wood	72 66 70 72 280
	G Day	71 67 65 70 273			W Austin	70 68 69 73 280
	F Lickliter	65 68 69 71 273			J Maginnes	71 67 67 75 280
	G Waite	69 65 71 69 274		T64	P Goydos	68 70 73 70 281
	D Pohl	68 65 70 71 274			N Henke	72 66 69 74 281
	K Gibson	69 67 67 71 274		T66	D Mast	68 69 74 71 282
T33	C Beck	71 68 67 69 275			W Grady	72 66 70 74 282
	B Gilder	65 68 71 71 275			C Beckman	69 69 69 75 282
	C Martin	70 69 66 70 275		T69	M Wiebe	69 69 72 73 283
	R Damron	66 69 68 72 275			D Morland	68 71 69 75 283
	D A Weibring	69 66 67 73 275		71	P Jacobsen	69 68 75 72 284
T38	P Moss	69 70 71 66 276		72	A Bean	65 70 74 77 286
	C Barlow	71 68 69 68 276		73	D Pooley	71 68 72 77 288
	S McCarron	73 66 69 68 276				

The main players to miss the cut (made at 3 under) were:–

M Springer (-2)	B Friend (-2)	S Murphy (-2)	G Chalmers (-2)
B Jobe (-2)	G Hnatiuk (-2)	B Henninger (-2)	T Pernice Jr (-2)
C Parry (-2)	K Clearwater (-2)	A Bengoechea (-2)	B Schwarzrock (-2)
M Hulbert (-2)	J Edwards (-2)	R Gamez (-2)	R Howison (-2)
P Blackmar (-1)	R Freeman (-1)	T Dodds (-1)	D Toms (-1)
D Sutherland (-1)	D Edwards (-1)	B Cheesman (-1)	E Aubrey (-1)
K Wentworth (-1)	K Fergus (-1)	J Smith (-1)	H Frazar (E)
C Paulson (E)	D Peoples (E)	S Gump (E)	M Brisky (E)
S Kendall (E)	E Booker (E)	M Standly (E)	J Delsing (E)
T Byrum (E)	J Green (+1)	B Tway (+1)	B Elder (+1)
D Forsman (+2)	C Rose (+2)	F Zoeller (+3)	M Bradley (+4)
D Stockton (+4)	P Jordan (+4)	M Goggin (+4)	G Hallberg (+4)
C Perks (+4)	B Gay (+5)	B Fabel (+6)	J Daly (+6)
C A Spence (+7)	M Donald (+8)	J Gallagher (+8)	G Boros (+12)
G Nicklaus (+13)			

Joey Sindelar (70) withdrew.

ROUND BY ROUND LEADERBOARD

FIRST ROUND

P Curry	8 under
B Gilder	6 under
J Gove	6 under
T Herron	6 under
A Bean	6 under
D Frost	6 under
F Lickliter	6 under
K Triplett	4 under
M CLARK	2 under

SECOND ROUND

D Frost	15 under
T Herron	12 under
B Glasson	10 under
P Curry	10 under
M CLARK	9 under
6 others at	9 under

THIRD ROUND

K Triplett	18 under
D Frost	16 under
M CLARK	15 under
C Riley	13 under
C Howell	13 under
T Herron	13 under
B Glasson	13 under

END OF PLAY SUNDAY

M CLARK	17 under (9)
S Lowery	16 under (18)
K Triplett	16 under (9)
S Micheel	15 under (16)
C Howell	15 under (10)
C Riley	15 under (9)

FINAL ROUND

M CLARK	19 under
K Triplett	19 under
C Howell	18 under
C Riley	17 under
S Lowery	16 under
S Micheel	16 under

Soft, young greens were exceptionally receptive. In such 'target' golf conditions there were a hundred sub-par rounds in R1 and a hundred and four in R2.

Heavy rain forced the suspension of the final round on Sunday with twenty-seven players still to complete. The tournament, after a further delay for rain and thunder, ended on Monday.

PUNTERS' POINTS

● Michael (who?) Clark The Second came first after a thrilling play-off win against Kirk Triplett. The 31-year-old went par-birdie-birdie and birdie again in the play-off to win and prove what a tough cookie he is mentally.

● Another triumph for the nappy factor! Clark became a first-time dad of a son, Austin, last year.

● Kirk Triplett birdied the last hole in his rain-delayed final round to force the play-off but couldn't add to his Nissan Open win earlier this season. It was his ninth top 10 in nineteen starts.

● Charles Howell really is a name to note. He's the 2000 NCAA champion, a long hitter with a good putting stroke who's left his studies unfinished to go on the tour. Here in just his third tour start he finished alone in 3rd place after a 16 under par finish over the last 54 holes.

● Disappointing final rounds by players in contention included Bill Glasson (+1), Joe Ogilvie (+3) and David Frost (+2).

● Sometimes the most profitable golf bets come when opposing a player. Here it had to be the favourite David Toms. Last week he was in serious contention for a major for the first time, playing alongside Tiger Woods in R3 in the British Open, and came on here suffering from MLD. He then lost his clubs (for two days) and missed the practice round. Not surprisingly he then missed the cut!

1999 RESULT		
1	125/1	J L Lewis
won at the fifth play-off hole		
2	100/1*	Mike Brisky
T3	100/1*	Brian Henninger
T3	66/1*	Kirk Triplett
T5	40/1*	Steve Jones
T5	150/1	Pete Jordan
T5	jt fav 16/1	Chris Perry

1998 RESULT		
1	jt fav 20/1	Steve Jones
2	66/1	Scott Gump
3	jt fav 20/1	Kenny Perry
4	66/1	David Toms
T5	jt fav 20/1	Fred Funk
T5	50/1	Brad Fabel
T5	33/1	Scott McCarron
T5	80/1	D A Weibring

WINNERS IN THE LAST TEN YEARS

1991	D A Weibring	1996	Ed Fiori
1992	David Frost	1997	David Toms
1993	David Frost	1998	Steve Jones
1994	Mark McCumber	1999	J L Lewis
1995	D A Weibring	2000	Michael Clark II

PUNTERS' GUIDE

- The new course is popular with the players and its large receptive greens made for really low scoring and a feast of birdies, with 62 (twice) and 63 (three times) the lowest scores.

- Although one or two players had played exhibitions here (including 7th-placed Tim Herron) this was a 'new' course that neutralised the usual course experience advantage that the seasoned pros have over the rookies. For that reason it was probably always going to be a 'tournament of shocks'.

- This year fourteen of the twenty-three players (61%) quoted from 50/1 - 80/1 inclusive were DYMs and the top 5 included a QYM (!!) Charles Howell, a TYM (!) Chris Riley and a DYM winner in Michael Clark.

  In the last two John Deeres of the thirteen players in the top 5 (or T5th) seven have been at least DYMs.

- The John Deere has also become an outsiders tournament over the last two years.

  > Of the thirteen players in the top 5 (or T5th) eight have been priced at or over 100/1!

- Any player who was in serious contention in the British Open must be avoided and opposed if coming straight on here (e.g. David Toms, the absurdly short favourite this year).

- Players whose profiles refer to this tournament include Steve Lowery, Scott Verplank, Steve Jones, Tim Herron, Neal Lancaster, Shaun Micheel, David Toms, Len Mattiace, Mark Hensby and Chris Riley.

THE INTERNATIONAL PRESENTED BY Q WEST

Date	3rd - 6th August
Course	Castle Pines, Castle Rock, Colorado
Par	72
Yardage	7,559
First Prize	$630,000
Total Purse	$3.5 million

THE TOURNAMENT

This is an unusual tournament as it is decided by points rather than strokes. Points are awarded as follows: An albatross (+8), an eagle (+5), a birdie (+2), par (zero), bogey (-1), a double bogey or worse (-3). The points accumulate over all four rounds. The field is cut to the lowest 70 plus ties after R2, and to the lowest 36 plus ties after R3.

THE COURSE

In the thin desert air of Colorado the ball travels an extra 10 - 15% on the 6,200-feet altitude Castle Pines course. At over 7,500 yards it is the longest on the tour. The greens are bentgrass and very quick.

2000 ODDS

jt fav	10/1	Ernie Els	50/1	Kirk Triplett
jt fav	10/1	Phil Mickelson	50/1	Robert Allenby
	12/1	David Duval	50/1	Stuart Appleby
	20/1	Vijay Singh	50/1	J M Olazabal
	25/1	Sergio Garcia	66/1	Brad Faxon
	28/1	Tom Lehman	66/1	Steve Jones
	28/1	Steve Flesch	66/1	Angel Cabrera
	40/1	David Toms (DC)	66/1*	Mark Calcavecchia
	40/1	Notah Begay	66/1	Mike Weir
	40/1	Stewart Cink	80/1	Adam Scott
	50/1	Justin Leonard	80/1	Steve Pate
	50/1	Steve Lowery	80/1	Robert Damron
	50/1	Chris Perry	80/1*	Charles Howell

2000 RESULT

1	jt fav 10/1	Ernie Els	15	19	6	8	48
2	jt fav 10/1	Phil Mickelson	10	8	14	12	44
3	50/1	Stuart Appleby	14	14	2	11	41
4	100/1*	Greg Norman	12	14	6	6	38
5	150/1	Craig Spence	6	10	6	10	32

T6	J Ogilvie	2	8	11	10	31		B Henninger	11	3	11	0	25
	G Hnatiuk	6	14	4	4	31	T24	E Aubrey	10	6	2	6	24
8	S Ames	15	2	7	6	30		M Reid	10	4	5	5	24
T9	V Singh	3	8	9	9	29		M Clark	12	8	1	3	24
	E Fryatt	2	12	14	1	29		F Langham	4	7	12	1	24
T11	P Stankowski	8	5	6	9	28	T28	B Friend	10	5	3	5	23
	D Pride	5	7	8	8	28		Kevin Sutherland	7	5	6	5	23
	G Chalmers	15	(-3)	8	8	28	30	J Delsing	10	12	0	0	22
T14	C Stadler	1	10	9	7	27	T31	R Allenby	(-1)	11	8	3	21
	C Riley	7	10	6	4	27		N Lancaster	7	6	5	3	21
	M Calcavecchia	7	11	5	4	27		B May	6	4	10	1	21
	A Magee	5	18	1	3	27		J Gove	13	4	6	(-2)	21
	S Garcia	8	13	9	(-3)	27	T35	C DiMarco	11	5	2	1	19
T19	M Weir	5	7	8	6	26		S Pate	11	0	8	0	19
	N Begay	4	14	6	2	26		K Triplett	7	10	4	(-2)	19
T21	S Jones	2	7	11	5	25	38	J Sindelar	7	5	10	(-5)	17
	M O'Meara	8	0	16	1	25							

The following players played in R3 on Saturday but failed to qualify for the final day.

B Mayfair	5	6	6	+17		J Leonard	(-3)	13	2	+12
W Austin	6	7	4	+17		B Bates	2	7	3	+12
T Scherrer	15	(-2)	4	+17		S Lowery	4	12	(-4)	+12
S Micheel	8	6	3	+17		B Geiberger	3	8	(-1)	+10
F Nobilo	6	6	4	+16		J Kaye	2	6	2	+10
O Browne	10	(-2)	8	+16		Jerry Smith	6	7	(-4)	+9
R Black	9	4	2	+15		J Van de Velde	(-1)	8	2	+9
D Dunakey	0	8	7	+15		J Maggert	4	3	2	+9
C Parry	6	1	8	+15		J Williamson	(-3)	10	2	+9
Chris Perry	2	10	2	+14		B Cheesman	4	4	0	+8
G Hallberg	5	7	2	+14		D Barron	3	4	1	+8
W Grady	11	3	0	+14		G Hjertstedt	7	1	(-1)	+7
J Haas	7	2	5	+14		David Sutherland	8	1	(-3)	+6
K J Choi	3	6	5	+14		S Gump	3	5	(-2)	+6
M Wiebe	2	5	7	+14		M Brisky	10	(-3)	(-2)	+5
M Brooks	6	6	1	+13		R Beem	8	(-1)	(-2)	+5
B Hughes	11	0	2	+13		K Wentworth	5	5	(-6)	+4
K Hosokawa	1	9	3	+13		H Haas	5	3	(-4)	+4
B Andrade	5	7	0	+12		T Lehman	15	8	W/D	

The main players to miss the R2 cut (made at 7pts) were:–

S Flesch (6 pts)	J D Blake (6 pts)	D Toms (6 pts)	L Mize (6 pts)
D Stockton (6 pts)	C Martin (6 pts)	T Pernice Jr (6 pts)	B Gay (6 pts)
S Gotsche (6 pts)	B Jobe (5 pts)	T Armour III (5 pts)	C Howell (5pts)
C Barlow (5 pts)	K Gibson (4 pts)	D Morland (4 pts)	J L Lewis (4 pts)
J Green (4 pts)	A Scott (4 pts)	D Frost (3 pts)	B Faxon (3 pts)
J Cook (3 pts)	N Faldo (3 pts)	B Chamblee (3 pts)	S Kendall (3 pts)
J Carter (3 pts)	M Gogel (2 pts)	D Waldorf (2 pts)	S Cink (2 pts)
T Dodds (2 pts)	T Purtzer (2 pts)	M Springer (1 pt)	J P Hayes (1 pt)
M Hulbert (1 pt)	J M Olazabal (1 pt)	B Estes (1 pt)	R Sabbatini (1 pt)
S McCarron (0 pts)	T Byrum (0 pts)	J McGovern (0 pts)	R Mediate (-1 pt)
C Beck (-1 pt)	H Frazar (-1pt)	P Goydos (-2pts)	R Fehr (-3 pts)
E Toledo (-4 pts)	W Wood (-5 pts)	C Rose (-5 pts)	Carl Paulson (-5 pts)
R Damron (-6 pts)	H Kuehne (-6 pts)	F Allem (-8 pts)	D Gossett (-9 pts)
F Lickliter (-9 pts)	G Nicklaus (-9 pts)	E Booker (-12 pts)	

Andy Bean, Grant Waite, Peter Jacobsen, Robin Freeman all withdrew.

ROUND BY ROUND LEADERBOARD

FIRST ROUND

E ELS	15 pts
T Scherrer	15 pts
T Lehman	15 pts
S Ames	15 pts
G Chalmers	15 pts
S Appleby	14 pts

SECOND ROUND

E ELS	34 pts
S Appleby	28 pts
G Norman	26 pts
A Magee	23 pts
T Lehman	23 pts
J Delsing	22 pts
S Garcia	21 pts

THIRD ROUND

E ELS	40 pts
P Mickelson	32 pts
G Norman	32 pts
S Garcia	30 pts
S Apleby	30 pts
E Fryatt	28 pts

FINAL ROUND

E ELS	48 pts
P Mickelson	44 pts
S Appleby	41 pts
G Norman	38 pts
C Spence	32 pts

Thunderstorms disrupted both the opening rounds, with players having to complete R1 on Friday and R2 on Saturday. R3 was completed on Saturday.

PUNTERS' POINTS

- Course specialist Ernie Els, heavily tipped for this tournament in his player profile last year, led from wire to wire to claim his first American win for seventeen months. Since his last US win the 'Big Easy' has had five 2nd places on the US tour with four of them to Tiger Woods.

- Phil Mickelson played very well in a format to which he's well suited, but 'desert fox' Lefty had to be content with 2nd place.

- 50/1 Stuart Appleby has come into form recently after a superb finish to the British Open, and has now posted two top 4 finishes here in the last four years.

● 100/1 DYM Greg Norman, who has had more hip surgery than the Queen Mother, made an impressive comeback here, swinging really well.

	1999 RESULT				1998 RESULT	
1	125/1	David Toms		1	33/1	Vijay Singh
2	12/1	David Duval		T2	200/1	Willie Wood
3	150/1	Stephen Ames		T2	18/1	Phil Mickelson
4	40/1	Chris Perry		4	fav 8/1	Tiger Woods
T5	100/1	Billy Mayfair		5	150/1	Rocco Mediate
T5	20/1	Ernie Els				

WINNERS IN THE LAST TEN YEARS

1991	J M Olazabal		1996	Clarence Rose	(31 pts)
1992	Brad Faxon		1997	Phil Mickelson	(48 pts)
1993	Phil Mickelson	(45 pts)	1998	Vijay Singh	(47 pts)
1994	Steve Lowery	(35 pts)	1999	David Toms	(47 pts)
1995	Lee Janzen	(34 pts)	2000	Ernie Els	(48 pts)

PUNTERS' GUIDE

● With aggressive play so crucial the key stats here are for total birdies, total eagles and par 5 birdies as well as the course form on this specialist's track.

> This year Phil Mickelson topped the total eagles stats and was 3rd for par 5 birdies, with Ernie Els 4th just behind him.

● If 'betting in running' do remember that the par 5 14th, and especially the par 5 17th, offer genuine birdie/eagle chances.

● The winner in each of the last three years has led, or been tied for the lead, after R1, R2 and R3. On that basis after R1 a 'bet in running', especially on a course specialist at the head of the leaderboard, should prove profitable. With a fast start so important it is interesting to note that five of the front 7 after R1 all had early-morning tee times this year on Thursday.

● Over recent years the best records are held by:

	2000	1999	1998	1997	Average
Phil Mickelson	44	29	41	48	40.5
Ernie Els	48	35	17	32	33.0
Andrew Magee	27	27	31	27	28.0
Kirk Triplett	19	31	31	23	26.0

● Players whose profiles refer to this tournament include Nick Faldo, Robert Allenby, Ernie Els, Phil Mickelson, Stuart Appleby, Greg Chalmers, Steve Flesch, Vijay Singh, Sergio Garcia, Ed Fryatt, Stephen Ames, Kirk Triplett and Andrew Magee.

THE BUICK OPEN

Date	10th - 13th August
Course	Warwick Hills, Grand Blanc, Michigan
Par	72
Yardage	7,105
First Prize	$486,000
Total Purse	$2.7 million

THE TOURNAMENT

This tournament has been held at Warwick Hills since 1978, and before that from its inaugural year 1958 to 1969. This is a well-established event with a well-established sponsor.

THE COURSE

This course has wide fairways encouraging aggression off the tee. The holes are straight without dog legs and the rough is not penal so the scoring is low and the event was called a 'putting contest' last year by Ernie Els. The bentgrass greens are very large.

2000 ODDS

fav	7/4	Tiger Woods	66/1	Chris Perry
	14/1	Phil Mickelson	66/1	Paul Azinger
	25/1	Vijay Singh	66/1	Shigeki Maruyama
	28/1	Davis Love	66/1	J M Olazabal
	33/1	Jim Furyk	80/1*	Kenny Perry
	33/1	Loren Roberts	80/1*	Lee Janzen
	40/1	Hal Sutton	80/1	Stephen Ames
	40/1	Steve Flesch	80/1	Brad Faxon
	40/1	Fred Couples	66/1	Tim Herron
	50/1*	Bill Glasson (non runner)	80/1	Dennis Paulson
	50/1	Stewart Cink	80/1	Jeff Sluman
	50/1	Justin Leonard		

2000 RESULT

1	100/1	Rocco Mediate	68 64 70 66 268
2	66/1	Chris Perry	67 69 65 68 269
3	40/1	Hal Sutton	67 67 69 68 271
T4	200/1	Woody Austin	63 67 73 70 273
T4	14/1	Phil Mickelson	69 71 65 68 273

T6	Carl Paulson	70 70 68 66 274		G Day	73 69 68 70 280
	Dudley Hart	70 65 70 69 274		S McCarron	74 68 68 70 280
	J Maggert	69 70 67 68 274		J Cook	71 69 69 71 280
	B Faxon	70 69 66 69 274		S Gotsche	73 68 68 71 280
	Joe Ozaki	66 69 69 70 274		F Couples	71 68 68 73 280
T11	S Verplank	69 70 70 66 275		P Goydos	69 70 67 74 280
	L Mize	70 66 72 67 275	T45	T Scherrer	71 71 70 69 281
	T Woods	70 70 67 68 275		R Black	69 72 70 70 281
	S Kendall	69 67 69 70 275	T47	D Berganio	73 68 74 67 282
	V Singh	66 71 68 70 275		B Gay	73 68 72 69 282
T16	L Roberts	68 73 69 66 276		M Bradley	73 66 74 69 282
	G Chalmers	70 71 68 67 276		B Mayfair	67 71 74 70 282
	J Furyk	69 70 69 68 276		J Gove	69 73 70 70 282
	G Hnatiuk	71 69 68 68 276		K J Choi	72 70 69 71 282
	Kenny Perry	71 68 68 69 276		T Herron	69 71 69 73 282
T21	J Williamson	73 65 73 66 277	T54	C Martin	68 73 74 68 283
	T Pernice Jr	72 65 72 68 277		G Kraft	70 70 72 71 283
	D Barron	68 73 68 68 277		S Murphy	70 71 71 71 283
	P Azinger	65 70 69 73 277	T57	J Carter	71 71 72 70 284
T25	S Flesch	73 67 71 67 278		M Wiebe	74 68 73 69 284
	Joel Edwards	72 66 72 68 278		N Lancaster	71 71 71 71 284
	Robin Freeman	72 68 67 71 278		D Peoples	72 69 68 75 284
T28	B Quigley	71 71 73 64 279	61	David Sutherland	69 71 73 72 285
	T Purtzer	70 71 69 69 279	62	P Jordan	71 70 70 75 286
	C Beckman	70 68 70 71 279	63	C Perks	74 68 72 73 287
	J Sluman	70 68 69 72 279	T64	Steve Hart	71 71 76 70 288
T32	T Nogami	72 70 72 66 280		A Bengoechea	68 73 74 73 288
	E Toledo	69 69 74 68 280		J Delsing	68 71 71 78 288
	J Maginnes	67 71 74 68 280	T67	C Bowden	70 71 78 70 289
	Tom Byrum	68 73 71 68 280		M Gogel	71 70 75 73 289
	J Roth	70 70 71 69 280		G Hjertstedt	69 68 80 72 289
	B Jobe	70 72 69 69 280	70	J Caron	74 68 71 78 291
	B Watts	71 70 69 70 280			

The main players to miss the cut (made at 2 under) were:–

R Fehr (-1)	S Gump (-1)	C Parry (-1)	D A Weibring (-1)
P H Horgan (-1)	S Micheel (-1)	M Springer (-1)	S Ames (-1)
D Stockton (-1)	E Aubrey (-1)	D Love (-1)	D Pride (-1)
J D Blake (-1)	R Howison (-1)	D Dunakey (-1)	M Goggin (-1)
M Hulbert (E)	J Van de Velde (E)	D Frost (E)	L Rinker (E)
J Kaye (E)	D Briggs (E)	B Andrade (E)	E Booker (E)
E Fryatt (E)	L Mattiace (E)	Ro Gamez (+1)	T Tryba (+1)
L Janzen (+1)	C A Spence (+1)	J McGovern (+1)	B Tway (+1)
C Barlow (+1)	A Magee (+1)	R Cochran (+2)	G Waite (+2)
B Hughes (+2)	W Grady (+2)	D Paulson (+2)	J Leonard (+2)
D Morland (+2)	F Allem (+3)	B Cheesman (+3)	O Uresti (+3)
N Henke (+3)	J P Hayes (+3)	T Armour III (+3)	C DiMarco (+3)
K Gibson (+5)	C Raulerson (+5)	J Green (+5)	J Sindelar (+5)
T Dodds (+5)	M A Jimenez (+6)	S Maruyama (+6)	S Cink (+7)
R Beem (+8)	J M Olazabal (+9)		

ROUND BY ROUND LEADERBOARD

FIRST ROUND

W Austin	9 under
P Azinger	7 under
Joe Ozaki	6 under
V Singh	6 under
C Perry	5 under
J Maginnes	5 under
B Mayfair	5 under
H Sutton	5 under
R MEDIATE	4 under

SECOND ROUND

W Austin	14 under
R MEDIATE	12 under
H Sutton	10 under
Joe Ozaki	9 under
P Azinger	9 under
D Hart	9 under

THIRD ROUND

C Perry	15 under
R MEDIATE	14 under
H Sutton	13 under
W Austin	13 under
P Azinger	12 under
Joe Ozaki	12 under

FINAL ROUND

R MEDIATE	20 under
C Perry	19 under
H Sutton	17 under
W Austin	15 under
P Mickelson	15 under

PUNTERS' POINTS

● 100/1 Rocco Mediate birdied the last hole while the leader throughout the final round Chris Perry made bogey, so that the 37-year-old with the broomstick 'stole' the tournament and notched his fourth tour win.

● So Chris Perry had once more played really well only to slip up when within sight of the winning post. He has still only one tour win.

● 'The Law of the Tiger' discussed in Part 1 certainly applied here. Never in contention, and with his game and mental approach well below par, he finished T11th.

● Jim Furyk amazingly made only one bogey yet could only finish T16th!!

1999 RESULT

1	150/1	Tom Pernice Jr
T2	100/1*	Bob Tway
T2	100/1	Ted Tryba
T2	25/1	Tom Lehman
5	66/1	Bob Estes

1998 RESULT

1	125/1	Billy Mayfair
2	66/1	Scott Verplank
3	100/1	Andrew Magee
T4	500/1	Eric Booker
T4	fav 11/2	Tiger Woods

WINNERS IN THE LAST TEN YEARS

1991	Bob Faxon	1996	Justin Leonard
1992	Dan Forsman	1997	Vijay Singh
1993	Larry Mize	1998	Billy Mayfair
1994	Fred Couples	1999	Tom Pernice Jr
1995	Woody Austin	2000	Rocco Mediate

PUNTERS' GUIDE

● If betting in running remember that holes 12, 13 and 14 are relatively easy and the 15th (a tough par 4) the course's hardest hole.

● In this tournament this year very unusually a late R1 tee time (and so an early R2 start) was an advantage.

● Three interesting stats:-

> In the last four years there have been twenty players who have finished in the top 4 (or T4th) with twelve of them starting at or over 100/1!!

> This is a 'catch-up' course so it's not surprising to find that only six third-round leaders have gone on to win.

> There have been eleven first-time winners here in the last twenty-six years.

● This year's result was clear confirmation that this is very much a course-specialists' tournament. There were eight players who had posted at least two top 20s here in the last three years and they included winner Rocco Mediate, 2nd Chris Perry and 3rd Hal Sutton, as well as T11th Vijay Singh. Not bad, eh!!

● In 2001 there will be ten players with at least two top 20s in the last three years and who made the cut in 2000.

	2000	1999	1998	
Loren Roberts	16	9	–	
Tiger Woods	11	–	4	
Rocco Mediate	Won	9	30	
Jim Furyk	16	9	-	
Hal Sutton	3	8	12	
Vijay Singh	11	72	8	(won 1997)
Chris Perry	2	15	23	
Skip Kendall	11	19	36	
Dudley Hart	6	25	12	
Scott Verplank	11	MC	2	
Woody Austin	4	15	30	

● Players whose profiles refer to this tournament include the above players (with the exception of Vijay and Tiger), Paul Azinger and Jeff Sluman.

THE 82ND USPGA CHAMPIONSHIP

Date   17th - 20th August
Course   Valhalla G.C., Louisville, Kentucky
Par   72
Yardage   7,167
First Prize $800,000
Total Purse $5 million

PLEASE SEE PART 6.

THE WORLD GOLF CHAMPIONSHIP NEC INVITATIONAL

Date	24th - 27th August
Course	South Course, Firestone G.C., Akron, Ohio
Par	70
Yardage	7,189
First Prize	$1 million
Total Purse	$5 million

PLEASE SEE PART 5.

THE RENO-TAHOE OPEN

Date	24th - 27th August
Course	Montreux G. & C.C., Reno, Nevada
Par	72
Yardage	7,552
First Prize	$540,000
Total Purse	$3 million

THE TOURNAMENT

This tournament was introduced last year to be played alongside the World Championship NEC Invitational. It is played at altitude in desert conditions.

THE COURSE

Designed by Jack Nicklaus, this a long course, although it plays shorter than the 7,500 figure suggests in the high altitude desert air. Swirling winds can play a part here although the smooth greens offer many birdie chances.

2000 ODDS

fav	14/1	Sergio Garcia	66/1*	Chris Riley
	25/1	Chris Perry	66/1*	John Cook
	25/1	David Toms	66/1	Tom Scherrer
	33/1	Mark Calcavecchia	66/1	Adam Scott
	33/1	Steve Flesch	66/1	Chris Howell
	33/1	Bill Glasson	80/1*	Jonathan Kaye
	33/1*	Lee Janzen	80/1	Kevin Sutherland
	33/1	Franklin Langham	80/1*	Duffy Waldorf
	33/1	Bob May	80/1**	Rocco Mediate
	40/1	Steve Lowery	80/1*	J P Hayes
	40/1	Jeff Sluman	80/1*	Frank Lickliter
	40/1	Scott Hoch	80/1	Craig Stadler
	50/1	Michael Clark	80/1*	Paul Stankowski
	50/1	Fred Funk	80/1	Olin Browne
	50/1	Dennis Paulson	80/1	Mark Brooks
	50/1	Joe Ogilvie	80/1	Russ Cochran
	66/1	Chris DiMarco	80/1*	Jerry Kelly
	66/1	Scott Verplank	80/1	Bob Estes
	66/1*	Tim Herron		

2000 RESULT

1	66/1	**Scott Verplank**	**69 68 71 67 275**	
		Verplank won at the fourth play-off hole		
2	100/1	**Jean Van de Velde**	**67 71 65 72 275**	
3	33/1	**Bob May**	**69 67 70 70 276**	
T4	125/1	**Scott McCarron**	**66 70 71 71 278**	
T4	150/1	**Doug Dunakey**	**74 68 64 72 278**	
T4	100/1	**Brian Henninger**	**71 63 71 73 278**	

T7	F Langham	75 68 71 66 279		B Glasson	71 73 75 68 287
	S Flesch	67 68 73 71 279		B Gay	71 71 76 69 287
	Tom Byrum	69 72 68 70 279		B Fabel	73 70 73 71 287
	D Waldorf	72 67 69 71 279		S Micheel	72 71 73 71 287
	D Toms	72 65 69 73 279		D Forsman	72 68 75 72 287
T12	Joe Ozaki	71 69 74 67 281		J Gove	70 71 73 73 287
	S Hoch	76 67 71 67 281		R Black	72 69 73 73 287
	A Magee	70 68 74 69 281		Jerry Smith	69 69 75 74 287
	T Herron	68 71 71 71 281	T51	P Goydos	71 71 78 68 288
	K-J Choi	70 68 69 74 281		J Ogilvie	69 70 76 73 288
T17	L Janzen	74 69 72 67 282		T Tryba	70 68 75 75 288
	S Garcia	72 67 75 68 282		Y Mizumaki	75 68 70 75 288
	J Kelly	71 72 70 69 282		B Schwarzrock	72 71 70 75 288
	R Beem	70 72 68 72 282		H Frazar	71 69 70 78 288
T21	D Peoples	71 72 71 69 283		M Goggin	69 67 72 80 288
	C DiMarco	71 71 72 69 283	T58	B Estes	73 72 74 70 289
	J Sluman	71 72 71 69 283		Bobby Cochran	73 69 75 72 289
	M Calcavecchia	70 70 73 70 283		J D Blake	72 73 72 72 289
	F Funk	72 70 71 70 283		C Howell	74 71 69 75 289
	J P Hayes	72 72 67 72 283	T62	M Brisky	72 73 74 71 290
T27	C Parry	73 72 72 67 284		Joel Edwards	71 71 75 73 290
	R Mediate	68 70 77 69 284		C Riley	73 70 71 76 290
	B Mayfair	70 71 74 69 284	T65	S Lowery	72 71 76 72 291
	G Waite	71 72 72 69 284		J L Lewis	70 73 73 75 291
	T Armour III	73 70 72 69 284	T67	M Wiebe	73 70 75 74 292
	David Sutherland	72 69 73 70 284		B Burns	69 72 74 77 292
T33	Chris Perry	73 67 75 70 285	T69	T Dodds	72 72 75 74 293
	J McGovern	69 72 72 72 285		P Jordan	71 74 74 74 293
	C Perks	78 67 68 72 285	71	Larry Rinker	73 69 80 72 294
T36	Carl Paulson	73 69 75 69 286	T72	E Aubrey	67 76 80 72 295
	R Howison	77 66 71 72 286		W Austin	68 73 76 78 295
	C Barlow	76 69 69 72 286	74	Robin Freeman	70 75 77 74 296
	M Sposa	68 75 70 73 286	T75	N Henke	69 76 75 78 298
	P Jacobsen	66 69 76 75 286		C Bowden	71 73 75 79 298
	J Rollins	68 71 73 74 286	77	J Durant	73 70 73 83 299
T42	S Gotsche	73 70 76 68 287			

The main players to miss the cut (made at 1 over) were:–

B Tway (+2)	O Browne (+2)	J Cook (+2)	B Watts (+2)
O Uresti (+2)	D Stockton (+2)	F Nobilo (+2)	B Hughes (+2)
J Kaye (+2)	A Scott (+2)	M Gogel (+3)	T Tolles (+3)
P Moss (+3)	B Lietzke (+3)	T Scherrer (+3)	B Andrade (+3)
J Delsing (+3)	C Beckman (+3)	B Quigley (+4)	R Gamez (+4)
C Stadler (+4)	R Cochran (+4)	S Katayama (+4)	D Briggs (+4)
J Daly (+4)	E Toledo (+4)	K Wentworth (+4)	M Reid (+4)
B McCallister (+5)	B Cheesman (+5)	M Brooks (+5)	L Mize (+5)
K Gibson (+5)	B Bates (+5)	B Heintz (+5)	C Martin (+5)
F Zoeller (+6)	M Springer (+6)	M Clark (+6)	D Paulson (+6)
P Stankowski (+6)	M Hulbert (+6)	P Curry (+6)	B Jobe (+7)
G Nicklaus (+7)	D Morland (+7)	D Gossett (+7)	S Stricker (+7)
D Pride (+7)	B Elder (+7)	E Fryatt (+8)	D Edwards (+8)
P Blackmar (+8)	R Zokol (+8)	S Gump (+8)	P H Horgan (+8)
C Pavin (+9)	S Murphy (+9)	J Maginnes (+9)	K Hosokawa (+9)
J Haas (+10)	F Lickliter (+11)		

Tim Loustalot (81) and Charles Raulerson (77) withdrew.

ROUND BY ROUND LEADERBOARD

FIRST ROUND
S McCarron	6 under
P Jacobsen	6 under
S Flesch	5 under
J Van de Velde	5 under
E Aubrey	5 under
S VERPLANK	3 under

SECOND ROUND
B Henninger	10 under
P Jacobsen	9 under
S Flesch	9 under
S McCarron	8 under
M Goggin	8 under
B May	8 under
S VERPLANK	7 under

THIRD ROUND
J Van de Velde	13 under
B Henninger	11 under
D Toms	10 under
B May	10 under
D Dunakey	10 under
S McCarron	9 under
K-J Choi	9 under
S VERPLANK	8 under

FINAL ROUND
S VERPLANK	13 under
J Van de Velde	13 under
B May	12 under
S McCarron	10 under
D Dunakey	10 under
B Henninger	10 under

Winds gusted between 15 - 25 mph during R3.

PUNTERS' POINTS

● Jean Van de Velde had a 12-foot putt at the last for his first US tour victory. However he missed and Verplank won the play-off with a birdie at the fourth extra hole.

● 66/1 Scott Verplank's win was his first since 1988, so ending the fourth longest drought between wins in USPGA history.

● Jean Van de Velde proved here what a fine start he's made to his career in America, although he'll always be a dodgy player to support when in really serious contention. It was his second runner-up position this year and both have come in desert tournaments.

● Bob May showed clearly here that his confidence was much higher than his tiredness after his massive effort in last week's USPGA.

1999 RESULT (inaugural year)

1	150/1	Notah Begay
T2	fav 12/1	Chris Perry
T2	40/1*	David Toms
T4	50/1*	Fred Funk
T4	50/1	John Cook
T4	50/1	Brandt Jobe

PUNTERS' GUIDE

● Three players have posted high finishes in this event in both years.

	2000	1999
> David Toms	T7	T2
> Fred Funk	T21	T4
> Duffy Waldorf	T7	T24 (last 7 rounds at or under par)
> Chris Perry	T33	T2

● In the tournament's two years there have been nine rounds of 65 or less. Eight of those players then shot a round at least 7 shots worse and collectively their next round averaged an over par 73.77. Streakers don't keep it up, a point to remember here in 2- and 3-ball betting.

● Is course experience here vital?

Yes, Scott Verplank played here last year (T50th)

No, Jean Van de Velde was making his Reno-Tahoe debut.

● However the key is probably proven success in desert tournaments.

> Jean Van de Velde was T2nd at the Tucson Open this year.

> Scott Verplank has a fine recent Phoenix Open record.

● Players whose profiles refer to this tournament include Steve Flesch, David Toms, Tom Byrum, Duffy Waldorf, Franklin Langham, Scott McCarron, Fred Funk, Tom Scherrer and J P Hayes.

AIR CANADA CHAMPIONSHIP

Date	31st August - 3rd September
Course	Northview G. & C.C., Surrey, British Columbia
Par	71
Yardage	6,893
First Prize	$504,000
Total Purse	$2.8 million

THE TOURNAMENT

Formerly the Greater Vancouver Open, this tournament was retitled in 1999. It was being played for the fifth consecutive year on the Northview course. This is the first leg of the two-week 'Canadian Swing'.

THE COURSE

The Northview course had been changed this year in three key ways – slightly narrower fairways, slightly smaller (bentgrass) greens and increased rough.

2000 ODDS

fav	14/1	Sergio Garcia	50/1	Michael Clark
	20/1	Jesper Parnevik	66/1	Stephen Ames
	20/1	Mike Weir	66/1	Brian Henninger
	20/1	Robert Allenby	80/1*	Retief Goosen
	22/1	Mark Calcavecchia	80/1	Glen Hnatiuk
	28/1	Greg Chalmers	80/1	Joe Ozaki
	33/1	Scott Hoch	80/1	Adam Scott
	33/1*	Fred Funk	80/1	Jonathan Kaye
	40/1	Bill Glasson	80/1	Brent Geiberger
	40/1	Tim Herron	80/1	Craig Parry
	50/1	Scott Dunlap	80/1*	Olin Browne
	50/1	Skip Kendall	80/1	Craig Stadler
	50/1*	Steve Lowery	80/1	Chris Riley
	50/1	Scott McCarron		

2000 RESULT

1	100/1	Rory Sabbatini	68 68 67 65 268
2	100/1	Grant Waite	65 67 68 69 269
3	22/1	Mark Calcavecchia	68 70 65 67 270
T4	125/1	Doug Barron	65 69 70 67 271
T4	50/1	Michael Clark	68 70 70 63 271
T4	fav 14/1	Sergio Garcia	68 67 69 67 271
T4	80/1	Chris Riley	71 64 68 68 271

T8	K-J Choi	68 68 68 68 272		R Fehr	72 69 73 66 280
	B Geiberger	71 65 69 67 272		P Jordan	70 70 70 70 280
	D Stockton	65 72 67 68 272		F Nobilo	70 68 68 74 280
T11	B Burns	67 69 70 67 273		T Tolles	66 72 68 74 280
	J L Lewis	67 66 68 72 273	T52	E Aubrey	71 70 67 73 281
T13	T Armour III	68 65 68 73 274		G Boros	70 71 74 66 281
	J Durant	71 65 66 72 274		M Brooks	67 71 69 74 281
	Joel Edwards	66 71 70 67 274		D Dunakey	69 72 72 68 281
	M Goggin	67 70 68 69 274		S Gump	70 70 71 70 281
	R Goosen	69 66 68 71 274		B Henninger	75 66 67 73 281
	J Kelly	67 68 68 71 274		J Kaye	69 71 72 69 281
	S Lowery	70 63 71 70 274		B McCallister	71 70 72 68 281
	J McGovern	73 65 67 69 274		Y Mizumaki	70 69 68 74 281
	S Micheel	67 69 68 70 274		D Pride	68 68 70 75 281
T22	S Dunlap	71 68 71 65 275		David Sutherland	69 72 67 73 281
	G Kraft	72 68 67 68 275	T63	K Gibson	74 66 70 72 282
	J Parnevik	66 65 70 74 275		P Goydos	70 69 72 71 282
	H Tanaka	68 67 68 72 275		C Martin	70 71 69 72 282
	E Toledo	69 69 70 67 275		R McMillan	71 69 68 74 282
T27	R Allenby	74 65 72 65 276		C Perks	70 71 68 73 282
	J Green	67 72 68 69 276		Larry Rinker	66 70 76 70 282
	S Hoch	69 69 70 68 276	T69	E Booker	72 66 74 71 283
	S McCarron	69 66 73 68 276		Steve Hart	71 69 71 72 283
T31	R Beem	69 70 70 68 277		D Mast	70 70 68 75 283
	J Buha	65 72 73 67 277		G Nicklaus	73 65 71 74 283
	G Chalmers	72 69 68 68 277	T73	J Delsing	72 68 70 74 284
	G Hjertstedt	72 69 68 68 277		Jim Gallagher	74 67 71 72 284
	P Jacobsen	71 69 69 68 277		G Hallberg	72 68 67 77 284
	Joe Ozaki	66 70 72 69 277		N Henke	70 71 75 68 284
	C Parry	66 73 70 68 277		B Jobe	67 73 69 75 284
T38	T Barranger	68 68 73 69 278		A Miller	72 67 72 73 284
	Bart Bryant	74 65 70 69 278		C Stadler	70 68 72 74 284
	J Gobe	73 68 70 67 278	T80	G Hnatiuk	72 69 73 71 285
	T Herron	70 69 64 75 278		Jerry Smith	67 73 69 76 285
	D Peoples	71 70 72 65 278	T82	J Coston	71 70 71 74 286
	M Weir	67 69 69 73 278		S Murphy	74 66 73 73 286
T44	Carl Paulson	70 69 69 71 279		J Ogilvie	69 72 72 73 286
	A Scott	73 67 68 71 279	T85	J Caron	72 69 74 72 287
T46	S Alker	71 67 73 69 280		W Wood	71 69 70 77 287
	O Browne	70 70 69 71 280	87	B Elder	70 70 77 71 288

The main players to miss the cut (made at 1 under) were:-

M Standly (E)	O Ulresti (E)	T Tryba (E)	M Reid (E)
C Barlow (+1)	B Cheesman (+1)	M Gogel (+1)	P Blackmar (+1)
C Beckman (+1)	P Curry (+1)	D Gossett (+1)	C Howell (+1)
C A Spence (+1)	L Mattiace (+1)	R Gamez (+1)	R Zokol (+1)
A Bean (+2)	B Fabel (+2)	B Hughes (+2)	J Maginnes (+2)
F Funk (+2)	T Dodds (+2)	M Hulbert (+2)	T Byrum (+2)
S Ames (+3)	T Pernice Jr (+3)	H Kuehne (+3)	D Forsman (+3)
K Hosokawa (+3)	D Morland (+4)	S Lyle (+4)	B Quigley (+5)
C Raulerson (+5)	B Cochran (+5)	P H Horgan (+5)	K Wentworth (+6)
S Kendall (+7)	R Freeman (+7)	B Friend (+7)	D A Weibring (+9)
E Fryatt (+12)			

R Black (73) withdrew.

ROUND BY ROUND LEADERBOARD

FIRST ROUND

D Barron	6 under
D Stockton	6 under
J Buha	6 under
G Waite	6 under
6 players at	5 under
R SABBATINI	3 under

SECOND ROUND

J Parnevik	11 under
G Waite	10 under
T Armour III	9 under
J L Lewis	9 under
S Lowery	9 under
D Barron	8 under
R SABBATINI	6 under

THIRD ROUND

G Waite	13 under
J Parnevik	12 under
J L Lewis	12 under
T Armour III	12 under
J Durant	11 under
R SABBATINI	10 under
6 others at	10 under

FINAL ROUND

R SABBATINI	16 under
G Waite	15 under
M Calcavecchia	14 under
D Barron	13 under
S Garcia	13 under
M Clark	13 under
C Riley	13 under

PUNTERS' POINTS

● Rory Sabbatini, having missed three of his previous five cuts and with poor course form (MC by 3 last year), gave bookies a superb 100/1 triumph.

● The 24-year-old made a 30-foot birdie putt on the last to beat Grant Waite narrowly and gain his first tour win. Starting the day 3 shots back, Sabbatini was a 33/1 chance on Sunday morning.

● Re tee times: Grant Waite made a fast beginning (65) off an early R1 start, while Sabbatini played 'catch up' from an afternoon tee time.

● There were disappointing final rounds by players in contention:-

> Tim Herron   T6 after R3 then shot 75 to finish T38

> Jesper Parnevik   T2 after R3 and 5/2 fav then shot 74 to finish T22

> J L Lewis   T2 after R3 then shot 72 to finish T11

> Tommy Armour III   T2 after R3 then shot 73 to finish T13
> Joe Durant   T5 after R3 then shot 72 to finish T13
> Retief Goosen   T6 after R3 then shot a par 71 to finish T13
> Jerry Kelly   T6 after R3 then shot a par 71 to finish T13

● Make a note of a guy finishing T73rd on level par, Andy Miller, son of top USPGA player Johnny Miller. Dad says, "I think he feels he has a great future, which I know he does."

1999 RESULT

1	33/1	Mike Weir
2	25/1	Fred Funk
3	jt fav 16/1	Carlos Franco
T4	80/1*	Scott McCarron
T4	jt fav 16/1	Payne Stewart
T4	150/1	Phil Tataurangi

1998 RESULT

1	40/1	Brandel Chamblee
2	20/1	Payne Stewart
3	150/1	Lee Porter
4	125/1	Brian Claar
T5	100/1	Omar Uresti
T5	20/1	Jeff Maggert
T5	80/1	Mike Weir
T5	25/1	Bob Estes
T5	25/1	Russ Cochran

WINNERS IN THE '90s

1996	Guy Boros
1997	Mark Calcavecchia
1998	Brandel Chamblee
1999	Mike Weir
2000	Rory Sabbatini

PUNTERS' GUIDE

● After five years we can draw certain conclusions:-

> This is an excellent tournament for first-time winners with four of the five winners (Calcavecchia was the exception) gaining their maiden victory at Northview.

> Course form, although always an advantage as 1999 winner Mike Weir (T5th 1996: T5th 1998) showed, is not a necessary condition for a selection as Calcavecchia (1997), Chamblee (1998) and Sabbatini (this year) had no form or poor form on the track.

> Current form. Sabbatini and Boros had poor current form whereas the other three winners had each recorded at least one top 10 in their previous three starts.

● In 2001 the best guideline will probably be to go for:-

> A young player seeking his first win who had been in serious contention earlier in the season in a tournament when he had then posted a top 5 finish. That criteria would have highlighted the winners in each of the last three years.

> One who is a 275-yard plus driver, as overall it is clear that the longer hitters have an advantage here.

● Best course records over the five years belong to

> Mark Calcavecchia   Won 1997, T21st 1999, 3rd 2000 from three starts

> Mike Weir   T5th 1996, T5th 1998, Won 1999, T38th 2000. All five starts

> Russ Cochran   T5th 1996, 4th 1997, T5th 1998

> Greg Kraft   12-44-27-22 (2000) in last four years

> Dave Stockton   51-20-35-8 in last four years

> Bob Estes   3rd 1997, T5th 1998, T10th 1999, DNP 2000

● Players whose profiles refer to this tournament include Mike Weir, Dave Stockton Jr, Greg Kraft, Brent Geiberger, Scott McCarron, Greg Chalmers, Michael Clark, Bob Estes, Tom Byrum, Gabriel Hjerstedt, Ian Leggatt, Mathew Goggin and Steve Lowery.

THE BELL CANADIAN OPEN

Date	7th - 10th September
Course	Glen Abbey G.C., Oakville, Ontario
Par	72
Yardage	7,112
First Prize	$558,000
Total Purse	$3.1 million

THE TOURNAMENT

This is the fourth oldest tournament on the tour. It has been played at Glen Abbey every year since 1977 (with the exception of 1980 and 1997).

THE COURSE

This is a Jack Nicklaus course (the first he designed) which tends to favour faders (left to right) of the ball. It is a tough course, especially when the wind blows, with small, bentgrass greens that place a premium on accuracy.

2000 ODDS

fav	5/4	Tiger Woods – 4/5 in a place	66/1	Lee Janzen (28/1)
	16/1	Hal Sutton (9/1)	66/1	Franklin Langham (33/1)
	20/1	Sergio Garcia (12/1)	66/1	Scott Verplank (40/1)
	28/1	Jesper Parnevik (16/1)	66/1	Greg Chalmers (40/1)
	28/1	Davis Love (16/1)	66/1	Scott Dunlap (33/1)
	33/1	Mark Calcavecchia (20/1)	66/1	Brad Faxon (50/1)
	40/1*	Justin Leonard (16/1)	66/1	Steve Jones (40/1)
	40/1	Paul Azinger (20/1)	80/1	Shigeki Maruyama (50/1)
	50/1	Mike Weir (28/1)	80/1	Mark O'Meara (40/1)
	50/1	Steve Flesch (28/1)	80/1	Jeff Sluman (50/1)
	66/1	Michael Clark (33/1)	80/1	Glen Day (50/1)

Please note: the odds in brackets were in the 'without Tiger' market.

2000 RESULT

1	fav 5/4	Tiger Woods	72 65 64 65 266
2	100/1	Grant Waite	69 64 68 66 267
3	20/1	Sergio Garcia	67 69 70 67 273
T4	66/1	Greg Chalmers	69 65 71 69 274
T4	150/1	Craig Perks	72 69 67 66 274

T6	S Flesch	71 68 68 69 276			R Gamez	70 73 70 69 282
	F Langham	73 67 68 68 276			S McCarron	71 72 70 69 282
	R Sabbatini	70 71 67 68 276		T42	S Dunlap	73 70 71 69 283
	S Verplank	72 67 68 69 276			D Gillespie	72 72 68 71 283
T10	P Azinger	73 65 68 71 277			C Howell	69 74 68 72 283
	K Fukabori	70 66 70 71 277			D Love	68 69 71 75 283
	B Jobe	70 68 68 71 277			C Pavin	73 65 74 71 283
	J L Lewis	67 70 65 75 277			J Sluman	71 72 69 71 283
	J McGovern	76 67 66 68 277		T48	J Buha	71 73 68 72 284
	S Micheel	69 67 72 69 277			M Calcavecchia	70 69 77 68 284
	C Stadler	71 70 69 67 277			J Delsing	72 72 67 73 284
	P Stankowski	72 67 67 71 277			L Janzen	71 70 71 72 284
	Kevin Sutherland	65 72 70 70 277			S Lyle	71 72 70 71 284
	H Sutton	72 72 65 68 277			M Standly	73 70 70 71 284
T20	C Barlow	69 68 73 68 278		T54	D Barron	70 72 71 72 285
	C Beckman	66 73 67 72 278			A Bengoechea	71 73 69 72 285
	O Browne	72 68 70 68 278			B Burns	76 68 68 73 285
	B Cheesman	74 65 68 71 278			S Maruyama	73 70 73 69 285
	S Gotsche	74 69 64 71 278		T58	B Claar	69 74 71 72 286
	L Mattiace	69 73 69 67 278			J Rollins	71 71 73 71 286
T26	T Dodds	69 70 69 71 279		T60	K-J Choi	75 68 70 74 287
	M Goggin	74 67 66 72 279			G Day	73 69 77 68 287
	J Leonard	68 73 68 70 279			G Nicklaus	74 70 74 69 287
	F Nobilo	73 70 69 67 279			C Raulerson	72 72 70 73 287
	J Parnevik	67 74 69 69 279			J Restino	70 72 71 74 287
	B Watts	67 68 71 73 279		T65	E Aubrey	74 70 69 75 288
T32	S Ames	68 71 63 78 280			P Curry	72 71 71 74 288
	M Bradley	71 69 70 70 280			B Fabel	72 72 73 71 288
	T Tolles	71 72 67 70 280			M Springer	72 72 70 74 288
T35	D Dunakey	70 71 73 67 281		69	C A Spence	72 72 74 71 289
	T Scherrer	74 67 66 74 281		70	M Weir	74 69 73 74 290
	J Sindelar	72 68 66 75 281		71	R Howison	72 72 73 74 291
T38	E Booker	72 70 71 69 282		72	J Green	74 69 74 76 293
	D Briggs	74 68 69 71 282		73	B Elder	70 71 82 72 295

The main players to miss the cut (made at level) were:-

T Armour III (+1)	M Brisky (+1)	B Bryant (+1)	K Gibson (+1)
D Paulson (+1)	G Sauers (+1)	B Tway (+1)	J Williamson (+1)
B Bates (+1)	D Morland (+1)	F Allem (+2)	C DiMarco (+2)
G Hjertstedt (+2)	S Jones (+2)	F Lickliter (+2)	A Magee (+2)
B Mayfair (+2)	S Murphy (+2)	M O'Meara (+2)	T Pernice Jr (+2)
C Riley (+2)	M Sposa (+2)	B Schwarzrock (+2)	G Hnatiuk (+2)
K Wentworth (+2)	B Faxon (+3)	B Friend (+3)	B Quigley (+3)
L Rinker (+3)	M Wiebe (+3)	R Zokol (+3)	H Frazar (+3)
R Beem (+3)	J Gove (+3)	T Purtzer (+4)	S Stricker (+4)
J Ogilvie (+4)	D Barr (+5)	J D Blake (+5)	D Stockton (+5)
A Scott (+5)	P H Horgan (+6)	M Hulbert (+6)	D Pride (+6)
D Sutherland (+6)	O Uresti (+6)	B Gay (+6)	K Hosokawa (+6)
D Gossett (am) (+6)	M Clark (+6)	B Gilder (+7)	B Andrade (+8)
B Cochran (+8)	W Levi (+13)		

Craig Bowden (76), Bradley Hughes (78) and Steve Hart (78) all withdrew.

ROUND BY ROUND LEADERBOARD

FIRST ROUND		SECOND ROUND	
K Sutherland	7 under	G Waite	11 under
C Beckman	6 under	G Chalmers	10 under
J L Lewis	5 under	B Watts	9 under
B Watts	5 under	S Garcia	8 under
S Garcia	5 under	S Micheel	8 under
J Parnevik	5 under	K Fukabori	8 under
T WOODS	level!	T WOODS	7 under

THIRD ROUND		FINAL ROUND	
T WOODS	15 under	T WOODS	22 under
G Waite	15 under	G Waite	21 under
S Ames	14 under	S Garcia	15 under
J L Lewis	14 under	G Chalmers	14 under
G Chalmers	11 under	C Perks	14 under

RESULTS IN OTHER MARKETS (without Woods)

1	66/1	Grant Waite
2	12/1	Sergio Garcia
T3	40/1	Greg Chalmers
T3	100/1	Craig Perks
T5	28/1	Steve Flesch
T5	33/1	Franklin Langham
T5	50/1	Rory Sabbatini
T5	40/1	Scott Verplank

PUNTERS' POINTS

- "I've had a wonderful summer." Too right he has, with five wins in seven tournaments, including three major championships to complete a career grand slam.

- It was the nineteenth time in twenty USPGA tour events that Tiger has won when he either held or had a share of the 54-hole lead!

- However here Grant Waite matched the Tiger shot for shot in a thrilling final round. Ahead by a shot on the last, Woods hit a brilliant 218-yard 6 iron out of bunker, over the water, at the flag to land 18 feet from the pin. Waite's putt narrowly missed, so Tiger had won again

- Grant Waite ("I gave him a run for his money") will certainly take confidence from his Tiger chase, and he was the only player to post four rounds in the 60s. By no means a course specialist, Waite certainly knew Glen Abbey where his recent form figures were 34-42-67.

- R4 nerves were shown on Sunday by
  > Stephen Ames   T3rd after R3, he shot 78 to finish T32nd!
  > J L Lewis   T3rd after R3, he shot 75 to finish T10th

> Brian Watts   T6th after R3, he shot 73 to finish T26th
> Joey Sindelar   T6th after R3, he shot 75 to finish T35th.

1999 RESULT			**1998 RESULT**		
1	fav 14/1	Hal Sutton	1	66/1	Billy Andrade
2	80/1*	Dennis Paulson	*won at the first play-off hole*		
T3	66/1	Dudley Hart	2	150/1	Bob Friend
T3	40/1*	Lee Janzen	3	150/1	Mike Hulbert
T3	16/1	Justin Leonard	T4	40/1	Hal Sutton
T3	125/1	David Sutherland	T4	125/1	Bradley Hughes
			T4	50/1	Glen Day

WINNERS IN THE LAST TEN YEARS

1991	Nick Price	1996	Dudley Hart (54 holes)
1992	Greg Norman	1997	Steve Jones
1993	David Frost	1998	Billy Andrade
1994	Nick Price	1999	Hal Sutton
1995	Mark O'Meara	2000	Tiger Woods

PUNTERS' GUIDE

● Best recent records in this tournament are held by

> Hal Sutton   T10 (2000) Won (1999) T4 (1998) T11 (1997)
> Justin Leonard   T26 (2000) T3 (1999) DNP (1998) T6 (1997)
> Greg Chalmers   T4 (2000) T15 (1999) in just two starts
> Kevin Sutherland   T10 (2000) T29 (1999) T36 (1998) T23 (1997)
> Scott Verplank   T6 (2000) MC (1999) T9 (1998)
> Scott Dunlap   T42 (2000) 7 (1999) T13 (1997) T3 (1996)

● Players whose profiles refer to this tournament include Hal Sutton, Mike Weir, Greg Chalmers, Scott Dunlap, Kevin Sutherland, Dudley Hart, Scott Verplank, Steve Flesch, Michael Bradley, Brandt Jobe and Shaun Micheel.

THE SEI PENNSYLVANIA CLASSIC

Date	14th - 17th September
Course	Waynesborough C.C., Paoli, Pennsylvania
Par	71
First Prize	$540,000
Total Purse	$3 million

THE TOURNAMENT

This is the latest tournament to be added to the USPGA tour being played for the very first time at Paoli. It will alternate between this course and the Laurel Valley Golf Club in future years. Pennsylvania is in the north east, sandwiched between New York State and West Virginia.

THE COURSE

The Waynesborough course is a par 71 (35:36) with a 539-yard par 5 closing hole. The signature holes are the par 4 9th (heavily sloped green) and 11th (small green). The fairways are fairly generous with difficult undulating bentgrass greens. It is important to stress that the wind can blow significantly in the afternoon. The course was highly praised this year.

2000 ODDS

fav	14/1	Jim Furyk	50/1	Scott Dunlap
	16/1	Tom Lehman	50/1	Dudley Hart
	25/1	Loren Roberts	50/1	Jeff Sluman
	25/1	Steve Flesch	50/1	Fred Funk
	25/1	Bob May	66/1	Glen Day
	28/1	Mark Calcavecchia	66/1	Steve Pate
	28/1	Chris Perry	66/1	Kevin Sutherland
	33/1	Grant Waite	66/1	Duffy Waldorf
	33/1	Scott Verplank	66/1*	Jerry Kelly
	33/1	Carlos Franco	66/1	Joe Durant
	40/1	Lee Janzen	66/1*	Jeff Maggert
	40/1	Scott Hoch	80/1	Scott McCarron
	40/1	Kirk Triplett	80/1	Shaun Micheel
	50/1	Bill Glasson	80/1*	Chris Riley
	50/1	Shigeki Maruyama	80/1	J P Hayes

2000 RESULT

1	100/1*	Chris DiMarco	68 67 66 69 270
T2	28/1	Mark Calcavecchia	68 66 70 72 276
T2	125/1	Brad Elder	69 69 68 70 276
T2	40/1	Scott Hoch	69 69 73 65 276
T2	125/1*	Jonathan Kaye	68 69 68 71 276
T2	28/1	Chris Perry	72 68 66 70 276

7	S Lyle	69 69 72 67 277			M Sposa	68 70 75 72 285
T8	J Maggert	69 69 72 68 278			W Wood	71 72 73 69 285
	L Roberts	67 71 66 74 278		T46	Dudley Hart	68 70 75 73 286
	S Verplank	72 68 70 68 278			T Tryba	70 70 74 72 286
11	J Carter	72 64 74 69 279		T48	E Booker	70 73 72 72 287
T12	C Franco	68 75 70 67 280			S Maruyama	73 70 74 70 287
	M Goggin	71 65 73 71 280			S Murphy	71 68 74 74 287
	F Lickliter	67 67 70 76 280			C Pavin	73 70 71 73 287
	C Perks	71 71 69 69 280			Jerry Smith	72 71 72 72 287
	T Purtzer	68 70 70 72 280			E Toledo	71 71 73 72 287
	J Rollins	71 71 66 72 280		T54	D Briggs	65 72 76 75 288
T18	E Aubrey	65 71 71 74 281			B Claar	71 69 74 74 288
	K-J Choi	70 69 73 69 281			J Gove	73 68 76 71 288
	L Mattiace	69 72 69 71 281			P Goydos	74 69 70 75 288
	D Morland	69 71 68 73 281			B Hughes	69 71 72 76 288
	J Sluman	70 69 71 71 281			J McGovern	71 72 74 71 288
	B Watts	70 73 69 69 281			C Riley	70 72 74 72 288
T24	C Barlow	75 67 68 72 282		T61	S Flesch	70 68 73 78 289
	D Barron	70 71 69 72 282			M Hulbert	70 72 73 74 289
	Carl Paulson	75 68 69 70 282			G Nicklaus	69 73 74 73 289
	M Springer	73 69 69 71 282			F Nobilo	72 70 72 75 289
T28	C Beckman	71 71 73 68 283		65	B Quigley	69 71 79 71 290
	O Browne	72 67 73 71 283		T66	R Burns	74 69 78 70 291
	T Lehman	73 67 73 70 283			R Howison	76 67 76 72 291
	T Scherrer	72 67 74 70 283			R Zokol	71 70 72 78 291
	Kevin Sutherland	76 65 73 69 283		T69	T Dodds	73 67 75 77 292
T33	M Bradley	71 70 71 72 284			D Dunakey	68 71 78 75 292
	Tom Byrum	71 69 72 72 284			Robin Freeman	74 68 68 82 292
	B Gilder	70 71 75 68 284			K Wentworth	73 70 74 75 292
	B Henninger	71 69 76 68 284		T73	S Gump	70 73 76 74 293
	R Mediate	72 67 73 72 284			B Heintz	74 69 75 75 293
	M Standly	71 72 68 73 284			D Pride	74 68 74 77 293
	G Waite	69 70 74 71 284			C A Spence	73 69 73 78 293
	D Waldorf	71 71 73 69 284		77	J Caron	70 73 78 74 295
T41	S Kendall	73 68 75 69 285		T78	N Lancaster	69 73 71 83 296
	J Maginnes	74 69 73 69 285			J Sindelar	73 69 77 77 296
	S Pate	69 66 73 77 285		80	K Kemp	75 68 79 77 299

The main players to miss the cut (made at 1 over) were:-

W Austin (+2)	C Bowden (+2)	R Cochran (+2)	J Daly (+2)
G Day (+2)	R Fehr (+2)	D Frost (+2)	J Furyk (+2)
R Gamez (+2)	K Gibson (+2)	P H Horgan (+2)	B May (+2)
S McCarron (+2)	J Williamson (+2)	C Martin (+2)	B Cochran (+2)
T Hatch (+2)	F Allem (+3)	M Brisky (+3)	M Brooks (+3)
B Chamblee (+3)	J Delsing (+3)	T Pernice Jr (+3)	M Reid (+3)
O Uresti (+3)	B Gay (+3)	M Gogel (+3)	P Curry (+3)
B Gage (+3)	J Durant (+4)	B Fabel (+4)	S Gotsche (+4)
S Hart (+4)	G Hjertstedt (+4)	L Janzen (+4)	D Paulson (+4)
D Sutherland (+4)	K Triplett (+4)	D A Weibring (+4)	H Frazar (+4)
A Bengoechea (+4)	A Scott (+4)	T Armour III (+5)	R Damron (+5)
J Kelly (+5)	B Mayfair (+5)	E Fryatt (+5)	S Dunlap (+6)
B Friend (+6)	J P Hayes (+6)	C Raulerson (+6)	G Sauers (+6)
T Tolles (+6)	B Bates (+6)	J Sullivan (+6)	N Napoleon (+6)
B Cheesman (+8)	P Jordan (+8)	P Moss (+8)	R Osberg (+8)
D Mast (+9)	Larry Rinker (+9)	B Tway (+9)	J Buha (+9)
C Anderson (+9)	M Wiebe (+10)	B Jobe (+10)	J Restino (+11)
P Blackmar (+13)			

Jay Haas (76), Fred Funk (77), Shaun Micheel (80) and Nolan Henke (80) all withdrew.

ROUND BY ROUND LEADERBOARD

FIRST ROUND		SECOND ROUND	
E Aubrey	6 under	M Calcavecchia	8 under
D Briggs	6 under	F Lickliter	8 under
L Roberts	4 under	C DiMARCO	7 under
F Lickliter	4 under	S Pate	7 under
C DiMARCO	3 under	E Aubrey	6 under
8 others at	3 under	J Carter	6 under
		M Goggin	6 under

THIRD ROUND		FINAL ROUND	
C DiMARCO	12 under	C DiMARCO	14 under
M Calcavecchia	9 under	M Calcavecchia	8 under
F Lickliter	9 under	B Elder	8 under
L Roberts	9 under	S Hoch	8 under
J Kaye	8 under	J Kaye	8 under
C Perry	7 under	C Perry	8 under
B Elder	7 under		

PUNTERS' POINTS

● 100/1 DYM Chris ("It's been such a long journey") DiMarco became the NINTH first-time winner on the USPGA tour this year with the biggest winning margin of them all.

● In 1998 (72.24 ranked T149th) and in 1999 (71.95 ranked T92nd) his final round scoring was poor, and he was awarded the bottle in last year's book. However this year, up to this tournament, he was 26th in R4 scoring averaging 70.12!

● However one reliable R4 'bottler' Frank Lickliter shot a 76 to continue his record of poor Sunday play. He's outside the top 150 for R4 scoring!!

- Two young players yet to win were impressive here:-
  - > T2nd Brad Elder in his rookie year
  - > T2nd Jonathan Kaye who was in contention for the third time this year.
- After two mega weeks, and going head to head with the Tiger so well last Sunday, the inevitable MLD hit Grant Waite (T33rd) here with a 3 over par final 36 holes.

PAST RESULTS AND RECENT WINNERS

This was the inaugural year for the Pennsylvania Classic.

PUNTERS' GUIDE

- In 2001 the tournament moves to the par 72 7,045-yard Laurel Valley Golf Club, so this year's course form will not be directly relevant until the Waynesborough course is again used in 2002.
- This was the second tournament this year to be played for the first time on a new course.

  The results provide interesting reading:-
  - > The John Deere Classic   Won by a 200/1** first-time winner, Michael Clark
  - > The Pennsylvania Classic Won by a 100/1* first-time winner, Chris DiMarco

  Last year, of course, we had the inaugural Reno-Tahoe Open won by a first-time winner, 150/1 Notah Begay.

  So it seems reasonable to conclude that tournaments on new courses (where the seasoned players don't enjoy the usual advantage of experience) give a real chance to players looking for a first-time win – and they're often DYMs.
- So at Laurel Valley in 2001 focus mainly on players looking for their maiden victory.
- Jim Furyk (MC) and Rocco Mediate (T33) were born in Pennsylvania and would dearly love to win this event.
- Players whose profiles refer to this tournament include Jonathan Kaye, Brad Elder, Mathew Goggin, Doug Barron, Craig Perks, Scott Verplank, Jeff Sluman and Rocco Mediate.

THE WESTIN TEXAS OPEN

Date	21st - 24th September
Course	LaCantera G.C., San Antonio
Par	70 (72 in the past)
Yardage	7,001
First Prize	$468,000
Total Purse	$2.6 million

THE TOURNAMENT

Started in 1922, this well-established tournament moved to its present venue in 1995 so this was the sixth successive year it had been played at the LaCantera course which was built on an old quarry.

THE COURSE

This year the course had been toughened with narrower fairways and the par reduced from 72 to 70 because the par 5 5th and 14th had been made into par 4s. This week the players face bermuda grass on the large greens.

2001 ODDS

fav	9/1	Hal Sutton	66/1*	Jonathan Kaye
	14/1	Loren Roberts	66/1*	Scott Dunlap
	16/1	Justin Leonard	66/1	Steve Elkington
	25/1	Carlos Franco	80/1*	Jay Haas
	25/1	Stewart Cink	80/1	Jim Carter
	33/1	David Toms	80/1	Mathew Goggin
	33/1	Bob May	80/1	Jerry Kelly
	40/1	Tim Herron	80/1*	Charles Howell
	40/1	Kirk Triplett	80/1	Brad Elder
	40/1	Bill Glasson	80/1	Andrew Magee
	50/1	Brent Geiberger	80/1	Tom Scherrer
	50/1	Steve Lowery	80/1	Ted Tryba
	50/1	Dudley Hart	80/1	Brian Watts
	50/1*	Duffy Waldorf (DC)	80/1	Scott McCarron
	50/1	J L Lewis	80/1	Frank Lickliter
	50/1	Brian Henninger	80/1	Len Mattiace

2000 RESULT

1	16/1	Justin Leonard	64 68 65 64 261
2	150/1	Mark Wiebe	64 70 65 67 266
T3	100/1	Blaine McCallister	65 68 67 69 269
T3	200/1*	Jim Gallagher	67 70 64 68 269
5	80/1	Frank Lickliter	68 65 70 67 270

T6	L Mattiace	65 67 73 66 271		S Utley	72 68 72 65 277
	E Toledo	68 67 69 67 271		J Williamson	68 71 66 72 277
	D Waldorf	69 67 69 66 271	T44	C Franco	69 70 69 70 278
T9	B Bates	67 70 67 68 272		S Lowery	69 71 70 68 278
	D Forsman	69 66 68 69 272		S Micheel	66 68 72 72 278
	C Pavin	66 72 66 68 272		R Thompson	70 69 66 73 278
	L Roberts	64 67 72 69 272	T48	D Dunakey	68 68 70 73 279
	B Watts	65 69 71 67 272		J Durant	71 69 72 67 279
T14	C Beckman	67 69 67 70 273		B Gilder	68 71 71 69 279
	B Claar	68 67 70 68 273		B Glasson	69 69 71 70 279
	C Howell	72 68 68 65 273		M Sposa	64 71 72 72 279
	J Kelly	66 67 70 70 273	T53	Bart Bryant	68 68 73 71 280
	B May	70 67 71 65 273		J Carter	71 69 72 68 280
T19	S Cink	66 71 69 68 274		D Pohl	67 71 68 74 280
	S Dunlap	72 67 70 65 274	T56	K Gibson	69 68 73 71 281
	Joel Edwards	69 68 68 69 274		D Ogrin	74 66 70 71 281
	R Fehr	67 70 71 66 274		J Rollins	66 69 70 76 281
	H Frazar	70 70 70 64 274		M Standly	69 64 75 73 281
	P Goydos	66 67 76 65 274		D A Weibring	69 68 73 71 281
	P Jordan	71 68 66 69 274	T61	A Bean	70 70 73 69 282
	J L Lewis	69 70 70 65 274		E Fiori	70 70 70 72 282
	S Murphy	67 70 71 66 274		S Gump	69 70 72 71 282
	B Quigley	70 68 67 69 274		G Kraft	71 69 73 69 282
	D Toms	69 68 71 66 274		S McCarron	67 70 75 70 282
T30	Dudley Hart	68 70 69 68 275		Y Mizumaki	71 67 74 70 282
	T Herron	68 67 68 72 275		C Rose	67 71 72 72 282
	J Kaye	70 67 70 68 275	T68	B Chamblee	71 66 73 73 283
T33	C Barlow	65 73 70 68 276		S Elkington	73 66 71 73 283
	R Beem	70 68 68 70 276		P H Horgan	71 69 71 72 283
	Steve Hart	70 67 73 66 276		S Lyle	72 67 76 68 283
	D Pride	67 71 70 68 276	T72	P Blackmar	67 72 74 71 284
	M Reid	67 69 68 72 276		J Buha	68 70 72 74 284
	Jerry Smith	73 64 71 68 276		K Clearwater	73 67 74 70 284
	T Tryba	72 65 67 72 276		M Heinen	66 73 75 70 284
T40	W Austin	67 71 73 66 277	T76	J Daly	69 70 73 74 286
	D Barr	69 68 69 71 277		D Morland	69 69 81 67 286

The main players to miss the cut (made at level) were:-

B Andrade (+1)	T Armour III (+1)	M Carnevale (+1)	R Cochran (+1)
B Estes (+1)	L Mize (+1)	K Triplett (+1)	R Zokol (+1)
B Jobe (+1)	C Perks (+1)	P Curry (+1)	B Cheesman (+2)
R Gamez (+2)	M Hulbert (+2)	L Rinker (+2)	M Sullivan (+2)
H Sutton (+2)	D Briggs (+3)	T Byrum (+3)	D Frost (+3)
B Geiberger (+3)	D Pooley (+3)	B Gay (+3)	D Gossett (am) (+3)
A Baddeley (am) (+3)	M Brisky (+4)	R Freeman (+4)	B Friend (+4)
S Gotsche (+4)	J Haas (+4)	D Hammond (+4)	B Henninger (+4)
R Howison (+4)	J Maginnes (+4)	J McGovern (+4)	J Ogilvie (+4)
C Byrum (+5)	J Delsing (+5)	N Henke (+5)	P Moss (+5)
M Goggin (+5)	J Gove (+5)	J Adams (+6)	R Black (+6)
G Boros (+6)	B Bryant (+6)	B Fabel (+6)	F Nobilo (+6)
T Purtzer (+6)	M Kuchar (am) (+6)	B Elder (+6)	M Brooks (+7)
W Wood (+7)	B Hughes (+8)	B Crenshaw (+9)	M Donald (+9)
E Booker (+10)	G Hallberg (+10)		

ROUND BY ROUND LEADERBOARD

FIRST ROUND		SECOND ROUND	
J LEONARD	6 under	L Roberts	9 under
L Roberts	6 under	J LEONARD	8 under
M Sposa	6 under	L Mattiace	8 under
M Wiebe	6 under	P Goydos	7 under
		J Kelly	7 under
		F Lickliter	7 under
		M Standly	7 under
		B McCallister	7 under

THIRD ROUND		FINAL ROUND	
J LEONARD	13 under	J LEONARD	19 under
M Wiebe	11 under	M Wiebe	14 under
B McCallister	10 under	B McCallister	11 under
J Gallagher	9 under	J Gallagher	11 under
		F Lickliter	10 under

PUNTERS' POINTS

● 16/1 Justin Leonard won for the first time since the 1998 Players Championship, and it was especially sweet for him as a proud, native-born Texan.

He proved conclusively that he's a fine front runner and an excellent R4 player (a brilliant 64 on Sunday) when in contention.

● T3rd Jim Gallagher Jr, a seventeen-year tour veteran, lost his tour card last year and has played in only eleven tournaments (T30th best finish) this season.

● Defending champion Duffy Waldorf proved once more that he loves this course. His form here in his six starts includes two wins, a 4th and T6th this year.

● The average score of the ten players in serious contention was 68.5 in R4 yet Tim Herron (72), Cameron Beckman (70) and Jerry Kelly (70) all played disappointingly on Sunday.

1999 RESULT

1	66/1*	Duffy Waldorf
won at the first play-off hole		
2	50/1	Ted Tryba
3	66/1*	Brent Geiberger
4	125/1	Rich Beem
T5	33/1*	Jay Haas
T5	125/1	Brian Henninger
T5	125/1	Mike Reid

1998 RESULT

1	33/1	Hal Sutton
T2	fav 16/1	Justin Leonard
T2	50/1	Jay Haas
T4	200/1	Mike Reid
T4	100/1	Steve Lowery
T4	28/1	Andrew Magee
T4	20/1	Loren Roberts

WINNERS IN THE LAST TEN YEARS

1991	Blaine McCallister	1996	David Ogrin
1992	Nick Price	1997	Tim Herron
1993	Jay Haas	1998	Hal Sutton
1994	Bob Estes	1999	Duffy Waldorf
1995	Duffy Waldorf	2000	Justin Leonard

Played at LaCantera G.C. since 1995.

PUNTERS' GUIDE

● In the last three years nineteen players have finished in the top 5 (or T5).

> nine (47.37%) started at or over 100/1

> twelve (63%) started at or over 66/1

So this is an outsiders' tournament.

● The LaCantera course has now been used for the last six years and the best records are held by

> Justin Leonard   2nd (1995), T11th (1996), T2nd (1998), Won (2000) in his four starts

> Duffy Waldorf   Won (1995 & 1999), 4th (1997), T6th (2000) in his six starts

> Loren Roberts   T3rd (1995), T14th (1997), T4th (1998), T9th (2000) in his five starts

> Corey Pavin   four top 12 finishes in the last five years

> Len Mattiace   T6th (2000), T29th (1999), T20th (1997), T4th (1996) in the last five years

> Mark Wiebe   2nd (2000), T12th (1999), T20th (1997), T9th (1995) in his five starts

> J L Lewis   T19th (2000), T12th (1999), T20th (1998), T18th (1996) in his last four starts

> David Toms   T19th (2000) T12th (1999), T20th (1997) in his last three starts

● It seems clear from the six-year history at LaCantera that this is very much a course-specialists' track that particularly suits the experienced, straight-hitting, but not necessarily long players.

● Players whose profiles refer to this tournament include Duffy Waldorf, David Toms, Mark Wiebe, Len Mattiace, Corey Pavin, Justin Leonard, J L Lewis, Stephen Ames and Dan Forsman.

THE BUICK CHALLENGE

Date	28th September - 1st October
Course	Callaway Gardens, Pine Mountain, Georgia
Par	72
Yardage	7,057
First Prize	$414,000
Total Purse	$2.3 million

THE TOURNAMENT

Started in 1970 it changed its venue from the Green Island course in Georgia to the Callaway Gardens course in the same state. It was renamed the Buick Challenge from 1995.

THE COURSE

This was the tenth successive year in which this course (owned by the Callaway Manufacturing Company family) has been this tournament's venue. It is an unusually hilly and undulating course with narrow fairways that place a premium on accuracy off the tee as the Bermuda rough may be only 3 inches deep yet it's thick enough to make balls disappear.

2000 ODDS

fav	11/1	David Duval	50/1	Greg Chalmers
	12/1	Justin Leonard (PWW)	66/1	Frank Lickliter
	14/1	Davis Love	66/1	Jerry Kelly
	25/1	Stewart Cink	66/1	Steve Elkington
	25/1	Chris Perry	66/1	Rory Sabbatini
	33/1	Nick Price	66/1	Bill Glasson
	33/1	David Toms (DC)	66/1*	John Huston
	33/1	Steve Flesch	80/1*	Chris DiMarco
	33/1	Paul Azinger	80/1	Jonathan Kaye
	40/1	Scott Hoch	80/1	Shigeki Maruyama
	40/1	Grant Waite	66/1*	Steve Pate
	40/1*	Notah Begay	66/1	Len Mattiace
	40/1	Franklin Langham	66/1	Jim Carter
	50/1	Fred Funk	66/1*	Scott Dunlap
	50/1	Jeff Maggert	66/1*	Charles Howell
	50/1	J L Lewis		

2000 RESULT

1	fav 11/1	David Duval	68 69 67 65 269
T2	50/1	Jeff Maggert	63 69 69 70 271
T2	33/1	Nick Price	70 68 65 68 271
4	125/1	Carl Paulson	70 67 69 67 273
T5	125/1	Joel Edwards	72 69 68 66 275
T5	100/1	Brent Geiberger	71 69 69 66 275
T5	40/1	Scott Hoch	67 71 68 69 275

T8	P Azinger	66 71 72 67 276			L Mattiace	70 70 73 71 284
	G Chalmers	69 70 68 69 276			P Moss	67 73 70 74 284
T10	B Andrade	71 72 68 66 277			T Pernice Jr	71 70 73 70 284
	J D Blake	72 68 67 70 277			T Scherrer	72 71 73 68 284
	S Elkington	70 73 66 68 277			J Sindelar	66 74 71 73 284
	P Goydos	69 70 68 70 277			E Toledo	70 73 70 71 284
T14	C Beckman	67 70 74 67 278		T48	N Begay	72 70 71 72 285
	Brian Gay	67 71 69 71 278			B Fabel	68 72 76 69 285
	G Hnatiuk	68 69 70 71 278			D Forsman	71 72 71 71 285
	G Waite	71 70 69 68 278			S Gotsche	71 72 70 72 285
T18	S Cink	67 71 71 70 279			J P Hayes	70 69 74 72 285
	D Dunakey	69 74 67 69 279			D Pride	69 70 72 74 285
	J Kelly	70 69 71 69 279			David Sutherland	71 72 70 72 285
	D Love	70 71 68 70 279		T55	S Kendall	69 74 72 71 286
	Chris Perry	69 70 69 71 279			J L Lewis	70 73 68 75 286
T23	C DiMarco	67 73 69 71 280			J Maginnes	69 73 70 74 286
	B Estes	70 69 72 69 280			L Mize	68 74 71 73 286
	C Raulerson	66 73 69 72 280			T Tryba	67 72 73 74 286
	R Sabbatini	68 72 72 68 280		T60	F Allem	72 69 71 75 287
T27	C Barlow	73 70 69 69 281			M Goggin	69 74 76 68 287
	Bobby Cochran	72 70 70 69 281			J Inman	72 68 74 73 287
	S Flesch	73 68 68 72 281		T63	Bart Bryant	73 70 75 70 288
	R Gamez	69 73 68 71 281			J Daly	72 71 73 72 288
	J McGovern	71 72 69 69 281			B Heintz	70 70 75 73 288
T32	D Barron	73 70 71 68 282			G Kraft	69 71 76 72 288
	M Bradley	71 71 67 73 282			F Lickliter	70 73 71 74 288
	R Damron	70 71 71 70 282		68	J Delsing	70 70 77 72 289
	B Glasson	73 68 72 69 282		69	Jim Gallagher	72 71 73 74 290
	G Hjertstedt	74 69 68 71 282		T70	F Langham	72 71 72 76 291
	B Hughes	73 68 68 73 282			C Strange	71 71 75 74 291
T38	J Cook	70 73 67 73 283		T72	M Hulbert	69 74 73 76 292
	J Durant	68 69 71 75 283			F Nobilo	68 73 75 76 292
	P H Horgan	68 72 71 72 283			B Schwarzrock	67 72 79 74 292
T41	F Funk	70 71 72 71 284		75	M Wiebe	71 72 73 78 294

The main players to miss the cut (made at 1 under) were:-

M Brisky (E)	B Chamblee (E)	Robin Freeman (E)	J Leonard (E)
S Lyle (E)	B Quigley (E)	L Rinker (E)	B Tway (E)
B Bates (E)	K Westworth (E)	E Fryatt (E)	C Perks (E)
E Aubrey (+1)	D Briggs (+1)	M Brooks (+1)	K Gibson (+1)
S Gump (+1)	G Hallberg (+1)	R Howison (+1)	P Jordan (+1)
S Micheel (+1)	D A Weibring (+1)	E Booker (+1)	D Morland (+1)
J Smith (+1)	P Curry (+1)	J Carter (+2)	E Fiori (+2)
J Green (+2)	J Haas (+2)	S Hart (+2)	N Lancaster (+2)
S Pate (+2)	M Springer (+2)	K Sutherland (+2)	M Sposa (+2)
K-J Choi (+2)	K Nolan (+2)	A Baddeley (am) (+2)	C Howell (+2)
B Burns (+3)	B Cheesman (+3)	S Dunlap (+3)	J Huston (+3)
D Toms (+3)	O Uresti (+3)	B Jobe (+3)	C Martin (+3)
B McCallister (+4)	M McCumber (+4)	J Ogilvie (+4)	K Hosokawa (+4)
D Gossett (am) (+4)	T Byrum (+5)	R Cochran (+5)	J Kaye (+5)
D Stockton (+5)	T Tolles (+5)	R Black (+6)	N Henke (+6)
B Crenshaw (+8)	B Friend (+8)	C A Spence (+8)	M Clark (+8)

Shigeki Maruyuama withdrew (injured wrist) after a 71.

ROUND BY ROUND LEADERBOARD

FIRST ROUND

J Maggert	9 under
P Azinger	6 under
J Sindelar	5 under
C Raulerson	6 under
8 players at	5 under
D DUVAL	4 under

SECOND ROUND

J Maggert	12 under
D DUVAL	7 under
P Azinger	7 under
J Durant	7 under
Carl Paulson	7 under
C Beckman	7 under
G Hnatiuk	7 under

THIRD ROUND

J Maggert	15 under
N Price	13 under
D DUVAL	12 under
S Hoch	10 under
Carl Paulson	10 under

FINAL ROUND

D DUVAL	19 under
N Price	17 under
J Maggert	17 under
C Paulson	15 under
J Edwards	13 under
S Hoch	13 under
B Geiberger	13 under

PUNTERS' POINTS

● He didn't touch a club from 3rd August to 16th September during which time he lay flat on his back for two weeks recovering from his back injury. "This is a spectacular week for me....and it's an absolute dream," were Duval's understandable comments after his 11/1 success.

● 50/1 Jeff Maggert did what he does so well. He hit fairways and greens and lost a R4 lead. In 72-hole stroke-play tournaments he's now been 2nd fourteen (yes fourteen) times, yet he's only won once.

● Does course form matter? Apparently not to T2nd-placed Nick Price who travelled straight from a wet fortnight in Japan to play for the first time ever at Callaway Gardens.

● Top of the 1999 BUY.COM tour, Carl Paulson posted his best-ever tour finish when 4th after a good final round.

● 1998 winner here Steve Elkington showed a welcome return to fitness and form finishing fast (10 under last two rounds) to secure T10th position.

1999 RESULT

1	50/1*	David Toms
2	50/1	Stuart Appleby
T3	150/1	Jay Delsing
T3	200/1	Craig Barlow
T3	fav 11/1	Davis Love

1998 RESULT

1	33/1	Steve Elkington
won at the first play-off hole		
2	28/1	Fred Funk
3	40/1	Bill Glasson
4	125/1	J L Lewis
5	100/1	Skip Kendall

WINNERS IN THE LAST TEN YEARS

1991	David Peoples	1996	Michael Bradley
1992	Gary Hallberg	1997	Davis Love
1993	John Inman	1998	Steve Elkington
1994	Steve Elkington	1999	David Toms
1995	Fred Funk	2000	David Duval

PUNTERS' GUIDE

● Players with the best recent records at Callaway Gardens include:-

	2000	1999	1998	1997
Davis Love	18	3	14	W
Paul Azinger	8	6	-	MC
David Duval	W	-	6	9
Grant Waite	14	20	39	9
Steve Elkington	10	MC	W	MC
Stewart Cink	18	6	MC	2
Chris Perry	18	13	8	21
Jeff Maggert	2	13	8	-

> Davis Love has now posted eighteen consecutive sub-par rounds here.

> Davis Love, Jeff Maggert and Chris Perry are the only players in the last three years to have posted consecutive top 20s.

● In the last seven years of the thirty-nine players in the top 5 (or T5th)

> fourteen (36%) started at or over 100/1

> nine (23%) started at or over 125/1

> five (12 ½%) started at or over 150/1

Also in six of the last seven years AT LEAST two players priced at 100/1 finished in the top 5.

So this has become very much an 'outsiders' tournament.

● Players whose profiles refer to this tournament include Paul Azinger, Grant Waite, Steve Elkington, Chris Perry, Davis Love, Bill Glasson, Stewart Cink, Jeff Maggert, Fred Funk and Notah Begay.

THE MICHELOB CHAMPIONSHIP

Date	5th - 8th October
Course	Kingsmill G.C., Williamsburg, Virginia
Par	71
Yardage	6,853
First Prize	$540,000
Total Purse	$3 million

THE TOURNAMENT

Known as the Anheuser-Busch Golf Classic up to 1995 after which it was retitled the Michelob Championship. This was the tournament that in 1997 started David Duval on his winning run.

THE COURSE

Kingsmill has been the venue since 1981. Not a long course it has three par 5s which are all reachable in 2 shots. It suits the short but straight-hitting players. The bentgrass greens are small (three-quarters of size of last week for example) and tricky to read.

2000 ODDS

fav	7/2	David Duval (PWW)	66/1	Fred Funk
	22/1	Jim Furyk	66/1*	Lee Janzen
	25/1	Loren Roberts	66/1	Dudley Hart
	25/1	Notah Begay (DC)	66/1*	John Huston
	33/1	Robert Allenby	66/1	Rory Sabbatini
	33/1	Paul Azinger	66/1	Frank Lickliter
	33/1	Mark Calcavecchia	66/1	Steve Lowery
	33/1	Scott Hoch	66/1	Mark O'Meara
	33/1	Scott Verplank	80/1	Carl Paulson
	33/1	Steve Flesch	80/1	Steve Pate
	40/1	Greg Chalmers	80/1*	Brian Watts
	40/1	Grant Waite	80/1*	Jean Van de Velde
	50/1	David Toms	80/1	Stephen Ames
	50/1	Mike Weir	80/1	Tom Scherrer
	50/1	Jeff Sluman	80/1	Charles Howell
	66/1*	Franklin Langham		

2000 RESULT

1	50/1	**David Toms**	**68 70 67 66 271**
		Toms won at the first play-off hole	
2	50/1	**Mike Weir**	**70 66 71 64 271**
3	66/1	**Frank Lickliter**	**67 69 68 69 273**
4	80/1	**Tom Scherrer**	**71 64 72 67 274**
T5	80/1	**Stephen Ames**	**69 69 70 67 275**
T5	150/1	**Bradley Hughes**	**68 63 72 72 275**
T5	150/1	**Sean Murphy**	**66 72 69 68 275**
T5	150/1	**Mike Reid**	**73 68 65 69 275**

T9	M Bradley	68 67 71 70 276		J Kaye	72 68 71 72 283
	S Hoch	70 70 70 66 276		S McCarron	70 71 71 71 283
	C Riley	69 67 68 72 276		D Peoples	72 69 71 71 283
T12	S Flesch	69 69 68 71 277		R Zokol	68 69 73 73 283
	C Parry	71 69 68 69 277	T48	F Allem	70 71 72 71 284
	J Sindelar	70 67 71 69 277		J Buha	68 73 70 73 284
T15	C Beckman	66 71 68 73 278		Tom Byrum	68 71 72 73 284
	P Moss	67 73 70 68 278		D Frost	70 68 75 71 284
	S Pate	66 69 72 71 278		J Huston	68 71 70 75 284
	David Sutherland	68 66 71 73 278	T53	O Browne	72 68 73 72 285
T19	J Cook	68 73 68 70 279		K Clearwater	67 70 76 72 285
	D Duval	70 65 69 75 279		T Dodds	69 69 73 74 285
	J Furyk	69 68 69 73 279		L Mattiace	71 70 71 73 285
	J McGovern	69 70 71 69 279		Kevin Sutherland	67 71 73 74 285
	L Roberts	69 66 70 74 279	T58	P Azinger	71 67 75 73 286
	J Van de Velde	69 70 70 70 279		J Delsing	73 67 71 75 286
T25	T Armour III	69 66 72 73 280		L Janzen	72 69 74 71 286
	M Calcavecchia	70 71 67 72 280		K Nolan	69 69 76 72 286
	Jim Gallagher	72 67 69 72 280	T62	R Allenby	72 69 73 73 287
	J Maginnes	71 70 67 72 280		F Funk	71 69 72 75 287
	G Waite	70 68 71 71 280		K Gibson	68 70 76 73 287
T30	R Damron	66 70 76 69 281	T65	Bobby Cochran	69 71 74 74 288
	S Dunlap	68 70 69 74 281		S Lyle	69 70 75 74 288
	B McCallister	68 70 74 69 281	T67	G Hnatiuk	69 70 75 75 289
	B Schwarzrock	69 69 74 69 281		C Howell	69 69 76 75 289
	M Sposa	70 71 69 71 281		F Nobilo	72 66 74 77 289
	C Strange	70 69 73 69 281	70	D Pride	71 70 71 78 290
T36	A Bengoechea	69 71 70 72 282	T71	J Caron	68 73 77 73 291
	J Byrd	72 68 70 72 282		S Gotsche	70 69 75 77 291
	Robin Freeman	68 71 71 72 282		Steve Hart	70 71 76 74 291
	B Tway	69 70 73 70 282	74	M Gogel	73 68 77 75 293
	S Verplank	71 68 69 74 282	T75	J D Blake	74 67 79 74 294
T41	M Clark	70 71 72 70 283		J Rollins	73 68 76 77 294
	S Gump	71 67 70 75 283	77	R Friend	69 72 76 78 295
	J P Hayes	66 69 71 77 283			

The main players to miss the cut (made at 1 under) were:-

B Andrade (E)	W Austin (E)	B Bryant (E)	B Burns (E)
G Day (E)	D Forsman (E)	G Chalmers (E)	C Martin (E)
B Faxon (+1)	J Green (+1)	S Lowery (+1)	C Paulson (+1)
T Pernice Jr (+1)	T Purtzer (+1)	D Stockton Jr (+1)	K Hosokawa (+1)
R Sabbatini (+1)	R Black (+2)	M Brisky (+2)	B Claar (+2)
D Hart (+2)	F Langham (+2)	D Ogrin (+2)	B Quigley (+2)
M Springer (+2)	K-J Choi (+2)	G Hallberg (+3)	J Sluman (+3)
W Wood (+3)	B Bates (+3)	K Wentworth (+3)	P Curry (+3)
D Barron (+4)	B Gilder (+4)	P Jacobsen (+4)	M O'Meara (+4)
C Raulerson (+4)	C Rose (+4)	D Gossett (am) (+4)	J Gove (+4)
B Cheesman (+5)	P Jordan (+5)	N Lancaster (+5)	N Begay (+5)
G Nicklaus (+5)	C A Spence (+5)	D Morland (+5)	B Heintz (+5)
C Perks (+5)	E Aubrey (+6)	R Howison (+6)	M McCumber (+6)
S Micheel (+6)	M Standly (+6)	O Uresti (+6)	C Pavin (+7)
L Rinker (+7)	N Henke (+8)	G Hjertstedt (+8)	B Mayfair (+8)
M Hulbert (+9)	T Tryba (+9)		

Brian Watts (73) and Mark Brooks (77) withdrew.

ROUND BY ROUND LEADERBOARD

FIRST ROUND		SECOND ROUND	
C Beckman	5 under	B Hughes	11 under
R Damron	5 under	D Sutherland	8 under
J P Hayes	5 under	T Armour III	7 under
S Pate	5 under	M Bradley	7 under
S Murphy	5 under	D Duval	7 under
D TOMS	3 under	J P Hayes	7 under
		S Pate	7 under
		L Roberts	7 under
		T Scherrer	7 under
		D TOMS	4 under

THIRD ROUND		FINAL ROUND	
B Hughes	10 under	D TOMS	13 under
D Duval	9 under	M Weir	13 under
C Riley	9 under	F Lickliter	11 under
F Lickliter	9 under	T Scherrer	10 under
D Sutherland	8 under	S Ames	9 under
D TOMS	8 under	B Hughes	9 under
C Beckman	8 under	S Murphy	9 under
L Roberts	8 under	M Reid	9 under

PUNTERS' POINTS

● 50/1 David Toms, a proven front runner, won his third USPGA tournament in the last fifteen months, beating Mike Weir with a par at the first sudden-death play-off hole.

● Mike Weir, playing for the first time in a month, shot a final round 64 (30 on the back nine). Last year he'd bogeyed the last to miss out on a play-off, this year he holed a 15-foot putt at the last for birdie.

● The 'Sunday shocker' was in-form course-specialist David Duval's 75. Tired after R3, he'd used the fitness trailer on Saturday evening. Nevertheless his final round was a struggle.

● Frank Lickliter went back to his old irons two months ago and, "it has really made a difference." Here he played a very good (and so very unusual) final round 69 to finish 3rd.

● Long-time leader Bradley Hughes (twelve missed cuts in his previous sixteen tournaments) has a poor R4 scoring record (182nd in 1999: T165th to Oct 8th this year) and again here he went over par on Sunday!

● On Sunday there were nineteen players within 4 shots of the lead and their average score was an above par 71.47. Any sub-par R4 round from a player in contention was therefore good.

1999 RESULT

1	80/1	Notah Begay
won at the second play-off hole		
2	100/1	Tom Byrum
3	40/1	Mike Weir
4	150/1	Barry Cheesman
T5	125/1	Jay Don Blake
T5	100/1	Nick Faldo
T5	125/1	Tom Scherrer

1998 RESULT

1	fav 9/1	David Duval
2	200/1	Phil Tataurangi
3	150/1	Barry Cheesman
T4	40/1	Payne Stewart
T4	100/1	Bradley Hughes

WINNERS IN THE LAST TEN YEARS

1991	Mike Hulbert	1996	Scott Hoch
1992	David Peoples	1997	David Duval
1993	Jim Gallagher Jr	1998	David Duval
1994	Mark McCumber	1999	Notah Begay
1995	Ted Tryba	2000	David Toms

PUNTERS' GUIDE

● Successful course experience seems to be important here if you examine the 'Kingsmill credentials' of this year's top 10.

		2000	Past Form
>	David Toms	Won	T15th in 1997
>	Mike Weir	2nd	3rd last year
>	Frank Lickliter	3rd	T6th in 1998
>	Tom Scherrer	4th	T5th last year
>	Bradley Hughes	T5th	T4th in 1998
>	Michael Bradley	T9th	4th in 1994: T11th in 1995 and T3rd 1996
>	Scott Hoch	T9th	won here in 1996 and was 5th in 1997

● Best recent Kingsmill records belong to:-

	2000	1999	1998	1997	1996
David Duval	19	8	Won	Won	-
Scott Hoch	9	24	22	5	Won
Frank Lickliter	3	24	6	MC	17
Tommy Armour III	25	MC	10	19	7
Tom Scherrer	4	5	-	-	MC
Robert Damron	30	17	-	MC	-
Stephen Ames	5	13	MC	-	-
Bradley Hughes	5	MC	4	36	-
Steve Pate	15	-	17	-	-
David Toms	Won	59	MC	15	-

● Players whose profiles refer to this tournament include Tommy Armour III, Michael Bradley, David Toms, Stephen Ames, Frank Lickliter, John Cook, Mike Weir, Brian Watts and Tom Scherrer.

THE INVENSYS CLASSIC IN LAS VEGAS

Date	11th - 15th October		
Course	TPC at Summerlin	Desert Inn	Southern Highlands
Par	72	72	72
Yardage	7,243	7,193	7,381
First Prize	$765,000		
Total Purse	$4.25 million (up by $1.65 million)		

THE TOURNAMENT

Formerly known as the Las Vegas International this is an unusual five-day, 90-hole tournament with the first three rounds following a pro-am format with one round at each of the three courses. The cut is then made before the final two rounds are played at the host Summerlin course. Twenty amateurs play R4, only pros play the final round. The other 90-hole, five-day tournament is the Bob Hope held in January in California.

THE COURSE

The courses are wide-fairway, desert, resort courses, so the ball flies a long way through the thin desert air. The greens are large and bentgrass. The wind can play an important part here, as it did in R4 last year. This year the longer (by 217 yards) Southern Highlands course replaced the easier Las Vegas course.

2000 ODDS

fav	10/1	Phil Mickelson	66/1	Stephen Ames
	16/1	Jim Furyk (DC)	66/1	Steve Elkington
	20/1	Justin Leonard	66/1	Lee Janzen
	20/1	Davis Love	80/1	Tim Herron
	25/1	Hal Sutton	80/1*	John Huston
	28/1	Mark Calcavecchia	80/1*	Jonathan Kaye
	33/1	Stewart Cink	80/1	Chris DiMarco
	33/1	Bob May	80/1*	Brent Geiberger
	33/1	Mike Weir	80/1	Jerry Kelly
	33/1	Steve Flesch	80/1*	Franklin Langham
	40/1	Chris Perry	80/1	John Cook
	40/1	Stuart Appleby	80/1	Steve Lowery
	40/1	Jeff Maggert	80/1	Chris Riley
	40/1	Fred Couples	80/1*	Rocco Mediate
	50/1	Scott Verplank	80/1*	Rory Sabbatini
	50/1	Robert Allenby	80/1*	Tom Scherrer
	50/1	Greg Chalmers	80/1	Jean Van de Velde
	50/1	Bill Glasson	80/1	Jeff Sluman
	66/1	Dudley Hart		

2000 RESULT

1	150/1	Billy Andrade	67 67 63 67 68 332
2	fav 10/1	Phil Mickelson	69 65 67 66 66 333
T3	33/1	Stewart Cink	68 68 67 65 66 334
T3	80/1*	Jonathan Kaye	68 70 67 67 62 334
T5	80/1	John Cook	65 70 65 68 67 335
T5	80/1	Chris DiMarco	66 69 70 67 63 335
T5	100/1	Scott McCarron	67 66 66 66 70 335
T5	150/1	Shaun Micheel	68 69 66 63 69 335

T9	Tom Byrum	65 65 65 69 72 336		J Maggert	68 69 67 69 71 344
	J Durant	66 71 66 67 66 336		J Maginnes	68 70 68 71 67 344
	S Flesch	66 71 66 67 66 336		K Triplett	68 69 70 67 70 344
T12	B McCallister	67 64 68 69 69 337		B Tway	70 67 64 75 68 344
	C Parry	71 67 68 67 64 337		J Williamson	71 69 65 69 70 344
	M Weir	67 68 63 72 67 337		C Martin	64 70 67 71 72 344
T15	L Janzen	65 67 69 68 69 338	T49	D Peoples	70 70 67 69 69 345
	S Verplank	70 66 68 66 68 338		R Gamez	69 67 68 69 72 345
T17	F Couples	69 68 66 67 69 339		Dennis Paulson	68 66 70 67 74 345
	J Furyk	70 68 67 67 67 339	T52	R Allenby	69 69 68 70 70 346
	S Lowery	71 69 66 63 70 339		S Elkington	67 67 71 70 71 346
	J Sluman	67 67 68 68 69 339		B Henninger	69 68 69 75 65 346
	P Stankowski	70 67 67 70 65 339		P Jacobsen	71 67 68 71 69 346
T22	O Browne	64 70 68 68 70 340	T56	J Delsing	69 69 66 71 72 347
	B Chamblee	71 69 66 69 65 340		T Dodds	71 68 67 75 66 347
	T Herron	67 70 70 67 66 340		E Fryatt	69 69 68 68 73 347
	J Leonard	68 69 70 64 69 340		Kevin Sutherland	70 67 66 73 71 347
	B May	65 69 69 67 70 340	T60	W Austin	71 66 67 70 74 348
T27	B Faxon	64 72 69 70 66 341		G Chalmers	68 70 69 68 73 348
	M Goggin	67 68 68 70 68 341		S Murphy	72 67 68 71 70 348
	Dudley Hart	70 67 66 67 71 341		C Raulerson	68 72 67 70 71 348
	S Kendall	65 69 72 67 68 341		M Wiebe	66 70 69 71 72 348
	J L Lewis	70 68 66 71 66 341	T65	D Dunakey	67 69 70 69 74 349
	R Mediate	71 66 65 68 71 341		F Funk	69 68 69 71 72 349
T33	K Gibson	70 70 67 68 67 342	T67	F Allem	70 69 68 71 72 350
	R Beem	70 65 66 70 71 342		J P Hayes	68 71 66 74 71 350
	B Mayfair	71 69 66 68 68 342	T69	B Fabel	71 68 66 72 74 351
T36	Jim Gallagher	71 68 67 67 70 343		D Waldorf	70 66 70 73 72 351
	M Gogel	71 69 63 71 69 343	71	M Springer	66 74 66 75 71 352
	B Lietzke	63 71 70 72 67 343	72	M Clark	70 66 70 76 74 356
T40	B Geiberger	71 70 65 70 68 344	73	R Sabbatini	73 68 66 74 78 359
	M Kirk	70 67 69 68 70 344	74	B Burns	72 64 71 76 77 360
	D Love	69 70 66 69 70 344			

The main players to miss the cut (made at 9 under) were:–

B Estes (-8)	M Bradley (-8)	M Calcavecchia (-8)	G Day (-8)
B Gay (-8)	E Aubrey (-8)	R Freeman (-8)	R Black (-8)
C Beckman (-8)	J Edwards (-8)	R Damron (-8)	J D Blake (-8)
J Sindelar (-8)	G Hjerstedt (-8)	E Fiori (-8)	R Fehr (-8)
J Carter (-7)	D Sutherland (-7)	G Kraft (-7)	J Gove (-7)
S Ames (-7)	H Sutton (-7)	J Van de Velde (-7)	C A Spence (-7)
E Toledo (-6)	T Scherrer (-6)	C Barlow (6)	S Maruyama (-6)
C Riley (-6)	G Nicklaus (-6)	B Jobe (-6)	T Armour III (-6)
T Tryba (-5)	T Pernice Jr (-5)	B Bates (-5)	B Friend (-5)
M Brooks (-5)	K Wentworth (-5)	C Perks (-5)	B Hughes (-5)
C Perry (-5)	C Howell (-5)	B Elder (-4)	F Langham (-4)
K-J Choi (-4)	J Kelly (-4)	D Morland (-4)	S Gump (-4)
S Appleby (-3)	J Haas (-3)	J Ogilvie (-3)	T Tolles (-2)
B Glasson (-2)	M Brisky (-2)	D Stockton (-1)	D Pride (-1)
M Reid (-1)	P Jordan (-1)	B Watts (E)	N Henke (E)
R Cochran (E)	E Booker (+2)	M Hulbert (+2)	B Cheesman (+4)
O Uresti (+7)	J Rollins (+8)		

Tom Purtzer (72-71) was disqualified.

ROUND BY ROUND LEADERBOARD

FIRST ROUND

B Lietzke	9 under
O Browne	8 under
B Faxon	8 under
C Martin	8 under
5 players at	7 under
B ANDRADE	5 under

SECOND ROUND

T Byrum	14 under
B McCallister	13 under
L Janzen	12 under
D Forsman	11 under
S McCarron	11 under
B ANDRADE	10 under
9 other players at	10 under

THIRD ROUND

T Byrum	21 under
B ANDRADE	19 under
M Weir	18 under
S McCarron	17 under
B McCallister	17 under
J Cook	16 under

FOURTH ROUND

B ANDRADE	24 under
T Byrum	24 under
S McCarron	23 under
S Micheel	22 under
P Mickelson	21 under
S Cink	20 under
J Cook	20 under
B McCallister	20 under

FINAL ROUND

B ANDRADE	28 under
P Mickelson	27 under
S Cink	26 under
J Kaye	26 under
J Cook	25 under
C DiMarco	25 under
S McCarron	25 under
S Micheel	25 under

PUNTERS' POINTS

- A bookies' paradise as out of form 150/1 Billy Andrade, 159th on the Money List, won for the fourth time. On the first three days he had the luck to play the courses on the 'right days', viz Summerlin (day one), Desert Inn (Thursday) and Desert Highlands (Friday with no wind), and Sunday he had the 'bottle' to hang on (despite a poor drive at the last) for a narrow win. He's now secured his card for 2001.

- Desert fox and 10/1 favourite Phil Mickelson let his chance slip when he bogeyed the par 5 9th on Sunday. He was the tournament's No. 1 for greens in regulation.

- Jonathan Kaye, whose flat fade is well suited here, shot 64 in R5 last year and a course record 62 in the final round this time.

- Scott McCarron has had two big finishes this year and both have been in Nevada where he and his wife have family and friends: 4th in the Reno-Tahoe Open and T5th here despite his poor 'broomstick' putting in R5.

- Course-specialist T5th John Cook loves these 90-hole events, after all he's won three, and he went very close here. He could well spring a surprise here in 2001.

1999 RESULT

1	fav 16/1	Jim Furyk
2	125/1	Jonathan Kaye
3	66/1	Dudley Hart
4	33/1	Chris Perry
5	80/1*	Andrew Magee

1998 RESULT

1	33/1	Jim Furyk
2	25/1	Mark Calcavecchia
3	80/1	Scott Verplank
4	50/1	Bob Tway
5	fav 12/1	Davis Love

WINNERS IN THE LAST TEN YEARS

1991	Andrew Magee	1996	Tiger Woods
1992	John Cook	1997	Bill Glasson
1993	Davis Love	1998	Jim Furyk
1994	Bruce Lietzke	1999	Jim Furyk
1995	Jim Furyk	2000	Billy Andrade

PUNTERS' GUIDE

● Players with the best recent records include:-

	2000	1999	1998	1997	1996
Jim Furyk	17	W	W	19	22
Jonathan Kaye	3	2	DQ	-	-
Mark Calcavecchia	MC	MC	2	4	3
Davis Love	40	-	5	30	2
Fred Couples	17	10	22	9	8
Brandel Chamblee	22	6	10	-	74
Stewart Cink	3	22	16	MC	12
Scott Verplank	15	61	3	-	-
Steve Flesch	9	32	-	-	-
Mike Weir	12	19	MC	-	-

● Before betting in this tournament do check out the US stats for total eagles. The top 20 players in that table provided

> in 1999 four of the tournament's top 5

> in 2000 three of the tournaments's top 5 (or T5)

● At this time of year check out the players 'on the bubble' who fall into either of the two categories that create special end of season incentives.

> Players who want to clinch a top 30 position on the Money List to secure a place in the mega-dollar Tour Championship.

> Players on and around the 125th place on the Money List keen to secure their tour cards so avoiding the dreaded trip to Q School.

● Players whose profiles refer to this tournament include Jonathan Kaye, John Cook, Brandel Chamblee, Steve Flesch, Mike Weir, Dudley Hart, Andrew Magee, Fred Couples and Scott McCarron.

THE TAMPA BAY CLASSIC

Date	19th - 22nd October
Course	Westin Innisbrook Resort (Copperhead Course), Tampa Bay, Florida
Par	71
Yardage	7,054
First Prize	$432,000
Total Purse	$2.4 million

THE TOURNAMENT

This was a new tournament on the USPGA schedule introduced to coincide with the Presidents' Cup.

THE COURSE

This is a wide fairway resort course that had been the venue for the (out of season) JC Penney Classic from 1990. The JC Penney was a man/woman pairs competition, so quite a few players had course experience. The course is long at 7,230 yards with Bermuda grass greens.

2000 ODDS

fav	14/1	Justin Leonard	66/1	Billy Andrade
	25/1	Scott Hoch	66/1*	Brent Geiberger
	25/1	David Toms	66/1	Scott Dunlap
	25/1	Steve Flesch (non runner)	66/1	Duffy Waldorf
	25/1	Fred Couples	66/1	Stephen Ames
	33/1	Chris Perry	66/1*	Craig Parry
	33/1	Bob May	66/1*	Nick Faldo
	33/1	Grant Waite	66/1	Steve Lowery
	33/1	Jeff Maggert	66/1	Blaine McCallister
	33/1	Lee Janzen	66/1	Tom Scherrer
	40/1	Chris DiMarco	80/1*	Joe Durant
	40/1	John Cook	80/1	Brad Faxon
	40/1	Frank Lickliter	80/1*	Steve Jones
	50/1	Tim Herron	80/1*	Steve Pate
	50/1	Jeff Sluman	80/1	Fred Funk
	50/1	Dudley Hart	80/1*	Jerry Kelly
	66/1	Bill Glasson	80/1*	Michael Bradley
	66/1*	John Huston	80/1	Paul Goydos
	66/1*	J L Lewis	80/1	Olin Browne
	66/1*	Kenny Perry	80/1	Joel Edwards

2000 RESULT

1	66/1*	John Huston	66 73 67 65 271
2	100/1*	Carl Paulson	66 66 70 72 274
T3	50/1*	Frank Lickliter	67 68 71 69 275
T3	100/1*	Len Mattiace	68 66 70 71 275
5	80/1*	Joe Durant	68 69 73 66 276

T6	B Faxon	70 71 71 65 277		F Funk	71 69 73 71 284
	L Janzen	67 71 71 68 277		Dudley Hart	70 68 72 74 284
	S Lowery	67 69 69 72 277		R Howison	72 70 72 70 284
9	T Herron	67 71 71 69 278		S Murphy	68 72 74 70 284
T10	C Barlow	70 70 71 68 279		D Toms	71 68 73 72 284
	D Barron	69 71 70 69 279		G Waite	69 72 69 74 284
	A Magee	73 68 66 72 279		B Watts	70 71 70 73 284
	B Tway	71 68 71 69 279	T48	C Parry	70 69 72 74 285
T14	F Couples	67 72 71 70 280		C Perks	71 67 75 72 285
	S Dunlap	70 70 71 69 280		J Sluman	72 66 71 76 285
	Robin Freeman	69 70 68 73 280	T51	S Ames	75 66 74 71 286
	J Leonard	70 71 68 71 280		T Armour III	71 72 74 69 286
	T Tolles	72 67 71 70 280		W Austin	74 69 70 73 286
T19	C Beckman	69 73 68 71 281		K Gibson	70 72 73 71 286
	Russ Cochran	72 68 69 72 281		J Maginnes	71 72 73 70 286
	P Curry	69 69 71 72 281	T56	F Allem	72 70 75 70 287
	S Gump	66 68 74 73 281		T Dodds	69 73 73 72 287
	J Kelly	69 73 71 68 281		N Lancaster	71 70 76 70 287
	G Kraft	70 69 75 67 281		C Riley	69 73 73 72 287
	J Maggert	73 67 69 72 281		M Wiebe	70 68 73 76 287
	O Uresti	71 72 69 69 281	T61	M Bradley	70 72 71 75 288
T27	B Burns	71 68 71 72 282		D Forsman	70 72 77 69 288
	R Friend	66 72 70 74 282	T63	B Bates	72 71 73 73 289
	S Kendall	70 73 72 67 282		M Gogel	72 69 75 73 289
	B Mayfair	71 69 72 70 282		K Wentworth	74 69 71 75 289
	D Peoples	71 67 72 72 282	T66	N Faldo	71 72 72 75 290
	Kenny Perry	67 70 73 72 282		G Morrison	69 73 76 72 290
T33	J Cook	71 70 72 70 283		C Raulerson	72 70 76 72 290
	C DiMarco	68 69 72 74 283		J Sindelar	71 71 71 77 290
	B Fabel	69 74 70 70 283		M Sposa	67 74 75 74 290
	B Gay	69 72 72 70 283	71	E Toledo	73 69 75 74 291
	M Hulbert	64 75 75 69 283	72	M Brisky	70 73 76 73 292
	B May	67 75 69 72 283	T73	J Haas	69 73 79 73 294
	Jerry Smith	71 72 70 70 283		S Micheel	72 70 73 79 294
T40	J Delsing	69 70 71 74 284			

The main players to miss the cut (made at 1 over) were:–

B Quigley (+2)	P Goydos (+2)	S Hoch (+2)	J Williamson (+2)
C Howell (+2)	G Hnatiuk (+2)	P Jacobsen (+2)	T Tryba (+2)
C Perry (+2)	D Paulson (+2)	G Day (+2)	C Pavin (+2)
R Damron (+2)	P Moss (+3)	R Beem (+3)	B McCallister (+3)
B Andrade (+3)	S Pate (+3)	J Edwards (+3)	K-J Choi (+3)
P Jordan (+4)	D Mast (+4)	C Rose (+4)	B Glasson (+4)
J McGovern (+4)	B Cochran (+4)	R Gamez (+5)	O Browne (+5)
M Springer (+5)	M Goggin (+5)	T Scherrer (+5)	E Booker (+5)
S Hart (+5)	S Gotsche (+5)	B Jobe (+6)	P H Horgan (+6)
J Gove (+6)	C Martin (+6)	B Elder (+6)	S Jones (+6)
J Ogilvie (+6)	G Hjerstedt (+7)	C A Spence (+7)	J Gallagher (+7)
D Stockton (+8)	F Zoeller (+8)	D Dunakey (+8)	B Cheesman (+8)
G Nicklaus (+8)	D Pride (+9)	J Carter (+9)	J L Lewis (+10)
B Heintz (+10)	K Nolan (+10)	N Henke (+12)	R Fehr (+14)

Mark Brooks (69-72-73) withdrew.
Please note: Steve Flesch, David Sutherland, Scott McCarron, Tom Byrum and Michael Clark all did not start.

ROUND BY ROUND LEADERBOARD

FIRST ROUND

M Hulbert	7 under
R Friend	5 under
S Gump	5 under
J HUSTON	5 under
S Pate	5 under
C Paulson	5 under
8 players at	4 under

SECOND ROUND

C Paulson	10 under
S Gump	8 under
L Mattiace	8 under
F Lickliter	7 under
S Lowery	6 under
J HUSTON	3 under

THIRD ROUND

C Paulson	11 under
L Mattiace	9 under
S Lowery	8 under
J HUSTON	7 under
F Lickliter	7 under
A Magee	6 under
R Freeman	6 under

FINAL ROUND

J HUSTON	13 under
C Paulson	10 under
F Lickliter	9 under
L Mattiace	9 under
J Durant	8 under

PUNTERS' POINTS

● Home advantage rules OK! 66/1 John Huston resides in the Palm Harbor area and has played the Copperhead course over a hundred times. His brilliant 65 in R4 brought him a well-deserved victory, his sixth on the tour.

● 100/1 Carl Paulson is best suited by a long, wider-fairway, four par 5 course, so he did well here until Huston passed him on Sunday.

● The lowest rounds this week were recorded by

64	Mike Hulbert (R1)
65	John Huston (R4), Brad Faxon (R4)

66   John Huston (R1), Carl Paulson (R1&R2), Len Mattiace (R2), Joe Durant (R4), Andrew Magee (R3), Scott Gump (R1), Bob Friend (R1), Jeff Sluman (R2)

● On Sunday Frank Lickliter, for the third successive tournament in which he has been in contention, shot less than the average of the top players. He will win in 2001.

● For the first time ever all the front 5 were DYMs!!

PAST RESULTS AND RECENT WINNERS

This was the inaugural Tampa Bay Classic.

PUNTERS' GUIDE

● When this course was used for the J C Penney Classic it was clear that it favoured the longer hitters, as the successes of Davis Love (twice with Beth Daniel) and John Daly (once with the big-hitting Laura Davies in 1999) illustrated.

● An analysis of the tournament this year also leads to the conclusion that long hitters who enjoy wider fairways do well here.

● This year Florida based players provided four of the first 5, with Carl Paulson being the exception.

● Players whose profiles refer to this event include Steve Lowery, Tim Herron, Andrew Magee, Carl Paulson, Frank Lickliter, Len Mattiace, Scott Dunlap and Brad Faxon.

THE NATIONAL CAR RENTAL GOLF CLASSIC AT WALT DISNEY

Date	26th - 29th October	
Course	Magnolia (host course)	Palm
Par	72	72
Yardage	7,190	6,957
First Prize	$540,000	
Total Purse	$3 million	

THE TOURNAMENT

The two courses are played on Friday and Saturday. The tougher course, the Magnolia, is then played in R3 and R4 making three times in all. For the first two days the pros play alongside amateurs till the halfway cut.

THE COURSES

The Magnolia course is the harder, although both are wide-fairway resort courses with course records of 61 (11 under par). The bermuda grass greens are large and generally flat.

2000 ODDS

fav	5/4	Tiger Woods (DC)	66/1	Dudley Hart
	22/1	Davis Love	66/1	Frank Lickliter
	25/1	Vijay Singh	66/1	Steve Lowery
	28/1	John Huston (PWW)	66/1	Jeff Maggert
	33/1	Mike Weir	66/1	Bob May
	40/1	Steve Flesch	66/1	Grant Waite
	50/1	Carlos Franco	80/1*	John Cook
	50/1	Scott Hoch	80/1	Scott Dunlap
	50/1	Lee Janzen	80/1	Brad Faxon
	50/1	David Toms	80/1	Jonathan Kaye
	50/1	Scott Verplank	80/1	Franklin Langham
	66/1	Stuart Appleby	80/1	Carl Paulson
	66/1	Paul Azinger	80/1	Kenny Perry
	66/1	Joe Durant	80/1	Jeff Sluman
	66/1	Chris DiMarco		

2000 RESULT

1	100/1	**Duffy Waldorf**	**65 66 69 62 262**
2	40/1	**Steve Flesch**	**63 65 66 69 263**
3	fav 5/4	**Tiger Woods**	**63 67 66 69 265**
T4	100/1	**Fred Funk**	**66 69 66 65 266**
T4	50/1	**Scott Verplank**	**69 67 65 65 266**

6	G Day	66 68 66 67 267			B Henninger	65 72 71 69 277
7	J Sluman	68 64 67 70 269			J L Lewis	71 65 68 73 277
T8	S Lowery	67 71 66 66 270			T Purtzer	68 71 71 67 277
	David Sutherland	68 71 65 66 270			P Stankowski	72 68 67 70 277
T10	P Azinger	67 69 67 68 271			J Maggert	70 69 69 69 277
	C Franco	65 66 71 69 271		T48	B Burns	69 69 71 69 278
	D Morland	66 69 70 66 271			S Dunlap	71 69 69 69 278
T13	B Chamblee	65 70 70 67 272			L Janzen	69 70 71 68 278
	D Love	69 67 65 71 272		T51	T Armour III	73 66 68 72 279
	B May	65 69 66 72 272			J Carter	69 71 69 70 279
	Chris Perry	66 70 67 69 272			J Daly	68 71 72 68 279
	E Toledo	66 71 69 66 272			G Hnatiuk	69 70 70 70 279
T18	B Hughes	67 71 64 71 273			L Mize	68 71 71 69 279
	B Jobe	65 70 70 68 273			T Tolles	72 67 70 70 279
	S Kendall	65 68 69 71 273		T57	D Barron	70 68 76 66 280
	V Singh	67 69 67 70 273			D Forsman	70 68 72 70 280
	C DiMarco	71 66 65 71 273			S Hoch	66 72 72 70 280
	D Toms	69 70 66 68 273			F Langham	66 71 74 69 280
T24	W Austin	68 71 66 69 274			D Pride	69 69 70 72 280
	J Buha	69 70 66 69 274		T62	R Black	69 71 70 71 281
	B Faxon	69 65 71 69 274			J Cook	68 72 71 70 281
	M Gogel	66 70 69 69 274			J Haas	67 73 68 73 281
	B Heintz	66 68 71 69 274			R Sabbatini	72 68 69 72 281
	S Murphy	67 69 66 72 274		T66	O Browne	69 71 71 71 282
	M Reid	67 69 71 67 274			Brad Bryant	71 69 69 73 282
	M Springer	64 69 70 71 274			D Dunakey	69 69 71 73 282
	G Waite	67 69 71 67 274			E Fryatt	68 70 73 71 282
	J Williamson	70 65 66 73 274			A Magee	70 67 75 70 282
T34	J D Blake	67 73 68 67 275			D Peoples	70 70 70 72 282
	Joel Edwards	69 70 69 67 275		T72	B Bates	69 70 73 71 283
	B Friend	68 68 71 68 275			B Watts	70 70 69 74 283
	G Kraft	69 69 69 68 275		74	S Pate	70 67 74 73 284
	Carl Paulson	73 66 72 64 275		75	J Maginnes	72 68 73 72 285
T39	B Glasson	64 72 69 71 276		T76	D Frost	68 72 69 79 288
	M Weir	69 68 69 70 276			J P Hayes	71 69 68 80 288
T41	S Appleby	71 67 73 66 277		78	C A Spence	70 69 76 76 291
	B Geiberger	70 69 69 69 277				

The main players to miss the cut (made at 4 under) were:–

P Goydos (-3)	G Hjertstedt (-3)	C Strange (-3)	C Beckman (-3)
C Barlow (-3)	J Ogilvie (-3)	R Beem (-3)	G Nicklaus (-3)
B Elder (-3)	K-J Choi (-3)	M Goggin (-3)	J Smith (-3)
E Aubrey (-2)	J Kaye (-2)	F Lickliter (-2)	C Raulerson (-2)
J Sindelar (-2)	T Tryba (-2)	B Tway (-2)	O Uresti (-2)
J Gove (-2)	J Rollins (-2)	J Durant (-1)	B Fabel (-1)
R Mediate (-1)	M O'Meara (-1)	T Pernice Jr (-1)	K Perry (-1)
B Gay (-1)	J Van de Velde (-1)	M Clark (-1)	C Perks (-1)
F Allem (E)	B Cheesman (E)	J Green (E)	J Huston (E)
P Jordan (E)	B Mayfair (E)	B McCallister (E)	K Triplett (E)
E Booker (E)	C Howell (E)	M Bradley (+1)	M Brisky (+1)
T Dodds (+1)	S Gotsche (+1)	P Jacobsen (+1)	J Kelly (+1)
R Fehr (+2)	N Henke (+2)	L Mattiace (+2)	S Ames (+3)
S Hart (+3)	N Lancaster (+3)	C Pavin (+3)	K Wentworth (+3)
C Martin (+3)	R Cochran (+4)	R Damron (+4)	T Scherrer (+4)
S Gump (+5)	S Micheel (+5)	D Stockton (+6)	J Delsing (+7)

RESULT IN THE 'WITHOUT WOODS' MARKET

1	50/1	Duffy Waldorf
2	33/1*	Steve Flesch
T3	66/1	Fred Funk
T3	33/1	Scott Verplank
5	50/1	Glen Day

ROUND BY ROUND LEADERBOARD

FIRST ROUND

T Woods	9 under
S Flesch	9 under
B Glasson	8 under
M Springer	8 under
D WALDORF	7 under
6 others at	7 under

SECOND ROUND

S Flesch	16 under
T Woods	14 under
D WALDORF	13 under
C Franco	13 under
J Sluman	12 under
S Kendall	11 under
M Springer	11 under

THIRD ROUND

S Flesch	22 under
T Woods	20 under
J Sluman	17 under
B May	16 under
D WALDORF	16 under
G Day	16 under

FINAL ROUND

D WALDORF	26 under
S Flesch	25 under
T Woods	23 under
F Funk	22 under
S Verplank	22 under

PUNTERS' POINTS

● I'd fancied Flesch at 15/8 to win the tournament on Sunday morning by holding off Tiger.....yet I hadn't counted on Waldorf coming up on the outside with a 62! "Obviously, it's a surprise to me".....and to me too Duffy baby!

- You had to feel for Steve Flesch who couldn't make a 7 footer for a play-off at the last green having played very well all week. Surely he'll get that first win in 2001.

- Tiger was not at his best yet still contended well, although those lumpy bets at 5/4 were lost.

- It's worth noting that outside the front 5 only three players shot four sub-70 rounds. They were 6th-placed Glen Day, who has a good record in this event, T10th Paul Azinger and, back in T34th place, Greg Kraft.

- MLD still rules, OK? After his brilliant Presidents Cup performance Kirk Triplett in R1 shot 76 with 40(!) on the back nine, his worst non-major score since April. Last week's winner John Huston shot 74 in R1. Both players missed the cut.

1999 RESULT			1998 RESULT		
1	fav 5/1	Tiger Woods	1	50/1	John Huston
2	20/1	Ernie Els	2	14/1	Davis Love
T3	200/1	Franklin Langham	3	100/1	Brent Geiberger
T3	66/1	Bob Tway	T4	200/1	Tom Purtzer
T5	40/1*	John Huston	T4	150/1	Rocco Mediate
T5	25/1	Vijay Singh	T4	50/1	Jesper Parnevik

WINNERS IN THE LAST TEN YEARS

1991	Mark O'Meara	1996	Tiger Woods
1992	John Huston	1997	David Duval
1993	Jeff Maggert	1998	John Huston
1994	Rick Fehr	1999	Tiger Woods
1995	Brad Bryant	2000	Duffy Waldorf

PUNTERS' GUIDE

- In the last six years of the twenty-nine players who have finished in the first 4 (or T4th) thirteen (i.e. 44.8%) have started at or over 100/1.

- Current form, accuracy and driving distance seem to be the three keys to the 'Disney'.

	Last 3 form figs	Driving Distance	GIR%
Duffy	33/6/69	18th 283 yards	T31 68.2
Flesch	27/12/9	33rd 279 yards	19th 69.8
Tiger	1/1/1	2nd 297 yards	1st 74.8

- With two courses each using a two-tee start the tee times in R1 and R2 are of minimal importance here.

- Over the last five years the following players have all posted at least three top 25s.

Tiger Woods Won 1996 & 1999: T7th 1998: 3rd 2000

Paul Azinger T18th 1996: T17th 1999: T10th 2000 in three starts

Vijay Singh   T12th 1998: T5th 1999: T18th 2000 in three starts

Glen Day   T13th 1996: T10th 1997: 11th 1998: T7th 1999: 6th 2000

Jeff Sluman   T18th 1996: T7th 1999: 7th 2000

● Players whose profiles refer to this tournament include John Huston, Paul Azinger, Steve Lowery, Jeff Sluman, Glen Day, Scott Verplank and Chris DiMarco.

THE SOUTHERN FARM BUREAU CLASSIC

Date	2nd - 5th November
Course	Annandale, Madison, Mississippi
Par	72
Yardage	7,199
First Prize	$396,000
Total Purse	$2.2 million

THE TOURNAMENT

This was the seventh successive year that the Annandale course had played host to this tournament known as the Deposit Guaranty Golf Classic from 1986 to 1998.

THE COURSE

This Jack Nicklaus-designed course is relatively easy. Faders are favoured here. The bent grass greens are of average size.

2000 ODDS

jt fav	20/1	Fred Funk	40/1	Len Mattiace
jt fav	20/1	Lee Janzen	50/1*	Paul Stankowski
	22/1	Scott Hoch	50/1	Billy Andrade
	25/1	Frank Lickliter	66/1*	Tom Byrum
	25/1*	Steve Lowery	66/1*	Blaine McCallister
	25/1	Brad Faxon	66/1	Joel Edwards
	25/1	Grant Waite	66/1	Bob Tway
	28/1	Jonathan Kaye	66/1	Paul Goydos
	28/1	Glen Day	66/1	Cameron Beckman
	33/1	Carl Paulson	80/1*	Greg Kraft
	33/1	Brian Henninger	80/1*	Tom Scherrer
	40/1	Skip Kendall	80/1*	David Sutherland
	40/1	Kenny Perry	80/1	Brian Watts
	40/1	Bill Glasson	80/1	Chris Riley
	40/1	Jerry Kelly	80/1*	Andrew Magee
	40/1	J L Lewis		

2000 RESULT

1	25/1*	**Steve Lowery**	**64 67 65 70 266**

Lowery won at the first extra hole

2	40/1	**Skip Kendall**	**67 68 65 66 266**
3	40/1	**Kenny Perry**	**69 65 65 68 267**
T4	25/1	**Brad Faxon**	**72 65 67 65 269**
T4	200/1*	**Pete Jordan**	**69 64 72 64 269**

T6	Tom Byrum	69 67 66 68 270			G Day	67 70 71 68 276
	B Elder	70 64 69 67 270			J Kaye	71 67 68 70 276
	F Funk	70 65 64 71 270		T43	L Janzen	67 70 71 69 277
	C Riley	69 67 67 67 270			L Mattiace	68 68 71 70 277
	G Waite	66 67 67 70 270			J Sindelar	69 69 70 69 277
T11	B Andrade	66 67 66 72 271			D Stockton	67 69 70 71 277
	B McCallister	68 69 66 68 271			J Gove	68 71 69 69 277
T13	Bobby Cochran	69 71 70 62 272			G Kraft	68 66 69 74 277
	B Jobe	66 66 70 70 272		49	B Henninger	70 69 70 69 278
	J Kelly	69 67 67 69 272		T50	R Black	69 70 73 67 279
	F Nobilo	68 66 66 72 272			J Daly	68 70 72 69 279
	E Toledo	69 67 68 68 272			B Hughes	68 69 71 71 279
T18	B Schwarzrock	69 70 64 70 273			D Pride	70 70 69 70 279
	B Watts	69 65 69 70 273			B Quigley	70 66 71 72 279
T20	J Buha	70 69 66 69 274		T55	E Fryatt	73 66 70 71 280
	Russ Cochran	69 66 69 70 274			G Hnatiuk	71 66 71 72 280
	D Morland	67 71 68 68 274			R Howison	70 70 74 66 280
	K Nolan	68 69 68 69 274			J L Lewis	68 70 69 73 280
	B Gay	66 71 66 71 274			O Uresti	70 67 73 70 280
	M Goggin	73 67 69 65 274		T60	D Barron	70 70 67 64 281
	C Perks	68 68 66 72 274			C Beckman	69 70 67 75 281
	B Tway	69 68 67 70 274			R Beem	68 69 71 73 281
	M Clark	66 71 72 65 274			C Martin	68 72 70 71 281
T29	M Bradley	67 68 71 69 275			L Mize	68 71 72 70 281
	T Armour III	68 68 69 70 275			C Raulerson	68 72 72 69 281
	K J Choi	70 70 69 66 275		T66	D Dunakey	71 68 71 72 282
	Jim Gallagher	70 65 68 72 275			David Sutherland	67 70 75 70 282
	B Glasson	67 67 71 70 275		T68	A Bengoechea	69 70 72 72 283
	T Scherrer	67 66 67 75 275			Bart Bryant	71 69 69 74 283
	F Lickliter	64 72 69 70 275			J Delsing	69 71 71 72 283
T36	S Hoch	68 70 68 70 276			S Murphy	70 69 72 72 283
	M Sposa	68 70 69 69 276		72	T Pernice Jr	65 74 70 75 284
	J Carter	68 64 71 73 276		T73	S Gump	71 69 72 74 286
	P Curry	70 69 70 67 276			T Purtzer	70 70 73 73 286
	P H Horgan	68 68 71 69 276				

The main players to miss the cut (made at 4 under) were:-

D Briggs (-3)	C Byrum (-3)	B Claar (-3)	J Edwards (-3)
D Hammond (-3)	C Paulson (-3)	L Rinker (-3)	S Utley (-3)
B Bates (-3)	E Booker (-3)	J Rollins (-3)	E Aubrey (-2)
B Fabel (-2)	D Forsman (-2)	B Gilder (-2)	M Hulbert (-2)
G Sauers (-2)	W Wood (-2)	C Barlow (-2)	J Caron (-2)
J Smith (-2)	R Gamez (-1)	S Gotsche (-1)	D Peoples (-1)
M Wiebe (-1)	R Zokol (-1)	B Heintz (-1)	J Quinney (-1)
M Brisky (E)	T Dodds (E)	D Frost (E)	K Gibson (E)
J Green (E)	J McGovern (E)	A Bean (E)	B Cheesman (+1)
R Fehr (+1)	S Lyle (+1)	A Magee (+1)	J Freeman (+1)
C A Spence (+1)	R Freeman (+2)	B Friend (+2)	N Henke (+2)
J Maginnes (+2)	D Mast (+2)	D Ogrin (+2)	G Nicklaus (+2)
R Crowder (+2)	G Hjertstedt (+3)	K Wentworth (+3)	B Burns (+4)
P Moss (+4)			

ROUND BY ROUND LEADERBOARD

FIRST ROUND		**SECOND ROUND**	
F Lickliter	8 under	S LOWERY	13 under
S LOWERY	8 under	J Carter	12 under
T Pernice Jr	7 under	B Jobe	12 under
B Andrade	6 under	B Andrade	11 under
M Clark	6 under	G Waite	11 under
B Gay	6 under	T Scherrer	11 under
B Jobe	6 under	P Jordan	11 under
G Waite	6 under		

THIRD ROUND		**FINAL ROUND**	
S LOWERY	20 under	S LOWERY	22 under
B Andrade	17 under	S Kendall	22 under
F Funk	17 under	K Perry	21 under
K Perry	17 under	B Faxon	19 under
S Kendall	16 under	P Jordan	19 under
F Nobilo	16 under		
T Scherrer	16 under		
G Waite	16 under		

On Thursday nine players had uncompleted rounds.

On Friday twenty-nine players had uncompleted rounds.

PUNTERS POINTS

● Steve Lowery had to make a birdie on the last to take Skip Kendall into a play-off, and having done that he needed to hole a 40-foot putt to win at the first extra hole.....and he did that too.

● Skip Kendall, yet to win on tour, was posting his third 2nd place, while in form Steve Lowery was recording his second tour win.

● Two key punter points emerged.

> An early tee time here is a real advantage as conditions were calm on Thursday morning whereas there was rain and gusty winds in the afternoon. Steve Lowery took advantage.

> Unusual to find one firm's tournament favourite (Corals had Lowery 12/1) is a DYM. Lowery gave the DYM system its seventeenth transatlantic triumph of its best-ever year.

1999 RESULT			1998 RESULT		
1	100/1*	Brian Henninger	1	12/1	Fred Funk
2	125/1	Chris DiMarco	T2	200/1	Tim Loustalot
T3	25/1*	Glen Day	T2	150/1	Franklin Langham
T3	125/1	Paul Stankowski	T2	66/1	Paul Goydos
T3	150/1	Perry Moss	T5	100/1	P H Horgan
			T5	80/1	John Maginnes

WINNERS AT THE ANNANDALE COURSE

1994	Brian Henninger (2 rounds and a play-off)
1995	Ed Dougherty
1996	Willie Wood
1997	Billy Ray Brown
1998	Fred Funk
1999	Brian Henninger (3 rounds only)
2000	Steve Lowery

PUNTERS' GUIDE

● Since 1980 this tournament has been weather reduced on six occasions. With volatile weather an early R1 tee time really is a bonus here.

● This year broke the mould of this tournament as an outsiders' paradise. Nevertheless the record of the seven years at Annandale is that of the forty-four players in the top 5 (or T5)

> twenty-one (47.7%) started at or over 100/1

> thirty (68.18%) started at or over 66/1

● With the tournament now firmly established as the last of the regular season it provides a 'last chance' saloon for players to make the top 125 on the M/L and so retain their cards.   So keep your eye on players from 120th - 140th on the Money list as they have a real incentive (e.g. Pete Jordan T4th at 200/1* this year moved from 126th to 107th on the M/L).

● Players with at least two top 20s in the last three years include

> Brian Henninger: W 1994 (2 rds): Won 1999 (3 rds): Top 20 in 1996,1997 and 1998

> Paul Stankowski:T3rd 1999: T18th 1998

> Jonathan Kaye: 6th 1999: T18th 1998
> Fred Funk: T6th 2000: Won 1998
> Skip Kendall: 2nd 2000: 13th 1997 in only two starts
> Steve Lowery: Won 2000: T27th 1998: T4th 1997
> Brad Faxon: T4th 2000: T17th 1999
> Blaine McCallister: 4th 1997: T9th 1999: T11th 2000
> Grant Waite: T11th 1998: MC 1999: T6th 2000

● Players whose profiles refer to this tournament include Blaine McCallister, Grant Waite, Glen Day, Brad Faxon, Brian Henninger, Jonathan Kaye, Mathew Goggin, Paul Stankowski and Brad Elder.

THE TOUR CHAMPIONSHIP

Date	2nd - 5th November
Course	East Lake Course, Atlanta, Georgia
Par	70
Yardage	7,108
First Prize	$900,000
Total Purse	$5 million

THE COURSE

This course was used for this event in 1998. It has a par 70 with only two par 5s, although a couple of the par 4s are really long and virtually par 5s. The greens are bentgrass.

2000 ODDS

fav	5/4	Tiger Woods	50/1*	Loren Roberts
	12/1	David Duval	50/1	Mike Weir
	14/1	Phil Mickelson	66/1	Notah Begay
	16/1	Ernie Els	66/1	John Huston
	25/1	Davis Love	66/1	Bob May
	33/1*	Vijay Singh	66/1*	Chris Perry
	33/1	Hal Sutton	66/1	David Toms
	40/1	Steve Flesch	80/1*	Mark Calcavecchia
	40/1	Scott Verplank	80/1	Chris DiMarco
	40/1	Justin Leonard	80/1	Robert Allenby
	40/1	Stewart Cink	80/1	Stuart Appleby
	50/1	Carlos Franco	100/1	Kirk Triplett
	50/1	Jesper Parnevik	125/1	Franklin Langham
	50/1	Paul Azinger		
	50/1	Nick Price		

ALL QUOTED

N.B. Jim Furyk was a late withdrawal (wrist injury)

2000 RESULT

1	14/1	**Phil Mickelson**	67 69 65 66	**267**
2	fav 5/4	**Tiger Woods**	68 66 66 69	**269**
T3	16/1	**Ernie Els**	64 72 68 69	**273**
T3	50/1	**Nick Price**	70 68 68 67	**273**
T3	33/1*	**Vijay Singh**	69 66 65 73	**273**

6	D Duval	65 68 74 67 274	T18	S Cink	73 68 72 68 281
7	S Appleby	73 65 68 69 275		C DiMarco	71 72 70 68 281
T8	Chris Perry	69 65 74 68 276		T Lehman	72 72 67 70 281
	K Triplett	69 69 70 68 276	21	M Weir	70 69 71 72 282
	D Love	66 71 71 68 276	T22	B May	71 72 70 70 283
T11	M Calcavecchia	72 67 71 67 277		J Parnevik	72 67 72 72 283
	P Azinger	69 66 73 69 277	24	C Franco	75 71 66 72 284
	D Toms	69 67 70 71 277	T25	J Huston	72 65 76 72 285
14	S Verplank	71 70 67 70 278		H Sutton	70 74 73 68 285
15	S Flesch	66 74 71 68 279	27	L Roberts	70 74 73 70 287
T16	R Allenby	68 69 70 73 280	28	F Langham	75 70 74 69 288
	J Leonard	69 69 73 69 280	29	N Begay	76 77 68 75 296

ROUND BY ROUND LEADERBOARD

FIRST ROUND

E Els	6 under
D Duval	5 under
S Flesch	4 under
D Love	4 under
P MICKELSON	3 under
T Woods	2 under
R Allenby	2 under

SECOND ROUND

D Duval	7 under
T Woods	6 under
C Perry	6 under
P Azinger	5 under
V Singh	5 under
P MICKELSON	4 under

THIRD ROUND

V Singh	10 under
T Woods	10 under
P MICKELSON	9 under
E Els	6 under

FINAL ROUND

P MICKELSON	13 under
T Woods	11 under
V Singh	7 under
E Els	7 under
N Price	7 under

PUNTERS' POINTS

● 14/1 Phil Mickelson deservedly won to end a really successful year for Lefty. Off to a fast start in R4 he played composed golf to beat Tiger who, playing with Vijay in the pair behind, could never find his usual spark.

● Woods' 2nd place ended his streak of nineteen straight USPGA tour wins when he owned at least a share of the lead entering R4.

● T3rd 50/1 Nick Price showed that he is a player for the mega-rich events with a solid performance.

● Tied with Tiger for the lead going into R4 Vijay's putting let him down as (Augusta excepted) it so often does.

● Jesper Parnevik was playing his first tournament since his hip operation.

1999 RESULT

1 fav	7/2	Tiger Woods
2	20/1	Davis Love
3	80/1	Brent Geiberger
4	33/1	Chris Perry
T5	66/1	Jeff Sluman
T5	40/1	John Huston
T5	50/1	Fred Funk
T5	100/1	Duffy Waldorf

1998 RESULT

1	40/1	Hal Sutton
2	20/1	Vijay Singh
T3	18/1	Jim Furyk
T3	33/1	Jesper Parnevik
T5	28/1	Steve Stricker
T5	25/1	Justin Leonard
T5	66/1	Scott Verplank

WINNERS IN THE LAST TEN YEARS

1991	Craig Stadler	1992	Paul Azinger
1993	Jim Gallagher Jr	1994	Mark McCumber
1995	Billy Mayfair	1996 T	om Lehman
1997	David Duval	1998	Hal Sutton
1999	Tiger Woods	2000	Phil Mickelson

PUNTERS' GUIDE

● In 2001 the Tour Championship returns to the Champions course at Houston, Texas where this tournament was last played in 1999 and 1997.

● The best 1999 and 1997 Champions course records are held by

	1999	1997	
> Davis Love	2	3	stroke average 68.5
> Tiger Wood	Won (by 4)	T12	stroke average 68.75
> Chris Perry	4	-	
> David Duval	T15	W	stroke average 69.12

N.B. Duval's winning score in 1997 would have resulted in a 2nd-place finish (by 4 shots) in 1999.

● Players with at least two top 10s in this tournament in the last three years are:-

	2000	1999	1998
> Chris Perry	T8	4	-
> Vijay Singh	T3	T9	2
> David Duval	6	T15	T8
> Davis Love	T8	2	T8
> Tiger Woods	2	W	T20

● Players whose profiles refer to this tournament include Davis Love, Tiger Woods and David Duval.

WORLD GOLF CHAMPIONSHIPS 2000   PART 5
THE ANDERSEN CONSULTING WORLD MATCH PLAY

Date	23rd - 27th February
Course	La Costa, Carlsbad, California
Par	72
Yardage	7,022
Winner	S1 million
Total Prize Money	$5 million

FORMAT AND DRAW

The format is a straight knock-out matchplay over 18 holes until the final which is over 36 holes. The 3rd-place play-off is also over 18 holes.

The draw is based on world rankings with No. 1 meeting No. 64, No. 2 meeting No. 63 and so on. There are four quarters to the draw so the golf punter can see the full draw laid out in advance. For the second successive year Jumbo Ozaki (WR 43) stayed at home to allow Michael Campbell (WR 65) to play.

THE COURSE

The Carlsbad course had been the venue for the season opening Mercedes tournament up to and including 1998 so there is plenty of course form to study. It is a resort course with wide fairways that places an emphasis on accurate iron play. The greens are bentgrass. This year the course had taken a lot of rain before the tournament so the greens were damp and the course played long.

2000 ODDS

fav	11/2	Tiger Woods	100/1*	Mark O'Meara
	18/1	David Duval	100/1*	Stewart Cink
	20/1	Colin Montgomerie	100/1*	Steve Pate
	20/1	Ernie Els	100/1	Andrew Magee
	20/1	Phil Mickelson	100/1*	M A Jimenez
	20/1	Davis Love	100/1*	Steve Stricker
	25/1	Vijay Singh	100/1	Rocco Mediate
	25/1	Jesper Parnevik	100/1*	Shigeki Maruyama
	33/1	Tom Lehman	100/1*	Bernhard Langer
	33/1	Sergio Garcia	100/1	Bob Estes
	33/1	Fred Couples	100/1	Duffy Waldorf
	40/1	Nick Price	100/1	Dudley Hart
	40/1	Hal Sutton	100/1	Glen Day
	40/1	Jim Furyk	125/1**	Bob Tway
	40/1	Lee Westwood	125/1	Brandt Jobe
	50/1	Justin Leonard	125/1	Fred Funk
	66/1	Lee Janzen	125/1	Retief Goosen
	66/1*	John Huston	125/1	Mark Calcavecchia

66/1*	Stuart Appleby	125/1*	Jeff Sluman
66/1	Michael Campbell	125/1	Craig Parry
66/1	Scott Hoch	125/1	Tim Herron
80/1*	Steve Elkington	125/1	Loren Roberts
80/1*	David Toms	125/1	Padraig Harrington
80/1*	Jeff Maggert (DC)	125/1*	Thomas Bjorn
80/1	Paul Azinger	125/1	Brian Watts
80/1*	Chris Perry	125/1	Angel Cabrera
80/1	Brent Geiberger	125/1*	Paul Lawrie
80/1*	Greg Norman	150/1	Dennis Paulson
80/1*	J M Olazabal	150/1	Billy Mayfair
80/1	Carlos Franco	150/1	Joe Ozaki
80/1	Mike Weir	150/1	Ted Tryba
80/1	Darren Clarke	200/1**	Olin Browne

There were 18 DYMs compared to 8 last year.

There were 2 TYMs compared to 0 last year.

2000 RESULT

TOP HALF OF THE DRAW

	R1	R2	R3	QF	SF
1	Tiger Woods *5&4*	Woods *1 up*			
64	Michael Campbell		Woods *4&3*		
32	Retief Goosen *4&2*	Goosen			
33	Stewart Cink			Woods *1 up*	
16	Justin Leonard *6&5*	Leonard			
49	Fred Funk		Maruyama		
17	John Huston	M'yama *1 up*			
48	Shigeki Maruyama *1 up*				Woods *5&4*
8	Nick Price	Calc' *4&3*			
57	Mark Calcavecchia *2&1*		Calcavecchia		
25	J M Olazabal *1 up*	Olazabal			
40	Craig Parry			Lawrie	
9	Phil Mickelson	Mayfair			
56	Billy Mayfair *1 up*		Lawrie *1 up*		
24	Chris Perry	Lawrie *3&2*			
41	Paul Lawrie *1 up*				

	R1	R2	R3	QF	SF
4	Davis Love III *2&1*	Love *3&2*			
61	Olin Browne		Love *3&2*		
29	Steve Elkington	Sluman			
36	Jeff Sluman *2&1*			Love *3&2*	
13	Jim Furyk *2&1*	Furyk *2&1*			
52	Rocco Mediate		Furyk		
20	Jeff Maggert	Tway			
45	Bob Tway *6&5*				Love
5	Ernie Els *2&1*	Els			
60	Bernhard Langer		Estes		
28	Bob Estes *1 up*	Estes *1 up*			
37	Steve Pate			Jiminez	
12	Tom Lehman *6&4*	Lehman			
53	Andrew Magee		Jiminez *2&1*		
21	M A Jiminez *1 up*	Jiminez *4&3*			
44	Brent Geiberger				

BOTTOM HALF OF THE DRAW

	R1	R2	R3	QF	SF
2	David Duval *4&3*	Duval *2&1*			
63	Angel Cabrera		Duval *2&1*		
31	Tim Herron *2&1*	Herron			
34	Dudley Hart			Duval *5&4*	
15	Sergio Garcia *1 up*	Garcia *7&6*			
50	Loren Roberts		Garcia		
18	Carlos Franco	Weir			
47	Mike Weir *4&3*				Duval
7	Lee Westwood *3&1*	Westwood			
58	Brandt Jobe		Hoch *2&1*		
26	Stuart Appleby	Hoch *1 up*			
39	Scott Hoch *1up*			Hoch	
10	Jesper Parnevik *2&1*	Parnevik *1 up*			
55	Padraig Harrington		Parnevik		
23	Fred Couples	Ozaki			
42	Jumbo Ozaki *1 up*				

R1	R2	R3	QF	SF
3 Colin Montgomerie *2&1*	Montgomerie			
62 Dennis Paulson				
		Bjorn		
30 Glen Day	Bjorn *1 up*			
35 Thomas Bjorn *1 up*				
			Clarke *1 up*	
14 Mark O'Meara *1 up*	O'Meara			
51 Greg Norman				
		Clarke *1 up*		
19 Darren Clarke *2&1*	Clarke *5&4*			
46 Paul Azinger				
				Clarke *4&2*
6 Vijay Singh	Waldorf *2&1*			
59 Duffy Waldorf *2&1*				
		Waldorf		
27 Steve Stricker *2&1*	Stricker			
38 Lee Janzen				
			Sutton	
11 Hal Sutton *4&3*	Sutton *1 up*			
54 Ted Tryba				
		Sutton *2&1*		
22 David Toms *1 up*	Toms			
43 Brian Watts				

SEMI-FINALS

Tiger Woods beat Davis Love III 5&4

Darren Clarke beat David Duval 4&2

THIRD PLACE PLAY-OFF (18 holes)

David Duval beat Davis Love III 5&4

FINAL (36 holes)

Darren Clarke beat Tiger Woods at the 38th hole

FINAL ORDER

1	80/1	Darren Clarke
2	fav 11/2	Tiger Woods
3	2nd fav 18/1	David Duval
4	20/1	Davis Love

PUNTERS' POINTS

● 'The couch potato against the athlete' was one American summary of the final. Nevertheless 'Sumo' Clarke's 18 stone outplayed the World No. 1 over the full 36 holes to give the bookies a smile as an 80/1 unconsidered outsider had won for the second time.

● Of the eleven 'Eurostars' playing Clarke was joint ninth in Hills' specialist list at 14/1.

● Last year's 'form' in this event was hardly worth a carrot as the four 1999 semi finalists (Maggert, Magee, Pate and Huston) were all defeated in R1.

● This year, with the greens softened by a lot of rain in the area leading up to the tournament, it was noticeable that Europeans fared well in R1. Excluding US tour player Parnevik, the Euros won nine of their twelve R1 matches for a LSP (pre tax) of 7.87 points and a 73.9% return. So a key punters' point is to back the incoming Euros if the greens are playing slow because of the weather!

● The rain-softened course also favoured the longer hitters this year. It was noticeable that the first 4 were all really long hitters. So the motto is clear at Carlsbad in the future - if the course is wet

> Follow the Euros in R1.

> Follow the big hitters in the outright.

1999 RESULT

1	80/1	Jeff Maggert
2	125/1	Andrew Magee
3	50/1	John Huston
4	125/1	Steve Pate

WINNERS SINCE THE TOURNAMENT STARTED

| 1999 | Jeff Maggert |
| 2000 | Darren Clarke |

PUNTERS' GUIDE

● With two WGC Match Plays behind us there is little clear pattern to the results.

> In 1999 every one of the nine players priced under 33/1 was knocked out in the first two rounds.

> In 2000 three of the first four were priced at or under 20/1 and were in the front six in the betting.

● The real 'value' must be in opposing favourites in the opening round. This year

> 16 of the 32 R1 matches were won by the outsider for a LSP (pre tax) of 4.1 pts and a 12.81% return.

> Sometimes 'value' can be outstanding, e.g. Duffy Waldorf had finished TEN shots ahead of Vijay Singh in the 1996 Mercedes here, and was T12th for greens in regulation compared to Singh's 31st. At 7/4 in a two-runner race he illustrated the 'value' on offer.

● With wide fairways not punishing errant tee shots the emphasis at Carlsbad is on accurate iron play. It is therefore interesting to note that the three top Americans were all in the top 10 for greens in regulation and all at or over 75%

> Davis Love   2nd 76.1%
> David Duval   3rd 75.8%
> Tiger Woods   T7th 75.0%

● It is worth noting that only eight players have won their first round in both years

> Tiger Woods   2nd 2000: QF 1999
> Bob Tway   R2 2000: R2 1999
> Shigeki Maruyama R2 2000: QF 1999
> Scott Hoch   QF 2000:R2 1999
> David Duval   3rd 2000: R2 1999
> Thomas Bjorn   R3 2000: R2 1999
> Justin Leonard   R2 2000: R2 1999
> J M Olazabal   R2 2000: QF 1999

● The two years compared

1999	GIR rank	% greens hit	Age
Jeff Maggert	14	71.9	35
Andrew Magee	T84	64.1	36
John Huston	2	76.5	37
Steve Pate	26	70.4	37
2000			
Darren Clarke	N/A	N/A	31
Tiger Woods	T7	75.0	24
David Duval	3	75.8	28
Davis Love	2	76.1	35

● Last year I suggested four criteria for the outright selection.

a) In cut-making form, especially in last tournament

b) Over 70% of greens in regulation

c) 50/1 or over

d) Age under 40

Woods, Love and Duval qualified under a), b) and d), Clarke under c) and d).

● In 2001 the tournament will be held at the Metropolitan club in Melbourne, Australia starting (wait for it) on 3rd January. There will undoubtedly be a number of qualified players who will simply choose not to play.

● In 2001 Aussie players whose domestic season will be well under way will have two key advantages

> They will be 'match fit' not rusty
> They will have 'home' advantage compared to some real jet-lagged European and American opponents.

● Four Aussie players who may qualify can therefore be noted as they all have recorded victories in Melbourne. They are
  > Robert Allenby   (1 win)
  > Craig Parry   (3 wins)
  > Greg Norman   (7 wins)
  > Stephen Leaney   (2 wins)

  However Greg Norman has indicated he will not play
● Players whose profiles refer to this tournament include Shigeki Maruyama, Bob Tway, Stephen Leaney and Craig Parry.

THE WORLD GOLF CHAMPIONSHIPS NEC INVITATIONAL

Date	24th - 27th August
Course	South Course, Firestone C.C., Akron, Ohio
Par	70
Yardage	7,189
First Prize	$1 million
Total Purse	$5 million

THE TOURNAMENT

This traditional tournament was renamed last year to become part of the World Golf Championships. This year the qualification rules were changed so that the top 12 in the European Order of Merit qualified rather than the Ryder Cup players, as a result Parnevik and Garcia were not qualified to play.

Only 37 players from the original 40 completed in the absence of Duval, Singh and Elkington. There is no halfway cut.

THE COURSE

The South course at Firestone has been used throughout this event's history (formerly called the World Series). It is long with a 625-yard par 5 (16th) and with half the par 4s over 450 yards, and demands skilful long-iron play. The bentgrass greens are small.

2000 ODDS

fav	11/8	Tiger Woods (DC)	66/1	Paul Azinger
	11/1	Phil Mickelson	66/1	Stewart Cink
	16/1	Ernie Els	80/1	Michael Campbell
	22/1	Lee Westwood	80/1	Kirk Triplett
	25/1	Davis Love	80/1	Carlos Franco
	25/1	Colin Montgomerie	80/1	Mark O'Meara
	40/1	Vijay Singh (non-runner)	80/1	Mike Weir
	40/1*	Notah Begay	100/1	Jeff Maggert
	40/1*	J M Olazabal	100/1	Padraig Harrington
	40/1	Jim Furyk	100/1	M A Jimenez
	40/1	Stuart Appleby	100/1*	Shigeki Maruyama
	40/1	Darren Clarke	125/1	Steve Pate
	50/1	Tom Lehman	150/1*	Retief Goosen
	50/1	Loren Roberts	150/1	Andrew Coltart
	50/1*	Hal Sutton	150/1	Gary Orr
	50/1	Thomas Bjorn	200/1*	Ian Woosnam
	50/1	Nick Price	250/1*	Paul McGinley
	66/1*	Greg Norman	250/1*	Phillip Price
	66/1	Justin Leonard		

ALL QUOTED

2000 RESULT

1	fav 11/8	**Tiger Woods**	**64 61 67 67 259**	
T2	66/1	**Justin Leonard**	**66 67 71 66 270**	
T2	250/1*	**Phillip Price**	**66 69 66 69 270**	
T4	40/1	**Jim Furyk**	**65 69 69 68 271**	
T4	11/1	**Phil Mickelson**	**66 66 69 70 271**	
T4	50/1*	**Hal Sutton**	**68 68 65 70 271**	

7	S Cink	72 69 68 63 272	23	P McGinley	71 72 71 67 281
T8	P Azinger	68 70 70 65 273	T24	R Goosen	69 74 73 67 283
	C Montgomerie	71 69 66 67 273		J Maggert	72 69 73 69 283
T10	J M Olazabal	67 73 69 65 274		M Weir	68 76 68 71 283
	T Bjorn	69 69 70 66 274	T27	C Franco	66 77 72 69 284
T12	R Allenby	69 69 70 67 275		P Harrington	76 65 71 72 284
	E Els	67 71 69 68 275		M O'Meara	71 71 70 72 284
14	L Roberts	67 69 66 75 277		G Orr	70 68 72 74 284
T15	M Campbell	71 69 70 68 278	T31	G Norman	68 71 76 70 285
	S Maruyama	71 70 68 69 278		T Lehman	71 74 70 70 285
T17	N Begay	74 66 69 70 279	T33	I Woosnam	73 72 72 69 286
	D Clarke	66 71 71 71 279		K Triplett	75 67 72 72 286
	A Coltart	69 69 69 72 279	35	D Love	75 72 70 70 287
T20	N Price	70 69 74 67 280	36	M Jimenez	69 74 72 73 288
	L Westwood	66 69 73 72 280	37	S Pate	75 73 69 75 292
	S Appleby	67 70 70 73 280			

ROUND BY ROUND LEADERBOARD

FIRST ROUND

T WOODS	6 under
J Furyk	5 under
D Clarke	4 under
J Leonard	4 under
Phillip Price	4 under
L Westwood	4 under
C Franco	4 under
P Mickelson	4 under

SECOND ROUND

T WOODS	15 under
P Mickelson	8 under
J Leonard	7 under
J Furyk	6 under
L Westwood	5 under
Phillip Price	5 under

THIRD ROUND

T WOODS	18 under
H Sutton	9 under
Phillip Price	9 under
P Mickelson	9 under
L Roberts	8 under
J Furyk	7 under

FINAL ROUND

T WOODS	21 under
J Leonard	10 under
Phillip Price	10 under
J Furyk	9 under
P Mickelson	9 under
H Sutton	9 under

There was a three-hour thunder-and-lightning delay on Sunday. During one spell of forty-five minutes an inch and a half of rain fell, making the greens very receptive.

RESULTS IN OTHER MARKETS

WITHOUT WOODS

T1	40/1	Justin Leonard	
T1	125/1	Phillip Price	
T3	25/1	Jim Furyk	
T3	fav 5/1	Phil Mickelson	
T3	28/1	Hal Sutton	1/4 odds 1-4

TOP AMERICAN PLAYER W/O WOODS

1	18/1	Justin Leonard	
T2	9/1	Jim Furyk	
T2	fav 5/2	Phil Mickelson	
T2	25/1	Hal Sutton	1/4 odds 1-3

TOP EUROPEAN PLAYER

1	66/1*	Phillip Price	
2	9/2	Colin Montgomerie	
T3	8/1	Thoms Bjorn	
T3	6/1	J M Olazabal	1/4 odds 1-3

TOP REST OF THE WORLD

T1	14/1	Robert Allenby	
T1	fav 9/4	Ernie Els	
T3	20/1	Michael Campbell	
T3	20/1	Shigeki Maruyama	1/4 odds 1-3

PUNTERS' POINTS

● Yes, he did it again.....took the lead, extended it and won in a canter unchallenged at 1.25 a.m. (GMT) early on Monday with the galleries holding candles in the near darkness.

● Tiger must have the record for the number of records he holds!

● Has Tiger improved or have the rest gone backwards? Simple....course ace Mickelson was a shot adrift of Tiger last year. This year 'Lefty' again shot 271.....only this time he was 12 back!!

● The 'shocks' were the guys in 2nd place

   > 250/1 DYM Welshman Phillip Price had lost his form and his motivation. However a session or two with sports psychologist Alan Fine turned him round and he played superbly (four sub-70 rounds).

   > Justin Leonard has had a disappointing season. However he 'caught fire' here to show his best form of the year.

● Course specialist Phil Mickelson was a disappointing 1 under for his last two rounds.

● The only player in the tournament to shoot each round progressively lower than its predecessor was Stewart Cink who shot a brilliant 63 in R4.

1999 RESULT

1	fav 6/1	Tiger Woods
2	20/1	Phil Mickelson
T3	100/1*	Craig Parry
T3	28/1	Nick Price
5	20/1	Ernie Els

1998 RESULT

1	20/1	David Duval
2	12/1	Phil Mickelson
3	14/1	Davis Love
4	40/1	John Cook
T5	50/1	Loren Roberts
T5	fav 7/1	Tiger Woods

WINNERS IN THE LAST TEN YEARS

1991	Tom Purtzer	1996	Phil Mickelson
1992	Craig Stadler	1997	Greg Norman
1993	Fulton Allem	1998	David Duval
1994	J M Olazabal	1999	Tiger Woods
1995	Greg Norman	2000	Tiger Woods

PUNTERS' GUIDE

● This tournament will be played at Firestone once more in 2001. However it will move to the Sahalee course in Redmond, Washington in 2002, the venue for Vijay Singh's 1998 USPGA win.

● The best recent records (top 10s only) on this track in this event belong to

	2000	1999	1998	1997	
That man again!	W	W	5	3	
Phil Mickelson	4	2	2	2	(Won 1996)
Davis Love	35(!)	10	3	9	
Jim Furyk	4	10	-	-	

● Phil Mickelson in the last five years has an amazing record

> from 1996 it reads W-2-2-2-4

> seventeen of those twenty rounds at or under par

> five-year stroke average of 68.4

● Shigeki Maruyama, put up here last year in the Rest of The World market, was T3rd at 20/1 this year. He was T2nd 25/1 in 1998 and 4th in 1999. He'll be thereabouts in this market again in 2000.

● Players whose profiles refer to this tournament include Phil Mickelson, Shigeki Maruyama, J M Olazabal, Stewart Cink, Robert Allenby, Notah Begay, Jim Furyk and Tiger Woods.

THE WORLD GOLF CHAMPIONSHIPS
AMERICAN EXPRESS STROKE PLAY CHAMPIONSHIP

Date	9th - 12th November
Course	Valderrama, Satogrande, Spain
Par	72
Yardage	6,791
First Prize	£690,400
Total Purse	$5 million

THE TOURNAMENT

This is the third and final World Golf Championship of the year with the prize money counting on the respective money lists of all the World's tours. The top 50 in the world rankings plus 'the best of the rest' from the five tours competed.

This year the number of acceptances was falling faster than the Euro as Mickelson, Duval, Sutton, Love, Azinger, Couples, Norman and ole uncle Tom Lehman all withdrew. All the fifty-five players receive a healthy cheque as there is no halfway cut.

THE COURSE

Beautifully maintained Valderrama provides a real test. The greens are fast, in great condition and bentgrass. The wind can get up in the afternoon and become a serious factor. As usual the 17th with its watery grave was crucial in R4.

2000 ODDS

fav	11/8	Tiger Woods (DC)	80/1	Dudley Hart
	12/1	Lee Westwood	100/1	Phillip Price
	16/1	Ernie Els	100/1*	Robert Allenby
	20/1	Colin Montgomerie	100/1	Mark Calcavecchia
	22/1	Darren Clarke	100/1	Jose Coceres
	25/1	Vijay Singh	100/1	Chris DiMarco
	33/1*	Michael Campbell	100/1	Scott Hoch
	33/1	Sergio Garcia	100/1	Jeff Maggert
	40/1	Nick Price	100/1	Gary Orr
	40/1	Padraig Harrington	100/1	Kirk Triplett
	40/1	M A Jimenez	125/1	Andrew Coltart
	50/1	Justin Leonard	125/1	Shigeki Maruyama
	50/1	J M Olazabal	125/1	Paul McGinley
	66/1	Steve Flesch	150/1*	Duffy Waldorf
	66/1	Angel Cabrera	150/1	Rocco Mediate
	66/1*	Pierre Fulke (PWW)	150/1	Mathias Gronberg
	66/1	Bernhard Langer	150/1	Franklin Langham
	66/1	Chris Perry	150/1	Joe Ozaki
	66/1	Jesper Parnevik	150/1	Dennis Paulson

66/1	Stuart Appleby	150/1	Peter Senior
66/1	David Toms	250/1*	Lucas Parsons
66/1	Thomas Bjorn	250/1*	Hidemichi Tanaka
66/1	Mike Weir	250/1**	Nobuhito Sato
80/1	Carlos Franco	250/1	Darren Fichardt
80/1	Retief Goosen	250/1	Kyi Hla Han
80/1	Eduardo Romero	300/1*	Nic Henning
80/1	Scott Verplank	500/1**	Tjaart Van der Walt
80/1	Bob May		

ALL QUOTED

2000 RESULT

1	66/1	**Mike Weir**	68 75 65 69 277
2	12/1	**Lee Westwood**	72 72 68 67 279
T3	28/1	**Vijay Singh**	71 70 71 68 280
T3	150/1*	**Duffy Waldorf**	70 69 72 69 280
T5	33/1	**Sergio Garcia**	69 74 74 64 281
T5	40/1	**Padraig Harrington**	66 72 73 70 281
T5	40/1	**Nick Price**	63 72 74 72 281
T5	fav 11/8	**Tiger Woods**	71 69 69 72 281

9	M Campbell	72 71 69 70 282			D Toms	70 75 72 72 289
10	M Calcavecchia	72 67 69 75 283			M A Jimenez	74 73 70 72 289
T11	S Flesch	71 72 73 68 284			C Montgomerie	75 67 73 74 289
	B May	71 69 72 72 284			J Leonard	72 74 69 74 289
	H Tanaka	71 66 70 77 284		T35	B Langer	75 69 76 70 290
T14	K Triplett	72 73 71 69 285	.		Joe Ozaki	72 76 71 71 290
	J Coceres	70 71 74 70 285			R Goosen	69 75 74 72 290
16	Chris Perry	68 72 75 71 286			P McGinley	70 77 70 73 290
T17	F Langham	68 74 76 70 288		39	J Maggert	72 71 75 74 292
	D Clarke	74 70 74 70 288		T40	D Fichardt	76 80 69 68 293
	A Coltart	67 75 74 72 288			T Bjorn	70 77 71 75 293
	Nic Henning	69 74 73 72 288		T42	P Fulke	75 77 73 69 294
	J M Olazabal	70 76 69 73 288			M Gronberg	74 70 79 71 294
	A Cabrera	74 74 67 73 288			P Senior	73 77 72 72 294
	S Hoch	67 76 71 74 288		T45	L Parsons	78 72 75 70 295
	Phillip Price	73 72 69 74 288			Dennis Paulson	75 71 72 77 295
T25	C DiMarco	74 74 73 68 289			C Franco	69 77 71 78 295
	S Appleby	72 76 71 70 289		T48	S Verplank	71 80 76 70 297
	G Orr	71 74 73 71 289			Dudley Hart	72 76 73 76 297
	R Allenby	69 76 73 71 289		T50	S Maruyama	71 77 78 72 298
	N Sato	73 73 72 71 289			T Van Der Walt	76 73 75 74 298
	E Romero	71 72 74 72 289		52	K H Han	75 74 77 77 303

R Mediate, J Parnevik and E Els all withdrew.

ROUND BY ROUND LEADERBOARD

FIRST ROUND

N Price	9 under
P Harrington	6 under
S Hoch	5 under
A Coltart	5 under
M WEIR	4 under
F Langham	4 under
C Perry	4 under

SECOND ROUND

N Price	9 under
H Tanaka	7 under
P Harrington	6 under
D Waldorf	5 under
M Calcavecchia	5 under
M WEIR	1 under

THIRD ROUND

H Tanaka	9 under
M WEIR	8 under
M Calcavecchia	8 under
T Woods	7 under
N Price	7 under
D Waldorf	5 under
P Harrington	5 under

FINAL ROUND

M WEIR	11 under
L Westwood	9 under
V Singh	8 under
D Waldorf	8 under
N Price	7 under
T Woods	7 under
P Harrington	7 under
S Garcia	7 under

RESULTS IN OTHER MARKETS

TOP REST OF THE WORLD

1	16/1	M Weir
2	7/1	V Singh
3	8/1	N Price

TOP EUROPEAN

1	fav 7/2	L Westwood
T2	12/1	P Harrington
T2	12/1	S Garcia

TOP (W/O TIGER)

1	33/1	D Waldorf
2	16/1	M Calcavecchia
T3	8/1	S Flesch
T3	12/1	B May

OUTRIGHT WITHOUT WOODS

1	50/1	M Weir
2	7/1	L Westwood
T3	16/1	V Singh
T3	66/1	D Waldorf
T5	18/1	N Price
T5	25/1	P Harrington
T5	20/1	S Garcia

PUNTERS' POINTS

● In-form 66/1 Mike Weir, star of the Internationals in the Presidents' Cup, recovered from a disappointing wind-swept 75 in R2 to shoot 10 under for the last 36 holes to deservedly win this World Championship event.

● Defending champion Tiger Woods, still not at his best, had his usual problems at the 17th and finished a well-beaten favourite.

● Nick Price was still in with a real chance until he visited the water twice at the 17th in R4 to take a triple bogey.

● Lee Westwood in trouble at the 17th in R4 (made a 'great six') deservedly won the European Order of Merit after a superb 68-67 finish.

WINNERS OF THE WGC AMERICAN EXPRESS STROKE PLAY CHAMPIONSHIP

1999   Tiger Woods
2000   Mike Weir

PUNTERS' GUIDE

● In 2001 this tournament moves to the Bellerive Country Club in St Louis, USA, and in 2002 to the Jack Nicklaus-designed Mount Juliet course in County Kilkenny in Ireland. So next year there will be no recent course form for punters to study.

● After two years the players with the best form (successive top 10s) in this tournament are :-

	1999	**2000**
Tiger Woods	W	T5
Nick Price	T4	T5
Lee Westwood	T4	2nd
Sergio Garcia	T7	T5

● A couple of players are worth noting in each of the speciality markets

> Top European

   * Lee Westwood 2nd 9/1 1999, Won 7/2 2000

   * Sergio Garcia 3rd 6/1 1999, T2nd 12/1 2000

> Top Rest of The World

   * Nick Price W7/1 1999, 3rd 8/1 2000

   * Vijay Singh 2nd 7/2 1999, 2nd 7/1 2000

THE MAJORS 20000   PART 6

THE 64TH US MASTERS

Date	6th - 9th April
Course	Augusta National, Augusta, Georgia
Par	72
Yardage	6,985
First Prize	$650,000
Total Purse	$3.5 million

THE TOURNAMENT

This is the only major to be held each year at the same venue. It has massive prestige with the winner receiving the coveted green jacket. However the 'Ayatollahs of Augusta' allow only limited TV coverage and this year changed the qualification rules so that Kiwi star Michael Campbell, together with seven winners from the previous twelve months on the USPGA tour, were not invited. The 96-strong field contained several 'ceremonial golden oldies' as well as six amateurs!

THE COURSE

There were further changes to Augusta this year. So since Woods's record-breaking runaway win in 1997 the course has been 'Tiger-proofed'. The fairways are narrower and the 'rough' (the second cut) has been introduced. The key to Augusta is the ability to position the ball on the right part of the very difficult, very fast undulating bentgrass greens and then to maintain your patience.

2000 ODDS

fav	5/2	Tiger Woods	50/1	Vijay Singh
	16/1	David Duval	66/1	J M Olazabal (DC)
	18/1	Colin Montgomerie	66/1	Darren Clarke
	22/1	Davis Love	66/1	Sergio Garcia
	25/1	Ernie Els	66/1	John Huston
	25/1	Phil Mickelson (PWW)	66/1	Greg Norman
	28/1	Jim Furyk	80/1	Bernhard Langer
	33/1	Tom Lehman	80/1*	Mark O'Meara
	33/1	Lee Westwood	80/1	Stewart Cink
	33/1	Nick Price	80/1	Lee Janzen
	40/1	Hal Sutton	80/1	Scott Hoch
	40/1	Jesper Parnevik	80/1	Carlos Franco
	40/1	Fred Couples	80/1	Steve Elkington
	50/1	Justin Leonard	80/1	Paul Azinger

28 players were best priced at or under 80/1.

2000 RESULT

1	50/1	Vijay Singh	72 67 70 69 278
2	25/1	Ernie Els	72 67 74 68 281
T3	125/1	Loren Roberts	73 69 71 69 282
T3	16/1	David Duval	73 65 74 70 282
5	fav 5/2	Tiger Woods	75 72 68 69 284

6	T Lehman	69 72 75 69 285			Jumbo Ozaki	72 72 74 75 293
T7	D Love III	75 72 68 71 286			N Faldo	72 72 74 75 293
	P Mickelson	71 68 76 71 286			T Bjorn	71 77 73 72 293
	C Franco	79 68 70 69 286			J Leonard	72 71 77 73 293
10	H Sutton	72 75 71 69 287			P Azinger	72 72 77 72 293
T11	N Price	74 69 73 72 288		T37	F Funk	75 68 78 73 294
	G Norman	80 68 70 70 288			J Haas	75 71 75 73 294
	F Couples	76 72 70 70 288			N Begay III	74 74 73 73 294
T14	D Paulson	68 76 73 72 289		T40	S Garcia	70 72 75 78 295
	J Furyk	73 74 71 71 289			M Brooks	72 76 73 74 295
	C Perry	73 75 72 69 289			J Parnevik	77 71 70 77 295
	J Huston	77 69 72 71 289			I Woosnam	74 70 76 75 295
18	J Sluman	73 69 77 71 290			D Clarke	72 71 78 74 295
T19	G Day	79 67 74 71 291			R Goosen	73 69 79 74 295
	P Harrington	76 69 75 71 291		T46	S Gump	75 70 78 73 296
	C Montgomerie	76 69 77 69 291			S Maruyama	76 71 74 75 296
	J Van de Velde	76 70 75 70 291		48	B Jobe	73 74 76 74 297
	B Estes	72 71 77 71 291		T49	S Pate	78 69 77 74 298
	S Stricker	70 73 75 73 291			M A Jimenez	76 71 79 72 298
T25	L Mize	78 67 73 74 292			D Toms	74 72 73 79 298
	C Parry	75 71 72 74 292		T52	R Mediate	71 74 75 79 299
	S Jones	71 70 76 75 292			S Elkington	74 74 78 73 299
T28	M Weir	75 70 70 78 293		T54	D Gossett (am)	75 71 79 78 303
	B Langer	71 71 75 76 293			J Nicklaus	74 70 81 78 303
	D Hart	75 71 72 75 293		56	S Kendall	76 72 77 83 308
	S Cink	75 72 72 74 293		57	T Aaron	72 74 86 81 313

The following players missed the cut (made at 148 - 4 over par)

J M Olazabal	72 77 149		Joe Ozaki	75 77 152
B Tway	77 72 149		L Westwood	77 75 152
D Green (am)	73 76 149		L Janzen	76 76 152
D Waldorf	78 71 149		Paul Lawrie	79 74 153
J Maggert	77 72 149		J Daly	80 73 153
A Baddeley (am)	77 72 149		Hunter Haas (am)	80 73 153
S Hoch	78 71 149		B Crenshaw	79 76 155
A Cabrera	74 76 150		C Coody	81 74 151
S-Y Kim (am)	75 75 150		K Triplett	76 79 155
C Pavin	80 70 150		T Tryba	75 81 156
S Appleby	73 77 150		F Zoeller	82 74 156
M O'Meara	75 75 150		B Watts	78 79 157
B Geiberger	76 74 150		R Floyd	80 78 158
G Player	76 74 150		T Herron	84 74 158
C Stadler	73 77 150		G Storm (am)	83 76 159
T Watson	75 76 151		A Palmer	78 82 160
S Lyle	79 72 151		S Ballesteros	81 81 162
G Hjertstedt	78 73 151		G Brewer	84 78 162

ROUND BY ROUND LEADERBOARD

FIRST ROUND		SECOND ROUND	
D Paulson	4 under	D Duval	6 under
T Lehman	3 under	P Mickelson	5 under
S Garcia	2 under	E Els	5 under
S Stricker	2 under	V SINGH	5 under
S Jones	1 under	S Jones	3 under
P Mickelson	1 under	T Lehman	3 under
R Mediate	1 under		
T Bjorn	1 under		
B Langer	1 under		
V SINGH	level		

WHEN PLAY WAS SUSPENDED ON SATURDAY EVENING

V SINGH	7 under thru 14
D Duval	4 under thru 14
E Els	3 under thru 15
L Roberts	3 under complete
P Mickelson	2 under thru 15
T Woods	1 under complete
M Weir	1 under complete
D Love	1 under complete

THIRD ROUND		FINAL ROUND	
V SINGH	7 under	V SINGH	10 under
D Duval	4 under	E Els	7 under
E Els	3 under	L Roberts	6 under
L Roberts	3 under	D Duval	6 under
T Woods	1 under	T Woods	4 under
D Love	1 under		
M Weir	1 under		
P Mickelson	1 under		

Thursday:	Rock-hard greens and a really swirling wind.
Friday:	Conditions were easier with scores one and a half shots per round lower.
Saturday:	Play was suspended for two hours by a thunder storm. On the resumption the swirling wind and slower greens made conditions very, very difficult for the leading players. The early pre-thunderstorm starters such as Love and Woods had the very best of conditions and so put themselves back in contention. Eight players had to finish R3 early on Sunday.
Sunday:	Conditions were much better, although final day pin placements inevitably caused difficulty.

PUNTERS' POINTS

● Vijay Singh thoroughly deserved his second major victory which was based on

> Being 9 under par on the par 5s.

> Being No. 1 in the tournament for greens in regulation.

> Putting really well, especially on Sunday morning when completing R3.

> Patience and mental control, especially after finding the water on the 11th in R4.

● David Duval once more played really well, but not quite well enough. Twice finding the water — firstly at the 12th in R3 (caused by a sudden gust of wind), and then particularly at the 13th in R4 (when indecisive with his club selection) — effectively killed off his chances.

● 'Boss of the Moss' T3rd Loren Roberts had 16 fewer putts than Singh and made seven of eight sand saves but his lack of length told in the end.

● If the tournament had been played only over the final three rounds the result would have been - 1st Vijay (10 under), 2nd Carlos Franco (9 under) and 3rd Greg Norman (8 under).

● Colin Montgomerie, subject of heavy pre-tournament betting had the worst of the weather from poor tee times in R1 and R2. Nevertheless he stuck it out well to post 69 in R4 to record his third successive top 20 finish. However on his own admission he has still to come to terms with the Augusta greens. His sand save stats (one out of eight) were particularly poor, and only one player had more putts than Monty.

● Phil Mickelson posted another high finish to reward spread backers who sold his finishing position. However he was frankly disappointing when "it really counted" as his game is made for Augusta.

● Tiger Woods was very lucky in R3 when he played early in the day in the very best of the weather whereas the leaders later on played in near impossible conditions. The truth is he never looked like winning.

● Some stats.

> Who was No. 1 for fairways hit? T46th Scott Gump at 82%.

> The best for sand saves? Glen Day with an amazing six out of six.

> For driving distance? Guess who at 300 yards.

> 4th for greens in regulation? T37th Notah Begay.

1999 RESULT			1998 RESULT		
1	66/1	J M Olazabal	1	66/1	Mark O'Meara
2	18/1	Davis Love	T2	33/1	David Duval
3	66/1	Greg Norman	T2	40/1	Fred Couples
T4	100/1*	Bob Estes	4	50/1	Jim Furyk
T4	100/1	Steve Pate	5	150/1	Paul Azinger

WINNERS IN THE LAST TEN YEARS

1991	Ian Woosnam	1996	Nick Faldo
1992	Fred Couples	1997	Tiger Woods
1993	Bernhard Langer	1998	Mark O'Meara
1994	J M Olazabal	1999	J M Olazabal
1995	Ben Crenshaw	2000	Vijay Singh

PUNTERS' GUIDE

● There are now only five players with successive top 20 finishes over the last three years when the course has been 'Tiger-proofed'.

> David Duval   T3rd 2000: T6th 1999: T2nd 1998

> Tiger Woods   5th 2000: T18th 1999: T8th 1998

> Phil Mickelson   T7th 2000: T6th 1999: T12th 1998

> Colin Montgomerie T19th 2000: T11th 1999: T8th 1998

> Jim Furyk   T14th 2000: T14th 1999: 4th 1998

● Does length off the tee really count at Augusta?

> No it doesn't if you look at the double triumph of Olazabal and the victories of Langer, Crenshaw and O'Meara. Indeed this year T3rd Loren Roberts averaged 249 yards off the tee, 51 yards behind Tiger, yet he finished ahead of the World's No. 1.

> Yes if you notice that seven of this year's front 9—Singh, Els, Duval, Woods, Lehman, Love and Mickelson—are all long drivers. Indeed Singh (10 under overall) was 9 under for the par 5s on which effectively he won the tournament.

● Last year I suggested that the 'new' toughened-up Augusta could develop a similar pattern to Sawgrass and the Players' Championship where in ten of the last eleven years the winner had been in the top 3 (or T3rd) after R1.

Here we have seen

> 1999: The first 5 at halfway included the front 3 at the finish.

> 2000: The first 4 at halfway included 3 of the first 4 at the finish.

It is clearly a course, like Sawgrass, where it is very, very difficult indeed to play 'catch-up'.

So the 'New Law of Augusta' is to select a course-proven, winning player who is in the first 3 (or T3rd) at halfway. The point is fully developed in Part 1.

● Overall the changes to the course have made a good start vitally important. So although there are effectively only eighty players in with a semblance of a chance an early R1 tee time is an advantage.

The ideal identikit for Augusta is a player with

> Proven course experience

> Patience

> A good pair of tee times over the first 36 holes
> A rock-solid short game
> Huge length off the tee

● This year only one player in the first 5, 125/1 Loren Roberts, started at or over 66/1. This was in marked contrast to the nineties when exactly half of the players in the first 4 started at 66/1 or greater.

On the 'Tiger-proofed' course in the last three years the winners' prices have been 50/1 2000, 66/1 1999 and 66/1 1998.

● Stanley's last year introduced the concession that stakes would be refunded on outright selections who missed the cut. Absurdly hailed as "the biggest single bookmaker concession in sports betting history" it really is a very minor concession. Last year of the front 18 in the market only Parnevik, and this year of the front 20 only Westwood (known to be ill) and Olazabal missed the cut!

● Players whose profiles refer to this tournament include

> US Players: Ernie Els, Fred Couples, David Duval, Tom Lehman, Carlos Franco, Davis Love, Phil Mickelson, Carlos Franco, Jim Furyk, John Huston, Mike Weir and Bob Estes

> Europeans: Colin Montgomerie, Lee Westwood and Bernhard Langer

---

RESULTS IN OTHER MARKETS

TOP AMERICAN PLAYER

T1	80/1*	Loren Roberts
T1	9/1	David Duval
3	13/8	Tiger Woods
4	20/1	Tom Lehman

1999 RESULT

1	14/1	Davis Love
T2	80/1*	Bob Estes
T2	80/1	Steve Pate
T2	fav 7/2	David Duval
T4	22/1	Phil Mickelson

1998 RESULT

1	33/1	Mark O'Meara
T2	20/1	David Duval
T2	22/1	Fred Couples
4	28/1	Jim Furyk

TOP EUROPEAN PLAYER

T1	7/2	Colin Montgomerie
T1	28/1	Padraig Harrington
T1	40/1*	Jean Van de Velde

1999 RESULT

1	11/1	J M Olazabal
2	fav 7/2	Lee Westwood
T3	11/1	Bernhard Langer
T3	11/2	Colin Montgomerie

1998 RESULT

T1	25/1	Darren Clarke
T1	6/1	Colin Montgomerie
T3	33/1	P-U Johansson
T3	8/1	J M Olazabal

TOP REST OF THE WORLD PLAYER (Non Europeans)

1	7/1	Vijay Singh
2	7/2	Ernie Els
3	14/1	Carlos Franco

1999 RESULT

1	11/1	Greg Norman
T2	40/1*	Carlos Franco
T2	5/1	Nick Price

1998 RESULT

1	3/1	Ernie Els
2	16/1	David Frost
3	14/1	Steve Elkington

TOP AMATEUR PLAYER

In a six-runner field the result was

1	10/3	David Gossett
T2	12/1	Danny Green
T2	7/4	Aaron Baddeley

ON THE HANDICAP

Surrey no longer offer a full handicap on the whole field. Multi-Sports, 50/1 the field, offered the only full handicap list. Their result was :-

1	V Singh
2	L Roberts
3	E Els
T4	D Duval
T4	D Paulson

TIGER WOODS SPECIAL

Corals offered 8/1 about Tiger Woods shooting all 4 rounds in the 60s. A poor price considering he had not shot a <u>single</u> round below 70 in the last two years. The bet lost.

CORALS EUROSTAR AND AMERICAN EXPRESS BETS

These are the special markets in which Corals' list four players to make the cut which they price from 4/1 to 15/2.

They offered four groups of Euro players, and four groups of American players. All eight groups contained at least one player who missed the cut so Corals had a 'skinner'.

PUNTERS' GUIDE TO THE SPECIALITY MARKETS

TOP AMERICAN PLAYER

● American players have won only four of the last eleven US Masters, so if you fancy an American player to do well it really is wise to consider backing him in the Top US Player market rather than in the conventional outright market.

- The player who has dominated this market with three consecutive top 4 finishes is David Duval T1st 9/1 2000, T4th 7/2 1999 and T2nd 20/1 1998.
- The other Americans with outstanding recent form in this market are:-
  > Phil Mickelson: T5th (unplaced) 14/1 2000: T4th 22/1 1999: Won 16/1 1996
  > Davis Love: T5th (unplaced) 14/1 2000: W 14/1 1999: T4th 14/1 1996
- This year Corals, Hills and Multi-Sports opened up a 'Top American without Tiger Woods' market, so expanding punter choice. In that market 8/1 Davis Love and 12/1 Phil Mickelson both finished T4th.

TOP EUROPEAN PLAYER

- Only two European players have been placed in this market in three of the last four years.
  > J M Olazabal: W 11/1 1999: T3rd 8/1 1998: T3rd 5/1 1997
  > Colin Montgomerie: W(dh) 7/2 2000: T3rd 11/2 1999: W(dh) 6/1 1998
- Two-times US Masters champion Bernhard Langer has now made seventeen successive cuts here, and twice in the last four years he's been 'in the frame' in this market — T3rd 11/1 1999 and 2nd 15/2 1997.

TOP REST OF THE WORLD PLAYER

- Canadian Mike Weir was T5th after R3 and I can see him making the frame in 2001. He'll be well worth backing in this market.

THE 100TH US OPEN

Date	15th -18th June
Course	Pebble Beach, Monterey Peninsula, California
Par	71
Yardage	6,846
First Prize	$900,000
Total Purse	$4.5 million

THE TOURNAMENT

This is the second major of the season. Each year it is held on a different course, although they all now meet the same extremely rigorous standards that have resulted in only one player beating par in the last two years. This year was only the fourth time that Pebble Beach had been the venue with 1992 the most recent.

THE COURSE

There was the usual exceptionally tough US Open layout—narrow fairways averaging 30 yards at point of landing, severe three-inch rough and the smallest (bentgrass) greens on the tour. The wind at Pebble added a further severe degree of difficulty. The course had been reduced to a par 71 within the easy par 5 2nd hole becoming a cruel par 4.

2000 ODDS

fav	3/1	Tiger Woods	50/1	Justin Leonard
	14/1	David Duval	50/1	Nick Price
	18/1	Colin Montgomerie	66/1	Fred Couples
	18/1	Phil Mickelson	66/1	Stewart Cink
	20/1	Ernie Els	66/1	Lee Janzen
	25/1	Davis Love	66/1	Greg Norman
	33/1	Jesper Parnevik	80/1*	Carlos Franco
	33/1	Vijay Singh	80/1	John Huston
	33/1	Tom Lehman	80/1	Mark O'Meara
	33/1	Jim Furyk	80/1	Chris Perry
	40/1	Sergio Garcia	80/1	Mike Weir
	40/1	Hal Sutton	80/1	Scott Hoch
	40/1	Lee Westwood	80/1*	Stuart Appleby
	40/1	Darren Clarke	80/1	J M Olazabal

28 players were best priced at or under 80/1

2000 RESULT

1	fav 3/1	Tiger Woods	65 69 71 67 272
T2	20/1	Ernie Els	74 73 68 72 287
T2	100/1	M A Jimenez	66 74 76 71 287
4	80/1	John Huston	67 75 76 70 288
T5	125/1	Padraig Harrington	73 71 72 73 289
T5	40/1	Lee Westwood	71 71 76 71 289

7	N Faldo	69 74 76 71 290
T8	S Cink	77 72 72 70 291
	D Duval	75 71 74 71 291
	L Roberts	68 78 73 72 291
	V Singh	70 73 80 68 291
T12	P Azinger	71 73 79 69 292
	M Campbell	71 77 71 73 292
	R Goosen	77 72 72 71 292
	J M Olazabal	70 71 76 75 292
T16	F Couples	70 75 75 73 293
	S Hoch	73 76 75 69 293
	J Leonard	73 73 75 72 293
	P Mickelson	71 73 73 76 293
	D Toms	73 76 72 72 293
	M Weir	76 72 76 69 293
22	N Begay III	74 75 72 73 294
T23	M Brisky	71 73 79 72 295
	T Lehman	71 73 78 73 295
	B May	72 76 75 72 295
	H Sutton	69 73 83 70 295
T27	H Irwin	68 78 81 69 296
	S Jones	75 73 75 73 296
	Nick Price	77 70 78 71 296
	S Stricker	75 74 75 72 296
	T Watson	71 74 78 73 296
T32	T Kite	72 77 77 71 297
	R Mediate	69 76 75 77 297
	Chris Perry	75 72 78 72 297
	L Porter	74 70 83 70 297

	R Zokol	74 74 80 69 297
T37	W Austin	77 70 78 73 298
	A Cabrera	69 76 79 74 298
	B Clampett	68 77 76 77 298
	L Janzen	71 73 79 75 298
	J Kelly	73 73 81 71 298
	L Mize	73 72 76 77 298
	C Parry	73 74 76 75 298
	T Tryba	71 73 79 75 298
	C Warren III	75 74 75 74 298
T46	T Bjorn	70 70 82 77 299
	S Garcia	75 71 81 72 299
	R Hartman	73 75 75 76 299
	C Montgomerie	73 74 79 73 299
	S Verplank	72 74 78 75 299
T51	M O'Meara	74 74 78 74 300
	W Schutte	74 75 74 77 300
T53	D Clarke	71 75 83 72 301
	K Clearwater	74 74 80 73 301
	J Coston	70 77 80 74 301
56	K Triplett	70 71 84 77 302
T57	D Eichelberger	78 69 77 79 303
	J Green	74 75 77 77 303
59	J Wilson (am)	74 72 82 76 304
60	J Furyk	72 74 84 75 305
T61	B Chamblee	70 77 82 77 306
	C Franco	74 75 75 82 306
63	R Damron	72 73 84 84 313

The following players missed the cut (made at 149 - 7 over par)

Note: The cut reduces the field to the lowest 60 scorers (and ties) and any player within ten strokes of the leader

B Estes	73 77 150
F Funk	76 74 150
Dudley Hart	77 73 150
B Henninger	77 73 150
T Herron	75 75 150
C Pavin	72 78 150
D Pooley	76 74 150
B Gay	72 78 150
M Burke Jr	77 73 150
R Imada	75 75 150
K Johnson	74 76 150
S Appleby	75 76 151
T Armour III	76 75 151
M Brooks	74 77 151

R Barnes	80 73 153
A Bean	77 77 154
D Berganio Jr	77 77 154
R Gamez	75 79 154
D Love III	75 79 154
S Pate	74 80 154
J Cook	79 76 155
J P Hayes	76 79 155
J Nicklaus	73 82 155
D Gossett	78 77 155
J Buha	80 75 155
M Harris	77 78 155
J Reeves	74 81 155
S Gump	74 82 156

B Geiberger	73 78 151	C Beckman	78 78 156
J Maggert	72 79 151	P Gow	77 79 156
F Nobilo	75 76 151	J Sanchez	77 79 156
C Stadler	79 72 151	Z Zorkic	80 76 156
B Jobe	72 79 151	B Langer	77 80 157
C Campbell	74 77 151	S Maruyama	77 80 157
M Slawter	77 74 151	J Sandelin	77 80 157
M Gogel	72 79 151	M Malizia	76 81 157
C Kaufman	76 75 151	G Day	77 80 157
B V Orman	76 75 151	J Lee	79 78 157
J Daley	83 69 152	J Levitt	79 78 157
D Frost	76 76 152	F Lickliter	81 77 158
J Kaye	74 78 152	J McLuen	79 79 158
J McGovern	76 76 152	E Whitman	82 76 158
J Sluman	78 74 152	J L Lewis	77 82 159
J Van de Velde	76 76 152	G Norman	77 82 159
E Fryatt	78 74 152	C A Spence	76 83 159
D Kestner	74 78 152	R Stimmel	76 83 159
P Goydos	71 82 153	G Davidson	81 79 160
A Magee	74 79 153	M Troy	79 81 160
J Parnevik	73 80 153	C Renner	85 76 161
B Quigley	75 78 153	C Strange	81 81 162
C Tidland	77 76 153		

*John Daly, after a 14 (!!) at the 18th in a R1 83, withdrew!

ROUND BY ROUND LEADERBOARD

FIRST ROUND

T WOODS	6 under
J Huston	4 under
B Clampett	3 under
H Irwin	3 under
L Roberts	3 under
N Faldo	2 under
H Sutton	2 under

SECOND ROUND

T WOODS	8 under
T Bjorn	2 under
J M Olazabal	1 under
K Triplett	1 under
J Huston	level
H Sutton	level
L Westwood	level

THIRD ROUND

T WOODS	8 under
E Els	2 over
P Harrington	3 over
M A Jimenez	3 over
P Mickelson	4 over
J M Olazabal	4 over

FINAL ROUND

T WOODS	12 under
M A Jimenez	3 over
E Els	3 over
J Huston	4 over
P Harrington	5 over
L Westwood	5 over

- On Thursday play was abandoned because of fog with seventy-five players still to complete R1.

- R1 was completed on Friday and R2 started but not completed again because of fog.

- On Saturday the tournament got up to date with itself as R2 and R3 were both completed. The wind, and so the scoring, was high.

- On Sunday there was little breeze with lower scoring as nineteen players shot par or better compared to just three in R3!!

FINAL DAY BETTING (without Tiger Woods)

Ernie Els	(+2)	9/4	T1st
Phil Mickelson	(+4)	6/1	
Padraig Harrington	(+3)	8/1	T4th
M A Jimenez	(+3)	8/1	T1st
J M Olazabal	(+4)	12/1	
Lee Westwood	(+5)	12/1	T4th
John Huston	(+5)	16/1	3rd

Place odds differed a lot — Stan James 1/4 1-4, Multi-Sports 1/5 1-4, Hill & Ladbrokes 1/4 1-3.

The winner, Tiger Wood's odds were

Pre Tournament	After R1	After R2	After R3
3/1	Evens	N/o	N/o; 14/1 anyone else to win!

PUNTERS' POINTS

● What a win! What a star! What an achievement! Tiger Woods' total domination of his sport was shown fully here with a stunning display.

> He led from start to finish

> He won by a record and breathtaking 15 (!!) shots

> He didn't shoot a single round over par despite the difficulty of the course and the windy 'impossible' conditions in R3.

● Let T2nd Ernie Els sum it all up. "The guy is unbelievable, man. I'm running out of words. Give me a break."

● The tournament was a triumph (Tiger apart) for the European tour players who filled three of the top 6 places, and that with Monty way back in T46th place.

> Padraig Harrington, T1st at 28/1 in the Top European market at Augusta, was T2nd at 20/1 in that category here. He called a penalty shot against himself in R2 or he would have finished T4th overall.

> Miguel Angel Jimenez played really well to finish 2nd at 100/1 after his fine top 20 finish last week in the Buick Classic.

> Lee Westwood was the only player (other than Tiger) to shoot only one round over par, to give him form figures of W-2-4-5! He seems to have cured his 'Americanitis' on this trip.

● 7th-placed Nick Faldo finished T4th here in the 1992 US Open and this time he was actually 3rd 'on the handicap'. His rejuvenated form was essentially based on his brilliant putting. Interesting that his sports psychologist, Kjell Enhager, acted as his caddie this week!

● Make a note of Stewart Cink for this tournament on the spreads and in match bets. This year he continued his impressive US Open record which now reads

T16th-T13th-T10th-T32nd-T8th and for the first time he was placed (T3rd at 40/1) in the Top US market.

- The well-fancied Jesper Parnevik's form here can be forgotten as he had a severe hip problem.
- The major effect of this tournament however will surely be to encourage the bookies to open up more 'without Tiger' markets.
  > This year in the outright betting only Corals and Ladbrokes did so.
  > In the Top American market only Hills and Ladbrokes.

So well done to Ladbrokes and let's hope that in future it will become routine for 'without Woods' markets to be created.

1999 RESULT

1	50/1	Payne Stewart
2	40/1	Phil Mickelson
T3	22/1	Vijay Singh
T3	fav 8/1	Tiger Woods
5	66/1	Steve Stricker

1998 RESULT

1	66/1	Lee Janzen
2	80/1	Payne Stewart
3	66/1	Bob Tway
4	66/1	Nick Price
T5	80/1	Steve Stricker
T5	20/1	Tom Lehman

WINNERS IN THE LAST TEN YEARS

1991	Payne Stewart	1996	Steve Jones
1992	Tom Kite	1997	Ernie Els
1993	Lee Janzen	1998	Lee Janzen
1994	Ernie Els	1999	Payne Stewart
1995	Corey Pavin	2000	Tiger Woods

PUNTERS' GUIDE

- The US Open course set up demands all-round skill with the emphasis on solid, accurate ball striking together with the patience and mental strength to accept a bad break or a lipped putt without throwing the toys out of the pram.
- This year the 'usual suspects' with some of the best US Open records, such as Maggert (MC), Furyk (60th), Montgomerie (T46th), Stricker (T27th), Lehman (T23rd) and Janzen (T37th), never got near the leaders.
- The most consistent records are held by
  > Ernie Els   T2nd 2000: W 1997: T5th 1996: W 1994: T7th 1993
  > Tiger Woods   W 2000: T3rd 1999: T18th 1998: T19th 1997
- The key statistical index for this tournament has surely become the all-round ranking – this is computed by totalling a player's rank in the eight major sets of stats.

All-round rank	Player	1999 US Open	
1st	Tiger Woods	T3rd	8/1
2nd	Phil Mickelson	2nd	40/1
3rd	Vijay Singh	T3rd	22/1
4th	David Duval	T7th	10/1

All-round rank	Player	2000 US Open	
1st	Tiger Woods	Won	3/1
2nd	Phil Mickelson	T16th	
3rd	David Duval	T8th	
4th	Ernie Els	T2nd	20/1

If all eight above had been backed each way (at 1/4, 1-5) there would have been a LSP of 9¾ pts, and if all eight had been sold on their finishing positions a tasty profit would have been made on each of the bets.

● Tiger Woods followed Payne Stewart last year as a R3 leader who went on to win. This 'double' broke the earlier pattern that the R3 leader usually lost.

The R3 leader has now lost in twenty-two of the last thirty-six US Opens i.e. 61.1%, equivalent to between 4/6 and 8/13 that the player heading the Sunday morning leaderboard does not win.

● With the US Open course set up so differently from Augusta it is perhaps not surprising that in the last eleven years only one US Masters champion has posted a US Open top 10 finish in the same season: Nick Faldo in 1990 was 3rd in the US Open.

● Last year (p28) I pointed to the useful form guide that is given by the Buick Classic when it was the tournament immediately before the US Open.

		Buick Classic	US Open
1993	Lee Janzen	T3rd	Won
	Payne Stewart	T7th	2nd
1994	Ernie Els	2nd	Won
1996	Tom Lehman	T2nd	T2nd
	Ernie Els	Won	T5th
and now			
2000	Ernie Els	T5th	T2nd
	M A Jimenez	T19th	T2nd

However Jesper Parnevik (T5th), John Cook (T5th) and Greg Norman (4th) were well placed in the Buick this year yet all missed the cut here.

● In 2001 the US Open moves to the Southern Hills Country Club in Tulsa, Oklahoma which played host to the Tour Championship in 1995 and 1996. The players performances then are referred to when relevant in their player profiles.

● The players whose profiles refer to this tournament include:

> US Players: Ernie Els, Steve Stricker, Vijay Singh, Tom Lehman, David Duval, Paul Azinger, Stewart Cink, Bob Tway, Justin Leonard, Scott Verplank and Tiger Woods.

> European Tour: Michael Campbell, Padraig Harrington, Colin Montgomerie, M A Jimenez, Lee Westwood.

RESULTS IN OTHER MARKETS

TOP AMERICAN PLAYER

2000 RESULT

1	15/8	Tiger Woods
2	40/1	John Huston
T3	40/1	Stewart Cink
T3	9/1	David Duval
T3	50/1	Loren Roberts

1999 RESULT

1	40/1	Payne Stewart
2	28/1*	Phil Mickelson
3	fav 5/1	Tiger Woods
4	50/1*	Steve Stricker

1998 RESULT

1	33/1	Lee Janzen
2	40/1	Payne Stewart
3	33/1	Bob Tway
T4	40/1	Steve Stricker
T4	14/1	Tom Lehman

TOP AMERICAN PLAYER WITHOUT TIGER WOODS

2000 RESULT

1	40/1	John Huston
T2	33/1	Stewart Cink
T2	8/1	David Duval
T2	40/1	Loren Roberts

TOP EUROPEAN PLAYER

2000 RESULT

1	22/1	M A Jimenez
T2	20/1	Padraig Harrington
T2	7/1	Lee Westwood

1999 RESULT

1	12/1	Darren Clarke
2	fav 9/4	Colin Montgomerie
3	9/1	Jesper Parnevik

1998 RESULT

1	9/2	Lee Westwood
2	10/1	Jesper Parnevik
T3	8/1	J M Olazabal
T3	fav 11/4	Colin Montgomerie

TOP REST OF THE WORLD PLAYER

2000 RESULT			1999 RESULT		
1	7/2	Ernie Els	1	9/2	Vijay Singh
2	11/2	Vijay Singh	2	6/1	Nick Price
T3	18/1	Michael Campbell	T3	25/1	Craig Parry
T3	40/1*	Retief Goosen	T3	25/1*	Carlos Franco
			T3	50/1	Esteban Toledo

ON THE HANDICAP - 50/1 THE FIELD

2000 RESULT		1999 RESULT	
1	Tiger Woods (scratch)	1	Payne Stewart (+5½)
2	M A Jimenez (+8)	2	Phil Mickelson (+3½)
3	Nick Faldo (+10½)	3	Vijay Singh (+2)
4	Padraig Harrington (+8)	4	Steve Stricker (+5½)
5	John Huston (+6)		

OUTRIGHT BETTING WITHOUT TIGER WOODS

It was disappointing that the only two leading firms priced up this market, so take a bow Corals and Ladbrokes.

2000 RESULT		
T1	12/1	Ernie Els
T1	40/1	M A Jimenez
3	33/1	John Huston
T4	40/1	Padraig Harrington
T4	20/1	Lee Westwood

PUNTERS' GUIDE TO THE SPECIALITY MARKETS

TOP AMERICAN PLAYER

● The best records over the last four years are held by

> Tom Lehman   T4th 14/1 1998: W 14/1 1997

> Steve Stricker   4th 50/1* 1999: T4th 40/1 1998

> Tiger Woods   W 15/8 2000: 3rd 5/1 1999

> Bob Tway   3rd 33/1 1998: T3rd 66/1 1997

● Do compare prices in this market and the outright market as a player may be only fractionally shorter to be Top American than he is to win the tournament.

TOP EUROPEAN PLAYER

● In the last four years the best records are held by

> Colin Montgomerie   2nd 9/4 1999: T3rd 11/4 1998: W 7/2 1997

> Lee Westwood   T2nd 7/1 2000: W 9/2 1998: 3rd 16/1 1997

> Jesper Parnevik   3rd 9/1 1999: 2nd 10/1 1998

> M A Jimenez   W 22/1 2000: 4th 16/1* 1999

> J M Olazabal   T3rd 8/1 1998: 2nd 8/1 1997

- Win bets on Monty in this market over the last three years would all have lost at short prices—7/2, 9/4 and 11/4. With a wider depth of players like Harrington and Jimenez with real chances, the big Scot is becoming poor value at a short price in this market.

- Next year the winds will probably blow at the Southern Hills course and they will improve Padraig Harrington's each-way chance in this market.

TOP REST OF THE WORLD PLAYER

- The best recent records in this market (which has excluded Europeans in the last two years) are held by
  > Ernie Els   W 7/2 2000
  > Vijay Singh 2nd 11/2 2000: W 9/2 1999

- In 2001 at Southern Hills, where Ernie Els and Vijay Singh have played well in the past, they must be expected to dominate this market again.

- However Michael Campbell's performance this year (without the ERC driver he uses in Europe) was eye-catching. He'll be suited to Tulsa and could be the 2001 each-way value in this market.

THE HANDICAP

- Sadly its 50/1 not 66/1 the field in this market in which only Multi-Sports priced up in 2000. Surely with every player given a handicap at least 60/1 the field could be offered in 2001.

- In four of the last five years the tournament winner has also been the winner 'on the handicap', so if you strongly fancy a player to win you can at least get 50/1 'on the handicap'.

- So if your mate tells you he backed Tiger Woods at 50/1 for the US Open.....remember he probably has an account with Multi-Sports.

- The winners' handicaps over the last five years have been Scratch 2000: + 5½ 1999: +6½ 1998: +9 1997: +10 1996.

THE 129TH BRITISH OPEN

Date	20th - 23rd July
Course	Old Course, St Andrews, Fife. Scotland
Par	72
Yardage	7,115
First Prize	£500,000
Total Purse	£2.75 million

THE TOURNAMENT

This is the most prestigious of all the majors and is held each year on a different links course. It provides a completely different examination compared to the US majors. The nature of the tournament is determined to a large extent by how much the wind blows.

THE COURSE

'The Old Lady' has wide fairways, 116 bunkers (many incredibly deep), no real rough and massive (often double) greens. This year the dry fairways meant the course played short and with benign conditions the course's only defences were the bunkers, the pin positions and the fast tricky undulating greens.

2000 ODDS

fav	5/2 Tiger Woods	40/1	Sergio Garcia
	16/1 Ernie Els	50/1	Retief Goosen
	20/1 Lee Westwood	50/1	J M Olazabal
	20/1 Colin Montgomerie	50/1	Nick Price
	25/1 David Duval	50/1	Justin Leonard
	28/1 Phil Mickelson	50/1	Notah Begay
	33/1 Tom Lehman	50/1	Michael Campbell
	33/1 Jim Furyk	66/1*	Hal Sutton
	33/1 Davis Love	66/1	Fred Couples
	40/1 Darren Clarke	66/1	Nick Faldo
	40/1 Vijay Singh	80/1	Padraig Harrington
	40/1 Jesper Parnevik	80/1	Robert Allenby

24 players were best priced at or under 80/1

2000 RESULT

1	fav 5/2	Tiger Woods	67 66 67 69 269
T2	16/1	Ernie Els	66 72 70 69 277
T2	100/1	Thomas Bjorn	69 69 68 71 277
T4	33/1	Tom Lehman	68 70 70 70 278
T4	150/1	David Toms	69 67 71 71 278

6	F Couples	70 68 72 69 279		T Yoneyama	74 69 70 73 286
T7	P Azinger	69 72 72 67 280		J Parnevik	73 69 72 72 286
	P Fulke	69 72 70 69 280	T42	G Orr	72 71 72 72 287
	L Roberts	69 68 70 73 280		R Goosen	72 72 71 72 287
	D Clarke	70 69 68 73 280		J Furyk	69 71 75 72 287
T11	D Duval	70 70 66 75 281		L Parsons	70 72 71 74 287
	M McNulty	69 72 70 70 281		N O'Hern	69 74 70 74 287
	D Love	74 66 74 67 281		J Maggert	72 71 69 75 287
	V Singh	70 70 73 68 281		J Moseley	70 71 70 76 287
	S Appleby	73 70 68 70 281		N Faldo	70 71 75 71 287
	B May	72 72 66 71 281		J Leonard	70 74 72 71 287
	B Langer	74 70 66 71 281		S Cink	69 73 76 69 287
	P Mickelson	72 66 71 72 281	T52	R Mediate	74 69 76 69 288
	Dennis Paulson	68 71 69 73 281		I Garbutt	68 75 70 75 288
T20	S Flesch	67 70 71 74 282		M Weir	75 68 70 75 288
	N Begay	69 73 69 71 282	T55	G Owen	70 74 72 73 289
	P Harrington	68 72 70 72 282		A Coltart	70 72 73 74 289
	S Pate	73 70 71 68 282		D Frost	73 71 71 74 289
	P McGinley	69 72 71 70 282		S Maruyama	68 76 69 76 289
	B Estes	72 69 70 71 282		T Watson	73 71 72 73 289
T26	M O'Meara	70 73 69 71 283	T60	C O'Connor Jr	69 75 72 74 290
	M Calcavecchia	73 70 71 69 283		J Sluman	72 68 75 75 290
	C Montgomerie	71 70 72 70 283		S Elkington	73 69 74 74 290
	M A Jimenez	73 71 71 68 283		K Triplett	73 71 74 72 290
	D Robertson	73 70 68 72 283	T64	D Botes	71 70 76 74 291
T31	J Sandelin	70 70 75 69 284		P-U Johansson	72 69 76 74 291
	S Jones	70 70 72 72 284		L Westwood	70 70 76 75 291
	J M Olazabal	72 70 71 71 284		I Poulter	74 69 73 75 291
	J Van de Velde	71 68 72 73 284	T68	I Woosnam	72 72 73 75 292
35	E Romero	71 68 72 74 285		G Brand Jr	69 72 80 71 292
T36	J Coceres	74 66 69 77 286	T70	T Kite	72 72 76 74 294
	S Garcia	68 69 73 76 286		K Hosokawa	75 69 77 73 294
	R Allenby	72 71 72 71 286	T72	L Alexandre	75 68 76 76 295
	C Parry	72 72 71 71 286		P Senior	71 71 74 79 295

The following players missed the cut (made at 144 - even par)

M Ilonen (am)	74 71 145		S Khan	76 72 148
K Tomori	73 72 145		C Franco	75 73 148
J Spence	74 71 145		S Katayama	71 77 148
S Verplank	72 73 145		J Daly	76 72 148
N Sato	75 70 145		R Chapman	75 73 148
M Campbell	72 73 145		P Rowe (am)	72 76 148
J Carter	72 73 145		C DiMarco	72 76 148
M Lafeber	73 72 145		P Sjoland	76 72 148
S Leaney	75 70 145		Y Mizumaki	74 74 148
H Miyase	72 73 145		A Cejka	78 70 148
F Funk	71 74 145		C Pavin	73 75 148
H Sutton	75 70 145		L Donald (am)	73 75 148
Y Imano	77 68 145		Joe Ozaki	79 70 149

M Farry	72 73 145	S Lyle	71 78 149
A Cabrera	74 72 146	D Gossett (am)	71 78 149
J Huston	76 70 146	T Herron	77 72 149
Phillip Price	75 71 146	Brian Davis	72 77 149
P Eales	74 72 146	Chris Perry	74 75 149
N Price	76 70 146	J M Carriles	77 72 149
S Dunlap	68 78 146	J Nicklaus	77 73 150
S Dyson	72 74 146	R Russell	74 76 150
J-F Remesy	69 77 146	S Watson	76 74 150
M Zerman	76 68 146	M James	76 75 151
Steve Webster	74 73 147	B Tway	73 78 151
A Scott	72 75 147	T Scherrer	77 74 151
David Sutherland	75 72 147	S Little	79 72 151
S Tinning	76 71 147	P Dwyer	76 75 151
L Janzen	75 72 147	K H Han	71 81 152
J Bickerton	75 72 147	Paul Lawrie	78 75 153
W-T Yeh	77 70 147	R Karlsson	80 73 153
T Tryba	73 74 147	A Da Silva	79 74 153
S Ballesteros	78 69 147	P Golding	78 75 153
J Randhawa	73 74 147	J Harris	76 78 154
A Oldcorn	71 76 147	T Johnstone	79 75 154
N Henning	78 69 147	G Emerson	79 76 155
S Stricker	73 74 147	F Jacobson	82 73 155
B Charles	72 75 147	G Player	77 79 156
M Brooks	74 73 147	L Trevino	80 77 157
S Torrance	72 75 147	D Fichhardt	81 76 157
B Marchbank	74 74 148	P Affleck	76 81 157
S Khan	76 72 148	C Gillies	80 80 160

ROUND BY ROUND LEADERBOARD

FIRST ROUND

E Els	6 under
T WOODS	5 under
S Flesch	5 under
S Dunlap	4 under
I Garbutt	4 under
S Garcia	4 under
P Harrington	4 under
T Lehman	4 under
S Maruyama	4 under
D Paulson	4 under

SECOND ROUND

T WOODS	11 under
D Toms	8 under
S Flesch	7 under
S Garcia	7 under
L Roberts	7 under
T Bjorn	6 under
F Couples	6 under
E Els	6 under
P Mickelson	6 under
T Lehman	6 under

THIRD ROUND

T WOODS	16 under
T Bjorn	10 under
D Duval	10 under
D Clarke	9 under
L Roberts	9 under
D Toms	9 under

FINAL ROUND

T WOODS	19 under
E Els	11 under
T Bjorn	11 under
T Lehman	10 under
D Toms	10 under

Tiger Woods' odds

Pre tournament	after R1	after R2	after R3
5/2	11/8	1/3	1/20

PUNTERS' POINTS

● Tiger Woods completed the career Grand Slam in great style. He took the lead early on the second day and was never caught. He plotted his way round St Andrews like an experienced chess grandmaster and by avoiding the bunkers he never looked in any danger.

● At one point on Sunday Duval, playing superbly, got within 3 of the Tiger. However he made bogey at 12th, found a bunker off the tee at the 13th and Tiger went clear. An 8 at the Road hole (17th) put Duval back to finish T11th. He was much, much better than that!

● The enigma of Big Ernie continues. A brilliant opening 66 from an afternoon tee time was followed by a 'poor' par 72. Lapses of concentration continued so he has now finished 2nd in each of this year's majors.

● Dave Toms was this year's 'shock' 150/1 outsider. Playing in his first Open he did well until the pressure told over the back nine in R4 when he came home in 39!

● Let's remember T4th Tom Lehman's performance here. He dropped 2 shots all week and one of those was at the very first hole. In benign, warm conditions the 1996 Open winner loves links golf.

● Monty's woes as usual were on the greens where he 'over-borrowed' with the regularity of a bankrupt beggar!

● Westwood, as predicted in last year's book, had 'his wrong head on' and never showed.

● Forget Parnevik's finish here (T36th). With his left hip playing up and his resultant confidence low it's form that can be completely forgotten.

1999 RESULT

1	150/1	Paul Lawrie

won 4-hole play off by 3 shots

T2	40/1	Justin Leonard
T2	150/1	Jean Van de Velde
T4	200/1	Angel Cabrera
T4	150/1	Craig Parry

1998 RESULT

1	40/1	Mark O'Meara

won 4-hole play-off by 2 shots

2	250/1	Brian Watts
T3	12/1	Tiger Woods
T4	28/1	Jim Furyk
T4	200/1	Raymond Russell
T4	500/1	Justin Rose (am)
T4	50/1	Jesper Parnevik

WINNERS IN THE LAST TEN YEARS

1991	Ian Baker Finch		1996	Tom Lehman
1992	Nick Faldo		1997	Justin Leonard
1993	Greg Norman		1998	Mark O'Meara
1994	Nick Price		1999	Paul Lawrie
1995	John Daly		2000	Tiger Woods

PUNTERS' GUIDE

● As defending champion Tiger will be a very, very short-priced favourite at Royal Lytham St Annes in 2001. 3rd in 1998, T7th 1999 and runaway winner in 2000, he will have an obvious favourite's chance.

● The last time the Open visited the Royal Lytham course was in 1996. The result then was:-

1	Tom Lehman	17 under	T11	Vijay Singh	10 under
T2	Mark McCumber	15 under	T11	Alex Cejka	10 under
T2	Ernie Els	15 under	T11	Darren Clarke	10 under
4	Nick Faldo	14 under	T14	David Duval	9 under
T5	Jeff Maggert	12 under	T14	Paul McGinley	9 under
T5	Mark Brooks	12 under	T14	Shigeki Maruyama	9 under
T7	Fred Couples	11 under	T14	Mark McNulty	9 under
T7	Greg Turner	11 under	T18	Padraig Harrington	8 under
T7	Greg Norman	11 under	T18	Loren Roberts	8 under
T7	Peter Hedblom	11 under	T18	Rocco Mediate	8 under

● Let's remember that the weather and particularly the presence (or absence) of winds is vital in analysing any British Open. This year the conditions were generally calm and conducive to good scoring (fifty-one players beat par).

● The best recent Open records are held by

> Tiger Woods   W2000: T7th 1999: 3rd 1998

> Davis Love   T11th 2000: T7th 1999: 8th 1998: T10th 1997

> Jesper Parnevik   T36th 2000 (ignore): T10th 1999: 4th 1998: T2nd 1997: 2nd 1994

> Tom Lehman   T4th 2000: W 1996

● This year's Loch Lomond form translated well to the links of the British Open.

	Loch Lomond	British Open
Ernie Els	Won	2nd
Tom Lehman	2nd	4th

Nevertheless so far no Loch Lomond winner has gone on to win the British Open.

● If you fancy a long shot in the British Open the recent stats are on your side.

In the last four years of the twenty-three players who finished in the top 5 (or T5th)

> nine (39%) started at or over 150/1

> eleven (47.8%) started at or over 100/1

> thirteen (56.5%) started at or over 66/1

> seventeen (73.91%) started at or over 50/1

● Players whose profiles refer to this tournament include

> US Players: David Duval, Tiger Woods, Ernie Els, Davis Love, Fred Couples, Tom Lehman, Nick Faldo, Loren Roberts, Shigeki Maruyama, Brad Faxon, Jim Furyk and Robert Allenby.

> European Tour: Jesper Parnevik, Darren Clarke, Paul McGinley, Padraig Harrington, Colin Montgomerie, Lee Westwood, Thomas Bjorn, Greg Turner and Mark McNulty.

RESULTS IN OTHER MARKETS

TOP AMERICAN PLAYER

2000 RESULT

1	fav 11/8	Tiger Woods
T2	16/1	Tom Lehman
T2	16/1	David Toms
4	33/1	Fred Couples

1999 RESULT

1	18/1	Justin Leonard
T2	14/1	Davis Love
T2	fav 11/4	Tiger Woods
T4	20/1	Jim Furyk
T4	125/1*	Scott Dunlap
T4	33/1*	Hal Sutton

1998 RESULT

1	22/1	Mark O'Meara
2	150/1	Brian Watts
3	fav 6/1	Tiger Woods
4	14/1	Jim Furyk

TOP AMERICAN PLAYER W/O TIGER WOODS

T1	12/1	Tom Lehman
T1	50/1	David Toms
3	20/1	Fred Couples
T4	40/1	Paul Azinger
T4	28/1	Loren Roberts

TOP EUROPEAN PLAYER

2000 RESULT

1	14/1	Thomas Bjorn
2	66/1	Pierre Fulke
3	14/1	Bernhard Langer
4	14/1	M A Jimenez

1999 RESULT

T1	66/1	Paul Lawrie
T1	100/1	Jean Van de Velde
3	10/1	Jesper Parnevik
4	fav 7/2	Colin Montgomerie

1998 RESULT

T1	150/1	Raymond Russell
T1	100/1	Justin Rose
T1	14/1	Jesper Parnevik
T4	25/1	Costantino Rocca
T4	14/1	Thomas Bjorn

TOP BRITISH & IRISH PLAYER

2000 RESULT

1	7/1	Darren Clarke
T2	33/1	Paul McGinley
T2	12/1	Padraig Harrington
T4	4/1	Colin Montgomerie
T4	66/1	Dean Robertson

1/4 1,2,3,4

1999 RESULT

1	66/1*	Paul Lawrie
2	fav 5/2	Colin Montgomerie
T3	28/1	Andrew Coltart
T3	4/1	Lee Westwood

1998 RESULT

T1	100/1	Raymond Russell
T1	250/1	Justin Rose
3	100/1	Gordon Brand Jr
T4	33/1	Peter Baker
T4	100/1	Des Smyth

TOP REST OF THE WORLD (excl. US & EUROPEANS) PLAYER

2000 RESULT

1	fav 7/2	Ernie Els
T2	10/1*	Vijay Singh
T2	40/1*	Mark McNulty
T2	22/1	Stuart Appleby

1/4 1,2,3,4

1999 RESULT

T1	40/1*	Angel Cabrera
T1	33/1	Craig Parry
3	20/1*	Greg Norman
4	40/1	David Frost

1998 RESULT

1	40/1	Greg Turner
T2	20/1	Robert Allenby
T2	11/1	Vijay Singh
T4	33/1	Peter O'Malley
T4	20/1	Stephen Ames

TOP AUSTRALASIAN PLAYER

2000 RESULT

1	9/1	Stuart Appleby
2	6/1	Robert Allenby
3	12/1	Craig Parry

1/4 1,2,3

1999 RESULT

1	9/1	Craig Parry
2	13/2	Greg Norman
3	16/1	Frank Nobilo
4	12/1	Peter O'Malley

1998 RESULT

1	14/1	Greg Turner
T2	10/1	Robert Allenby
T2	fav 9/2	Vijay Singh

ON THE HANDICAP

Sadly not a single bookie had a full-field handicap!

PUNTERS' GUIDE TO THE SPECIALITY MARKETS

TOP AMERICAN MARKET

● Not surprisingly Tiger 3rd 6/1 1998: T2nd 11/4 1999: Won 11/8 2000 has the best recent record.

● However in 2001 Tom Lehman will be defending his title at Royal Lytham where he led by 6 after R3, and then cruised home to win by 2 in 1996. Especially in the w/o Woods market he must be the selection particularly after his fine effort (only two bogeys) this year.

TOP EUROPEAN PLAYER

● Only two players have posted two top 4 finishes in the last three years

> Jesper Parnevik: 3rd 10/1 1999: T1st 14/1 1998

> Thomas Bjorn: W 14/1 2000: T44th 14/1 1998

● Ignore Parnevik's lack lustre display this year and in 2001 expect Jesper to resume normal service in this market.

TOP BRITISH ISLES PLAYER

● This year Clarke 7/1 and McGinley 33/1 finished 1st and T2nd, and at Royal Lytham back in 1996 Darren finished 2nd at 40/1 and Paul 3rd at 50/1 in this market.

● They must both go well again in 2001 on the shores near Blackpool.

TOP AUSTRALASIAN PLAYER

● The best recent records are held by

> Craig Parry: 3rd 12/1 2000: W 9/1 1999

> Robert Allenby: 2nd 6/1 2000: DNP 1999: T2nd 10/1 1998

● However let's remember that in 1996 at Royal Lytham Greg Turner, who is a fine links player, was T7th in the overall tournament and the highest placed Aussie by some distance. Keep him in mind for a 'shock' in this section in 2001.

The 1996 Royal Lytham & St Annes main speciality market results were:-

TOP US PLAYER			TOP BRITISH PLAYER		
1	20/1	Tom Lehman	1	fav 7/2	Nick Faldo
2	50/1	Mark McCumber	2	40/1	Darren Clarke
T3	33/1	Mark Brooks	3	50/1	Paul McGinley
T3	33/1	Jeff Maggert	T4	500/1	Michael Welch
			T4	66/1	Padraig Harrington

THE 82ND USPGA CHAMPIONSHIP

Date	17th - 20th August
Course	Valhalla G.C., Louisville, Kentucky
Par	72
Yardage	7,167
First Prize	$800,000
Total Purse	$5 million

THE TOURNAMENT

This is the final major of the season. It is the least prestigious of the four and the lightest betting major of all. The field includes twenty-five US club professionals. It is held in humid, sticky conditions so prevalent in August. This year in the event of a play-off there would be a 3-hole mini-tournament, and there was!

THE COURSE

The Valhalla course was last used for the USPGA in 1996. This year the rough had grown and, together with the lightning-fast greens, the course initially provided a test in the usual very warm, very humid conditions. However after heavy rain on Thursday, the temperature dropped and the course was there for the taking if the players found the fairways.

2000 ODDS

fav 7/4	Tiger Woods		50/1	Nick Price
14/1	Ernie Els		66/1	Darren Clarke
16/1	Phil Mickelson		66/1	Fred Couples
28/1	Lee Westwood		66/1	Notah Begay
28/1	Colin Montgomerie		66/1	Greg Norman
33/1	Vijay Singh		80/1*	Loren Roberts
40/1	Tom Lehman		80/1	Paul Azinger
40/1	Davis Love		80/1	Justin Leonard
40/1	Jim Furyk		80/1	Stuart Appleby
50/1	Jesper Parnevik		80/1	Michael Campbell
50/1*	Hal Sutton		80/1	John Huston
50/1	Sergio Garcia			

NOTE: David Duval and Steve Elkington were late withdrawals.

2000 RESULT

1	fav 7/4	**Tiger Woods**	**66 67 70 67 270**

Woods won the 3-hole play-off by a single shot

2	150/1	**Bob May**	**72 66 66 66 270**
3	125/1	**Thomas Bjorn**	**72 68 67 68 275**
T4	80/1	**Stuart Appleby**	**70 69 68 69 276**
T4	100/1	**J M Olazabal**	**76 68 63 69 276**
T4	150/1	**Greg Chalmers**	**71 69 66 70 276**

7	F Langham	72 71 65 69 277			J Sluman	73 69 72 73 287
8	N Begay	72 66 70 70 278			P Stankowski	75 72 68 72 287
T9	D Clarke	68 72 72 67 279			D Toms	72 68 72 75 287
	S Dunlap	66 68 70 75 279		T46	B Henninger	70 74 71 73 288
	F Funk	69 68 74 68 279			B Langer	75 69 73 71 288
	D Love	68 69 72 70 279			S Maruyama	77 69 71 71 288
	P Mickelson	70 70 69 70 279			M O'Meara	71 72 70 75 288
	T Watson	76 70 65 68 279			D Waldorf	75 70 71 72 288
T15	S Cink	72 71 70 67 280		T51	A Coltart	74 71 73 71 289
	C DiMarco	73 70 69 68 280			G Day	76 71 71 71 289
	L Westwood	72 72 69 67 280			N Faldo	79 68 69 73 289
	M Clark	73 70 67 70 280			J Kaye	69 74 71 75 289
T19	R Allenby	73 71 68 69 281			S Lowery	73 74 73 69 289
	J P Hayes	69 68 68 76 281			J Parnevik	72 74 70 73 289
	L Janzen	76 70 70 65 281			B Watts	72 74 73 70 289
	T Kite	70 72 69 70 281			J Ogilvie	73 73 71 72 289
	A Cabrera	72 71 71 67 281		T59	P Harrington	75 72 69 74 290
T24	P Azinger	72 71 66 73 282			Dennis Paulson	72 75 70 73 290
	S Jones	72 71 70 69 282			L Roberts	74 72 71 73 290
	J Sandelin	74 72 68 68 282			C Strange	72 70 76 72 290
T27	B Faxon	71 74 70 68 283			C Franco	72 74 74 70 290
	S Kendall	72 72 69 70 283		T64	B Glasson	73 74 71 73 291
	T Pernice Jr	74 69 70 70 283			W Grady	71 74 68 78 291
T30	S Ames	69 71 71 73 284			J Haas	73 74 68 76 291
	K Perry	78 68 70 68 284			C Stadler	74 69 71 77 291
	M Weir	76 69 68 71 284			M A Jimenez	70 77 74 70 291
	J Van de Velde	70 74 69 71 284		T69	G Kraft	71 73 75 73 292
T34	M Calcavecchia	73 74 71 67 285			K Triplett	76 71 73 72 292
	E Els	74 68 72 71 285		71	J Huston	75 72 74 72 293
	B McCallister	73 71 70 71 285		T72	J Furyk	74 71 74 75 294
	Chris Perry	72 74 70 69 285			P Lawrie	75 71 73 75 294
	S Garcia	74 69 73 69 285		T74	R Damron	72 74 81 70 297
T39	C Montgomerie	74 72 70 70 286			S Hoch	73 70 75 79 297
	T Izawa	73 73 71 69 286			B Mayfair	74 73 76 74 297
T41	J Leonard	73 73 71 70 287		77	R Sabbatini	74 71 76 78 299
	S Pate	75 70 74 68 287		78	Jumbo Ozaki	74 71 76 79 300

The following players missed the cut (made at 147 - 3 over par).

J D Blake	73 75 148	T Smith	78 73 151
B Estes	74 74 148	G Norman	75 77 152
J Kelly	74 74 148	M Gronberg	78 74 152
A Magee	75 73 148	Phillip Price	77 75 152
J Maggert	73 75 148	E Terasa	76 76 152
J Nicklaus	77 71 148	B Geiberger	75 78 153
P O'Malley	74 74 148	E Romero	75 78 153
V Singh	77 71 148	S Stricker	80 73 153
Kevin Sutherland	74 74 148	J Freeman	76 77 153

I Woosnam	73 75 148	R Gaus	76 77 153
S Flesch	76 72 148	C Pavin	79 75 154
R Goosen	75 73 148	J Coceres	75 79 154
E Fryatt	69 79 148	G Turner	77 77 154
G Orr	77 71 148	S Brady	78 76 154
J Blair	75 73 148	B Sherfy	80 74 154
M Brown	71 77 148	R Wilkin	76 78 154
T Dunlavey	76 72 148	C Parry	80 75 155
M Brooks	78 71 149	J Woodward	78 77 155
F Couples	79 70 149	S Katayama	76 79 155
T Herron	72 77 149	J Daly	74 82 156
P McGinley	74 75 149	Joe Ozaki	81 75 156
Nick Price	77 72 149	B Gaffney	79 77 156
H Sutton	74 75 149	M Campbell	84 73 157
T Tryba	75 74 149	M Gill	81 77 158
S Verplank	75 74 149	K Burton	80 79 159
H Frazar	75 74 149	L Wadkins	76 83 159
B Boyd	74 75 149	S Torrance	82 78 160
R Cochran	74 76 150	R Morton	84 78 162
B Tway	77 73 150	R Stelten	85 79 164
E Sabo	78 72 150	T Thelten	85 79 164
S Kelly	74 77 151	J Elliott	87 79 166
K Kimball	75 76 151	T Kelley	84 83 167

Tom Scherrer (77), Rocco Mediate (77), Dudley Hart (79), Tom Lehman (82), Ben Crenshaw (83) and Jim Carter (85) all withdrew

The play-off scores were

	16th hole	17th hole	18th hole
Tiger Woods	Par	Par	Par
Bob May	Bogey	Par	Par

So Tiger Woods won by 1 shot in an exciting, yet poor-quality, birdieless play-off.

ROUND BY ROUND LEADERBOARD

FIRST ROUND

T WOODS	6 under
S Dunlap	6 under
D Clarke	4 under
D Love	4 under
S Ames	3 under
E Fryatt	3 under
F Funk	3 under
J P Hayes	3 under

SECOND ROUND

T WOODS	11 under
S Dunlap	10 under
J P Hayes	7 under
F Funk	7 under
D Love	7 under
B May	6 under

THIRD ROUND

T WOODS	13 under
B May	12 under
S Dunlap	12 under
J P Hayes	11 under
G Chalmers	10 under
T Bjorn	9 under
S Appleby	9 under
J M Olazabal	9 under

FINAL ROUND

T WOODS	18 under
B May	18 under
T Bjorn	13 under
S Appleby	12 under
J M Olazabal	12 under
G Chalmers	12 under

Eighteen players had to complete R1 early on Friday

Ten players had to complete R2 early on Saturday

The winner, Tiger Woods's, best odds through the tournament were:-

Pre-tournament	After R1	After R2	After R3	Before play-off
7/4	4/7	1/4	4/9	4/9

EUROPEAN TOUR PLAYERS' PERFORMANCES

Made the cut	Missed the cut
3rd Thomas Bjorn	Sam Torrance (+16)
T4th J M Olazabal	Michael Campbell (+13)
T9th Darren Clarke	Jose Coceres (+10)
T15th Lee Westwood	Greg Turner (+10)
T19 Angel Cabrera	Eduardo Romero (+11)
T24th Jarmo Sandelin	Phillip Price (+8)
T30th Jean Van de Velde	Mathias Gronberg (+8)
T34th Sergio Garcia	Paul McGinley (+5)
T39th (!) Colin Montgomerie	Retief Goosen (+4)
T46th Bernhard Langer	Ian Woosnam (+4)
T51st Andrew Coltart	Peter O'Malley (+4)
T51st Jesper Parnevik	Gary Orr (+4)
T59th Padraig Harrington	
T64th M A Jimenez	
T72nd Paul Lawrie	

PUNTERS' POINTS

● A below-par Tiger Woods still managed to win his third successive major when he successfully defended his USPGA title. Ultimately it was Bob May's tendency to push his shots from the tee when faced with the winning post that cost him dear over the last 3 holes and in the play-off.

● Tiger's achievements are now truly staggering (please see his Player Profile) and, like a good football team that wins when not playing well, he relied on his in-built 'hate to lose' competitiveness to finally secure his win.

● Nevertheless three successive 66s was a superb effort from Bob May who had only just returned from Britain after a first-class defence (T5th) of his Victor Chandlers British Masters title.

● Thomas Bjorn recorded his second successive top 3 in a major after finishing a distant T2nd to Tiger in the British Open.

● Two players in contention felt the pressure in R4.

> Scott Dunlap T2nd after R3 played with Tiger, shot 75 in R4 to finish T9th

> J P Hayes 4th after R3, shot 76 to finish T19th.

● Jose Maria Olazabal had missed his last three USPGA cuts, and his last two cuts this year, yet he found his form and the fairways after the Thursday rain to be the clear 'winner' over the final 54 holes at 16 under, including that brilliant 63 in R3.

1999 RESULT			1998 RESULT		
1	fav 7/1	Tiger Woods	1	50/1	Vijay Singh
2	66/1*	Sergio Garcia	2	66/1	Steve Stricker
T3	100/1	Stewart Cink	3	100/1	Steve Elkington
T3	150/1	Jay Haas	T4	20/1	Nick Price
5	33/1	Nick Price	T4	33/1	Mark O'Meara
			T4	100/1	Frank Lickliter

WINNERS IN THE LAST TEN YEARS

1991	John Daly	1996	Mark Brooks
1992	Nick Price	1997	Davis Love
1993	Paul Azinger	1998	Vijay Singh
1994	Nick Price	1999	Tiger Woods
1995	Steve Elkington	2000	Tiger Woods

PUNTERS' GUIDE

● In the last three years seventeen players have finished in the top 5, eight (or 47%) have started at or over 100/1 and eleven (64.7%) at or over 66/1.

In the pre-Tiger days this was traditionally the tournament for upsets and clearly it still is.

● The pre-Tiger (pre-1999) formula for finding the USPGA winner was well proven.

> An experienced player in his thirties

> A player seeking his first major win

> A player with sound recent form

There had been eleven first-time winners, and eleven winners in their thirties in the thirteen years up to and including 1998.

● This tournament clearly does provide a stage for experienced, in-form players yet to win a major to perform well, as May, Bjorn, Chalmers and Appleby showed again this year.

● This year an early R1 tee time was so important in providing momentum for players. In 2001 make sure if you have a pre-tournament outright bet that he has a nice, early start on day one.

● Best recent tournament records (two top 20s in the last three years) are held by six players:-

	2000	1999	1998
> Guess who?	W	W	10
> Lee Westwood	15	16	MC
> Nick Price	MC	5	4
> Stewart Cink	15	3	MC
> Davis Love	9	49	7
> Robert Allenby	19	MC	13

● There were three players this year who had shown the greatest improvement in their all-round stat ranking in the three months leading up to the USPGA—T7th Franklin Langham, T4th Greg Chalmers and T15th Chris DiMarco. It's a stat attack to remember in 2001.

● Players whose profiles refer to this tournament

> European Tour: Lee Westwood, Thomas Bjorn, P-U Johansson, M A Jimenez and Angel Cabrera

> American Players: Robert Allenby, Stuart Appleby, Notah Begay, Stewart Cink, David Duval, Steve Flesch, Jesper Parnevik, Phil Mickelson, Vijay Singh, J P Hayes, Mike Weir and you know who!

RESULTS IN OTHER MARKETS

TOP AMERICAN PLAYER

2000 RESULT

1	fav 10/11	Tiger Woods
2	80/1	Bob May
3	100/1	Franklin Langham
4	33/1	Notah Begay

2000 RESULT (w/o Woods)

1	80/1	Bob May
2	80/1	Franklin Langham
3	28/1	Notah Begay
T4	80/1	Fred Funk
T4	fav 6/1	Phil Mickelson
T4	20/1	Davis Love
T4	100/1	Scott Dunlap
T4	125/1	Tom Watson

1999 RESULT

1	fav 4/1	Tiger Woods
T2	50/1	Stewart Cink
T2	80/1	Jay Haas
4	100/1	Bob Estes

1998 RESULT

1	40/1	Steve Stricker
T2	20/1	Mark O'Meara
T2	80/1	Frank Lickliter
T4	50/1	Billy Mayfair
T4	20/1	Davis Love

TOP EUROPEAN PLAYER

2000 RESULT

1	33/1*	Thomas Bjorn
2	20/1	J M Olazabal
3	12/1	Darren Clarke
4	5/1	Lee Westwood

1999 RESULT			1998 RESULT		
1	16/1	Sergio Garcia	1	33/1	P-U Johansson
2	fav 11/4	Colin Montgomerie	2	14/1	Ian Woosnam
T3	28/1	M A Jimenez	3	jt fav 7/2	Colin Montgomerie
T3	15/2	Jesper Parnevik			

TOP REST OF THE WORLD PLAYER (excl. US & European)

2000 RESULT

T1	16/1	Stuart Appleby
T1	40/1	Greg Chalmers
T3	20/1	Robert Allenby
T3	40/1	Angel Cabrera

1999 RESULT			1998 RESULT		
1	13/2	Nick Price	1	8/1	Vijay Singh
2	66/1	Mike Weir	2	22/1	Steve Elkington
3	50/1	Greg Turner	3	jt fav 3/1	Nick Price
4	40/1*	David Frost			

PUNTERS GUIDE TO THE SPECIALIST MARKETS

Top American Player

> Davis Love, T4th (w/o Woods) 20/1 2000: T4th 20/1 1998: W 22/1 1997, and of course Tiger himself W 10/11 2000: W 4/1 1999 have the best recent records.

> Stewart Cink, T2nd 50/1 in 1999, and T15th in the outright this year, must be considered in this market (without Woods) in 2001, especially as the tournament will be played in Georgia where he lives.

Top European Player

Two players to consider at big prices in this market in 2001 would be :-

> Per-Ulrik Johansson. Did not qualify this year. However in this market in his last four USPGAs he has a solid record—2nd 40/1 1996 and Won 33/1 1998.

> Miguel Angel Jimenez. Nowhere near his best (T64th) this year. However his USPGA record in this market on his three previous starts T3rd 28/1, 3rd 40/1 and 2nd 25/1, suggests he will be worth a little each way in 2001.

Rest of The World Player

The players with the outstanding records in this market Nick Price (missed cut this year) and Steve Elkington (rarely fit these days) may give way from now on to 'younger bloods'.

> Angel Cabrera. Progressive form in this event T41st (1999) and T19th (2000) on his only starts, and T3rd at 40/1 in this market this year.

> Robert Allenby. A real 'class act'. T3rd at 20/1 this year in this market and he'll be past 30 at tee time (let's hope it's early) for the 2001 USPGA and in with a real chance.

THE PRESIDENTS CUP   PART 7

Date	19th - 22nd October
Course	Robert Trent Jones G.C., Lake Manassas, Virginia
Par	72
Yardage	7,315

THE TOURNAMENT

This is a match-play competition with ten foursomes (alternate shots) and ten fourballs before the twelve final-day singles. Hence there are 32 points at stake, so 16.5 is a winning total. Unlike the Ryder Cup, however, a tie is not possible because if the final score was level at 16 each the tie would be settled by a sudden-death play-off between two players designated in advance by the captains.

THE COURSE

This course was used for the previous two American stagings of this tournament and at 7,315 it is very long. The signature hole is the par 3, 190-yard 11th across water. The sloping, bentgrass greens were ludicrously quick, especially on the first day.

THE TEAMS (with the Players' odds to be top points scorer alongside each name)

UNITED STATES		INTERNATIONALS	
2/1	Tiger Woods	3/1	Ernie Els
5/1	David Duval	13/2	Vijay Singh
7/1	Phil Mickelson	10/1	Nick Price
11/1	Davis Love	12/1	Greg Norman
14/1	Hal Sutton	12/1	Stuart Appleby
16/1	Jim Furyk	12/1	Michael Campbell
16/1	Loren Roberts (wild card)	12/1	Mike Weir
16/1	Tom Lehman	16/1	Shigeki Maruyama
25/1	Stewart Cink	16/1	Retief Goosen
25/1	Paul Azinger (wild card)	16/1	Robert Allenby (wild card)
33/1	Notah Begay	20/1	Steve Elkington (wild card)
50/1	Kirk Triplett	20/1	Carlos Franco

Team Captains: Ken Venturi and Peter Thompson

ODDS 1/2   United States
          15/8 Internationals

DAY BY DAY RECORD

Thursday Foursomes (US names first)

P Mickelson and T Lehman beat G Norman and S Elkington 5 and 4

H Sutton and J Furyk beat S Appleby and R Allenby 1 up

S Cink and K Triplett beat M Weir and R Goosen 3 and 2

D Duval and D Love beat C Franco and N Price 1 up

N Begay and T Woods beat V Singh and E Els 1 up

FIRST DAY SCORE   United States 5   Internationals 0

Friday morning Fourballs

H Sutton and P Azinger lost to M Campbell and R Goosen 4 and 3

T Lehman and L Roberts lost to M Weir and S Elkington 3 and 2

J Furyk and D Duval lost to N Price and G Norman 6 and 5

T Woods and N Begay lost to C Franco and S Maruyama 3 and 2

P Mickelson and D Love beat V Singh and E Els 2 and 1

SECOND MORNING SCORE   United States 1   Internationals 4

TOTAL SCORE   United States 6   Internationals 4

Friday afternoon Foursomes

S Cink and K Triplett beat R Allenby and S Appleby 2 and 1

P Azinger and L Roberts beat C Franco and S Maruyama 5 and 4

T Woods and N Begay beat V Singh and E Els 6 and 5

H Sutton and T Lehman beat M Campbell and R Goosen 3 and 2

P Mickelson and D Duval lost to M Weir and N Price 6 and 4

FRIDAY AFTERNOON SCORE   United States   4   Internationals 1

END OF SECOND DAY SCORE   United States 10   Internationals 5

Saturday afternoon fourballs

H Sutton and J Furyk beat G Norman and M Campbell 6 and 5

T Lehman and P Mickelson beat M Weir and S Elkington 2 and 1

D Duval and D Love beat N Price and E Els 3 and 2

K Triplett and S Cink beat R Allenby and C Franco by 1 hole

T Woods and N Begay lost to R Goosen and V Singh 2 and 1

SATURDAY SCORE   United States 4   Internationals 1

GOING INTO THE SINGLES

THE SCORE WAS   United States 14 Internationals 6

Final day singles

Paul Azinger lost to Robert Allenby 2 and 1

David Duval beat Nick Price 2 and 1

Loren Roberts beat Stuart Appleby 3 and 2

Phil Mickelson lost to Mike Weir 4 and 3

Davis Love beat Ernie Els 4 and 3

Tom Lehman lost to Steve Elkington 1 hole

Tiger Woods beat Vijay Singh 2 and 1

Stewart Cink beat Greg Norman 2 and 1

Hal Sutton lost to Carlos Franco 6 and 5

Jim Furyk beat Shigeki Maruyama 5 and 4

Kirk Triplett halved with Michael Campbell

Notah Begay beat Retief Goosen 1 up

SINGLES SCORE	United States 7½	Internationals 4½
FINAL MATCH SCORE	United States 21½	Internationals 10½

INDIVIDUAL POINTS SCORER BETTING

US Points Scorer					**International points Scorer**			
T1	25/1	Stewart Cink	4 pts		1	12/1	Mike Weir	3 pts
T1	11/1	Davis Love	4 pts		T2	20/1	Carlos Franco	2 pts
3	50/1	Kirk Triplett	3½ pts		T2	10/1	Nick Price	2 pts
					T2	16/1	Retief Goosen	2 pts
					T2	20/1*	Steve Elkington	2 pts

MATCH SCORE BETTING

US to win 21½ - 10½ was 50/1

PUNTERS' GUIDE

● The results in this competition have been

1994 Lake Manassas USA 20 - Internationals 12

1996 Lake Manassas USA 16½ - Internationals 15½

1998 Melbourne   USA 11½ - Internationals 20½

2000 Lake Manassas USA 20½ - Internationals 11½

The winning margins have been much greater than in the (always tightly contested) Ryder Cup.

1998 Internationals winning 20½ - 11½ was 150/1**

2000 USA winning 20½ - 11½ was 50/1

● The new player making his debut has been the one to back as the teams' top points scorer at big odds in the recent Presidents Cup.

Internationals 1998 Shigeki Maruyama (debut) Won 40/1* 5 pts

2000 Mike Weir (debut) Won 12/1 3 pts

USA   2000 Stewart Cink (debut) won (dh) 25/1 4 pts

2000 Kirk Triplett (debut) 3rd 50/1 3½ pts

● The 2002 match will be held in South Africa. What odds Gary Player as the Internationals' captain?

PLAYER PROFILES   PART 8

Golf Form Symbols

The symbols and letters are used to indicate features about different players.

🗿 Nappy factor. Child born last year or due this year.

☼ Player at his best in sunny, dry conditions

⛅ A very good player in bad weather

🐎 Proven front runner, well able to take a lead and go on to win a tournament

🍾 Has appeared to lack 'bottle' in a tournament in the last year or two by allowing the final round pressure to effect his play

🎂 Has a significant birthday in 2001, i.e. 29 or 39; 30 or 40, or had one recently in 2000

A Still an amateur

CT On the 'comeback trail' after illness, or after a winless spell

D Disappointing in 2000

F Plays particularly well when fresh after a break

FT Expected to win for the first time in the next year or two

G Almost certain to go on to win tournaments

g Likely to go on to win tournaments

M Has the ability to win a major for the first time in the next year or two

PB Probably past his best and won't win again

S Streak player, capable of low scores when 'on fire'

Y Young player, under 30, of real promise and potential

y Young player, under 30, of some promise and potential

V A 'virgin' golfer ... one who has not yet experienced the thrill for the first time ... of a tour win.

These symbols are used for players on both the European and USPGA tours.

COMMENTARY

1 This year the profiles cover
   * the top 115 on the European Order of Merit
   * the top 125 on the US Money List
   * six players from the BUY.COM tour in America, including the top 3
   * the top 3 players from the Challenge tour in Europe
   * selected other 'name' or promising players

2 The players have been placed in the main tour in which they played in 2000, even if they may switch tours in 2001. So the European tour includes, J M Olazabal, M A Jimenez and Sergio Garcia, and the American tour includes Ernie Els, Nick Faldo, Bob May, Jesper Parnevik and Jean Van de Velde

3. The key abbreviations used include

OM	Order of Merit	T	Tied eg. T4th
ML	American Money list	R	Round eg. R2
*	DYM player	GIR	Greens in regulation (i.e. 2 shots on a
MLD	Mental let down		par 4)
BEF	Best ever finish	PMA	Positive mental association
NIC	Never in contention	FP	Finishing position

4. ECLECTIC means the summation of the player's best individual rounds over a particular period of time, e.g. R1 from one year with best R2 from a different year, and R3 and R4 from a third year.

5. The BUY.COM tour (USA), formerly the NIKE tour, and the Challenge Tour (Europe) are the 'feeder' tours from which players graduate to the main tours.

6. The key stats for The American players include the Tour Championship (but not the American Express tournament). Other stats used are from mid October unless stated.

USING THIS SECTION

I hope you will find the comments, analysis and predictions really helpful. However in using them you should always keep up to date by studying the recent tournament form and the 2001 season's developing stats to spot the players who are improving, suffering a loss of form, improving their putting or slipping down the greens in regulation stats.

Please remember if a player has been highlighted for a particular tournament, and Tiger looks to be a strong favourite, then you can use the 'without Woods' market.

THE EUROPEAN TOUR PLAYERS

STEPHEN ALLAN

Age 27   **Born** Melbourne, Australia **Lives** Bagshot or Melbourne

European tour wins 1, 1998 German Open **Order of Merit** BEF 16th 1998

A problem of stiffening in his hips meant that he didn't post a top 60 finish until mid June when he found his form, subsequently posting high finishes in the Compaq European Grand Prix (T6th), the European Open (T21st), the Loch Lomond (T4th at 125/1 and Top Aussie at 20/1), the Dutch Open (T7th after being R2 leader) and the Victor Chandler British Masters (T11th).

'Babyface' can be very wayward off both tee and fairway although he is a fine putter and a very long (290-yard plus) hitter.

> He's a must each-way bet in the Compaq European Grand Prix where in just two starts his stroke average is 70.62, seven of his eight rounds have been at or under par, and he was T6th in 2000 and T11th in 1997.

> Must have a serious chance in the Wales Open where he finished well this year to be T21st.

> A good links player he obviously enjoys the Noordwijke course where he was T7th in this year's Dutch Open after leading at halfway. Worth following in match bets there and as an outsider (80/1 this year) with a squeak.

> He's at his peak when in continuous play, especially in July to mid August when year in year out he is unquestionably at his best, viz:-

  * 1998 he won his only tournament

  * 1999 two best finishes of the year

  * 2000 two of his three top 10s (T4th and T7th).

Key stat   Ranked 5th (at 290.5 yards) for driving distance.

PETER BAKER   D

Age 33   **Born** Shifnal   **Lives** Wolverhampton

European tour wins 3 – the 1988 Benson and Hedges International after a play-off; 1993 British Masters and 1993 Scandinavian Masters (after a play off) **Ryder Cup** 1993 (4 pts from 5!) **Dunhill Cup** 1993 **Order of Merit** BEF 7th 1993

From 1995 through 1999 he was consistently in the top 35 of the O/M with the prospect of a return to his brilliance of 1993.

However 2000 has been a disappointment. He has posted high finishes in the Alfred Dunhill (T14th), the Qatar Masters (T19th), the Deutsche Bank Open (T17th), the Belgacom Open (T18th) and the Turespana Masters (T15th). His 'big' tournaments were the Spanish Open, where he was T3rd at 100/1*, and the Italian Open, where he was T5th at 66/1.

Always high in greens in reg at 70% plus. His short game, particularly his putting, is like his team Wolves, getting gradually worse each year.

An optimistic 8/1 to make the Ryder Cup side.

> His best chance will be when coming from 'off the pace' as he showed in the Spanish Open with a course record 64 to finish T3rd, whereas in the (rain-reduced) Alfred Dunhill he was T4th after R2 then shot 72 to finish T14th, and in the Belgacom Open he was T5th after R3 then shot 73 to finish T18th.

> His recent record in the Deutsche Bank Open (17th 2000) makes him one to note in match bets and on the spreads in that tournament, especially as he played really well when T4th when the tournament last visited the St Leon Rot course in 1999.

> Could well post a top 5 finish early in the season in the Alfred Dunhill in South Africa where his accurate iron play has resulted in successive top 20 finishes.

> He must have a good chance in the Italian Open in early November. 5th in 1998 and T5th this year on the Is Molas course proves he enjoys the tournament and the course.

Key stat   Ranked 119th for total putting.

SEVE BALLESTEROS   PB D

Age 42   **Born** Spain   **Lives** Spain

Record 80 Worldwide wins incl. 5 majors **Order of Merit** Top 1986, 1988 and 1991

Poor ole' Seve has been given the PB in each of the last four years and sadly he's earned it again in 2000.

His form has been consistent—consistently poor.

At 18 over par (two rounds of 81) the 1980 and 1983 US Masters Champion missed the cut this year at Augusta for the fourth successive year.

In the British Open he missed the cut for the fifth time in a row.

Without doubt he is still charismatic, exciting to watch and the world's Number 1 from car parks, jungle, and assorted undergrowth. His ability to create and make recovery shots is still awesome. Sadly his ability to put himself in need of them still continues. The sad fact is he rarely makes a cut nowadays and he's outside the top 180 for driving accuracy (32%).

Off the tee he is on the wild side of erratic. Ewen Murray's analysis is that his problems essentially start with his address position.

However his short game and his putting is still very good. Indeed he was Europe's No. 1 in both 1998 and 1999 both for average putts per round and putts per green in reg.

> Whenever there is any premium on the accuracy he can be opposed with confidence in 3-ball betting as, in effect, you are backing in a two-runner race.

> It appears that he is too proud to accept the advice that could improve his driving off the tee which in essence is the heart of his problem. Let's hope he can find one big finish from somewhere, although I very much doubt it.

> He was quoted at a joke price of 100/1 to gain a 'wild card' place from Sam Torrance. Surely 1,000,000/1 would be more like the true odds!!

Key stat   This season Seve has not had a single top 50 finish.

JORGE BERENDT   D

Age 36   **Born** Formosa   **Lives** Argentina

European tour wins BEF 2nd 1993 Portuguese Open (lost in play-off) **Challenge tour wins** 2 **World Cup of Golf** 1996 **Order of Merit** BEF 69th 1993

Jorge rejoined the tour, via the Challenge tour, in 1999 when he was 109th on the O/M. He struggled again in 2000 to retain his card. He started the season well with his best finishes of the year in his first five tournaments when he was T13th in the Dubai Desert Classic, T4th at 80/1 in the Rio de Janiero Open and T13th in the Sao Paulo Open.

From April he couldn't get into the top 35 in a single tournament.

He is one of the shortest drivers at just 264 yards. He is very accurate off the tee, although his approach play and his putting (again!) have let him down. Faces a trip to Q School

> Let's remember his straight hitting led to two 5th-place finishes in 1999 and he could well 'make the frame' in 2001 whenever there is a premium on accuracy.

> His game is all about straight driving so he can be considered for match bets in the Dubai Desert Classic (T13th 2000) even though it's moved back to the Emirates course.

Key stat   Ranked 15th for driving accuracy.

JOHN BICKERTON   V FT

Age 31   **Lives** Crowie, Worcs   **Born** Redditch

European tour wins BEF 2nd in 1999 Portuguese Open, and 1999 Compass Group English Open **Challenge tour wins** 1 in 1994 **Order of Merit** BEF 20th 1999

After a stellar year in 1999 he has had a disappointing start to the new millennium.

High finishes were recorded in the Heineken Classic (T18th), the Portuguese Open (T18th), the Dubai Classic (T20th), the English Open (T23rd), the Dutch Open (T17th), the German Masters (T22nd) and the Italian Open (T7th).

His best finish came in the weakly contested Madeira Island Open (T5th at 12/1).

In the Seve Ballesteros Trophy he lost all his three matches, including his singles to Jarmo Sandelin (2 and 1).

His poor year stems from his very poor putting because he is very accurate from tee and fairway. A skinny 4/1 to make the 2001 Ryder Cup side.

> Became a first-time father of a son in late 1999. Expect the 'nappy factor' to kick in in 2001, especially if he can improve his putting. He will then give himself real winning chances, especially when there is a premium on accuracy.

> He'll have an obvious chance at a short price in the Madeira Island Open given his four-year record (T5-T4-T14-T13).

> Can be seriously fancied for the Portuguese Open where he was T16th 1998, 2nd 1999 and top 20 this year when fatigued after the Malaysian Open.

> Worth support in match bets, and as an outsider with a squeak in the Dubai Desert Classic (T20 2000: T15 1999) where his accuracy is so important.

> He will surely win the 2001 Italian Open if he putts better than he did this year. 2nd for greens in reg, he was 46th for putts per GIR. He knows the course from his Challenge tour days so he'll be worth support at 80/1 (this year's price) in Sardinia in early November.

Key stat   3rd (at 78%) for driving accuracy.

THOMAS BJORN   M G 🏇 ⛏

Age 29   **Lives** London   **Born** Denmark

European tour wins 5, 1996 Loch Lomond Invitational, 1998 Heineken Classic and 1998 Spanish Open, 1999 Sarazen World Open, 2000 BMW International **Challenge tour wins** 4, all in 1995 when he was No. 1 on Money list. **World Cup of Golf** 1996, 1997 **Ryder Cup** 1997 in winning team **Order of Merit** BEF 5th 2000

It's been a very good 'nappy factor' year for the Great Dane. 1999 ended really well when he won the Dunlop Phoenix in Japan beating Sergio Garcia in a play-off.

This year he won his fifth European tour event in September when he landed the BMW International at 16/1. He also posted top 5 finishes in the Heineken Classic (2nd at 40/1*), the Canon European Masters (2nd at 10/1) and the German Masters (5th at 22/1).

He also had high finishes in the Dubai Desert Classic (13th), the English Open (17th), the European Open (8th), the Loch Lomond (T19th), the Scandinavian Masters (T23rd) and the Lancome Trophy (T16th).

In America he was T22nd in the Players Championship.

In the Andersen World Match Play he beat Glen Day (1 hole) and Monty (2 and 1) before losing (5 and 4) to the eventual winner Darren Clarke. He finished T10th in the WGC NEC Invitational.

In the Coral Eurobet Seve Ballesteros Trophy he was T2nd top European points scorer at 6/1, scoring 3 points from five matches, although he lost by 1 hole to Lee Westwood in the singles.

In the autumn in the Cisco Matchplay he lost in R1 to Retief Goosen.

However it was in the majors that he made a mega impact. 28th in the US Masters. He was 2nd at halfway in the US Open, then playing with Tiger in near-impossible conditions in R3 he shot 82 and finished the tournament T46th.

Later with that experience actually boosting his confidence he shot four sub-par rounds to finish T2nd at 100/1 in the British Open, and 3rd at 125/1 in the USPGA.

A long hitter at 285 yards he's hit 70% of his greens in reg. His driving accuracy stats (ranked outside top 55) don't reflect the improvement in his driving as a result of the work he has done with his coach Peter Cowen over the second half of the season.

His weakness remains his short game where his sand save stats are poor (outside top 85) and he tends to hit putts rather than stroke them and he can be over-aggressive on the greens.

His neck injury that troubled him in February seems now to be OK. Withdrew from the Belgacom Open (after 3 holes!) with an inflamed left foot.

> 2000 has seen Bjorn take his game to a new higher level so that he is now a world-class player with his confidence really high after a season in which he's won, virtually secured his Ryder Cup place, made every major cut, and posted two top 4 major finishes. There is every reason to expect Thomas will maintain his form in 2001 (especially as he's 30 in February), even if the impact of the 'nappy factor' is reduced.

> This year saw the arrival of 'Major Tom' as he made every cut, shot twelve of his sixteen rounds at or under par and was T2nd in the British Open and 3rd in the USPGA. With his driving now so good he must be given the M symbol as he'll have a serious chance in the last three majors, Tiger permitting.

I believe his best 2001 Major chances will lie in the heat and humidity of the USPGA and at Royal Lytham in the British Open. He can be backed in both tournaments to be the top European.

> This year in the top European markets he's been 2nd 33/1 Players Championship, Won 14/1 British Open, Won 33/1* USPGA and 2nd 6/1 Seve Ballesteros Trophy. That's some record, so do remember him!

> He has real PMAs with the Loch Lomond tournament that gave him his first win. He's well suited to the course so I expect him to play really well in 2001. However as it's the week before the British Open he may be 'tuning up' rather than going flat out.

> Worth backing for the 2001 Dubai Desert Classic. He's lived in Dubai where he met his wife so he'll feel at home at the Emirates course.

> In the first week in February back Bjorn to win the Heineken Classic. 2nd in 2000 and the winner in 1998, he will have an obvious chance.

> He's a certainty for the Ryder Cup in which he's already scored plenty of points.

> Pity he was disappointed when his fellow and wiser Danes opposed the Euro in their September 2000 referendum.

Key stat   His stroke average of 69 for the last two majors in 2000 was bettered only by you know who.

DIEGO BORREGO   D

Age 28   **Born** Malaga   **Lives** Marbella

European tour wins 1, 1996 Turespana Masters **Challenge tour wins** 2, 1993 and 1995 **Dunhill Cup** 1996 **World Cup of Golf** 1996 **Order of Merit** BEF 30th 1996

His 72nd placing in the 1999 O/M was his best since his 'glory' year of 1996 with his stroke average (71.48) his best ever.

However in 2000 he has managed only three significant finishes in the Madeira Island Open (T24th), the Victor Chandler British Masters (T23rd) and notably in the Scandinavian Masters (T4th at 150/1 when 10th in the tournament's putting stats).

Short off the tee at just 270 yards his strength is his driving accuracy, his weakness his short game particularly his bunker play.

Coached by Costa del Sol neighbour, Miguel Angel Jimenez.

> Inconsistent, yet he has posted three punter-friendly top 4 finishes (100/1, 125/1, and 150/1) in the last two seasons when his putter was hot.

> His best chance will be in the weakly contested Madeira Island Open (T4th 1999: T24 2000).

Key stat   110th for putts per round.

GORDON BRAND JR

Age 42   **Born** Scotland   **Lives** Bristol

European tour wins 8, but only one in the nineties, the 1993 GA European Open. **World Cup of Golf** 7 times, last 1994 **Ryder Cup** 1987, 1989 **Dunhill Cup** 10 times, last 1997 **Order of Merit** BEF 4th 1987

Found form from June, making six cuts from his next eight tournaments including T8th in the Wales Open, T14th in the Dutch Open, T68th in the British Open, T22nd in the Compaq European Grand Prix and T25th in the BMW International.

His big tournament came in late October when he finished 2nd at 150/1 in the Italian Open and then the following week finished T14th in the Volvo Masters.

A fine player in bad weather. Plays quickly (refreshing change!).

> His victory in the 1993 European Open was achieved in very heavy rain and we must remember he's a fine wet-weather player.

> He can be noted in match bets and 3 balls for the Dutch Open on the Noordwijkse course where he was 2nd in 1992 and where he shot 63 in R4 when T14th this year.

> Showed by his good form in the Italian Open that he is a fine pressure player (despite a last-hole bogey in R4 66), that he can suddenly find his form (his 2nd place came after three missed cuts) and that he must be given a serious chance of recording his ninth win in 2001.

> His fine end to the season marks him down as a player who is now to be taken seriously again. He topped the greens in reg stats in the Volvo Masters. He could well land a 'shock' win in 2001 when the big names are missing and his putter works.

Key stat   Shot same score 281 in the Volvo Masters at Montecastillo in 2000 as he did there in 1994 when 3rd in the Turespana Masters.

MARKUS BRIER

Age 32   **Born** Vienna, Austria   **Lives** Vienna

European tour BEF T2nd 2000 Spanish Open

Markus is the first Austrian golfer to make the full European PGA tour. He qualified via the 1999 Challenge tour where he was 2nd twice and 3rd three times.

In 2000 he was T13th in the Heineken Classic, T14th in the Qatar Masters, T7th in the Madeira Island Open and then secured his card when T2nd at 150/1* in the Spanish Open in late April. Finished T25th in the Turespana Masters and T13th in the Canon European Masters (four sub-par rounds).

His form from May onwards was generally disappointing.

His stats are uniformly poor for the whole season with putting his main problem.

Uses Claude Grenier as his coach, and former pro cyclist Harry Maier as his mental skills advisor.

> If he can recapture his early season form, and especially his accuracy, he should achieve his goal of retaining his tour card.
> Clearly at his best in the early months of the season.
> His best play this year was in Spain (R1 Turespana Masters leader and T2nd in the Spanish Open).

Key stat   143rd (!!) in putts per green in reg.

ANGEL CABRERA   G V FT

Age 31   **Born** Cordoba, Argentina   **Lives** Cordoba, Argentina

European tour wins BEF 2nd 1996 Oki Pro-Am, 1999 Irish Open, (T2nd) 1999 Benson & Hedges, 2000 European Open **International wins** 2 **Alfred Dunhill Cup** 1997, 1998, 2000 **World Cup of Golf** 1998, 1999 **Order of Merit** BEF 10th 1999

'Pato' is the 31-year-old Argentinian who uses his one-time sponsor Eduardo Romero as his role model. Joined the tour in 1996 and has progressed steadily since.

In late 1999 he started the European tour season well when T9th in the Johnnie Walker Classic, and in the World Cup of Golf he finished T3rd at 50/1 in the individual rankings

In 2000 he played in the World Match play losing 4 and 3 to Duval in R1. Also played in the WGC AmericanExpress at Valderrama, when he was T17th. In the majors he missed the cut in the Masters and the British Open. He finished T37th in the US Open and posted his first US major top 20 when T19th in the USPGA.

On the European tour itself he posted three top 5 finishes when 2nd at 50/1 in the European Open, T3rd at 33/1 in the Dutch Open and T5th at 50/1 in the Volvo Masters.

He also posted top 10s in the Murphy's Irish Open (T10th), the Benson and Hedges (T9th) and the Canon European Masters (T10th), and top 25s in the Rio de Janiero Open (T21st), the Qatar Masters (T14th), the Spanish Open (T21st), the Deutsche Bank Open (T23rd), the Lancome Trophy (T16th), the German Masters (T11th) and the Turespana Masters (T12th).

Scored three wins in his four matches as he helped Argentina reach the Dunhill Cup semi-finals

Hits the ball miles, well 290 yards actually. His one key problem remains his erratic play off the tee where he still hits only five out of every nine fairways.

His putting has also let him down many times shown by his putts per round ranking outside the top100.

Nevertheless he is a very strong, long-hitting, fast-improving and most competitive player.

> With four 2nds already only the occasional wayward tee shot and some errors of course management are holding him back from his first tour win. Expect him to strike gold and land a victory in 2001!

> He simply must be supported in the European Open given his form figures of 2nd 2000: T6th 1999 and T5th 1998. Have a little Angel delight at the K Club and back Cabrera in the outrights and in match bets.

> He obviously enjoys two tournaments in which he's posted high finishes on different courses in each of the last two years.

  * Dutch Open T3rd 2000: T8th 1999

  * Irish Open 10th 2000: 2nd 1999

He'll be worth an each-way bet in both events.

> The Qatar Masters is a tournament for first-time winners and it would be no surprise to see him notch his first victory there in 2001 (T14th 2000: T17th 1998) if he gets an early tee time.

> The wider fairways of the USPGA suit him well. Having posted a fine top 20 this year expect him to do well again in 2001, so support him in match bets and in the Rest of the World market where he was T3rd at 40/1 this year.

> He'll have a very big chance in the 2001 German Masters for two key reasons. Firstly, it'll start just four days after the Ryder Cup, and secondly, Cabrera's length is well suited here as he showed with three rounds in the 60s this year.

> He must have a big chance in the Volvo Masters. The forgiving fairways and four par 5s suit him (No. 1 for driving distance there in 2000). T5th this year, better course management could see him win at 40/1 in 2001 at Montecastillo.

Key stat   2nd for driving distance, 8th for GIR, yet 108th for total putting.

MICHAEL CAMPBELL   G 🐌 💀

Age 31   **Born** New Zealand   **Lives** New Zealand

European tour wins 3, 1999 Johnnie Walker Classic, 2000 Heineken Classic, 2000 German Masters (three rounds only) **ANZ tour wins** 3, 1993 Canon Challenge, 2000 NZ Open, 2000 Ericsson Masters **Challenge tour wins** 3 – all in 1994 **Majors** Famously T3rd 1995 British Open **Dunhill Cup** 1995, 1999, 2000 **World Cup of Golf** 1995 **Presidents Cup** 2000 **Order of Merit** BEF 4th 2000

It's been a mega year for 'Cambo'. It started with his first win on the European tour when he won the Johnnie Walker Classic at 66/1 in November 1999. It continued in January 2000 when he won the New Zealand Open (at 10/1), his own national open "in front of 100 of my relations", and then the Heineken Classic (at 33/1) by 6 shots the very next week. His fourth win since November 1999 followed when he landed the Ericsson Masters at 16/1 on the ANZ tour. He ended the season 'down under' Number 1 on the ANZ Order of Merit.

On the European mainland he had three 2nd places, in the English Open (2nd at 33/1), the Scandinavian Masters (2nd at 25/1) and the Lancome Trophy (T2nd at 25/1) before he won the German Masters at 25/1 in early October. Ahead after R3 the tournament was abandoned giving him his first win on European soil and his FIFTH win in twelve months. Posted another high finish in November when T3rd at 20/1 in the Volvo Masters (63 in R4).

He also had high finishes in the French Open (T7th), the Volvo PGA (T11th), the Loch Lomond (T9th) and the Canon European Masters (T10th).

In the Andersen World Match Play he lost to Tiger Woods (5 and 4) in R1. He finished a very creditable T12th in the US Open. Missed the cut in the British Open, and the USPGA before finishing T15th in the WGC NEC Invitational. Won one of his three games in the Dunhill Cup in the losing New Zealand team. In the Presidents' Cup he scored 1½ points, halving his singles with Kirk Triplett....and did the Haka, and did it well, before the tournament started.

Finished the season with 9th place in the WGC American Express at Valderrama.

His stats reflect the overall excellence of his play. Not overly long at 277 yards off the tee, he's accurate (68-70% for both driving accuracy and GIR) and a brilliant putter, although his sand saves stats (ranked outside top 170) are poor. He must improve his bunker play.

Coached by Jonathan Yarwood. His swing is all poise, balance and rhythm.

Caddie is Michael Waite. Loves playing in the wind and rain.

> Campbell has fully justified the huge confidence shown in his profile last year. Inspired by the 'nappy factor', safely past 30 and now a proven winner there's every reason to expect that he will continue to fulfil his huge potential.

> However, despite having posted five wins in twelve months on three continents doubts remain as, like Geronimo, I have reservations:-

  * Motivation. He admitted that before June, "I'd been lacking a little motivation", so with his family expanding he may find it difficult to get himself really up for some 'ordinary' tournaments.

  * R4 scoring. His nervy final-round play when in contention had dogged him for some years and this year in the French Open (74 in R4) and in the English Open (lost lead over the back nine) those doubts resurfaced.

> Having, self confessedly, been inspired by the birth of his son Thomas he may find that the birth of his second child in November/December 2000 will cause some distraction early in 2001.

> Probably at his best when in continuous play as he can be 'rusty' when returning to Europe after a break, e.g. 77 in R1 at the K Club in the European Open after a two-week break.

> The 2000 Lancome Trophy was won by the fastest finisher over the last three rounds the previous year. If that pattern is repeated you must back Campbell for the 2001 Lancome Trophy (13 under par last 54 holes this year).

> He'll probably return to Europe for the European Open in the first week of July and then, with 'the cobwebs blown away', he'll be a very sound bet for the 2001 Loch Lomond (T9th 2000: T7th 1999) the following week.

> In the Volvo Masters in the last two years he's finished T7th and T3rd. However he shot 70 in R1 (1999) and 73 (this year) so back him after R1 after he's removed the rust!

> He can be followed in match bets and on the outrights for

  * The Scandinavian Masters. 2nd 2000 and 14th in 1999 on the Barseback course which is next year's venue.

  * The Omega European Masters. T10th (2000), T15th (1999).

> In 2000 in mainland European non-majors tournaments he had opened with a round in the 70s eight times, and then followed up with a round in the 60s on seven of those eight occasions for an astonishing R2 stroke average of 68.14.

  It confirms my belief that he's at his best when coming from 'off the pace' so in 2001 the message is clear and potentially very profitable.

  * Back Campbell in R2 3 balls, but only when he has shot 70 plus in R1.

Key stat   2nd for putts per GIR.

EMANUELE CANONICA G Y V

Age 29   **Born** Torino   **Lives** Lucca, Italy

European tour wins BEF 2nd 2000 Deutsche Bank Open **Dunhill Cup** 1996, 1999 **Order of Merit** BEF 27th 2000

Hit his best-ever tour form in a five-week spell from mid-May during which he was a brilliant 2nd at 200/1* in the mega-rich Deutsche Bank Open (67 in R4) and T3rd at 100/1* in the Compaq European Grand Prix (68 in R4).

He notched his third top 5 finish in the BMW International (T5th at 150/1) in early September.

His other high finishes were in the Portuguese Open (9th) and the Spanish Open (T27th).

He's one of the 'diddymen' at 5 foot 2 yet he's a monster driver, finishing top of the driving distance stats (over 295 yards) in both 1998 and 1999. However his accuracy off the tee is improving although it often does not match his length. His putting and sand save stats point to the key ares for improvement. Only 8/1 to make the 2001 Ryder Cup side.

> He's showed improved form over the last two years. Three top 10s in 1999, and his best ever Order of Merit finish after three top 5s in 2000, show he's a player to note. Past 30 in January, he hopes to play in the States in future. Keep your eye on him. He's coached by Butch Harmon and he's a guy improving fast who has considerable potential and could well post his first win in 2001.

> His game is tailor made for the Is Molas course, new home of the Italian Open. He made a fine start (66.69) this year and must be backed at 66/1 in 2001.

> Worth an interest in the Dimension Data Pro-Am in South Africa where he shot his lowest ever round (63) in 1999, and where he finished T3rd at 100/1 in 2000.

> His most consistent form has unquestionably been in the Compaq European Grand Prix on a track suited to his big hitting. His record (T3rd 2000, 11th 1999,

19th 1997) is very good with nine of his last twelve rounds at or below par. Worth noting therel in 3 balls, match bets and as an 80/1 chance with a 'squeak'.

Key stat: Top-ranked player for driving distance in 1999 and 2000.

DAVID CARTER g

Age 28   **Born** South Africa   **Lives** Englefield Green

European tour wins 1, 1998 Irish Open (in a play-off) **International wins** 1, 1996 Indian PGA **Dunhill Cup** 1998 **World Cup of Golf** 1998 (winners) **Order of Merit** BEF 19th 1998

After finishing 33rd (1996 and 1997), 19th (1998) and 27th (1999) on the O/M he has struggled in 2000.

He has posted just three top 25s in the Qatar Masters (T14th), the Compaq European Grand Prix (T22nd) and the Irish Open (T10 and No. 1 for GIR) although his accurate approach play ensured he made the cut in fifteen of his first seventeen events.

His key problem, as usual, has been his (broomstick) putting, although his accuracy from the tee had fallen to slightly below 60% by late summer.

12/1 to make the 2001 Ryder Cup side.

> He 'burst' into form in May and June 1999 when he reduced the use of his shoulders when putting. I expect him to find similar form in 2001. So keep an eye on his putting stats and when they improve.....Get Carter!

> He'll be worth an each-way interest in both the English Open (T3rd, 1999: T26th 2000) and the Compaq European Grand Prix (6th 1997: 2nd 1999: T22nd 2000).

> He simply loves the Irish Open, the tournament that gave him his only win. His record, 10th 2000: 21st 1999: Won 1998: T15th 1997 on different courses, speaks for itself and suggests he's match-bet material in 2001.

> He's posted high finishes (T20th 1997: T14th 1999) when Barseback has been the recent venue for the Scandinavian Masters. He could well cause an 80/1 shock there in early August.

Key stat 28th for greens in reg.

FRANCISCO CEA ☼ g y

Age 26   **Born** Malaga, Spain   **Lives** Malaga, Spain

European tour BEF T3rd 2000 Italian Open **Challenge tour wins** 1, in 1996 **Order of Merit** BEF 58th 1999

2000 had been a really disappointing season for Francisco with just a couple of top 25s, in the Brazil Rio de Janeiro Open (T21st) and the Compaq European Grand Prix (T18th), until he played brilliant golf at the end of October.

He looked a certainty to lose his card and head for Q School. However in the Turespana Masters he finished T5th, and then went on to the Italian Open where he had to post a top 5 finish to save his card. Showing real skill and nerve he recorded his best-ever finish when T3rd at 100/1* including 63 in R2. In both events the weather was good.

Last year he did really well getting into the top 60 on the O/M. However he's tried to readjust his swing and had a bad season until relaxing and reverting to his natural fade. If his end of season putting continues in 2001 he'll have a superb season.

Very short off the tee. At his best in dry warm conditions.

> Let's remember this guy was No. 1 on the stats for driving accuracy in 1999, and has a lot of natural ability. With his confidence high after ending the season with eight consecutive sub-par rounds and successive top 5 finishes and with him back to his natural fade he could well 'breakthrough' in 2001. Highly rated by his peers. Let's keep our eyes open for Cea in 2001.

> Diego Borrego was a Malaga-born guy in his mid twenties when he won the Turespana Masters, and I think Malaga-based Francisco Cea can follow his footsteps and land the 2001 Turespana Masters in mid March.

> He has a fine record in the Italian Open (T6th 1999, T3rd 2000) and he was brilliant on the greens this year (averaged under 25 putts per round) although short off the tee (267 yards). Worth support in R1 3 balls and match bets, and as an outsider with a squeak.

Key stat   This year he finished T5th and T3rd (with a stroke average of 67.75) in his last two tournaments to save his tour card.

ALEX CEJKA   🎂 G D

Age 30   **Born** Marienbad, Czech   **Lives** Prague

European tour wins 3, all in 1995 **Challenge tour wins** 4 **Dunhill Cup** 1994,95,97,98 **World Cup of Golf** 1995,96,97,99 **Order of Merit** BEF 6th 1995

Chay-ka has had a really disappointing year posting only three top 25s, in the Heineken Classic (T18th), the French Open (T22nd) and the BMW International (T25th) before he played well in the Lancome Trophy in September to finish T4th at 100/1.

In the Seve Ballesteros Trophy he lost to Phillip Price 2 and 1, and scored just 1½pts from five games as his putting failed him.

Missed the cut in the British Open.

This year he has struggled because his putting continues to be below the standard of his approach play although his greens in reg figure (78% when he was Europe's No. 1 in 1998) has fallen by 10% in the last two years as his confidence has dropped.

> He will need to recover the putting touch of five years ago if he is to recapture former glories. He is working really hard on his short game with coach Peter Karz.

> He'll be 30 in December 2000 so he could well show improved form early in 2001 and he must surely enter into calculations for the Heineken Classic (T25th

1998: T13th 1999: T18th 2000 after being T3rd after R3) especially in match betting and as a big-priced outsider with a squeak.

> He now suffers from 'contention rust' when in with a serious winning chance as he showed this year in the Heineken Classic when he was T3rd after R3 only to shoot 77 in R4 and finish T18th, and in the Lancome Trophy where he led by 2 shots after R3 then shot par 71 in R4 to finish T4th.

> This year he played a restricted schedule before September because his aim in 2001 is to make the Ryder Cup side so, "I am going to play in every tournament to try to achieve my goal," for which he's started as a 14/1 chance.

> Overall I expect him to win in 2001 as he is a straight-hitting, hard-working and highly motivated player with a definite goal!

> The premium on accuracy now at Crans suits Cejka (3rd 1999: T5th 1998) where he'll have a leading chance in 2001.

> He has an excellent recent record in the Lancome Trophy (T4th 2000: T10th 1999: T11th 1998) in which he can be followed in match bets and as a 66/1 outsider with a real chance.

> He must be put into the serious contender category for the 2001 German Masters as it'll be played right after the Ryder Cup (in which I don't expect him to play) and his stroke average over the last two years (T22nd 2000: T6th 1999) is 69.43. A 'must' for R1 3 balls as he's shot 69 (2000), 66 (1999) since the course was changed.

Key stat   18th for shot accuracy he's 123rd (!) for total putting.

ROGER CHAPMAN   S

Age 41   **Born** Kenyan   **Lives** Windlesham

European tour wins 1, 2000 Brazil Rio de Janiero 500 Years Open. **Order of Merit** BEF 17th 1988 **Dunhill Cup** 2000

Roger Michael, after eighteen successive years on the tour, lost his card in 1999 after his worst-ever year when 125th on the O/M with just one top 10. He regained his card at Q School when 12th.

This year he landed his first win when he beat Padraig Harrington in a play-off to land the Rio de Janiero Open at 150/1 in after shooting 65 in R4. It was his first victory after twelve 2nd places worldwide and six on the European tour.

He also had high finishes in the Moroccan Open (T22nd), Volvo PGA (T13th), the Victor Chandlers British Masters (T23rd), the Scottish PGA (T24th), the Canon European Masters (T23rd), the German Masters (T14th) and the Volvo Masters (T17th).

Won one of his three games on his Dunhill Cup debut for a woeful England side in October.

Had laser surgery after his win in April.

A short hitter at 272 yards, his strength has always been his accuracy to the green.

> He can be followed with some confidence in the Moroccan Open in match bets and as a player who could win from 'off the pace' as his recent record 2nd in 1997, 9th in 1998, DNP 1999 and T22nd 2000 is very good.

> A streaker who can shoot very low numbers in early rounds, and in R4 as he showed this year with 66 (Portuguese Open) and 65 (Rio de Janiero and Victor Chandler British Masters)

> His consistent ball striking makes him a player who should not be opposed in match bets. Made seventeen of first twenty cuts this year.

Key stat   Hit 70% of his greens in regulation (32nd).

DARREN CLARKE M G

Age 32   **Born** Dungannon   **Lives** Sunningdale (next door to Paul McGinley)

European tour wins 6, 1993 Alfred Dunhill Open, 1996 German Masters, 1998 Benson & Hedges, 1998 Volvo Masters, 1999 English Open, 2000 English Open **Majors** T2nd 1997 British Open, **World Golf Tournaments** Winner 2000 Andersen Consulting World Match Play **Ryder Cup** 1997, 1999 **Dunhill Cup** 1994-1999 incl. **World Cup** 1994,95,96 **Order of Merit** 2nd 1998 and 2000

What a year for Darren! He won the Andersen Consulting World Match Play at 80/1 and en route he beat opposition of real quality. In R1 he beat Paul Azinger (2 and 1) who was already a winner this year, in R2 he beat O'Meara (5 and 4), in R3 he beat the tough Thomas Bjorn (1 up), in the QF he faced Hal Sutton who'd beaten him in the Ryder Cup singles and having gone 3 down he fought back to win 1 up. In the semi-final he beat David Duval 4 and 2, before playing Tiger Woods in the final and beating him 4 and 3.

In the Majors he was T40th in the Masters, T53rd in the US Open, T7th in the British Open and T9th in the USPGA.

In the Coral Eurobet Seve Ballesteros Trophy he won 2½ out of his 5 points to finish T2nd at 9/2 as top British scorer. He'd halved his singles with Garcia.

In the Cisco World Matchplay at Wentworth he had a titanic battle with Nick Faldo in R1, eventually beating him at the 40th hole with an eagle. In the QF he lost, when tired, to Vijay Singh 5 and 4.

In the WGC NEC Invitational he finished T17th, and another T17th finish in the WGC Amex at Valderrama meant that Darren had finished 2nd on the European Order of Merit for the second time.

On the European tour he won for the sixth time as he successfully defended his English Open title at 9/1. He also posted six top 5 finishes, in the Volvo PGA (T2nd 16/1), the Compaq European Grand Prix (T3rd at 6/1), the Canon European Masters (3rd at 10/1), the Lancome Trophy (T2nd at 12/1), the Turespana Masters (4th at 10/1) and the Volvo Masters (2nd at 12/1).

He also had high finishes in the Dubai Desert Classic (T17th), the Benson and Hedges (22nd), the Deutsche Bank Open (T15th), the European Open (7th), the Dutch Open (T17th) and the Scandinavian Masters (T23rd).

His stats are uniformly impressive as you'd expect. He's a long hitter with a fine all round game although he can be a little errant off the tee. He's a great medium-range (8-20 foot) putter.

> Cigar smoking Darren is a player I love to watch. He has style, charm, and enormous talent. Yet stablemate Lee Westwood has won as many European tournaments this year as Darren in his career! So you do feel, despite the brilliance of his Andersen World Match Play win, he is an under achiever and he admits it himself "I've had the potential for the past few years but I've had a tendency not to finish things off. I've let a lot of tournaments slip through my fingers."

> Became a father of a second son, Conor Matthew, in late September so 2001 will be his second 'nappy factor' year and I expect Darren to celebrate big style when he wins the 2001 British Open at Royal Lytham.

He finished T11th there when it was last the venue in 1996 when he was 2nd top Brit at 40/1. He's a links player in every way. Brought up on the sandhills of Northern Ireland, "links golf is in my blood....and I'm even sponsored by a links course, the Portmarnock Hotel and Golf Links near Dublin." When the wind gets up Clark is built well to play well.

Let's remember when T2nd in the 1997 British Open he was only half the player he is today. He must have a big chance and can be backed in the outright with a 'saver' on Darren to be top Brit.

> Expect Darren to make a bold bid for the 2001 US Masters. He likes the set up, the fast greens and, of course, he won the Match Play in the States last year. His best eclectic score over the last three years at Augusta is 9 under (72-71-67-69) which would place him firmly in contention.

> He can be fancied for the valuable Deutsche Bank Open as it will be played on the Heidelburg course where he finished 7th when it was last the venue in 1999.

> He will be going for a three-peat in the English Open. He loves the Forest of Arden course where his record is first class (T4th in 1993,1995 and 1996: Won 2000). Monty won three Volvo PGAs 'on the bounce' so Darren could well do the same in the English Open in 2001.

> Whisper it.......an Irishman hasn't won an Irish tournament on the European tour since 1982! However he'll have a mega chance at the K Club in early July. Form figures of 7-2-4 for a three-year stroke average of 70.16, including a course record 60 (R2 in 1999), surely suggest that Irish eyes will be smiling after the European Open ends on 8th July!

> In early September I expect Darren to walk away with the Omega European Masters. This year he missed countless putts yet still finished 3rd, next year I can visualise him holing a few early on before strolling to an easy win....now that's confidence for you, or is it just stupidity??

> He cries out to be backed each way for the Volvo Masters. In the last three years he's finished 1st, T5th and 2nd with nine of his twelve rounds in the 60s for a stroke average of 68.08!

> He's a certainty to make the Ryder Cup side for the Belfry where he'll be a most important part of Sam's team.

Key stat   He beat both the World No. 1 (Tiger Woods) and the World No. 2 (David Duval) when winning the 2000 Andersen Consulting World Match Play Championship.

RUSSELL CLAYDON   D

Age 35   **Born** Cambridgeshire   **Lives** Cambridgeshire

European tour wins 1, 1998 BMW International **Dunhill Cup** 1997 **Order of Merit** BEF 20th 1997.

After two years in the top 25 in the O/M 1997 and 1998 (when he won for the first time) his form has slipped over the last two years.

In 2000 he posted just one top 25 when finishing 8th in the Dubai Classic.

The problem has been his long game off tee and fairway with driving accuracy and greens in reg stats in 'intensive care' outside the top 150. However his bunker play and putting are still very good.

His poor form may be linked to the new Claydon diet - "you eat badly for ten years and then sensibly for six months and it falls off you".

Looks intelligent but supports Spurs. Now he must go to Q School.

> 1994-1998 he was permanently in the top 40 on the O/M so it is sad to see the new slimline Russell doing so poorly.

> If his early season driving accuracy and greens in reg stats show him in the top 60, his fine short game will ensure that he posts high finishes again.

> In the hope that that happens he retains the streaker symbol as he can shoot very low numbers, and let's also remember his 1998 victory came after three missed cuts in his previous four starts so he can strike form very quickly especially on a wide fairway, receptive green course.

Key stat   166th for driving accuracy.

JOSE COCERES   G

Age 37   **Born** Argentina   **Lives** Argentina

European tour wins 2, 1994 Catalonian Open and 2000 Dubai Desert Classic **International wins** 6 Dunhill Cup 1993,95,97, 2000 **World Cup of Golf** 1989,1997 **Order of Merit** BEF 13th 2000

It's been a brilliant year for Jose. He was T2nd in late 1999 in the Argentinian Open (his ambition is to win it!) and followed a fitness regime in the winter.

He then exploded onto the European tour to win his first event the Dubai Desert Classic at 125/1 leading throughout. He followed that with a T7th in the Qatar Masters, and 3rd at 20/1 in the Rio de Janiero Open.

He maintained his form later when T3rd at 50/1 in the Benson and Hedges after which he led the tour's stroke averages. T13th in the French Open, T13th in the

European Open, T22nd at Loch Lomond, T23rd at the Canon European Masters, T16th in the Lancome Trophy and T26th in the Belgacom Open were his other big finishes before he finished 2nd at 80/1* in the rain-reduced German Masters. In the Dunhill Cup he won three of his four matches as he helped Argentina reach the semi finals. Went on to finish T14th in the WGC Amex at Valderrama.

Finished T36th in the British Open (77 in R4) and missed the cut by a mile in the USPGA on his debut in a US major.

Jose has two really great strengths - his accuracy off both tee and fairway and his low ball flight which makes him a superb player in the wind. His weakness has always been his putting.

> Jose will surely find in 2001 that his accurate approach play will once more put him in serious contention.

> Must be followed in the European Open (13th 2000: 6th 1999: 20th 1998) especially if the wind blows.

> He is 'unexposed' in the Dutch Open at Noordwijkse having missed the cut there this year when very tired after the British Open. He was T2nd in 1993 on the Noordwijkse track and he'll worth a serious bet there in 2001 if not in contention the previous week in the British Open.

> If he gets an early tee time he could well land the 2001 Qatar Masters at a big price in the gusty conditions at Doha.

> He's a must for match bets in the Lancome Trophy where his recent record (T16-T15-T18 in the last three years) suggests he'll also be worth a couple of bob each way at 80/1 in the outrights.

> He can be backed with confidence for the 2001 German Masters. With the top Euros suffering post-Ryder Cup let down and on the course where he was 2nd in 2000 (with a three-round stroke average of 66) Jose could well be the 50/1 winner.

Key stat   2nd for driving accuracy and 3rd for greens in reg.

ROBERT COLES

Age 28   **Born** Hornchurch   **Lives** Hornchurch
European tour BEF T7th 2000 French Open **Order of Merit** BEF 111th 1996

Regained his card at the 1999 Q School. However 2000 has been a struggle although he's had two top 10s, in the French Open (T7th) and the Wales Open (T8th). He also posted top 20s in the Rio de Jainero Open (T17th) and the North West of Ireland Golf Classic (T11th), and a top 25 in the Portuguese Open (T24th).

Inaccuracy off the tee has been Robert's main problem this year although his game all round can obviously be considerably improved.

Badly injured in a late-1998 car crash (fractured ribs) he is now fully fit. Looks intelligent but supports West Ham and Joe Cole! Must now go to Q School.

> Up to September he'd made eleven cuts and had a final round in the 60s in six of them which is encouraging should he get into serious contention in 2001.

> Must come into calculations for the Welsh Open where he was brilliant in three of his four rounds this year. He led after a 64 in R1 then went 79(!)-67-69 to finish T8th. So with the 'big guns' missing he could reward each-way support in the 2001 Welsh Open.

> He clearly loves the French Open, where he's posted two top 10s (T7th 2000: T8th 1997) so keep him in mind for 3 balls and match bets even though the tournament moves to a new venue in 2001.

> He'll have a sound chance in the weakly contested West of Ireland Golf Classic (T11th 2000).

Key stat   124th for driving accuracy.

ANDREW COLTART   G 🌧

Age 30   **Born** Dumfries   **Lives** Richmond

European tour wins 1, 1998 Qatar Masters **Challenge tour** 1, 1994 Scottish PGA **International tour wins** 2, Australian PGA in 1994 and 1997 **Dunhill Cup** 1994,95,96,98, 2000 **World Cup** 1994,95,96,98 **Ryder Cup** 1999 **Order of Merit** 7th 1996

In 1998 he won for the first time on the European tour and for the second time on the ANZ tour, and then last year he made his Ryder Cup debut and became a first-time dad, of a daughter.

In 2000 Andrew had four top 5 finishes, in the Greg Norman Holden International (T3rd at 66/1*), the Benson and Hedges (T3rd at 66/1), the Volvo PGA (T2nd at 66/1) and the Victor Chandler British Masters (T5th at 50/1).

He also posted top 20s in the Spanish Open (17th), the Wales Open (14th), the Compaq European Grand Prix (18th) and the Volvo Masters (T10th), and top 25s in the Heineken Classic (25th) and the Scandinavian Masters (T23rd).

He was T55th in the British Open, T51st in the USPGA, a promising 17th in the WGC NEC Invitational and T17th in the WGC Amex at Valderrama. Won two of his three games in the Dunhill Cup to give him a career record of twelve from seventeen.

His stats paint a picture of a player who is very accurate with his irons (72% greens in reg), yet misses countless birdie chances (not in the top 140 for putts per GIR).

Not a long hitter at 268 yards. Can be over self-critical.

> A player with a sound swing he has now posted eleven punter-friendly top 5 finishes in the last three years on the European tour. If he can regain his putting touch he can win again in 2001.

> He can be supported for the 2001 Heineken Classic in a tournament in which he's played well in recent years (T25th 2000: T13th 1999: T15th 1998).

> Coltart will have a serious chance in three big tournaments that all start in May 2001.

> * Worth each-way support for the 2001 Benson and Hedges. T3rd this year when his final three rounds (8 under par) were the second best in the

tournament. The Belfry suits his straight hitting.....if his putter works he could win!

* Last year I nominated the Volvo PGA as his 'best chance', and so it proved when he was T2nd at 66/1. So having a good recent record, (T5th 1998 and 2nd 2000) on a course suited to his straight hitting, he can be supported for the 2001 Volvo PGA in match bets, on the spreads, and each way in the outrights.

* T5th in The Victor Chandler British Masters this year he'll be suited by the new Marquess course when that tournament starts on the last day of May.

> In the last three years at Montecastillo he's finished T10th (2000), T26th (1999) and 2nd (1998) for a three-year stroke average of 69.25. Keep him in mind there especially for match bets.

> He'll have a really big chance in the weakly contested Wales Open where he finished T14th this year, after a 65 in R3.

> 7/4 to make the 2001 Ryder Cup team, and 10/1 to be given a 'wild card'.

Key stat   10th for greens in regulation.

BRIAN DAVIS   g y

Age 26   **Born** London   **Lives** Enfield

European wins 1, 2000 Spanish Open **Dunhill Cup** 2000 **Order of Merit** BEF 29th 2000

In his rookie year, 1997, he had three top 10s; 1998 four top 20s, and in 1999 two top 10s and in 2000 he notched his first tour victory in April in the Spanish Open at 100/1*.

This win followed good early season form when T3rd at 100/1* in the Portuguese Open, T5th at 80/1* in the Qatar Masters, T10th in the Alfred Dunhill (R1 leader after) and T16th in the South African Open.

He went on to finish T13th in the Deutsche Bank Open, T6th in the English Open and T25th in the BMW International. Lost all his three matches representing England for the first time in the Dunhill Cup.

Missed the cut in the British Open.

His success this season has been based on superb putting.

His bunker play has been poor, and he has hit only five out of every nine fairways this year as he did last. Long hitter 280 yards+. 10/1 to make the 2001 Ryder Cup side

Born in London, the poor lad supports Arsenal.

> Having represented England at boy, youth and top amateur levels he has progressed consistently over recent years and will continue to do so, especially if he can improve his accuracy off the tee.

> He has a sound record in Germany and will be an outsider with a squeak in the 2001 Deutsche Bank Open (T13th 2000) when it returns to the St Leon Rot course where he was T5th in 1999.

> Worth an interest in the English Open (T6th 2000) where he was 11 under par for his last three rounds this year.
> He could well 'make the frame' at a big price in the 2001 Scandinavian Masters having finished fast (T9th) when the Barseback course was last the venue in 1999.

Key stat   6th for total putting.

MARK DAVIS

Age 36   **Born** Essex   **Lives** Essex

European tour wins 2, both in Austria, the last in 1994 **Order of Merit** BEF 31st 1994

Mark didn't play for ten months in 1999 following a serious knee injury. After visiting specialist Volker Smasal he underwent extensive surgery and physio, and this year he has played on a medical exemption.

He was T2nd in the Madeira Island Open and had three other high finishes, T14th in the Moroccan Open (66 in R4), T10th in the Irish Open (9 under last 54 holes) and T13th in the European Open. Disqualified in the Scandinavian Masters (wrong drop from a water hazard) in August. Troubled by a wrist injury in the autumn that forced him to withdraw from the BMW International (after 6 holes at level par) in September and to pull out on the eve of the Turespana Masters in October.

Very erratic off the tee, he gets 'up and down' from bunkers only four times in every nine attempts. His strength has always been his putting, indeed he was Europe's No. 1 in 1994.

Became a first-time father of a son last year. Will probably start 2001 on a medical exemption.

> Very good, often brilliant, putting and 'nappy factor' inspiration could enable Davis to make his Mark in 2001 with at least a top 5 finish and, just maybe, a win.
> Fits the bill for the Madeira Island Open (T2nd 2000) as an experienced player in his thirties with course form.
> He must be considered in two tournaments with which he has PMAs
  * The Portuguese Open (T2nd 1996: T10th 1995)
  * The Moroccan Open (T4th 1998: T14th 2000)

Key stat   171st for driving accuracy.

BRADLEY DREDGE

Age 27   **Born** Wales   **Lives** Newport, Gwent

Challenge tour wins 2, 1997 & 1998 **European tour** BEF T6th 2000 Irish Open.

Started on the tour in 1998 but lost his card after missing the cut in fifteen of his twenty-two starts. In 1999 he regained his playing privileges after finishing 8th on the Challenge tour following a season which included a victory.

In 2000 Brad has struggled to retain his card for the first time, although he did post his first-ever tour top 10s, in the Madeira Island Open (T7th), the Moroccan Open (T8th) and the Irish Open (T6th). He also had a top 25 in the Portuguese Open (T24th).

A member of Barry Hearn's Matchroom Golf Management group.

A longish hitter at 275 yards, his inconsistent performances are reflected in his stats in all of which he's outside the top 120.

> He has a very poor R1 scoring record with only a single sub-70 start in his first twenty-one tournaments.

> He was in the top 20 in the 1999 South African Open and he'll be keen to make a fast start in 2001 by doing so again.

Key stat   Only 141st in the all-round ranking.

PAUL EALES

Age 36   **Born** Epping   **Lives** Preston

European tour wins 1, 1994 Extremadura Open **Challenge tour wins** 1 in 1991 **Order of Merit** BEF 35th 1994

Paul has struggled for much of this year, although he played well early on in the South African Open (T13th) and the Rio de Janiero Open (T13th). It was all downhill (no top 35 finishes) after that for Preston Paul until he was T30th in the Lancome Trophy in September and T30th in the rain-reduced German Masters on 1st October. Paul saved his card when T12th in the Italian Open in late October.

Missed the cut in the British Open.

His stats tell the full story of a player who from tee to green is still in the top 20 on the tour. However on the putting surface he's totally lost it! Very, very short off the tee at 262 yards.

> A thorough professional and a doting, devoted dad to son Joshua, it's now a question of putting. If Paul can get the flatstick working again he can make an impact as he's a very, very straight hitter and a fine player in windy conditions.

> Maybe in his late thirties he's thinking of an alternative career as he's started radio broadcasting.

> Let the pressure get to him in this year's South African Open where he was joint halfway leader and 3rd after R3 only to finish T13th.

Key stat   14th for driving accuracy yet 164th (!) for total putting.

OLIVIER EDMOND

Age 30   **Born** France   **Lives** France

European tour BEF T2nd 1998 French Open **European Challenge tour wins** 1, in 1997 **Dunhill Cup** 1998 **Rookie of the Year** 1998 when 93rd on O/M.

2nd place in his native Paris in the French Open in 1998 was the basis for his 93rd place on the O/M and his award as the Rookie of the Year in which he'd made eleven of fifteen cuts.

In 1999 however he made just two cuts in eleven starts after illness curtailed his season, so he returned this year on a medical exemption.

He's posted three top 20s in the Portuguese Open (T18th), the Qatar Masters (T14th) and the Volvo PGA (a creditable T7th).

Ranked in top 40 for length, his problem has been his inaccuracy off the tee. A good bunker player.

Third child, and second son born in 1999.

> Having overcome testicular cancer he'll be keen to follow the example of Trevor Dodds on the USPGA tour who also overcame the illness and then landed his first victory.

Key stat   143rd for driving accuracy.

GARY EMERSON **V**

Age 36   **Born** Bournemouth   **Lives** Salisbury

European tour wins BEF T5th 1995 Canaries Open **Challenge tour wins** 1 in 1998 **Order of Merit** BEF 96th 2000

Gary's annual struggle to retain his card has continued in 2000. He had five top 25s, in the Malaysian Open (T23rd), the Volvo PGA (T17th), the Compaq European Grand Prix (T12th), the Belgacom Open (T12th) and the Turespana Masters (T25th), and a top 10 in the North West of Ireland Classic (T7th).

He achieved his seventh career hole in one in the Heineken Classic where he finished T64th.

A long hitter at 280 yards and a solid putter, his waywardness off the tee (not in top 150 for driving accuracy) is still his major problem.

> When he got into serious contention for the Belgacom Open (T5th after R3) he shot 72 in R4 to finish T12th.

> There is only one tournament in which Gary can be expected to play really well, and in which he can be backed place only and supported in match bets.

  It's in the weak field in the West of Ireland Classic where in its two years he's finished T6th 1999 and T7th 2000.

Key stat   In over 135 starts he's yet to post a top 4 finish.

GARY EVANS **V**

Age 31   **Born** Rustington   **Lives** Worthing

European tour wins BEF 2nd 1992 Turespana Masters **Order of Merit** BEF 35th in 1992 (Rookie year)

Gary's had an 'interesting' year having travelled to the Portuguese Open to find he'd not entered: travelled to Brazil hurt his back and came home, and after R2 the

Spanish Open his hotel room was burgled, he was up till 2 a.m., and then shot 77 in R3 before finishing T7th.

His other high finishes were in the Heineken Classic (T25th), the Greg Norman Holden International (T17th), the English Open (T17th), the Belgacom Open (T26th), the Turespana Masters (T19th) and the Italian Open (T21st), with his top 10s in that Spanish Open (T7th, 2nd after R2 when burgled) and the European Open (T8th).

Short off the tee at 258 yards. His bunker play has been good this year. Still seeking his first win.

> Undoubtedly has the ability to land his first European tour win in 2001 in one of the lesser events.

> He's shown sufficient form in the Compaq European Grand Prix (T4th 1996, 6th 1997, T3rd when abandoned 1998) to suggest he'll have an each-way chance in 2001.

> Career record of 57% cuts made makes him a dodgy match bet proposition.

Key stat   175th for driving distance at 261.4 yards.

MARC FARRY   D V

Age 41   **Born** France   **Lives** France

European tour wins 1, rain-reduced 1996 BMW International **Dunhill Cup** 4 times latest 1999 **World Cup of Golf** 6 times, latest 1999. **Order of Merit** BEF 49th 1999

After his best-ever year in 1999 Marc has struggled in 2000. He took six weeks to recover from bronchitis early in the season. Later he posted top 20s in the English Open, where he was T12th after a fast finish (8 under for his last three rounds), and in the Lancome Trophy (T16th) and had three other top 30s, in the Wales Open (T29th), the European Open (T28th) and the Victor Chandler British Masters (T23rd).

Saved his card when he was T7th in the Belgacom Open in late September.

He missed the cut in the British Open.

Fairly long off the tee at 276 yards. His greens in reg stats (outside top 150 at 60%) and his putts per greens in reg (outside top 100) give the reasons for his disapointing season.

> It is virtually impossible to see Marc winning his first 72-hole tournament in 2001 given his poor stats and the likelihood that when in serious contention he will let the pressure get to him as it did in the 1999 French Open where he hooked under pressure after leading by 2 shots with 20 holes to play to finish T8th.

> He has played steadily at Gut Larchenhof in the last two years (T17th 1999: T30th 2000) with a R1 68, R3 66 and R4 69, so he must be noted in 3 balls for the German Masters.

Key stat   145th for shot accuracy.

NICLAS FASTH

Age 28   **Born** Sweden   **Lives** Sweden

European tour wins 1, 2000 Madeira Island Open **Challenge tour wins** 4, 1 in 1999 and 3 in 1993 **Order of Merit** BEF 45th 2000

Made a big mistake in 1998 when having gained his US tour card he tried to play both tours. However, totally focussed on Europe a year later he won on the Challenge Tour in 1999 and finished 2nd at Q School to regain his card.

In 2000 posted his first win at 66/1* in the Madeira Island Open, leading from start to finish, and he played very well to be 4th at 125/1 in the Canon European Masters. He also had high finishes in the Portuguese Open (T14th), the Spanish Open (T7th), the Benson and Hedges (T22nd), the Loch Lomond (T29th), the Victor Chandler British Masters (T20th) and the BMW International (T25th with four sub-par rounds).

His two key weaknesses are driving accuracy (outside top 125) and sand saves (outside top 150). 7/1 to make the 2001 Ryder Cup side.

> Plays well on the Iberian Peninsula where he's been top of the Q School in 1996 at San Roque, and last year had good finishes in the Spanish (T7th) and Portuguese (T14th) Opens, so keep him in mind as a long shot in those tournaments.

> Finished well to make the top 25 this year in the Benson and Hedges. He could make the frame at a huge price next year in that event.

> 14 under par over the final 54 holes (2nd best in the tournament) when 4th in this year's Canon European Masters he will be worth each-way support at Crans in 2001.

Key stat   133rd for driving accuracy.

ALISTAIR FORSYTH   S

Age 24   **Born** Glasgow   **Lives** Paisley

Winner 1999 Mastercard Tour Order of Merit and Tartan Tour money list **European tour** BEF T3rd 2000 Heineken Classic

Alistair (all 6 foot 2 of him) was the top player at the November 1999 Q School to earn his 2000 tour card.

He consolidated well in his rookie year, making six of his first seven cuts including a superb 3rd at 150/1 in the Heineken Classic, and top 10s in the Dubai Desert Classic (T9th) and the Brazil Rio de Janiero 500 Years Open (6th).

After such a fast start there was a reaction until top 25s were recorded in the Murphy's Irish Open, (T23rd), the Victor Chandler British Masters (T23rd) and the Scottish PGA (T7th).

In late September he shot four sub-70 rounds in the Belgacom Open to finish T5th at 100/1.

Part of Ian Doyle's Cuemasters team. Has a contract to wear Pringle.

Not long at 270 yards. His strength is his accuracy off tee and fairway.

A superb player of short irons. Disappointing sand save stats (not in top 150).

Supports Glasgow Rangers. 6/1 to make the 2001 Ryder Cup side.

> Threw away two big winning opportunities this year.

   * In the Rio de Janiero he was the 2-shot halfway leader, then 75-73 to finish T6th

   * In the Scottish PGA, T2nd at halfway he shot 71-75 to finish T7th.

Clearly best when coming from 'off the pace' (65 in R4 in the Victor Chandler British Masters).

> After a fine first season it will be difficult to consolidate in a Ryder Cup year but his all-round stats (except sand saves) suggest he will do so.

> Showed with a 62 in R2 in Brazil (22 putts and 2 chip-ins) that he can be a streak player.

> Could well land a 'shock' win in 2001 in a lesser tournament when coming from 'off the pace', possibly in the Scottish PGA.

> Shot a sub-70 score in R2 in one third of his first twenty-one starts in 2000 so keep him in mind for Friday 3-ball betting.

Key stat   20th for shot accuracy.

PIERRE FULKE **G**

Age 29   **Born** Sweden   **Lives** Sweden

European tour wins 3, 1999 Lancome Trophy, 2000 Scottish PGA, 2000 Volvo Masters **Challenge tour wins** 2, 1992 **Order of Merit** BEF 12th 2000

After winning his first tournament in September last year he later sustained a serious wrist injury in the Belgacom Open and was sidelined for seven months. With the help of Swedish chiropractor Michael Jansch he rejoined the tour for the Wales Open (T29th) in mid June.

He hit form in the British Open where he was T7th after four par or sub-par rounds, finishing 2nd top European at 66/1.

In his next three tournaments he was T17th in the Scandinavian Masters, T11th in the Victor Chandler British Masters and then he won the Scottish PGA at Gleneagles at 16/1. He finished T14th in the German Masters, T19th in the Turespana Masters and T7th in the Italian Open. He then landed the Volvo Masters at 50/1, leading throughout he played brilliantly to hold off Darren Clarke.

He continues to be an accurate player who has now significantly improved his putting although his bunker play (68th) can be improved. Tends to draw the ball. He'll be 30 in February 2001.

> I had made him my 'best bet' on 1st November at 50/1 to land the Volvo Masters, so, although delighted when he won, 'the cat was out of the bag' as everyone realised what a really good player he is.

> I had planned to make him my 'surprise' player for the New Year before his Volvo Masters win. I really do fancy him to do really well in 2001 for three key reasons.
  * He'll be 30 in February and this often acts as a spur to a player.
  * His stats are absolutely stunning - 5th for driving accuracy, 2nd for total putting, 17th for shot accuracy and 10th for sand saves.
  * He's mentally really tough. After all he's won three times in just over a year in different countries, and at Montecastillo he went head to head in R4 down the stretch with Darren Clarke and outplayed him!

So in 2001 expect Pierre to win again, to have a good year and to play well in the Ryder Cup (originally a 5/1 chance to make the Belfry).

> Early in the season I can see him landing the 2001 Dubai Desert Classic at 33/1. Attached to a club in Dubai he'll feel 'at home' in the event.

Key stat   5th in the overall ranking.

STEPHEN GALLACHER   y g

Age 26   **Born** Scotland   **Lives** Scotland

Challenge tour wins 1, 1998 KB Golf Challenge **European tour** BEF T4th 2000 Dubai Desert Classic **Order of Merit** BEF 56th 2000

Stephen, nephew of former Ryder Cup Captain Bernard Gallacher, clinched two close-season deals with Top Flite Strata balls and Ben Hogan golf bags.

An up and down season for Stephen. The positive side came when he posted his best-ever tour finish in the Dubai Desert Classic (T4th at 150/1 after a fast finish) and in the Benson and Hedges (T5th at 125/1).

However his poor putting has been the big negative as he has made only four other top 25s, in the Heineken (T18th), the Irish Open (T23rd), the Lancome Trophy (T22nd) and the Turespana Masters (T19th).

A very long hitter, in the top 30 for driving accuracy, he has a sound swing. However it's on the greens where he has really struggled.

> Let a real chance slip in this year's Lancome Trophy. T2nd after R3, in R4 he shot 75 (!) in R4 to finish T22nd.

> A very good links player with a host of amateur titles to his credit and a member of the winning 1995 Walker Cup side, he's still just 26. With his first child due in February 2001, especially if it's a son, expect 'the law of the nappy factor' to kick in. In 2001 Stephen could post some high finishes, even a first win, in the second half of the year if he can handle the back nine on a Sunday better than he did this year in the Lancome.

> The Qatar Masters is a first-time winners event and let's remember he was T3rd after R3 there in 1999 (missed cut 2000) so he could go close at 125/1 in 2001 if he has an early tee time.

> He'll be worth a bet in both the West of Ireland Classic and the Scottish PGA at Gleneagles as both have 'weak' fields and are held on links courses on which he plays so well.

> With some top Euros having post-Ryder Cup let down the 2001 Belgacom Open will present a sound opportunity for Gallagher. T6th in 1999 and T47th this year, his two-year eclectic score (68-68-66-68) is 14 under which places him in the top 5 at the very least.

Key stat   147th for total putting.

IAN GARBUTT   V

Age 28   **Born** Doncaster   **Lives** Doncaster (Sunny Donny)

European tour wins BEF T7th 1998 Dutch Open **Challenge tour wins** 1, in 1996 when No. 1 on the tour. **Order of Merit** BEF 51st 1999

This year the guy from Donny has posted three top 10s, in the Greg Norman Holden International (T8th), the English Open (T10th) and the Wales Open (T8th). He also had high finishes in the Victor Chandler British Masters (T16th), the BMW International (T13th), the Canon European Masters (T17th) and the Lancome Trophy (T24th).

Briefly led the British Open during R1, finishing T52nd.

It really is amazing that a guy who can be in the top 5 for greens in regulation can't finish higher than T7th on the tour....and yes, you've guessed, it's because of his putting which continues to plague him although he's tried shorter putters.

A member of Chubby Chandler's 'stable'. Talented player, he was off scratch at 16 and the English Amateur Champ at 18. 10/1 to make the Ryder Cup side.

> Did not take advantage of two opportunities this year when
>   * T3rd after R3 in the Wales Open, he then shot 73 to finish T8th.
>   * T4th after R3 in the Victor Chandler British Masters, he then shot 74 to finish T16th.

> Superficially at least a 'cold putter', and poor R4 scoring when in contention suggest that especially in a Ryder Cup Ian will continue winless. However another non-winning, cold-putting, fairways-and-greens player, Pierre Fulke, has found two wins in two years and 'Garby' might do so, too.

> Attached to the Le Meridien course he'll be very keen to do well in the Portuguese Open. His missed cut this year came when he was in very poor form. Must be noted in match bets in 2001.

> He has a solid bank of form in the English Open (10-25-15-12) in the last four years. Worth support in match bets and as an 'off the pacer', in-running bet after R2, as his 67 in R4 this year was encouraging.

> T25th (1999) and T17th (2000) his last seven rounds have all been at or under par at the European Masters. Worth noting in match bets at Crans in 2001

Key stat   Top 5 in the last two years for greens in regulation, yet his best finish is still T7th. 172nd (!!) for total putting.

SERGIO GARCIA   G ☼

Age 20   **Born** Spain   **Lives** Spain

European tour wins 2, 1999 Irish Open, 1999 German Masters **Majors** 2nd 1999 USPGA **Dunhill Cup** 1999 **Ryder Cup** 1999 **Order of Merit** BEF 3rd 1999

2000 has been a disappointing year for Sergio. He did not win and he didn't post even a top 30 finish in any Major. In late 2000 he lost in a play-off to Bjorn in the Dunlop Phoenix. On the ANZ tour he was 3rd in the Ericsson Masters at 12/1. On the European tour he was 5th at 25/1 in the Volvo PGA, 12th in the Spanish Open, 10th in the Irish Open, 17th in the rain-reduced German Masters and 13th in the Volvo Masters.

On the USPGA tour he posted three top 5 finishes, in the Buick Classic (3rd at 33/1), the Air Canada (T4th at 14/1) and the Canadian Open (3rd at 20/1). He also finished T15th in the Byron Nelson Classic, T14th in the International and T17th in the Reno-Tahoe Classic. In a floodlit, made-for-TV event he beat a fatigued Tiger Woods by 1 hole at Little Bighorn.

In the Andersen World Match Play he beat Loren Roberts and Mike Weir before losing to David Duval in R3. Finished T5th in the WGC Amex (64 in R4) in November.

In the Cisco World Matchplay he beat Adam Scott before being beaten by Lee Westwood.

Fanny Suneson became his caddie after leaving Nick Faldo. However they split up after he missed the cut in the Players Championship. Corals had quoted 2/1 that Fanny would lose her job with him during 2000!

> A long hitter, he is a player who has massive natural ability. Off scratch at 13, he had a brilliant amateur record. However his putting has been a cause of real concern. In 1999 he was 59th in putts per round and 53rd for putts per GIR in Europe, and in America in eight starts on average he probably was 2 to 3 putts per tournament behind the top putters. This season after another poor start on the greens he's moved to a left-below-right grip.

  His results later in the year, especially the successive top 4 finishes on the 'Canadian Swing', suggest he's now improving on the greens.

> He will surely go on to win many tournaments and to become a real world star.

> However it does seem that he currently has three major problems.

  * Firstly, technically his swing with fast hands can lead to variations in ball speed so making for occasional errant tee shots with distance control a problem.

  * Secondly, he is still immature as he showed again this year with his completely unacceptable behaviour in R3 of the British Open. T3rd at halfway he felt he was unlucky as his ball landed in an old divot, he made a poor shot and then hacked lumps out of the fairway as his temperament let him down big style. He walked out of the pro-am on the eve of the Volvo Masters when unable to diffuse a situation with one of the amateurs in his group.

* Thirdly, listening to Butch Harmon, it appears that he is over controlled by his manager and his father. Tiger, age for age, was a far more mature man.

So with technical, temperament and personal-control issues it is perhaps not surprising that the 'wonderkid' has been overhyped and underpriced as he overreacted and underperformed in 2000.

> Indeed his temperament now seems to provide us with a clear betting opportunity. The bad breaks and dodgy bounces that are all part and parcel of links golf really upset him as he showed twice this year.

Firstly, in the Irish Open he went into R4 the favourite just 2 shots off the lead. He shot 77 and after a poor shot at the 9th stormed, "What kind of caddy are you?" to his bagman.

Secondly, last year on his British Open debut he finished plumb last after missing the cut following 89-83. This year after a fine start he shot 73-76 to finish T36th.

He had a fine amateur links record and he does have massive talent, yet I firmly believe he can be opposed on links courses

> Plans to play a lot in America where he is well suited by four key factors

   * The generally warm weather

   * The fast greens

   * The 'target golf' in which 'bad luck' is not the factor it can be on links courses

   * The galleries that enjoy his smile, enthusiasm and ability

> In America he can be followed with confidence in the Byron Nelson Classic. T15th (2000) and T3rd (1999) for a two-year stroke average of 68.12, and where he shot 62 in 1999 in R1.

> He could yet give Sam Torrance a headache if he doesn't automatically qualify for the Ryder Cup side because he plays so much in the States. No wonder Chandlers only go 5/2 for the young Spaniard to receive a 'wild card'.

> Can be backed with confidence at Castle Pines in the R2 3 balls for the International. He scored 16 pts in R2 in 1999 and 13 pts in 2000, and that's very good scoring!

Key stat   His British Open stroke average is 76.3 for his six rounds!

IGNACIO GARRIDO

Age 28   **Born** Madrid   **Lives** Madrid

European tour wins 1 - 1997 German Open **Challenge tour wins** 4 **Dunhill Cup** 1995, 96 **World Cup of Golf** 1995,97 **Ryder Cup** 1997 **Order of Merit** 6th in 1997

The 1997 Ryder Cupper has had an average year with top 25 finishes in the Alfred Dunhill (T22nd) and the Rio de Jainero Open (T11th).

His big finishes were in the European Open when T5th at 125/1, after coming from 'off the pace' with 69 in R4, and the BMW International where he was 4th at 125/1.

His other top 10s came when he was T8th in the Moroccan Open (after being the R3 leader) and in the German Masters (T6th).

Off the tee he is very long (286 yards) and very wayward (hits just five fairways in nine). This year his putting has been poor.

If he is to recapture his 1997 form he must become straighter off the tee and hole more putts. An 8/1 DYM to make the 2001 Ryder Cup side.

> The Moroccan Open this year was the fifth time in the last three years when he has entered the final round in the lead or in 2nd place. Sadly, his finishing positions have been 15th-35th-6th-2nd-8th after an over par R4 score each time, so Ignacio retains the bottle.

If he enters the final round leading or in 2nd place oppose him with confidence in the 2-ball betting.

> If he's to land a second victory it will be (like Jamie Spence) when he comes from 'off the pace' to set a target.

Key stat   In the last three years he's led or been 2nd after R3 on five occasions. His R4 average has then been 75.8 (!) and he didn't win any of them!

DAVID GILFORD   PB D

Age 35   **Born** Crewe   **Lives** Crewe (someone has to!)

European tour wins 6, last in 1994 **Ryder Cup** 1991,95 **Dunhill Cup** 1992 **World Cup of Golf** 1992, 93 **Order of Merit** BEF 7th 1994

It's difficult to remember that just five years ago David was Europe's joint top points scorer in the Ryder Cup in America, difficult because he is now struggling to maintain his career at the highest level.

In 2000 laid low by a viral infection he started the season in late April. His best finish came in his second tournament when T7th in the French Open; later he was T21st in the European Open and T23rd in the Scandinavian Masters.

He was joint R1 leader in the BMW International (64) then faded to finish T55th!

His game's key features are unchanged. He's short (272 yards) yet very accurate off the tee, however his putting and in particular his chipping, pitching and bunker play continue to be weak. A crazy 12/1 (should be 112/1!!) to make the 2001 Ryder Cup side.

> He does seem to be past his best now and it really is very difficult to see him winning again, although he might post a top 5 finish if coming from 'off the pace' on a track where there is a premium on accuracy.

> His long, loose swing is unsuited to breezy conditions, so he can be opposed in 3-ball betting when the wind blows.

Key stat   When last in contention, T3rd at halfway in the 1999 European Open, he shot 79-72 to finish T55th.

TOM GILLIS V

Age 32   **Born** Michigan   **Lives** Michigan

European Tour BEF T3rd 2000 Belgacom Open **Order of Merit** BEF 78th 2000

Gained his card in 1998 and retained it when 116th on the O/M.

In 1999 had early tendonitis and ultimately lost his card which he regained when 8th at Q School.

This year he equalled his top finish when T6th in the Scandinavian Masters. Made five other high finishes in the Alfred Dunhill (T22nd), the Dubai Desert Classic (T29th), the Moroccan Open (T22nd), the Benson and Hedges (T22nd) and the English Open (T26th).

His really big week came late in September when, after a week's holiday fishing and golfing in the States, he finished T3rd at 125/1 in the Belgacom Open to secure his card with his best-ever finish.

His iron play has been a key weakness this year.

> In the Moroccan Open he was T6th in 1998 and T22nd in 2000 on different courses, so he clearly enjoys the tournament. Could 'pop up' in the frame at 125/1 in 2001.

> Has shown nerves when the winning post appears, e.g. he shot 78 in R4 of the 1998 Madeira Open to finish T10th and a bogey-bogey finish this year in the Scandinavian Masters.

Key stat 123rd for greens in regulation.

THOMAS GOGELE V

Age 30   **Born** Germany   **Lives** Germany

European tour BEF T2nd 1996 German Open **Dunhill Cup** 1996,97,98, 2000 **World Cup of Golf** 1998 **Order of Merit** BEF 46th 1998

Top 90 on the Order of Merit from 1996 to 1999, Gurg-e-lay has had another disappointing year. He posted high finishes in the Dubai Desert Classic (T17th), the Spanish Open (T21st), the Volvo PGA (T20th), the BMW International (T13th) and the Canon European Masters (T13th), and a top 10 in the Madeira Island Open (T7th). In the Dunhill Cup he won one of his three games for a career record of six wins in twelve matches.

Uses Dennis Pugh as his coach.

A long hitter at 281 yards. His all-round stats have not progressed in the last couple of years.

He'll be 30 in November 2000.

> Notably, his best 1999 finish was when coming from 'off the pace' with a 65 in R4, and in 1998 he was not convincing when in contention at halfway in three tournaments (South African Open, Madeira Open, Moroccan Open).

> His best winning chance will be in the Madeira Island Open where his record, 12th 1996, 8th 1997, T4th 1998 and T7th 2000, is very good.

> Must enter into calculations for the BMW International held in Germany ("I enjoy playing on home soil") on a wide-fairways course. He was 3rd at 125/1 in 1998 and T13th this year, so he'll be an outsider who could 'shock' with an 'off the pace' win in 2001.

> I can see him going really close from 'off the pace' in the 2001 Italian Open. He's a big hitter ideally suited to the long, wide, four par 5 course at Is Molas where he shot 65 in R3 this year when only 2 shots 'out of the frame'. Back Gogele in Sardinia at 100/1 in early November.

Key stat   167th (at 54.1%) for driving accuracy.

RICARDO GONZALEZ

Age 31   **Born** Argentina   **Lives** Argentina

European tour BEF T2nd 2000 South African Open **Challenge Tour Wins** 2, 1990 and 1998 Dunhill Cup 1998 **World Cup of Golf** 1996, 1998 **Order of Merit** BEF 34th 2000

Established himself on the tour in 1999, his nappy factor year (first son born 1998), with three top 10s finishing 61st in the O/M.

In 2000 he has built on that platform with two big finishes, in January when T2nd at 100/1 in the South African Open, in which he missed an eagle putt on the last to force a play-off, and in June when T4th at 150/1 in the English Open.

He also had a top 10 in the Volvo Masters (T7th), top 20s in the Alfred Dunhill (T18th), the Scandinavian Masters (T11th) and the Italian Open (T12th), and a top 25 in the French Open (T22nd).

He is a massive hitter at 291 yards, ranked in the tour's top 10 in both 1999 and 2000. Driving accuracy (53-55% in the last two years) can be improved, yet his greens in reg stat is very solid (top 40). However his putting overall is on the poor side of weak.

> His most consistent performance in the last couple of years (T28th 2000: T15th 1999) has been on different courses in the Irish Open.

> 'Match fit' from playing in South America late in the year, he can be noted early on in South Africa where he putted well this year when T18th in the Alfred Dunhill, and, in his BEF, when T2nd in the South African Open.

> To be avoided in opening round 3-ball betting as a problem has been his poor R1 scoring. His R2 scoring has been better than R1 in thirteen of his first eighteen tournaments and by an average of 2.2 shots!!

> He thrives on long, wide-fairway courses, so it's no surprise that he enjoys the Italian Open (T6th 1999 and T12th 2000). He was the longest driver in this year's tournament at 301 yards. In early November the Is Molas course will give him his big chance.

Key stat   173rd (at 52.1%) for driving accuracy

RETIEF GOOSEN

G

Age 32   **Born** South Africa   **Lives** South Africa/Surrey UK

European tour wins 4, 1996 Slaley Hall Northumberland Challenge, 1997 French Open, 1999 French Open, 2000 Lancome Trophy **International wins** 6, all in South Africa, latest 1995 South African Open. **Dunhill Cup** 1995,1997,1999,2000 **World Cup** 1993,95,98 **Presidents Cup** 2000 **Order of Merit** BEF 5th 1999

Retief has had another successful season in which he won his fourth European tournament, the Lancome Trophy at 33/1 in September. He also posted four top 5 finishes, in the Alfred Dunhill in South Africa (4th at 10/1), the South African Open (T5th at 12/1), the Malaysian Open (T5th at 9/1) and the Loch Lomond (T4th at 50/1*).

He also had high finishes in the Greg Norman Holden (T16th), the Deutsche Bank Open (T13th) and the Irish Open (T21st). On the US tour he finished T13th in the Canadian Open.

In the majors he was T40th in the US Masters, T12th in the US Open, 41st in the British Open and he missed the USPGA cut.

In the Andersen World Match Play he beat Stewart Cink in R1 before losing by just one hole to Tiger Woods in R2.

In the Cisco World Matchplay he beat Thomas Bjorn before losing to Ernie Els 2 and 1 in the Q-F. Scored 2½ points from his five games played for runners up South Africa in the Dunhill Cup. He had a career record of 17½ pts from twenty-four games.

In the Presidents Cup he lost to Notah Begay (1 hole) in the singles and overall scored 2 pts from five games.

His stats show his strengths as he's hit 72% of GIR, and knocks the ball a long way (281 yards plus). However not in the top 150 for sand saves, or top 100 for putts in GIR identify his obvious weakness. In sum, he's long, accurate to the green where he misses far too many putts.

He's had laser eye surgery which he feels has improved his putting.

Had a mid season slump after "my caddy sacked me in America I had four different caddies in four tournaments." Admits he struggled with his motivation before his September victory.

> Retief has now won in each of the last two years, and during that time he's also posted TEN other top 5 finishes so he's clearly a serious player.

> However he's yet to win one of the bigger tournaments and has yet to get into serious contention in a major. I do feel that fundamentally he lacks self belief and confidence.

> He also had a lower back problem from October which caused him to play with a reduced swing.

> With three of his four wins in France it's clear that "I have sort of taken the country to heart". His victories have also come on three different courses so the new Lyon venue for the 2001 French Open will suit him. He's won the

tournament in the last two odd years (1997 and 1999) so back Retief for a third French Open success in early May.

> In January 'in his own backyard' he'll have obvious chances in the Alfred Dunhill and South African Open.

> He can be fancied for three important European tournaments.

* The Deutsche Bank Open. He was 2nd in 1999 when the 2001 venue, the St Leon Rot course in Heidelbury was last used.

* The Volvo PGA. T7th 2000: T4th 1999 and he played well at Wentworth in the Cisco Matchplay in October. If his putting improves he could go very close in 2001.

* The Loch Lomond. In his last three starts he's got a stroke average of 68.58 after finishing 3rd (1997), T10th (1999) and T4th (2000). However Ladbrokes' generous 50/1 quote this year will not be available in 2001.

> There's one surefire way to profit from 'the goose' and it is to oppose him on the spreads and in match bets in the tournament the week after he's won.

After his win this year he finished T66th in the German Masters. So after his last 3 wins (all in France) his record in the following week now reads MC-MC-66!

Key stat   138th for total putting.

RICHARD GREEN   FT G 🎂

Age 29   **Born** Melbourne   **Lives** Melbourne

European tour wins 1, 1997 Dubai Desert Classic **Order of Merit** BEF 34th 1996

"I over celebrated after winning in Dubai and rode on that success for too long." Indeed he missed thirteen of his sixteen cuts in 1998, and in 1999 he was 102nd on the O/M with two top 10s and twelve missed cuts in twenty-two starts.

However in 2000 he had high finishes in the South African Open (T19th), the Benson and Hedges (T18th), the Wales Open (T17th), the Compaq European Grand Prix (T18th) and the Loch Lomond (T22nd, after being T1st at halfway).

His best finishes were T5th in the Volvo PGA, after which he was 2nd on the driving accuracy stats, and T3rd at 125/1 in the Italian Open in late October.

Left hander who uses Dale Lynch as his swing coach. He is remarkably accurate both off the tee (although short at 265 yards) and the fairway. His short game however lets him down a lot.

30 in February 2001.

> Richard is a remarkably accurate player from both tee and fairway. However it's on the green that Richard struggles. For example in the Italian Open he was top (91%) for driving accuracy, 4th for greens in reg yet 32nd for putts per GIR. As a result he finished 3rd. However such an accurate player sooner or later has a good putting week so I expect Richard will win in 2001.

> I fancy him a lot for the 2001 Wales Open. T17th this year he finished fast (7 under for the last 54 holes) and can be backed to win next year.

> T7th at the Belfry this year (and T18th 1999 on a different course) he could well be the surprise 80/1 winner of the 2001 Benson & Hedges.

Key stat   No. 1 on tour for driving accuracy at 79.5%.

MATHIAS GRONBERG   G F

Age 30   **Born** Sweden

European tour wins 2, 1998 European Open (by 10) and 1995 European Masters **Challenge tour wins** 1 **Dunhill Cup** 1998, 2000 **World Cup of Golf** 1998 **Order of Merit** BEF 10th 1998

Mathias went to the US Q. School in Autumn 1999 only to miss his full US tour card by a single shot.

In 2000 on the European tour he started the season superbly in South Africa. After finishing T14th in the Alfred Dunhill he won the South Africa Open the following week at 66/1 coming from 5 'off the pace' with 67 in R4.

He went on in July to post top 5 finishes in the European Open (4th at 100/1) and the Dutch Open (T3rd at 66/1).

He also had a top 10 in Rio de Janiero Open (T6th) and top 20s in the Malaysian Open (T11th), the English Open (T12th) and the Victor Chandler British Masters (T18th).

Missed the cut by 8 in the USPGA. Won two of his three games for Sweden in the Dunhill Cup.

A top 20 driver for distance (283 yds) his problem is still inaccuracy off the tee. A brilliant player of fairway woods. He was 30 in March 2000.

> Married to an American he clearly wants to gain his US card and if he does he will have to improve his accuracy off the tee. Nevertheless he is solid all round with a proven ability to win and can be expected to go on to further success on the European tour.

> A proven front runner he can be backed both in the outrights, and especially in final round 2-ball betting if he is leading after R3 as he's won both the tournaments when he went into Sunday ahead.

> He loves the K Club and the European Open which he won (in a canter) in 1998 and was 4th in 2000. So he'll be worthy of support both in matchbets and the outrights.

> With two top 10s in the three years since Seve redesigned the course Mathias clearly enjoys golf at Crans so he can be supported in the European Masters in match bets and as a 50/1 chance with a squeak.

> Worth each-way support in South Africa where he's won already particularly in the Alfred Dunhill (T14th 2000: T22 1999: 9th 1998).

> Quoted at 9/2 to make the 2001 Euro Ryder Cup starting line up, and 20/1 to get a 'wild card' place.

Key stat   126th (at 59.5%) for driving accuracy.

JOAKIM HAEGGMAN

Age 31   **Born** Sweden   **Lives** Monaco

European tour wins 2, 1997 Scandinavian Masters, 1993 Spanish Open
European Challenge tour wins 2, 1992 and 1990 **Ryder Cup** 1993 **Dunhill Cup**
1993, 1997 **World Cup Golf** 1993.94.97 **Order of Merit** BEF 15th 1993

Joakim lost his form after being a fixture in the top 60 on the O/M from 1992-1997. This year however there have been signs of a revival with high finishes in the Malaysian Open (T16th when 2nd for putting), T11th in the Portuguese Open (when 4th for driving accuracy), T22nd in the Moroccan Open, and T17th in the Dutch Open.

His big finish came in the Rio de Janeiro Open (T4th at 80/1*).

His putting has been first class compensating to some extent for his erratic driving. Poor Sand Save stats.

> It's really difficult to see him winning again given his erratic long game.
> At his best on easy courses where his putting can shine and his wayward driving can be hidden.

Key stat   122nd for shot accuracy.

CRAIG HAINLINE   🐑 D

Age 30   **Born** Kansas   **Lives** Texas

European tour BEF T5th twice in 1998 **Challenge tour wins** 1 in 1997 **Order of Merit** BEF 41st 1998

In his third full year on the tour Craig has really struggled. He made a fine start when T16th in the Greg Norman Holden International and followed up, two weeks after his 30th birthday, with a superb T2nd at 66/1 in the Malaysian Open. However apart from the T35th in the Qatar Masters he couldn't even post a top 50 finish in the rest of the season.

His main problem has been on the greens where his putting has been on the bad side of atrocious. Must now go to Q School.

> Coming from Wichita, USA, he's a fine player when the winds really blow.
> Showed in this year's Malaysian Open (T2nd) that he's at his best when coming from 'off the pace', and as he lost final day leads twice in 1998 he's not a good front runner.
> His most consistent tournament has been the Loch Lomond International where he's made three successive cuts for an eclectic score of 13 under. If his putter's working by July remember him in 3-ball betting there (66 R2: 67 R1: 68 R4) as he's had some good rounds.
> Proved this year that he enjoys the heat and humidity of the Malaysian Open when T2nd. He could go close again in that tournament in mid February.

Key stat   158th for total putting.

CHRISTOPHER HANELL   FT g

Age 27   **Born** Sweden   **Lives** Sweden

European tour BEF 3rd 1999 Victor Chandler British Masters **Order of Merit** BEF 65th 2000

He made a very bright start to his professional career in 1999 when 62nd on the O/M including T5th in the Qater Masters, and 3rd in the Victor Chandler British Masters.

In 2000 he has consolidated really well with a series of high finishes in the South African Open (T13th), the Heineken Classic (T25th), the Greg Norman Holden International (T13th), the Madeira Island Open (T14th), the English Open (T26th), the European Open (T13th), the Scandinavian Masters (T11th when T2nd at 33/1 in the Top Scandinavian market), the BMW International (T13th) and the Canon European Masters (T23rd).

> He has made a very sound start to his career, he has solid stats all round although he's short off the tee. 'Bottled' it at the Loch Lomond, where he was a shot off the lead at halfway to finish T41st.

> With two successful years experience behind him, high finishes on 3 continents, and solid overall stats he's every chance of winning his first tournament in 2001 so he gets the FT symbol.

> He is 'must bet' material in the Madeira Open. In two starts he was R1 leader in 1999, and T14th in 2000 in a tournament in which the Swedes have a first class record.

> He started his two tour years very well as he gets 'match fit' quickly so he's one to have on your side in match bets before April.

Key stat   125th for total driving.

ANDERS HANSEN   g y

Age 30   **Born** Denmark   **Lives** Denmark

European tour wins BEF T6th 1999 West of Ireland Golf Classic **Order of Merit** BEF 53rd 2000

Went to the University of Houston where he posted two collegiate wins. 3rd place at Q School gained Anders his card for 1999 in which he finished 107th on the O/M.

In 2000 his straight-hitting consistency saw him make sixteen of his first twenty-one cuts and post a series of high finishes. They came in the Heineken Classic (T25th), Spanish Open (T21st), French Open (T15th including 65 in R2), Benson and Hedges (T14th), Volvo PGA (T20th) and Lancome Trophy (T12th) with top 10s in the Alfred Dunhill (T10th), the Sao Paulo Open (T8th) and the Greg Norman Holden International (T6th).

His stroke average continues to fall. However his stats point conclusively to the reasons for his consistency (high in driving accuracy stats) and his absence of 'being in contention' finishes (poor putting). 8/1 to make the 2001 Ryder Cup side.

> With Thomas Bjorn as a role model and safely past 30 in September 2000 Anders can win if he improves his putting. So keep an eye on his early season putting stats for any improvement as a 'shock' first win in 2001 is probable..

> Making 76% of his cuts he's not one to oppose in match bets.

> Could be well suited to the new course for the 2001 Victor Chandler British Masters.

> With a favourable tee time could make the front five at a big price in the Alfred Dunhill Championship in South Africa (T10th 2000: T30 1999) where his last six rounds have been under par on a course suited to his straight driving.

Key stat   16th for shot accuracy and 9th (at 72.3%) for driving accuracy.

SOREN HANSEN   g y

Age 26   **Born** Copenhagen   **Lives** Copenhagen

European tour BEF T7th 2000 Belgacom Open **Challenge tour wins** 1 in 1998 **World Cup of Golf** 1998 **Order of Merit** BEF 73rd 2000

Graduated from the 1998 Challenge tour to finish 112th on the O/M in his rookie year (1999) on the main tour.

In 2000 he has posted high finishes in the Alfred Dunhill (T22nd), the Greg Norman Holden International (T22nd), Malaysian Open (T11th), Qatar Masters (T14th), the English Open (T26th), the BMW International (T25th after being T6th after R2), the Canon European Masters (T23rd), with top 10s in the French Open (T7th) and the Belgacom Open (T7th).

No relation to Anders Hansen although the two Danes are good buddies.

Sound greens in reg stats. However his putting is on the poor side of dreadful!

> Tasted serious contention for the first time in the Belgacom Open when T2nd after R3. He then shot 72 to finish T7th. It was an experience that he can draw on next year.

> In the last two years he has posted top 25s in Ireland, Malaysia, Spain, the Middle East, Australia, South Africa and mainland Europe. He is now firmly in the 'winner about to happen' category.

Key stat   133rd for total putting

PADRAIG HARRINGTON   G 🐦 ⛪

Age 29   **Born** Dublin   **Lives** Dublin

European tour wins 3, 1996 Spanish Open, 2000 Sao Paolo Open, 2000 Turespana Masters **Dunhill Cup** 1996,1997, 1998, 1999, 2000 **World Cup** 1996,97,98 **Ryder Cup** 1999 **Order of Merit** BEF 7th 1999 and 2000

It's been a real yo-yo year for Padraig. He won the Sao Paolo Open at 12/1 on the tour's 'Brazilian Swing', and he posted top 5s in the Malaysian Open (T2nd at 25/1), the Rio de Janeiro Open (2nd at 16/1), the Belgacom Open (T3rd at 33/1) and the German Masters (T3rd at 25/1).

He also had high finishes in the Deutsche Bank Open (T17th), the Volvo PGA (T17th), the BMW (T20th) and the Volvo Masters (T14th).

In the Andersen World Match Play he lost 2 and 1 in R1 to Jesper Parnevik.

In the Coral Eurobet Seve Ballesteros Trophy he beat Jimenez (1 up) in the singles, scored 2½ out of 4 points, and finished T2nd at 8/1 as top British points scorer. In the Cisco World Matchplay he beat Bob May (6 and 5) in the QF, before losing to Monty (5 and 3) in the SF.

In the WGC NEC Invitational he finished T27th. However at Valderrama in the WGC Amex he finished T5th at 40/1.

In the Majors he was T19th in the US Open, a superb T5th at 125/1 on his debut in the US Open, T20th British Open, and T59th in the USPGA.

Won two of his three games in the Dunhill Cup to give him a career record of nine wins from fifteen games.

However he's never allowed to forget the dreadful moment in the Benson and Hedges when 5 shots ahead going into R4 he was disqualified for not signing his card 2 days earlier!

Won for the second time this year when he landed the Turespana Masters at 16/1 in October on the Club de Campo course where he won his first tournament (the Spanish Open) in 1996.

His stats are good for greens in reg (top 10), putts per GIR (top 15), although his driving accuracy at just 63% indicates the area most in need of improvement. Increased his length off the tee to 279 yards. He putts left hand below right. His chipping can still be improved. David McNeely is his inspirational caddie.

Credits his coach Bob Torrance for much of his improvement this year.

He has suffered from neck, and upper spine problems this year. He'll be 30 in August 2001.

His sportsmanship was shown when in R2 of this year's US Open he called a penalty on himself as his ball moved on the putting surface.

> There must be a question mark over Padraig's ability to 'clinch the victory' when in contention. For example

 * Before his win in Sao Paolo this year he'd had 7 second places in the previous 11 months.

 * In the 2000 Malaysian Open he led with 2 to go then bogeyed both those final 2 holes to finish T2nd.

 * In the 2000 Rio de Janeiro Open he lost in a play-off in which he bogeyed both holes (3 putt and found the water).

 However he surely would have won the Benson & Hedges, he won his Ryder Cup singles, and his positive reaction after this year's shattering disqualification were all signs of a tough mental attitude so let's give him the benefit of the doubt.

> Padraig (my elder lad calls him Porridge) is an improving player who will surely qualify for the Ryder Cup side on merit (3-1 on) so long as the problems with his neck do not resurface. I just can't see him needing a wild card (8/1).

536 • Elliott's Golf Form 2001

> Last year in his profile you'll remember the immortal words..."Worth a bet to be a 'shock' 40/1 winner in May at the Belfry in the Benson and Hedges.." This year let's hope his pen works and his signature's in place so we may collect because I expect him to compensate us for last year's 'shock' by winning the 2001 Benson & Hedges at 33/1.

> He must be noted in the top European market for the majors. This year his record was first class, viz. T1st 28/1 US Masters, T2nd 22/1 US Open, T2nd 12/1 British Open and lost USPGA, to give a very tidy profit on the season of £265 for a £10 each-way stake on each major.

> His 69-67 finish this year gave him his third top 20 in five years for the Volvo PGA. He must be noted at Wentworth for match bets in late May.

> Surprisingly perhaps he can be opposed in the Irish Open. His T28th this year followed three missed cuts in the previous four years.

> Well worth a bet just after Valentine's Day for the 2001 Malaysian Open where his recent record (T2nd 25/1 2000: T4th 125/1 1999) is first class.

> He must be expected to go close in the BMW International Open as his record 2nd (1999), 9th (1997), 3rd (1996) is very solid. However it will be the last tournament for Ryder Cup points. IF he needs points then he must be backed although I expect his place will be secure by then.

> His record in the German Masters at Gut Larchenhof in the last two years (T3rd 2000: T2nd 1999) for a stroke average of 68.29 is stunning....so should you back him in 2001?........as this tournament starts just four days after the Ryder Cup I'd be wary as win, lose or draw there's bound to be a mega-big, post-Ryder MLD.

> In the 'odd years' (2nd 1997: 2nd 1999) he's played well at Montecastillo where the forgiving fairways do not punish his occasional wayward driving. In 2001 (another odd year) he could go close once again in the Volvo Masters.

Key stat   6th for both greens in regulation and putts per GIR yet 85th for driving accuracy.

DAVID HIGGINS

Age 28   **Born** Cork   **Lives** Co. Kerry

European tour BEF T3rd 1996 BMW International **European Challenge tour wins** 3, all in 2000

David has had a superb year on the Challenge tour winning 3 times, the NCC Open in Sweden in June, the Gunther Hamburg Classic in July in a play-off, and the Rolex Trophy (pro-am) in Switzerland in August to give him a glorious summer!

However he can't be accused of consistency as he's posted only a couple of other top 10s including T3rd in the Touquet Challenge in France.

> A talented player, Irish Amateur Champion as a 22-year-old he's shown this year that he knows how to win but that he does not know how to achieve a consistent level of performance.

> He'll be looking to retain his card which will clearly be difficult in Ryder Cup year. His best chance will surely be in the weakly contested West of Ireland Classic.

Key stat   On the 2000 Challenge tour he won 3 times in 3 months yet posted only 3 other top 25s before November.

DAVID HOWELL   g

Age 25   **Born** Swindon   **Lives** Swindon (still a poor football team)

European tour wins 1 - 1999 Dubai Desert Classic **International tour wins** 1998 Australian PGA **Order of Merit** BEF 32nd 1998 **Dunhill Cup** 1999

The 25-year-old has been on the tour from 1996, and has made very steady progress on the O/M from 54th (1996) to 47th (1997) to 32nd (1998) and 22nd in 1999 when he won his first tournament, the Dubai Desert Classic.

However this year has been disappointing.

He was still troubled by his ankle problem when as defending champion he finished T64th in the Dubai Desert Classic.

In the Seve Ballesteros trophy he won two of his three matches losing 2 and 1 in the singles to Robert Karlsson.

He posted a top 10 in the Deutsche Bank Open (T9th) and had top 25s in the English Open (T23rd), the BMW (T20th), the German Masters (T22nd), the Turespana Masters (T15th) and the Italian Open (T21st).

However his big finish came when he was 2nd at 50/1* in the Wales Open after shooting 14 under for the last 54 holes.

His stats reflect his disappointing year with his putting in need of artificial respiration, and he's also been inaccurate off the tee. Tends to draw the ball.

Looks sensible yet supports Swindon Town.

> Let's make no mistake David is a very good player who has posted twelve top 5 finishes (including a 66/1 win in Europe and a 25/1 win in Australia) in the last five years and he's only 25!

> He's a versatile player who has played well in every month of the year, on every continent and every type of course. However if he's to really move to that next higher level he really must improve his putting.

> David really must be backed in the 2001 Wales Open. The big names will be missing, he was a fast finishing 2nd this year and he practices on the Celtic Manor course in the winter. At 33/1 each way he'll be a rock solid each-way bet.

> Keep him in mind for match bets in the South African Open (T9th 1998: 4th 1996).

> 15/8 to make the 1999 Ryder Cup his odds this time round are a very skinny 5/2.

Key stat   92nd on the overall ranking.

FREDRIK JACOBSON   FT V

Age 26   **Born** Sweden   **Lives** Sweden

European tour BEF 2nd 1998 Belgacom Open (lost in a play off) 2nd 2000 Compaq European Grand Prix, 2nd 2000 Irish Open **Order of Merit** BEF 25th 2000

127th on the 1999 O/M 'Freddie' regained his tour card when 7th at Q School in November 1999. A month later he injured his thumb in an ice skating fall. Returned to the tour in mid-March 2000 posting four really big finishes in French Open (T4th at 125/1) and then in successive tournaments the Wales Open (T3rd at 125/1), the Compaq European Grand Prix (2nd at 100/1) and the Irish Open (2nd at 66/1 including 63 in R2).

He also had high finishes when T17th in the Dutch Open, on a links course, T17th in the Canon European Masters and T10th in the Volvo Masters. Missed the cut in the British Open.

His putting has been first class this year although his accuracy off the tee continues to be by far his biggest problem. 6/1 DYM to make the 2001 Ryder Cup side.

> Off scratch at 15 he now needs to notch his first win. He showed real nerves with a bogey bogey finish in the Irish Open when 1 up with 2 to play. Not a player to follow when there is a premium on accuracy.

> His ambitious plan is to go to US Q School in November 2000 to try to secure his 2001 tour card

> He will have a major chance in the Madeira Island Open (T10th 1999, T10th 1998, 2nd 1997) in which Swedes do so well especially if he is in regular play before the tournament.

> His game is really well suited to the wider fairways of links golf shown by his 2nd in the 1998 Belgacom Open, T9th 1999 Scottish PGA and 2nd in the 2000 Irish Open, and he can be followed in three 'links' tournaments:-

* The Irish Open: 2nd in 2000
* The Scottish PGA: T9th 1999
* The Dutch Open: 10 under par last three rounds when top 20 this year

Key stat   107th for shot accuracy yet 11th for total putting.

RAPHAEL JACQUELIN   V

Age 27   **Born** France   **Lives** France

European tour BEF 3rd 1999 Turespana Masters **Challenge tour wins** 3, all in 1997 **Dunhill Cup** 2000 **Order of Merit** BEF 88th 1998

This year 'Jacquo' secured his card when he finished 3rd at 125/1 in the Scottish PGA. He had started well, from an early tee time, to shoot 64 in R1. In September he finished well to be T24th in the Lancome Trophy.

He had struggled up to then having posted just a couple of top 25s, in the Alfred Dunhill (T22nd) and the Heineken Classic (T25th) very early in the season and a solid T13th in the Volvo PGA (65 in R4).

Made his Dunhill Cup debut in October winning one of his three games before finishing T12th in the Turespana Masters.

In the top 50 for Driving Distance, he shows up well (top 50) for greens in regulation. However his putting continues to be a really serious weakness.

> Raphael is clearly a difficult player to read as he can find form very suddenly. This year, for example, he had eight consecutive missed cuts before his season's best when 3rd in the Scottish PGA.

> Clearly enjoys the Turespana Masters. 3rd 1999, and T12th this year he has an eclectic score over the last two years of 20 (!) under par. If 'off the pace' he can be supported in the final day 2 balls after 65 (1999) and 66 (2000).

Key stat   115th in putts per GIR.

MARK JAMES

Age 47   **Born** Manchester (regular rain)   **Lives** Ilkley (more regular rain)

European tour wins 18, latest 1995 Moroccan Open, 1997 Spanish Open **Dunhill Cup** 7 times, last 1999 **World Cup** 9 times, last 1997 **Ryder Cup** 7 times, last 1995, and Captain 1999 **Majors** 4 top 5s in the British Open. **Order of Merit** 3rd 1979

The 1999 Ryder Cup at Brookline was to follow 'Jesse' throughout the first seven months of 2000 before he was inevitably asked to resign as Sam Torrance's 2001 Ryder Cup assistant. The publicity and book sales won, the image of golf lost.

In 2000 on the golf course in the week when serialisation of his book started he was a fine T2nd at 125/1 in the English Open. Later he posted a top 10 in the Wales Open (T8th).

His long game remains in good shape. Short off the tee at 265 yards.

> Diagnosed with lymphoma in the Autumn. Everyone will wish Mark well and like Paul Azinger let's hope he can overcome this cancer and come back to win again....even if in Mark's case it maybe on the Seniors Tour.

> Put a few bob away in the Piggy bank to use to back James on the Seniors Tour from 2003.

> In the meantime remember he missed many makeable putts in the English Open this year when T2nd as he suffered from 'contention rust'.

> Past his best he maybe yet in 2001 he'll be determined to do well so expect him to post at least one high finish possibly in the Wales Open where he played so well this year when T8th.

Key stat   Ranked 82nd overall.

MIGUEL ANGEL JIMENEZ   ☼ G

Age 36   **Born** Malaga   **Lives** Malaga

European tour wins 6, 1992 Piaget Open, 1994 Dutch Open, 1998 Turespana Masters, 1998 Lancome Trophy, 1999 Turespana Masters, 1999 Volvo Masters

Dunhill Cup 10 times, latest 2000 **World Cup** 1990,92,93,94 **Ryder Cup** 1999
Order of Merit 4th 1998

Miguel started 2000 late after a bout of flu. He showed in the US Open when he was T2nd at 100/1, that he is a serious player on the World stage.

On the European tour he had top 10 finishes in the Deutsche Bank Open (T6th), the Benson and Hedges (T9th), the German Masters (T6th) and the Turespana Masters (T7th as defending champion), and high finishes in the Buick Classic in America (T19th) and the Canon European Masters (T21st).

In the majors he was T49th in the US Masters, that brilliant T2nd in the US Open, T26th British Open and T72nd in the USPGA.

In the Andersen World Match Play he beat Brent Geiberger (1 hole), Tom Lehman (5 and 4) and Bob Estes (2 and 1), before losing in the quarter-finals to Davis Love 3 and 2.

In the Coral Eurobet Seve Ballesteros Trophy he got 2½ points from five matches losing by 1 hole to Padraig Harrington. Won three of his five games as he helped Spain retain the Dunhill Cup

Jimenez is in essence a straight, but not long, hitter, at his best in hot, humid conditions. When he putts well he is a player who merits real respect.

> He aims to secure a US tour card for 2001. If he succeeds I think he will do very well for 4 key reasons.

    * He's a proven player in hot, humid conditions.

    * The 'target golf' so often needed on the US tour will suit his straight hitting style.

    * As a Spaniard he will enjoy the fast US greens as he proved at Pebble Beach in this year's US Open.

    * His record in America in recent years in the US Open (2nd 2000), the USPGA (T10th 1999) and the Buick Classic (top 20, 2000) is very encouraging.

If he plays in America I expect he'll do well, and, like Van de Velde, he may prove to be very successful in 'desert tournaments'.

> In the majors he can be followed in the Top European speciality markets in two US majors.

    * The US Open T28th 1995, T23rd 1999, T2nd 2000 in three starts. He was the top Euro this year at 22/1.

    * The USPGA T13th 19995: T10th 1999: T72 (when out of form) 2000. In his first three USPGAs he finished T3rd at 28/1, 3rd at 40/1 and 2nd at 25/1 in the Top Euro market.

> On the European tour he can be given big chances in three tournaments in which he's played consistently well in each of the last three years.

    * The Canon European Masters T21st (2000), T6th (1999), T7th (1998).

    * The Lancome Trophy T24th (2000), T10th (1999), Won (1998)

    * The Deutsche Bank Open T6th (2000): T7th (1999 on the course to be used in 2001): T7th (1998).

In these tournaments he can be followed on the spreads, in matchbets and each way in the outright markets.

> The venue for the 2001 Turespana Masters has still to be decided. However he loves the tournament (Won in 1999 and 1998: T7th 2000). If he plays next year take the hint and have a little Angel delight.

Key stat   3rd for shot accuracy.

PER-ULRIK JOHANSSON

Age 34   **Born** Sweden   **Lives** Marbella (very hot), Spain

European tour wins 5, last the 1998 European Open **Ryder Cup** 1995 & 1997 **Dunhill Cup** 1991,92,95,97,98 **World Cup of Golf** 1991, 1992, 1997 **Order of Merit** 11th 1997

Once more it's been a mixed year for the experienced Swede. As in 1999 he posted four top 5 finishes, in the Greg Norman Holden International (T3rd at 66/1), the European Open (3rd at 100/1), the Victor Chandlers British Masters (2nd at 33/1) and the Turespana Masters (3rd at 33/1).

He also posted high finishes in the Malaysian Open (9th), the Loch Lomond (15th), the Scandinavian Masters (17th) and the German Masters (22nd).

Won all his 3 games in the Dunhill Cup to give him a career record of 14 wins from 21 games.

He finished T64th in the British Open.

For the third successive year he suffered (in late August) from dizziness and headaches.

He has a solid all round game and a rounded golf swing. His stats are solid all round with a marked improvement in his bunker play. He's in the top 30 for shot accuracy, total putting and total driving.

> Illness, dizziness and a hip problem (last year) have dogged the progress of this fine player with the back to front caps. I wouldn't mind having a bet that next year he follows Norman, Elkington and Parnevik in having arthroscopic hip surgery.

> Without a win in the last two years during which time he's been dogged by illness he's nevertheless notched 6 punter friendly top 5 finishes. If he can have a full illness and injury free year he could well win again....however it's a big if!

> He can be followed with real confidence in the 2001 European Open. His record is first class, he won in 1996 and 1997, was jetlagged in 1998, missed the cut in 1999, and finished a superb 3rd this year. So in early July at the K (Club) go for PUJ.

> He'll have PMAs with the Victor Chandler British Masters after his fine 2nd place this year. If fit he will have a big chance on the Marquess course in early June.

> He obviously enjoys the Turespana Masters (3rd 2000: T5th 1999) in which he must have a leading chance if he plays in mid March.

> 2/1 to make the 2001 Ryder Cup side, and 12/1 to be given a 'wild card'.

Key stat   8th in the overall ranking.

RICHARD S JOHNSON

Age 24   **Born** Sweden   **Lives** Sweden

European tour BEF T2nd 2000 Madeira Island Open **Challenge tour wins** 1, in 1999 **Order of Merit** BEF 96th 2000

Earned tour card at 1999 Q School and made an impression with a top 10 in his first tournament, the Portuguese Open (T6th) and later when T2nd in the Madeira Island Open, 11th in the Sao Paulo Open and T11th in the Victor Chandler British Masters.

Outside the top 80 in all the stats he obviously can improve his all-round game.

> A win in 1999, and a 2nd place in his rookie year is a solid platform on which he can build.

> After his fine T2nd this year and in a tournament in which Swedes excel he must be expected to do well in the 2001 Madeira Island Open.

Key stat   115th in putts per GIR.

TONY JOHNSTONE

Age 44 and counting   **Born** Zimbabwe   **Lives**   UK

European tour wins 5, last one the 1998 Alfred Dunhill South African PGA **International wins** 16, last in 1994 **Order of Merit** BEF 7th 1992 **Dunhill Cup** 1993-1998 incl., 2000

Ended 1999 well when T7th in the individual World Cup of Golf ranking.

In 2000 he posted his best finish in two years when T3rd at 66/1* in the Portuguese Open. He also had high finishes in the Dubai Desert Classic (T20th), the English Open (T17th) and the Lancome Trophy (T12th). Missed British Open cut (sixth successive time).

Won two of his three games in the Dunhill Cup for a career record of 10½ points from twenty-six games.

Like 'Laurence of Arabia' he's at his best in sand. His key weakness has been his putting in recent years. A good player in poor weather.

> "Apart from two weeks I've putted like a moron for five years." (The two weeks were his 1998 victory and this year's T3rd.) Indeed he's thought of quitting over the last two years. Acquired a new effective 80-year-old (!) putter at St Andrews in October and expects his putting to improve. He's also got a new driver, and new ball and now hits it further than he's ever done before.

> With renewed confidence because of his new equipment Tony is really looking forward to the new season so keep an eye on him especially early on in South Africa.

Key stat   Top player on tour, as in 1999, for sand saves.

OLLE KARLSSON

Age 31   **Born** Sweden   **Lives** Marbella (lucky lad!)

European tour wins BEF T2 1998 English Open **Order of Merit** BEF T51st 1995

In a career disrupted regularly by injury and accident Olle played in 2000 initially on a medical exemption.

He made three top 20s in the Compaq European Grand Prix (T14th), the North West of Ireland Open (T11th) and the Scottish PGA (5th at 66/1).

A long hitter Olle's problem continues to be erratic play off the tee. Must now go to Q School.

> He's shown signs of nerves when in contention in the final round in recent years — in the 1996 Portuguese Open (77 in R4), the 1999 Moroccan Open (74 in R4) and the N W of Ireland Golf Classic (74 in R4 to slip from T2nd to T11th).

> Clearly best when coming from off the pace as in this year's Scottish PGA where he closed 69-66 to finish T5th. It's the one tournament for which he can be recommended in 2001.

Key stat   40th for shot accuracy.

ROBERT KARLSSON

Age 31   **Born** Sweden   **Lives** Monaco

European tour wins 3, 1995 Mediteranean Open, 1997 BMW International (play-off) and the 1999 Belgacom Open **Dunhill Cup** 1992 **Order of Merit** 10th 1997

The tallest player on the tour at 6 foot 5 inches (in old money), Karlsson had the disappointment in 1999 of not receiving Mark James' second wild card for the Ryder Cup. It went inexplicably to Coltart who was behind him in the Ryder Cup table. If Karlsson had been born in St Andrews instead of St Malm he would surely have got the nod.

This year he has really struggled after three successive years in the top 20 on the O/M.

Took a long winter break then played three tournaments in America and one on the Buy.Com tour before moving to South America when the European tour had its 'Brazilian Swing' in late March. He was T30th in the Rio de Janiero Open and T13th in the Sao Paolo Open. His only other top 25 finishes came in the Volvo PGA (T13th) and the Irish Open (T31st).

In the Seve Ballesteros trophy he got 1½ points from 4 beating David Howell in the singles 2 and 1.

In January he went on a body cleansing fast to boost energy!

He is a fine putter and a long driver at 278 yards. However inaccuracy off the tee (outside top 150 for driving accuracy) and poor approach play (outside top 100 for Greens in reg) have been his main problems.

> Will probably go to Q School in America in November to get his 2001 US tour card.

> Twice this year he has let good chances slip.
  * In the Rio de Janiero Open, T3rd after R3 he shot 78 (!) in R4 to finish T30.
  * In the Volvo PGA, T3rd after R2 he shot 74-71 to finish T13th.
  Let's hope these were not signs of an emerging late round 'bottler'.

> Be wary of Karlsson in R1 3-ball betting as he rarely makes a fast start and in 2000 in R1 he broke 70 only twice in his first thirteen events.

> He's an absolute must bet if the 2001 Moroccan Open returns to the Golf d'Agadir course.
  In successive starts he's been in the top 4 five times, so it's no wonder, "I just get a good feeling when I come here."

> At his best on easy courses where there is a reduced premium on driving accuracy, so he can be expected to play well in the 2001 Belgacom Open. He won it in 1999, was T3rd in 1998, and his T60th this year can be overlooked as he was not in form at the time. He'll be worth a bet at the Royal Zoute course next year.

Key stat   145th for driving accuracy.

SOREN KJELDSEN   g

Age 25   **Born** Denmark   **Lives** Denmark

European tour BEF T2nd 1999 Qatar Masters **Challenge tour wins** 1 in 1997 Order of Merit 56th 1999 World Cup of Golf 1998

Joined tour in 1998 and kept his card in that year (115th on O/M) and in 1999 (56th).

This year he has had top 25 finishes in the Moroccan Open (T22nd), the European Open (T25th), the Wales Open (T21st) and the Dutch Open (T17th after poor 72 in R4).

He also had top 10s in the Qatar Masters (T7th) and the Deutsche Bank Open (T9th, he was 14 under for last 54 holes).

His big problem continues to be his putting. His strength is his accuracy off the tee. 6/1 to make 2001 Ryder Cup side.

> On a course where first time winners win he can be supported in the Qatar Masters. T2nd in 1999, T7th in 2000 his game and his patience are well suited to the windy conditions. If he gets an early R1 tee time have an each-way bet.

> His finish (67,66,69) in this year's Deutsche Bank was the best in the tournament. Must be noted in this tournament in 3-ball betting and as an 100/1+ outsider with a 'squeak' if he gets a good R1 tee time when the tournament moves to the St Leon-Rot course in 2001.

> Often starts poorly before improving significantly in R2 - a point to remember in 3-ball betting.

Key stat   136th for putts per GIR.

MAARTEN LAFEBER

Age 26   **Born** Holland   **Lives** Holland

Challenge tour wins 1 in 1999 **European tour** BEF T5th 1999 Dutch Open **Order of Merit** BEF 85th 2000

Former Swiss, Dutch and Spanish (beating a younger Garcia) Amateur champion who returned to the main tour via the 1999 Challenge tour where he was 7th on the O/M.

In 2000 he had high finishes in the Alfred Dunhill (T22nd), the English Open (T12th), the Wales Open (T17th) and the Lancome Trophy (T24th including 66 twice!), and a top 10 when T6th in the Scandinavian Masters.

Made seven consecutive cuts from very late May.

Top 50 for driving distance, its inaccuracy off the tee (94th) and poor bunker play (142nd) that are his key weaknesses.

> His record shows clearly that he's at his best when relaxed after an ordinary start as in the 2000 English Open, 1999 Dutch Open and 2000 Wales Open. However when 3rd after R2 in the 2000 Scandinavian Masters this year he then shot 72 -71 to finish T6th, and on the 1999 Challenge tour in the Beazer Homes he led after R3 then shot 74 to finish 2nd.

Key stat   42nd for total driving.

BARRY LANE D PB

Age 40   **Born** Middlesex   **Lives** Woking

European tour wins 4, last in 1994 **Anderson World Champion** 1995 (£1M) **Ryder Cup** 1993 **Dunhill Cup** 4 times **World Cup of Golf** 1996 **Order of Merit** 5th 1992

This year once he blew out the 40 candles on his cake in June Barry's form improved making consecutive cuts including a T11th in the Scandinavian Masters (2nd at halfway), and later he posted another T11th in the BMW International in September.

Earlier he'd had high finishes in the Qatar Masters (T19th), and the Portuguese Open (T23rd). Became a father of a son, Elliot (well named eh?) in late September.

His stats overall in every category paint the same picture. At his best he's superb when the wind blows. Working to improve his fitness.

> Nevertheless the improved form in the second half of the season suggest that he could post a top 5 finish in 2001 although he may not win. After all he let winning chances go in the 1998 Irish Open, the 1998 Benson and Hedges as well as this year's Scandinavian Masters.

> So it's difficult to see him winning in Ryder Cup year.

Key stat   Last win was in 1995 when he pocketed $1 million for landing the Andersen Consulting World Match Play.

BERNHARD LANGER

Age 43   **Born** Germany   **Lives** Germany

European tour wins 37 (!) last in 1997 **International wins** 4 **Majors** 1985 and 1993 US Masters **Ryder Cup** 1981 and on 9 occasions, last in 1997 **Dunhill Cup** 1992, 2000 **World Cup of Golf** 11 times **Order of Merit** 1st 1981 and 1984

This year, back to his blade irons from cavity backed clubs, Bernhard started the European season brightly with three top 20s in his first four starts when T14th in the Alfred Dunhill, T10th in the South African Open and T16th in the Malaysian Open.

He posted further top 20s in the Benson and Hedges (T18th), the Volvo PGA (T17th), and the Volvo Masters (T14th), and a top 10 in the Irish Open (T10th),

He came close to winning in late July in the Dutch Open (2nd at 28/1) and in late August in the BMW International (2nd at 25/1). Finished T6th in the German Masters.

In the majors he was T28th in the US Masters, a creditable T11th in the British Open (after a superb final three rounds), T46th in the USPGA, and he missed the cut in the US Open.

In America for the 'Florida Swing' he was T36th in the Doral Ryder Open, T18th in the Bay Hill, and T42nd in the Players Championship.

In the Seve Ballesteros trophy he won three of his four matches, beating Ian Woosnam 4 and 3 in the singles. He was T2nd top European scorer at 5/1.

Won two of his three Dunhill Cup games in October.

He continues to be the ultra professional, a brilliant iron player and as mentally tough as anyone who has ever played the greatest game.

If his back problems are really over now he will make a real effort to regain his Ryder Cup place for which he was best priced at 15/8.

If his consistency, attitude and accurate iron play are his strengths his weakness is inaccuracy off the tee. As he started to earn Ryder Cup points in September he was in the top 20 for greens in regulation, (7th 1999), and putts per green in reg, top 20 for sand saves, yet outside the top 100 for driving accuracy.

Pete Coleman, his long serving caddie, is a master of his craft, and one of the reasons for Langer's continued success.

> May play more in the States in 2001.

> Romero's win in September proved that golden oldies like Langer can notch victories after many winless years. "I play well but someone else seems to play better" and he's right with his inference that he could win again in 2001. I hope he does although I doubt it as his lack of length and occasional erratic tee shots may continue to be too big a handicap. Nevertheless he loses the PB symbol.

> He can be supported with confidence in match bets in which he must never be opposed. Throughout the nineties he made the cut in 87% of his tournaments, and in 2000 in ten of his first eleven European tour (non majors) events.

> He's made the cut in the US Masters every year from 1984 and finished in the top 40 every time so look out for suitable match bets for Langer at Augusta.

> He'll be very keen to pick up Ryder Cup points in South Africa early in the year. With two top 20s there in 2000 he can be supported in 2001 especially in match bets in the South African Open (T10th 2000: T27th 1999: T4th 1998).

> With a home in Florida Bernhard enjoys the 'Florida Swing' in the States. He can be supported in the Bay Hill Invitational in the speciality markets.
  * 10/1 top Euro 2000: Top Euro 1998 when T4th in the outright
  * 16/1 2nd top non American 2000: Top non-US player 1998

> He has a fine record at the Royal Zoute course (T3rd 1994: T4th 1993; T14th 1999) and, if in form, he must enter into calculations for the 2001 Belgacom Open.

> At Nordwijkse he will have a first class chance in the 2001 Dutch Open as "I love the course" having won there in 1992, and finished 2nd at 28/1 this year.

> He was 4/1 to make the 1999 Ryder team which he failed to do. To return to the side in 2001 he's best priced at 15/8, and he's 10/1 to gain a 'wild card'.

Key stat   98th for driving accuracy.

PAUL LAWRIE MBE

Age 31   **Born** Aberdeen   **Lives** Aberdeen

European tour wins 2, 1996 Catalonian Open, 1999 Qatar Masters **Major wins** 1, the 1999 British Open (will we ever forget it?) **World Cup** 1996 **Dunhill Cup** 1999 **Order of Merit** BEF 6th 1999

1999 was one of those 'change your life' years for Paul when he won the Qatar Masters before he landed that unforgettable British Open in a play-off. From 'journeyman' to millionaire, from Paul who? to an M.B.E. he's taken it all in his stride.

This year he's had niggling neck and groin injuries. Nevertheless he's posted two top 5 finishes, in the Dubai Desert Classic (T4th at 40/1) and the Victor Chandler British Masters (T5th at 50/1*). He also had high finishes in the Deutsche Bank Open (T15th), the European Open (8th), the Loch Lomond (T19th), the Lancome Trophy (T12th), the German Masters (T17th) and the Volvo Masters (T17th).

Missed the cut in the US Masters, didn't play in the US Open because of his groin problem, finished T72nd in the USPGA; and missed the cut as defending champion in the British Open. Finished T73rd in the States in the Players' Championship.

In the Coral Eurobet Seve Ballesteros Trophy he scored 2½ points beating Van de Velde, 5 and 4, in the singles.

Played well twice in America, firstly when T8th in the Mercedes, and then when T5th in the World Match Play when he beat Chris Perry, Billy Mayfair and Mark Calcavecchia before losing to Tiger Woods in the quarter-finals.

His big problem has been his inaccuracy off the tee. His approach play to the greens (80th in mid Oct.) could also be improved. His putting however has been first class.

He's now a big hitter, over 281 yards off the tee.

> He can be followed in match bets in the European Open. He's got PMAs with the K Club having finished 8th-15th-10th-14th in the last four years for a four-year stroke average of 70.75.

> Must have a leading chance in the Lancome Trophy in which he's got a good record (T12th 2000: T18th 1999: 8th 1997). His eclectic score over the last two years is 12 under par, which is almost a winning total.

> He's 5/2 to make the Ryder Cup team and just 9/2 for a 'wild card'. If he doesn't make the side he could well win the 2001 German Masters (T17th in 2000) in the week after the Belfry when the top bananas will be really jaded. This year his 66 (R2) and 68 (R3) were impressive rounds.

Key stat   7th for total putting.

STEPHEN LEANEY   G 🐎

Age 31   **Born** Australia   **Lives** Australia, Camberley when in UK

European tour wins 3 – 1998 Moroccan and Dutch Opens, 2000 Dutch Open **Australia tour wins** 7 – the Western Australian Open (4 times), the Victoria Open (1995 and 1997) and the 1998 ANZ Players' Championship **Dunhill Cup** 1999, 2000 **Order of Merit** BEF 11th 1998

Shot to prominence in 1998 with two victories, then in 1999 he had three top 4 finishes to establish himself as a leading player on the tour.

In 2000 he made a fast start when 5th at 40/1 in the Heineken Classic. He then missed the cut in the Greg Norman Holden International after which he played in a charity cricket match at the famous Melbourne cricket ground sustaining a hairline fracture of a finger on his left hand.

He rejoined the tour in March for 'the Middle East swing' missing the cut in Dubai, before finishing T3rd at 66/1* in the Qatar Masters.

Later he was T22nd in the Loch Lomond before he won for the third time in Europe when he landed the Dutch Open in late July at 66/1*.

In the Dunhill Cup he won two of his three games to give him a career record of four wins from six.

Missed the cut in the British Open.

Not long off the tee (267 yards) he is an accurate driver (69%) whose putting has often let him down this year.

> I am a big fan of this guy. He is a fine ball striker, a winner in Asia, Australia and Europe and a proven front runner. Goes to US Q School in November and if he obtains his US tour card I expect he will eventually be successful drawing on the experience of his friends Robert Allenby and Stuart Apleby.

> "I've only lost once in nine tournaments as a pro when I've been leading in the final round". So if he's in the lead or joint lead after R3 back him in 2 balls, and in the outrights to win.

> If he stays on the European tour I think he could well be the surprise 66/1 winner of the Volvo PGA in 2001. 16th (1998), T4th (1999) on his first two appearances he was a disappointing T43rd this year.

> He can be supported at Loch Lomond where his recent record is solid with 6 of his last 7 rounds at or under par, and this year (if we conveniently exclude his 77 in R2) he was only a shot behind the winner.

> Clearly he enjoys golf in Holland having won the Dutch Open twice (1998 and 2000) and on different courses. He was T15th when last he defended his Dutch title so he may be better followed in match bets rather than in the outrights in 2001.

> In the last couple of years he's finished T32 and T15 in the Irish Open (on different courses) with 7 of those 8 rounds at or below par. So have a punt or two each way on Leaney for the Irish Open in 2001.

> Can be backed at 50/1+ in the 2001 Victor Chandler British Masters as his relative inexperience will be nullified by the fact that it will be played on the new Marquess course at Woburn.

> Although he won his first European tournament, the 1998 Moroccan Open after a 5 week break I believe he is best when in continuous play having cleared away 'the rust'.

Key stat   30th for shot accuracy.

DAREN LEE

Age 35   **Born** Cockney   **Lives** Harlow

European tour BEF 5th 2000 BMW International **European Challenge tour** BEF 2nd, 1998 Galea Open

It's been a year of real struggle for the experienced Daren (yes, only one R in it) as he's hovered around that crucial 115th place on the O/M.

He'd posted two top 25s, in the Madeira Island Open (T18th) and the Compaq European Grand Prix (T22nd), and two top 30s, in the Dutch Open (T28th) and the Scandinavian Masters (T29th), before he made a big cheque when T5th in the BMW International, his best-ever finish.

Very short at 263 yards, he's accurate off the tee (top 25), but not from the fairway (outside top 125 for GIR).

> As a 35-year-old without a win on any tour, and just one top 5 it's not easy to find a significant betting opportunity.

> However a 66 in both R1 and R3 this year in the BMW suggest that he must be noted for 3 balls at the Golf Club Munchen in late August.

Key stat   75th in overall ranking.

THOMAS LEVET

Age 32   **Born** Paris   **Lives** Paris

European tour wins 1, 1998 Cannes Open **Challenge tour wins** 1 **Dunhill Cup** 1992, 98, 2000 **World Cup of Golf** 1998 **Order of Merit** 69th 1998

Playing on the Challenge tour in 1998 he got a sponsors' exemption for the Cannes Open and won it as a 'no hope' 250/1 outsider.

In 1999 he had a top 10 and four top 25s.

In 2000 he had top 25s in the South African Open (T16th), the Irish Open (20th) and the Sao Paulo Open (T22nd). His big finish came when he was T2nd at 80/1* in the Moroccan Open which secured effectively his card.

Threw away his chance in the BMW International in September — T4th at halfway, he then shot 73 and 77 to finish T46!

Lost all three games in the Dunhill Cup to give him a career record of two wins from nine games.

His approach play to the greens is sound. However he is very wayward off the tee and has putted poorly.

> Very difficult to find a betting opportunity for the Frenchman who may struggle to retain his card in 2001.

Key stat   69th for driving accuracy yet he's 12th for greens in reg.

JONATHAN LOMAS

Age 32   **Born** Chesterfield   **Lives** Ayrshire

European tour wins 1, 1996 Czech Open, Won 1996 Novotel Perrier Pairs (with S Bottomley) **Challenge tour wins** 3 **Order of Merit** 20th 1996 **Dunhill Cup** 1996

Joined via the Challenge tour in 1994 and has kept his card ever since. Was Rookie of the Year in 1994.

In 2000 he had a hole in one early on when T22nd in the Alfred Dunhill. Secured his card with a fine performance when 2nd at 150/1 in the French Open playing well alongside Monty in R4.

Also had high finishes in the Benson & Hedges (T9th) and the Scottish PGA (T16th).

> Well suited to links golf (he was T11 in the 1994 British Open) he will surely have a chance in the weakly contested Scottish PGA (67 in R4 this year when T16th) in August.

> Worth noting in any match bets in the Benson and Hedges tournament, (T16th 1999 and T9th 2000 on different courses).

Key stat   143rd in putts per green in reg.

PETER LONARD   S

Age 33   **Born** Sydney   **Lives** UK Sunningdale

European tour BEF T2nd 1997 Johnnie Walker Classic, and T2nd 1999 Heineken Classic. **Order of Merit** 48th 1997 **International wins** 1997 Australian Masters

Peter made 10 of his first 11 cuts this year including three top 25s in the Johnnie Walker Classic (17th), the Alfred Dunhill (22nd), the South African Open (26th) and the Brazil Rio de Janiero 500 Years Open (17th).

Later he was 5th at 125/1 in the Irish Open.

His iron play has become inaccurate this year although he still hits two thirds of his fairways.

> Match fit from the ANZ tour he can be noted in the early season tournaments in South Africa where he'll be worth supporting in match bets against 'rustier' European players.

> He's led two tournaments this year after R1, the Madeira Open (67) and the Brazil Rio de Janiero (62, with 29 on the back nine) so he's awarded the streaker symbol.

> Clearly enjoys Ireland, and who can blame him? In the Irish Open over the last three years on two different courses he was 5th (2000) and 8th (1998) so keep him in mind for that tournament in 2001.

Key stat   55th for greens in reg.

SANTIAGO LUNA   ☼

Age 38   **Born** Madrid   **Lives** Madrid

European tour wins 1, 1995 Madeira Open **International wins** 1, 1998 Hassan Trophy **Dunhill Cup** 1991, 1998 **World Cup of Golf** 1995,1998 **Order of Merit** BEF 31st 1998

Although 'Santi' made ten cuts in his first thirteen tournaments he could only post three high finishes, in the Moroccan Open (T14th), the French Open (T15th) and the Brazil Rio de Janiero 500 Years Open (T6th). Later he was T7th in the Dutch Open, T9th in the Turespana Masters, and T21st in the Italian Open.

Finished T16th in the BMW International.

A poor year for the experienced Spaniard with his stats all round disappointing especially his (broomstick) putts per GIR (outside top 100). Tends to draw the ball.

> Joins the European tour when it reaches Europe. Didn't break 70 this year till his 15th round so he is 'rusty' in early season.

> He can be followed on the spreads as a big priced outsider and in match bets in the French Open (T15th 2000, T3rd 1999, T8th 1998) where his last eleven rounds have been shot at 28 under par on two different courses so another new course in 2001 will not faze him.

> If the 2000 tour schedule allows 'Santi' some tournaments to sharpen up before the Portuguese Open he'd be a player to note on the Le Meridien course (T3rd 1999, T6th after R3 1998) which he loves so much.

> Worth noting in match bets in the BMW International (T16th 2000: T21st 1999) in September where he's been underpar in 7 of his last 8 rounds.

Key stat   17th for total driving.

DAVID LYNN

Age 27   **Born** England   **Lives** England

European tour BEF T2nd Austrian Open 1996 **Challenge tour** 1 win, 1997 **Order of Merit** BEF 63rd 2000

Gained his card at 1999 Q School birdieing the first extra hole to win a seven man play-off for five places.

Big impact in 2000 with three top 10s, in the Alfred Dunhill (T5th), the Madeira Island Open (T7th) and the English Open (T9th), and two top 20s in the Wales Open (T12th) and the European Open (T12th for his biggest cheque).

For a player with this record his stats are not impressive so his great strength is simply scoring! His solid all round game can clearly be improved in all departments.

> His strong finish in this year's Madeira Island Open (7 under last two rounds) makes him a player to consider on that quirky course in 2001.

> With his consistent cut making record he's not one to oppose in match bets.

Key stat   Made the cut in his first 17 tournaments in 2000.

MALCOLM MACKENZIE   **PB**

Age 39 (dodgy age!) **Born** Sheffield   **Lives** Barrow-on-Soar

European tour BEF 2nd, 1990 and 1991 Order of Merit 25th 1990 Majors T5th 1992 British Open

Finished 9th at the 1999 Q School to earn his tour card for his eighteenth successive season, in which he posted a top 10 and four top 20s.

His high finishes were in the Moroccan Open (T8th), the Alfred Dunhill Championship (T14th), the Portugues Open (T14th), the Qatar Masters (T19th) and the NW Ireland Golf Classic (T15th).

275 yards off the tee. Inaccuracy off both tee and fairway (not in top 100 for greens in reg or driving accuracy) continue to be his problem. Supports Sheffield Wednesday who also don't shoot straight!

He'll be 40 in Sept 2001.

> Off scratch at 15, Malcolm is a talented player, although his best days were in the early nineties. Difficult to see him winning for the first time now although his best chance will surely be in the West of Ireland Golf Classic as he's a fine links player (5th in the 1992 British Open), enjoys Ireland (T7th 1999 Irish Open) and was T15th in the tournament this year.

Key stat   Not a single top 3 finish in the last ten years.

MIGUEL ANGEL MARTIN ☼

Age 38   **Born** Spain   **Lives** Spain

European tour wins 3, including 1997 Heineken Classic and 1999 Moroccan Open **Dunhill Cup** 1991, 1994, 1997, 2000 **World Cup of Golf** 1997, 1998 **Ryder Cup** 1997 (qualified, DNP) **Order of Merit** BEF 17th 1996

Miguel, who chews tee pegs (I wonder if a manufacturer could start strawberry flavourings) for concentration ended 1999 in fine form when T3rd in the individual rankings in the World Cup of Golf and 3rd in the Hassan Trophy.

In 2000 he made his first eleven cuts and had five high finishes in the Dubai Desert Classic (T17th), the Qatar Masters (T5th at 40/1), the Sao Paulo Open (T8th after being 3rd at halfway), the Spanish Open (T12th), the French Open (T20th) and the Deutsche Bank Open (T17th). Won four of his five games to help Spain retain the Dunhill Cup in October. His victory in the final over David Frost was crucial and followed a 50-foot putt at the last which took the game to the 19th hole where he won. Before 2000 he'd lost all his seven Dunhill Cup games.

A freak serious injury at Loch Lomond stopped him playing in the British Open. Finished T5th in the BMW International in September and followed up when 7th in the Lancome Trophy (64 in R1).

Keeps his head amazingly still off the tee, Draws the ball. He's a very deliberate player. Accuracy off the tee, his usual strength, has let him down badly this year (not in top 150). 8/1 to play in the 2001 Ryder Cup having qualified for the side in 1997 before being controversially ruled out as unfit. 33/1 to get a 'wild card' from Sam Torrance.

> At his best in very warm, dry and still conditions.

> Worth considering in match bets in the Spanish Open (T12th-T25th-T11th last three years).

> His lack of length at 38 years of age is going to be an increasing handicap against the big-hitting younger 'gorillas' on the tour.

Key stat   165th for driving distance at just 264 yards.

PAUL McGINLEY   G

Age 34   **Born** Dublin   **Lives** Sunningdale (very posh)

European tour wins 2, last 1997 Oki Pro-Am **Dunhill Cup** 6 times, last 1999 **World Cup of Golf** 5, last 1999 **Order of Merit** BEF 15th 1996

Paul's close season went well as he made deals with Adidas and Taylor Made and finished T4th in the Australian Open.

He made a fast start in 2000 when he had high finishes in the Alfred Dunhill (T5th at 40/1), the Heineken Classic (T18th), the Portuguese Open (T3rd at 25/1), the Dubai Desert Classic (T2nd at 50/1) and the Qatar Masters (T7th).

He actually missed Cheltenham races (great Gold Cup, Paul!) to play in the Madeira Open to earn the twenty grand he needed to make the Seve Ballesteros Trophy. He failed!

Later he had top 25s in the Benson and Hedges (T18th), the Volvo Masters (T20th), the European Open (T13th) and the Lancome Trophy (T16th), and top 10s in the Deutsche Bank Open (T9th, after 65 in R2) and the Belgacom Open (T7th). He also had top 5 finshes in the Irish Open (T3rd at 50/1) and the Turespana Masters (T5th at 40/1).

In the British Open he shot four rounds at or under par to finish T20th, and was T2nd at 33/1 to be Top Brit. Missed the cut in the USPGA before finishing T23rd (of 37) in the WGC NEC.

Won two of his three Dunhill Cup games to give him a career record of twelve wins from twenty-two games.

Not long off the tee at 274 yards, he has sound all-round stats apart from sand saves (outside top 150). Paul has worked hard this year on his fitness.

3/1 to make the Ryder Cup team and 20/1 to be a 'wild card' choice.

> Paul is very much like a hold-up horse who mustn't hit the front too soon. At his best when coming from 'off the pace', as in this year's Irish Open, when T3rd after a 63 in R4, and in the Lancome Trophy (65 in R4).

  By contrast, in the European Open at the K Club after R3 he was T4th then shot 76 to finish T13th.

> He must be followed in March on the 'Middle East swing'.

  * Qatar Masters. T7th 2000: T16th 1999: T21st 1998, he can be supported with confidence, if he has an early tee time, in match bets and each way in the outrights.

  * The Dubai Desert Classic. T2nd 2000: T3rd 1999 with seven of his last eight rounds at or under par. In 2001 the tournament moves to the Emirates course which suits Paul who was T6th there in 1997.

> When the British Open was last held at Royal Lytham in 1996 Paul was 3rd top Brit at 50/1, and the tournament's halfway leader. The talented Irishman will be worth an each-way bet in the 2001 top Brit market (T2nd at 33/1 this year).

> He will have a leading chance in the Portuguese Open after his T3rd this year in his first start for three years.

> He can be noted for the German Masters (T14th 2000: T17th 1999) in match bets and 3 balls (64 in R3 this year), although he may not have the length to win.

> Clearly Paul has PMAs with the Turespana Masters. If he makes the starting tape in mid March he'll have a first-class chance (T3rd 1998: DNP 1999: T5th 2000).

Key stat   12th in the all-round ranking.

ANDREW McLARDY

Age 26   **Born** Zimbabwe   **Lives** Johannesburg

European tour BEF 5th 1999 Scandinavian Masters **Order of Merit** BEF 84th 1999

84th on the O/M, with three top 10s, in his 1999 Rookie year.

In 2000 he has struggled to retain his card with four top 25s, in the Greg Norman Holden International (T22nd), the Irish Open (T23rd), the Scandinavian Masters (T23rd after 73 in R4) and the Scottish PGA (T20th).

He had a top 20 in the Sao Paolo Open (T13th).

A long hitter at 280 yards his accuracy from tee and fairway have been his biggest problem.

> He has a consistent record in his two years in three tournaments.

* The Irish Open T23rd, 2000: T25th 1999.

* The Scandinavian Masters T23rd 2000: he was 5th at the Barseback course when it was last the venue in 1999.

* The Scottish PGA T20th 2000: T6th 1999. With his parents coming from West of Scotland and with Andrew a fine player if the winds blow this is one tournament in which he'll have an each-way chance and where he can be noted for match bets.

Key stat   142nd for shot accuracy.

MARK McNULTY

Age 47   **Born** Zimbabwe   **Lives** Sunningdale

European tour wins 15 – last the 1996 Volvo Masters **International wins** 23 – last 1998 South African Players Champ. **Dunhill Cup** 8 times, last 2000 **World Cup of Golf** 6 times last 1998 **Presidents Cup** 1994 and 1996 **Majors** BEF T2nd 1990 British Open **Order of Merit** 2nd 1990 and 1987

Won the Swaziland Open for the fifth time in early February coming from 7 shots back with a final round 61.

Laid low after that with illness (105 degrees!) so did not join the European tour till mid May. However on his return he has regained his form and confidence. He had two really big finishes, first when T5th at 50/1* in the Welsh Open, and later when 4th at 100/1* in the Victor Chandler British Masters.

Played well in the British Open to finish T11th, and T2nd at 40/1 in the Rest of the World market.

Posted top 20s in the English Open (T17th) and the German Masters (T17th). Very short off the tee (256 yards) he compensates through his accuracy and fine putting especially his lag putting. In the Dunhill Cup he won 2 of his 3 games to give him a career record of 17 from 26 games. Most definitely at his best in warm, dry weather.

> Used David Leadbetter, his coach, before his fine effort in this year's Victor Chandlers British Masters. With his PMAs with this tournament (T4th 2000: T18th 1999) he can be supported on the new course in 2001 especially in match bets.

> Back in 1996 Mark was T14th at Royal Lytham in the British Open. It was hot then, and if the sun shines there again in 2001 he can be supported in 3 balls, match bets, and in the Rest of the World betting (T2nd 40/1 in 2000).

Key stat   8th for driving accuracy.

PETER MITCHELL ☼

Age 42   **Born** Camberwell   **Lives** Kent

European tour wins 3 incl. 1997 Madeira Island Open & 1998 Portuguese Open **World Cup of Golf** 1996 **Order of Merit** BEF 12th 1996

From 1991 Peter has been in top 52 on the O/M, so 2000 has been a very disappointing year for him. Without a top 10 he has made just six top 25 finishes, in the Portuguese Open (T18th), the Dubai Desert Classic (T20th), the Deutsche Bank Open (T17th), the Irish Open (T21st), the German Masters (T22nd) and the Turespana Masters (T25th).

He's had rib problems over the last year or two. However he ended this year feeling physically O.K.

The key reason for his poor year has been the putter. It seems that his poor putting has also affected his traditional accuracy as he's not in the top 65 in either greens in reg or driving accuracy.

Fader of the ball.

> He has performed consistently well on Portuguese territory in recent years.

* Won 1997 Madeira Island Open
* Won 1998 Portuguese Open
* T5th 1999 Estoril Open
* Second-best finish in 2000 was T18th in the Portuguese Open.

So whenever Peter goes to Portugal take note, especially in the Portuguese Open where his record in the last three years (18th-19th-Won) is superb.

Key stat   2000 was his first year since 1988 without a top 10 finish.

COLIN MONTGOMERIE MBE   G 🏇

Age 37   **Born** Scotland   **Lives** Surrey (massive house)
Weight   Falling fast

European tour wins 23, 1989 Portuguese Open, 1991 Scandinavian Masters, 1993 Dutch Open, Volvo Masters, 1994 Spanish Open, English Open, German Open, 1995 German Open, Lancome Trophy, 1996 Dubai Desert Classic, Irish Open, Canon European Masters, 1997 Compaq European Grand Prix, Irish Open, 1998 Volvo PGA, British Masters, German Masters 1999 The Benson & Hedges, The Volvo PGA, The Loch Lomond Invitational, The Scandinavian Masters, and The BMW International, the Cisco World Matchplay, 2000 French Open, 2000 Volvo PGA **US Tour wins** Nil **Major wins** BEF 2nd 1995 USPGA, 2nd 1997 US Open, T2nd 1994 US Open **Ryder Cup** 5, last 1999 **Dunhill Cup** 10, last 2000 **World Cup** 6, last 1998 **European Order of Merit** No. 1 for 7 successive years from 1993 - 1999 inclusive!

It's been an unusual year for Monty. He won only twice and lost form because weight for it....he was slimming. However he never got into contention in a single major.

On the European tour he won the French Open with Pete Coleman as his caddie (at 13/2), and the Volvo PGA, for the third successive year (at 5/2). He also posted five top 5 finishes in the Spanish Open (5th at 13/2), the Benson and Hedges (T5th at 6/1), the Loch Lomond (3rd at 8/1), the Victor Chandlers British Masters (3rd at 7/2) and the German Masters (T3rd at 12/1).

He also had top 10 finishes in the Deutsche Bank Open (T6th), the English Open (8th), the European Open (T8th) and the Volvo Masters (9th), and a top 20 in the Scandinavian Masters (T17th).

His weight loss affected him in the Scandinavian Masters (T17th) where he had headaches and his form was really poor in September when he followed his T46th in the Lancome Trophy with T26th in the Belgacom Open. However he recovered with his swing back in the groove in the German Masters (T3rd) and the Cisco World Matchplay where he was rather unlucky to lose to Westwood in the final (at the 38th) having earlier defeated Harrington (5 and 3) and Singh (5 and 4).

In the Coral Eurobet Seve Ballesteros Trophy he acted as player captain of the British side scoring only 2 points after playing in all five matches. Lost in a mega-shock to Seve in the singles when 5/1 on.

In the Andersen World Match Play he beat Dennis Paulson (2 and 1) before losing to Thomas Bjorn.

In the WGC NEC Invitational he finished fast to secure 8th place.

In the majors he was T19th (NIC) in the US Masters, T46th in the US Open, T26th in the British Open and T39th in the USPGA.

In the Dunhill Cup he won only 1 of his 3 games to give him a career record of 20 points from 34 games.

Monty is now back to his best. He has a superb swing with a beautiful rhythm. Although he continually moans about his putting he has a good putting stroke. However his superbly accurate approach play does give him countless birdie chances so when he doesn't take them it makes him appear to be a poor putter. Nevertheless if he was in the Loren Roberts-Brad Faxon class on the greens he would be virtually unbeatable.

His other technical problem may be when clipping from off the green which still seems to be below the standard of the rest of his game.

> Monty is contender for 'Slimmer of the Year'. He'd been, on his own admission, on a rotten diet before he began to focus on fruit and vegetables. Trouble was Monty lost too much too fast as 25 lbs in eight weeks vanished so did his rhythym as his weight transference in his swing went awry. However by October after overcoming poor form he was stronger physically and better mentally ("increased my self esteem").

> I have stressed my admiration for Monty many times in the past. He has his values clear, with his family coming first, second and third and he definitely will not be joining the USPGA tour. Indeed in October 2000 Monty announced that he will be following a reduced European tour schedule in 2001. It will he said represent a new phase in the lives of myself and family. "My days of rushing from one tournament to another without ever having time to stop and smell the

flowers along the way are over".

> The big question with Monty is whether he will win a major. I really do now think that it's most unlikely for four key reasons.

Firstly, I really do wonder now if he's hungry enough. I say this because this year he had a corporate engagement on the Monday of the week of the USPGA. So why was that in the diary if he was really determined to win that coveted first major? His preparation was clearly suboptimal and he finished T39th.

Secondly, he finds it difficult to handle disappointment so that one bad hole has often been followed by another. This inability to handle disappointment is undoubtedly a real problem....if only he had Lee Westwood's temperament.

Third, three of the majors are 'across the pond' and he has still not solved the problem of his relationship with the American galleries. He is all too easily distracted for as Dennis Paulson said, "we tease him that he's put off by a fart two fairways away", and Butch Harmon has spoken of his 'rabbit ears' picking up every small sound.

Fourth, his style and record suggests that he's most unsuited to the one British major, the British Open where his record of one top 10, and five missed cuts in the last ten years is poor.

So overall it's not easy to see Monty landing that elusive first major although I wouldn't rule it out as he now has one big advantage because in 2001 the new slimline fitter Monty will be better able to handle the heat and humidity in America.

> In America his best chances will lie in

* The Players Championship. The tough Sawgrass course demands accuracy. If he can get a good pair of tee times he will surely go close as he's been 2nd 3rd and 7th in eight starts, including his 3rd place in 2000.

* The US Masters. I can't see Monty winning because of his putting on the slick Augusta greens. However, 8th-11th-19th form figures in the last three years on a course where the recent changes emphasise accuracy (his key strength) suggest his finishing position can be sold on the spreads.

* The US Open. In nine starts he's made every cut and has three top 5 finishes (3rd 1992: T2nd 1994: 2nd 1997) and three other top 20s. It's the tournament 'made for Monty' because of its emphasis on accuracy. However for reasons already given I can't see him winning although he must be considered for match bets.

> He can be opposed in 2 tournaments in each of which he's got a poor record.

* European Open. Form figures over the last five years of 8th-15th-MC-22nd-27th, with only eight of those eighteen rounds under par, is un-Monty-like. Worth taking him on in match bets.

* The British Open. His record of 26th-15th-MC-24th-MC-MC-8th-MC-MC-26th in the last ten years is unimpressive although it's improved recently.

> He clearly could win virtually any tournament he enters. Nevertheless I would nominate him specifically for three:-

* The Loch Lomond. 3rd (2000), Won (1999), 10th (1997) are good figures, and he has had fourteen of those sixteen rounds under par for a stunning stroke average 68.75.

* Volvo PGA. Winner in each of the last three years, he played beautifully in the Cisco World Matchplay including an estimated 61 in one round. "I feel I'm one up on the first tee every time I play here.....I feel I am going to win when I come through the driveway. It's close to home and suits my game."

* Victor Chandler British Masters. The week after the Volvo PGA it will be played on the new Marquess Course at Woburn. 3rd 2000, 2nd 1999, Won 1998 is a fine record and Monty could well win it again in 2001.

> He will be a tower of strength in the Ryder Cup where he's bound to be heavily involved in the foursomes and let's remember he's not lost a singles match in his five Ryder Cups

Key stat   No. 1 on the European Order of Merit for seven successive years from 1993-1999 inclusive — a record that will surely NEVER be equalled, let alone beaten!

JARROD MOSELEY

Age 27   **Born** Australia   **Lives** Australia

European tour wins 1, 1999 Heineken Classic **Order of Merit** 16th 1999

His shock 250/1 win on a sponsors' exemption in the 1999 Heineken Classic earned Jarrod an exemption till the end of 2001 and he built on that success with three top 3 finishes to finish the season 16th on the O/M.

In 2000 he has found it difficult to maintain his progress as he didn't post a top 30 finish till his 13th tournament when he was T22nd in the Loch Lomond. Then a week later he was T42nd in the British Open. He maintained his form when T14th in the Dutch Open on a links course, T11th in the Victor Chandler British Masters, T8th in the Canon European Masters, and T22nd in the German Masters.

He is a very sound putter. However he is outside the top 100 for driving accuracy, and his greens in reg ranking (not in top 150) is very poor.

> His best form, after his Heineken success, has clearly been in July and August in which he's posted his three top 3 finishes in 1999, and his two top 20s in 2000.

> He obviously enjoys playing in Holland where in two starts he's finished T3rd in 1999 at Hilversum, and T14th in 2000 at Noordwijkse. So keep him in mind for the 2001 Dutch Open.

> His poor R4 scoring record this year (one sub 70 round to Sept) and the fact that he made four successive bogeys when he actually led the British Open in R2 suggest he may be feeling the pressure in his second season.

Key stat   22nd for total putting.

ROLF MUNTZ

Age 31　　　**Born** Holland　　　**Lives** Belgium

European tour wins 2000 Qatar Masters **Challenge tour wins** 4 **World Cup of Golf** 1999 **Order of Merit** BEF 58th 2000

Bookies cheered home Rolf this year when he landed his first tour win in the Qatar Masters at 150/1. Then after six successive missed cuts he 'popped up' at 125/1 when 3rd in the Irish Open.

In his other tournaments Rolf was consistent, consistently poor. His only solid stat is for greens in reg showing his solid iron play is sandwiched between waywardness off the tee and woeful putting on the greens.

Draws the ball, and finds it difficult to move it the other way (left-right). 7/1 to make the Ryder Cup side.

> His three massive finishes in the last two years have been on links courses (1999 Scottish PGA T2nd, and 2000 Irish Open T3rd) and in wind (won 2000 Qatar Masters).

  He is clearly at his best on wide fairway links tracks and when the breezes blow as he showed when winning the British Amateur Championship in 1990 at Muirfield links.

> In the weakly contested 2001 Scottish PGA (T2nd 1999: T20th 2000) he must have a real chance especially if the wind gets up.

Key stat　　　In the last two years he's had just three top 10s yet they've all been 'biggees' with a win, a T2nd and a 3rd.

GERRY NORQUIST

Age 34　　　**Born** Arizona　　　**Lives** Arizona

European tour wins 1, 1999 Malaysian Open **International wins** 8, last the 1998 Volvo Asian Matchplay **Order of Merit** BEF 88th 1999

Played the Asian tour from 1991 winning the Benson and Hedges Malaysian Open in 1993 and again when it was cosanctioned with the European tour he won it again, from the front, in 1999. That win earned him a two-year exemption.

In 2000 he has played mainly on the Brazilian, Far Eastern and Australian parts of the European tour. He was 2nd at 125/1 in the Brazil Sao Paolo 500 Years Open after birdieing the last 3 holes, and was T16th as defending champion in the Malaysian Open.

Accuracy off the tee and a good putting touch are his great strengths.

> He clearly enjoys the Far East and especially the Malaysian Open (winner twice and T16th 2000) in which he can be followed with confidence in match bets and in the outrights in mid February.

Key stat　　　He won 9 tournaments in 5 different countries in the nineties.

HENRIK NYSTROM

Age 31 **Born** Sweden **Lives** Sweden

European tour BEF 2nd 2000 Scottish PGA **Order of Merit** BEF 109th 2000

In 1999 156th on the O/M meant a trip to Q School where he finished 35th. Henrik has shown much improved form this year with three top 20s, in the Wales Open (T12th), the Compaq European Grand Prix (T14th) and the BMW International (T20th). However his big tournament, and career-best finish, came when he was 2nd at 100/1* in the Scottish PGA.

Also played on the Challenge tour this year posting three top 10s in four starts.

An accurate driver (22nd) his approach play has been poor on occasions so he's lowly ranked for greens in reg (130th).

> It's been a really important year for Henrik as he's been in serious contention twice and he's retained his card for the first time.

* Wales Open. T3rd after a 64 in R3 he shot 75 in R4 to finish T12th. "I learned a lot from that. I learned to stay calm."

* Scottish PGA. 2nd after R3, he led during R4, he finished 2nd.

> He must enter into calculations for the

* Wales Open. T12th 2000 including 64 in R3.

* Compaq European Grand Prix. T14th including 67 in R3.

Key stat He made the cut in nine tournaments (from sixteen) and in R3 he was under par on eight of the nine occasions, including rounds of 64, 67, 68 and 68.

GEOFF OGILVY   G Y

Age 23 **Born** Adelaide **Lives** Melbourne

European tour BEF T3rd Scandinavian Masters **ANZ tour** Rookie of the Year 1998-99 **Order of Merit** BEF 48th 2000

65th on the O/M 1999, in his European rookie year.

He was 2nd at 100/1 on the Johnnie Walker Classic in November 1999, and later had high finishes in the South African Open (T26th), the Benson and Hedges (T14th), the Deutsche Bank Open (T6th) and the Belgacom Open (T18th).

He uses his least reliable club, his driver, far too often. "I try to hit them harder and harder.....that's the way I am." A long hitter at 290 yards. Uses Dale Lynch as his coach.

> A talented player (off scratch at 16), he has posted three top 5 finishes on the European tour in his first 2 seasons. Needs to "play the percentages" off the tee more.

> Needs to improve his mental skills. He bust his putter in this year's South African Open then putted with his driver. "Mentally I get a bit impatient"....once he improves in this regard he'll do really well.

Key stat 159th for driving accuracy.

NICK O'HERN G

Age 29   **Born** Perth, Australia   **Lives** Perth, Australia

European tour BEF T5th 2000 Wales Open. **ANZ tour** 2000 Coolum Classic **Dunhill Cup** 2000 **Order of Merit** BEF 42nd 2000

On the ANZ tour in 1997/8, and 1998/9 he made eighteen cuts in twenty starts, and in 1999/2000 he was 'Mr Consistency' with top 10s in six tournaments, the Ford Open (T8th), the Australian PGA (T3rd), the ANZ Players (T7th), the Australian Open (T2nd), the Coolum Classic (Won) and the Canon Challenge (T3rd).

On the European tour he made the cut in fifteen of his first seventeen starts with high finishes in the French Open (T15th), the Volvo PGA (T11th after being R1 leader with 65), the English Open (T12th), the Wales Open (T5th at 40/1) and the Irish Open (T6th). Later he was T7th in the Lancome Trophy

42nd in the British Open. Played very impressively to win all three games in the Dunhill Cup on his debut.

A natural right hander he plays left handed. In one-handed sports he's right handed, in two-handed games he's left handed!

Wife acts as his caddy. A fine putter and very accurate driver, his iron play can still be improved. Very low hands when addressing the ball. He'll be 30 in October 2001.

> This guy is a seriously good and fast improving player who must now be placed firmly in 'the winner about to happen' category. I expect him to win in 2001.

> Must ALWAYS be considered in match bets and on the spreads as his consistency is tremendous.

> Turning high finishes into his first win won't be easy in a Ryder Cup year and when he's short off the tee. However he can be fancied for three tournaments in 2001:-

  * The English Open, T12 2000, where accuracy is the key
  * The Irish Open, four sub-par rounds when T6th 2000
  * The Wales Open, T5th this year, will provide a big opportunity

> Nick is usually 'very fast out of the traps'. This year for example he shot an opening round in the 60s in eight of his first seventeen tournaments, and in the Dunhill Cup he shot a sparkling 65 on day one. So never oppose him in R1 3 balls and look for suitable opportunities to back him.

> Well suited to the Nom-la-Breteche course, Nick had a back problem over the last two rounds in this year's Lancome Trophy when T7th. In 2001 with the top Euros' minds on the Ryder Cup back him at 66/1 or more to cause a shock in Versailles.

> In the Irish Open (T6th), the Belgacom Open (T30th) and especially in the Dunhill Cup (stroke average of 68!) he showed he's a fine links player. Could well provide a shock in the 2001 Belgacom Open when the top Euros are having a Ryder Cup hangover.

Key stat   16th (at 70.2%) for driving accuracy.

JOSE MARIA OLAZABAL   S ☀

Age 34   **Born** Spain   **Lives** Spain

European tour wins 18, latest 2000 Benson and Hedges, and 1998 Dubai Desert Classic **International wins** 4, last 1994 NEC World Series **Major wins** 2, the US Masters in 1994, and again in 1999 **Dunhill Cup** 9 times, last 2000 **World Cup** 1989 **Ryder Cup** 6 times, latest 1999 **Order of Merit** 2nd 1989

It's been a mixed year for 'Olly' in which he secured another win in the most bizarre circumstances. After R3 of the Benson and Hedges he was 5 strokes behind the leader and odds on favourite Padraig Harrington. However the disqualification of the Irishman gave him his chance and he took it with a last round 66 to win at 40/1.

On the European tour he had top 10s in the Greg Norman Holden (T8th), the Irish Open (T10th) and the Loch Lomond (T9th after 66 in R4).

In the majors he missed the cut as the defending champion at Augusta and finished 31st in the British Open. However he played really well to finish T12th in the US Open and T4th at 100/1 in the USPGA. Finished T10th in the WGC NEC Invitational after 65 in R4 and T17th in the WGC Amex at Valderrama.

In the World Match Play he beat Craig Parry before losing to Mark Calcavecchia.

In the Coral Eurobet Seve Ballesteros Trophy he scored 2½ points from five matches, beating Gary Orr 2 and 1 in the singles. In the Dunhill Cup in October he won four of his five games as he helped Spain retain the trophy.

A brilliant mid-to-long iron player, Olly's weakness, as always, has been his driving accuracy at 55%. However his putts per GIR (top 20) and sand saves (top 10) are testament to the continued excellence of his skill on and around the greens.

> Olly will focus on the US tour next year. However, although he will enjoy the heat and the fast greens his driving inaccuracy will surely continue to be a handicap especially on the tighter courses.

> Like Van de Velde however I expect he'll do very well in any desert tournaments he enters as he'll enjoy the heat, the fast greens and the wider fairways.

> His game is, as we know, tailor made for Augusta. He was below par in 2000 when he missed the cut. Nevertheless before that he had two victories, a second place and two other top 10s in his previous ten starts in which he'd made every cut. This profile tipped him for his 66/1 success in 1999, however in 2001 I suggest he's best backed in the top European market.

> Must be seriously considered for match bets in the Irish Open where his recent record is most consistent (6th 1997: T9th 1998: DNP 1999: T10 2000).

> 5/2 ON to make the Ryder Cup side are not tempting odds as I have very serious doubts whether he will qualify for the side given his US tour decision. If he doesn't Sam Torrance will I expect make him a 'wild card' choice as his recent Ryder Cup record (1997 and 1999) is 4½ pts from 8, and he proved in 2000 when he won the Benson & Hedges that he can play the Belfry course really well. Worth a bet at 7/2 with Victor Chandlers to receive a wild card.

> With his brilliant short game Olly is undoubtedly a streaker as he proved this year when he'd shot seven rounds of 66 or under by mid October including that brilliant 63 in R3 of the USPGA.

> He had a superb record at the Firestone course in the WGC-NEC Invitational in the early nineties (Won 1990, Won 1994) and this year he played well to finish T10 (last two rounds 69.65). Worth noting each way in the top European market (T3rd at 6/1 this year).

> The forgiving fairways at Montecastillo in the Volvo Masters suit Olly. 3rd in 1997, 7th in 1998 and T5th this year he has a 68.91 stroke average for those years. A must for match bets.

Key stat   156th (!) at 56% for driving accuracy.

ANDREW OLDCORN

Age 40   **Born** Bolton   **Lives** Edinburgh (classy city)

European tour 2, last 1995 Jersey Open **Order of Merit** BEF 34th 1996

Another disappointing year for the Bolton-born Scottish resident. He had one big finish when 5th at 125/1 in the Compaq European Grand Prix, a top 10 in the Italian Open (T7th) and three other top 20s in the Portuguese Open (T11th), the Wales Open (T17th) and the Scottish PGA (T11th).

He had a top 25 in the BMW International (T25th).

Andrew's great strength is his accuracy off the tee. However his lack of length (262 yards) is a mega handicap these days. His sand saves stats are very poor.

Recovered from a wrist injury sustained in April. He was 40 in March 2000.

> Soon to be a first time dad. 2001 will be Andrew's 'nappy factor' year.

> Living 'up the road' in Edinboro he obviously enjoys the Compaq European Grand Prix with two top 5 finishes in its four years (4th in 1996, and T5th 2000). Worth noting there in match bets and as a place-only bet.

> Finished well (7 under last three rounds) this year in the Scottish PGA (T11th) to suggest he'd go close again in his other 'home' tournament in 2001.

> In the Portuguese Open he has a solid recent record (T11th 2000: T25th 1999) and can be noted there in the 3-ball betting especially in R3, 67 (2000) 69 (1999).

Key stat   6th for driving accuracy.

PETER O'MALLEY

Age 35   **Born** Sydney, Australia   **Lives** Sydney and Bracknell (UK)

European tour wins 2, last 1995 Benson & Hedges **International wins** 2, last 1998 Canon Challenge (ANZ tour) **World Cup of Golf** 1992, 1998 **Dunhill Cup** 1999, 2000 **Order of Merit** BEF 10th 1995

'Pom' has played consistently as usual this year posting five top 20s, in the Johnnie Walker Classic (T12th), the Heineken Classic (T18th), the Greg Norman Holden International (T16th), the Dutch Open (T14th) and the Victor Chandler British Masters (T20th), and four top 10s in the French Open (T7th), the Benson & Hedges (T9th), the Volvo PGA (T7th) and the English Open (T10th).

In the Dunhill Cup he won one of his three games to give him a career record of two wins from six.

His accuracy off both tee and fairway are the basis for his consistency. His putting has prevented him turning his high finishes into top 5s let alone a victory.

One always feels that he has more talent than achievement probably because under severe R4 pressure he hooks the ball.

> He retains the bottle

* 2000 T3rd after R3 in the Heineken Classic, he shot 72 in R4 to finish T18th.

* In 1999 3-shot leader after R3 of the ANZ tour championship, shot 78 to finish T11th.

* In 1998 dropped 3 shots in last 2 holes to lose the Johnnie Walker Classic.

  If he's to win again it will surely be when backing into the winners' enclosure from the 'off the pace'.

* In the vital Dunhill match against Coceres he dropped 5 shots from the 15th - 17th inclusive to shoot 76 and lose the game so Argentina reached the sem finals.

* His accuracy and consistency make him solid match bet material particularly in four tournaments:-

> European Open: Successive top 20s in 1999 and 2000.

> French Open: 7th in 1995, and 7th 2000.

> Greg Norman Holden International: T17th 2000; T4th 1999, T11th 1998

> Heineken Classic: successive top 20s in 2000 and 1999

Key stat   Top 20 for both driving accuracy and greens in reg in each of the last two years

GARY ORR   G

Age 33   **Born** Scotland   **Lives** Weighbridge

European tour BEF T2nd 1998 Volvo PGA **Dunhill Cup** 1998, 1999, 2000 **Order of Merit** BEF 10th 2000

The 33-year-old Scot joined the tour in 1993 finishing every year since in the top 72 on the O/M. However over the course of 1998, when 28th on the Order of Merit, and 1999, when 21st, Gary established himself as a leading tour player, although he entered 2000 without that elusive first victory.

However this has been breakthrough time for Gary with a couple of wins. He eagled the last in February to win the Portuguese Open at 22/1, and in early August he won the Victor Chandler British Masters at 50/1.

Apart from the Heineken Classic he made every cut through to September posting top 20s in the Loch Lomond (T13th) and the South African Open (T16th), top 10s in the Greg Norman Holden International (T8th), the Spanish Open (6th), the Deutsche Bank Open (T9th) and the English Open (T6th), and a top 5 in the Alfred Dunhill (T2nd at 50/1). Came from 'off the pace' to finish 2nd at 50/1 in the Turespana Masters in October.

In the Seve Ballesteros Trophy he scored 1½ points from four matches, losing 2 and 1 to Olazabal in the singles.

In the British Open he finished 41st, and he missed the cut (by 1 shot) in the USPGA. Finished 27th (of 37) in the WGC NEC Invitational. Lost all three games in the Dunhill Cup for a career record of three wins from nine games.

Not long off the tee at 275 yards his great strength is his unerring accuracy off both tee and fairway. His putting looks mechanical yet has clearly improved, especially under pressure. A back problem forced him to withdraw from the Dutch Open.

Tends to draw the ball.

Became a first-time father in April this year.

> Last year I suggested he'd post his first win this year encouraged by Paul Lawrie's success, as Gary must have known he was at the very least as good a player as his fellow Scot. Well he's now got two wins and the challenge is to maintain his all-round consistency and to earn a Ryder Cup place for which he was best priced at 15/8 (he's 10/1 to get a 'wild card'). I expect Gary to qualify for the Belfry.

> From the start of the 1999 season - Sept 2000 Gary had made the cut in an amazing forty-two (93%) of his forty-five European tournaments. So, as I pointed out last year, you can make a handy second income by supporting him in match betting, especially if there is any premium on accuracy.

> Gary simply cries out to be backed to be the 50/1 winner of the 2001 Volvo PGA for three key reasons:-
  * The course is tailor made for his accuracy
  * His course record 7th in 1996, 2nd in 1998, and then consecutive top 30s is very good.
  * This is his local course as he lives nearby.

> He has a stroke average of 70.5 over the last three years at Loch Lomond where he's finished T13th 2000, T46th 1999 and T7th 1998. He is a must for match bets and he'll be worth an each-way interest at 66/1 on the Bonnie Banks in 2001.

> He has shown superb recent form in the English Open. T6th in 2000, and T7th in 1999 on different courses he's now posted three top 10s in the last four years. A must for match bets and on the spreads he could well be the 50/1 winner of the 2001 English Open.

> He can be backed with confidence for the 2001 Greg Norman Holden International played again on the tough Lakes course. It places a premium on diriving accuracy so playing to his great strength as he showed this year when T8th after the second best final 54 holes in the tournament.

> T14th at Barseback when it was last used for the Scandinavian Masters in 1999 he must be considered a serious candidate in 2001.

> In mid March he will be a solid each-way bet in the Turespana Masters (T8th 1999: 2nd 2000).

Key stat   Top (at 77.7%) for greens in reg.

HENNIE OTTO

Age 24   **Born** South Africa   **Lives** South Africa

Challenge tour wins 1, 1999 Philips Challenge **South African wins** 2 **European tour** BEF 6th 2000 Scottish PGA

Hennie made a good start to his European tour career when he won on the 1999 Challenge tour and with a total of four top 4 finishes he earned his 2000 tour card.

This year he had one high finish when in the top 10 in the Scottish PGA (T6th). However he didn't post any other top 30 finish in a disappointing year until September when he was T22nd in the Belgacom Open after a 64 in R1.

Clearly this year has been tough for him as he embarked on the tough learning curve of the European tour.

He is long off the tee as 280 yards, however all his other stats see him ranked outside the top 100. Must go to Q School.

A member of Chubby Chandler's group.

> Will want to get off to a fast start in his native South Africa where his best chance will be in the South African Open (T5th 1999: T34th 2000) where his eight rounds over the last two years have all been at or under par.

> In the Belgacom Open he was T5th after R3 then shot a poor 74 to finish T22nd to suggest that he's not yet ready to win on the European tour in Europe.

> Called a 'star of the future' by Ernie Els last year it will be interesting to study his early season stats to see if he is going to develop his potential.

Key stat   Only one sub-70 opening round in his first twenty-five tournaments in 2000.

GREG OWEN   FT g

Age 28   **Born** Mansfield   **Lives** Mansfield (poor side!)

European tour BEF T3rd 1999 Lancome Trophy: T3rd Sao Paolo Open **Challenge tour wins** 1, in 1996 **Order of Merit** BEF 39th 2000

Spent the winter with martial arts expert, Ron Cuthbert to strengthen and stretch his muscles.

Got off to a fast start this year with five top 20 finishes before May in the Portuguese Open (T6th), the South African Open (T10th), the Dubai Desert Classic (T13th, when 3rd for GIR) and the Sao Paolo Open (T3rd).

He went on to post further high finishes in the Spanish Open (T17th), the European Open (T21st), the Dutch Open (T7th), the Victor Chandler British Masters (T20th) and the Turespana Masters (T15th). Finished very well in the BMW International in September (T5th at 100/1) and was placed T17th in the Volvo Masters.

55th in the British Open.

A long hitter at 285 yards he is accurate off both tee and fairway. However his putting and bunker play regularly let him down.

A member of Barry Hearn's management group. 6/1 chance to make the Ryder Cup side which is one of his goals.

> His R4 scoring in Rio (73) and in the Victor Chandler Masters (73) were disappointing. However "nerves don't frighten me, I enjoy them and love the excitement of being up there competing" so let's hope this progressive player will win his first tournament in 2001. If so he must improve his putting. Nevertheless he merits the FT symbol.

> He clearly enjoys the Victor Chandler British Masters (T20th 2000: T4th 1999: T7th 1998) and in 2001 he can be expected to do well again especially as the older players' experience advantage will count for nothing on a new course.

> In mid March Greg could well spring a surprise in the Turespana Masters. He's had two successive top 20s and has a solid record in Spain.

Key stat   2nd for total driving, 5th for greens in regulation yet 142nd (!) for total putting.

DAVID PARK

Age 26   **Born** Wales   **Lives** Wales

European tour wins 1 1999 Compaq European Grand Prix **Challenge tour wins** 2 **World Cup of Golf** 1999 **Dunhill Cup** 2000 **Order of Merit** BEF 40th 1999

Burst onto the scene in 1999. He led the Challenge tour after a victory, a second and a fourth when he played the Moroccan Open finishing 2nd after a play-off, to Martin. He then went on to the Compaq European Grand Prix which he won at 100/1.

In 2000 he had a high finish early on when T5th at 125/1 in the Greg Norman Holden International. He went on to be 16th in the Malaysian Open, T13th in the Brazil 500 Years Open, T17th in the Sao Paolo Open, 22nd in the French Open, 21st in the Wales Open, and a fine T7th in the Belgacom Open. Missed the cut as defending champion in the Compaq European Grand Prix.

On his debut for Wales in the Dunhill Cup helped his side reach the semi finals winning two of his four games.

Short off the tee at 269 yards his iron play and putting (both outside top 100) have been poor this season. Very good from sand (top 10). 8/1 to make the Ryder Cup side.

> Since his successes in 1999 he's had some disappointing R4s in the 1999 BMW International (80), the 2000 Greg Norman (74 in R4 when T1st after R3) and the Sao Paolo Open (R3 joint leader then 76 in R4) to merit the 'bottle'.

> So best chance will be when coming from 'off the pace' in one of the lesser tournaments, possibly in the Wales Open (T21st this year) which he'd dearly love to win.

Key stat   32nd for driving accuracy.

LUCAS PARSONS

Age 31   **Born** New South Wales   **Lives** Sydney

European tour wins 2000 Greg Norman Holden Intl. **Challenge tour wins** 2, both in 1999. **International wins** 3, on ANZ tour.

Lucas won the Greg Norman Holden International, before his local crowd, at 100/1 to earn a two-year exemption.

However since then he's failed to notch a top 25 finish although he was 41st in the British Open.

His big problem has been his long game where he has been inaccurate off both tee and fairway, and poor from bunkers. A long hitter at 280 yards.

> With just one high finish (and that a win!) on the European tour Parsons is not a player to rely on. Nevertheless he has won somewhere in each of the last three years.

> If his early season accuracy stats show an improvement he can then be noted as he has been a consistent cut maker before this year.

> Will face a tough task as defending champion in the 2001 Greg Norman Holden International.

Key stat   99th on the overall ranking.

VAN PHILLIPS

Age 28   **Born** Southall   **Lives** Maidenhead

European tour wins 1, 1999 Portuguese Open **Challenge tour wins** 1 in 1996 **Order of Merit** 50th 1998

Made his breakthrough victory in the 1999 Portuguese Open. However in 2000 he'd not really consolidated as he'd posted just five top 25s, in the Dubai Desert Classic (T13th), the Qatar Masters (T19th), the Spanish Open (T10th), the French Open (T22nd) and the Canon European Masters (T13th), until he played really well in the Italian Open (T5th at 125/1).

Has improved his strength and fitness in the gym.

Short off the tee at 268 yards. His game has been based on accurate approach play.

> In each of the last four seasons his best form has been early and he made his usual fast start in 2000 with four top 25s in his first nine starts in which he made eight cuts.

> He enjoys the French Open (T22nd 2000, T23rd 1998, T3rd 1997) where eleven of his last twelve rounds have been at or under par. However it moves to a new course in 2001.

> He will be in with a chance if he gets a good tee time in the Qatar Masters (T19th 2000; 4th 1998).

> He was 14 under par on the par 5s in the Italian Open when T5th this year. Must have a solid each-way chance next year at 100/1.

Key stat   31st on the overall ranking.

IAN POULTER   FT

Age 24   **Born** Hitchen   **Lives** Luton (poor team)

European tour BEF T2nd 2000 Moroccan Open **Challenge tour** 1 win in 1999
Order of Merit BEF 31st 2000

In his rookie year Ian has sure made an impact. He made 4 cuts in his first 5 events
including high finishes in the Portuguese Open (T18th), the Alfred Dunhill (T22nd),
the Malaysian Open (T23rd) and the Qatar Masters (T11th). Then in successive
tournaments he was T3rd in the Sao Paulo Open, and T2nd at 100/1 (when my
selection) in the Moroccan Open.

Later he was T22nd in the Benson and Hedges, and T17th in the Deutsche Bank
before tendonitis caused by too much golf set in. He returned for the Compaq
European Grand Prix (T14th). T64th in his first British Open. 8/1 to make his Ryder
Cup debut in 2001.

His breakthrough came in the Italian Open in late October which he won at 100/1
on a course he knew from the Challenge tour. 3 birdies in the last 6 holes brought
him his first win and almost certainly the 'Rookie of the year' title.

Long (280 yards) although not always accurate off tee, he has putted well this year.

> 'Second seasons' are always tough yet this lad is a class act and he's not afraid
> of winning. Could well post another success in 2001 probably when the big
> names are missing.

> He can be fancied for the Compaq European Grand Prix after his promising play
> (69 in R1, and T14th finish) this year when 'rusty'.

> If the Golf D'Amelkis course is used again for the 2001 Moroccan Open he will
> have a first class chance after his T2nd this year after shooting 4 sub seventy
> rounds, including the back nine in 31 (!) in R4.

Key stat   28th for total putting.

PHILLIP PRICE   G

Age 34 (going ever greyer)   **Born** Pontypridd   **Lives** Pontypridd

European tour wins 1, 1994 Portuguese Open **Dunhill Cup** 1991,1996, 2000
World Cup of Golf 5 times, last 1998 **Order of Merit** BEF 8th 2000

He may not have won this year yet Phillip has really established on the world stage
after a brilliant display in the World Golf Championship NEC Invitational in which he
played superbly posting four rounds in the 60s to finish T2nd at 250/1.

On the European tour he had four top 5 finishes, in the Alfred Dunhill (T2nd at 50/1),
the Portuguese Open (2nd at 28/1), the Benson and Hedges (2nd at 66/1) and the
Wales Open (T5th at 20/1).

He also had top 10s in the Johnnie Walker Classic (7th), the Greg Holden
International (T8th), the Canon European Masters (T6th) and the Lancome Trophy
(T6th), and high finishes in the Spanish Open (17th), the Volvo PGA (T20th), the
European Open (T13th), the Loch Lomond (T19th) and the German Masters
(T22nd).

Missed the cut in the British Open and the USPGA. In the Coral Eurobet Seve Ballesteros Trophy he scored 2½ pts (from four matches) beating Alex Cejka 2 and 1 in the singles. In the Dunhill Cup helped Wales reach semi finals winning 3½ points from his four games to finish as the tournament's 4th top points scorer at 50/1. He subsequently finished T17th in the WGC Amex at Valderrama.

Not long at 268 yards his greens in reg and driving accuracy percentages are both 65-66%. He's had a brilliant season on the greens. Draws the ball. New coach is Dennis Sheedy.

> His much-improved form this year can be attributed to two key factors.

* His marriage at Xmas 1999 to Sandra which he believes has been so important to his improved play.

* His use of sports psychologist Alan Fine before the WGC NEC tournament.

> Phillip is an expectant first-time father, so 2001 will be his 'nappy factor' year.

> His confidence should be much higher as a result of his fine WGC NEC T2nd place at Firestone and his superb Dunhill Cup. That brilliant American finish earned him £290,000, not quite enough to secure his US tour card. However he will play in all the big-money events, which could make his initial odds to make the Ryder Cup team look attractive as Phillip was a nice Price at 9/4.

> The fact is he's got only one tour win and that was well over six years ago. However he now has the confidence to put that right, so I expect him to win in 2001.

> A low ball hitter with his irons, he must be followed when it's cold and wet as, "I'm a good grinder....I've had my best results in cold and windy conditions." So he'll be well worth a bet 'in running' if he's within 4 shots of the lead and the weather's bad.

> Born in Newport, he'd love to win the 2001 Wales Open (T5th 2000 including 65 in R4) held at Celtic Manor in Newport. He'll have 'home' advantage in the week before the USPGA and if his putter works he'll win!

> He can be followed with some confidence in the Alfred Dunhill. 6th in 1998 and T2nd this year, he'll be worth a bet at 50/1 at Houghton in mid January.

> He has PMAs with the Portuguese Open which gave him his first win in 1994. 2nd in 2000 he'll probably go close again in 2001.

Key stat   5th for total putting.

IAIN PYMAN   D

Age 27   **Born** Whitby   **Lives** Leeds

European tour wins T2nd German Open, 2 1997 Oki Pro-Am **Order of Merit** 56th 1996 **Challenge tour wins** 2, 1999 Russian Open, 1999 Challenge de France Beyer

Iain regained his card via the 1999 Challenge tour where he won twice. However he has struggled in 2000 with only 3 noteworthy finishes, in the Spanish Open (T12th), the Compaq European Grand Prix (T22nd) and the Loch Lomond (T27).

His stats tell the story of a player who is a fair putter, 275 yards off the tee, yet who continues to struggle for accuracy off both tee and fairway. Must go to Q School.

> A talented player off scratch at 17 and English Amateur Champ when 20.

> He's posted a couple of high finishes on the quirky course used for the Madeira Open (T8th 1996: T4th 1995) where he could spring a 100/1 shock in 2001.

Key stat   157th for shot accuracy.

PAOLO QUIRICI

Age 33   **Born** Switzerland   **Lives** Switzerland

European tour BEF T2 1999 Sarazem World Open **Challenge tour wins** 1 in 1993 **Dunhill Cup** 1991 **World Cup of Golf** 8 times **Order of Merit** 54th 1998

Tall Swiss guy who had four top 10s in 1998 and just one in 1999 when he posted his best-ever finish when T2nd in the Sarazen World Open.

In 2000 he was 11th in the Rio de Janiero 500 Years Open, T10th in the Spanish Open, T22nd in the Benson and Hedges, T11th in the Dutch Open, T23rd in the Scandinavian Masters, T16th in the Victor Chandlers British Masters (in which he was ranked top for driving accuracy and 4th for putts per GIR), T13th in the Canon European Masters and T12th in the Belgacom Open.

A very long hitter at 286 yards. He's putted well this year and his driving accuracy stats are much improved. If the stats paint a true picture he's one of Europe's top 10 players!!!

A diabetic whose condition is now stable. He uses a pump attached to his belt (like Scott Verplank in the States).

> Showed his most consistent form this year in July and August

> In his home country in the Canon European Masters he was T3rd after R3, then shot 74 to finish T13th suggesting that he may not be at his best when near the lead as the winning post approaches.

> Well worth each-way support at 100/1 for the 2001 Spanish Open on the course where he was T10th this year (despite a 78 in R2), T2nd in the 1999 Sarazen World Open, and where seven of his last eight rounds have been under par.

> Worth noting in the Scandinavian Masters where his record over the last four years (23rd-21st-7th) is very solid.

Key stat   6th (!!) in the overall ranking!!

JEAN-FRANCOIS REMESY

Age 36   **Born** Nines   **Lives** Cannes

European tour 1 - 1999 Estoril Open **Challenge tour wins** 1 in 1994 **Dunhill Cup** 1999, 2000 **World Cup of Golf** 1999 **Order of Merit** 57th 1999

After his breakthrough victory last year Jean-Francois (he used to be known as Jeff) has consolidated in 2000 with four top 10s, in the South African Open (T5th at 125/1), the Sao Paolo Open (T8th), the Benson and Hedges (T9th) and the

Belgacom Open (T7th). He also had a high finish in the Dubai Desert Classic (T24th).

Lost all his three Dunhill Cup matches for a career record of no wins in six games.

Accuracy off the tee is his trademark (12th). However his record is one of inconsistency. His stats are overall better than his scoring.

> His exemption for winning ends at the end of 2001 so he will be very keen to secure his card.

> With four top 10s in 2000 he is clearly a player who could well post a top 5 or two next year, although he often has one disappointing round per tournament.

> Accuracy off the tee is the key to the Dubai Desert Classic and its Remesey's strong point. T24th in 2000, keep him in mind there for suitable match bets even though the tournament moves to the Emirates course next year.

Key stat   145th (at 267.3 yards) for driving distance.

WAYNE RILEY   PB D

Age 38   **Born** Australia   **Lives** Camberley

European tour wins 2–1995 Scottish Open, 1996 Portuguese Open **International wins** 4, last in 1991 **Dunhill Cup** 1996 **World Cup of Golf** 1997 **Order of Merit** 11th 1995

A shadow of his former self once again this year in which he posted four top 20 finishes, in the Malaysian Open (T11th), the Portuguese Open (T60, the Qatar Masters (T19th) and the English Open (T17th).

His problems are his inaccuracy off both tee and fairway as well as his continued dodgy putting.

On three occasions in 1999 he got into serious contention and each time 'blew' his chance so he was awarded the 'bottle' in last year's volume.

> At his best early in the season when fresh and mentally strong

  * In 2000 he made his first ten cuts during which he shot his season's two best finishes

  * 1999 six top 30 finishes in his first eight starts

> Best chance will probably be in the early season Portuguese Open (T6th 2000: T7th 1998: Winner 1996) in a tournament that provided his last victory

> Worth support in 3-ball betting before the cut in the BMW International especially if juicy odds are available (65 in R1 in 2000: 63 in R2 in 1999).

Key stat   166th for shot accuracy!

JOSE RIVERO   PB

Age 45 and counting   **Born** Madrid   **Lives** Madrid

European tour wins 4, last in 1992 **Ryder Cup** 1985-1987 **Dunhill Cup** 1986-95 incl. **World Cup** 8 times, last 1994 **Order of Merit** BEF 19th 1988

Jose has only once, in 1996, finished outside the top 100 on the O/M. However he has struggled this year to retain his card. He had just three top 20s, in the Dutch Open (T7th), the Dubai Desert Classic (T11th) and the Sao Paolo Open (T17th).

With his stats well outside the top 75 for both driving accuracy and greens in reg and outside the top 150 for driving distance it's not difficult to see his problems. His putting is still solid. Kept his card....just, he was 114th on the O/M.

> Let's remember that when last in contention in the 1998 Turespana Masters he shot 78-76 after he was T3rd after R2, and in the 1998 European Masters when he got into real contention, he took 40 on the back nine in R4. So given those dodgy stats it look certain that he won't win again.

Key stat   128th for driving accuracy.

DEAN ROBERTSON

Age 30   **Born** Scotland   **Lives** Scotland

European tour wins 1, the 1999 Italian Open **World Cup of Golf** 1999 **Order of Merit** 25th 1999

Caught a virus in the World Cup of Golf in Malaysia in late 1999. He flew to Australia for the Greg Norman International only to return without hitting a shot.

In his first tournament back he was R1 leader (65) in the Spanish Open before finishing T12th.

Later he was T22nd in the Compaq European Grand Prix, T13th in the European Open, T10 in the Canon European Masters, T7th in the Lancome Trophy, and T5th at 80/1 in the Belgacom Open.

Had a good British Open finishing T26th, and at 66/1 he was T4th in the Top Brit. market.

Driving accuracy continues to be a problem although his putting has been really solid (10th). A good player in windy conditions. Brian Byrne is Deano's caddie.

> Excessive leg movement in his golf swing has caused his inconsistency off the tee "my legs are like chicken legs." Nevertheless Dean's a fine player and no chicken!

  Indeed he's a much underrated golfer who could well post a second win in 2001

> Must be considered, especially in match bets for the Compaq European Grand Prix (T22nd 2000: T6th 1999) where he's only had one round over par (R2 this year in poor weather) in the last two years.

> If he wins again he must be opposed in his following tournament. After his 1999 Italian Open success he 'celebrated' with Stephen Hendry (a fellow member of Ian Doyle's Cuemaster team) and then withdrew from his next tournament after a 79!!

> He really must be noted in 3 balls and match bets at Crans in the European Masters where he's finished T10th (2000) and T15th (1999) in the last two years including that 63 in R3 this year.

> With Ryder Cup hangover reducing the threat from the top Euros I think he has a big chance in the 2001 Belgacom Open where he played very impressively this year with four sub-70 rounds. He'll be worth support at Royal Zoute.

Key stat   118th (at 60.1%) for driving accuracy.

COSTANTINO ROCCA   D PB

Age 44   **Born** Bergamo   **Lives** Bergamo, Italy

European tour wins 5 latest 1999 West of Ireland Golf Classic **Ryder Cup** 1993.95.97 **Dunhill Cup** 7 times, last 1999 **World Cup of Golf** 9 times **Majors** BEF 2nd 1995 British Open **Order of Merit** 4th 1995 and 1996

It really is sad to see such a one time Ryder Cup player fall on such hard times.

To analyse his record this year is to intrude into private grief...let's just say he's not had a top 25 finish with his T28th in the Benson and Hedges his season's best.

As you'd expect no matter what stat you name his record is very poor. Not surprisingly his confidence looks shattered. The PB symbol is clearly merited.

> His demise was shown in the European Open where his record at the K Club is very good yet he missed the cut at eleven over par by 8 shots!

> Every golf fan will hope that he will come storming back in 2001. However being Ryder Cup year with so many young big hitters coming through it will be very, very difficult.

Key stat   168th in the overall ranking.

CARLOS RODILES   ☼ g y

Age 25   **Born** Malaga   **Lives** Florida

European Challenge tour BEF 2nd **European tour** BEF T4th 2000 West of Ireland Classic

Carlos is an articulate American educated player who we must keep our eye on. On this year's Challenge tour he's played consistently with three top 4 finishes in the Challenge de Espana (2nd), Gunther Hamburg Classic (2nd) and the Le Touquet Challenge (2nd after losing a play-off) to finish 3rd on the Money list.

His play-off record after losing the Le Touquet Challenge this year is played four lost four!

On the main tour he posted three really impressive finishes in six starts when T4th at 66/1 in the West of Ireland Classic in August, T7th in the Spanish Open on 1st May and T7th in the French Open the following week.

> Let's just pause and reflect on the quality of those 7th-place finishes in the Spanish Open and the French Open, with six of those rounds under par. However he had his first taste of serious contention when T4th after R3 in the Spanish Open he shot 73. It will stand him in good stead next year.

> When in Spain I enjoy drinking Carlos1....it's a Brandy I can recommend. However Carlos could well become the Number 1 in mid March in the Turespana

Masters. Four years ago an unknown guy (Diego Borrego) from Malaga won the tournament at 80/1. Next year make a 'killing on Carlos' as he'll be a helluva bet at 100/1 in 2001.

> Having posted four sub-par rounds in the West of Ireland Classic this year he'll have a really bright chance in that weakly contested event in 2001.

Key stat   In 2000 in six starts on the full European tour he made all six cuts and had three top 7 finishes.

EDUARDO ROMERO   G F 🐎

Age 46   **Born** Cordoba, Argentina   **Lives** Cordoba, Argentina

European tour wins 6, last in 1994 **International wins** 6, all in South America **Dunhill Cup** 8 times, latest 2000 **World Cup of Golf** 10 times **Order of Merit** BEF 11th 1990 **Majors** T7th 1997 British Open

The 'grandfather of Argentinian golf the 46-year-old with the dodgy 'tache is affectionately known as 'El Gato' (the cat).

Apart from 1995 (when he only played 8 events) he's been a fixture in the top 30 on the O/M.

This year he had three top 5s, in the Qatar Masters (T3rd at 50/1 after a brilliant last 36 holes), in the Sao Paolo Open (T3rd at 25/1 after a final hole eagle) and the Spanish Open (T3rd at 50/1*), and a top 10 in the Irish Open (T6th).

He also had a top 25 in the Dutch Open (T11th).

In the British Open he finished T35th and he missed the cut in the USPGA for the third successive year.

Then in early September after a six-week break he was the 50/1 winner of the Canon European Masters. Leading throughout he won in a canter by 10 shots, shooting a course record 62 in R3. It was his first victory since he won this tournament back in 1994. The following week he finished T22nd in the Lancome Trophy.

He went on to finish 2nd at 40/1 in the Belgacom Open. In the Dunhill Cup won three of his four games helping Argentina to the semi finals before finishing T7th in the Turespana Masters (NIC).

Up to that victory it had been the usual story for Eduardo as he's in the top 20 for greens in reg. and outside the top 100 on all the putting stats. He is the ultimate 'straight hitting doesn't make enough putts player' who regularly posts high finishes yet rarely wins. This year his use of the new ERC Callaway driver has "given me a new life" and he's now in the top 35 for driving distance.

At his best in warm dry conditions, (and in Swiss mountains).

> Having dropped 5 shots over the final 4 holes in the British Open he knew he must improve his concentration so he returned to Yoga which clearly has worked judged by his runaway win in the European Masters and his belief that he's "a completely different man this year".

> He proved what a fine links player he is with big finishes in the Belgacom Open (2nd), Irish Open (T6th), the Dutch Open (T11th) and the British Open (top 10 after 68 holes!).

> Eduardo's game reminds me so much of American Tom Watson - a superb tee to green straight hitter whose putting within 8 feet is very dodgy. However Tom won at 100/1 (the 1998 Colonial) when 48 so I still think there could be another European tournament left in 'El Gato' especially as he now hits the ball so far.

> He cries out for support in the Spanish Open where he's been a 'gift' over recent years with no fewer than FIVE top 6 finishes in the last six years, and he won it in 1991. On the spreads and in match bets Romero cries out to be backed in the 2001 Spanish Open, and he'll be worth an each-way wager on the outrights too.

> In the 2001 Omega European Masters he will be the defending champion. "I love the course....I live at altitude in Argentina," and with many top Euros then already qualified for the Ryder Cup he could well win again. He'll sure be a must for match bets.

Key stat 97th for total putting.

RAYMOND RUSSELL

Age 28 **Born** Edinburgh **Lives** Nottingham

European tour wins 1996 Cannes Open Dunhill Cup 1996 and 97 **World Cup of Golf** 1997 **Order of Merit** 14th 1996: 16th 1997

94th on the OM last year he nevertheless ended the year well when 2nd in the Ford Open on the ANZ tour. Later he was T3rd in the ANZ Players Championship.

This year apart from finishing T13th in Rio de Janiero Open he was in poor form until late June/early July.

He sparked into life at the Loch Lomond (T13th), and then prequalified for the British Open where he missed the cut. two weeks later he was 3rd at 150/1* in the Scandinavian Masters (only player to shoot four sub-70 rounds) and then T10th in the Victor Chandler British Masters. Finished T15th in the Turespana Masters.

He has struggled this year from tee and fairway. If he 'finds' his long game he'll be a force again because he has a superbly smooth putting stroke, and proven bottle.

> At his best with wider fairways on links course do look out for him in the betting to prequalify for the British Open. This year he was my Saturday 'best bet' when T1st at Lundin at a generous 33/1 when he was in top form after Loch Lomond.

> I am planning to keep an eye on his early season stats for driving accuracy and greens in reg. because if they improve he'll be a brilliant putter available at 'value' prices.

> Although he's not figured yet in the weakly contested Scottish PGA it will surely provide a big opportunity for him in August. Watch out for him then!

Key stat 169th for total driving yet 12th for total putting.

JARMO SANDELIN   D

Age 33   **Born** Finland   **Lives** Monaco

European tour wins 4, 1995 Turespana Open, 1996 Madeira Island Open, 1999 Spanish Open, 1999 German Open **Dunhill Cup** 1995, 1996, 1999 **World Cup** 1995, 96 **Ryder Cup** 1999 **Order of Merit** 9th 1999

It's been a disappointing year for the guy with the neat line in Crocodile skin shoes and Italian leather belts.

He's posted just one top 5 finish, in the European Open (T5th at 80/1), and three other top 10s, in the Irish Open (T10th), the Loch Lomond (T7th) and the Victor Chandler British Masters (T8th). His other high finishes came in the BMW International (T13th), the Dubai Desert Classic (T24th) and the Rio de Janeiro Open (T25th).

In the Coral Eurobet Seve Ballesteros Trophy he scored 2 points from three matches, defeating John Bickerton 2 and 1 in the singles.

He missed the cut in the US Open and e finished T31st in the British Open and T24th in the USPGA.

He is a very long hitter. However it seems that he rarely uses a 'stock' safe shot off the tee, too often seeming to go 'for broke'. This is reflected in his poor driving accuracy percentage which is just 59% (only 62% in 1999).

However he's a good putter even if, like his driving, he can be too agressive.

He's a proven front runner who knows how to win.

He ended the season really poorly with four successive missed cuts.

> His erratic play and inconsistency was superbly illustrated in this year's French Open. He hit absolutely every single fairway and green in R1, he was the tournament joint leader after R2, shot 78(!) in R3, then in R4 annoyed by his poor putting he bent his putter over his knee and proceeded to use it...so he was disqualified for using a club whose characteristics he'd changed!!

> So it's not surprising to find two top golf odds compilers, Don Stewart (Victor Chandlers) and John Wright (Coral Eurobet) differing widely in their assessment of Sandelin's chance of making the 2001 Ryder Cup side.

  Coral Eurobet went 3/1 ON while Victor Chandlers went 7/2 AGAINST. So Corals reckon his chance is 75%, Chandlers 22.2%. Personally, I agree with Don.

> His girlfriend Linda is expecting their first baby on Xmas Eve this year. IF IT'S A BOY then I really do expect 'Daddy' Sandelin to be 'nappy factor' inspired in 2001, to show a more mature approach in harnessing his massive talent, and to win.

> His best chances will probably be in

  * The European Open. His long hitting is suited here as he showed when T5th this year, and it's a tournament Swedes have won in three of the last five years.

* The Lancome Trophy. His form figures were 2nd-6th-6th before he missed the cut this year when 'his swing had gone'. Expect normal service to be resumed in 2001 and for Jarmo to win the Lancome!

* The BMW International. He's posted two top 15 finishes in three starts and he could well surprise at a tasty price.

> He's a player who thrives on confidence so that one good finish creates another, just as it did this year in July when he posted his season's first top 10 in Ireland (T10th Irish Open) and then followed up with a T5th and T7th in successive weeks.

Key stat   130th (59.2%) for driving accuracy.

MASSIMO SCARPA

Age 30   **Born** Venice   **Lives** Venice

European tour wins 1, 2000 North West of Ireland Classic **Challenge tour wins** 4, all in 1998 **Dunhill Cup** 1999 **Order of Merit** 99th 1999

99th on the O/M last year with just one top 10 finish although he made sixteen cuts in his twenty-five tournaments.

In 2000 he had a poor season until late June after his 30th birthday when he was 12th in the Compaq European Grand Prix, shot 63 in R2 in the Irish Open (T59th) the next week, and then in early July he was T28th in the European Open.

In August a steady 36th, with four sub-par rounds, in the Victor Chandler British Masters was a solid preparation for the weakly contested North West of Ireland Classic the following week, which he won at 50/1.

Massimo plays mainly right handed then switches to left handed for shot from within 60 yards. He now carries four wedges, two left handed and two right. After his poor performances pre June his stats are uniformly poor.

> Clearly a more confident and successful player now he's past 30 he has a one year exemption for his win so he has no worries about securing his card in 2001. This should relax him and ensure he has a satisfactory season.

> He has shown consistent form in the Compaq European Grand Prix (T16th 1999: T12th 2000) where he can be noted in suitable match bets.

Key stat   168th for greens in regulation.

ADAM SCOTT   G Y FT ▐

Age 20   **Born** Australia   **Lives** Las Vegas

College   Las Vegas University (left after 18 months)

European tour BEF 5th 2000 Benson & Hedges

This is the guy who's been dubbed the 'next Tiger Woods'. He won a scholarship to the University of Las Vegas at 17, hit 62 to be leading qualifier in the 1997 US Junior Championship, won the 1997 World Junior title, and has made a massive impression over the last 12 months.

Shot to prominence early this year with a 63 in R2 in the Greg Norman Holden International going on to finish T37th as an amateur.

On the European tour he was T6th in the Moroccan Open, and T5th at 125/1 in the Benson & Hedges so after two top 6 finishes in his first two starts he turned pro, making his debut when T61st in the Compaq European Grand Prix.

He finished T10th in the Irish Open, missed the European Open cut before finishing T12th in the Loch Lomond. He missed the cut in the British Open.

He had high finishes later in the season when T12th in the Belgacom Open and T6th in the rain-reduced German Masters. Lost in R1 of the Cisco World Matchplay at Wentworth to Sergio Garcia 2 and 1.

His stats (on Oct. 1st), even after such a brief career, show three key features. Firstly, he drives further than Michael Schumacher and was 2nd for driving distance. Secondly, he hit 69% of greens, and thirdly, not surprisingly, his putting on the slower European greens sees him outside the top 100. The IMG group will manage him from now on.

> He has a swing like Tiger, a massive driving distance, the world's best coach in Butch Harmon, a sound all-round game and he's made a brilliant start to his career. With four top 12s in his first six 'ordinary' European tournaments he's got his 2001 European tour card.

> This guy, believe me, is a seriously good player, clearly better than fellow young Aussies like Brett Rumford, Brad Lamb and Aaron Baddeley, and in Dave Renwick he's got a seriously good caddie.

> However beware! His form must carry a punters' wealth warning after two interesting tournament finishes this year.

  * 'Down under' on the ANZ tour he led the Victorian Open by 3 shots with 4 to play only to slump to a T3rd finishing position after a 75 in R4.

  * Similarly in the Loch Lomond he bogeyed the last 4 holes in R4 to finish T12th having been the joint halfway leader.

  Sorry, it may be his first year as a pro and he may be destined to be a world top 10 player, but the simple fact is that twice this year he's "blown it", so he's awarded the bottle.

> Once he learns how to win as a professional he'll have the full set of tools to go 'all the way'.

> I expect him to play really well in late April on the 'Iberian Swing'.

  * He enjoys Portugal where he has friends and will look forward to the Portuguese Open.

  * His huge hitting will be well suited to the Catalunya course, home of the Spanish Open.

> Make a careful note in your diary now to back Adam Scott in the first couple of weeks of October 2001.

  * The German Masters. His length is ideal here as he proved with a brilliant 65-68 in R2 and R3 this year when he finished T6th in the rain-reduced tournament.

* The Belgacom Open. T12th this year he was top for driving accuracy (83.9%), 5th for greens in reg. (81.9%) only to be let down by his putting (T55th).

And remember his main opponents will be jaded after the Ryder Cup. Great SCOTT it's an opportunity not to be missed!

Key stat   4th for total driving and 14th in the overall ranking.

JOHN SENDEN

Age 29   **Born** Brisbane, Australia   **Lives** Brisbane, Australia

European tour T6th 1999 European Open **Challenge tour wins** 2, both in 1998 **International wins** 1, 1996 Indonesian PGA **Order of Merit** BEF 69th 1999

On the ANZ tour he was T3rd at 50/1 in the Coolum Classic, and 7th in the Canon Challenge.

On the European tour he has had a number of high finishes with his T4th at 125/1 in the French Open the highlight. He posted 6 other top 25s, in the Alfred Dunhill (T22nd), the Benson and Hedges (T14th), the Wales Open (T14th), the Scandinavian Masters (T10th) the Scottish PGA (T11th) and the Lancome Trophy (T24th).

His approach play to the greens is impressive. However his putting is on the dreadful side of poor!

30 in April 2001.

> After a fine year (two wins) on the 1998 Challenge tour 'Sendo' has established himself on the tour. Safely past 30 he could well be a 'shock' winner in 2001 if he improves his putting.

> His best chances of a win on mainland Europe will probably be in the

* Wales Open: T14th 2000 incl. 69 (R1) and 68 (R4), and

* The Scottish PGA: T11th 2000

In both tournaments there are weak fields and he'll be worth support.

> 'Down Under' he could go close in the Heineken Classic (T25 2000: T10th 1999) where 7 of his last 8 rounds have been under par.

Key stat   4th for shot accuracy he's 176th (!!!) for total putting.

PETER SENIOR

Age 41   **Born** Singapore   **Lives** Queensland

European tour wins 4, last the 1992 Benson & Hedges **ANZ tour wins** 18, last one 1997 Canon Challenge **International win** 3, all in Japan

Made a fine start to the season T5th in the Johnnie Walker Classic, T13th in the Heineken Classic, and a brilliant 2nd at 66/1* in the Greg Norman Holden International. Played well to finish T10th in the Volvo Masters.

Disappointing 72nd (plumb last) in the British Open after a 79 in R4.

Out driven off the tee by the younger guys. His short game has been "killing me".

One of the first users of the 'broomstick' putter. He even owns a boat called Broomstick, would you believe?

> A superb player in blustery conditions when he can be supported with confidence in 3-ball betting.

> Cries out to be backed in the outright market, on the spreads and in match bets in the Greg Norman Holden International as he has the best tournament record (Won 1996: 11th 1998: 7th 1999: 2nd 2000) of any player over its last four stagings, and he says himself, "it's a very special event to me."

Key stat   174th for total driving.

PATRIK SJOLAND   g

Age 29   **Born** Sweden   **Lives** Marbella

European tour wins 2, 2000 Irish Open,1998 Italian Open (three rounds only) **Challenge tour wins** 1 in 1995 **Dunhill Cup** 1996,1998, 1999, 2000 **World Cup of Golf** 1995,96,98 **Order of Merit** 5th 1998

In late November 1999 he won the Hong Kong Open on the Asian PGA Davidoff tour.

In 2000 he showed some early season form when T13th in the Heineken Classic, T23rd in the Malaysian Open, a superb T2nd at in the Dubai Desert Classic, T19th in the Qatar Masters and T14th in the Moroccan Open.

Then he became a first time father of a son in April. Nappy factor inspired he won the Irish Open at 100/1* just seven weeks after little Hugo Sjoland entered the world.

Missed the cut in the British Open.

Later he was a fine T8th (four sub-70 rounds) in the Victor Chandler British Masters, and he finished T17th in both the German Masters and the Volvo Masters. In the Dunhill Cup won 1 of his 3 matches for a career record of 7½ points from 14 games.

A fine putter especially from the 12 foot range, his weakness is his erratic, and rather short, driving. Tends to draw the ball

He'll be 30 in May 2001.

> Will try for his US tour card in Autumn 2000.

> He does tend to pull shots off the tee under pressure when in contention. Indeed he did so in this year's Irish Open win in which really Jacobson 'handed' him the tournament.

   Best chance of a third win may well be coming from 'off the pace' after a storming hot putting R4.

> With an early tee time he'll be worth support in each-way bets, and in suitable match bets, in the 2001 Qatar Masters where he's the only player to have recorded three successive top 20s (19th-11th-2nd).

> Worth noting in match bets and as an outsider with a squeak in the 2001 Victor Chandler British Masters as his tournament record (8th 2000: T26th 1999: T8th 1997) is solid.

Key stat 165th for total driving.

DES SMYTH PB

Age 47 **Born** Drogheda, Ireland **Lives** Drogheda, Ireland

European tour wins 7, last in 1993 Ryder Cup twice **Dunhill Cup** 5 times, latest in 2000 **World Cup of Golf** 5 times **Order of Merit** 7th 1988

It's been a year of struggle for the 'old timer' with only one high finish when T6th in the Irish Open. His other top 30s were in the French Open (T22nd), the Volvo PGA (T26th) and the Turespana Masters (T25th). In the Dunhill Cup he won one of his three matches to give him an impressive career record of 8½ points from twelve games.

Woefully short off the tee at 267 yards he's still accurate off the tee (67.7%) and to the greens (66.5% GIR). However his putting is now definitely in 'intensive care'.

Still a fine player in blustery conditions.

> In each of the last two years his best finishes have been on home soil, and it's a safe bet 'history will repeat itself' in 2001.

* The Irish Open. T6th in 2000, he'll go well at the Fota Island course in Cork.
* The West of Ireland Open. T3rd in 1999, he disappointed in 2000. However he could go close again in 2001.

Key stat 140th for total putting.

JAMIE SPENCE S G

Age 37 **Born** Tunbridge Wells **Lives** Tunbridge Wells

European tour wins 2, 1992 Canon European Masters (p/o) and 2000 Moroccan Open **Challenge tour** 1, in 1989 **Dunhill Cup** 1992, 2000 **Order of Merit** BEF 10th 1992

It's been a first-class year for the Arsenal fan with a victory and two other top 4 finishes.

His second tour win came in the Moroccan Open at 33/1* after a brilliant 64 in R4 and superb work by his caddy Janet Squire.

His other big finishes were in the Dubai Desert Classic (T4th at 100/1) and the Scandinavian Masters (T4th at 80/1).

He was T6th in the Compaq European Grand Prix, and T17th in the Wales Open. He also had two holes in one, in the Qatar Masters and in Morocco.

Played poorly at St Andrews (three defeats) in the Dunhill Cup.

His brilliant putting compensates for his lack of length off the tee. A real streak player capable of very low scoring because of his skill on the greens. Fades the ball.

A keen punter, Jamie is a regular writer for the Racing Post. 14/1 to make the Ryder Cup side.

> He is a must in match and spread bets in the Compaq European Grand Prix in which his record is first class, viz. T6th 2000, T11th 1999, T3rd of R2 finishers when abandoned 1998, T6th 1997 and T9th 1996. He'll merit an each-way bet in the outright market, too

> Must be noted in 2-ball betting in R4 when 'off the pace' as his brilliant putting in the past (60(!) in 1992 European Masters), and this year, (66 Scandinavian Masters: 64 Moroccan Open) have led to really low numbers.

> Like a 'hold up' horse he is best when coming from 'off the pace' as he has shown in his two victories.

Key stat   2nd for putts per GIR in 1999 he was 4th in 2000.

HENRIK STENSON   y g

Age 24   **Born** Gothenburg   **Lives** Malmo

European tour BEF T11th 2000 Scandinavian Masters **European Challenge tour wins** 4, 1999 Grand Final, 2000 Luxembourg Open, 2000 Gula Sidorna Grand Prix (Sweden), 2000 Cuba Challenge Tour Grand Final.

21st on the Challenge tour as a 23-year-old in 1999 after two second places he's now progressed to earn his 2001 tour card following a splendid season on the Challenge tour in which he's been most consistent with three wins, two 2nds and a T3rd.

On the European tour he was 18th in the Madeira Island Open, T11th in the Scandinavian Masters, T11th in the NW of Ireland Open and, T11th in the Scottish PGA.

> Henrik is the latest in the seemingly never-ending line of really promising young Swedish players. With four top 20s in four starts (in the admittedly weaker events) this year on the full European tour, he's a player of real promise who could well cause a 'shock' in 2001.

> He really must be followed in the 2001 Scandinavian Masters as a 125/1 outsider with a real chance and in the top Scandinavian player market. There are four key reasons:-

* In the last two years all his eight rounds have been under par in this tournament.

* He won in Sweden ("it is special to win on home soil and in front of so many friends") on the Challenge tour this year so he can handle home crowd 'pressure'.

* In 2001 the tournament moves to the Barseback Club to which he is attached so he sure will have 'home' advantage.

* This year in the tournament he finished T11th after four sub-par rounds and just 3 shots off T4th place. He was T2nd at 66/1 in the Top Scandinavian player speciality market.

Key stat   In the last two years he's won four times on the Challenge tour.

SVEN STRUVER   g 🥀

Age 33   **Born** Germany   **Lives** Germany

European tour wins 3, 1996 South African PGA (three rounds), 1997 Dutch Open, 1998 Canon European Masters (play-off) **Dunhill Cup** 1994,95,96,98, 2000 **World Cup of Golf** 1993,94,95,97,98 **Order of Merit** 13th 1998

This has been Sven's most disappointing year since he fully established himself on the tour in 1992.

He has posted just three top 25s, in the South African Open (T19th), the Heineken Classic (T25th) and the Spanish Open (T21st). Struck form at St Andrews in October winning all his three Dunhill Cup games.

His card is secure however until 2003 following his European Masters five-year exemption in 1998.

Short off the tee at 270 yards he has putted badly this year.

Became a first-time father (of a daughter) in late 1999.

> His two 72-hole wins came after making six cuts in a row (1998 Canon European Masters) and after missing six cuts in a row (1996 Dutch Open) so he's not a guy you can easily 'read'.

> A 'shock' win in 2001 would be no surprise as he'll be determined to get back to form and he's a real 'closer' when he gets the chance.

> He has a sound early season record in South Africa where he can be noted in match bets in both the South African Open (T19th 2000: 4th 1999: T9th 1997) and the Alfred Dunhill (Won 1996), and he'll be worth a speculative each-way punt at 100/1 in the South African Open.

Key stat   2000 was his first season without a top 10 finish.

CARL SUNESON   g

Age 33   **Born** Las Palmas   **Lives** Las Palmas

European tour BEF 3rd 2000 BMW International **Challenge tour wins** 4, 3 in 1999 **Order of Merit** BEF 48th 1996

Carl topped the 1999 Challenge tour after three wins to earn his tour card for 2000.

This year he had two top 20s in the Portuguese Open (T14th where he was No. 1 for GIR yet 42nd for putts per GIR) and the Qatar Masters (T19th). He also had top 25s in the Wales Open (T21st) and the European Grand Prix (T22nd). Then in late October he posted his best finish of the year in the Italian Open (T7th).

Then in early September he secured his card when 3rd at 125/1 in the BMW International after his first visit to psychologist Jos Vanstiphout.

Soon-e-son is a huge hitter (top 10 for driving distance) and has good greens in regulation stats (top 40). However his problem has been his putting. 10/1 to make the 2001 Ryder Cup side.

> With both his diabetic and thyroid problems now under control and with mental skills advice working after it was first received in early September there is a real chance that this long hitter could be set for a successful 2001.

> Well worth a bet in the Wales Open in 2001. T6th after R3 this year then his second son was born before R4 so his late lapse of concentration (dropped 4 shots in the last 5 holes) on Sunday was perhaps excusable.

> When the Moroccan Open was last played at the Royal Golf D'Agadir course in 1999 Carl was tops for driving accuracy, however his putting let him down so he finished T14th. If that course is used again in 2001 he'll be a match bet must, and you can then put each-way cash on Carl with confidence.

> Well suited to the Is Molas course. This year he was 4th for driving distance and top 10 for greens in reg to be let down by his putting. Worth the risk as a 100/1 outsider in the 2001 Italian Open.

Key stat   150th for total putting.

DES TERBLANCHE

Born South Africa   **Lives** South Africa   **Weight** Unknown!

European tour BEF 2nd 2000 Malaysian Open

Big Des has secured his tour card after two top 5 finishes. The first came in the Malaysian Open, where he was T2nd at 100/1* after four sub-par rounds, and the other when 5th at 40/1 in the Moroccan Open.

He also posted four top 20s, in the Alfred Dunhill (T18th), the South African Open (T19th), the Madeira Island Open (T18th) and the North West of Ireland Classic (T19th).

In early September he finished 3rd in the Johnnie Walker Taiwan Open.

His great strength is his putting, his great weakness his erratic (if huge at 285 yards) driving.

No stranger to the sweet trolley Des is to weight watchers what Jack the Ripper was to door to door salesmen!

> With his putting touch he could well make further top 5 finishes in 2001.

> It is noticable that his R4 scoring is disappointing with just one sub-70 round before September, and that in the Malaysian Open.

> Indeed the Malaysian Open (T2nd this year) will provide an early season opportunity in mid February.

Key stat   7th for putts per GIR.

STEEN TINNING   G

Age 38   **Born** Copenhagen   **Lives** Denmark

European tour wins 1, 2000 Wales Open **Dunhill Cup** 1998 **World Cup of Golf** 5, last 1995 **Order of Merit** BEF 30th 2000

Gave an early indication of what was to come when T9th in the Johnnie Walker Classic in November 1999.

In 2000 he was T13th in the South African Open early in the year. Posted a top 20 in the Madeira Island Open (T18th).

His big moment came in June when he won the Wales Open at 100/1*. It was his first win in 292 tournaments and indeed it was his first top 3 finish!

Later he was T17th in the Dutch Open, T6th in the Scandinavian Masters, T23rd in the Victor Chandler British Masters, T19th in the Turespana Masters, and T21st in the Italian Open.

Poor form in his early thirties followed a car crash in 1990.

Steen has solid all round stats this year although his accuracy to the greens is his stock in trade.

Uses Arne Niellson as his mental adviser. 6/1 to make the 2001 Ryder Cup side.

> With his personal confidence increased following his win and with Danish golf improving rapidly he could well get into the winners enclosure again in 2001 in one of the lesser tournaments as he showed commendable 'bottle' in his victory.

> He can be backed in the Top Scandinavian market in the Scandinavian Masters (W 16/1 2000: 3rd 1999: DNP 1998 in this market).

> Obviously at home on the Noordwijkse course where he's finished T17th (2000) and T6th (1993). He can be supported in the Dutch Open on that track in 2001.

> Steen is just the sort of experienced player to lift the 2001 Madeira Island Open where he recorded his best ever finish (before 2000) when T4th in 1995. Top 20 in 1999 he'll have a big chance next year.

> Has the accuracy to do well in the South African Open (top 20, 2000) where he can be noted in suitable match bets.

Key stat   47th in the overall ranking.

SAM TORRANCE MBE   PB

Age 47   **Born** Largs, Scotland   **Lives** Wentworth

European tour wins 21, last 1998 French Open **Ryder Cup** 1981-1995 inclusive **Dunhill Cup** 9 times, latest 1999 **Majors** BEF 5th 1981 British Open **Order of Merit** 2nd 1984 and 1995

On the course Sam had one memorable tournament, the Compaq European Grand Prix which he led after a 66 (incl. a hole in one) in R1. However in poor weather he followed it with a 79 and finished T14th.

Prequalified for the British Open he then missed the cut. Also missed the cut (by 13 shots!) in the USPGA.

Finished T16th in the Scottish PGA, T16th in the Lancome Trophy and T6th in the German Masters. Has putted very well this year. Off the course he showed more loyalty than judgement in supporting his friend Mark James in the controversy over Jesse's book. James' ultimate and inevitable resignation could have come much earlier if Sam had not helped to prolong the matter. Let's hope Sam's memoirs do not appear in 2002!

> Well 2001 is the year for Smokin' Sam, the year when he hopes to captain the European team to victory in the Ryder Cup at the Belfry. His chance of success has been diminished by the decision to keep the European selection procedures unchanged. (a point developed in Chapter 2).

> His son Daniel will win eventually on tour, and Dad on the Seniors tour, but in the meantime sorry but it's the inevitable PB symbol for Sam.

Key stat   152nd for total driving yet 14th for total putting.

GREG TURNER   F

Age 37   **Born** New Zealand   **Lives** UK – Sunningdale

European tour wins 4, last 1997 British Masters **International wins** 6   **Dunhill Cup** 10 times, last 2000 **World Cup of Golf** 10 times **Presidents Cup** 1998 **Order of Merit** Top 35 1993-1999 incl. BEF 18th 1997

After his first son was born he won the Australian PGA in December 1999 on a tough course at 22/1. It was his 6th international win. Then in January 2000 he started the European tour, after recovering from a left wrist injury, with a fine 6th in the Heineken Classic after a poor 74 in R1.

Then he had his poorest year on the European tour since 1992 with 5 other top 20s, in the English Open (T12th), the Compaq European Grand Prix (T9th), the Scandinavian Masters (T11th), the BMW International (T20th) and the German Masters (T17th).

He played poorly in the USPGA missing the cut by 7 shots! Won 2 of his 3 Dunhill Cup games so his career record is 12 wins in 28 games.

Short off the tee at 264 yards he's had problems reaching the greens in regulation this year (outside top 125). Fades the ball. His short putting can be dodgy.

> In 2001 he can be noted particularly in suitable match bets in three tournaments.

  * The Compaq European Grand Prix where he's had only four of his twelve rounds over par and he's finished T40th 1997, T31st 1999 and T9th 2000.

  * The BMW International T20th 2000: T12th 1997 in his two starts.

  * The Scandinavian Masters where he's had four successive top 20s with T9th (1999) and T11th (2000) his most recent finishes. At Barseback, the 2001 venue, he finished T20th (1997) and T9th (1999).

> He can be followed at the Forest of Arden in the British Open. In his last six tournaments there he's had a win (1997) and four top 20s so he's a confident choice for suitable match bets and worth an each-way punt at big odds in the outright.

> A fine links player with a solid British Open record he finished T7th the last time the tournament was held at Royal Lytham, its 2001 venue. He was then top Aussie at 18/1 and he was again top in that market in 1998, so in 2001 he'd be worth a small each-way nibble to be top Aussie.

> He has an excellent record on the Royal Zoute course (T10th 1993: T17th 1994: T3rd 1998: T4th 1999) and we can forget his performance this year (T60th) when out of form. So if he's in steady form back Greg each way for the 2001 Belgacom Open.

> "I guess I run good fresh!". Guess he's right as 2 of his last 4 wins in the Balearic Open (1995, after a 12 week break) and the New Zealand Open (1997, after a 5 week break) have come when fresh.

Key stat   164th (at 264 yards) for driving distance.

NICOLAS VANHOOTEGEM

Age 28   **Born** Brussels (expensive restaurants!)   **Lives** Knokke, Belgium

Challenge tour wins 1, 1995 **European tour** BEF T6th 2000 Rio de Janiero Open **Order of Merit** BEF 98th 2000

Earned his card when 3rd at the 1999 Q School.

However he's struggled to retain it although he's had two top 10s in the Rio de Janiero Open (T6th including 63 in R4) and the Compaq European Grand Prix (8th), and a top 20 in the French Open (T15th after 66 in R4). He had a top 25 in the Greg Norman Holden International (T21st).

Short off the tee at 270 yards his main problem has been on the greens. Overall his stats are fairly solid for a player so low on the OM.

> His performance in the 2000 Compaq European Grand Prix was very impressive. He was one of only three players to shoot four rounds at or under par when he finished 8th so he must enter calculations at Slaley Hall in 2001.

> His nerve when in contention has still to be tested as two of his best finishes this year came from 'off the pace' thanks to a superb final round (Rio de Janiero 65: French Open 66).

> Attached to the Royal Zoute (home of the Belgacom Open) as the Club professional. However his form T55th (1998), T22nd (1999) and T81st (2000) so far is not impressive.

Key stat   51st in the overall ranking.

ANTHONY WALL

Age 25   **Born** London   **Lives** Sunningdale

European tour wins 1 2000 Alfred Dunhill Championship **Order of Merit** BEF 44th 2000

Match fit from the ANZ tour, where he'd finished 6th in the Australian PGA, the young Londoner secured his first tour win in the three-round Alfred Dunhill in South Africa. He came from behind to win as a 100/1 DYM. "....ever since I started playing golf, when I was 4, this is what I've dreamed of".

He was T14th in the Portuguese Open, T17th in the English Open, T19th in the Turespana Masters, and a fine T5th at 125/1 in the Benson and Hedges.

A superb long-iron player. His putting (71st) and especially his bunker play (90th) can be improved. 8/1 to make the Ryder Cup side.

> From 'Wonder Wall' to serious illness in the same rollercoaster season it's been an interesting year for the young Londoner. Suffered from glandular fever this season which forced his withdrawal from the Dubai Classic and the Dutch Open. The virus tends to 'hang around' and explains Anthony's inconsistent season. Let's hope he can have a fully fit season in 2001.

> His 69-69 finish this year in the English Open when T17th suggest he will be a longshot with a serious chance in 2001.

> He really must be supported at the Belfry in the 2001 Benson and Hedges after his first-class effort (T5th) this year.

> He has a fine record on the Iberian peninsula and can be supported each way and in match bets in two successive tournaments in April:-
  * Portuguese Open (T14th 2000: 6th 1999)
  * The Spanish Open (W/D 2000: T7th 1999)

Key stat   30th in the overall ranking

STEVE WEBSTER   g y FT V

Age 25   **Born** Nuneaton   **Lives** Atherstone

European tour BEF T2nd 1998 German Open **Order of Merit** 37th 1998

Steve has posted six top 25s this year in the Qatar Masters (T11th), the Deutsche Bank Open (T23rd), the English Open (T23rd), the European Open (T13th), the Scandinavian Masters (T17th including 64 in R2) and the Victor Chandler British Masters (T23rd).

His big finish came when he was T3rd at 50/1 in the Sao Paolo Open.

On the ANZ tour 'down under' he posted top 10s in the Ford Open (T6th), the Australian Open (9th) and the Eriksson Masters (T7th).

A long hitter and fader of the ball. Once more driving accuracy, sand saves and putting are the areas in need of improvement.

The wide fairways of links golf are well suited to his long hitting game. 10/1 to make the Ryder Cup side.

> This promising young player has now had seven top 5 finishes in the last four years and he's just 25!

> 64 in R2 in the Victor Chandler British Masters, and a course-record 63 in the Australian Open shows his talent, while a 77 in R4 of the Volvo PGA and 80 in R1 of the Benson and Hedges show his occasional waywardness.

> He has played in all three Qatar Masters and was T11th in 2000. In a tournament for first time winners he must be given a real chance if he gets an early tee time.

> Starts the season early and is usually match fit from 'Aussie' when the Alfred Dunhill starts. Form figs. of 22nd-T3rd-32nd show he knows the course and he'll have an each-way chance at Houghton in 2001.

> Steve could well be the surprise winner of the 2001 Italian Open. Only T44th this year yet he finished well (10 under last three rounds) enough to suggest he's well suited to the long, wide-fairway course at Is Molas.

Key stat 107th for driving accuracy.

ROGER WESSELS

Age 39 **Born** South Africa **Lives** South Africa, UK Marlow

European tour BEF T2nd 1995 South African PGA **International wins** 2, latest 1994 Canadian Masters **World Cup of Golf** 1994 **Order of Merit** BEF 35th 2000

Improved form from the South African this year with three top 10s, in the French Open (T4th at 150/1), the Irish Open (T10th) and the Dutch Open (T6th).

He also had five top 25s, in the Johnnie Walker Classic (T15th), the Greg Norman Intl (T13th), the Wales Open (T21st), the European Open (T13th) and the Belgacom Open (T22nd).

In the Lancome Trophy he went from R1 leader (63) to missing the cut (after 81 in R2)! On the Vodacom tour in mid October he won the three-round Observatory Classic by 6 shots before he finished T9th in the Turespana Masters, T7th in the Italian Open and T7th in the Volvo Masters in successive weeks.

Tends to draw the ball. Still a solid putter. However his greens in reg stats can be improved a lot.

Will be 40 in March 2001.

> In 2000 he's tended to start slowly with only a single R1 sub-70.

> Watch out for this guy in 2001. After hard work with Scott Cranfield he has improved his mental skills, his diet and his results as his end of season form showed. In mid January he's a must bet as an 80/1 outsider in the Alfred Dunhill tournament in South Africa. He's a member at the Houghton course and he's better now than when he was T2nd in 1995.

> Worth noting at Noordwijkse for the Dutch Open as he clearly enjoys the links course there (T6th 2000 when 14(!) under for his last three rounds).

> He's awarded the streaker symbol after his 63 (R1) in the Lancome Trophy, and 64 (R2) in the Belgacom Open.

Key stat In his final three tournaments he finished T9th-T7th-T7th with eight of those twelve rounds in the 60s, all at or under par for a stroke average of 68.58!

LEE WESTWOOD G M 🐎 Y S 👑

Age 27 **Born** Worksop **Lives** Big House, Worksop

European tour wins 14, 1996 Scandinavian Masters, 1997 Volvo Masters, 1998 Deutsche Bank Open, 1998 English Open, 1998 Loch Lomond Invitational, 1998 Belgacom Open, 1999 Dutch Open, 1999 European Open, 1999 Canon European Masters, 2000 Deutsche Bank Open, 2000 Compaq European Grand Prix, 2000

European Open, 2000 Scandinavian Masters, 2000 Belgacom Open **International wins** 8, incl. 1998 Compaq Classic (USA) **Ryder Cup** 1997,1999 **Dunhill Cup** 1996-99 incl. **Majors** T5th 2000 US Open **Order of Merit** 1st 2000

Lee has had a crackin' year on the European tour as he became Europe's No. 1 so ending Monty's seven-year reign. However he still could not win his first major.

On the European tour he achieved five victories, in the Deutsche Bank Open (at 33/1!!), the Compaq European Grand Prix (at 9/2), the Smurfit European Open (at 7/1), the Volvo Scandinavian Masters (at 13/2) and the Belgacom Open (at 7/1).

He also posted top 5s in the Dubai Desert Classic (T4th at 12/1), the Volvo PGA (T2nd at 10/1), the English Open (T4th at 9/1), the Dutch Open (T3rd at 9/2), the Volvo Masters (T3rd at 7/1) and he sealed his O/M win at the WGC Amex (2nd at 12/1).

High finishes were also recorded in the South African Open (T10th), the Lancome Trophy (T7th), the rain-reduced German Masters (T11th) and the Italian Open (T12th).

Blamed his lack of concentration when T21st in the Canon European Masters on his move to his big new home near Worksop.

In the Coral Eurobet Seve Ballesteros Trophy he scored 4 points from 5 games, beating Thomas Bjorn (1 up) in the singles, to finish as the top British scorer at 5/1.

In the Andersen World Championship Match Play he beat Brandt Jobe 3 and 1 before losing by 1 hole, to Scott Hoch. In the WGC NEC Invitational he was a disappointing T20th.

He won the Cisco World Matchplay at Wentworth in the Autumn beating Sergio Garcia 2 and 1, Ernie Els 1 up, and then Monty at the 38th hole of a tremendous final. It was his 6th European win of the year.

In the majors he missed the cut in the US Masters, finished a fine T5th in the US Open, a poor T64th in the British Open, and a fast finishing T15th in the USPGA.

His great strengths are his long straight driving, accurate iron play and superb putting. Indeed his all round game is now first class as he's improved his bunker play a lot over the last couple of years. His chipping is one area with further scope for improvement.

Lee has a fine temperament with that priceless asset of not dwelling on a mistake, a poor shot or a bogey. If only he could have bottled that and sold it to Monty!. He's had laser eye surgery.

Moved into a massive house with its own driving range in the Autumn. He married Laurae Coltart (Andrew's sister) in January 1999. He's due to become a first-time father in 2001

> Lee has avoided the fashion for golfers to lose weight and use weights. "If I'd wanted to be an athlete then I'd have taken up 400 metres running. I don't like being called an athlete and I'd sooner be called a professional golfer".

> When following Lee in the 'non majors' it is wise to back him win only as his wins to starts ratio on the Euro tour from the start of 1998 to mid October is 22.2% equivalent to win odds of 7/2!!

> He has now won twelve European tournaments and one in America in the last three years and has won on all four major tours. That truly phenomenal record has undoubtedly been underappreciated because of Monty's seven-year reign as Europe's No. 1. It is quite clear that Lee will go on to post many, many more wins on the European tour. He could, of course, win any event at any time. However he can be nominated for four tournaments:-

* The Smurfit European Open. The course suits his long straight driving and this year this tournament was the first time he'd ever successfully defended a title. It's in the calendar at an ideal time between the US and British Opens and so expect Lee to win it for the third time in a row at 11/2 in early July.

* The Dutch Open. Coming a week after the British Open he can be followed IF, and only IF, he was not in contention at Royal Lytham. His tournament record is first class (3rd-W-3rd in last three years) and on the Noordjwijkse course he finished T3rd this year when below his best.

* The Volvo PGA. He played superbly in the Autumn at Wentworth when he beat Garcia, Els and Monty to land the Cisco World Matchplay. T2nd this year he can be backed to win the 2001 Volvo PGA at 9/1.

* Back Lee to land the 2001 Volvo Masters. He won it in 1997 and his final 36 holes this year (65.65) were easily (by 6 shots!) the best in the field.

> I'd be wary of backing Lee in three European tour events, and one major.

* His first tournament of the year. Lee invariably on his own admission is 'rusty' when the season starts so do oppose him in match bets, and if a suitable spread opportunity arises.

* The Compaq European Grand Prix. He won it in 2000 after he arrived jet lagged from the US Open and he has a crackin' record on a course tailor made for his game. Form figures of W-5-3 with a stroke average of 69.25 is mighty impressive. However once again he'll play after returning jet-lagged. I can't see history repeating itself in 2001 and at 4/1 favourite thanks but no thanks!

* The English Open. He never looked at ease this year when T4th and his overall record at the Forest of Arden is unimpressive for a player of his quality.

* The British Open. Links golf does not really suit him and he's yet to post a top 10 finish.

> "I never play well straight after a two-week break," said by Lee about his poor performance in the Italian Open, applies generally. Take him on after a break in 3 balls, matches and on the spreads.

> Is Lee really suited to America? Well, the jury must be out. The case for the prosecution would point to his illness on the eve of the 2000 US Masters, his high temperature and dehydration more than once in 1999, and the fact that "when I play in America it feels like I'm going to work".

However he has won in the States, played brilliantly at least once in each of the last three years and loves the fast greens. In 1998 he won the Compaq Classic, and was T5th in the Players Championship, in 1999 he was T6th in the same tournament and in 2000 he was T5th in the US Open and his 69-67 USPGA final rounds took him to T15th place.

I suggest Lee has now overcome his 'allergy to America', learnt the lessons of dehydration, and so in 2001 fired up in Ryder Cup year and in the American's own backyard I suggest he can be backed in three tournaments.

* The US Masters. Let's forget his missed cut when ill this year and remember his brilliant final three rounds in 1999 (6 under par) that took him to T6th place. Back him to be top European, in suitable match bets and in the outrights without Tiger.

* The Players Championship. T6th in 1999, T5th in 1998 his accuracy is tailor made for this really tough track. If he gets a good pair of tee times he should be backed to be top Euro (Won 7/1 and 7/2 in 1998 and 1999).

* The US Open. 5-MC-7-19 is an impressive bank of form for a 27-year-old so he can be backed in matchbets, in the top Euro market, and in the outrights.

> He's a certainty to play in the Ryder Cup. However his 2000 form on the Belfry was his worst of the year (T54th in the Benson and Hedges). However that was almost certainly a 'one-off' and can be forgotten.

> He has to be the choice to win the 2001 European Order of Merit. Clarke won't have his World Match Play winnings in 2001, Monty is to play less, so I expect Lee to be Europe's No. 1 again in 2001.

Key stat   Europe's top-ranked putter, Lee has the best stroke average of any European player.

ROGER WINCHESTER   V

Age 31   **Born** Exeter   **Lives** Wimbledon (up and under team)

European tour BEF T3rd 1999 Scottish PGA **Challenge Tour wins** 2, latest 1998 **Order of Merit** BEF 82nd in 1999 and 2000

Roger has not posted a single top 10 in 2000. However he has had six top 25s, in the Dubai Desert Classic (T20th), the Moroccan Open (T14th), the Volvo PGA (T20th after going 7 under over the last two rounds), the Scottish PGA (T24th), the BMW International (T20th), the Dutch Open (T17th) and the Belgacom Open (T18th).

He posted a top 30 when T26th in the English Open.

His putting stats are encouraging, however for driving accuracy and greens in reg (both outside the top 130) his stats are depressing.

> In these last two years on tour he's let good positions slip. In the 1999 Loch Lomond he was T3rd after R3, he then faltered to finish T10th, and in the 2000 BMW International he was T5th after R3, he then shot 75 in R4 to finish T20th.

And let's remember his Challenge tour win came when he went 5 under over the last 7 holes so he's clearly best when playing 'catch-up' from off the pace.

> He's well suited to links courses and can be noted in two tournaments.

* The Scottish PGA in which he'll probably have his best chance of the year (T3rd 1999: T20th 2000).

* The Dutch Open is held on the links course at Noordwijkse where he was under par in every round when T17 this year. Look for him in match bets and R1 3 balls (67 in R1, 2000).

Key stat   29th for total putting.

IAN WOOSNAM MBE

Age 42   **Born** Oswestry   **Lives** Jersey

European tour wins 28, last the 1997 Volvo PGA **International wins** 10 **Majors** 1991 US Masters **Ryder Cup** 1983-97 incl. **Dunhill Cup** 9 times latest 2000 **World Cup of Golf** 14 times **Order of Merit** 1st 1990

In late 1999 he was 2nd in the Hong Kong Open on the Asian Davidoff tour, and T2nd in the Argentinian Open.

On the European tour in 2000 he posted top 10s in the Portuguese Open (T9th after 66 in R4) and the Volvo PGA (T7th), and top 4 finishes in the Qatar Masters (2nd at 20/1), the Deutsche Bank Open (T3rd at 80/1) and the Wales Open (T3rd at 11/1). He also had top 20s in the Victor Chandler British Masters (T11th) and the Volvo Scandinavian Masters (T17th), and finished T24th in the Lancome Trophy.

In the majors he was T40th in the US Masters, T68th in the British Open and he missed the cut in the USPGA.

In the Seve Ballesteros Trophy he won only one of his four matches, losing 4 and 3 in the singles to Bernhard Langer. In the Dunhill Cup he won three of his four matches, helping Wales to reach the semi finals.

He continues to complain about his putting although he's ranked 40th for putts per GIR. Indeed after taking 126 putts in the US Masters he threatened to quit the game!

His iron play is still superb although his stats suggest his driving remains erratic. Draws the ball. His dodgy back was playing up again during the Turespana Masters in October.

> It's been three years since his last win and it showed in the 2000 Wales Open when Woosie suffered from 'contention rust'. The tournament leader going into the last day, as 4/6 favourite, he shot 73 ("I felt the pressure") to finish T3rd. Could well make amends by winning the Wales Open at his second attempt in 2001.

> A brilliant player in windy conditions, if he gets an early tee time have a bet on Woosie to land the 2001 Qatar Masters where his recent record (2nd 2000: T8th 1999: T9th 1998) is first class.

> Making 'Woosie for Wentworth' your slogan for the 2001 Volvo PGA could well reap a rich reward on the course where he won his last tournament in 1997, and where he finished T7th this year.

> 7/2 to regain his Ryder Cup place in 2001.

Key stat   141st (at 57.8%) for driving accuracy.

WEI-TZE YEH   D

Age 34   **Born** Taiwan

European tour wins 1, 2000 Malaysian Open

Wei who? won the Malaysian Open as an unknown rank outsider coming from well off the pace to shoot 12 under par for the last 54 holes to win by a shot.

Since then he has failed to reach the leaderboard at any stage of any other tour event.

> Obviously, in tournaments in the steamy heat in the Far East, he can be expected to be at his best.

> His win secured a three-year tour exemption. However on the evidence so far there's no reason to anticipate a top 5 finish in that time.

Key stat   He hasn't shot a sub-70 round on tour since his Malaysian Open victory.

THE AMERICAN TOUR PLAYERS

ROBERT ALLENBY G Y M

Age 29   **Born** Melbourne, Australia **Lives** Florida

US tour wins 2, 2000 Shell Houston Open, 2000 Western Open **European tour wins** 4, 3 in 1996 **International wins** 5, all in Australia **Presidents Cup** 2000 **Money list** BEF 16th 2000

This year it's been 'breakthrough' time for Allenby as he won his first, and then his second USPGA tournaments when he landed the Shell Houston Open (at 100/1*) and the Western Open (at 100/1), and had top 20s in the Bob Hope (T12th), the Doral Ryder Open (T12th) and the Canon Greater Hartford Open (T14th).

T36th in the British Open and T19th in the USPGA. He finished T12th in the WGC NEC Invitational. Played in the Presidents Cup, winning his singles against Azinger (1 point from four matches). T16th in the Tour Championship.

Robert is a player I have always liked and this year he's justified his G symbol. His great strength is his driving which is very long at 285 yards and his accuracy off the tee is up 2% to 72%. His putting has improved with experience in the States. Last year he was 182nd for putting, this year he is in the top 70. He's a fine player in windy conditions.

> In the first week of the New Year do back Allenby for the WGC Andersen World Match Play. He lives and was born in Melbourne where the tournament takes place at the Metropolitan Golf Club. With some big names missing I can recommend Allenby with some confidence and he'll be a big price!.

> He'll be 30 on 12 July 2001 and that can often provide a player with a real spur, and that date is also the first day of the Loch Lomond Invitational. He's had four top 15s including T2nd 1998 and 3rd 1996 for a stroke average of 69.69, so he's a must for match bets and worth a 'nibble' in the outrights.

> I have always believed that one day he'd win a major so he's definitely given the M symbol.

> I really do believe he has a British Open in him and given good tee times I could see him winning at Royal Lytham at 80/1 in a place. Back him as a long shot and to be the top Aussie (2nd 6/1 2000).

> Often a player in his thirties seeking his first major wins the USPGA and I think Allenby could well do so in 2001. At a big price he'll be worth a nice each-way bet to land a big-priced surprise.

> On the USPGA tour as a Florida resident he can be backed in two tournaments on the 'Florida Swing'

>   * The Bay Hill Invitational. His long hitting is suited here. T29th this year he can leave that form behind in 2001.

>   * The Doral Ryder Open. T12th this year with four sub-par rounds he could well be the 'Doral Man' next year.

> I really do fancy him for the 2001 Compaq Classic. He didn't play in 2000 yet he ended with a 64 in R4 in 1999 (T28th) and this is a real 'driver's course' that's tailor made for him.

> A little each way on Allenby at 100/1+ for the 2001 US Money list (w/o Woods) could well pay a huge dividend. As you've just read, I rate this guy highly and he could well have a stellar year.

Key stat   No 1 player for total driving in 2000.

STEPHEN AMES   G V ❙

Age 36   **Born** Trinidad   **Lives** Calgary, Canada

US tour BEF 3rd 1998 Nissan Open, 3rd 1999 Sprint International **BUY.COM tour wins** 1, in 1991 **European tour wins** 2, 1994 and 1996 Benson & Hedges Internationals **Money list** BEF 63rd 2000

Having overcome visa problems Stephen was starting his first full USPGA season (started in May last year) and he's established himself by easily retaining his card.

He posted top 5 finishes in the Compaq Classic (T4th at 100/1) and the Michelob (T5th at 80/1). He also had top 10s in the Doral Ryder Open (8th) and the International (8th), and top 25s in the Tucson Open (T17th), the Honda Classic (T19th), the Shell Houston Open (T17th), the Western Open (T15th incl. 63 in R2) and the John Deere Classic (T23rd).

Played really well in the Bob Hope Classic being T3rd after R4 when he had to withdraw.

He finished T30th in the USPGA.

In many ways his stats are impressive as he's in the top 25 for birdie conversion and fifth for par 3 birdies. A good putter (top 50) his big weaknesses are in sand saves and R4 scoring (both outside the top 170).

> A naturally talented player off scratch within six months of taking up the game he has now 'bedded' in to the USPGA tour. However his key problem has been his final round scoring especially when in contention.

In each of the last two years he's let winning opportunities slip.

* 1999 International. In the lead on the back nine in R4. Finished 3rd.
* 1999 Texas Open. Led after R3, shot 75 in R4 to finish T8th.
* 2000 Tucson Open. T2 after R3, shot 76 in R4, to finish T17th
* 2000 Doral Ryder Open. 3rd after R3, shot 72 in R4, to finish 8th.

Last year I said that he'd learn from his R4 disappointments and so he was not awarded the bottle. Sadly this year it's merited.

Surely his best chance for his first US win will be when coming from 'off the pace', when he is clearly most comfortable, as he showed in both his top 5 finishes this season in which he came from 'off the pace' in R4 with a 68 in the Compaq Classic, and 67 in the Michelob.

> I still believe a player of his huge talent will win on the tour and once he gets the first win one or two others could well follow.

> I really do fancy him for the Michelob as I can see him winning when coming from 'off the pace'. T13th in 1999 and T5th this year his last seven rounds have all been under par for a stroke average of 68.86!

> He's got a superb record in the International where he was 8th (30 pts) this year, and 3rd (43 pts) in 1999 for an average of 36½ points. He'll be a stormin' match bet, worth support on the spreads and in the R1 betting 15 pts (2000): 11 pts (1999).

> He's very well suited to courses where there's no premium on driving accuracy so he can be followed in match bets, and in the outrights in two tournaments.

   * The Bob Hope Classic where he shot three brilliant rounds (66-63-64) out of four before he withdrew this year when T3rd.

   * The Las Vegas Invitational where he was 9th in 1999.

> Proved in the 1999 Texas Open that he can overcome the LaCantera course when he was 16 under par and the 2-shot leader after R3. A non runner this year if he 'goes to post' back him to win the 2001 Texas Open

> Remember him in the top non-American markets during the Florida Swing (T3rd 16/1 Honda Classic: 3rd 20/1 Doral Ryder Open).

Key stat   171st (!) for R4 scoring.

BILLY ANDRADE

Age 36   **Born** Rhode Island   **Lives** Rhode Island & Atlanta, Georgia

US Tour wins 4, 1991 Kemper Open, Buick Classic, 1998 Canadian Open, 2000 Invensys Classic in Las Vegas **Money list** BEF 14th 1991

2000 was on course to be Billy's worst year since his days as a rookie back in 1988. When he teed off in Vegas for the Invensys Classic in mid October he lay 159th on the money list and Q School beckoned. However, he shocked punters and himself when he won at 150/1 to give bookmakers a real skinner. His massive first prize of $765,000 (!) shot him up to 43rd on the M/L.

Before then his season had been very, very disappointing as he'd missed seventeen of his first twenty-seven cuts, managing just one top 10, in the Buick Challenge (T10th), and four top 25s, in the Bay Hill (T22nd), the Byron Nelson (T25th), the Colonial (T24th) and the Southern Farm Bureau (T11th).

His poor form was caused in essence by his poor long game. Outside the top 120 for both driving accuracy and greens in reg in 1999 he's outside the top 100 for both in 2000.

His putting remains solid although his sand saves have slipped from 61% to 48%. Great friend of Brad Faxon.

> Billy traces his troubles back to early 1999 when he took the whole of May off and never shook off the 'rust' that that absence created. Clearly a much better player when in continuous play, and let's remember his two wins in 1991 came back to back.

> Expect a steadier year from Andrade in 2001 with his best chance probably coming in the Greater Milwaukee Open where from 1996-1998 incl. he averaged 67.8. Worth support at Brown Deer Park in 2001.

Key stat 172nd for driving accuracy.

STUART APPLEBY

Age 29   **Born** Cohuna, Australia   **Lives** Florida

US Tour Wins 3, 1997 Honda Classic, 1998 Kemper Open & 1999 Shell Houston Open **International Wins** 1, 1998 Coolum Classic in Australia **BUY.COM Tour Wins** 2, in 1995 **US Money List** BEF 18th 1997: **The Presidents Cup** 1998 and 2000 **Dunhill Cup** 1997,1998,1999

Who will ever forget his press conference before the 1998 USPGA when he returned to the US tour following his wife's tragic accidental death earlier in the year in London?

In 1999 he won for the first time since his tragedy landing the Shell Houston Open at 80/1 and finished the year 25th on the M/L.

This year he has posted a series of high finishes. On the ANZ tour he was T22nd in the Greg Norman Holden and T13th in the Ericsson Masters.

On the US tour he had top 10s in the Sony Open in Hawaii (2nd at 40/1), the Kemper Open (7th) and the International (3rd at 50/1), and top 20s in the Mercedes (15th), the Nissan Open (T18th), the Honda Classic (T12th), the Compaq Classic (T11th), the Memorial (T17th), the Western Open (T20th).

In the World Match Play he lost by 1 hole to Scott Hoch. In the Presidents Cup he didn't score at all losing in the singles to Loren Roberts (3 and 2)

In the majors he missed the cut in the US Masters and US Open. He finished a creditable T11th in the British Open and was a brilliant T4th at 80/1 in the USPGA, and T22nd in the Players Championship (the 'fifth major'.)

Finished T20th in the WGC NEC Invitational, and a solid 7th in the Tour Championship..

Very long off the tee at 287 yards. He has a solid all round game although his driving accuracy remains at just 63% (outside top 150) for the second successive year. Also for the second successive year his best scoring round is easily R3.

A very good player in tough windy conditions.

> Safely past 30 on Mayday 2001 his strong all round game, proven bottle, and considerable experience mark him down most definitely as a player to follow in 2001 when he could well win one or more tournaments.

> Very early in January forget your hangover and back Appleby for the World Match Play. Held at the Metropolitan Club, Melbourne and with one or two big names missing he'll have a 'helluva' chance on home soil.

> On the ANZ tour he has a good record both in the Greg Norman Holden International (T3rd 1998) and on the tough Lakes course (T4th 1995) so he'll be worth each-way support in early February in that tournament.

> In America he can be followed with real confidence in three tournaments

 * The Kemper Open. A very good player at TPCs, his record here (7th-6th-W-14th-18th, with sixteen of his last twenty rounds under par, for a stroke average of 69.25) makes him an outstanding bet.

 * The Honda Classic. Gave him his first US win in 1997. Since then he's finished T4th-T9th-T12th. A first-class chance at Heron Bay in 2001.

 * The International. His long hitting is suited to this points-scoring event. 3rd with 41 pts in 2000, and 2nd with 41 pts in 1997, he merits support at Castle Pines in 2001.

> Keep an eye on him in the speciality markets.

 * 2nd top non American in the Honda Classic.

 * Top Aussie at 9/1 in the British Open

 * Top Rest of The World player at 16/1 in the USPGA.

 * His form figures (20:13:9:7) over the last four years seem to be going the wrong way, yet four successive top 20s mark Appleby down as a sound outright bet in the Western Open and a must in match betting.

 * He has a fine record in the Sony Open in Hawaii (2nd-T16th-9th-31st) where he plays well in the wind; and in the Colonial (35th-11th-10th) where he's shot enough good rounds to be long shot with a live chance.

Key stat   17th on the all-round ranking.

TOMMY ARMOUR III   D

Age 41   **Born** Denver, Colorado   **Lives** Dallas Texas

US Tour Wins 1, the 1990 Phoenix Open **BUY.COM Tour Wins** 2 in a row, both in 1994 **US Money List** BEF 35th 1990:

After two consecutive years in the top 55 on the M/L 2000 has been disappointing for Thomas Dickson.

He's made only 4 prominent finishes. However his T5th at 150/1 in the Nissan Open (worth $105K) virtually secured his card. He posted a top 10 in the Byron Nelson Classic (T10th), and top 25s in the Western Open (T23rd), the Air Canada (T13th) and the Michelob (T25th). Missed the cut in the US Open.

This year he's missed the cut in 60% of tournaments with his poor form compared to last year caused by his poor putting. Top 15 for putting average last year he's outside the top 175 in 2000. A long hitter at 282 yards although driving accuracy ranking is outside top 100 again.

> He can be noted for match bets in the Western Open where his form figures (23rd-13th-17th) in the last three years are solid.

> He has a sound record in the Nissan Open in recent years, T5th this year at Pacific Palisades he was T6th at Valencia in 1998.

> Twice this year he's let final round pressure get to him.

 * Air Canada. T2nd after R3 he shot 73 in R4 to finish T13th.

 * Nissan Open. T2nd after R3 he shot 71 in R4 to finish T5th.

> He simply must be supported in the 3-ball betting in R1 of the Michelob where his opening day record on the Kingsmill course is first class - 69 (2000), 69 (1999), 70 (1998), 67 (1997), 67 (1996) for an amazing R1 stroke average of 68.4 in the last five years!

Key stat   T13th for putting average in 1999, he's 187th (!) in 2000.

WOODY AUSTIN

Age 36   **Born** Florida   **Lives** Minnesota

College University of Miami

US Tour Wins 1, 1995 Buick Open in the year he was USPGA tour Rookie of the Year. **Buy.com Tour Wins** None, yet he was No. 1 for Scoring Average (69.91) on 1998 Nike Tour with nine top 10s. **US Money List** BEF 32nd in 1996

In 2000 the former bank teller made two top 10s, in the Tucson Open (T7th) and the Bay Hill Invitational (9th) and earned over $118K when T4th at 200/1 in the Buick Open (R1 leader with 63).

He also posted top 25s in the Greater Milwaukee Open (T22nd) and the NCR Classic at Disney (T24th).

Short off the tee at 274 yards Woody's perennial problem remains his putting (outside top 150 for total putting)

> He has struggled to retain his card since his two-year exemption from winning the Buick Open expired at the end of 1997.

> Woody simply loves the Buick Open where his record is amazing. He won it in 1995, 3rd 1996, T6th after R3 in 1998, T15th 1999 and T4th in 2000.

  * However more detailed analysis is very revealing over the last three years

1998	69-69	69-74
1999	68-69	73-67
2000	63-67	73-70

    His six pre-cut rounds have a stroke average of 67.5

    His six post cut rounds have a stroke average of 71.00

  * So back Woody Austin in the R1 and R2 3 balls in the Buick Open with real confidence, and support him in any available match or spread bets.

  * On the outrights with three top 5 finishes in the last six years he's well worth an each-way bet, especially if a lazy compiler once more offers the staggering 200/1 on offer this year!

Key stat   In the last three years he has a stroke average, before the cut, of 67.5 in the Buick Open.

PAUL AZINGER

Age 40   **Born** Minnesota   **Lives** Florida

US Tour Wins 12, 5 in 1980s, 6 from 1990-93 incl. and the 2000 Hawaiian Open **Major wins** 1, 1993 USPGA **Euro Tour Wins** 2, BMW International Open in 1990 and 1992 **US Money List** BEF 2nd 1987 and 2nd 1993: From 1987 - 1993 incl. only once out of top 10 when 11th in 1988 **Ryder Cup** 3 times **The Presidents Cup** 1994 and 2000

Started 2000 brilliantly winning his first tournament of the year, and his first for seven years when he led all the way from an early tee time to win the Hawaiian Open at 80/1 by 7 shots!

After missing his next cut he then went on a run of fourteen successive cuts posting a series of high finishes with top 10s in the Memorial (T5th), the British Open (T7th), the WGC NEC Invitational (T8th), the Bell Canadian Open (T10th) and the the NCR Classic at Disney (T10th). Top 25s came in the Players Championship (T17th), the MCI Classic (T25th), the US Open (T12th), the Fedex St Jude Classic (T20th), the Buick Open (T21st) and the USPGA (T24th). Finished T8th in October in the Buick Challenge.

His 2000 major record T28th (Masters), T12th (US Open), T7th (British Open) and T24th (USPGA) is impressively consistent. In the Presidents Cup he scored 1 point, losing to Allenby in the singles. Finished T11th in the Tour Championship

His driving accuracy (down 2½%) and greens in reg (down almost 2%) have been compensated for by his truly brilliant putting this year (top 5 compared to T111th last year). Uses Butch Harmon.

> Having overcome cancer he now goes, 'to every touarment with a lot of confidence,' and if he maintains the improved putting he showed this year he can go on to further success.

> He must have a big chance in the AT&T. Suited by the wider fairways and often windy conditions his record is first class—T10th (1999): T3rd (1998): 7th (1997): 3rd (1992) and he won it (1991). Make 'Azinger for the AT&T' an early season slogan.

> He also has a fine record in another pro-am celebrity event, the NCR Classic at Walt Disney. In his last three starts he's finished T10th (2000), T17th (1999) and T18th (1996), so he's a must for match bets and worth noting as an outsider with a squeak.

> He has fond memories of Warwick Hills where he returned to the tour in 1994 after he was diagnoised with lymphoma. T21st this year (65 in R1) in a tournament won by experienced players Azinger could win the 2001 Buick Open at 66/1.

> Worth noting in two tournaments in 3 balls, matches and as a long priced outsider.

 * The Memorial. T5th (2000), T19th (1999) and he won it in 1993.

 * The St Jude Classic. A stroke average of 68.5 over the last three years with form figures of 20th-6th-7th.

> Landed a nice touch in a match bet 'rick' this year to beat a woefully out of form Maggert in the US Open. He's posted three successive top 15s in that major, so keep an eye on Paul in the match betting.

> He will fancy his chances in the Buick Challenge after consecutive top 10s (T7th 2000: T6th 1999). He can be supported at Calloway Gardens in match bets and as a 40/1 chance.

Key stat T111th for putting last year he's 4th in 2000.

DOUG BARRON   V

Age 31   **Born** Memphis, Tennessee **Lives** Memphis, Tennessee
College Mississippi State Univ.

US Tour wins BEF T4th 2000 Air Canada Championship **BUY.COM Tour wins** BEF T3rd in 1996 **Money list** BEF 108th 2000

This was Doug's fourth year on the tour and his previous three have resulted in money list positions of 116th (1997), 109th (1998) and 123rd (very close to losing his card, in 1999).

2000 has seen Doug again struggle to retain his card. However he has posted two top 5s including his best ever finish when T4th at 125/1 in the Air Canada. He was T5th at 150/1 in the Canon Greater Hartford Open.

His other high finishes were in the Greater Milwaukee Open (T18th), the Fedex St Jude Classic (T25th), the Buick Open (T21st), the Pennsylvania Classic (T24th), and a top 10 in the Tampa Bay Classic (T10th).

Short off the tee at 269 yards. His greens in reg. show a 2% improvement, however his putting average has slipped from 65th to outside the top 120.

> Yet to win on either tour it must be remembered he 'blew up' (79 in R4) in the 1999 Honda Classic when in serious contention.

> As stated last year he has definitely been at his best from June onwards. This year he missed nine of thirteen cuts before late June when he proceeded to make eight of his next nine cuts, including all his six top 25 finishes.

> His form at Brown Deer Park is very consistent. T18th (2000), T17th (1999), 6th (1998), 26th (1997). So in 2001 he'll be a 125/1 outsider with a squeak.

> Could go well in the Honda Classic where he was T6th in 1999, and where he shot 68 (R1) this year before he missed the cut.

Key stat 144th (at 268.6 yards) for driving distance.

NOTAH BEGAY   G Y

Age 28   **Born** Albuqueque, New Mexico **Lives** Albuqueque, New Mexico
NIKE tour 4 second places on 1998 Nike Tour. **US Tour wins** 3, the 1999 Reno-Tahoe Open, 1999 Michelob Championship, 2000 Fed Ex St Jude Classic, 2000 Canon Greater Hartford Open. **Presidents Cup** 2000 **Money list** BEF 20th 2000

Notah made a sensational start to his full USPGA tour career in 1999 when he won twice and earned over $1 million.

He started the 2000 season well when T4th at 125/1 in the AT and T. However the following month in early March he served seven days in custody following a second drink driving conviction.

On his return he missed the cut in the Bay Hill Invitational. He finished T15th in the MCI Classic. Found his form in June when after finishing 22nd in the US Open he won the Fedex St Jude Classic at 80/1, and followed that up the very next week by winning the Canon Greater Hartford Open at 40/1. Trying for a third win in a row he finished T4th at 40/1 in the Loch Lomond before finishing T20th in his first British Open.

He went on to be T19th in the International and 8th in the USPGA. Finished T37th in the US Masters and T17th in the WGC NEC International. Played alongside his old University friend Tiger Woods in the Presidents Cup. Won 3 pts from five matches, defeating Goosen (1 hole) in the singles.

Missed the cut when defending his Michelob title. Finished a poor last (adrift by 8 shots) in the Tour Championship.

A deceptively long hitter his greatest strength is his ability and courage to 'close out' a tournament when he has a sniff of success.

He putts L-R putts left handed and he goes right handed for R-L putts.....and it sure works.

He is the only American Indian on the PGA tour and is a role model to so much American Indian youngsters. Uses his younger brother Clint as his caddy.

> A streak player capable of shooting low numbers. Shot 59 in 1998 on the BUY.COM tour, 63 (R3 Reno-Tahoe) and 64 (R4 Canon Greater Hartford Open) in 1999, and 64 twice this year when winning the Canon Greater Hartford Open.

> With four wins (all after late June) in two seasons, a proven 'closer', a long hitter and a 'streaker' there's every reason to expect the earring wearing Notah to go on to further success.

> Last year his profile nominated him for just two tournaments, the Fedex St Jude Classic and the Canon Greater Hartford Open and he won both at 80/1 and 40/1.

So this year I suggest you can back him in three tournaments:-

* The International. He's played twice making the first cut in 1999, and finishing in the top 20 in 2000. A winner already in the desert his long hitting could form the basis of a 50/1 win in Colorado at his favourite time of the year.

* The AT&T. T4th this year at a time when he wasn't mentally 100% he could well spring a 50/1 surprise win in the 2001 AT and T.

> 4th in the greens in regulation stats for the 2000 US Masters he was last (131 putts!) for putting. Once he gets used to the greens he'll become an interesting contender at Augusta.

> However his best chance in a major will probably be in the USPGA. Held at his time of the year, in hot humid conditions and with slightly wider fairways, he was 8th this year on his debut after a brilliant final three rounds.

> Maybe worth opposing in the Buick Challenge where in two starts he's finished T48th this year, and T61st in 1999 posting just two sub-70 rounds in the eight played.

Key stat   Won 4 of his first 34 USPGA non-major tournaments.

JAY DON BLAKE

Age 42   **Born** Utah   **Lives** Utah

College Utah

US Tour Wins 1, 1991 **International Wins** 1, 1991 **Money list** BEF 21st 1991. In top 90 1991-1998 inclusive

Another steady year for Jay Don in which he's posted three top 10s, in the Bell South Classic (T5th at 100/1*), the Doral Ryder Open (T9th) and the Buick Challenge (T10th), and five top 20s in the AT&T (T11th), the Buick Invitational (T14th), the Colonial (T20th), the Kemper Open (T13th) and the Canon Greater Hartford Open (T18th).

Short off the tee at 265 yards Jay was the tour's top putter in 1991, 3rd in 1992 and he can still use the flatstick very well. Accuracy to the green is his problem (141st).

Fades the ball.

> In each of the last four years he's posted a top 5 finish, and at big prices
  * 1997 Hawaiian Open (T4th), St Jude Classic (T5th)
  * 1998 Bell South Classic (2nd)
  * 1999 Michelob (T5th)
  * 2000 Bell South Classic (T5th)

> He cries out to be backed in match bets and as an each-way long shot in the 2001 Bell South Classic as his record (5th-16th-2nd-28th) in just four starts is superb.

> He may not have the length to win the Buick Invitational but his LT stroke average (69.87) is hugely impressive. The winner in 1991, T4th in 1993 and T14th this year, he's a must for match bets.

> He missed the cut this year, but he had previously (1997-99 inclusive) averaged 69.3 in the Fedex St Jude Classic where he must be noted in 2001.

Key stat   165th (at 266 yards) for driving distance.

MICHAEL BRADLEY   G ☼ CT

Age 34   **Born** Florida   **Lives** Florida

College Oklahoma State University

US Tour wins 2, 1996 Buick Challenge, 1998 Doral Ryder Open **Internatl wins** 2, in 1989 and 1990 both in Canada **Money list** BEF 20th 1996

Michael was a really good player in 1996 when he was 20th on the M/L having his maiden win and three other top 5s. In 1997 he had three top 10s to finish T47th on the M/L. However in 1998 although he did me a favour winning the Doral Ryder Open at 80/1 he had back surgery for a herniated disc in June.

His career since then has been 'on hold'. In 1999 146th on the M/L he retained his card because of his two-year exemption gained for his 1998 win.

This season he missed his first nine cuts and didn't post a top 40 finish until September. However he then showed consistent form with three successive top 35 finishes (32nd-33rd-32nd) before playing well to finish T9th in the Michelob.

After such a disastrous season to September his stats are poor. Although his sand save stats are good and when he's got to Sunday his R4 scoring is in the top 50.

> His exemption has now expired so he'll probably have to go to Q School where I would expect him to secure his 2001 tour card.

> Let's be absolutely clear this guy is a good player, with a fine swing who is a proven winner, a long hitter and now, free from his back problems, firmly on the comeback trail. As a result of his poor recent form he'll be at nice prices next year when I think he'll represent some genuine value.

> A born and bred Floridian he has already won in the heat and humidity of his home state, and indeed both his wins have been on bermuda grass greens so in early March 2001 raid your piggy bank and back Bradley big style in his three home-state tournaments for which he'll be on offer at big prices and represent genuine 'value'.

* The Doral Ryder Open T2nd 1996: Won 1998

* The Honda Classic 2nd 1997

* The Bay Hill Invitational T6th 1997

> Outside his home state he can be backed with real confidence in two tournaments.

* The Fedex St Jude Classic 6th (1996), T5th (1997), T12th (1998)

* The Michelob T4th (1994), T11th (1995), T3rd (1996) for a three-year stroke average of 68.58, and T9th this year.

Key stat   Posted just one top 10 from January 1999 to October 2000 in forty-six starts.

MARK BROOKS

Age 39   **Born** Fort Worth, Texas   **Lives** Fort Worth, Texas

US Tour Wins 7, one in 1988: In '90s, Greater Greensboro Open (1991), Greater Milwaukee Open (1991), Kemper Open (1994), Bob Hope Chrysler Classic (1996), Shell Houston Open (1996) **Major Wins** 1, 1996 USPGA **Money list** BEF 3rd in 1996

Mark has generally struggled since his magic year (1996) when he was 3rd on the Money list after winning three tournaments including his first major, the USPGA.

His subsequent Money list positions (108th-129th-74th) show his decline. 2000 has seen no real progress with just three high finishes in the Shell Houston Open (T5th), the Compaq Classic (T17th) and the Byron Nelson Classic (T7th) in successive weeks in May, and an earlier top 10 in the AT&T (T7th). He missed the cut in the US Open, the British Open and the USPGA. He finished T40th in the US Masters.

Accuracy off the tee is his strength (top 50 last two years for driving accuracy), but his iron play lets him down (outside top 125 for GIR last two years).

However his putting has improved a lot this year. Draws the ball. He'll be 40 in March 2001. Withdrew from the Tampa Bay Classic and the NCR Disney Classic with a bad back in late October.

> Once players blow out the 40th candle on their birthday cake they often show much improved form and this could well happen to Mark after March 2001.

> He has a warm feeling towards the Canon Greater Hartford Open which gave him his first win in 1988. He's played sufficiently well 'in snatches' there recently with an opening 65 in R1 this year, and a solid T12th in 1998 to merit consideration especially in the early 3-ball betting, and as a 100/1 'shock' outsider.

> As a Texan he enjoys the Shell Houston Open (winner 1996: T5th 2000) held in his home state where he can be supported in match bets and as a big priced outsider with a genuine chance.

Key stat   30th for putting average.

BOB BURNS

Age 32   **Born** California   **Lives** Tennessee
BUY.COM tour wins 2, both in 1998 **US tour** BEF T5th 1994 Buick Classic

In 1999 Bob lost his card when 177th on the M/L after posting just three top 25s in thirty-one starts. This year however he has shown better form.

Made a fast start when T9th in the Sony Open in Hawaii, he went on to post another top 10 in the Compaq Classic (T6th).

He also had high finishes in the Kemper Open (T20th) and the Air Canada (T11th).

Quite long at 276 yards he shows in the top 30 for par 3 birdie leaders. Uses left-below-right putting technique.

> Although his best scoring round this year is R4 it was noticeable that his swing quickened under the pressure on Sunday in the Compaq Classic.

> His most consistent performance this year (four rounds at or under 70) came in the first event, the Sony Open in Hawaii in which he'll probably do well again in 2001.

Key stat   28th for par 3 birdies.

TOM BYRUM   D

Age 40   **Born** South Dakota   **Lives** Texas
US Tour wins 1, 1989 Kemper Open **Money list** BEF 32nd 1989

Tom has had a steady year, highlighted by three top 10s, in the Reno-Tahoe Open (T7th), the Invensys Classic in Las Vegas (T9th) and the Southern Farm Bureau (T6th). He had three other top 25s in the Tucson Open (T13th), the Compaq Classic (T24th) and the Byron Nelson Classic (T25th).

His lack of length off the tee (266 yards) is a big handicap. This year his sand saves (down 8%) and putting (72nd to outside top 115) are the main causes for his poor record.

His great strength continues to be his accuracy off the tee (75%) in which he's usually in the top 15.

Tends to draw the ball. Was 40 in September 2000.

His younger brother Curt is also a tour player.

> After his disappointing final round in the Invensys Classic at Las Vegas (72) I can't see him winning again. However this year his three top 15 finishes have all been in desert tournaments which he clearly enjoys.

> A straight hitting player Tom Elliott's (crackin' middle name) best chance will probably be in the Buick Classic (made cut 2000: T10th 1999: T5th 1998) as it places a premium on driving accuracy.

> In the Air Canada his eclectic score in 1996 and 1997 was 19 under par (including 63 and 64) to prove he has the ability to win the tournament. He'll be a 125/1 outsider with a squeak in 2001.

Key stat   Tom's last win was over 280 tournaments ago in 1989.

MARK CALCAVECCHIA

Age 40   **Born** New England   **Lives** Florida

US Tour wins 9, 5 in the 1980s incl. 1989 Phoenix Open, and 4 in the nineties - 1992 Phoenix Open, 1995 Bell South Classic, 1997 Greater Vancouver Open and 1998 Honda Classic **Major wins** 1, 1989 British Open **International wins** 4, last, the 1997 Subaru Sarazen World Open **Money list** BEF 5th in 1989

Calc has had a really successful, if winless, year in 2000. He's posted four top 5 finishes, in the Greater Greensboro Classic (T3rd at 66/1), the Canon Greater Hartford Open (2nd at 40/1), the Air Canada (3rd at 22/1) and the Pennsylvania Classic (2nd at 28/1).

He also had top 10s in the Phoenix Open (T7th), the Honda Classic (T7th) and the Colonial (T8th), and top 25s in the AT&T (T20th), the International (T14th), the Reno-Tahoe Open (T21st) and the Michelob (T25th). Finished T11th in the Tour Championship.

In the World Match Play he beat Nick Price (2 and 1) in R1 before losing to Olazabal. 10th in the WGC American Express Championship. Finished T26th in the British Open and T34th in the USPGA. Uses Butch Harmon.

His excellent year has been based on improvement in total driving (6th from T43rd), in putting (136th to top 70) and crucially in greens in reg. (up 2½% to top 30). A fine iron player who fades the ball. He was 40 in June 2000.

> Calc is a consistent highly experienced guy who knows how to win. His accuracy gives him birdie chances and when his putter works he's a formidable competitor. Without a win for two years I expect him to win in 2001 as he's never gone winless for three years (although that was pre-Tiger).

> "I'm a transplanted Northeastener," so he loves the Canon Greater Hartford Open where he's had an amazing four top 5s in the last five years for a stroke average of 67.25. At 33/1+ he'd be a crackin' bet, so make 'Calc for the Canon' your slogan in midsummer.

> A real desert fox Mark Calc down as a must bet for the 2001 Phoenix Open at 40/1+. He's had seven top 10s and two wins in thirteen starts for a long-term stroke average of under 69.

> He loves the Greater Milwaukee Open where he's posted nine top 10s in twenty-one starts, so with fourteen of his last sixteen rounds in the 60s he'll be worth a bet at Brown Deer Park in 2001.

> His game is well suited to the Air Canada where in three starts he's got form figures of 3rd-21st-Won. Worth an each-way 'nibble' at the Northview course.

> Can be backed with confidence for the 2001 Honda Classic. A Florida resident, Calc won it in 1998 and finished T7th this year.

Key stat   He's posted at least one top 3 finish every year since 1986.

JIM CARTER

Age 39   **Born** North Carolina   **Lives** Scottsdale, Arizona

US Tour wins 1, 2000 Tucson Open **BUY.COM Tour wins** 1 in 1994 **Money list** BEF 33rd in 1989

What a start to the new millennium for Jim Laver Carter who gained his first ever win, in the Tucson Open at 80/1, on his 292nd start.

Since then he's recorded four top 20s, in the Doral Ryder Open (T15th),the Players Championship (T13th winning $112K), the Buick Classic (T11th) and the SEI Pennsylvania Classic (11th).

Arizona Jim also visited Scotland missing the cut in the British Open having finished T27th the previous week at Loch Lomond.

Short off the tee (265 yards) his putting has been his real strength this year. A fine bunker player (top 30 last two years). He'll be 40 in late June 2001.

> There's one definite way to 'get Carter'. It's to back him in the Buick Classic in match bets and particularly in the R1 3 balls. In his last three starts he's finished 13th (2000), 5th (1999) and 5th (1997) for a stroke average of 69.58 (!), and his R1 scoring has been 69 (2000), 67 (1999), and 69 (1997) for a first-day stroke average of 68.33. With two top 5 finishes in the last three starts he definitely merits place-only support at 20/1+.

Key stat   163rd (at 266.4 yards) for driving distance.

GREG CHALMERS   FT F Y G S

Age 27   **Born** Sydney, Australia   **Lives** Perth, W. Australia

US Tour wins BEF T2nd 2000 Kemper Open **International wins** 1997 ANZ Players Championship and 1997 Challenge Tour Championship **European Challenge Tour** 1 win in 1997 **Majors** BEF T4th 2000 USPGA **Money list** BEF 41st 2000

Greg earned his tour card by finishing T4th at the 1998 Q School. He retained it in 1999 posting seven top 25 finishes in his Rookie year.

In 2000 he progressed further. He posted top 4 finishes in the Kemper Open (T2nd at 150/1) and the Canadian Open (T4th at 66/1), and top 25s in the Nissan Open (T18th), the Tucson Open (T25th), the MCI Classic (T25th), the International (T11th), the Buick Open (T16th), the Buick Challenge (T8th) and the Players Championship (impressive when T9th).

He finished T4th at 150/1 in the final major, the USPGA.

His stats this year are really impressive and show improvement in every main category apart from sand saves. Left handed player.

> This guy is now, without question, firmly in 'the winner about to happen' category. He has a really impressive progressive record.

* 1997 European Challenge tour. One win and seven top 10s, and he won the ANZ Tour Championship.

* 1998 Rookie on the European tour. Eight top 20s including two 2nds to finish 25th on O/M. Wins Australian Open. T4th at US Q School.

* 1999 Rookie on the US tour. Posts seven top 25s to retain his card.

* 2000 He establishes himself with a series of fine performances. In his 3rd major he finishes T4th. In the top 20 for birdie conversion, all round Ranking, and R4 scoring.....and he was only 27 in October 2000!

> His excellent temperament is shown by his bounce-back rating (measures reaction on next hole after a bogey)

A streak player capable of shooting low (remember his 61 in R3 of the 1998 English Open?), and also by contrast a good player on tough courses.

He will surely continue to play really well again in 2001 when I expect him to post his first US tour win.

> Always keep him in mind in the 'top rest of the world' markets in which he was T4th at 33/1 in the Nissan Open, and the 40/1 winner in the USPGA.

> He must be followed 'in the fall' on the Canadian swing

* Canadian Open T4th (2000), T15th (1999) where his last five rounds have all been under par for a stroke average of 68.4.

* Air Canada. T21st (2000), T31st (2000) where his two-year eclectic score (68-69-65-68) at 16 under could win!

> He shows a real liking for two desert tournaments:-
>
>   * The International. T11th 2000 on his second appearance, scoring 15 pts in R1, I believe this event suits him really well and make him an outsider with a really good chance in 2001.
>   * The Tucson Open. 12 under par for his last 54 holes to finish T25th this year was very promising.
>
> When the tour makes the Florida swing follow him in two tournaments.
>
>   * I think he'll represent a 'value' bet in the 2001 Doral Ryder Open despite his T45th finish this year. However he was T10th in 1999 after being 2nd at halfway and he'll be worth an each-way wager.
>
> His T8th finish in this year's Buick Challenge on his second start at Calloway Gardens suggests he'll do well there again in 2001.

Key stat   8th in the all-round ranking.

BRANDEL CHAMBLEE

Age 38   **Born** Minnesota   **Lives** Phoenix, Arizona

College University of Texas

US Tour wins 1, 1998 Air Canada Championship **Buy.com Tour wins** 1, 1990 New England Classic **Money list** BEF 37th in 1998

Apart from his best year in 1998 (37th M/L) he has never finished in the top 70 on the Money list, and 2000 has been another disappointing year although he has posted three top 10s, in the Nissan Open (T10th), the Bay Hill Invitational (T10th) and the Byron Nelson Classic (T7th after 65 in R4). He also posted top 20s when T18th in the Phoenix Open and T13th in the NCR Classic at Walt Disney.

T61st in the US Open.

Short off the tee at 272 yards. His greens in regulation stats have improved from 110th last year to top 30 by mid-September this season.

For the second successive year his sand save stats are outside the top 100 and his putting average outside the top 95.

> He's been awarded the 'bottle' in the past as his R4 scoring average has never been his strength because he has shown nerves when in or close to the lead. Undoubtedly at his best when coming from 'off the pace'.
>
> His victory came on the back of 'hot' form figures 12th (previous tournament) - 8th - 26th.
>
> Living in Arizona he's clearly well suited to the Invensys Classic in Las Vegas where he's finished T10th in 1998, T6th in 1999 and T22nd this year for a 68.26 stroke average. Keep an eye on him in match bets and as an outsider with a squeak.

Key stat   21st for greens in regulation.

K J CHOI

Age 30   **Born** Seoul, Korea   **Lives** Seoul, Korea

US Tour BEF T8th 2000 Air Canada

Choi (let's call him Choy) qualified for the US tour when 38th at the 1999 Q School.

Posted just one high finish before August when T21st in the Doral Ryder Open (T21st). Found his form from August with solid finishes in the Reno-Tahoe Open (T12th), the Air Canada (T8th) and the Pennsylvania Classic (T18th).

His big problem has definitely been his putting especially before August. His temperament is good as he's in the top 20 for 'bounce-back'.

> In the Reno-Tahoe Open he was T6th after R3, then he shot 74 to finish T12th to suggest that he will need more experience at the top of the leaderboard on a Sunday.

> Four straight 68s in this year's Air Canada mark Choi as a player to note in 3 balls and as a place-only prospect at massive odds in British Columbia in 2001.

Key stat   59th for total driving, he's 161st for putting.

STEWART CINK   G Y

Age 27   **Born** Alabama   **Lives** Georgia

US Tour wins 2, 1997 Canon Greater Hartford Open, 2000 MCI Classic **BUY.COM tour wins** 3, incl. the Tour Championship in 1996 **Majors** T3rd 1999 USPGA **Presidents Cup** 2000 **Money list** BEF 10th in 2000

Stewart Ernest is the big guy (6 foot 4 in his socks) from Alabama who lives in Georgia and this year he secured his second tour win when he landed the MCI Classic at 40/1. He also posted three top 5 finishes in the Nissan Open (T5th at 66/1), the Colonial (T2nd at 40/1) and the Invensys Classic in Las Vegas (T3rd at 33/1). He also had high finishes in the Phoenix Open (T10th), the Bay Hill (T6th), the Bell South Classic (T10th), the Kemper Open (T20th), the Canon Greater Hartford Open (T14th), the Texas Open (T19th) and the Buick Challenge (T18th).

In the Andersen World Match Play he lost in R1 to Retief Goosen 4 and 2.

He finished T41st in the British Open, a fast finishing T8th in the US Open, T28th in the US Masters, and T15th in the USPGA. Finished very well in the WGC NEC Invitational to secure 7th place after 63 in R4.

On his debut in the Presidents Cup he played superbly. Partnered Kirk Triplett to three wins before he beat Greg Norman in the singles. Finished tied top US pts scorer at 25/1. Finished T18th in the Tour Championship.

Average length at 277 yards. In the last two years he's outside the top 150 for driving accuracy which fell 3% to 64% in 2000. A fine iron player (top 20 GIR) he is once more in the top 15 for scoring in R3, and in R4.

> Cink is clearly not a 'front runner'. He bogeyed 3 of the last 4 holes in this year's Colonial to hand the tournament to Mickelson. However his MCI Classic success by contrast came from 'off the pace' as he birdied 3 of the last 4 holes on his course debut.

> He is a fine player who will go on to win again especially after his confidence boosting form in the Presidents Cup. If his early season stats show an improvement in driving accuracy take note!

> A very consistent player, making twenty-one of his first twenty-five cuts. He's therefore a sound candidate for match bets.

> His US Open record is really solid (8th-32nd-10th-13th-16th) with four successive top 16 finishes and his BEF in 2000. He can certainly be followed in match bets and on the spreads.

> There are three tournaments in which Cink has built a really solid bank of form.
  * The Canon Greater Hartford Open. T14th (2000), T8th (1999), T2nd (1998), Won (1997) give him a stroke average of exactly 67 with every round in the 60s.
  * The Colonial. 2nd this year at 40/1 he has a stroke average of 68.75 over the last four years.
  * The Phoenix Open. Last two years he finished T10th each time for a stroke average of 69.62.
  He can be supported in them on the spreads, in match bets and in the outrights.

> He will be looking forward in 2001 to three tournaments that will be held in home state of Georgia.
  * The Bell South Classic. Form figures of 10th-2nd-5th are good. This is his 'home' track as his house is adjacent to the 14th fairway. Must have the early tee times he was denied this year.
  * The Buick Challenge. 18th-6th-MC-2nd-9th are solid form figs in this home state tournament.
  * His big major chance in 2001 will surely be the USPGA which will be played at Atlanta. T15th in 2000, T3rd in 1999 he could well be the 'pop-up' young outsider at a tasty price in mid August.

> If you bet in R3 3 balls remember Stewart Cinks a lot of putts. He averaged 69.86 in R3 in 1999 and 69.76 to mid October 2000.

> The wider fairways of the three courses used in the Invensys Classic suit him really well. T3rd-T22nd-T16th in the last three years he could well win the tournament from 'off the pace' in 2001.

> He is a confident each-way selection at 40/1 in the without Woods market for the WGC-NEC Invitational. His final 54 holes this year were the best (Tiger apart) in the tournament and his 63 in R4 was superb.

Key stat   152md (!) for driving accuracy.

MICHAEL CLARK   G

Age 31   **Born** Tennesse   **Lives** Georgia

BUY.COM tour wins 2, 1996 and 1998. **US tour wins** 1 1, 2000 John Deere Classic **Money list** BEF 56th 2000

Served his 'apprenticeship' for four full years from 1996 on the BUY.COM tour. In 1999 he posted eight top 10s on that tour. Finished 11th at the 1999 Q School to earn his card. Became a first-time father of a son in 1999 so 2000 was his nappy factor as well as his rookie year. In it he's posted his first win, in the John Deere Classic as a 200/1* outsider after beating Kirk Triplett in a play-off, and in his first major he finished a creditable T15th in the USPGA.

He also had a top 5 in the Air Canada (T4th at 50/1) and top 25s in the Compaq Classic (T13th), the Kemper Open (T20th), the International (T24th) and the Southern Farm Bureau (T20th).

Nevertheless he's been very inconsistent missing thirteen cuts in his first twenty-two non-major tournaments.

A long hitter at 282 yards his strength has been his final round scoring, his weakness Greens in reg (outside top 125).

> This guy sure knows how to finish.

   * He's posted 63 twice in R4 (Kemper Open and Air Canada) and once in R3 (John Deere Classic).

   * He beat the experienced Triplett to gain his first win with three birdies and a par in the 4 play off holes.

   * By late September he was 7th for R4 scoring.

   So on that evidence he can be followed with some confidence in R4 2 ball betting where as an 'unknown' he'll often be overpriced.

> Keep an eye on him in the Compaq Classic where this year he posted four sub-par rounds when T13th. He could well cause a shock there in 2001.

> Worth a bet in the 2001 Air Canada Championship after finishing T4th this year (four sub-par rounds) and posting that 63 in R4!

Key stat   14th for R4 scoring.

TIM CLARK

Age 25   **Born** South Africa   **Lives** North Carolina
University   North Carolina

BUY.COM tour wins 2, both in 2000, Fort Smith Classic and Boise Open

Joined the BUY.COM tour in 1999 finishing T46th on the M/L. This year he's won twice, the BUY.COM Fort Smith Classic in August, and the BUY.COM Boise Open in mid September. He also posted top 5 finishes in the BUY.COM Mississippi Gulf Coast Open (T5th) and the BUY.COM Monterey Peninsula Classic (T3rd).

His stats suggest his approach play is good (15th at 69% in GIR) while his putting is not (89th for putting and 95th for birdie conversion).

> When the tour takes the 'Canadian Swing' it may be worth remembering that Tim won back-to-back events on the 1998 Canadian tour.

> He was jt. leader of the 1999 NIKE tour Dominion Open before falling away to finish T10th. However this year his R4 scoring average (69.67) is top 10, impressive and he clinched his wins this year with low final rounds (66 and 67).

> A North Carolina resident he won a three-round tournament in 1997 as an amateur in Greensboro in his home state without a bogey. So keep an eye on his progress as he will sure be looking to the Greater Greensboro Classic on his home state course in April.

Key stat   95th for birdie conversion on the 2000 BUY.COM tour.

RUSS COCHRAN   D

Age 42   **Born** Kentucky   **Lives** Kentucky

US Tour wins 1, 1991 Western Open **Money list** BEF 10th in 1991

After a poor 1999 when he only just saved his card in 2000 Russell Earl has putted well enough to make four top 10s, in the Nissan Open (4th at 150/1), the Doral Ryder Open (T6th), the Fedex St Jude Classic (T4th at 100/1) and the Greater Milwaukee Open (T7th).

He also posted top 25s in the Colonial (T24th), the Buick Classic (T24th), the Tampa Bay Classic (T19th) and the Southern Farm Bureau (T20th).

His brilliant putting this year took him to top position on the putting average stats by early May. His problems are highlighted by the fact that he's not in the top 125 for either driving accuracy or total driving. A good player when the wind blows.

> An inconsistent player, in the last two seasons he's only made the cut in half his tournaments so he can be opposed in match bets.

> His brilliant putting can lead to low scoring especially in the early rounds (he was R1 leader twice in 1999) so don't oppose him easily in R1 3-ball betting.

> At his best on wide fairway courses such as those used for the Bob Hope (top 20, 1999) and the National Car Rental at Disney (T7th, 1999).

Key stat   Top for putting in early May he finished the season ranked 75th.

JOHN COOK   D

Age 43   **Born** Ohio   **Lives** California

US Tour wins 10, 3 in the eighties. Then 1992 Bob Hope Classic, 1992 Hawaiian Open, 1992 Las Vegas International, 1996 St Jude Classic, 1996 CVS Charity Classic, 1997 Bob Hope Classic, 1998 GTE Byron Nelson Classic. **International wins** 2 **Major wins** BEF T4th 1994 USPGA and 5th 1994 US Open **Money list** BEF 3rd 1992

He has had a disappointing year in which he missed thirteen of his first twenty-three cuts. He's posted three top 10s when T5th at 125/1 in the Buick Classic, T5th at 80/1 in the Invensys Classic in Las Vegas, and T8th in the Colonial. He also had top 25s in the Hawaiian Open (T22nd) and the John Deere Classic (T12th).

Short at 266 yards he is still accurate off the tee (top 30) and fairway (12th for greens in reg) however his putting has again been on the dreadful side of really bad and is the root cause of his poor performance this year.

> His exemption for winning the 1998 Byron Nelson has now expired so Cooky must secure his card in 2001, and his putting will hold the key. Let's remember this guy is a straight hitting class act who's got ten wins on the board.

> He will represent superb value at 100/1 for the 2001 Mastercard Colonial. His last win was in Texas, and his straight hitting has given him an excellent record here in recent years - 8th in 2000, 11th in 1999, and 5th in 1998 for a three-year stroke average of 68.3. He's not a 'name' and so will be on offer at juicy odds and if his putter's hot he will do really well. Make 'Cooky for the Colonial' your slogan at Fort Worth in May.

> His straight short hitting is tailor made for the Kingsmill course where he was T19th this year, and 7th in 1997. 125/1 in a place this year at anything like that price he'd be crackin' each-way value for the 2001 Michelob.

> Must be supported for the 2001 Invensys Classic in Las Vegas. T5th this year he's won three 90-hole tournaments in his career including the Las Vegas event in 1992. At 66/1 next year he'll represent solid each-way value.

Key stat   175th (!) for putting.

FRED COUPLES

Age 41   **Born** Seattle   **Lives** Los Angeles

US Tour wins 13, 3 in the '80s then 1990 LA Open, 1991 St Jude Classic, 1991 BC Open, 1992 Nissan Open, Nestle Invitational, 1993 Honda Classic, 1994 Buick Open, 1996 Players Championship, 1998 Bob Hope Classic, 1998 Memorial **European tour wins** 2, 1995 Dubai Classic; 1995 Johnnie Walker Classic **International wins** 3, last in 1995 **Major wins** 1, 1992 US Masters **Ryder Cup** 1989-1997 inclusive (5 times) **Presidents Cup** 1994, 1996, 1998 **Money list** Top in 1992. Best finish since in 1996 when 6th

In late 1999 he partnered Duval to win the Shark Shootout as 5/2 favourites.

This year Frederick Stephen (answers to Fred) has posted two top 5 finishes, in the Buick Invitational (T4th at 40/1) and the Nissan Open (T5th at 25/1). He posted high finishes in the Memorial (T8th), the Buick Classic (T16th), the Western Open (6th), the Colonial (T24th), the Invensys Classic in Las Vegas (T17th) and the Tampa Bay Classic (T14th).

In the majors he was T11th in the US Masters, T16th in the US Open, 6th in the British Open and he missed the USPGA cut. In the World Match Play he was a shock R1 loser to Joe Ozaki by 1 hole.

Long off the tee (284 yards) Fred is always high in greens in regulation although his driving accuracy (60-61%) is poor. Sand saves up 18% this year. His short (within 5 feet) putting can be very dodgy. Fades the ball.

> Last year I nominated him for the Nissan Open (T5th at 25/1) and I do so again. He's the only player with a sub-70 long term stroke average, the course suits his fade and, "I think I can beat Tiger or Duval on my favourite course."

> He's a big tournament player and rock-solid match bet material in two majors in which he can be followed on the spreads if his back's OK.

* The US Masters. He's made every cut, T11th this year and eight top 10s previously including 2nd (1998) and, of course, his 1992 victory.
* The British Open. eight top 10s in thirteen starts including an impressive 6th this year. He was T7th at Royal Lytham in sunny weather in 1996 and if the weather's warm Fred looks sure to go close again in 2001.

> He enjoys the Invensys Classic in Las Vegas in which his impressive form figures (17th-10th-22nd-9th-8th) make him match-betting material.

Key stat   In the last twenty-seven majors he's made twenty-four cuts including thirteen top 10s.

ROBERT DAMRON   V

Age   28   **Born**   Kentucky   **Lives**   Florida

US Tour wins BEF T3rd 1997 Fedex St Jude Classic, 1997 Buick Classic **Money list** 53rd 1997

In his fourth year on the tour Robert overall has struggled. However, he saved his card with one mega-finish in the Players Championship when he was T3rd at 200/1* to win over $270,000.

He had top 10s in the Honda Classic (T7th) and the Fedex St Jude Classic (T7th), and top 25s in the Doral Ryder Open (T12th), the Compaq Classic (T17th) and the Memorial (T25th).

Joint R1 leader (66) in the Michelob before finishing T30th.

Finished plumb last (63) in the US Open and T74th in the USPGA. Long at 278 yards, his greens in reg stats are still poor although his putting average is a really good top 40 for second successive season.

> He is clearly at his best during the Florida swing in March on the Bermuda greens he knows so well.

> Although he missed the cut this year in the Bay Hill Invitational he can be expected to make amends in 2001. Living next to the course his record is solid, 4th 1999: T29th 1998: T11th 1997 so have a little each way and keep him in mind in the 3 balls.

> Still to win he's best when coming from 'off the pace' as he showed with his best in the tournament 10 under par for the last three rounds in this year's Memorial after a 78 (!) in R1.

> Worth a small each-way investment in the 2001 Fedex St. Jude Classic where he's finished (T7th 2000: T7th 1998: 3rd 1997) in the top 7 in three of the last four years.

Key stat   11th in 1999 he was 33rd for putting average this year.

GLEN DAY

Age 35   **Born** Alabama   **Lives** Arkansas

US Tour wins 1, the 1999 MCI Classic **International wins** 1, 1990 Malaysian Open **Money list** BEF 15th in 1998

His best ever Money list placing (15th) in 1998 was followed by his first tour win in 1999. But 2000 has been an ordinary year for the guy from Little Rock, Arkansas.

He started well with a top 10 in the all winners Mercedes Championship (T8th), and had top 25s in the Bob Hope (T16th), the AT&T (T20th), the Compaq Classic (T13th), the Byron Nelson Classic (T13th), the Fedex St Jude Classic (T25th) and the John Deere Classic (T23rd). Posted a top 10 in October in the NCR Classic at Walt Disney (6th).

He missed the cut in the US Open although he was T19th in the US Masters. In the WGC Andersen Consulting he lost in R1, by 1 hole, to Thomas Bjorn.

From T12th in 1999 for total driving he's outside the top 100 this year. His putting however remains very solid. Fader of the ball. His driving accuracy percentage has fallen this year.

> He can be backed with confidence in the MCI Classic where his recent record is very good. He was 2nd in 1998, winner in 1999 and this year as defending champion he perhaps understandably finished down the field.

> He has built up such a solid bank of form in the Compaq Classic (T13th 2000: T7th 1999: T3rd 1998) so he'll be well worth support on the spreads, in match bets and each way in the outright market in New Orleans in 2001.

> He really loves the NCR Classic at Walt Disney in which his record over the last five years is consistently good, viz. 13th 1996, 10th 1997, 11th 1998, 7th 1999, 6th this year for a stroke average of 68.85. So back Glen in match bets, on the spreads and as an outsider with serious place prospects.

> Must be noted for the Southern Farm Bureau Classic, 12th in 1996, 3rd in 1999 and T36th this year he has a 68.18 stroke average with everyone of his eleven rounds there under par.

Key stat   14th for putting average.

CHRIS DiMARCO   G

Age 32   **Born** New York   **Lives** Florida

US Tour wins BEF 1, 2000 Pennsylvania Classic **BUY.COM Tour wins** 1, 1997 Ozarks Open **Money list** BEF 19th 2000

It's been a breakthrough year for Christian Dean (call me Chris) with a series of good performances before his first win in the Pennsylvania Classic at 100/1* by 6 shots. He also had four top 5 finishes, in the Tucson Open (T2nd at 80/1), the Fedex St Jude Classic (T2nd at 150/1*), the Canon Greater Hartford Open (T5th at 80/1) and the Invensys Classic in Las Vegas (T5th at 80/1).

He also had high finishes in the Hawaiian Open (T22nd), the AT&T (T18th), the Renoe Tahoe (T21st), the Buick Challenge (T23rd) and the NCR Classic at Walt Disney (T18th).

He missed the cut in the British Open. Finished a very creditable T15th in the USPGA and T18th in the Tour Championship.

Moderate length off the tee at 277 yards. This year he's improved both driving accuracy (by 5%), greens in reg. (by 1.5%) and putting average (from 154th to top 40).

> He's now learned how to win after some nervy R4 play, especially in 1998.

> Can be followed with confidence in all markets for the Canon Greater Hartford Open. In three starts he's progressively improved his position 25th (1998), 20th (1999), 5th (2000) and his total strokes from 274-272-268 for a three-year stroke average of 67.83 with ten of his twelve rounds under par.

> Well worth an each-way bet in the Fedex St Jude Classic (2nd 2000 with four sub-70 rounds).

> Worth an each-way 'nibble' at a tasty price for the Hawaiian Open where he played well (T22nd) this year when a poor R3 ruined his chance.

> He's posted consecutive top 20s (T17th 1999: T18th 2000) in the NCR Classic at Walt Disney. Worth noting in match bets among the magnolias in October.

Key stat   27th for greens in regulation.

DOUG DUNAKEY **S**

Age 37   **Born** Iowa   **Lives** Florida

US Tour wins BEF T3rd 1999 Honda Classic **NIKE Tour**, 1, the 1999 Cleveland Open

Lost his card after finishing 133rd on the 1999 M/L when ironically he recorded his best ever finish in the Honda Classic.

Regained his card when 29th at Q School.

This year he made only one cut in his first ten tournaments yet he made it count for $109,000 when T5th at 150/1 in the Greater Greensboro Classic.

Later he was an impressive T4th at 150/1 in the Reno-Tahoe Open, and posted top 20s in the Fedex St Jude Classic (T20th), the BC Open (T18th) and the Buick Challenge (T18th).

Played occasionally on this year's BUY.COM tour, finishing T8th as defending champion in the Cleveland Open.

A long hitter (279 yards) his stats make grim reading. Proven in windy conditions.

> In the last two years he's missed a whole bunch of cuts (over 60%) yet he's posted three top 5s so he's one of those players who can suddenly find form big style. At his most consistent from late August this year.

> A streak player. He shot a 59 on the 1998 BUY.COM tour and a 64 (R3 Reno-Tahoe Open) and 65 (R2 Fedex St Jude Classic) this year.

Key stat   152nd for driving accuracy.

SCOTT DUNLAP   **V**

Age 37   **Born** Pensylvania   **Lives** Georgia

US Tour wins BEF T3rd 2000 Players Championship, T3rd 1996 Canadian Open
International wins 5, in Argentina, Canada and South Africa **Money list** BEF 44th 2000

In late 1999 he won the Argentinian Open from Coceres and Woosnam.

Scott has really established himself this year with a series of high finishes. His 'big' finish came when he won $270,000 when T3rd at 200/1* in the Players Championship. He also had top 10s in the Sony Open in Hawaii (6th), Byron Nelson Classic (T10th), the Canon Greater Hartford Open (T9th) and notably in the USPGA (T9th).

He posted top 25s in the Nissan Open (T12th), the Tucson Open (T25th), the MCI Classic (T15th), the Greater Greensboro Classic (T16th), the Air Canada (T22nd), the Texas Open (T19th) and the Tampa Bay Classic (T14th).

31st for driving accuracy and top 25 for greens in reg, his accuracy is the basis of his consistency. Strangely he's not in the top 125 for par 3 birdies yet he's 12th for par 4 birdies. Short putting (within 5 feet), can be dodgy.

He's played in South Africa and Canada and is now a highly experienced player.

> His record reminds me a bit of Tom Lehman (before he broke through) as a straight-hitting, highly travelled, highly experienced guy in his mid-late thirties looking for his first win.

> There is absolutely no doubt that Scott has the ability and the experience to get into winning positions. However he is being held back by his R4 scoring when under pressure.

  * Hawaiian Open. T4th after R3, he shot 70 in R4, to finish T6th.

  * The Colonial. 3rd after R3, he shot 7 over in R4, to finish T35th.

  * Buick Classic. 3 off lead after R3, he shot 5 over in R4, to finish T33rd.

  * USPGA. T2nd after R3, playing in last group (with Tiger) in R4, he shot 75 to finish T9th.

  Once he learns how to handle the pressure on a Sunday he'll win.

> He's made a top six finish before mid February in each of the last three years in either South Africa or America. Early on he'd be worth an each-way bet, if 80/1 is available, for the 2001 Sony Open in Hawaii.

> His eclectic score over the past two years (68-69-68-68) would put him into a top 4 finish in the MCI Classic. On a course suited to his accuracy he could go very close at Hilton Head in 2001.

> 2nd on the Canadian O/M in 1995 Scott is at home in the land of the Maple Leaf and can repay each-way support in the Canadian Open (42nd 2000: 7th 1999: 13th 1997: 3rd 1996).

> He plays out of the Sugarloaf course, home of the Bell South Classic. His form 23rd 1999: 25th 1998 and a missed cut this year is not impressive, yet he knows the track and his total driving stat marks him out as just the sort of player to do well there. At 80/1 he'd be worth a speculative nibble.

Key stat   20th for greens in regulation.

JOE DURANT   D

Age 36   **Born** Florida   **Lives** Florida

US tour wins 1, 1998 Western Open **BUY.COM Tour wins** 1, 1996 Mississippi Gulf Coast Classic **Money list** BEF 43rd 1998

Due-Rant was a lowly 157th on the Money list last year yet retained his card having secured a two-year exemption when winning the 1998 Western Open.

This year has again been disappointing overall with three top 10s, in the Compaq Classic (T9th), the Greater Milwaukee Open (T7th) and the Invensys Classic at Las Vegas (T9th), and top 20s in the Fedex St Jude Classic (T11th), the Canon Greater Hartford Open (T18th), the Air Canada (T13th), until he finished 5th at 80/1* in the Tampa Bay Classic.

Joe is a truly classic example of a player whose accuracy from tee to green is truly first class, yet he is let down big style by both his poor putting and bunker play.

> Joe's other weakness has been his R4 scoring (T90th in 1999 and outside top 100 in 2000). For example this year T5 after R3 in the Air Canada he shot 72 in R4 to finish T13th.

> Nevertheless a player with his continued astonishing accuracy from tee to green creates countless birdie chances (outside top 120 for birdie conversion), and he could win again when his putter has a 'hot' week and his nerve holds.

> In his last two starts on the Southwind course Joe has finished 11th (2000) and 12th (1998) for a stroke average of 69 with five rounds in the 60s, so he can be backed in match bets and each way for the 2001 Fedex St Jude Classic.

> Joe's accuracy is tailor made for Brown Deer Park with its five par 3s and its premium on accuracy. After making three consecutive cuts he was T7th at 66/1 there this year and he'll be worth an each-way wager at 66/1+ in the 2001 Greater Milwaukee Open.

> With driving accuracy the key to the River Highlands course, home of the Canon Greater Hartford Open, Joe must have a first class chance there in 2000. He's posted three top 20s there in the last four years with fifteen of his last sixteen rounds at or under par.

Key stat   2nd in 1999 and again in 2000 for greens in regulation. 187th in 1999 and 134th in 2000 for putting average.

DAVID DUVAL   ☘ G M CT

Age 29   **Born** Florida   **Lives** Florida

US tour wins 12—1997 Michelob Championship at Kingsmill, Walt Disney Oldsmobile Classic, The Tour Championship: 1998 Tucson Chrysler Classic: 1999 Mercedes Championship, Bob Hope Chrysler Classic, Players Championship, Bell South Classic, 2000 Buick Challenge **Major wins** T2nd 1998 US Masters **Nike tour wins** 2, 1993 Nike Wichita Open and NIKE tour championship **Presidents Cup** 1996, 1998, 2000 **Money list** 2nd 1997, 1st in 1998, 2nd in 1999

It's been a most unusual year for David Duval. After four wins in 1999 he had to wait until 1st October to win his first tournament this century when he landed the Buick Challenge at (11/1). He also had top 5 finishes in the Mercedes (3rd at 5/1), the Bob Hope (T5th at 7/1), the Buick Classic (2nd at 12/1 losing to Dennis Paulson in a play-off) and the Doral Ryder Open (T4th at 8/1). He also had high finishes in the Players Championship (T13th), the Byron Nelson Classic (T20th), the Memorial (T25th) and the Michelob (T19th).

In the Andersen World Match Play he beat Angel Cabrera (4 and 3), Tim Herron (2 and 1), Sergio Garcia (2 and 1) and Scott Hoch (5 and 4) before he lost to the eventual winner Darren Clarke. He beat Davis Love (5 and 4) to finish 3rd. He did not play in the WGC NEC Invitational.

In the majors he finished T3rd at 16/1 in the US Masters, T8th in the US Open, and T11th in the British Open. He did not play in the USPGA. Finished 6th in the Tour Championship

He had been troubled by a back injury for some time yet it didn't stop him playing until he withdrew from the International during R1 with a back injury. As a result from 3rd August to 16th September he never touched a club and spent over two weeks flat on his back. Before then the big question was whether his form, and particularly his putting, had been adversely affected by his change in lifestyle.

In November 1999 he embarked on a rigorous fitness programme. So that this year Duval had become a real lean machine. He reckoned he'd improved his leg and arm strength by 75% and gained half a club in distance. However his putting has been criticised and many thought he'd lost 'feel' because of all his pumping of iron.

After his injury he returned to win the Buick Challenge in early October and then played in the Michelob the following week. He had clearly fully recovered from his back injury. However the question was whether his back had been a casualty of his fitness fanaticism. However by October he had given up the lifting part of that fitness programme. In the Presidents Cup he beat Nick Price (2 and 1) and scored 3 points overall.

Duval is a very, very long and straight driver, a fine iron player and he's a proven winner. He is best suited by long par 72 courses on which he can 'murder' the par 5s.

His sand save percentage is up 9% to 53.8% yet it could still be improved. Sleeps very poorly after long flights so he restricts his overseas trips.

Parted company with Mitch Knox his caddy over the past two-and-a-half years early in the season, and later he fired Greg Rita in late August.

Duval behind the glasses and the stone face is an introspective guy who has a poor public image. Behind that frosty appearance I detect a warm, thoughtful guy with a decent set of values. Main relaxation is skiing and snowboarding in Sun Valley, Idaho.

He'll be 30 in November 2001.

> So what are we to make of Duval in 2001?

* Well there is the school of thought that suggests that his putting is so dodgy that he really won't win especially in the majors. Put simply and in Shakespearian language this is pure garbage! Reputations are easy to develop and writers latch on to them as if they are true, so now the accepted wisdom is Duval can't putt. Really? Well I know it can be annoying to refer to facts yet here goes.

* This year at the time of the Presidents Cup his % for par 4 birdies (+0.1%), and par 5 birdies (+1.6%) were both better than in 1999, while his birdie conversion % overall was only 1.4% lower.

* Because of the accuracy of his long game he is on the putting surface in or under regulation far more often than nearly everyone else. This is shown by the fact that his putts per greens in reg ranking is usually 50-70 places higher than his putts per round.

* He showed in the Presidents Cup in October that his putting was in every way superb. In 2001 I expect his birdie conversion rate to increase, especially on par 3s (his key weakness this year) where his birdie percentage has dropped by 3.8%.

* His long game is still magnificent. This year he's 2nd for total driving, his greens in reg percentage is up 0.5% and his driving accuracy is up 1.5%.

In sum In 2001 expect David Duval to have a sensational season in which he bounces back big style. He has a superb all round game, an excellent temperament and a burning desire to shake 'the Tiger' by the tail. So next year I expect him to record multiple wins including his first major.

> However my researches have highlighted one glaring weakness in his record - his R1 scoring record in big tournaments. In normal events its good as you'd expect. However in the majors it's not.

	US Masters	US Open	British Open	USPGA
1990	-	72	-	-
1992	-	76	-	-
1995		70	71	72
1996	73	75	76	74
1997	78	74	73	70
1998	71	75	70	76
1999	71	67	79	70
2000	73	75	70	70
Stroke avg R1	73.2	73	73.16	72
1998-00 avg R1	71.66	72.3	73	72

* Of twenty-five opening rounds in majors he's only ever shot one round under 70.

* In the US Masters, for example, he's shot four sub-70s yet none in R1.

* This year at St Andrews he was 1 over par after just 9 holes!

It's crystal clear that he's a slow starter so this must be improved in future if he's to land his first major.

> As with all the top players his focus will be on the majors and I really do give him a mega chance at Augusta. In the last three years he's finished T3rd (2000), T6th (1999) and T2nd (1998) for a stroke average of 70.58. Understandably Tiger will be 'all the rage' however I think Duval will shock the golfing world by winning the 2001 US Masters. However as I've already stressed he must get off to a quick start.

> In 1996 when the British Open was last held at Royal Lytham he finished T14th. However he had his customary slow start (76!) before he produced the best final

three rounds of the tournament. To win he'll need to recover from a long flight and to get off to a quick start. Overall I think a top 10 finish is most probable.

> In the US Open he's produced (T7th-T7th-T8th) three successive top 10 finishes and there's every reason to expect him to go very close at Tulsa next year especially if he can get a nice pair of tee times.

> In the non majors he can be followed with confidence in six tournaments.

   * The Mercedes. Winner (1999), he was 3rd in 2000. His eclectic score (67-63-67-68) over those two years would guarantee a nice easy win in 2001.

   * The Bob Hope. He really is a very, very, very (now that's three of them!) strong fancy to win the 2001 Bob Hope Chrysler Classic. T5th (2000), Won after a 59 in R4 (1999), T4th (1998) is a superb recent course record and he's a must finishing position sell.

   * The Players Championship. Sawgrass is his local course and he won there in 1999. Needs a good pair of tee times.

   * The Bell South Classic. Sugarloaf is a 'driver's course' ideal for Duval as he proved when winning in 1999, and he went to University at Georgia Tech.

   * The Buick Classic. 10th (1999), 2nd (2000) with seven of his last eight rounds under par.

   * The Memorial. Three top 3 finishes in five starts. However, as in the majors, he never makes a good start. His R1 scoring average is 72.8 yet it's 68.4 for R2 and 67.6 for R3. So in 2001 I suggest first you back him in 3 and 2 balls in R2 and R3, and second you back him each way and on the spreads AFTER R1.

> However there is one (early season) tournament in which he can be opposed. In the Phoenix Open he finished T30th at 7/1 in 2000, and T18th at 13/2 in 1999. The crowds heckle him and if he plays he can be opposed with confidence.

> He looks a cast iron each-way bet for the US Money list (without Woods) although there are two points to remember. First his back injury might reoccur and he may not play in the World Match Play in January.

> Can be seriously fancied for the 2001 Tour Championship to be held on the Champions course where he won in 1997.

Key stat   He's ranked 2nd for total driving.

JOEL EDWARDS

Age 39   **Born** Texas   **Lives** Texas

College Texas

US tour BEF T2nd 1992 BC Open **BUY.COM tour wins** 1, 1999 **Money list** BEF 73rd 2000

Had a brilliant 1999 when 2nd on the BUY.COM tour, winning the Mississippi Golf Coast tournament and having three 2nd-place finishes and one 3rd.

In 2000 he's built on that by securing his card in his best ever year in which his big finishes came when he was T3rd at 150/1 in the Shell Houston Open winning

$162K, and T5th at 125/1 in the Buick Challenge winning $84,000. He also had high finishes in the Hawaiian Open (T19th), the Compaq Classic (T17th), the Fedex St Jude Classic (T15th), the Colonial (T13th), the Buick Open (T25th), the Air Canada (T13th) and the Texas Open (T19th).

His much improved play over the last couple of years is based on his accuracy off the tee (top 50) and to the green (top 30), although his putting rank is still outside the top 100.

He'll be 39 (a dodgy age!) in November 2000.

> He had one big opportunity this year and let it slip big time:-

* T4th after R3 in this year's Compaq Classic he then shot 74 in R4 to finish T17th. Nevertheless his early round scoring suggest he can be followed there in 3-ball betting in 2001.

> If he's to 'make the frame' at a big price it will probably be in either:-

* The Fedex St Jude Classic. T15th this year when he was one of only seven players to shoot four sub-par rounds.

* The Shell Houston Open. Held in his home state he was an impressive T3rd this year.

Key stat   16th for total driving.

BRAD ELDER   g y

Age 25   **Born** Tulsa, Oklahoma   **Lives** Texas
College Texas

Buy.com tour wins 2, the 1999 Wichita Open, and the Inland Empire Open **US Tour** BEF T2nd 2000 Pennsylvania Classic **Money list** BEF 68th 2000

11th place on the BUY.COM tour in 1999 earned Brad his card for his rookie year in 2000,

He's secured his card with six top 20 finishes, in the AT&T (T20th), the Honda Classic (T16th), the MCI Classic (T11th), the Memorial (12th) and the Western Open (T15th), and a top 25 in the Greater Greensboro Classic (T21st). Finished T2nd in the inaugural Pennsylvania Classic in September and T6th in the Southern Farm Bureau Classic.

In the top 45 for total driving. However his sand save stats (four saves in nine attempts) are very poor. He's made twelve eagles (ranked 7th).

> T5th after R3 in the Memorial Brad shot 73 in R4 to finish 12th. He also had a disappointing 73 in R4 in the Tucson Open. However players have to learn how to win on the full tour and they'll be part of his 'learning curve'.

> He is a very talented player, was 1997 Jack Nicklaus College Player of the Year and he can be expected to establish himself as a very fine player over the next few years, and he may well post a 'shock' win in 2001.

> He really must be noted for the MCI Classic where from a dreadful set of tee times he played well (68-68 in R3/R4) to finish T11th. He can be expected to play

well there again in 2001 where he can be backed in match bets, and as an each-way 100/1+ outsider with real prospects.

> Four sub-par rounds this year when T15th give Brad a genuine chance in the 2001 Advil Western Open.

> With the elder players away at the British Open Brad will have a big chance in the 2001 BC Open after he shot two 69s when posting a top 30 on his course debut this year.

> Can be backed at a big price for the 2001 Marconi Pennsylvania Classic for two reasons. First, it'll be on a new course which means no advantage for the experienced players, and second he was T2nd in this tournament this year.

> Well worth backing for the Southern Farm Bureau Classic where he finished brilliantly (16 under for last 54 holes) this year to be T6th.

Key stat   11th for par 3 birdies.

STEVE ELKINGTON   G

Age 38   **Born** Australia   **Lives** Texas or Sydney

US Tour wins 9, all in the nineties, 1990 Greater Greensboro Open, 1991 Players Championship, 1992 Tournament of Champions, 1994 Buick Southern Open, 1995 Mercedes Championship, 1997 Doral Ryder Open, the Players Championship, 1998 Buick Challenge, 1999 Doral Ryder Open **Majors** 1, 1995 USPGA **International** 2, in Australia and Asia **Presidents Cup** 1994, 1996,1998 and 2000 **Dunhill Cup** 4 times **Money list** 5th 1995

'The Elk' has once more had a season of sinuses, allergies, infections and missed putts.

He made twelve of his first fourteen cuts to October yet could only post a single high finish in a 'normal' tournament when he finished T10th in the Buick Challenge.

He withdrew before the start of the Players Championship, the US Open and the USPGA with infection and sinus problems.

In the World Match Play he lost 2 and 1 to Jeff Sluman in R1. Finished T60th in the British Open, and finished T18th in the Mercedes.

His stats tell the story as he hits 68.7% of his greens and then proceeds to miss putts. He's outside the top 160 for heavens sake for both putting average and birdie conversion. Tends to draw the ball.

He has probably the most beautiful swing on the tour and when fit and healthy his approach play is good although his putting has let him down big style this year.

Dragged down by so many injuries that he lost count the 'Elk' has taken the advice of fellow Aussie Greg Norman and had arthroscopic hip surgery in August. "It's like being 15 again. It's hard to believe it feels so good".

He returned to the tour in late September and in his second tournament back posted his best finish of the year in the Buick Challenge (T10th). In the Presidents Cup he beat Tom Lehman in the singles, and with 3 pts was T2nd top scorer at 20/1.

> So here we now have a player who, in the last six years despite all manner of ailments, has won six tournaments including a major (the USPGA) and who now feels better physically than he has ever done before. He is surely the classic case of a player on the 'comeback' trail in 2001 when I expect him to win.

> In 2001 he must be expected to do really well in three 'ordinary' tournaments.

* The Shell Houston Open. He lives in Houston, Texas and would love to win this. In 1999 he was 5 shots off the pace with a round to go when he had to withdraw. With home advantage he must be strongly fancied for the 2001 Shell Houston Open.

* The Doral Ryder Open. Winner in 1997 and 1999 he must have an outstanding chance of keeping up his run of victories in alternative years. Make 'the Elk at Doral' your slogan during the 2001 Florida swing.

* The Buick Challenge. His best finish this year (T10th) came at Callaway Gardens in the tournament he won in 1998. I can see him winning the 2001 Buick Challenge.

> In these three tournaments he can also be supported 'in running' after R3 if he's within 5 shots off the lead as he's a fine record of shooting low numbers (64 in R4 1999 Doral Ryder: 65 in R4 1998 Buick Challenge: and 65 in R3 1999 Shell Houston Open) in these tournaments, and half of his ten wins have come from 'off the pace'.

> 'The Elk' will be delighted that the US Open next year will be held on the tough Southern Hills course where he finished T2nd in the 1995 Tour Championship. He was ranked T1st then for Greens in reg. so on that track if his putter works he will surely go close in 2001

> "I always feel comfortable playing this tournament" and Elk's USPGA record tells us why

* 3rd 1998: T3rd 1996: Won 1995: T7th 1994: T14th 1993 and T18th 1992

* Average position from 1992-1998 was 13th.

* He has not played in the last two years.

I can visualise him doing really, really well at the Atlanta Club in the 2001 USPGA.

Key stat   165th (!) for birdie conversion.

ERNIE ELS   G ☀ F

Age 31   **Born** South Africa   **Lives** South Africa, Florida & Wentworth

US Tour 6 wins, 1995 Byron Nelson Classic, 1996 Buick Classic, 1997 Buick Classic, 1998 Bay Hill Invitational, 1999 Nissan Open, 2000 The International **Majors** 2, US Open in 1994 and 1997 **International wins** 23, latest 1998 Sth African Open, 1999 Sth African PGA 2000 Loch Lomond Invitational **Dunhill Cup** 9, latest 2000 **World Cup** 4, latest 1997 **Presidents Cup** 1996, 1998, 2000 **Money list** BEF 3rd 2000

Towards the end of 1999 Ernie finished T4th in the Players Championship in South Africa before he won the Sun City Million at 11/2, his first Sun City victory.

In 2000 in the States he made a fast start finishing 2nd at 14/1 in the Mercedes, losing in a play-off at the 2nd extra hole to Tiger Woods....and that finish summarised the season ahead for the 'Big Easy' as he was often to play 'second fiddle' to Tiger.

He had top 5 finishes in the Hawaiian Open (T5th at 9/1), the MCI Classic (T3rd at 12/1), the Memorial (T2nd at 20/1) and the Buick Classic (T5th at 12/1) before he won the International (scoring 48 points, at 10/1).

He also had high finishes in the Doral Ryder Open (T15th), the Bay Hill Invitational (T14th) and the Players Championship (T20th).

In the Andersen World Match Play he beat Bernhard Langer (2 and 1) before he suffered a 'shock' defeat by 1 hole to Bob Estes. In the WGC NEC Invitational he finished T12th.

He had an amazing year in the Majors as he finished 2nd at 25/1 in the US Masters, 2nd at 20/1 in the US Open, and T2nd at 16/1 in the British Open. However the 'Grand Slams' of seconds eluded him as he finished (from poor tee times) a disappointing T34th in the USPGA. T3rd at 16/1 in the Tour Championship.

On the European tour he was 4th at 13/2 in the Heineken Classic. Later the week before the British Open, he won the Loch Lomond Invitational at 12/1.

In the Dunhill Cup he returned to St Andrews where he'd finished 2nd in the British Open to play brilliantly. He won all his five games as he led South Africa to finish 2nd. At 8/1 he was the tournament's top player shooting all five rounds in the '60s for a stroke average of 68. His nine rounds at St Andrews this year averaged 68.55! His Dunhill Cup career record was twenty-six wins in thirty-five matches.

Completely out of sorts in the Presidents Cup he lost ALL FIVE matches being beaten by Davis Love (4 and 3) in the singles.

Ernie is a long-hitting accurate player so relaxed he's almost horizontal. He is particularly strong on the par 5s. The standards on the US tour are shown by the fact that his sand saves percentage is up 1.3% yet his ranking has slipped from T18th to 27th. He is a consistent player who makes few mistakes. Gone back to using David Leadbetter as his coach.

Ernie has had occasional back problems which surfaced again and forced him to withdraw from the WGC American Express in November. Became a first-time father of a daughter in May 1999.

> Although a proven winner Ernie does let really good winning chances slip away. He did so four times in 1999 in the Heineken Classic, the US Masters, the Doral Ryder Open and the NCR Classic at Disney. Indeed he was awarded the bottle again!

 This year it was the same old story in the MCI Classic. Ahead by 2 after R3 Ernie was 4/9 yet he 'bottled' it shooting 74 (3 over) to finish T3rd.

 However by contrast in the Loch Lomond he was the joint leader after R3 and went on to win the tournament.

 So overall one can say that obviously Ernie knows how to win as he's had plenty of practice, however when ahead after R3 and he's at odds-on he's a dodgy proposition and is best avoided.

> As with so many of the leading players Ernie will focus on the Majors as he tries to build on his US Open wins by eventually securing a career Grand Slam.

  * US Masters. He really does have the ideal game for Augusta and this year he showed it when he was 2nd. His overall form is 2nd-T27th-T16th-17th-T12th-MC-T8th.

  * US Open. He's won this event twice (1994 and 1997) and has twice finished in the top 5 (2nd 2000, T5th 1996) so he's had two wins and two top 5s in the last seven years.

In 2001 he really will have a good chance because the tournament moves to the Southern Hills course where back in 1996 he was ranked as the No. 1 putter, and in 1996 as the No. 1 for greens in reg. So if 1995's putting and 1996's approach play merge big Ernie will win his third US Open in 2001.

  * The British Open. Royal Lytham clearly suits him and he'll remember his last visit there when T2nd in 1996. A better player now than then he's sure to be a very serious contender for the 2001 British Open.

The big question will be asked of Ernie when he goes head to head with Tiger down the stretch. It could well happen in any of the 2001 Majors and when it's asked it will be interesting to see if Ernie really has sufficient inner steel to outbattle the Tiger. I doubt very much if he has.

Ernie is best supported in the majors in the 'Without Woods' markets and definitely on the spreads as there's every reason to expect him to continue the fine major form he showed this year.

> There are six tournaments World wide in which you can expect him to play really well in 2001.

  * In Australia his form in the Heineken Classic T4th (2000), T2nd (1999) and T3rd (1998) with three consecutive top 4 finishes is superb.

  * On the European tour in two starts at Loch Lomond he's been 2nd (1997) and Won (2000) with seven of his eight rounds in the 60s for a truly staggering stroke average of 67.87! He'll be defending champion in 2001.

  * On the USPGA tour he will be defending the International title. His game is ideal for Castle Pines where he has made it to the final day in each of the las four years for an average of 33 pts.

  * The Riviera course suits Ernie. T3rd on it in the 1995 USPGA, he won the Nissan Open there in 1999 and the Kikuyu grass fairways (as in South Africa) suit him. Back Ernie for the 2001 Nissan Open.....or Els!

  * The Buick Classic suits Ernie. He won it in 1996 and 1997 and, "I know how to score round here."

  * The Memorial. His five-year form figures of 2nd-7th-7th-38th-6th are impressive.

So in 2001 I suggest you support Ernie on the spreads and with win bets in these six tournaments.

Key stat Ernie has won a USPGA tournament in each of the last seven years. This is the longest winning streak of any active player.

BOB ESTES   D

Age 34   **Born** Texas   **Lives** Texas
College Texas
US Tour wins 1, 1994 Texas Open **Money list** BEF 14th 1994

Top 30 on the Money list in 1998, and again in 1999 when he made twenty-seven of twenty-eight cuts and posted nine top 10s Bob has followed in 2000 with a most disappointing year.

He has played well in three big events. In the WGC Andersen Consulting Match Play he beat Steve Pate by 1 hole, then created a mega shock knocking out Ernie Elso also by 1 hole, before losing 4 and 3 to Jimenez. He also posted top 20s in the US Masters (T19th) and the British Open (T20th). He missed the cut by a single shot in the USPGA.

In three consecutive tournaments from late April he was T13th in the Greater Greensboro, 6th in the Byron Nelson Classic and T6th in the Colonial. Finished T23rd in the Buick Challenge in October.

This year his approach play has become inaccurate and with his putting also poorer it is clear that he's lost the metronomic consistency that was his trademark in the last couple of years. His lack of length (268 yards) is a big disadvantage so it's no surprise to see him outside the top 150 for par 5 birdies. Fades the ball. Probably best when in continuous play. Unusually does not wear a golf glove. Payne Stewart's caddie Mike Hicks joined Estes early in the year. He switched back from a metal driver to persimmon from August this year.

> There are now two big question marks hanging over Bob.

* Can he regain his accuracy and so his consistency?

* If so, can he then turn high finishes into a second win?

The answers are probably yes to the first, and probably no to the second.

> He can be noted for three tournaments which he didn't play this year and where his recent record is very good indeed.

* The Bay Hill Invitational. T5th 1999, T2nd 1998 for a two-year stroke average of 69.75.

* The Buick Classic. T10th 1999: 6th 1997 on his last two starts for a stroke average of 69.92.

* Air Canada. T10th 1999 for a three-year (1997-99) stroke average of 67.92.

Key stat   170th (!) for greens in regulation.

NICK FALDO   PB

Age 43   **Born** England   **Lives** Florida
US Tour wins 3, 1984 Sea Pines Heritage Classic, 1995 Doral Ryder Open, 1997 Nissan Open **International wins** 7, the 1994 Million Dollar Challenge at Sun City was the last **European tour wins** 23, the 1994 Alfred Dunhill Open was the last

Major wins 6, the US Masters in 1989, 1990 and 1996; and the British Open in 1987, 1990 and 1992 **Ryder Cup** 11 times **NOT** 1999 **Money list** BEF 12th in 1996

Nick's had an interesting year in which he and Mark James seemed to be at each other's throats for much of the summer as Nick reacted angrily to Jesse's revelation that he'd binned Faldo's good luck message sent to the 1999 Ryder Cup team at Brookline.

In America in ten non-majors to October the simple fact is he posted just one top 30 finish when T21st in the Doral Ryder Open.

In the Majors he finished T28th in the US Masters, a creditable 7th in the US Open, T41st in the British Open and T51st in the USPGA.

On the European tour he was T9th in the Loch Lomond and then with Ryder Cup points at stake he was T6th in the Canon European Masters, T12th in the Lancome Trophy, and T30th in the German Masters.

He played superbly in the Cisco World Matchplay before losing to a Darren Clarke eagle at the 40th (!) hole.

Nick's US stats are not surprisingly poor although they emphasise his driving accuracy (76%) which is his great strength. However he's very short off the tee (267 yards). Parted company with long time caddie Fanny Suneson who was replaced by Murray Lott.

> This year at Loch Lomond he was just a shot off the lead after R3 however he dropped 3 shots at the first two holes in R4 before he finished T9th. It showed conclusively that he now suffers from 'contention rust' when he has a serious chance of winning a tournament.

> He's clearly a more relaxed man since his engagement in late 1999 to Valerie Belcher and he's playing better golf in the second half of 2000 than he's done for at least three years. However, I really can't see Nick winning again because he's too short off the tee and he now (as at Loch Lomond) clearly suffers from 'contention rust'.

> He was top ranked for putting when he played so well to finish T7th in the US Open. However I really believe it had a lot to do with the fact that his Pebble Beach caddie was Kjell Enhager, his sports psychologist. I suspect that Faldo associated Kjell's company with deep focus, concentration and a positive mental approach......... he should use him more often!

> Corals initial odds of 8/1 for Nick to play in the 2001 Ryder team were quickly cut to 5/1. However (as I've said) I can't see him winning again so it's going to be very difficult indeed therefore for him to qualify on merit and as I can't see Sam Torrance making him a 'wild card' pick (10/1 on offer for that from Chandlers) I don't see Nick making it to the Belfry.

> Expect Nick to talk up his chances for the British Open at Royal Lytham where he finished T4th in 1996. However in the five years since then he's gone backwards as a whole host of younger players have moved on. I expect he'll play well, make the cut and finish mid division as he did this year.

> This year Nick played the International in Colorado in August. Not surprisingly he missed the cut as the points system used rewards aggressive birdie/eagle

makers who knock the ball miles. Faldo's the exact opposite a steady par making guy. If he returns to Castle Pines in 2001 he can be opposed in match bets and on the spreads with real confidence.

Key stat   9th for driving accuracy, he's 155th for birdie conversion.

BRAD FAXON

Age 39   **Born** New Jersey   **Lives** Rhode Island

US Tour wins 7, 1986 Provident Classic, 1991 Buick Open, 1992 New England Classic, The International, 1997 Freeport McDermott Classic, 1999 BC Open, 2000 BC Open **International wins** 1, 1993 Australian Open **Ryder Cup** 1995 & 1997 **Major wins** BEF 5th 1995 USPGA **Money list** 8th in 1996

In the 'close season' Bradley John went on a weights and exercise programme to increase his strength and athleticism for the new season.

He's had a mixed season with top 20s in the Tucson Open (T17th), the Kemper Open (T16th) and the AT&T (T20th), and top 10s in the Mercedes (T8th), the Buick Open (T6th) and the Tampa Bay Classic (T6th). He missed the cut in the US Open and finished T27th in the USPGA.

However his big moment came after he failed to prequalify for the British Open. He flew straight back to defend his BC Open title. Putting brilliantly and getting favourable bounces off trees he overcame jetlag to win at 25/1*.

A world class putter, brilliant at birdie conversion, he was top for putting in 1999 and again this year.

However his greens in reg. figures (outside top 135 for last two years) tell their own story. Short and regularly wayward off the tee. He'll be 40 in August 2001. Great friend of Billy Andrade.

> He must be opposed in the US Open (yet to make the top 30) where his erratic approach play is severely punished.

> In 2001 he simply cries out for attention in the third week of July....but in which tournament?

  * British Open. He loves this 'Olympics of Golf' and his last five starts show four top 20 finishes. So if he prequalifies he can be supported on the Royal Lytham course, where he shot 67 (R1) and 68 (R3) in 1996 when T32nd, in match bets and as top US player without Woods.

  * BC Open. If he fails to qualify for Royal Lytham he'll go for a "threepeat" BC Open although I can't see him being as lucky in 2001 as he was this year.

> If he doesn't make the Tour Championship he's sure to do well in the Southern Farm Bureau Classic where in two starts recently he's finished T17th last year and T4th in 2000 for an eclectic score of 22 under par good enough to win!

Key stat   No 1 for putting average in both 1999 and 2000.

STEVE FLESCH   FT V G

Age 33   **Born** Ohio   **Lives** Kentucky
College   University of Kentucky

US Tour wins BEF 2nd 1998 Freeport McDermott Classic **BUY.COM tour wins** 1, 1997 BUY.COM Tour Championship **Money list** BEF 13th 2000

In his third year on tour Steve has performed very consistently throughout the year although he hasn't secured his first breakthrough victory.

He has posted four top 5s in the Nissan Open (T5th at 100/1), the Memorial (T5th at 50/1), the Canon Greater Hartford Open (T5th at 33/1) and the NCR Classic at Walt Disney (2nd at 40/1), and nine top 10s in the Phoenix Open (T7th), the Buick Invitational (T10th), the Tucson Open (T7th), the Bell South Classic (T10th), the Compaq Classic (T6th), the Western Open (T9th), the Reno-Tahoe Open (T7th), the Canadian Open (T6th) and the Invensys Classic in Las Vegas (T9th).

He also had high finishes in the Honda Classic (T19th), the Bay Hill (T18th), the Fedex St Jude Classic (T20th), the Buick Open (T25th), the Michelob (T12th) and the Tour Championship (T15th).

T11th in the WGC American Express Championship. He finished T20th in his first British Open and missed the cut in the USPGA. Left handed player who fades the ball and is in the top 35 for driving distance.

> His stats have all moved in the right direction this year.
   * Driving accuracy up over 1%
   * Greens in reg up over 4%
   * Sand saves up over 11%
   * Birdie conversion up 3%
   * Putting 82nd to top 10.

> After such an ultra consistent year he has already improved nearly all aspects of his game. However, he has still to win and there have been some disturbing signs.
   * Buick Invitational, T4th after R3 he shot 73 in R4 to finish T10th.
   * Bay Hill. 3rd after R2 he finished T18th.
   * Western Open. Joint leader after R3, he shot 75 to finish T9th.
   * Reno-Tahoe Open. T2nd after R2 he shot 73-71 to finish T7th.

So he clearly has not yet learned how to 'close the deal'. However let's remember Duval played consistently well, appeared a 'bottler' then once he won he couldn't stop winning.....and that might just happen to Steve Flesch.

> I suggest you back STEVE in the five tournaments in which he's shown really good form, and as they are all on television you can watch him play well in the FLESCH.
   * The International. 10th in 1999. 6th 1998. His ability to shoot birdies and eagles is ideal here.

* The Bell South Classic. 10th (2000), 36th (1999) and 3rd (1998) he's well suited to the drivers' course at Sugarloaf.
* Compaq Classic. T6th-T20th-T2nd in three visits tells its own story.
* Tucson Open. In two starts (T7th 2000: T13th 1999) his stroke average is 69.12.
* Nissan Open. T5th this year. His last seven rounds average exactly 69 on a course that suits his fade.

A level-stake each-way bet on each of the above five should show a profit.

> He's played really well in Nevada this year so keep your eye on him for both the Reno-Tahoe Open (T7th) and the Invensys Classic in Las Vegas (T9th this year after T32nd in 1999).

> A 'young' player often pops up at a big price 'in the frame' in the USPGA and in 2001 Steve Flesch looks just the type of solid, all-round player who fits the bill.

Key stat   2nd (to guess who) in the all-round ranking.

DAN FORSMAN

Age 42   **Born** Wisconsin   **Lives** Utah

US Tour wins 4, 1985 Quad Cities Open, 1986 Bay Hill Classic, 1990 Shearson Lehman Open, 1992 Buick Open **Money list** BEF 10th 1992

Daniel Bruce (call him Dan) has had a disappointing year overall with one big finish when T3rd at 150/1 in the MCI Classic. He had a top 10 in the Texas Open (T9th) and top 25s in the Shell Houston Open (T17th) and the Canon Greater Hartford Open (T25th).

Usually an accurate iron player his ranking has fallen this year. However his putting (from T65 to outside top 120) has been the main problem. Must now go to Q. School.

> He's twice led tournaments (MCI Classic and Canon Greater Hartford Open) this year and his R1 and R2 scoring is usually his best. Indeed he was awarded the bottle last year after poor final rounds when in contention.

> Experienced course specialists do well at the LaCantera course (T9th 2000: T23rd 1999) so he must enter into calculations for the Texas Open although I can't see him winning the tournament.

Key stat   Eight and a half years and over 200 tournaments since his last win.

CARLOS FRANCO   ☼ G

Age 35   **Born** Paraguay   **Lives** Paraguay

US Tour wins 3, 1999 Compaq Classic and 1999 Greater Milwaukee Open, 2000 Compaq Classic **International wins** 30 worldwide, incl. 5 in Japan **Dunhill Cup** 1999 **Majors** T6th 1999 US Masters **Presidents Cup** 2000 **Money list** BEF 11th 1999

Rookie of the Year in 1999 with twp wins and three 3rds he has carried on the good work in 2000 with a third victory when he successfully defended the Compaq Classic at 25/1 winning in a play-off. He also posted top 10s in the Mercedes (T6th), the Sony Open in Hawaii (T9th), the Honda Classic (T7th), and top 25s in the MCI Classic (T15th), the Shell Houston Open (T11th) and the NCR Classic at Walt Disney (T10th).

In the World Match Play he lost to Mike Weir in R1 by 4 and 3, and finished T27th in the WGC NEC Invitational.

In the majors he was T7th in the Masters, T61st in the US Open, T58th in the USPGA and he missed the British Open cut. In the Presidents Cup he scored 2 points and played superbly (9 under for 13 holes) to hammer Hal Sutton (6 and 5) in the singles! Poor 24th in the Tour Championship.

His driving accuracy remains poor and anchored at 60%, and his greens in reg ranking remains outside the top 100. However this guy has great feel, a fine short game and he sure knows how to take his chances as his birdie conversion stats prove. Average sort of length at 274 yards.

> Carlos' is a brilliant story of a guy who's gone from extreme poverty (and I mean extreme poverty) to millionaire status. Proud of his roots he's very much his own man who rarely uses the practice range. A naturally talented player who was off scratch at 14. I expect his short game and his ability to take his chances will lead to further success. I sure hope so.

> "It seems almost like my home course and it's very hot." So he clearly has a love affair with the Compaq Classic and in 2001 he goes for his third win in a row. With a 67.37 stroke average over the last two years he's sure to do well again.

> I really do fancy him for the 2001 Honda Classic. T7th this year with tendonitis, and T3rd in 1999 he has a stroke average for his last seven rounds of 68.7!

> His Augusta record really is impressive.

* In 1999 he was T6th, and in 2000 T7th.

* Six of his eight rounds have been par or better

* This year for his last three rounds he was second best (at 9 under) of all the players.

* His two-year stroke average is a sub-par 71.37.

He's very much like Olazabal as a player who enjoys the wide Augusta fairways and has a natural feel in his short game.

So I suggest two bets -

First, in the top Rest of The World market in which he's been 3rd at 14/1 this year, and T2nd at 40/1* in 1999.

Second, in the outright 'without Tiger' market.

> His game seems to me clearly ill suited to the tight layout at the TPC Avenel. 80th this year (when in form, he'd been T20th the week before) he can be opposed in the 2001 Kemper Open.

Key stat   11th for birdie conversion.

HARRISON FRAZAR   V 🎂

Age 29   **Born** Texas   **Lives** Texas

US Tour wins BEF T2nd 1998 Byron Nelson Classic, T2nd 1999 Compaq Classic
BUY.COM Tour wins 1, 1997 South Carolina Classic **Money list** BEF 63rd 1998

After finishing 63rd (1998) and 79th (1999) on the Money list this year was Richard Harrison's third on the tour.

He's had two really big finishes when T3rd at 125/1 in the Bell South Classic, and 3rd at 80/1* in the Compaq Classic. He also had top 20s in the Doral Ryder Open (T15th) and the Memorial (T20th), and top 30s in the Honda Classic (T28th), the Shell Houston Open (T29th) and the Advil Western Open (T29th).

His great strength is off the tee where he's been in the top 7 for driving distance (290 yards) both last season and this. This year his driving accuracy has risen from 65% to over 70%. As a result he is always high on the stats for eagles. His putting (not in top 95) and sand saves (not in top 100 again) must be improved.

Uses Justin Leonard's coach Randy Smith. He self confessedly relishes the life of a pro golfer (who wouldn't?).

Became a father for a first time son in December 1999. He'll be 30 in late July 2001.

> Harrison is a strong fit player whose strength is in his driving. So far in his three years on tour he's posted five top 5 finishes yet he's yet to make his breakthrough first victory.

  * 2nd 1998 Byron Nelson Classic
  * 4th 1998 Colonial
  * T2nd 1999 Compaq Classic
  * T3rd 2000 Bell South Classic
  * 3rd 2000 Compaq Classic

> He's shown real signs of nerves under pressure this year

  * 2000 Compaq Classic. He was the leader on the 17th tee in R4, and then made double bogey. He finished 3rd.
  * 2000 Memorial. 2nd at halfway he partnered Tiger in R3 and shot 78. He finished T20th.

> The Sugarloaf course suits players high in the stats for total driving, and it sure suits Harrison Frazar (T3rd 2000) who will be worth each-way support in the 2001 Bell South Classic.

> His game is clearly well suited to the Compaq Classic where he's posted consecutive top 3 finishes (3rd 2000: T2nd 1999) for a two-year stroke average of 67.75. So when Harrison plays at English Turn in 2001 turn to your bookie and back Frazar!.

> He must enter into calculations when the tour makes the 'Texas Swing' in late April and May. A born-and-bred Texan resident he'd have 'home' advantage in the Byron Nelson (2nd 1998), the Colonial (4th 1998) and the Shell Houston Open (8 under after R2 in 2000).

> He may have been distracted by his baby son's illness when missing the cut this year in the Phoenix Open where his big hitting took him to T6th in 1999. Worth noting there early on in 2001.

Key stat   4th for total driving and 8th in holes per eagle.

ROBIN FREEMAN   V

Age 41   **Born** Minnesota   **Lives** California

US tour BEF 2nd 1995 Byron Nelson Classic **Money list** BEF 68th 1995

Regained his tour card when finishing 9th at the 1999 Q School.

This year he's had one 'big' finish when 3rd at 250/1 in the Nissan Open winning over $210,000. His other top 25s were in the Bell South Classic (T22nd), the Buick Open (T25th) and the Tampa Bay Classic (T14th).

His stats not surprisingly are poor all round.

> If there's one tournament that he'll look forward to as a resident Californian it will surely be the Nissan Open where he was 6th in 1997, and 3rd in 2000. However I'm not brave enough to suggest he'll win it at 150/1!

Key stat   156th (!) in the all-round ranking.

DAVID FROST   PB D

Age 42   **Born** South Africa   **Lives** Texas

US Tour wins 10, incl. three in 1980s then 1990 USF&G Classic, 1992 Buick Classic, Hardee's Golf Classic: 1993 Canadian Open, 1993 Hardee's Golf Classic, 1994 Canon Greater Hartford Open, 1997 Mastercard Colonial **International wins** 12, latest the 1999 South African Open **Dunhill Cup** 9 times, latest 2000 **Money list** BEF 5th 1993

Frosty has had a really poor year. In South Africa he was T5th at 16/1 in the Alfred Dunhill, and 3rd at 14/1 in the Dimension Data Pro-Am.

In the majors he was T55th in the British Open, and he missed the US Open cut.

In the Dunhill Cup he scored 3 points from five matches as he helped South Africa to the final. His career record in the tournament is 24 pts from thirty-six games.

However on the US tour he's had a desperately poor year in which he's made the cut in only seven of his twenty-three starts and apart from finishing T8th in the John Deere Classic he's not posted another single top 30 finish.

His stats as you'd expect after such a poor year are really bad. Indeed he's not in the top 100 in any of the main categories including putts per green in reg (12th 1999) and sand saves (2nd 1999), and for total driving and greens in reg he's outside the top 180!!

He's now built a thriving wine business.

> Last year Frosty's long game was in poor shape however he retained the magic of his short game. This year that magic, too has gone. So it may well be that we are seeing a career facing terminal decline.

> Even if his game were to improve he would surely suffer from 'contention rust' as he showed when the halfway leader (15 under par) in the John Deere Classic, he then shot 70-73 to finish T8th.

> That tournament, the John Deere is one to which he will look forward in 2001. It does not attract a strong field, will once more be held at the end of July, and he's proved he can play well on the Deere Run course after his 65-62 pre-cut start in 2000.

> The early season events in his home country South Africa are the ones in which he's done consistently well in recent years. His record in the Alfred Dunhill Cup, 2nd 14/1 1997: T3rd 25/1 1999: T5th at 16/1 2000, suggests one area in which Frosty can be followed in mid January.

Key stat   Frosty was ranked 12th for putting average in 1999 yet he slipped to 103rd in 2000. Similarly 2nd for sand saves last year he was also 103rd in 2000.

ED FRYATT   S 🎂

Age 29   **Born** Rochdale (Cyril Smith & Gracie Fields territory)

Lives Las Vegas, Nevada   **College** Las Vegas, Nevada

BUY.COM Tour wins 1, 1999 Nike Hershey Open **US tour** BEF T3rd 2000 MCI Classic **International wins** 4, 1996 Indonesian Open, 1997 Indian Open, 1998 China Open and 1998 Malaysian Open **Money list** BEF 77th 2000

Ed from Rochdale was 2nd on the Far East Omega tour O/M in 1998, then in 1999 he was 5th on the BUY.COM tour O/M having posted ten top 10s and notched a victory.

This year as a rookie on the full tour he has consolidated, retained his card and posted his best ever finish when T3rd at 150/1 in the MCI Classic. He also posted a top 5 in the Canon Greater Hartford Open (T5th at 125/1). He also notched three top 10s, in the Phoenix Open (T7th), the Doral Ryder (T9th) and the International (T9th).

Missed the cut in the USPGA after a 69 in R1 (then 79!) and the US Open. Uses Butch Harmon's coaching.

> He'll be 30 in April 2001. His R4 scoring average is good, and let's remember he'd won in everyone of the four previous years until 2000, so be prepared for Ed to post a high finish or two in 2001.

> He's awarded the streaker symbol after shooting a USPGA record equalling eight (yes, eight!) consecutive birdies in a 62 in R2 of the Doral Ryder Open.

> Worth a bet in the MCI Classic. When T3rd this year he lost the tournament at the par 4 8th (triple bogey in R2: double bogey in R4). If he can handle that hole in 2001 he'll have a leading chance.

> Living in Vegas he relishes desert golf and can be followed in desert tournaments:-
  * The Phoenix Open (T7th 2000)
  * The International (T9th 2000).

Key stat   136th for par 5 birdies

FRED FUNK

Age 44   **Born** Maryland   **Lives** Florida

US Tour wins 5, 1992 Shell Houston Open, 1995 Ideon Classic at Pleasant Valley, 1995 Buick Challenge, 1996 BC Open, 1998 Deposit Guaranty Classic **International wins** 1, 1993 Mexican Open **Money list** BEF 16th 1999

Fred has posted his usual series of high finishes although he's not had a single really big week until he finished T4th at 100/1 in the NCR Classic at Walt Disney in October.

He had top 10s in the Bob Hope (T7th) and the Southern Farm Bureau (T6th), and top 25s in the Players Championship (T13th), the MCI Classic (T25th), the Shell Houston Open (T17th), the Colonial (T13th), the Western Open (T20th) and the Reno-Tahoe Open (T21st).

He finished T37th in the US Masters, T9th in the USPGA and he missed the British and US Open cuts. In the World Match Play he lost to Justin Leonard by 6 and 5 in R1.

Fred is the archetypal, straight-hitting guy whose putter lets him down, a sort of Florida-based Eduardo Romero! He hits 80% of fairways and is in the top 10 for greens in reg, yet his putting is never up to the standard of his approach play. Draws the ball. Uses Fanny Suneson as his caddie.

> He's finding his lack of length an increasing handicap, so he may find it difficult to post his sixth tour win. Nevertheless he's so accurate that if he has a putting week it could well happen.

> 'Fairway Fred', despite the arrow-like accuracy of his driving, is probably at his best on easy courses. So I suggest he'll be worth an each-way interest in the Bob Hope where he's finished T7th 2000 and T4th 1999 in the last two years.

> He has a fine record at Callaway Gardens where he won in 1995, was T2nd in 1996, 17th 1997, 2nd in 1998 and then mid division T37th (1999) and T41st (2000) in the last two years. At 50/1 he'll be worth a little each way for the 2001 Buick Challenge.

Key stat   Top ranked for driving accuracy in both 1999 and 2000.

JIM FURYK   G 🐦 🏖

Age 30   **Born** Pennsylvania   **Lives** Florida
College Arizona

US Tour wins 5, 1995 Las Vegas Invitational, 1996 Hawaiian Open, 1998 and 1999 Las Vegas Invitational, 2000 Doral Ryder Open **BUY.COM wins** 1, 1993 NIKE Mississippi Gulf Coast classic **International wins** 1, 1997 Argentine Open **Ryder Cup** 1997, 1999 **Presidents Cup** 1998, 2000 **Money list** 3rd 1998, 4th 1997

James Michael, Jim to his mates, has the oddest swing on the planet but it works and this year it brought him his fifth tour success when during the Florida Swing he won the Doral Ryder Open at 33/1. He also posted five top 5 finishes in the Mercedes (T4th at 16/1), the Honda Classic (T4th at 14/1), the Canon Greater

Hartford Open (4th at 22/1), the Western Open (T3rd at 25/1) and the WGC NEC Invitational (T4th at 40/1).

He also had high finishes in the AT&T (T18th), the Byron Nelson (T20th), the Colonial (8th), the Memorial (T25th), the Buick Open (T16th), the Michelob (T19th) and the Invensys Classic in Las Vegas (T17th as DC).

In the Andersen World Match Play he beat Rocco Mediate and Bob Tway before losing to Davis Love.

In the majors he finished T14th in the US Masters, 60th in the US Open, T41st in the British Open, and T72nd in the USPGA. In the Presidents Cup he scored 3 points, easily beating Maruyama (5 and 4) in the singles.

His stats are very consistent year to year as he is short off the tee although he has been working on his distance and has added 3 yards this year on the official stats.

Accurate off the tee hitting three quarters of his fairways he has increased his greens in reg percentage by 3 points to 68%. A very solid X-handed putter. His accuracy and putting combine for a top 15 placing for par 3 birdies. His sand save percentage needs improving (from 58%) if he's to move to that higher level. A fader of the ball.

Fluff, Tiger's former caddy, is now Furyk's bagman.

He did not play in the lucrative Tour Championship as his wrist injury was obviously serious.

> Jim was 30 this year, so he enters his fourth decade after his poorest year yet in the majors. His overall record now in twenty starts is nineteen cuts, thirteen top 20s and seven top 10s including five top 5 finishes. I would expect him to resume normal service next year by posting top 20 major finishes, assuming his end-of-season wrist injury clears up.

> His five-year record in the US Masters T14th-T14th-4th-T29th-T29th is very solid and the course changes emphasising accuracy have helped him. He hasn't the length to win, but there is little downside to selling his finishing position for the 2001 US Masters with a nice profit in prospect.

> From the start of 1999 to mid October 2000 his stats are (from forty-nine tournaments)
  * forty-seven cuts made i.e. 95.9% equivalent to odds of 22/1 ON
  * sixteen top 10s made i.e. 32.65% equivalent to odds of just over 2/1
  * thirty-one top 25s made, i.e. 63.26% equivalent to odds of just over 7/4 ON

  So Jim is an absolutely ideal candidate as a consistent straight hitter who can be supported in match bets and whose finishing position can usually be sold with confidence on the spreads.

> Jim's win this year came from way 'off the pace' with a stunning 65 in R4 with five birdies in the last 7 holes, and I do think that he's better coming with a late run rather than as a front runner.

> Top 15 for pre-cut scoring last year, and top 10, this year Jim can be followed in R1 and R2 3-ball betting and must never be opposed.

> I think Furyk's best chances in 2001 will lie in three tournaments to which he is well suited and where he has a good record. He can be supported on the spreads, in match bets and in the outrights.

  * The Sony Open in Hawaii. Suits him because it emphasises accuracy off the tee and it's become a course specialist tournament, top 20 in 1999, T2nd in 1997 and he won it in 1996.

  * The Colonial. T8th (2000), T55th (1999), 2nd (1998) and 8th (1997). He's shot a 64 (1997) on this accurate-hitter's track.

  * The Honda Classic. He won in Florida (where he lives) last year and in just two starts his record (T4th 2000 and T12th 1998) is impressive for a stroke average of 68.28.

> His consistent record means that he has a very solid bank of form in a large number of tournaments. However I suggest you follow him in match bets and on the spreads in these three events.

  * Greater Greensboro Classic. T42nd (2000), 2nd (1999), T12th (1998), T14th (1997), T7th (1996)

  * AT&T. 18th (2000), MC (1999) 3rd (1998), 4th (1997) good in the wind at Pebble Beach

  * Buick Open. Four top 16s in five starts for a cumulative 52 under par, including a round of 62. He can be supported in match bets.

> A certainty for the American Ryder Cup side where he must be backed in the singles as his Presidents and Ryder Cup singles record is PL 4 W 4—by 3 and 2, 4 and 2, 4 and 3, and 5 and 4, and that is mega impressive as he's yet to step on the 17th tee!!.

> Played consistent golf (four rounds in the 60s) to be T4th in this year's WGC NEC Invitational and after a T10th in 1999 he has a two-year stroke average of 68.75 so he can be supported on the spreads and 'without Woods'.

Key stat From the start of last season to 11th October 2000 he posted sixteen top 10s in forty-nine tournaments and missed just two cuts!

BRIAN GAY

Age 29 **Born** Fort Worth, Texas **Lives** Orlando, Florida

College University of Florida

US tour BEF T4th 2000 Honda Classic

In 1999 he missed the cut in eighteen of his twenty-six events to lose his card, which he regained when T10th at Q School.

In 2000 he showed much improved form with seven top 20s, in the Tucson Open (T13th), the Kemper Open (T20th, after 64 in R4), the Greater Milwaukee Open (T14th), the Fedex St Jude Classic (T20th), the BC Open (T5th), the Buick Challenge (T14th) and the Southern Farm Bureau (T20th).

He had his big finish (worth $127K) when T4th in the Honda Classic in March. Missed the cut in the US Open.

His improved performances have been based on improved putting (top 25) and accuracy off the tee (74%: top 20). However his iron play is poor as he's outside the top 130 for Greens in reg, and outside the top 170 for par 3 birdies. 30 in December 2001.

> Let three very promising chances slip this year.

   * Greater Milwaukee Open. T4th after R3, shot 72 to finish T14th.

   * BC Open. T5 after R2, then shot 74-70 to finish T18th and he was T2nd after R3 before finishing T4th in the Honda.

   It's probably fair to conclude therefore that if he's to gain his first win it will be when his superb putting takes him from 'off the pace' to the clubhouse lead.

> Best chance will be in the weakly contested BC Open where he played so well this year in the first two rounds (T5th at halfway) on the way to finishing T18th.

> Worth noting in the St Jude Classic in the 3 and 2-ball betting (68-68-69 finish this year) if coming from 'off the pace'.

Key stat   24th for putting average.

BRENT GEIBERGER   G

Age 32   **Born** California   **Lives** California

US Tour wins 1, 1999 Canon Greater Hartford Open **Money list** BEF 19th 1999

Brent Andrew entered 2000 for his fourth year on the tour having shown progressive M/L finishing positions of 62nd, 49th and 19th last year when he won his first tournament.

However this year has been disappointing for the son of eleven-time tour winner Al.

Started the year well when he was 4th after R3 in the all-winners Mercedes Tournament. He then had a back injury, shooting 76 in R4 to finish T8th.

He posted top 25s in the Bob Hope (T12th including 61 in R2), the Buick Invitational (T10th), the Colonial (T24th) and the Canon Greater Hartford Open (T18th), and a top 10 in the Air Canada (T8th), and had his best finish in the Buick Challenge (T5th at 100/1).

In the WGC Andersen Match Play he lost by 1 hole to Jimenez. He missed the cuts in the US Masters, the US Open, and the USPGA for a sad hat-trick.

The key reason for Brent's decline is his putting which has gone from top 50 to outside the top 90. If, and when, he can regain his touch with the flatstick he will surely be in contention regularly.

> Worth keeping an eye on Brent's early season putting stats. I expect them to improve and so signal a return to form for this promising player who could well win again in 2001.

> He can be backed in match bets, and as an each way 80/1 chance in the Air Canada Championship where his form (T8th 2000: made cut 1999: 11th 1998:

12th 1997) shows three top 12 finishes and an eclectic score of 18 under over the last four years.

> Born and bred in California he merits support in the Buick Invitational where in just three starts (T10th 2000: 6th 1998: T25th (1997) he's 25 under par.

> His form in the Colonial is solid yet unspectacular (24-39-41-33). However his final 54 holes in 2000 were completed in 11 under par to make him an outsider with a real squeak in 2001.

Key stat   Putting average has slipped from 47th in 1999 to 94th this year.

BILL GLASSON

Age 40   **Born** California   **Lives** Oklahoma

US Tour wins 7, 1985 Kemper Open, 1988 BC Open, Centel Classic, 1989 Doral Ryder Open, 1992 Kemper Open, 1994 Phoenix Open, 1997 Las Vegas Invitational
Money list BEF 17th 1994

Bill is the guy who must speak to his doctor more often than he does to his caddie. He's had all manner of injuries (knee, elbow, back, forearm) and health (sinuses) problems that have continually dogged his career.

In 2000 he has consistently had high or fairly high finishes yet has been unable to convert any into a win, and only one (BC Open) into a top 5 finish.

He has had top 25s in the Compaq Classic (T24th), the Colonial (T24th), the Memorial (T20th), the Kemper Open (T10th), Fedex St Jude Classic (T15th), the Advil Western Open (T15th) and the John Deere Classic (T12th). His big finish came when he won $116K when T3rd as the 16/1 fav. in the BC Open.

His putting, really poor (138th) last year is much better (top 40) in 2000. His strengths are his length off the tee at 282 yards and as he hits the ball a long way in the air so he has a length advantage on wet courses. This year he was in the top 40 for greens in regulation as he was in 1999.

> With his record of injury and ill health he must only be backed when he is clearly fit.

> Was at his best in May, June and July this year when he made nine consecutive top 30 finishes.

> He'll be really keen to qualify for the 2001 US Open in Oklahoma where he lives. If he does Bill has the ability to 'make the frame'. as he did when T4th in 1995 on his second last start in the tournament.

> However if there's one tournament in which Bill can be backed with real confidence it simply must be the 2001 Kemper Open. He's won this event twice (1992 and 1985) on different courses, was T2nd in 1999 and T10th this year with all his last 8 rounds under par so with that record, if he's fit, he's a must to follow at the TPC at Avenel in 2001.

> He must also be noted in match bets and in the outrights in three other tournaments:-

   * The BC Open. T3rd this year as favourite in a weak field

* The Compaq Classic: 2nd 1997 and 24th 2000.
* The Buick Challenge. 3rd in 1998.

Key stat   36th for greens in regulation.

MATT GOGEL

Age 29   **Born** Colorado   **Lives** Kansas

College Kansas

BUY.COM Tour wins 6, 1996, 1997, two in 1998 (both in play-offs), two in 1999 **US tour** BEF, 2nd 2000 AT&T National Pebble Beach pro-am

Earned his 2000 card through the 1999 BUY.COM tour where he was 7th on the M/L.

In 2000 he got off to a flier in his second tournament when T7th in the Bob Hope, and then two weeks later he secured his card winning $352K when T2nd at 125/1 in the AT&T.

He then made only 6 cuts in his next twenty-one tournaments. However he did post a top 20 in the Shell Houston Open (T11th), and top 30s in the Honda Classic (T28th) and the NCR Classic at Walt Disney (T24th).

His stats for driving distance, driving accuracy, greens in regulation and sand saves are all outside the top 135 and make very grim reading. He'll be 30 in February 2001.

> He has been fortunate this year to secure his card on two wide fairway courses early in the season.

> Although he became the first player in BUY.COM tour history to win in four consecutive years (from 1996-1999 incl) he really 'choked' big time this year.

* Bob Hope: 2nd after R4, he had a poor par R4 to finish T7th.

* AT&T: 7 shots ahead with 7 holes to play he 'went to pieces' shooting 40 on the back nine in a final round 81 to lose and finish T2nd to Tiger.

> He'll find it really difficult to retain his card in 2001 although his best chances will clearly be in the wide fairway celebrity events in which he started so well this year.

Key stat   7 ahead with 7 to play he finished 2nd in the 2000 AT&T

MATHEW GOGGIN   g y

Age 26   **Born** Hobart, Tasmania   **Lives** Hobart, Tasmania

European Challenge Tour wins 2, 1996 Dutch Challenge, and 1997 Sao Paolo Open **Australian tour wins** 1, 1998 ANZ Tour Championship **BUY.COM Tour wins** 2, both in 1999

Mathew had an absolutely disastrous start to his rookie year making only two of his first seventeen cuts!! However from July he began to find some form posting four high finishes, notably in the Greater Milwaukee Open (T3rd at 125/1), the BC Open

(9th) and, in September, in the Air Canada (T13th), the Pennsylvania Classic (T12th) and the Southern Farm Bureau (T20th).

He's a huge hitter at 286 yards. However his putting average and sand save rankings are 'off the scale' (outside top 170) and they together with some inaccurate driving (118th) explain his disappointing season.

> As a long hitting winner every year from 1996 (as a 22-year-old) through 1999 I put him up last year in Part 2 as an unknown who could post a shock win in 2000. Well I was clearly too ambitious. However, let's not give up on this guy who had shown immense courage to comeback after his absolutely dreadful start to his Rookie year.

> 9th this year on his BC Open debut from the worst possible tee times (last out pm R1: last out am R2) he must have a very sound chance at a big price in the weak field at En Joie in 2001.

> Worth noting for the Air Canada after his solid T13th finish from four sub-par rounds on his debut there this year.

> There are three reasons for suggesting that Goggin will be worth each-way support in the 2001 Pennsylvania Classic:-

  * The tournament will be held on a brand new course which will nullify the usual advantage held by the experienced players.

  * He won in Pennsylvania on the BUY.COM tour in 1999.

  * He was a solid T12th in this year's inaugural Pennsylvania Classic.

> The forgiving fairways and four par 5s at Annandale suit Mathew as he showed with a very fast finish (T20th) this year when shooting 15 under for his last three rounds after getting the very worst of the weather. Well worth a bet at 80/1 to land the 2001 Southern Farm Bureau Classic if he gets an early tee time.

Key stat   29th for greens in regulation.

PAUL GOW   S

Age 30   **Born** Sydney, Australia   **Lives** Sydney, Australia

BUY.COM tour wins 2, 1997 Permain Bairn Open, and 2000 BUY.COM Hershey open **US tour** BEF T32nd 2000 Canon Greater Hartford Open **International wins** 1, 2000 Canon Challenge (ANZ tour)

Paul started the year well finishing 3rd at 25/1 in the New Zealand Open in late January. Three weeks later he won his first ANZ tournament, the Canon Challenge at 25/1 'in my own backyard'.

In the States he played well enough on the BUY.COM tour to secure his full US tour card having won the BUY.COM Hershey open. He also posted two other top 4 finishes, in the BUY.COM Steamtown Classic (T3rd) and the BUY.COM Ozarks Open (T4th). Form fell away from September missing five of his next six cuts.

On the US tour he missed the cut in the US Open and finished a very respectable T32nd in the Canon Greater Hartford Open.

An accurate player with solid greens in reg. stats his bunker play (80th) must be improved. Coached by Gary Edwin.

> Paul is a consistent player who posted eight top 10s in his first fifteen BUY.COM events this year, and made twenty-five consecutive ANZ cuts before his victory this year. He's also now a proven winner (two tournaments) this year with an excellent BUY.COM R4 scoring average.

Accuracy + consistency + 'bottle' = Paul Gow, so keep your eye on him in 2001.

> Expect him to make a bold defence of his Canon Challenge title in late January in his native city.

> Because of his accuracy he's probably at his best on tough course as his winning score in his BUY.COM victory this year was just 3 under.

Key stat   This year on the BUY.COM tour he had a R4 scoring average of 69.07 (ranked 2nd).

PAUL GOYDOS   D

Age 36   **Born** California   **Lives** California

US Tour wins 1, 1996 Bay Hill Invitational BUY.COM Tour wins 1, 1992 Yuma Open **Money list** BEF 44th 1996

This year Paul has made 70% of his cuts yet has only made five top 20s in the Bay Hill (T10th), the Buick Classic (T16th), the BC Open (T10th), the Texas Open (T19th) and the Buick Challenge (T10th).

He missed the cut in the US Open.

In his poorest season since 1995 his stats are not pleasant. Short off the tee at 263 yards and top 35 for driving accuracy his iron play has been poor as his greens in reg rating has slumped.

However his putting has improved a lot this year to the top 30.

> With his short driving a handicap and his greens in reg ranking outside the top 100 it's not easy to see Paul adding win number 2 to his CV.

> His best chance in 2001 may well be in the weak field for the BC Open where he finished very fast (11 under last 54 holes) to finish T10th this year.

Key stat   146th for greens in regulation.

JIMMY GREEN

Age 31   **Born** Minnesota   **Lives** Alabama

BUY.COM tour wins 1, 1996 Buffalo Open

Regained his tour card when T19th at Q School.

Got his season off to a 'flier' when, in his second tournament, he won $165K when T4th in the AT&T Pebble Beach Pro-Am in which he shot 68 in both his rounds at Pebble Beach.

Later he had top 20s in the Greater Greensboro Classic (T16th) and the Buick Classic (T13th), and top 30s in the Kemper Open (T28th) and the Air Canada (T27th).

He prequalified for the US Open, made the cut and finished T57th.

Short off the tee at 271 yards his putting stats are really poor. To late September he'd only ever made two consecutive cuts to illustrate his inconsistency.

> Jimmy will just be pleased to retain his card and avoid going back to Q School again.

> Worth noting in the three and two ball betting in the AT&T after his 68-68-68 finish this year.

Key stat   154th for putting average.

DUDLEY HART

Age 32   **Born** New York   **Lives** Florida

College Florida

US Tour wins 2, 1996 Canadian Open, 2000 Honda Classic **International Wins** 1, 1998 Sarazen World Open **Money list** BEF 29th 1999

Howard Dudley has had a successful, if injury threatened, year.

Making four cuts in his first five tournaments he then won the Honda Classic at 50/1 in March. He also had a big finish when T3rd at 33/1 in the Greater Greensboro Classic.

He posted a top 10 in the Buick Open (T6th) and high finishes in the AT&T (T20th), the MCI Classic (T25th) and the Kemper Open (T20th).

In the majors he finished T28th in the US Masters, missed the cut in the US Open, and withdrew from the British Open (after R2) and the USPGA (after R1).

In the World Match Play he lost in R1 to Tim Herron by 2 and 1.

The key this year has been his improvement in greens in reg and in driving accuracy (both up a massive 6%). On that basis he clearly does well when he putts well which he did in his Honda Classic win as he birdied the last 4 holes.

> The key punter point about Dudley to remember is that he withdrew three times this year during tournaments as he has a potentially serious back problem (bulging discs). So we must tread warily, however let's remember that in the last two years he's been nominated here for four tournaments and he played in three, with good each-way results 4th 50/1, T3rd 66/1, T3rd 33/1.

> Dudley cries out to be backed for the 2001 Greater Greensboro Classic where he's finished T3rd 33/1 (2000), 4th 50/1 (1999), T12th 80/1 (1998). His putting let him down this year however with his price contracting every year 33/1 might be the best odds on offer.

> Living 20 miles away, the Honda Classic is his local tournament. He'll be defending champion in 2001 and I don't expect him to win. However his recent R4 scoring record (65-69-69) demands that he must be backed in the final-day 2-ball betting if he's 'off the pace'.

> Dudley likes the Glen Abbey course ("it sets up well for my game") where he won in 1996 and was T3 in 1998. He missed the event this year because of his back. In 2001 take HART and back DUDLEY to win the Canadian Open.

> Remember him for the Invensys Classic in Las Vegas. He enjoys the warmth, was 3rd in 1999, top 30 this year and T12th in 1996.

Key stat   Withdrew with a back problem from three tournaments in 2000.

J P HAYES   S

Age 35   **Born** Wisconsin   **Lives** Texas

US Tour wins 1, 1998 Buick Classic **BUY.COM tour wins** 1, 1996 Nike Miami Valley Classic **Money list** BEF 51st 1998

J.P. has posted a couple of really big finishes this year when T2nd at 80/1 in the Honda Classic, and T3rd at 66/1 in the Greater Milwaukee Open.

He also had top 10s in the Buick Invitational (T10th), the Nissan Open (T10th) and the Memorial (T10th), plus top 25s in the Buick Classic (T19th), the Western Open (T23rd) and the Reno-Tahoe Open (T21st),

He missed the cut in the US Open. However in the USPGA he finished T19th.

Inaccuracy off the tee last year and this has been his main problem. A solid putter.

> He's now posted a win and four top 5 finishes in the last three years so as he's not a 'name' he can often represent fair value.

> His stats show consistently that his R3 scoring is definitely his best. So do remember J.P. in 2-ball betting on Saturdays!

> A Texan he must be considered for the Shell Houston Open (5th 1999: 8th 1997 including 64 in R3) where he's made four successive cuts.

> His stroke average over the last three years for the Buick Classic is 69.82. His only tour win came in the tournament in 1998, he was T28th as defending champ and T19th in 2000. He merits match bet support at the very least.

> In the last two years he's started like a train in the USPGA: 68 in R1 in 1999, and he started 69-68 in 2000. So back J.P. in R1 of the 2001 USPGA.

> He's also been very high on the early leaderboards in 'ordinary' tournaments.

* R1 joint leader (7 under) Honda Classic, and also R2 leader (2 under)

* R1 leader (7 under) Nissan Open

So if there's a 'who will lead after R1 or at halfway' market remember J.P.

Key stat   30th for putting average.

BRIAN HENNINGER   S ▮

Age 38   **Born** California   **Lives** Oregon

US Tour wins 2, 1994 Southern Farm Bureau Classic (rain shortened), 1999 Southern Farm Bureau Classic (3 rounds only) **BUY.COM Tour wins** 3, all in 1992 when 2nd on the BUY.COM Money list **Money list** BEF 55th 1999

Brian Hatfield (what a classic middle name) has had an average year after his best ever in 1999.

He's posted two top 10s in the Advil Western Open (T6th) and the Reno-Tahoe Open (T4th at 100/1) that together earned him $224K to secure his card.

He also posted four top 25s, in the Honda Classic (T12th), the Bell South Classic (T15th), the Greater Greensboro (T21st) and the International (T21st). He missed the cut in the US Open and finished T46th in the USPGA.

He is a superb putter, his problem however is hitting the greens in regulation (outside top 95 this year and last).

> A streak player, at his best when there is a minimum premium on accuracy and a maximum premium on putting. Capable of very low rounds, he led two tournaments after R1 this year (Honda Classic 65: Greater Greensboro Classic 66), and twice shot 63 (R2 Reno-Tahoe Open and R2 Western Open). So remember him in 3-ball betting, and, if a market is formed, to be R1 leader.

> However when faced with the winning post he's let good chances slip this year on three occasions and last year once. So he's awarded the bottle.

   * Reno-Tahoe Open. Leader at halfway, he shot 71-73 to finish T4th.
   * Greater Greensboro Classic. T5th after R3, he shot 76 in R4, to finish T21st.
   * Western Open. T1st after R3, he shot 74 in R4 to finish T6th.
   * 1999 John Deere Classic: R3 leader by 3, shot an over par 71, to finish T3rd.

   So he must be opposed in final round 2 ball betting if in serious contention.

   Let's remember he was not put to the test in his 1999 Southern Farm Bureau win which came when he was the R3 leader and the tournament was then cancelled with him the winner.

> So given his poor R4 record when in contention his best winning chance will surely be when he comes from off the pace.

> Must be noted in 2- and 3-ball betting in the Western Open. He's shot 63 in R2 (2000), 67 in R2 and R3 (1999) in the last couple of years in which he's finished T6th and 9th.

> If he gets an early tee time he'd have an outside chance in the Bell South Classic (15th 2000: 19th 1999: 36th 1998: 2nd 1997).

> He's well suited to the Southern Farm Bureau where he's won twice in reduced tournaments so remember him at Annandale in November.

Key stat   15th for putting average

MARK HENSBY   ≜ G y

Age 29   **Born** Melbourne   **Lives** Chicago, Illinois

BUY.COM tour wins 2, 1998 NIKE Fort Smith Classic, 2000 BUY.COM Carolina Classic (after a play-off) **US Tour** BEF T41st 1996 Quad City Classic

Joined the BUY.COM tour in 1997. He won for the first time in 1998 and this year he posted his second win in the BUY.COM Carolina Classic in July in a play-off, he also had four other top 5 finishes in the BUY.COM Florida Classic (2nd), the BUY.COM Monterrey (Mexico) Open (2nd), the BUY.COM Cleveland Open (T5th) and the BUY.COM Permian Basin Open (2nd).

His stats are really impressive as he's No. 1 for greens in reg (71.6%), 15th for putting, and 11th for birdie conversion. A long hitter (288 yards) he's 5th for par 5 birdie leaders. However his bunker play is in 'intensive care' (112th!).

He's shot a number of low rounds incl. 65 to win in 1998, and his record includes two course records - 62 (R2 Fort Smith Classic 1998) and 64 (Lehigh Valley Open 1999) as well as 63 this year in R1 of the Utah Classic. So he sure is a streaker!

He'll be 30 on 29th June 2001.

> Players often show much improved form once they're past 30. Hensby passes that Mark in late June. He can be followed in early July in the Western Open. He's a member of the host club at Cog Hill and the long course suits him well.

> The other tour event held in his home state of Illinois is the John Deere Classic. He'll know the course and as this will be only the second time the course has been used his opponents' experience advantage will be minimised.

  Make a note of his name. It's Hensby so Mark him down for his two home-state tournaments, the Western Open and the John Deere Classic once he's blown out that 30th candle on his birthday cake.

Key stat   No. 1 player for greens in reg on the 2000 BUY.COM tour

TIM HERRON   G

Age 30   **Born** Minnesota   **Lives** Arizona

US Tour wins 3, 1996 Honda Classic, 1997 Texas Open, 1999 Bay Hill Invitational
Majors BEF 6th 1999 US Open **Money list** BEF 22nd 1999

Timothy Daniel (answers to 'Lumpy') burst onto the scene in 1996 and has become a well established player ever since.

In 2000 he's not had a really big finish although he has posted four top 10s, in the Bay Hill (T10th), the Kemper (T7th), the John Deere Classic (7th) and the Tampa Bay Classic (9th). He also recorded top 20s in the Canon Greater Hartford Open (T18th), the Colonial (T13th) and the Reno-Tahoe Open (T12th).

He missed the cut in all the four majors.

In the World Match Play he beat Dudley Hart in R1 (2 and 1) before losing 4 and 3 to Duval in R2.

Top 15 for driving distance yet not in top 120 for driving accuracy. His all-round ranking has slipped to 54th in 2000 from 21st in 1999.

Fades the ball. He was 30 in February 2000.

> With three wins in five years, including his all-the-way win first in just his seventh tournament, Lumpy proved himself a good 'closer'. However in the second half of 2000 he twice let good opportunities slip on a Sunday.

  * Texas Open. T5th after R3 he shot 72 to finish T30th!

  * Air Canada. T6th after R3 he shot 75 to finish T38th!

This is disturbing and unexpected evidence of final-round pressure. Which Lumpy will we see in 2001—the one who knows how to win or this R4 'bottler'?

> A really good player in wet weather keep him on your side when the rains come down as they do in the AT&T where he was top 20 in 1998 and T10th in 1999.

> He must be backed to win the 2001 Bay Hill Invitational where he was T10th this year as defending champion having won in 1999.

> The new Deere Run course suits him judged by his 65-65 start this year when T7th, so in 2001 lump on Lumpy for the John Deere Classic. He has played exhibitions there and knows this new course well.

> If we ignore his poor effort this year (T75th) he can be given a real chance in the Fedex St Jude Classic where he shot a 63 in 1996, and where his form 13th (1997); 12th (1998) and 2nd (1999) is very solid indeed. Have a few bob on Tim at Southwind in 2001.

> "I'm really comfortable on this golf course" and he's proved it at the LaCantera track, where he's been T6th (1996), won (1997) and posted successive top 30s in the last two years. At 50/1+ he'll represent a solid each-way bet for the 2001 Texas Open.

Key stat   12th (at 285 yards) for driving distance.

GABRIEL HJERSTEDT

Age 29   **Born** Sweden   **Lives** Sweden

US Tour wins 2, 1997 BC Open: 1999 Tucson Open **Dunhill Cup** 1999 **Money list** BEF 41st 1999

Yetstet has had a disappointing year with just three top 20 finishes, in the Phoenix Open (T18th), the Bell South Classic (T15th) and the Greater Hartford Open (T14th).

Missed the cut in the US Masters for the third successive time.

His poor greens in regulation stats tell the story of poor approach play which has been his biggest problem especially on the par 4s.

> However his tour exemption for winning the 1999 Tucson Open expires at the end of 2001 so he will have the extra incentive of securing his card next year.

> Once past 30 in May it could well be that his form will improve. Let's remember Gabriel Steig Johan Eric has won twice in the last four years, and his birdie conversion ratio is still very good.

> Would have a realistic chance in the Air Canada where he was T13th in 1999, and T31st this year with seven of his last eight rounds in the 60s.

Key stat   146th for greens in regulation.

GLEN HNATIUK

Age 35   **Born** Canada   **Lives** Florida

College University of S.Mississippi

BUY.COM tour wins 4, latest in 1999 **US tour** BEF T3rd 2000 BC Open

Regained his tour card when 8th on the 1999 BUY.COM tour.

In 2000 he had three top 20s, in the Fedex St Jude Classic (T11th) and the Buick Open (T16th), and the Buick Challenge (T14th), and two card-saving top 10s when a career-best T3rd at 125/1 in the BC Open and T6th in the International at altitude.

NATch-ik is a classic example of a very, very accurate, short hitting player with a cold putter. His lack of length (263 yards) is an obvious handicap playing alongside guys hitting it miles (well 25 yards+) further.

> Most really straight hitters (Joe Durant, Olin Browne et alia) eventually have a week when their putters warm up and they gain a big-odds victory.

  Having four wins on the BUY.COM tour and having shown plenty of bottle in this year's BC Open he could spring a surprise in 2001.

> His best form this year was unquestionably from late June.

> His best chance will surely be in the BC Open where he was very impressive this year when T3rd.

Key stat   T6th for greens in regulation.

SCOTT HOCH

Age 45   **Born** North Carolina   **Lives** Florida

US Tour wins 8, four in 1980s, then 1994 Bob Hope Classic, 1995 Greater Milwaukee Open, 1996 Michelob Championship at Kingsmill, 1997 Greater Milwaukee Open **International wins** 6, last the 1995 Dutch Open **Ryder Cup** 1997 **Presidents Cup** 1994, 1996, 1998 **Major wins** None - Has 12 career top 10s in US Majors, BEF US Masters 2nd 1989 **Money list** BEF 6th 1997

Scott has had his usual (by recent standards) year in which he made 80% of his cuts, didn't win, yet posted a series of consistent finishes to earn well over a million dollars!

His highest finish came when he was T2nd at 40/1 in the inaugural Pennsylvania Classic. He also posted top 10s in the Shell Houston Open (T7th), the Compaq Classic (T9th), the Western Open (T9th), the Buick Challenge (T5th) and the Michelob (T9th). He also had top 25s in the Nissan Open (T25th), the Bay Hill (T14th), the Players (T13th), the MCI Classic (T15th), the Memorial (T13th), the Fedex St Jude Classic (T20th), the Greater Milwaukee Open (T22nd) and the Reno-Tahoe Open (T12th).

He missed the cut in the US Masters, and finished T16th in the US Open and T74th in the USPGA.

In the World Match Play he beat Stuart Appleby (by 1 hole), Lee Westwood (by 1 hole), before losing at the 19th to Jesper Parnevik in R3. T17th in the WGC American Express Championship.

The stats show the same broad Hoch picture....of a short hitting (270 yards) accurate player with consistent all round stats.

> It's now almost a hundred tournaments since Scott won, and it could be that his short hitting is now too big a handicap. However he may just have one last win in him.

> His astonishing consistency is shown by two key facts over the last six years that make him a player to always consider (and never oppose) in match bets
  * He's made 88% of his cuts
  * He's posted a top 25 finish in 52% of his tournaments
> He can be followed on the spreads (selling his finishing position) and in match bets in four tournaments where he is very much Mr Consistency:-
  * The Western Open. 9th (2000), MC (1999), 7th (1998), 13th (1997)
  * Compaq Classic. T9th-T12th-T12th-T11th over the last four years
  * Players Championship. 3rd-6th-5th-2nd over the last four years
  * Nissan Open 25th-7th-3rd in the last three years and his LT stroke average is among the top 8.
  If he's to win again it will probably be in one of those events.
> At his best in warm humid conditions. Self confessedly does not enjoy playing in wind or rain. Despite his T9th finish this year it is noticeable that his form in the Michelob has deteriorated since the tournament moved from summer to early October.
> His steady iron play gives him a lot of close matches (which he wins) in the opening round of the World Match Play. Indeed he's won in R1 in each year to date.

Key stat   He's posted a top 25 finish in more than half his tournaments in the last five years.

BRADLEY HUGHES

Age 33   **Born** Australia   **Lives** Florida

US Tour wins BEF T2nd 1998 CVS Charity Classic **International wins** 5, all in Australia latest 1998 Australian Masters **Presidents Cup** 1994 **World Cup** 1996, 1997 **Money list** BEF 80th 1998

Brad has had a most inconsistent year in which he missed eighteen of his first twenty-eight cuts up to early October.

This year he'd been struggling with only three top 20 finishes, in the Bob Hope Chrysler Classic (T12th), the Buick Invitational (T8th) and the Nissan Open (T5th at 125/1) until he won $105K to secure his card when T5th at 150/1 in the Michelob. Finished T18th in the NCR Classic at Disney in October.

His stats show clearly that he's really struggled both in his approach play and particularly on the greens.

He's a fine player in windy conditions.

> His most consistent tournament over the last two years has undoubtedly been the Nissan Open (T5th 2000: T15th 1999) in which he's shot eight successive rounds at or under par for a stroke average of 69.25. He'll be worth a small each-way interest in the top Rest of The World market (won 16/1 this year) for the 2001 Nissan Open.

> Clearly he enjoys the Kingsmill course where he's been 'in the frame' in two of the last three years (T5th 2000, T4th 1998) and he shot a 63 (his best ever) in R2 this year. Worth a place-only bet if 25/1 is again on offer in 2001.

> His R4 scoring record is truly dreadful. Ranked 182nd in 1999 (73.68 per R4) he was again outside the top 150 this year. When in contention, as in the Michelob this year (over par 72 in R4), he can be opposed on Sunday.

Key stat   170th for putting average.

JOHN HUSTON **g**

Age 39   **Born** Illinois   **Lives** Florida

US Tour wins 6, 1990 Honda Classic, 1992 Walt Disney Classic, 1994 Doral Ryder Open, 1998 Hawaiian Open, Walt Disney Classic, 2000 Tampa Bay Classic **Major wins** BEF T3rd 1990 US Masters **Money list** BEF 10th 1998

Johnny Ray (yes it's his real name!) has had a good season winning well over a million dollars. He made four really big top 5 finishes, in the Sony Open in Hawaii (T3rd at 20/1), the Bell South Classic (T5th at 33/1), the Byron Nelson Classic (T4th at 50/1) and most significantly in the US Open (4th at 80/1). However his sixth tour win came in late October at his local Copperhead course when he won the Tampa Bay Classic at 80/1*

He also had top 10s in the Bob Hope (T7th), the MCI Classic (T9th) and the Canon Greater Hartford Open (T9th).

He had a top 25 in the Colonial (T20th).

In the US Masters he finished T14th, missed the cut in the British Open, and was 71st in the USPGA. In the World Match Play he lost in R1 to Maruyama. T25th in the Tour Championship.

Not long at 272 yards he has always had a good short game and this year his putting (up from T86th to top 30) has been the basis for his success as his accuracy percentages are virtually unchanged. In the top 40 for birdie conversion and 7th for par 4 birdies. He'll be 40 in June 2001. Bothered by a bad back

> Five of his six wins have come in his native Florida. His best chance in his home state next year may well be in the Doral Ryder Open in which he was the winner in 1994, and the 2nd in 1998.

> He simply must be backed at 33/1 to win the NCR golf classic at Walt Disney in early November. He won it in 1998, was T5th in 1999, and let's forget his missed cut this year as he had MLD having won the week before.

> He simply loves the Waialae course in Honolulu. "I feel I don't have to play my best to do well. You have to keep the ball down and you don't have to drive it really far". No wonder his form figures are T3rd-T12th-Won (by 7 shots). So make 'Huston for Hawaii' your slogan when the Sony Open is played in Honolulu early in 2001.

> He has the best four-year stroke average (68.72) of any player for the Bell South Classic and with form figures of 5th-3rd-5th-DNP he's an each-way must bet at Sugarloaf in 2001.

> T7th (2000): 3rd (1999): T10th (1998) are impressive finishes in the Bob Hope Classic in the last three years so back Huston with a few BOB in the HOPE that he wins at 33/1.

> He can be backed with confidence especially in match bets for the MCI Classic where he's posted three successive top 10s (9th-5th-10th) for a three-year stroke average of 69.25.

> His record in the US Masters, in which he's made all eleven cuts, is impressive. I can't see him winning but he's worth supporting in suitable match and spread bets.

Key stats   T30th for putting average.

LEE JANZEN   ▌

Age 36   **Born** Minnesota   **Lives** Florida

US Tour wins 6 – 1992 Northern Telecom Open, 1993 Phoenix Open, 1994 Buick Classic, 1995 Players Championship, Kemper Open, Sprint International **Major wins** 2, US Open in 1993 and 1998 **Presidents Cup** 1998 **Dunhill Cup** 1995 **Ryder Cup** 1993, 1997 **Money list** BEF 3rd 1995

20th (1998) and 48th (1999) on the Money list in the last two seasons his gradual decline continued in 2000.

He posted two top 10s in the Players Championship (T9th) and the Tampa Bay Classic (T6th), and seven top 20s, in the Phoenix Open (T18th), the Nissan Open (T12th), the Kemper Open (T16th), the Advil Western Open (T15th), the Renoe-Tahoe (T17th), the Invensys Classic in Las Vegas (T15th) and in the season's final major, the USPGA (T19th).

In the US Open he was T37th. He missed the cut in the British Open and in the US Masters (first time in nine years). In the WGC Match Play he lost in R1 to Steve Stricker 2 and 1.

From 1996 to 1999 Lee had been in the top 12 for putting whereas this year he's outside the top 65, and his all round ranking is the lowest it's been since 1994. His R4 scoring (167th in 1999) is again just outside the top 100.

> In the last three years he's let winning chances slip on four occasions showing a tendency to hook under pressure.

  * 1999 Canadian Open. 76 in R4 to lose the lead and finish T3rd
  * 1998 Players Championship. 3-shot leader after R3, he shot 79 in R4, to finish T13th.
  * 1998 Shell Houston Open. Leader with 7 to play he finished T4.
  * 2000 Western Open. 3rd after R3 he shot 75 in R4 to finish T15.

So he may be an eight-time tour winner with two US Opens to his credit yet in 'ordinary' tournaments he clearly merits the 'bottle'.

In non majors he can be opposed in R4 2-ball betting if he's in the top 4 after R3.

> Showed his best form this year in his home state of Florida.

> Worth following in match bets in the Phoenix Open where he's posted four consecutive top 20s in the tournament he won in 1993.

> Lee's last non-major USPGA win was way back in 1995. If he's to change that he must improve his all round game, regain his putting touch, improve his final round scoring and possibly have a greater desire.

> His record shows he's best on tough courses (where par is a good score) especially in the summer (five of his eight wins).

Key stats   T13th for birdie conversion last year he slipped to 50th this year.

BRANDT JOBE   V D

Age 35   **Born** Oklahoma   **Lives** Texas

US tour BEF 4th 1999 Reno-Tahoe Open, T4th 2000 Phoenix Open **International wins** 9, 2 in Canada, 1 in Thailand and 6 in Japan including 3 in Japan in 1998.

Moving from the Canadian tour Brandt played successfully on the Japanese tour up to and including 1999.

In 1999 on the US tour he was 4th in the Reno-Tahoe Open. This year he made a fast start winning $132,000 in the Phoenix Open (T4th at 125/1) and had high finishes in the Bell South Classic (T22nd), the Canadian Open (T10th), the NCR at Walt Disney (T18th) and the Southern Farm Bureau (T13th).

He missed the cut in the US Open, and finished 48th in the US Masters. In the World Match Play he lost in R1 to Lee Westwood (3 and 1).

Long hitter at 280 yards he's been inaccurate off the tee and very ineffective (168th) with the putter this year.

> His best chance will probably be in the Canadian Open. He's won twice in Canada in the early nineties when he won the Order of Merit. He led after 63 in R1 in 1999 when T48th, and he was T10th this year.

Key stat   167th for driving accuracy.

STEVE JONES

Age 42   **Born** New Mexico   **Lives** Montana

US Tour wins 7, four in 1980s, and three in nineties - 1997 Phoenix Open, 1997 Canadian Open, and 1998 Quad City Classic **Major wins** 1, 1996 US Open **Money list** BEF 20th 1997

In 2000 Steven Glen (you can call him Steve) has played consistently, regularly making cuts. He's posted two top 5 finishes, in the Tucson Open (T5th at 66/1*) and in the Bell South Classic (T5th at 80/1).

He's also posted top 25s in the Sony Open in Hawaii (T22nd), the John Deere Classic (T12th) and the International (T21st).

He's played consistently to make the cut in all 4 majors, finishing T25th in the US Masters, T27th in the US Open, T31st in the British Open, and T24th in the USPGA.

His bunker play is still poor and let him down for example in the US Masters. A long hitter at 279 yards. He's hitting fewer greens this year. His putting has improved a lot and has been the main basis for his consistency.

> Yet to win in Florida he's probably at his best on bent grass greens.

> He had a fine record in the John Deere Classic (Won 1998, 5th 1999, 3rd 1996) before it moved to the Deere Run course where he finished T12th this year. Steve will have a real chance in one of his favourite tournaments in Illinois in 2001.

> He has a good desert record, and will be worth a bet in the Tucson Open where he was T5th this year.

> Steve is just the sort of player who enjoys 'giggle-golf' and could post a shock win in the 2001 Bob Hope Chrysler Classic (T4th 1998-T9th 1997).

Key stat   147th for sand saves last year he was 140th this year.

PETE JORDAN   V

Age 36   **Born** Illinois   **Lives** Florida
US tour wins BEF 2nd 1996 BC Open **Money list** BEF 107th 2000

In 2000 Pete has posted two really big finishes when T4th at 125/1 in the Fedex St Jude Classic, and T4th at 200/1 in the Southern Farm Bureau Classic to save his card! He also had top 25s in the Tucson Open (T25th), the Honda Classic (T19th), the Shell Houston Open (T11th) and the Texas Open (T19th).

However he's been making 70% of his cuts because he has been accurate off the tee hitting a very good 76% of his fairways.

However, he's short off the tee at 262 yards and his putting average is poor, outside the top 150.

> After two hundred tournaments Pete has posted only eight top 10s, so it's 24/1 against him posting a top 10 on that basis and therefore it's difficult to nominate him with any confidence.

> However in 3-ball betting when 'off the pace' in R4 of the Fedex St Jude Classic he can be followed as his 63 (1999) and 66 (2000) show. If he's to have a big 2001 finish it will surely be at Southwind, as his recent form there (T4th 2000: T18th 1999) is clearly good.

Key stat   T9th for driving accuracy

JONATHAN KAYE   V

Age 30   **Born** Colorado   **Lives** Phoenix, Arizona
US Tour wins BEF 2nd 1995 Quad City Classic, T2nd 2000 Pennsylvania Classic
Money list BEF 40th 2000

Having finished in the top 50 on the M/L last year Jonathan Andrew has maintained his form in 2000 although his first win still eludes him.

He had three big finishes in the Greater Greensboro Classic (T5th at 80/1) the Pennsylvania Classic (T2nd at 125/1*) and in the Invensys Classic in Las Vegas (T3rd at 80/1*). He also had top 25s in the Tucson Open (T17th), the MCI Classic (T11th), the Shell Houston Open (T11th), the Bay Hill (T14th), the Memorial (T25th), the Canon Greater Hartford Open (T18th) and the BC Open (T18th).

Missed the US Open cut. Finished T51st in the USPGA.

Driving Accuracy has improved this year (by 6%) so he's in the top 15 for Total driving. A sound putter who's in the top 20 for birdie conversion. Hits a flat fade. He was 30 in August 2000. Girlfriend Jennifer (a good player herself) acts as his caddie.

> He looks to be in the 'winner about to happen' category having had two successive successful years. However a couple of warning signs about R4 pressure were shown this year.

  * Tucson Open. T4th after R3 he shot 75 in R4 to finish T17th.

  * Honda Classic. T2nd after R3 he shot 70 in R4 to finish 6th.

> He must be expected to go close in the Canon Greater Hartford Open (18th 2000: 26th 1999) in a tournament won by first timers in three of the last four years.

> His best chance will probably be in the BC Open with its weaker field. Top 20 this year, 4th in 1999 Jonathan could win at the En Joie the course in 2001. O'Kaye?

> His bare form in the Kemper Open (T28th in last two years) is not really special. However he's shot four of his last five rounds in the sixties so he'll merit each-way support on the TPC at Avenel in 2001.

> Keep an eye on him for the 2001 Shell Houston Open in a first-timers tournament he's got first class recent form (T11th 2000: T5th 1999).

> Living in Arizona he's a good desert player, and must be noted for the Tucson Open (T17th this year) and particularly for the Invensys Classic in Las Vegas where he's shot final rounds of 64 (1999) and 62 (this year). 2nd in 1999 and T3rd this year he loves the set up which suits his flat fade. Could well win in Vegas from 'off the pace' in 2001.

> He can be backed with confidence at 50/1 for the Southern Farm Bureau Classic if he gets an early tee time. 18th in 1998, 6th in 1999 he got the worst of the weather when T36th this year for a three-year stroke average of 69.10.

Key stat   T10th for birdie conversion.

JERRY KELLY   V

Age 34   **Born** Wisconsin   **Lives** Wisconsin

US Tour wins None, BEF 2nd 1996 Greater Milwaukee Open **BUY.COM tour wins** 2, both in 1995 when he was top of NIKE Money list **Money list** BEF 59th in 1996 and 2000

Jerome Patrick (you can call him Jerry) has had a very consistent year, making a 'whole bunch of cuts (fifteen from seventeen) from late March to early September.

He posted two lucrative top 5 finishes in the AT&T (T4th at 125/1) and the BC Open (T5th at 50/1), and a top 10 in the Sony Open in Hawaii (T9th).

He also had top 25s in the MCI Classic (T15th), the Memorial (T25th), the Reno-Tahoe Open (T17th), the Air Canada (T13th), the Texas Open (T14th), the Buick Challenge (T18th), the Tampa Bay Classic (T19th) and the Southern Farm Bureau (T13th).

In the majors he finished T37th in the US Open and missed the cut in the USPGA.

Not long off the tee (274 yards), he has a sound short game.

> His R4 scoring continues to be his problem and explains why he's still to win. Last year I listed six tournaments in 1999 in which he finished poorly when in serious contention. This year in the Hawaiian Open (72 in R4), the MCI Classic (71 in R4), the Greater Greensboro Classic (77 in R4), the Air Canada (71 in R4) and especially in the BC Open (71 in R4) he has shown once more his 'achilles heel'.

He clearly has the talent to win. However if he's to do so it will surely be when coming from 'off the pace' as in this year's AT&T where he finished T4th after 67 in R4.

> His reliable consistency as a poor R4 scorer and a good pre cut R1 and R2 scorer do provide genuine first class betting opportunities.

* He cries out to be backed in the opening rounds of the Greater Milwaukee Open. In the last five years his scoring average before the cut is 67.6, and in R2 it's an amazing 67! He's certainly a must for match bets in this his local tournament (3rd 1999: T8th 1997: 2nd 1996).

* In the Greater Greensboro Classic he must be opposed in R4 2-ball betting if he's in the top 12 after R3. In three of the last four years he's been in the front dozen on Sunday morning and then shot 77 (2000), 76 (1998) and 77 (1997)!

> In the Shell Houston Open his form figures (17th-17th-6th-6th) in the last four years are very consistent with thirteen of those sixteen rounds under par. With a reputation for first-time winners he could come from 'off the pace' and be the shock winner at the Woodlands in 2001.

Key stat   His R4 scoring is still poor although it's improving—viz 150th (1997), 128th (1998), 105th (1999) and 99th (2000).

SKIP KENDALL   V

Age 36   **Born** Wisconsin   **Lives** Florida

US Tour wins BEF 2nd 1998 Buick Invitational **BUY.COM tour wins** 2, both in 1994 **Money list** BEF 32nd 1998

Jules (let's call him Skip) Kendall had had a steady year with one big finish when he won over $200,000 when 3rd at 125/1 in the Bay Hill Invitational until he finished 2nd in November in the Southern Farm Bureau Classic, losing to a 40-foot putt on the first extra play-off hole.

He also posted top 25s in the Honda Classic (T19th), the Colonial (T13th), the Buick Open (T11th) and the NCR at Walt Disney (T18th), and a top 10 in the Greater Milwaukee Open (T9th).

He was 56th (of 57) in the US Masters, and T27th in the USPGA. Short, at 270 yards off the tee, Skip's all round ranking (22nd in 1999) has fallen this year. He's a very good putter, and is always highly ranked for birdie conversion at 31-32%.

Still looking for that elusive first win after over one-hundred-and-ninety starts.

> Born in Wisconsin his 'home' tournament is the Greater Milwaukee Open. His form is very solid, T9th 2000: 6th 1999: 23rd 1998: 12th 1997. He can be backed each way as a big-priced outsider, or, if he's off the pace on Sunday, do back him in the 2 balls in R4 (68-65-65 in R4 in the last three years).

> Must be noted for match bets in the Buick Open (11th-19th-36th-49th) where his recent form is solid.

> Can be followed in the Canon Greater Hartford Open (2nd 1999: T32nd 2000) on a course suited to his game.

Key stat   T18th for birdie conversion.

GREG KRAFT   V S

Age 36   **Born** Michigan   **Lives** Florida

US Tour wins BEF 2nd 1993 Walt Disney Classic, 1994 Western Open, 1999 Doral Ryder Open, 1999 Colonial **Money list** BEF 52nd 1999

Greg entered 2000 having notched four 2nd places but no wins in his 234 USPGA starts. By the end of the season that elusive first win is still coming.

He's had one really big finish in the Advil Western Open (T3rd at 125/1 after 68 in R4) to win $156K.

He also had a top 10 in the Colonial (T6th) and top 25s in the Players Championship (T22nd), the Memorial (T13th), the Air Canada (T22nd) and the Tampa Bay Classic (T19th).

Greg is very much a streak player capable of shooting really low numbers. His lack of length (267 yards) is a big handicap. Ranked outside the top 140 in the last two years for total driving.

> When winning chances have presented themselves he's tended to be over aggressive, notably at the 1999 Doral Ryder Open.

> Last year I nominated him for the Western Open where he finished fast to be T3rd at 125/1. It was his third top 5 finish in the tournament in the last seven years (T5th 1998 2nd 1994). So although it's now blindingly obvious he'd be worth support at Cog Hill in 2001.

> In the last four years he's finished 12th-44th-27th-22nd in the Air Canada Championship for an eclectic score of 16 under. In a tournament that's thrown up four first-time winners in the last five years GREG could by a KRAFTy bet there in 2001.

Key stat   In over 300 starts on the BUY.COM and USPGA tours he's yet to win.

NEAL LANCASTER

S

Age 38   **Born** North Carolina   **Lives** North Carolina

US tour wins 1, 1994 Byron Nelson Classic **Money list** BEF 58th 1994

Having lost his card in 1999 when 139th on the M/L he played superbly when 3rd at Q School to regain it.

In 2000 he's retained his card with one big finish when T4th in the Bay Hill Invitational winning $132K. He also had a top 10 in the John Deere Classic (T8th), and top 25s in the Bob Hope (T23rd), the AT&T (T15th) and the Buick Invitational (T21st).

His perennial problems remains inaccuracy off the tee. Although inconsistent his putting can be sensational. Indeed he's shot 29 for the inward half, and also 29 for the outward half (in the 1995 US Open when T4th) in different tournaments.

> Living in North Carolina the Greater Greensboro Classic is his home tournament. Ten of his last twelve rounds have been under par and he's finished 4th (1998), 12th 1999 (all under par) and T34th in 2000 (69 in R4) so he can be followed in 3-ball betting, and as a 125/1 outsider who could make the frame for the second time in four years.

> A small investment on 'streaker' Neal in the 2001 John Deere Classic could pay a rich dividend. On the new course this year he was T8th (5 off the leader) after four sub-70 rounds.

> Neal could well create a 100/1 shock in the 2001 AT&T where he's finished T15th (2000), 8th (1999), T20th (1997) and where his stroke average in the last two years (70.28) is impressive.

Key stat   142nd for driving accuracy.

FRANKLIN LANGHAM

V FT

Age 32   **Born** Georgia   **Lives** Georgia

US Tour wins BEF T2nd 1998 Southern Farm Bureau Classic, 2nd 2000 Doral Ryder Open, 2nd 2000 Kemper Open, 2nd 2000 Greater Milwaukee Open. **BUY.COM tour wins** 1, in 1993 **Money list** BEF 26th 2000

James Franklin has had a truly stunning 'nappy factor' year. He posted no fewer than three 2nd place finishes, in the Doral Ryder Open (2nd at 150/1), the Kemper Open (T2nd at 125/1) and the Greater Milwaukee Open (2nd at 50/1). He also had top 10s in the Western Open (T6th), the Renoe-Tahoe Open (T7th) and the Canadian Open (T6th), and top 25s in the Bell South Classic (T15th), the Compaq Classic (T11th), the Byron Nelson (T20th) and the International (T24th).

In his very first major he finished a most creditable 7th in the USPGA. 28th (of 29) in the Tour Championship. T17th in the WGC American Express Championship.

His stats are very good although he's shortish off the tee at 274 yards. His improvement is based on improved driving accuracy (up 3%) and some really brilliant putting (birdie conversion up 3%).

> He 'blew it' big style in the Doral Ryder Open when he lost a 6 shot lead with 6 to play to lose by 2 shots to Jim Furyk, and in the Greater Milwaukee Open he shot a disappointing over par 72 in R4. The jury therefore is 'still out' on his final round scoring when under pressure as his scoring on Sunday overall is very good.

> At his very best this year from June after which he shot six top 10 in seven starts.

> He can be followed in four tournaments in 2001 in which his recent form is really good.

* The Western Open. 6th 2000: T17th 1999 for an eclectic score of 15 under par which would have won this year.

* The Kemper Open. A first time winners' tournament. His last 5 rounds, all under par, average 68.4(!). 2nd this year he could win it in 2001.

* The Compaq Classic. 15 under par for his last 54 holes this year. He shot 74 in R1 in both 1996 (T15th) and 1999 (T51st) so in 2001 I suggest you back him AFTER R1 if he's off to a sound start.

* The Reno-Tahoe Open. Played in both years (T7th 2000) and his eclectic total, 18 under par, is a winning one!

Key stat   T12th for putting average.

IAN LEGGATT

Age 35   **Born** Ontario, Canada   **Lives** Ontario, Canada
University   Texas

BUY.COM Tour wins 1, 2000 BUY.COM Dayton Open **US tour** BEF T56th 1998 Air Canada

Ian has had a really successful year on the BUY.COM tour having qualified via BUY.COM Q school. He's earned his full tour card for 2001.

In 2000 he hit form in June finishing 2nd in the BUY.COM Steamtown Classic (65 in R4) before he won the BUY.COM Dayton Open after a play-off the following week. He also had top 4 finishes in the BUY.COM Louisiana Open (T2nd) and the BUY.COM Richmond Open (T3rd).

On the USPGA he played on the 'Canadian Swing' in September missing the cut in both the Air Canada and the Canadian Open.

His BUY.COM stats show him to be a long (289 yards) but not accurate (70th) driver.

> Played really well for Canada in the 1998 World Cup in New Zealand finishing T8th in the individual rankings. So he has proved himself at a high level.

> A born and bred Canadian he will look forward to the 'Canadian Swing' where he should post his BEF in the Air Canada as I expect he'll make the 2001 cut after his 69 in R2 this year.

Key stat   70th for driving accuracy on the 2000 BUY.COM tour.

664 • Elliott's Golf Form 2001

TOM LEHMAN

G F 🏇 ☉

Age 41   **Born** Minnesota   **Lives** Arizona

College Minnesota

US Tour wins 4, 1994 Memorial, 1995 the Colonial, 1996 Tour Championship, 2000 Phoenix Open **Major wins** 1, 1996 British Open **International wins** 2, 1993 Casio World Open (Jap), 1997 Loch Lomond (Europe) **Ryder Cup** 1993,97,99 **Dunhill Cup** 1999, 2000 **Presidents Cup** 1994,1996,1998, 2000 **World Cup** 1996 **Money list** Top 1996

Tom, fresh from his dancing on the 17th at Brookline, was on the comeback trail this year. He won a non USPGA event, the Williams Challenge at 20/1 in Scottsdale, Arizona to give us warning of his determination. He then secured his 'comeback' win before his home crowd when he landed the Phoenix Open at 28/1, also in Scottsdale, Arizona.

He also posted a top 5 finish in the MCI Classic (2nd at 18/1) and high finishes in the Sony Open in Hawaii (T6th), the AT&T (T7th), the Players Championship (8th), the Greater Greensboro Classic (T16th) and the Kemper Open (T13th).

In the Andersen World Match Play he beat Magee (5 and 4) before losing to Jimenez (4 and 3). In the WGC NEC Invitational he finished a poor T31st and was T18th in the Tour Championship.

In the majors he was 6th at Augusta, T23rd in the US Open and T4th in the British Open. He withdrew from the USPGA after an 82 in R1. Won two of his three games in a weak USA team in the Dunhill Cup. In the Presidents Cup he scored 3 pts losing to Elkington (1 hole) in the singles.

Tom's great strength is his accuracy to the putting surface where he's hit 70% of his greens in reg. this year. However his putting has never been his strength and his birdie conversion ranking (T163 in 1999) remains low. His stock shot is a draw and he finds it difficult to vary from it.

> He had a knee operation in the late summer and so he's once more in a sense, on the comeback trail. Assuming he'll be fully fit he'll be a profitable player to follow in 2001 as the following points show.

> "I like firm conditions, there's no question about that....I think it forces you to be really patient, first of all, and to be very focused and I guess when I focus well I play well. The hard conditions and the big tournaments really narrow my focus".

So expect Tom to be at his best in the really big tournaments and on firm going!!

> Tom fell in love with Sawgrass at Q school in 1983. "I always look forward to playing there", where his record of six top 15s in eight starts is first class. 8th (2000), MC (1999 when unfit), 2nd (1998) and 6th (1997) is a superb recent bank of form. Tom must be backed each way for the 2001 Players Championship and given serious support in match bets and on the spreads.

> Lehman could well become 'Major Tom' in 2001 as two of the majors, the US and British Open, return to courses where he's won before.

> There are two key reasons for thinking that Tom can do really well in the 2001 US Open.

First, it will be played at Southern Hills in Tulsa. Oklahoma and when that course was last used for the 1996 Tour Championship Tom won by 6 shots, and was ranked top for greens in reg and T3rd for putting. (Tiger, of course, was then still an amateur).

Second, the US Open set up is all about accuracy which is Tom's strength and explains why he had a sequence from 1995 to 1998 of 3rd-T2nd-3rd-T5th in this major.

The reason I can't see him winning is that his inability to deviate from his stock draw shot can be a handicap. Nevertheless he must be expected to play well and he can be supported in match bets, on the spreads, and in the 'without Tiger' markets.

> He'll be 'defending champion' at Royal Lytham in the 2001 British Open having won there in 1996 in hot, dry conditions. T4th this year I expect Tom to have a big tournament next year if it's hot and dry again. He can be supported each way to be top American (without Woods) in which market he won this year at 12/1.

> He has a proven record at Augusta T3rd (1993), 2nd (1994) and 6th this year when he was ranked 2nd for greens in reg. Of course, you'd expect his putting will let him down and prevent Tom from winning. However that was said (OK, by me, I know!) before Vijay Singh's win this year.

> He loves the week before the British Open. He takes his family over to Scotland for the Loch Lomond where in three starts he has a stroke average of 68.41 having won in 1997, finished 9th a year later, and 2nd this year.

He was top US player at 9/2 this year. At that price in 2001 he'd be an each-way 'steal'.

> There are three USPGA tournaments in which he must be expected to play well and in which he can be supported in match bets and on the spreads.

* The AT&T. He's in the top 10 for his long-term stroke average. In his last three starts (7th 2000, 9th 1998, 20th 1997) he has a stroke average of 69.36 and Pebble Beach is his favourite course.

* The Sony Open in Hawaii. In eight starts he's finished in the top 6 five times. Ignore his 69th in 1999 when he had his shoulder problem. He's a must sell in the finishing positions on the spreads.

* The Greater Greensboro Classic. Three starts in the last five years have given him solid form figures of 16-5-11.

> However he really can be opposed in the Nissan Open held on the Riviera course that doesn't suit his stock shot, a draw. He's had only eight of his twenty-three rounds there below par.

Key stat   Tom's not taking his chances. 163rd for birdie conversion last year he's 151st (!) this year.

JUSTIN LEONARD   G Y

Age 28   **Born** Texas   **Lives** Texas
College Texas

US Tour wins 4, 1996 Buick Open, 1997 Kemper Open, 1998 Players Championship, 2000 Texas Open **Major wins** 1, 1997 British Open **Ryder Cup** 1997, 1999 **Presidents Cup** 1996, 1998 **Dunhill Cup** 1997 **World Cup** 1997 **Money list** BEF 5th 1997

Charles Garret are his middle names Justin case you're wondering, and after a winless 1999 he's notched tour win number 4 this year. It came in his home state when he won the Texas Open at 16/1. He also had a couple of top 5 finishes in consecutive weeks in the Memorial (T2nd at 80/1) and the Kemper Open (T2nd at 20/1). He also posted high finishes in the Phoenix Open (T23rd), the AT&T (T15th), the Greater Greensboro Classic (T16th), the Invensys Classic in Las Vegas (T22nd) and the Tampa Bay Classic (T14th).

In the Andersen World Match Play he beat Furyk 6 and 5 before losing to Maruyama. In the WGC NEC Invitational he recorded his third second place of the year when finishing T2nd at 66/1.

In the Majors he finished T28th in the US Masters, T16th in the US Open, T41st in the British Open and T41st in the USPGA so he'd made every cut yet he had never been in contention. T16th in the Tour Championship

Short at 270 yards off the tee. He's improved his driving accuracy to 73%. However in an inconsistent season his other stats have slipped so his all round ranking 17th last year has fallen considerably. Top 10 for sand saves in the previous two years he's outside the top 80 in 2000.

> This year he's been re-adjusting his swing in order to achieve greater length. This, in essence, accounts for his inconsistent form.

  It could also be that his concentration on his swing has been to the detriment of his short game as his rankings for birdie conversion (outside top 100), sand saves (outside top 80) and putting (not in top 40) have deteriorated sharply.

> Justin finished 6th in 1996 as a 24-year-old when the Tour Championship was played at Southern Hills so he'll be happy to return there for the 2001 US Open. T15th in 1999 and T16th in 2000, he can be fancied for a third successive top 20 so remember him for match bets and on the spreads.

> In the last couple of years Justin has the second best stroke average for the AT&T after having a poor record before 1999. T15th 2000: T4th 1999 so keep an eye on him at Pebble Beach.

> He'll be the defending champion for the Texas Open in 2001. Won 2000, 2nd 1998, 11th 1996, and 2nd 1995 in four starts speaks for itself. However the pressures of being home state defending champion may just prevent him from winning it again. However he will not defend his title if he's in the Ryder Cup side.

Key stat   112th (at 272.1 yards) for driving distance.

J L LEWIS

Age 40   **Born** Kansas   **Lives** Texas

College Texas

US Tour wins 1, 1999 John Deere Classic (after play-off) **BUY.COM tour** BEF three 2nd places **Money list** BEF 66th 1999

Big John (he's 6 foot 3 in his slippers) made the breakthrough in 1999 with his first win in the John Deere Classic to end the year 66th on the M/L.

So 2000 has been a disappointment with just one really big finish in the Bob Hope where he was T3rd at 125/1 winning $174K.

He made two other top 20s, in the Doral Ryder Open (T15th) and the Air Canada (T11th), and one top 10 when T10th in the Canadian Open. Missed the cut in the US Open.

He finished T27th (of 30) in the all-winners Mercedes Championship.

A long hitter at 278 yards his strength is accuracy to the greens, his weakness his poor R4 scoring especially when in contention. He was 40 in July 2000.

> He had two good winning chances in consecutive weeks in September yet he couldn't take them
>   * Air Canada. T2nd after R3, he shot a par 72 in R4 to finish T11th.
>   * Canadian Open. T3rd after R3, he shot 75 in R4 to finish T10th.
>
> On that evidence he can be opposed when in the top 4 after R3 in normal 72-hole tournaments.

> Wide fairway courses suit his long, if not always accurate, driving so his T3rd in the Bob Hope this year was not too surprising. Worth noting there in 2001.

> He is clearly very well suited to the La Cantera course which favours experienced course specialists. In his last four starts he's posted successive top 20 finishes so he's a must for match bets and at 66/1 J.L. will represent each-way value for the 2001 Texas Open.

Key stat   T41st for greens in regulation.

FRANK LICKLITER   V

Age 31   **Born** Florida   **Lives** Ohio

US Tour wins BEF 2nd 1999 AT&T **BUY.COM Tour wins** 1, in 1995 **Money list** BEF 44th 1999

Franklin Ray (answers to Frank) was in his fifth successive year on tour during which time he's progressively improved his ML position.

In 2000 he posted three top 5 finishes, when T5th in the Texas Open at 80/1, 3rd in the Michelob at 66/1 and T3rd at 50/1 in the Tampa Bay Classic.. He also had top 10s in the Phoenix Open (T10th), the Western Open (T9th) and the Greater Milwaukee Open (T9th), and top 25s in the MCI Classic (T25th), and the Pennsylvania Classic (T12th).

Missed the cut in the US Open.

A short hitter at around 268 yards he's accurate off the tee (top 25 last year and this). 3rd in putting last year he's slipped back to outside the top 60 this season which in essence explains his less impressive season.

His sand save stats (55%) are still poor (outside top 70 last three years) and need improvement. A fader of the ball.

Credited his fine form from mid September to the fact that he went back to his old irons and "it has really made a difference". Frank has got a degree in Sociology - that's the subject that studies people who don't need studying by people who do!

> His big problem has been his R4 scoring. 163rd at 72.48 in 1998, he improved to be 84th in 1999 at 71.86, and in 2000 he's outside the top 140 again.

His shakiness when near the lead showed in

* The Bob Hope. T7th after R4. He shot 74 in R5 to finish T28th.
* The Phoenix Open. R3 leader, he shot 74 in R4 to finish T10th
* Greater Milwaukee Open. Tied 1st at halfway, he finished T9th.
* John Deere Classic. T5th after R3, he finished T23rd.
* Pennsylvania Classic. T2nd after R3 then 76 to finish T12th.

However in the Autumn he got into contention three times and uncharacteristically did very well in R4 each time:-

* Texas Open. Shot 67 in R4 when 'contention average' was 68.5. Finished T5th.
* Michelob. Shot 69 in R4 when 'contention average' was 71.47. Finished 3rd.
* Tampa Bay Classic. Shot 69 in R4 when 'contention average' was 71.22.

Following these autumnal final rounds I think he'll definitely gain that elusive first win in 2001.

> Capable of low numbers as he showed this year with a career low 62 (Bob Hope R4), 64 (Phoenix R2), 65 (Bell South R2), 65 (Greater Milwaukee Open, R1) and 65 (Texas Open R2). So he's definitely a streaker!

> A very good low scorer in early rounds he must never be opposed in R1 or R2 3-ball betting.

> His short yet accurate driving is tailor made for the Kingsmill course (3rd 2000: T6th 1998) where he could win for the first time in the 2001 Michelob Championship.

> He has such a consistent record in the Western Open (9th-17th-17th in the last three years) that he merits match bet support.

Key stat   24th for driving accuracy.

DAVIS LOVE   G S

Age 35   **Born** North Carolina   **Lives** Georgia

US Tour wins 12, 1987 MCI Classic, 1990 The International, 1991 MCI Classic, 1992 Players Championship, MCI Classic, Greater Greensboro Open, 1993 Tournament of Champions, Las Vegas Invitational, 1995 The Compaq Classic,

1996 Buick Invitational, 1997 Buick Challenge, 1998 MCI Classic **Majors** 1, 1997 USPGA **Ryder Cup** 4, last 1999: **Dunhill Cup** 1992 **World Cup** 5, last 1997 **Presidents Cup** 1994,1996, 1998, 2000 **Money list** 2nd 1992: 3rd 1997

For the second successive year Davis has failed to reach the winner's enclosure. However he has posted no fewer than five top 5 finishes, in the Buick Invitational (4th at 20/1), the Bay Hill Invitational (2nd at 20/1), the MCI Classic (T3rd at 12/1), the Byron Nelson Classic (T2nd at 25/1) and the Colonial (T2nd at 14/1). He had high finishes in the Phoenix Open (T18th), the AT&T (T20th), the Honda Classic (T19th), the Greater Greensboro Classic (T21st), the Buick Challenge (T18th) and NCR Classic at Disney (T13th).

Played really well in the WGC World Match Play to finish 4th having beaten Ohlin Browne (2 and 1), Jeff Sluman (3 and 2), Jim Furyk (3 and 2) and Miguel Jimenez (3 and 2) before he lost heavily (5 and 4) in the SF to Tiger.

In the WGC NEC Invitational he was in poor form finishing 35th. T8th in the Tour Championship.

In the Majors he finished T7th in the US Masters, missed the US Open cut, was T11th in the British Open and T9th in the USPGA. In the Presidents Cup (4 points in four games) he beat Ernie Els (4 and 3) in the singles. He was joint top US points scorer at 11/1.

His stats paint an interesting picture. His birdie conversion rate is up 2%, his putting rank is still top 30. However his inaccurate approach play has let him down big style with his driving accuracy down 5%(!). Sand saves are also down by 4%. Can be a really dodgy putter inside 5 feet.

Davis plays a restricted schedule (focussing on the majors and the world tournaments) because of his lumbar problems.

He has a high, wide swing which had been shortened by the end of the season, and drives the ball miles, well 287 plus yards. Brother Mark acts as his caddie

> In 1992 and 1993 he won five tournaments, whereas in the last couple of years he's not won one! Indeed he's shown disappointing form this year in final round(s) on a couple of occasions.

  * Greater Greensboro Classic. T5th after R3, shot 76 in R4, finished T21st.
  * MCI Classic. 1 shot leader after R2 shoots only 1 under par for last 36 holes to finish T3rd.

  So 'contention rust' may be setting in with Davis.

> There are three majors in which he can be supported.

  * The British Open. He's built a very consistent record in the British Open, 4th (1995), T2nd (1996), T16th (1997), MC (1998), T12th (1999) and T11th (2000). I can't see him winning at Royal Lytham yet he does appeal for match bets and as a finishing position sell.

  * The USPGA. In 2001 the venue is in his home state of Georgia and in the tournament that gave him his only major victory he will probably play well. His recent record (W (1997), T7th (1998), T49th (1999), T7th (2000)) is solid, so he must enter calculations.

* The US Masters. He will focus all his early season efforts on 'getting it right' at Augusta. "I want to win this one very badly." With seven of his last eight rounds at or under par, and superb figures of 2nd (1995), T7th (1996), T7th (1997), T33rd (1998), 2nd (1999), T7th (2000) his finishing position MUST be sold on the spreads, he can be followed in match bets and backed each way in the outrights.

> He simply loves the Harbour Town course the week after Augusta. "It's kind of strange that for some reason after the Masters I always come here and play well". Indeed four of his twelve wins, including both his first and his last, were in the MCI Classic. I expect Davis to win his 5th MCI Classic in 2001 so he can be supported on the spreads and in the outrights. However should he win or have been in really serious contention at Augusta I would not support him. Remember the Law of Hilton Head!

> His record from 1992 in the Bay Hill Invitational is amazing. T8th-T8th-T2nd-T16th-T13th-T9th-T17th-3rd-2nd for an average position of 8th-9th yet he's never won and never had a R4 in the 60s! Nevertheless I can see him landing the 2001 Bay Hill and with that record he must warrant support in matches, on the spreads and as a 20/1 win bet.

> There are two other tournaments (both Buick sponsored) in which he has a really consistent record.

* Buick Invitational. His LT stroke average is 69.81, and he was T3rd in 1998 and he won it in 1996.

* Buick Challenge. He's posted eighteen consecutive sub-par rounds for form figures of 18th-3rd-14th-Won-2nd.

> He'll be looking forward to the Tour Championship to be held at the Champions course where he finished 2nd in 1999, and 3rd in 1997 with a stroke average of 68.5.

Key stat   136th for driving accuracy.

STEVE LOWERY   S

Age 40   **Born** Alabama   **Lives** Alabama

US Tour wins 2, 1994 Sprint International, 2000 Southern Farm Bureau Classic
BUY.COM Tour wins 1, in 1992 **Money list** BEF 12th 1994

Moved back to Alabama after his Florida home was burnt down in early 1999.

In his first full season since the fire and his move back to his native Alabama Steve has performed really well posting three top 5 finishes, in the Memorial (T5th at 125/1), the Kemper Open (T2nd at 80/1*) and the John Deere Classic (T5th at 33/1), before in November he won the Southern Farm Bureau Classic at 25/1* with a 40 foot birdie putt at the first extra hole.

He also posted top 10s in the Tucson Open (T7th), the Shell Houston Open (T7th), the Buick Classic (10th), the Tampa Bay Classic (T6th) and the NCR Classic at Disney (T8th), and top 25s in the Bay Hill (T22nd), the MCI Classic (T11th), the Western Open (T20th), the Air Canada (T13th) and the Invensys Classic (T17th).

Steve's improvement is shown in his stats which are much improved for driving distance (up 4 yards to 275 yards), driving accuracy (105th - top 50), greens in reg. (up 2½%), sand saves (up 4%) and birdie conversion (up 2.5%).

An aggressive player he's in the top 20 for par 5 birdies.

> Steve is very much a 'streak' player capable of shooting low numbers especially in final rounds when 'off the pace'. This year 63 (R2 Air Canada), 64 (R2 MCI Classic), 64 (R1 Kemper Open), 63 (R4 John Deere Classic), 63 (R4 Invensys Classic) and 64 (R1 Southern Farm Bureau) kept up his record big time!

> He clearly enjoys the new Deere Run course after his T5th finish this year. Worth following in the 2001 John Deere Classic at 50/1+.

> OK so he missed the cut this year in the Compaq Classic however his earlier record 3rd (1998), 7th (1997), 4th (1996) mark him down as a player with a real chance at the English Turn course in 2001.

> With 7 of his last 8 rounds under par, including a 63, he must have a serious each-way chance in the Canadian Open after finishing T13th (2000) and T10th (1999) in the last two years.

> Worth a bet at 66/1 for the Tucson Open where he's finished T7th (2000), T20th (1999) and 4th (1998) in the last three years.

> Steve is just the sort of aggressive player who can be expected to play well in the NCR Golf Classic at Walt Disney. T11th (1999) and T8th this year he can be supported to play well again in 2001.

Key stat   7th on all-round ranking.

ANDREW MAGEE

Age 38   **Born** Paris, France   **Lives** Arizona

US Tour wins 4, in 1988, 1991 Nestle Invitational, 1991 Las Vegas Invitational, and 1994 Northern Telecom Open. **Money list** BEF 5th 1991

Magee joined the tour in 1985 and has retained his card every year since. In 2000 he had one big finish when 2nd at 100/1 in the Greater Greensboro Classic after which he had tendonitis.

He recorded top 10s in the Bob Hope (T10th), the AT&T (T7th) and the Tampa Bay Classic (T10th), and top 20s in the Byron Nelson Classic (T15th), the Memorial (T20th), the International (T14th) and the Reno-Tahoe Open (T12th).

In the World Match Play (2nd in 1999) he lost in R1 to Tom Lehman (5 and 4). He missed the cuts in the US Open and USPGA.

His stats for putting average, and driving accuracy are both this year, as last year, outside the top 100. A long hitter at 279 yards.

> He's posted nine punter friendly top 5 finishes in the last four seasons so he's a player to note. However, as he showed in this year's Greater Greensboro Classic, he can strike form when not playing well, and on a course where he'd shown no previous form.

> Nevertheless he's suited to two types of events.

First, with two of his four wins in deserts, and living in Arizona, he can be noted for the Tucson Classic (T6th 1998: T10th 1997). However it's the International (5 successive top 20s) in which he's a must to follow on the spreads, in match bets and as an 80/1 outsider.

Second, wide-fairway, five-round tournaments suit him really well so remember him in the Bob Hope (T1st after R4 in 1998 when he finished 3rd), back him for the Invensys Classic in the Las Vegas (5th in 1999 and he won it in 1991), and remember he's very well suited to the Tampa Bay Classic (T10th incl 66 in R3 in 2000) when it returns in 2002.

Key stat   T139th for driving accuracy last year he was T144th in 2000.

JEFF MAGGERT   D

Age 36   **Born** Missouri   **Lives** Texas

College Texas

US Tour wins 1, 1993 Walt Disney Classic **WGC wins** 1, 1999 Andersen Consulting World Match Play **Majors** BEF T3rd 1995 & 3rd 1997 USPGA **Ryder Cup** 1995,97,99 **Presidents Cup** 1994 **Money list** BEF 9th 1994 and 9th 1999

Jeffrey Allan has had a very mixed year playing inconsistently. His big finishes came in the Players Championship where he was T3rd at 100/1*, and in the Buick Challenge where he was T2nd at 50/1.

He also posted top 10s in the Sony Open in Hawaii (T9th), the Western Open (T6th), the Buick Open (T6th) and the Pennsylvania Classic (T8th). Top 25s were recorded in the Mercedes (T16th), the Phoenix Open (T23rd), the Shell Houston Open (T17th) and the Tampa Bay Classic (T9th).

In the WGC tournaments he lost 6 and 5 in R1 to Bob Tway, and he finished T24 in the NEC Invitational.

In the majors he finished T41st in the British Open. He missed the cut in each of the three US Majors.

Last year T28th for putting, this year outside the top 140 tells its own story. If his 2001 early season stats are back to normal expect Jeff's accurate driving to give him the basis for some very high finishes.

> Once again this season Jeff let a winning position slip. In the Buick Challenge he led by 2 after R3. However he bogeyed 16th and 17th to finish 2 shots back to Duval in T2nd place.

> Never say "just a second" to Jeff as he's been 2nd fourteen times, led nine times into R4....and won just once. If he's to win again it will surely be when coming from "off the pace" to set a clubhouse target, or if he's in the lead on a rain reduced tournament.

> Admits that motivation can be a problem. "There's a lot more things that are enjoyable than chasing a ball around 30 weeks of the year and living in a hotel room".

> Lives on the Woodlands course where he can be backed for the 2001 Shell Houston Open (he's finished 2nd three times) in match bets and in the outrights.

> The course in Hawaii has been changed over the last couple of years and this suits Jeff's straight hitting (T9th 2000: T2nd 1999). With a 68.5 stroke average for those eight rounds back Jeff for the Sony Open in Hawaii early in 2001.

> Lost his form completely in May and June this year. However with his focus restored in 2001 let's remember this guy has a very solid US Open record with finishes from 1994 reading T9th-T4th-T97th-4th-T7th-T7th before this year's missed cut. So with five top 10s in the last seven years, if he's shown steady form he can be supported in match bets, and each way without Tiger.

> In the last three seasons he's finished T2nd (2000), 13th (1999) and 8th (1998) at Callaway Gardens for a brilliant three-year stroke average of 68.3 including two rounds of 63. He's a 'must' for match bets and support on the spreads for the 2001 Buick Challenge although he may not win after his experience this year!

Key stat   142nd for putting average.

SHIGEKI MARUYAMA   V S G

Age 31   **Born** Georgia   **Lives** Japan

Japanese tour wins 7, incl. three in 1997 and 1 in 1999 **Presidents Cup** 1998 and 2000 **US tour** BEF T2 2000 Buick Invitational **Money list** BEF 37th 2000

The guy with the permanent smile has had a successful year with three top 4 finishes, in the Buick Invitational (T2nd at 125/1), the Doral Ryder Open (T4th at 66/1) and the Western Open (T3rd at 80/1). He also had top 10s in the Sony Open in Hawaii (T9th), the Greater Greensboro Classic (T8th) and the Memorial (T10th), and top 25s in the Bay Hill (T18th), the Byron Nelson Classic (T20th) and the Colonial (T13th).

In the World Match Play he beat John Huston in R1 before losing by just 1 hole to Justin Leonard. He missed the US Open cut, finished T46th in both the US Masters and the USPGA. T55th in the British Open and T15th in the WGC NEC Invitational.

Shot 58 in R1 in prequalifying for the US Open at the Woodmont course in Maryland to prove that he can be a real streaker!

Injured his wrist in the Buick Challenge in early October (W/D after 71 in R1). In the Presidents Cup he lost to Furyk (5 and 4) in the singles and scored only 1 point.

A long hitter at 281 yards he is in the top 30 for par 5 birdies. His sound temperament is shown by his top 20 placing for 'bounceback'. His putting average has deteriorated this year.

Shot to fame in the 1998 Presidents Cup when he won all his five matches to help the Rest of The World team trounce America.

> Still inexperienced in the States having played only around fifty tournaments. Nevertheless he's posted ten top 10s in his thirty-one events from January 1999 including three top 4s, so he's a player we must take very seriously indeed as he could well notch his first US win in 2001.

> After his T9th this year in the Sony Open in Hawaii he must be expected to do well at the Waialae course again in 2001.

> In the World Match Play he was T5th in 1999 and got to R2 this year. He could well cause a shock by reaching the semi finals in Melbourne in the first week of January.

> His long hitting is clearly well suited to the Cog Hill course. T3rd this year Shigeki merits each-way support for the 2001 Western Open.

> A fine links player who has shot good rounds in the British Open particularly in the first and third rounds. Let's remember that in 1996 at Royal Lytham (the 2001 venue) he was T5th after R3 after 68 (R1) and 69 (R3). He's a helluva better player now than then so back him in the Rest of The World market for the 2001 British Open, and in the 3 balls in R1 and R3.

> Worth remembering Shigeki in the Rest of The World market for the WGC NEC Invitational as T3rd at 20/1 2000, 4th in 1999 and T2nd at 25/1 in 1998 is a solid record.

Key stat   In non majors from January 1999 to August 2000 he posted nine top 10s in nineteen tournaments.

LEN MATTIACE   V ▮

Age 33   **Born** New York   **Lives** Florida

US Tour wins BEF T2nd 1996 Buick Challenge **Money list** BEF 61st 2000

Len had posted four top 10s, in the Players Championship (T9th), the Colonial (T8th), the John Deere Classic (T10th) and the Texas Open (T6th). He also had high finishes in the Canadian Open (T20th), the St Jude Classic (T25th) and the Pennsylvania Classic (T18th) before he finished T3rd at 100/1* in the Tampa Bay Classic in late October.

Moo-tees can be a fine putter. His overall stats reflect his Money List position.

> Still to gain his first win after over 180 attempts. He's shown real nerves in the 1997 Walt Disney (74 in R4), the 1998 Players Championship (an 8 at the 17th in R4) and the 1999 Buick Classic (75 in R4) so it would be surprising if he secured his first win in 2001.

  Can therefore be safely opposed in final round 2-ball betting if he's in the top 4, or T4th after R3.

> He can be noted in match bets for the Colonial where he's had high finishes (T8th 2000: T11th 1999) in the last couple of years.

> He played very well in the last couple of rounds on the new course this year in the John Deere Classic to suggest that he could be a factor there in 2001.

> The Players Championship is the tournament in which Len has 'home' advantage. T9th in 2000, and famously T5th in 1998 he can be followed in 3 balls and in match betting.

> Unlucky to shoot a triple bogey on the 6th in R4 this year in the Tampa Bay Classic when T3rd. In his home state he'll have every chance when it's next played in 2002.

> He could well cause a shock 100/1 win in the Texas Open. 33 under par for the last four years, 4th 1996 and T6th this year he likes the Bermuda greens.

Key stat   189th for par 3 birdies!

BOB MAY   ☼ **G**

Age 32   **Born** California   **Lives** Las Vegas

European tour wins 1, 1999 Victor Chandler Masters **US tour** BEF T2nd 2000 Fedex St Jude Classic **Majors** BEF 2nd 2000 USPGA **Money list** BEF 29th 2000

What a year it's been for the 32-year-old guy from Vegas. He secured his tour card when T12th at Q School and he's played on both the US and European tours.

On the European tour he was T13th in the Volvo PGA, T15th in the Loch Lomond and, as defending champion, finished T5th at 33/1 in the Victor Chandler British Masters.

In America he had three top 4 finishes, in the Fedex St Jude Classic (T2nd at 100/1), the Reno-Tahoe Open (3rd at 33/1) and famously in the USPGA (2nd at 150/1 losing to Tiger in a play-off).

He also had top 25s in the Texas Open (T14th), the Invensys Classic in Las Vegas (T22nd), the NCR Classic at Disney (T13th) and the WGC American Express Championship (T11th).

In the majors he was T23rd in the US Open, T11th in the British Open and, of course, that 2nd place in the USPGA. T22nd in the Tour Championship.

Solid all-round stats, with 70% for greens in regulation especially notable, although his putting rank is poor because of his early season cold putter.

Bob has a lot of head movement off the tee (compare for example Spain's Miguel Martin). Tends to draw the ball. Putts left hand below right.

> Having gone head to head with Tiger and only lost in a photo finish (2000 USPGA) Bob sealed his growing reputation as a straight hitting tough competitor who has now moved his game to a higher level. However his American experience is limited and although we must not get carried away he now looks to be firmly in 'the winner about to happen' category.

> "I'd love to win a PGA tour event. I think as long as I keep on playing good and consistent golf, it will come" and so do I......indeed Bob it May be in 2001.

> Definitely at his best in warm conditions (he lives in Vegas remember) and from June onwards. So have a few BOB on MAY for the 2001 Reno-Tahoe Open where he was T3rd this year in the desert.

> He'll be delighted the 2001 US Open is to be held in Oklahoma where he went to University. T23rd this year he must enter into calculations at Southern Hills in June.

> He can be backed in the top American market for the Loch Lomond (T4th 2000: Won 7/1 1999) where he's finished 7th in 1999 and 15th this year for a two-year stroke average of 69.5.

Key stat   T10th for greens in regulation.

BILLY MAYFAIR D

Age 34　　　**Born** Scottsdale, Arizona　　**Lives** Scottsdale, Arizona

US Tour wins 5, 1993 Greater Milwaukee Open, 1995 Western Open, 1995 Tour Championship, 1998 Nissan Open, 1998 Buick Open **Money list** BEF 2nd 1995

Billy has had poorest year since 1994. He's posted a couple of top 10s in the Phoenix Open (T10th) and the Bay Hill Invitational (T10th), and top 25s in the Players Championship (T17th), the Nissan Open (T25th), the Greater Greensboro (T21st). He created a big shock when he beat Phil Mickelson in R1 of the WGC Andersen World Match Play, before losing to Paul Lawrie in R2.

Missed the cut badly in the US Open, and finished T74th in the USPGA.

Billy's great strength has always been his driving accuracy and his great weakness his putting and this year has, as usual, followed that pattern.

> Became a father for the first time of a son in late 1999. I expect the law of the 'nappy factor' to click into gear in 2001 as I expect him to show much improved form.

> Let's make no mistake this guy sure knows how to win when the chance comes along having made five victories from 1993 through 1998 and also posted 7 seconds in that spell.

> Back in 1995 Billy won the Tour Championship at the tough Southern Hills course when he was the only player not to exceed par. So he'll be really delighted that the US Open will be played there next year. An accurate driver, proven on the course (where he was top in 1995 for both fairways hit and greens in reg), he could go really well in the 2001 US Open at a massive price.

> When he does strike 'hot' form he can be followed as he has proved that he can post high finishes in consecutive tournaments.

> The tightening of the fairways for the Phoenix Open really suit Billy's straight hitting. Living nearby in Scottsdale Arizona I would give him a serious chance at 80/1+ to land the 2001 Phoenix Open. 4 shots off the winner when T10th this year he'll be worth a bet.

Key stat　　　11th for driving accuracy in 1999, he's 23rd in 2000

BLAINE McCALLISTER

Age 42　　　**Born** Texas　　　　　**Lives** Florida

US tour wins 5, last was the 1993 BC Open **Money list** BEF 15th 1989

Blaine finished top player at the 1999 Q School to retain his card after finishing 134th on the Money list in 1999.

In 2000 he had two crucial card saving big finishes (won $367,000) when 2nd at 125/1 in the Compaq Classic which he lost at the 2nd play-off hole, and T3rd at 100/1 in the Texas Open (winning $150,000).

He also had top 25s in the Bell South Classic (T10th), the MCI Classic (T25th) and the Byron Nelson Classic (T25th after being joint R1 leader), the Invensys Classic in Las Vegas (T12th) and the Southern Farm Bureau (T11th).

T34th in the USPGA.

Driving accuracy, and greens in reg are Blaine's strengths however in the bunkers and on the greens he has struggled.

> He lost his form in the late nineties as his wife's rapidly failing eyesight and family illness problems understandably distracted him. However, being No. 1 at Q School in 1999 has rejuvenated him.

> Since his wife's illness he says that he now really fully appreciates the life of a golf pro and so has a relaxed attitude on course.

> At his best in a 'purple' patch in May this year.

> 2001 will probably see Blaine fighting once more to retain his card. His consistency this year (seventeen cuts cuts in first twenty-three tournaments) if repeated next year will give him a fighting chance.

> He can be nominated at 66/1 for the Southern Farm Bureau. He knows the course really well and was T4th in 1997, T9th in 1999 and T11th this year.

Key stat   22nd for driving accuracy and 26th for greens in regulation.

SCOTT McCARRON   D

Age 35   **Born** California   **Lives** California
College California

US Tour wins 2, 1996 Compaq Classic, 1997 Bell South Classic **Money list** BEF 25th 1997

2000 was Scott's sixth successive year on the tour, and it's been an inconsistent one for the Californian. He's posted two big finishes when he won $124K when T4th in the Reno-Tahoe Open, and $149K when T5th at 100/1 in the Invensys Classic in Las Vegas..

However he's had only two other top 25s, in the Greater Greensboro Classic (T21st) and the Compaq Classic (T17th).

The key to his problem is very simple and very basic. He's inaccurate off the tee (just 60%) and his greens in reg ranking is also still outside the top 150.

His strengths are his long hitting (288 yards and top 10 ranked each year) and his putting (T6th this year: 4th in 1999).

> When he finds the green he's got both the putting touch and the bottle to take his chances. After all he was No. 1 on tour in 1999 for birdie conversion and he's top 20 again in this disappointing year.

> If his stats for greens in reg show early season improvement he would be a player to note as he's got lots of courage.

> He simply loves playing golf in Nevada (next door to his own state of California) where he's supported by his wife's family and lots of friends who live in Reno. "It's really neat to play in front of your hometown crowd". His two top 5s this year came in the states' two tournaments in which he can be supported:-

*   Reno-Tahoe Open. T4th 2000

*   The Invenys Classic in Las Vegas. T5th 2000

> "I had good feelings stepping on the first tee..." no wonder Scott said that before starting this year's Compaq Classic as it gave him his first win in 1996 and he finished T17th this year. He must enter calculations at New Orleans next year.

> He'll have a real chance in the Air Canada where he was in the top 30 this year after finishing T4th in 1999 after shooting a course record 61.

Key stat   184th for driving accuracy in 1999 and 180th this year.

SPIKE McROY

Age 32   **Born** Alabama   **Lives** Alabama

US tour BEF T6th 1998 Buick Invitational **BUY.COM tour wins** 2, 2000 BUY.COM Dakota Dunes Open, 2000 BUY.COM Tour Championship

Played the main tour unsuccessfully in 1997 and 1998. In 1999 he played the BUY.COM tour with a T3rd his best finish. 2000 was his 'nappy factor' year after the birth in 1999 of his first child, a son and he's been very successful finishing top of the BUY.COM tour money list after two wins and a 2nd. He won the BUY.COM Dakota Dunes Open in July, and the season ending BUY.COM Tour Championship in October. He finished T2nd in the BUY.COM Knoxville Open in July.

6th for greens in reg shows his strength while 104th for total driving, and 88th for driving accuracy show his weakness. Finished runner-up in the 1997 Compaq World putting championship.

> At his best when coming from 'off the pace' as he showed by his confidence-boosting win in the BUY.COM Tour Championship (74 in R1 then 64-65-69).

> Having made his BEF in the Buick Invitational in 1998 he'll be really looking forward to San Diego in February.

Key stat   Finished T6th for greens in regulation on the 2000 BUY.COM tour.

ROCCO MEDIATE

Age 38   **Born** Pennsylvania   **Lives** Florida

US Tour wins 4, 1991 Doral Ryder Open, 1993 Greater Greensboro Open, 1999 Phoenix Open, 2000 Buick Open **International wins** 1992 French Open **Money list** 15th 1991

Rocco had a very good 1999 with his first win for six years when he finished 37th on the M/L, and he's improved on that in 2000.

He landed his fourth tour win at 100/1 in the Buick Open in August, and he also had two other top 4 finishes, in the Colonial (T4th at 100/1) and as defending champion in the Phoenix Open (2nd at 66/1).

He also notched top 25s in the Mercedes (T16th), the Bob Hope (T16th), the Nissan Open (T18th) and the Memorial (T13th). In the World Match Play he lost in R1 to Jim Furyk 2 and 1. In the majors he was T32nd in the US Open (69 in R1) and T52nd in the British Open. Withdrew from the USPGA after a freak accident falling through a chair (honest!).

Not long at 271 yards it's his accuracy that is still Rocco's trademark. His driving accuracy (up 3% to 75%) and greens in reg (up to 67%) are very solid, and he's improved his bunker play (top 10 this year for sand saves). His putting overall has still let him down. Draws the ball.

> He's now won a tournament in each of the last two years, and both at 100/1.
> .There are two tournaments that unquestionably suit Rocco.
  * The Buick Open. W-9th-29th-8th are first-class form figures for a four-year stroke average of 68.94 with fifteen of his last sixteen rounds under par.
  * The Phoenix Open. The tightened course suits his accuracy. Winner in 1999 and 2nd in 2000.

Being defending champion in the Phoenix this year (2nd 2000) didn't faze him so he could well win the Buick Open again in 2001. Back him for both must be the message!

> Could surprise at a big price in the 2001 MCI Classic. OK, he missed the cut this year but he'd averaged 69.75 in the previous four years with three top 20s and a top 10 from 1996-1999,
> He would love to win the Pennsylvania Classic having been born in the State. T33rd this year and on a fresh course next year he'd have a real chance at 100/1.

Key stat   4th for driving accuracy.

SHAUN MICHEEL

Age 31   **Born** Florida   **Lives** Tennessee
College Indiana

BUY.COM Tour wins 1, 1999 Greensboro Open **International wins** 1, 1998 Singapore Open **US Tour** BEF T5th 2000 John Deere Classic, T5th 2000 Invensys Classic in Las Vegas **European tour** BEF T4th 1999 B&H Malaysian Open **Money list** BEF 104th 2000

Muh-Keel earned his 2000 tour card after finishing 9th on the 1999 BUY.COM tour money list on which he won the Greensboro Open.

Missed eight of his first ten cuts and didn't post a top 20 finish until late July. However he then improved to secure his card for 2001.

Shaun has posted a couple of top 5 finishes, in the John Deere Classic (T5th at 150/1) and in the Invensys Classic in Las Vegas (T5th also at 150/1).

He also has high finishes in the Air Canada (T13th) and the Canadian Open (T10th).

An accurate iron player Shaun was ranked in the top 20 for par 3 birdies in mid October. Average length at 278 yards he has been erratic off the tee (outside the top 100) and his putting has been variable at best (outside top 90).

> Shaun can 'streak' with the best of them having once shot a 58 (!) in a pro-am, a 63 in R4 in this year's Invensys Classic in Las Vegas, and a final round 65 in the 2000 John Deere Classic.

> Loves hot conditions as he has shown by his win in the Singapore Open (1998), his BUY.COM tour win in mid July (1999) and his two top 5s (in August, and in the heat of Vegas) this year.

> When first in contention this year in the Shell Houston Open he 'blew it'! 4 off the lead when T8th after R3 he shot 78 to finish T53rd.

Whereas later he showed commendable R4 composure when he was twice within 4 shots of the lead after R3.

* Air Canada. Shot 70 in R4 when the average in contention score was 69.86

* Invensys Classic. Shot 69 in R4 when the average in contention score was 68.6

> A winner in 1998 and 1999 he could well cause a 'shock' in 2001. If so it could well be in the John Deere Classic where he was an 'off the pace' T5th this year, where (on the new Deere run course) his inexperience is not a disadvantage, and it's held on the heat of summer.

Key stat   125th for driving accuracy.

PHIL MICKELSON   M G 🏇

Age 30   **Born** California   **Lives** Arizona
College Arizona

US Tour wins 16, 1991 Northern Telecom Open (as an amateur), 1993 Buick Invitational, 1993 The International, 1994 Mercedes, 1995 Northern Telecom Open, 1996 Nortel Open, 1996 Phoenix Open, 1996 Byron Nelson Classic, 1996 NEC World Series, 1997 Bay Hill Invitational, 1997 Sprint International, 1998 Mercedes, 1998 AT&T, 2000 Buick Invitational, 2000 Bell South Classic, 2000 Mastercard Colonial **Major wins** None (!) BEF 2nd 1999 US Open, 3rd 1994 USPGA, 3rd 1996 US Masters **Ryder Cup** 1995,97,99 **Dunhill Cup** 1996 **Presidents Cup** 1994,1996,1998,2000 **Money list** 2nd 1996 and 2000

It's been a brilliant year for 'Lefty' with four tournament wins, although he couldn't land his first major. His victories came in the Buick Invitational (at 20/1), the Bell South Classic (at 22/1), the Mastercard Colonial (at 14/1) and the Tour Championship (at 14/1 after 66 in R4). He also posted three top 5 finishes in the Byron Nelson Classic (T2nd at 22/1 after losing in a three-man play-off), the International (2nd at 10/1) and the Invensys Classic in Las Vegas (2nd at 10/1).

He also had high finishes in the Bob Hope (T16th), the Phoenix Open (T10th), the Doral Ryder Open (T21st), the Compaq Classic (T17th), the Buick Classic (T13th) and the Buick Open (T4th).

In the Andersen World Match Play he suffered a 'shock' R1 defeat by Billy Mayfair (1 hole). In the WGC NEC Invitational he finished T4th at 11/1.

In the majors he was T7th in the US Masters, T16th in the US Open, T11th in the British Open, and T9th in the USPGA. In the Presidents Cup he scored 3 points although he lost to Mike Weir (4 and 3) in the singles.

Phil is a very long hitter at 288 yards. He has a superb putting stroke which has worked really well this year. Sand saves up by 3% in 2000. His length and accurate iron play gives him many birdie and eagle chances and he takes them. 6th for birdie conversion in 1999 he's up by almost 2% this year. His weakness continues to be erratic driving off the tee shown by his continued ranking outside the top 120.

Became a first-time father of a daughter, Amanda, in June 1999. He was 30 in June 2000.

> Last year's profile was very keen on Phil......."I really do believe 2000 will be a mega-big year for Phil as I expect him to win at least once, and to make a breakthrough major victory. So he'll be worth a bet in the early exchanges on the US. Money list after the Mercedes".

Well he sure was nappy factor inspired after his winless 1999 as he landed those four wins (20/1, 22/1, 14/1, 14/1), and the 33/1 money list each-way bet was a success. However although his major record was impressive (four top 16 finishes) he did not achieve that first major breakthrough.

> Let's just reflect....Phil is 30 yet he's won sixteen (yes, sixteen) US tournaments and that's phenomenal. Alongside Duval, Monty and Westwood he's clearly one of the best players yet to win a major, so the big question is whether he can win that first major?

> The doubt is certainly not his ability, rather whether he has the nerve to reach out and take the major prize when it gets close. Phil is an enigma because although he won three times in 2000 he did wilt under R4 pressure on four occasions this year.

* Phoenix Open. Dropped 4 shots in last 8 holes in a R4 73 to finish T10th.
* Buick Classic. T2nd after R3, shot 75 in R4, to finish T13th.
* US Open. T5th after R3, shot 76 in R4 to finish T16th.
* Byron Nelson Classic. Needed par at the last to win, made bogey and then lost the play-off.

> The US Masters provides him with his very best chance in the majors. His whole game is absolutely tailor made for Augusta. He has the length, the wider fairways, the magical, imaginative short game and the putting touch. His recent course record T7th (1995), 3rd (1996), MC (1997 when ill with a virus), T12th (1998), T6th (1999) and T7th (2000) is very good. He must be a finishing position sell (FP of 22-25 in 2000), a match bet must, and at 25/1 he's worth each-way support.

> Last year I nominated him for the WGC NEC Invitational at Akron Ohio, he finished T4th at 11/1. His form on the Firestone course is really good, viz won 1996, 2nd 1997, 2nd 1998, 2nd 1999 and T4th 2000 for a five-year stroke average of 68.2. Sure to play well there in 2001, he can be sold on the finishing positions (FP 9-11 in 2000)

> It's an important and interesting fact that Phil has never successfully defended any of the thirteen championships that he has won, so that suggests that in 2001 we don't back him to win the four titles he'll be defending - the Buick Invitational, the Bell South Classic, the Colonial or the Tour Championship.

> However he can be followed in four 'ordinary' tournaments.

* The Byron Nelson Classic. T2nd (2000), MC (1999), 6th (1998), 12th (1997), Won (1996) is fine form.

* The Phoenix Open. Dropped 4 shots in the last 8 holes this year. A real 'desert fox' he will have a leading chance in his resident state in 2001.

* The International. He averages an astonishing 40.5 points over the last four years in which he's been 2nd twice and won once. He also won in 1993. Everything about Castle Pines is tailor made for Lefty!

* Bay Hill Invitational. Winner in 1997, T5th in 1999, Phil can continue his excellent recent record in 'odd' years by winning the 2001 Bay Hill Invitational.

> Well worth an each-way bet in the 'without Woods' market for the 2001 Money list. Tipped here successfully for the Money list this year he will surely do well again next year as he'll focus on all the big-money tournaments.

Key stat   3rd for par 5 birdies and 4th for birdie conversion.

LARRY MIZE

Age 42   **Born** Georgia   **Lives** Georgia

College Georgia

US Tour wins 3, one in 1983, and 1993 Northern Telecom Open and 1993 Buick Open. **International wins** 4, last in 1993 **Major wins** 1, 1987 US Masters (who could ever forget it?) **Money list** BEF 6th 1987 **Ryder Cup** 1987 **Dunhill Cup** 2000

Larry Hogan has had a year in which he had one big finish when T3rd at 125/1 in the MCI Classic (65 in R3). He also had top 20s in the Hawaiian Open (T14th) and the Buick Open (T11th), and top 25s in the US Masters (T25th with a 67 in R2) and the Memorial (T25th).

He finished T37th in the US Open. Won one of his three games on his Dunhill Cup debut (at 42) in October.

He now follows a reduced schedule to be with his family. His stats always tell the same story of a straight accurate driver (top 10 again this year) and a solid putter (top 50) who is severely handicapped by a lack of length (264 yards).

> Without a win in the last seven years, short off the tee and 42 years of age it's difficult to see Larry winning again. However he can be noted in match bets in three tournaments.

* The Hawaiian Open. He's made the cut in all his thirteen starts, and has posted a top 15 finish in each of the last three years, and shot 63 in R2 this year.

* The Memorial. T19th in 1999 and T25th this year.

* The US Masters. Fifteen cuts in seventeen starts, and ten top 30 finishes in his last twelve.

Key stat   7th for driving accuracy last year and 5th in 2000.

GARY NICKLAUS

Age 31 (dad's now 60) **Born** Florida **Lives** Florida
College Ohio State University
US tour BEF 2nd, 2000 Bell South Classic **Money list** BEF 119th 2000

Amazingly Gary at 31 was a rookie on the 2000 USPGA tour. He had tried for his card without success many times before finishing T12th at the 1999 Q School.

He'd missed five cuts (out of nine) and not posted a top 25 when he secured his card when 2nd at 150/1 in the Bell South Classic, winning over $302K. He lost at a par 3 in a play-off to Phil Mickelson. He then missed nine of his next twelve cuts although he was T25th in the Memorial.

Caddied for his dad (you must have heard of him) at dad's final US Open.

With only two significant tournaments his stats are uniformly poor.

> Being the son of a legend cannot be easy if your father is one helluva nice guy. So it's good that Gary has a chance in 2001 really to establish himself.

> On the basis of this year however it's not really possible to identify any betting opportunities.

Key stat   He may be 31 yet he's retained his tour card for the first time, finishing 119th on the Money List.

GREG NORMAN

Age 45   **Born** Australia   **Lives** Florida
US Tour wins 18, the last six being the 1995 Memorial, 1995 Canon Greater Hartford Open, 1995 NEC World Series, 1996 Doral Ryder Open, 1997 Fedex St Jude Classic, 1997 NEC World Series **International wins** 54, last the 1998 Greg Norman Holden International **Majors** British Open in 1986 and 1993 **Money list** Top 1990 and 1995 **Presidents Cup** 1994 (W/D), 1996,1998 and 2000 **Dunhill Cup** 10 times

On the ANZ tour he finished T2nd in the Australian Open and T7th in the Heineken Classic, but missed the cut in his own Greg Norman Holden International.

On the US tour he was T12th in the Doral Ryder Open, and 4th at 66/1 in the Buick Classic.

He finished T11th in the US Masters and missed the cut in the US Open. He missed the British Open as he recovered from hip surgery. In the Presidents Cup he lost to Stewart Cink (2 and 1) in the singles, and scored just 1 point.

Returning to the golf course he was 4th at 100/1* in the International before missing the cut in the USPGA, and finishing T31st (of 37) in the WGC NEC Invitational.

> Having made a full recovery from shoulder surgery (1998) and hip surgery (2000) Greg is keen to continue to play competitive golf which he still enjoys.

   * He must be noted for the 2001 US Masters. In the last six years he's been in the top 3 three times and in 2000 he was the third best in the tournament over

the final 54 holes. He won't beat Tiger but in match bets and at a nice price each way in the 'without Woods' market he'll be worth a wager at Augusta.

Key stat   He's won the same number of majors (two) as John Daly!

JOE OGILVIE

Age 26   **Born** Lancaster, Ohio   **Lives** Lancaster, Ohio

BUY.COM tour wins 2, both in 1998 **Money list** BEF 92nd 2000

Oh-gil-vee earned his card when 24th at the 1999 Q School having lost it when 137th on the M/L.

In 2000 he's secured it with two high finishes. He was T4th at 150/1 in the Fedex St Jude Classic and T6th in the International.

He also had solid finishes in the AT&T (T20th), the Tucson Open (T25th), the Canon Greater Hartford Open (T25th), the Greater Milwaukee Open (T14th), and he posted a top 10 in the BC Open (T10th),

Inaccuracy off both tee and fairway have been his main problems this year. Quite long at 275 yards.

> He has shown signs of pressure this year so he's awarded the 'bottle'.

* BC Open. T5th after R3, then 71 to finish T10th.

* John Deere Classic. 11 under par after R3 two shots off 4th place, he shot 74 to finish T38th.

* Fedex St Jude. T2nd at 9 under after R2 he then went only 2 under over the final 36 holes to finish T4th.

On the other hand from 'off the pace' he was brilliant twice

* AT&T. After 77 (very bad weather) in R1 he went 10 under last 54 holes

* The International. 29 of his 31 pts came in the last three rounds.

So it's pretty clear that he can be opposed when in serious contention.

> Best chance will surely be in the BC Open. T10th this year, and 36th in 1999 seven of his last eight rounds have been under par.

Key stat   128th for driving accuracy he's 63rd for putting

MARK O'MEARA   D

Age 43   **Born** Nth Carolina   **Lives** Florida (next door to Tiger)

US Tour wins 14, 4 in 80s; 1990 AT&T, 1990 Texas Open, 1991 Walt Disney Classic, 1992 AT&T, 1995 Honda Classic, 1995 Bell Canadian Open, 1996 Mercedes, 1996 Greater Greensboro Classic, 1997 AT&T, 1997 Buick Invitational **Major wins** 2, 1998 US Masters, 1998 British Open **International wins** 7, latest 1998 Cisco World Matchplay, 1997 Lancome Trophy **Ryder Cup** 5, latest 1999 **Dunhill Cup** 7, latest 1999 **Presidents Cup** 1996, 1998 **Money list** 2nd 1984, 5th 1996

O'Meara made his Mark big style in 1998 when he won both the US Masters and the British Open thanks to a lot of luck and a very hot putter. Since then he's been understandably keen to cash in on those successes. Partly as a result in 1999 he slipped to 45th on the M/L, and this year the decline has continued.

In 2000 he's played a limited schedule posting a top 10 in the Players Championship (T9th), and a top 25 in the International (T21st).

In the US Masters he missed the cut, in the US Open at his favourite Pebble Beach he was T51st, he was T26th in the British Open, and T46th in the USPGA.

In WGC World Match Play he beat Greg Norman in R1 before losing 5 and 4 to the eventual winner, Darren Clarke, in R2.

His stats are uniformly poor this year although he's still in the top 55 for putting. He is a superb putter, an excellent course manager, and a brilliant player of his mid irons.

Neighbour and close friend of Tiger Woods.

> The big question now, at 43, is whether he can rekindle the old fire and desire to chalk up another win.

> His victories have mainly been on the West Coast (8th) and early in the year (six in February) so he must surely be followed for the Bob Hope Chrysler Classic (2nd in 1991 and 1992: 4th in 1997: T6th in 1998) in match bets and as an each-way contender.

> In these last two lean years he's nevertheless posted two very solid finishes in the lucrative Players Championship (T6th 1999 and T9th 2000) so at Sawgrass in 2001 he'll be worth support especially in match bets.

Key stat   193rd (!!) for greens in regulation.

NAOMICHI 'JOE' OZAKI   V

Age 44   **Born** Japan   **Lives** Japan

US Tour BEF T2nd 1997 Buick Open **International wins** 31 all in Japan **Money list** 66th 1995

Joe is the younger brother of Jumbo Ozaki and this year he's posted one top 10, in the Buick Open (T6th), and three top 25s in the Buick Invitational (T14th), the Kemper Open (T20th) and the Reno-Tahoe Open (T12th).

In the World Match Play he created a shock when he beat Couples by 1 hole in R1 (at odds of 2/1) before losing in R2 to Parnevik (2 and 1).

He missed the cut in the US Masters and the USPGA.

Very short off the tee he has improved both his driving accuracy (by 2%) and his greens in reg stat (by 5%) this year. His putting however remains in intensive care outside the top 125. Troubled by a bad back in October he withdrew from the Tampa Bay Classic after nine holes.

> 'Joe' is an unusual player in that he's a proven multiple winner in Japan yet whenever he's been in contention in the US he's let the pressure get to him and, as a result, he was awarded the bottle in each of the last two volumes.

> He does provide one annual serious betting opportunity - it is to back him in the R1 3 balls in the US Players Championship. In 1998 he shot 69, in 1999 he shot 68, and he shot 70 and landed a 7/4 bet in 2000.

> If a firm such as Multi-Sports quote odds on the halfway leader in the Players Championship have a small investment on Joe Ozaki who was halfway leader in 1998 and 1999!!

Key stat   139th for putting average.

JESPER PARNEVIK   G F

Age 35   **Born** Sweden   **Lives** Florida

College Florida

US Tour wins 4, 1998 Phoenix Open, 1999 Greater Greensboro Open, 2000 Bob Hope Chrysler Classic, 2000 Byron Nelson Classic **International wins** 4, last 1997 **European tour wins** 4, 1993 Scottish Open, 1995 Scandinavian Masters, 1996 Lancome Trophy, 1998 Scandinavian Masters **Dunhill Cup** 4, last 1997 World Cup 1994,95 **Ryder Cup** 1997, 1999 **Majors** 2nd 1994 British Open, T2nd 1997 British Open **Money list** BEF 8th 2000

The charismatic Swede has had a highly successful season with a couple of victories, first in the Bob Hope Chrysler Classic (at 25/1) and later in the Byron Nelson Classic in a play-off (at 33/1). He also had top 5s in the Sony Open in Hawaii (T3rd at 25/1), the Nissan Open (2nd at 33/1) and the Buick Classic (T5th at 22/1).

He also had high finishes in the Mercedes (T6th), the MCI Classic (T9th) and the Greater Greensboro Classic (T8th).

In Europe he finished T23rd in the Deutsche Bank Open, and T11th in the Scandinavian Masters.

In the Andersen World Match Play he beat Padraig Harrington (2 and 1), Joe Ozaki (1 up) before losing to Scott Hoch (1 hole).

In the majors he was T40th in the US Masters, missed the US Open cut, was T36th in the British Open and T51st in the USPGA.

Troubled by a hip problem his form in June and July notably in the US and British Opens can be safely ignored. In the autumn he had arthroscopic hip surgery and returned to finish T22nd in the Tour Championship. However, still not 100% fit, he withdrew during the WGC American Express tournament.

Given his injury disturbed season his stats for 2000 are not too meaningful. However they confirm that he is a winner as his birdie conversion ratio is up 2.5%, he's 6th for putting, and was top for par 3 birdies at the time of his operation. Tends to draw the ball.

Has a quirky reputation. Allegedly he eats volcanic dust (why not?) and he advertises in the nude!

> The simple fact is that, despite his hip problems from early June this year he's won four US tournaments in the last three years, plus one in Europe. This guy

is a world class player so he simply MUST play in the Ryder Cup side for which he was originally priced at 5/2 on. However in case his American commitments prevent him making the side he's 6/5 ON to get a 'wild card'.

> This year he credited his excellent start to the year 6th (Mercedes), T3rd (Hawaii), Won (Bob Hope) to being totally relaxed after a ten-week lay-off so in 2001 I hope to see Yespair rejuvenated by the operation that was so successful for both Greg Norman and Steve Elkington.

> So he can be supported in suitable match and spread bets for the Mercedes where he played so well this year when T6th after being the R1 leader.

> Back Jesper Parnevik each way for the 2001 British Open. Ignore his 2000 form when he was injured and remember his form figures from 1994 to 1999 (2nd-T24th-T44th-T2nd-T4th-T10th) which are very good. The low, drilling, punched-type of shots needed are his stock in trade. He's sure to go close at Royal Lytham.

Must be also backed to be top European (3rd 10/1 1999: T1st 14/1 1998).

> Jesper fits perfectly the profile of the traditional USPGA winner as a proven winner in his thirties who's yet to land a major. Must have a serious chance in Georgia in August and he'll be a nice price.

> Can be given a serious chance in the Buick Classic where in two starts (T5th 2000: T10th 1998) he's had five of his seven rounds under par for a 69.71 stroke average.

> The MCI Classic suits his style and he will be well worth each-way support at Hilton Head in 2001. 2nd in 1997 and T9th 2000.

> In 2001 back him to be the 20/1 winner of the Greater Greensboro Classic, winner in 1999, and T8th this year he has a stroke average over the last two years of 68.37!!

> On the European tour in early August I can see him winning the Scandinavian Masters at 12/1 at the Barseback course where he won in 1995. Winner again in 1998 and 2nd in 1999 he'll be looking to his home tournament for Ryder Cup points.

Key stat   Parnevik has won more US non majors (four) than any other current European player.

CRAIG PARRY   F D 🦆

Age 34   **Born** Australia   **Lives** Florida and Australia

US Tour wins BEF 2nd 1994 Honda Classic, 1995 Colonial, 1996 Byron Nelson Classic, T2nd 1996 Buick Classic **International wins** 17, last in 1997 **World Cup** 1989, 1990, 1991 **Dunhill Cup** 1993, 1995, 1996, 1998, 1999 **Presidents Cup** 1994, 1996, 1998 **Money list** BEF 39th 1999.

It's been Craig's worst full year on the US tour with only one top 10 finish in the Fedex St Jude Classic (T7th), and top 25s, in the Players Championship (T22nd), the US Masters (T25th), the Michelob (T12th) and the Invensys Classic in Las

Vegas (T12th). In the other majors he finished T37th in the US Open, T36th in the British Open, and he missed the USPGA cut.

On the ANZ tour he was T3rd three times, in the Australian PGA, the ANZ Players Championship and the Coolum Classic.

In the World Match Play he lost by 1 hole to Olazabal in R1.

It's surprising with such a record to note that his driving accuracy (76%) is first class. However his putting has been the root cause of his problems. Fader of the ball.

> Still seeking his first US tour win. His problem has been his poor R4 scoring when in serious contention e.g. the 1992 US Masters and the 1990 and 1999 British Opens. This year he really 'bottled' it in the 2000 Australian PGA over the last 4 holes after which "I felt like an amateur". As a result he gets the 'bottle' symbol.

  So if he's to win in America it will surely be in a rain ruined tournament, or by coming from 'off the pace' to set a clubhouse target.

> He can be followed each way in the top non-American markets for the Bay Hill Invitational (L 2000: W 18/1 1999: 3rd 25/1 1998).

> A fine links player, he warrants each-way support in the top Aussie market for the British Open (3rd 12/1 2000: Won 9/1 1999).

> He must have good chances in two tournaments on the ANZ tour.

  * The (co-sanctioned) Heineken Classic: eleven of his last twelve rounds at or below par and he finished 18th 2000: 6th 1999: T10th 1998.

  * The Greg Norman Holden. He's got a good record on the Lakes course (Won 1995 and top 15s in each of the last two years) and he's a Sydney resident.

Key stat   T131st for putting average, 13th for driving accuracy.

STEVE PATE

Age 39   **Born** California   **Lives** California
College California

US Tour wins 6, 3 in 80s, then 1991 Honda Classic, 1992 Buick Invitational, and the 1998 CVS Charity Classic **Majors** T3rd 1991 US Masters **Ryder Cup** 1991, 1999 **Dunhill Cup** 1991 **Money list** 6th 1991

With a win in 1998 and 13th place (winning over $1¾m) in the 1999 Money list when he was a member of the successful US Ryder Cup side perhaps 2000 was always going to be a bit of an anti-climax.

His big finish came in the Greater Milwaukee Open (T3rd at 33/1) and he also had top 20s in the Buick Invitational (T14th), the MCI Classic (T15th), the Buick Classic (T11th), the Fedex St Jude Classic (T11th after being T1st at halfway) and the Michelob (T15th).

He was T20th in the British Open and T41st in the USPGA. In the WGC Andersen World Match Play (remember his 4th in 1999) he lost in R1 to Bob Estes by 1 hole.

His ability to score well and earn dollars is shown by the fact that in 1999 his Money list ranking was 73 places higher than his all-round ranking, and in 2000 it was 56 places higher by mid September. His bunker play continues to be a problem.

> A big tournament player he can be noted in two of the majors

  * The US Masters. In his last five starts he's made the top 6 three times - (T3rd 1991: T6th 1992: T4th 1999), and he made a magnificent seven successive birdies in a R3 65 in 1999. Worth a small interest in the 'without Woods' market each way.

  * The British Open. He's made five cuts in six starts so can be noted in match bets.

> A born-and-bred Californian he enjoys the Buick Invitational which he won in 1992, where he's played many good rounds, and where he was T14th in 2000. He'll be worth support in match bets, and in the 'without Woods' market at Torrey Pines in 2001.

Key stat   His Money list placing in the last two years has been at least 50 places higher than his all-round ranking.

CARL PAULSON   D

Age 30   **Born** Virginia   **Lives** Virginia
College South Carolina
BUY.COM tour wins 2, 1999 Utah Classic, 1999 Boise Open **US Tour** BEF T7th in 1995 Walt Disney Classic **Money list** BEF 64th 2000

It had been another year of struggle for Carl with two top 10s, in the Western Open (T9th) and the Buick Open (T6th), and three top 25s, in the Colonial (T24th), the Shell Houston Open (T17th) and the Pennsylvania Classic (T24th), until he finished 4th at 125/1 in the Buick Challenge winning $110K to secure his card.

He was 2nd at 100/1 in the Tampa Bay Classic in late October when he so nearly notched his first tour success.

A huge hitter he's in the top 10 for driving distance and par 5 birdies. However his putting rank outside the top 100 is his key problem.

> Having finished No. 1 on the 1999 BUY.COM tour it's been a disappointing year for Carl.

> Long par 72 courses on which he can attack the par 5s really suit Carl. So he can be followed at big prices in two such events in 2001:-

  * The Western Open. Four sub-par rounds when T9th this year.

  * The Buick Challenge. 13 under for his last three rounds when 4th in 2000.

Key stat   T11th for par 5 birdies.

DENNIS PAULSON

Age 38   **Born** California   **Lives** California

US Tour wins 1, 2000 Buick Classic, **International wins** 1990 Philippines Open **BUY.COM tour** 1, 1998 Huntsville Open **Money list** BEF 27th 1999

Last year Dennis made a big impact with a couple of 2nd-place finishes, and this year he's made the breakthrough securing his first win (at 100/1) in the Buick Classic, beating David Duval in a play-off at the 4th extra hole.

The rest of his form has been ordinary with just two top 25s, in the Buick Invitational (T21st) and the Nissan Open (T18th).

In the WGC World Match Play he lost 2 & 1 to Monty in R1. In the US Masters he was the R1 leader (68) before finishing T14th. He was T11th in the British Open, T58th in the USPGA and withdrew from the US Open after missing the cut.

Big Den's overall stats make grim reading, and being outside the top 170 for driving accuracy for the second successive year is not encouraging. A massive hitter at 282 yards. His putting this year has worsened considerably.

Wears flamboyant shirts. Much calmer on course now.

> Dennis' 100/1 win justified the prediction last year that he would win in 2000. However he must improve his driving accuracy and rediscover his 1999 putting touch if he's to continue to progress.

> Although he missed the cut this year at the English Turn course I think we should remember that he was T4th in 1999 and T4th in 1994 including a course record 62. So Dennis must have a big chance in the 2001 Compaq Classic on one of his favourite Jack Nicklaus designed courses so back him each way at 66/1+.

> He'll find it very difficult to defend his Buick Classic title although his stroke average is 69 for his last eight rounds there.

Key stat   175th for driving accuracy this year and 172nd last year!

DAVID PEOPLES

Age 40   **Born** Maine   **Lives** Florida

US tour wins 2, 1991 Buick Challenge, 1992 Michelob Championship **Money list** BEF 25th 1992

2nd at the 1999 Q School David has secured his card for 2001. He posted top 20s in the Fedex St Jude Classic (T11th), the Compaq Classic (T17th) and the Bell South Classic (T15th), top 25s in the Reno-Tahoe Open (T21st) and the Doral Ryder Open (T21st), and a top 10 in the Kemper Open (T7th).

A good iron player his putting has let him down this season.

> Ranked in the top 20 for scoring before the cut he can be noted in early 3-ball betting as he shot at least one pre-cut round in the 60s in fifteen of his first seventeen tournaments in 2000.

> Having shot 65 in R1 (and in R4) this year in the Fedex St Jude Classic keep him in mind for R1 3-ball betting at Southwind in 2001.

Key stat   37th for birdie conversion.

CRAIG PERKS

Age 33　　　**Born** New Zealand　　　**Lives** Los Angeles

BUY.COM tour BEF 2nd, in 1996 and 1999

Craig earned his tour card when 39th at Q School. He made a poor start in 2000 missing nine of his first twelve cuts and not posting a single top 50 finish.

Finished 2nd at 150/1 to Michael Campbell (losing in a play-off) in January for the New Zealand Open after a brilliant 65 in R4.

However he started making cuts from August and in successive weeks, in September, earned over $200,000 when T4th in the Bell Canadian Open, and T12th Pennsylvania Classic. Finished T20th in the Southern Farm Bureau (72 in R4)

Played unsuccessfully on the BUY.COM tour in 2000.

His stats not surprising make very gloomy reading with the glowing exception of sand saves as he's clearly a brilliant bunker player.

> His progressive scoring (72-69-67-66) in this year's Canadian Open mark him down as a player to note at Glen Abbey in the Autumn.

> After his superb performance when 2nd this year he must be considered for the New Zealand Open in mid January.

Key stat　　　4th for sand saves: he's 174th for par 5 birdies.

TOM PERNICE JR

Age 41　　　Born　Missouri　　　**Lives** Missouri

College California

US Tour wins 1, 1999 Buick Open **Money list** BEF 55th 1998

Having won over a million dollars in his last two years including his first win last year Tom entered the new Millenium full of hope. However 2000 has been disappointing.

He's had one top 5 finish when T5th at 150/1 in the Bell South Classic. He also had a top 10 when T8th in the all-winners season opening Mercedes Championship incl. a tournament best 65 in R3.

He also posted top 25s in the Phoenix Open (T23rd), the Bay Hill Invitational (T22nd) and the Buick Open (T21st as defending champion).

T27th in the USPGA.

Outside the top 130 for both greens in reg and total driving. His strength has been his final-round scoring.

> Tom's just the sort of guy to make the frame popping up at 125/1 on the wide fairways of the Bob Hope Chrysler Classic where he was T28th this year and T13th in 1999.

> Unusually in each of the last two years his scoring average is lowest of all......on a Sunday in R4!

Key stat　　　150th for greens in regulation.

CHRIS PERRY

Age 39   **Born** North Carolina   **Lives** Ohio

College Ohio

US Tour wins 1, 1998 BC Open **BUY.COM tour** 1, 1994 Utah Classic **Money list** BEF 5th 1999

James Christopher has had his usual year with a whole bunch of high finishes, over a million dollars in earnings but without a win.

He's had four top 5 finishes in the Greater Greensboro Classic (T5th at 40/1), the Buick Classic (T5th at 50/1), the Buick Open (2nd at 66/1) and the Pennsylvania Classic (T2nd at 28/1).

He also posted top 10s in the Bell South Classic (T10th), the Greater Milwaukee Open (T9th) and the Tour Championship (T8th), with top 25s in the Phoenix Open (T23rd), the Doral Ryder Open (T15th), the MCI Classic (T15th), the Memorial (T17th), the Buick Challenge (T18th) and the NCR Classic at Disney (T13th).

In the majors he was T14th in the US Masters, T32nd in the British Open, missed the cut in the British Open, and was T34th in the USPGA.

In the World Match Play he lost to Paul Lawrie by 1 hole. 16th in the WGC American Express Championship.

Chris has a strong all-round game based essentially on very accurate approch play and solid ("I've always been a good putter") putting. His driving accuracy is up 5% and greens in regulation by ½%. Fader of the ball. He was 39 in September 2000.

> His weakness has been his inability to convert serious winning chances into victories. After all he'd posted (up to October this year) forty-three career top 10s and one-hundred-and-thirteen top 25s yet he'd won only once....

  Indeed there have been two classic cases of Chris' ability to lose from a winning position in the last two years.

  * 1999 MCI Classic. 1 shot leader with 2 to play. Shoots bogey-bogey to finish 4th.

  * 2000 Buick Open. 2 up with 3 to play he lost to Mediate. So the bottle is awarded.

> So over the last 4 or 5 holes when he's in the lead he'd been well worth opposing when betting 'in running'.

> Chris's consistent run of high, if non-winning, finishes are ideal for match betting and for selling his finishing position on the spreads.

  He can be followed in those markets in four tournaments in all of which he's been in the top 25 in each of the last three years.

  * The Buick Classic. 5th-3rd-10th-17th-24th are his last five years' progressive form figures.

  * The Buick Open. 2nd-15th-23rd in the last three years

  * The Memorial. T17th-T24th-T6th in the last three years

  * The Buick Challenge T18th-T13th-T8th in the last three years

> Born in Carolina he can be seriously fancied for the two tournaments held in that state.

    * MCI Classic: T15th this year from poor tee times and T4th 1999 when ahead after 70 holes!

    * Greater Greensboro Classic: T5th-25th-38th in the last three years on a course that suits him.

> He simply cries out to be backed in the Greater Milwaukee Open.

    * If he has an early tee time sell his finishing position (FP 25-28 this year) on the spreads as his 9th (2000), 6th (1999) and 3rd (1998) finishes are impressive.

    * Back him in R1 and R2 3 balls. His stats in this event reflect his overall play very well.

	2000	1999	1998	Stroke Average
R1	66	65	68	66.3
R2	67	68	62	65.6
Compare				
R4	70	70	71	70.33

Key stat   In the last two years he's posted thirteen (!) top 5 finishes yet he's not won.

KENNY PERRY ☼ F

Age 40   **Born** Kentucky   **Lives** Kentucky
College Kentucky

US Tour wins 3, 1991 Memorial, 1994 New England Classic, 1995 Bob Hope Classic **Presidents Cup** 1996 **Money list** 13th 1996

The tall guy (he's 6 foot 1 in his slippers) from Kentucky has achieved a solid M/L placing this year based on three top 3 finishes. They came in the Bell South Classic (T3rd at 80/1*), the Greater Milwaukee Open (T3rd at 40/1) and the Southern Farm Bureau (3rd at 40/1).

He also had top 25s in the Phoenix Open (T23rd), the AT&T (T20th), the Tucson Open (T13th), the Western Open (T15th) and the Buick Open (T30th).

He finished T30th in the USPGA.

A consistent player who is regularly in the top 10 for greens in regulation. However his putting and bunker play let him down. He was 40 in August 2000.

> "I'm a hot weather player" so he can be backed in match bets and in the outrights in the desert in the Phoenix Open (three top 10s last five years) and the Tucson Open (T13th 2000: T13th 1999: T31st 1998).

> The hot, humid conditions surrounding the Greater Milwaukee Open suit him. T3rd this year (including 64 in R1) he could do well again there in 2001.

> If he qualifies for the 2001 US Open his 4th-place finish on the Southern Hills course in 1996 in the Tour Championship will give him PMAs for Oklahoma in June.

Key stat   T9th for greens in regulation in 1999 he was 3rd in 2000.

NICK PRICE

Age 43   **Born** South Africa   **Lives** Florida

US Tour wins 14 (!), 1983 World Series, 1991 Byron Nelson Classic, Canadian Open, 1992 Texas Open, 1993 Players Championship, Canon Greater Hartford Open, Western Open, St Jude Classic, 1994 Honda Classic, The Colonial, Western Open, Canadian Open, 1997 MCI Classic, 1998 Fedex St Jude Classic **European tour** 4, latest 1997 South African PGA **Major wins** 3, 1992 and 1994 USPGA: 1994 British Open **International wins** 18 latest 1998 Million Dollar Challenge **Dunhill Cup** 8, latest 2000: **Presidents Cup**1994, 1996, 1998 and 2000 **World Cup** 1993 **Money list** Top 1993 and 1994

Nick has had another year in which he's proved that even when he's well into his forties he can play good golf at the very highest level.

In 2000 he posted six top 5s, in the Doral Ryder Open (3rd at 25/1), the Players Championship (T3rd at 33/1), the Western Open (2nd at 33/1 losing in a play-off), the Buick Challenge (T2nd at 33/1), the Tour Championship (T3rd at 50/1) and the WGC American Express (T5th at 40/1).

He had top 25s in the Byron Nelson (T15th) and the Fedex St. Jude Classic (T25th).

In Europe he finished T17th in the Deutsche Bank Open. In the majors he finished 11th in the US Masters, T27th in the US Open, and he missed the cuts in both the British Open and the USPGA.

In the World Match Play he lost in R1 to Mark Calcavecchia 2 and 1, and he finished T20th in the WGC.NEC Invitational. In the Dunhill Cup he lost all three games to give him a career record of thirteen wins in twenty-six matches. In the Presidents Cup he lost to Duval (2 and 1) in the singles, scoring 2 points overall.

He now plays a restricted schedule and plays relatively few 'ordinary' tournaments because he spends a lot of time, especially in the summer, with his family. Focuses on the big-money events.

Nick's great strength is his accurate driving and approach play and his form therefore tends to depend mainly on his putting. It was brilliant in his prime from 1993-1994, and in his three major wins however it's variable now as he's outside the top 60 for putting.

At his best in warm weather.

> Back Nick in the 2001 Players Championship in match bets, on the spreads, and in the outrights for three key reasons.

* His record is first class. 3rd - 3rd-8th in the last three years, he won it in 1994 and has posted seven top 10s in eleven years.

* It's held in Florida where he lives.

* He focuses on mega-dollar tournaments like this.

> Worth support in match bets for the Doral Ryder Open. T10th last year and 3rd this year when his brilliant approach play was let down by some ordinary putting.

> If he's not in contention at Augusta he will have serious prospects the following week in the MCI Classic where from 1996-1998 he averaged 68.3 and of course he won there in 1997.

> At Southern Hills in 1994 he won the USPGA by 6 shots so he'll be delighted that it is the venue for the 2001 US Open. If he putts well he'll post a high finish. Keep an eye on Nick at Tulsa in July.

> In Europe he may well come over for the valuable 2001 Deutsche Bank especially as it will be held on the Heidelberg course where he was 3rd (after a brilliant 65-65 finish) in 1999.

Key stat 17th for total driving in 1999, and T24th in 2000.

CHRIS RILEY   g y

Age 27   **Born** California   **Lives** Las Vegas

US Tour BEF T7th 1999 Sony Open in Hawaii. T7th 1999 Buick Invitational **Money list** BEF 71st 2000

Earned his 1999 tour card via Q School and he retained his status when 112th on the M/L after three top 10s in his rookie year.

In 2000 he's improved his position thanks to a good run of form in the second half of the season during which he hit form with top 20s in the Canon Greater Hartford Open (T18th), the BC Open (T15th), the International (T14th), the Michelob (T9th) and the Southern Farm Bureau (T6th), and he posted two card-saving top 5 finishes in the John Deere Classic (4th at 150/1**) and the Air Canada Championship (T4th at 80/1), winning $242K with those performances.

Chris is a good putter whose problems early in the season were waywardness off both tee and fairway. A fine bunker player

> What an enigma! 'Hot' early season form in 1999 followed by a tailspin in the later months, whereas this year all his big finishes came after July.

> On the basis of his form in the second half of this season he could well gain a 'shock' first victory at big odds in 2001.

> He can be fancied to make 'the frame' at juicy odds in the two tournaments in which he's shown his most consistent form in the last two years.

* The Sony Open in Hawaii T7th 1999: T26th 2000.

* The Honda Classic T28th 2000: T9th 1999.

> He loves the heat (living in Las Vegas) and he sure loves the new Deere run course where he was an impressive 4th this year (with four rounds at or below 68) in the John Deere Classic. Chris could well win this tournament in 2001.

Key stat   104th (at 272.9 yards) for driving distance.

LOREN ROBERTS   G ○ 🏇

Age 45   **Born** California   **Lives** Tennessee

US Tour wins 7, 1994 Bay Hill Invitational, 1995 Bay Hill Invitational 1996, MCI Classic, 1996 Greater Milwaukee Open, 1997 CVS Charity Classic, 1999 Byron Nelson Classic, 2000 Greater Milwaukee Open. **Majors** BEF T2nd 1994 US Open **Ryder Cup** 1995 **Presidents Cup** 1994, 2000 **Money list** 6th 1994

Loren could not have realised after he finished next to the last in the Mercedes Championship just what a year lay ahead because he went on to notch his 7th tournament win when he was the runaway 8 (!) shot winner of the Greater Milwaukee Open.

However that was only part of his mega season as he posted three other top 5s, in the Bay Hill Invitational (T4th at 80/1), the Shell Houston Open (T3rd at 40/1) and in the US Masters (T3rd at 125/1 in his BEF at Augusta). He also had top 10s in the US Open (T8th) and the British Open (T7th).

In 'ordinary' USPGA tournaments he had high finishes in the Buick Invitational (T21st), the Nissan Open (T18th), the Byron Nelson (T25th as defending champion), the Fedex St Jude Classic (T7th), the Buick Open (T16th), the Pennsylvania Classic (T8th), Texas Open (T9th) and Michelob (T19th).

He finished 14th in the WGC NEC Invitational, while in the Andersen World Match Play he lost in R1 to Sergio Garcia at the 20th. Finished T58th in the USPGA. In the Presidents Cup he scored 2 points beating Appleby (3 and 2) in the singles. 27th (of 29) in the Tour Championship.

He is extremely short off the tee at 257 yards (ranked 191st in 1999 and similarly this year). His great strengths are his accurate driving (77% of fairways in 1999, and 79% this year) and legendary putting (known as 'Boss of The Moss' for his beautifully smooth putting action). This year his sandsaves (49% in 1999) are much improved at 62%, including seven out of eight in the US Masters. He's a real course strategist. At his best in warm dry conditions.

Although a proven winner Loren twice shot poor final rounds (74 in both cases) when in contention in the Pennsylvania Classic, and the Michelob Championship in the final third of the season.

> With six wins in the last six years 45-year-old Roberts knows how to win and whenever there is warm dry weather, an emphasis on driving accuracy and putting he'll always do well, and a seventh win, despite his lack of length, is definitely possible.

> He's won two tournaments (Bay Hill and the GMO) twice each and I think he could well make it three in 2001 as I can see him winning the 2001 Byron Nelson Classic again. It's played on two par 70 courses where the emphasis on accuracy and putting rather than length suits him ideally. Winner in 1999, and with all rounds at or under par as defending champion this year he loves this track.

> His other really big chance will surely be in the 2001 Greater Milwaukee Open ("the course fits my game"). Winner by 8 this year and let's remember the first

time he defended a title (1995 Bay Hill) he won so he could well retain his GMO title next year.

> There are four tournaments in which he has a good recent record and where you can see him finishing high enough to justify match bet support.

* The Buick Open. A 'putting contest', T16th (2000), 9th (1999).

* The Shell Houston Open. T3rd at 40/1 this year, after T5th at 80/1 in 1999 suggest a place only bet may yield a return.

* The Bay Hill. Course has been lengthened since his back to back wins in 1994 and 1995. Nevertheless he was T6th in 1997, and T4th in 2000.

* Buick Invitational. Over the last two years (T7th 1999, T21st 2000) he has a stroke average of 69.5.

> IF it's hot and dry at Royal Lytham next year back him in the R1 and R2 3-ball betting. On the course in 1996 he shot 67 (R1) and 69 (R2), and this year too in benign conditions he shot 69 (R1) and 68 (R2).

Key stat   4th for driving accuracy.

RORY SABBATINI   G Y

Age 24   **Born** Durban, South Africa **Lives** Tucson, Arizona

US Tour wins 1, 2000 Air Canada Championship **Money list** BEF 36th 2000

Rory Mario Trevor Sabbatini has sure made an impact in 2000.

In just his second tournament he was 2nd in the Bob Hope Chrysler Classic at 125/1, and later in early September he won the Air Canada at 100/1 after a 65 in R4 when he started Sunday as a 33/1 outsider.

He also had a top 10 in the Canadian Open (T6th), and top 25s in the AT&T (T11th), the Nissan Open (T12th), the Honda Classic (T16th) and the Buick Challenge (T23rd). He missed the cut in the US Open and finished 77th in the USPGA.

His stats show two key features. He's a very, very long hitter and he's in the top 10 for birdie conversion, par 5 birdies and eagles made. However he can be very inaccurate as both his driving accuracy and greens in reg rankings for last year and this are outside the top 150. He is trying to become less self critical.

> Let's be clear, in just two seasons on tour this 24-year-old guy (with twenty-four letters in his name) has had a win and three other top 3 finishes.

> Rory will merit each-way support in the weakly contested BC Open where on his only start he was T3rd in 1999.

> He must be backed for the 2001 Bob Hope Chrysler Classic where the set up of wide-fairway, par 72 (each with four par 5) courses suits him ideally. 2nd this year, when he dropped shots in R4 after arguing with a marshall, he must have a big chance next year.

> His long hitting is well suited to the Heron Bay course (T16th 2000 with four rounds at or below 70) so he'll have a real chance at a massive price in the 2001 Honda Classic.

Key stat   Three top 3s and a win in his first two years on tour.

TOM SCHERRER

Age 30   **Born** New York   **Lives** Florida

US Tour wins 1, 2000 Kemper Open **BUY.COM Tour wins** 2, 1998 Upstate Classic, 1995 Knoxville Open **Money list** BEF 35th 2000

It's been a 'breakthrough' year for 6 foot Thomas Cregg Scherrer who won his first tournament on the full tour when he landed the Kemper Open at 125/1.

He had already shown real promise when T2nd at 100/1* in the Tucson Open.

He later posted his third big finish of the season when 4th at 80/1 in the Michelob

His other high finishes were in the Bell South Classic (T22nd), the MCI Classic (T25th), the Greater Greensboro Classic (T16th) and the Fedex St Jude Classic (T7th).

He missed the cut in the British Open and withdrew after R1 of the USPGA.

His key stats are very similar to last year. His improved M/L position is based simply on having two really massive weeks. Safely past 30 in July 2000.

> Runner-up to Justin Leonard in the 1992 US Amateur and a member of the 1991 Walker Cup side, this guy has a sound amateur record, a good putting touch and now he's a winner in his 'nappy factor' year.

> Tom is very much a 'desert fox' with a really solid record in desert tournaments. He could spring an 80/1 surprise in the Reno-Tahoe Open where he was T9th last year after being 2nd after R3.

> Must enter into calculations for the Fedex St Jude Classic where six of his last eight rounds have been in the 60s as he's finished T7th (2000) and 25th (1999).

> He cries out to be backed for the 2001 Michelob. 4th in 2000 and T5th in 1999 he has a two-year stroke average of 69, including 64 in R2 this year.

Key stat   108th for driving accuracy.

JOEY SINDELAR   D

Age 42   **Born** New York   **Lives** New York

US Tour wins 6, latest 1990 Hardee's Golf Classic **Money list** BEF 3rd 1988

Joseph Paul (answers to Joey) has had a poor year. However when he has hit form he has made it pay, posting a couple of top 5s in the Bell South Classic in April (T5th at 150/1*) and in the Buick Classic (T5th at 125/1) in June. He also had top 20s in the Greater Milwaukee Open (T18th) and the Michelob (T12th).

He missed the cut in twelve of his first fourteen tournaments, then from early June he made eight of his next nine cuts.

Not surprisingly his stats reflect his inconsistent disappointing year. However they do point to his strength as he hits two thirds of his greens in regulation (up 2%). However he is short off the tee at 271 yards and still can't make the top 150 for sand saves. He remains a dodgy putter when within 4-6 foot of the hole. Just retained his card.

> Without a win for ten years, short off the tee and in his forties it's not easy to see Sindelar posting win number 7. However, he has proved this year that he can suddenly 'catch fire' and post a top 5 finish.

> 'Contention rust' may be present as two examples this year show.

　* Bell South Classic. Halfway leader, he then shot 74 in R3 before the tournament was abandoned with him in T5th place.

　* The Canadian Open. T6 after R3 he shot 75 in R4 to finish T35th!

　So if he's in the top 6 after R3 in 2001 he can be opposed in R4 betting.

> His best chance will probably be in the Greater Milwaukee Open where he's posted three top 10s and a top 20 in the last seven years. The course suits his short, straight hitting.

> Plays well in his native North East as he showed this year when T5th in New York in the Buick Classic.

Key stat　　　　T53rd for greens in regulation.

VIJAY SINGH　　　　　　　　　　　　　　　G ☼

Age 37　　　　**Born** Fiji　　　　　　　**Lives** Florida

US Tour wins 7, 1993 Buick Classic, 1995 Phoenix Open, 1995 Buick Classic, 1997 Memorial, 1997 Buick Open, 1998 Sprint International, 1999 Honda Classic **Major wins** 2, 1998 USPGA, 2000 US Masters **International wins** 12, latest Taiwan Open **European tour wins** 7, latest 1997 Sth African Open **Presidents Cup** 1994,96,98, 2000 **Money list** 2nd 1998

This year has been most unusual for Vijay as he didn't win a single 'ordinary' tournament yet he did win the US Masters, the one major he seemed least likely to win.

The keys to his 50/1 Augusta triumph were his much improved putting, his No. 1 ranking in greens in reg, and the fact that he went 9 under par on the par 5s.

He has posted four top 5s, in the AT&T (T2nd at 33/1), the MCI Classic (T3rd at 16/1 after 64 in R4), the Tour Championship (T3rd at 33/1*) and the WGC American Express (T3rd at 28/1), and he also had top 10s in the Mercedes (T8th) and the International (T9th). Other high finishes were recorded in the Sony Open in Hawaii (T19th), the Nissan Open (T18th), the Buick Classic (T24th), the Buick Open (T11th) and the NCR Classic at Disney (T18th).

In the majors after his US Masters 50/1 success he finished T8th in the US Open, T11th in the British Open, and he missed the USPGA cut after playing R1 and R2 with Tiger.

In the Andersen World Match Play he lost (2 and 1) to Duffy Waldorf in R1.

In Europe he finished T4th at 14/1 in the Lancome Trophy after he won the Johnnie Walker Taiwan Open in the Far East after a play-off. In the Presidents Cup he scored 1 point before losing to Tiger (2 and 1) in the singles.

Vijay is a very long hitter at 285 yards who creates plenty of birdie and eagles opportunities on the par 5s. He's in the top 10 for par 5 birdies which were the basis of his US Masters triumph. His sand save stats have improved a lot (now 60%) over the last couple of years. His putting as usual is most inconsistent and he's ranked outside the top 100. This year he's used the longer putter and went back to the broomstick for the US Open. His putting is undoubtedly his achilles heel, he even 3 putted from 4 feet in the NCR Classic. Once again he's not in the top 100 for driving accuracy.

Fades the ball. He has a fine temperament and is reputedly the hardest worker on the range on the tour. Paul Tesori is his new caddie.

> In the last four years he's won seven US tournaments including two majors and, as I say every year, I expect him to go on to win again.....and again!

Take a ride on Vijay in the Magnificent Seven in 2001. There are seven tournaments in which you can make out a very solid case for Vijay next year. They are all par 72 (four par 5) courses, and he's won four of them already.

An each-way bet on the Fijian in each of them should show a nice profit and give us something to Singh about.

* The Phoenix Open. He's a strong fancy to win this in 2001, Winner in 1995 his LT stroke average was best of all up to this year when he finished T41st (76 in R4).

* The AT&T. Suits his long hitting. 2nd 2000: T10th 1999 for a two-year stroke average of 69.57 which is the best of all!

* The Doral Ryder Open. 2nd in 1997, and 12th in 1998 the course suits Vijay who is based in Florida. His T36th this year (new clubs) and MC (1999 when putting very badly) can probably be ignored.

* The Memorial. The course suits him. Winner in 1997 and 2nd in 1999.

* The Buick Classic. 5th in 1999, he's won this twice, in 1993 and 1995.

* The Western Open. 4th 1999, 2nd 1998, T8th 1996 so forget his missed cut this year and expect Vijay to play really well at Cog Hill in 2001

* The International. Won 1998, 19th 1999, 9th 2000 where the points system suits his long hitting, and his ability to make eagles and birdies on par 5s is so vital

> With the USPGA and the US Masters already won Vijay will be aiming for a career grand slam by adding the British and US Opens to his tally.

* The British Open. At Royal Lytham in hot conditions in 1996 he was T3rd after R3 before a disappointing 73 left him in T11th place. If the weather's hot again he'll go close although his high ball flight can be a disadvantage if the winds blow.

* The US Open. At Southern Hills he was 6th in the 1995 Tour Championship (when 5th for putting) so he'll welcome that course being the 2001 venue. Form figures from 1995 of T10th-T7th-T77th-T25th-T3rd and T8th this year are encouraging. With five top 25s, and four top 10s in the last six years he must have a serious chance if he can improve his accuracy off the tee. Looks a solid finishing position sell.

* The USPGA. The wider fairways and hot humid conditions of the USPGA suit Vijay as his record of three top 5s, including his 1998 victory shows. Ignore his missed cut this year when below par and drawn alongside Tiger.

Key stat   7th for par 5 birdies.

JEFF SLUMAN

Age 43   **Born** New York   **Lives** Illinois

US Tour wins 3, 1997 Tucson Classic, 1998 Greater Milwaukee Open, and 1999 Sony Open in Hawaii **Major wins** 1, 1988 USPGA **Order of Merit** 14th 1992

Jeffrey George, Jeff to his friends, has had another steady year consistently making nice cheques without notching a single 'big' finish.

He's had top 20s in the Mercedes (14th), the Sony Open in Hawaii (T14th as defending champion), the Players Championship (T17th), the Colonial (T13th), the Pennsylvania Classic (T18th) and the NCR Classic at Disney (7th). He also posted top 25s in the Bob Hope (T23rd), the Buick Invitational (T21st), the Doral Ryder (T21st), the Memorial (T25th), the Canon Greater Hartford Open (T25th), the John Deere Classic (T23rd), the Reno-Tahoe Open (T21st) and the Invensys Classic in Las Vegas (T17th).

In the World Match Play he beat Steve Elkington in R1 (2 and 1), then lost in R2 to Davis Love (2 and 1).

He finished T8th in the Masters, T41st in the USPGA, T60th in the British Open and he missed the US Open cut.

He is an accurate iron player with a sound short game. Lack of length is becoming a real handicap.

> Jeff's consistency, making four cuts in every five, marks him as a player to be followed in match bets for tournaments such as these:-

* Buick Open. Stroke average of 69.5 over the last twenty-four rounds.

* Colonial. 13th-2nd-3rd-13th-2nd are mighty impressive form figures.

* The Buick Invitational. 21st-18th-16th-15th-15th in his last five starts.

* The Sony Open in Hawaii. Won 1999-13th 2000 for a two-year stroke average of 68.37.

* The NCR Classic in Disney. 7th in each of the last two years.

> In the outrights have a little each way on Jeff in the 2001 Colonial (w/o Woods, of course) and in the Pennsylvania Classic (T18th 2000 played in, 'his part of the world').

> In the Buick Open back him in the R1 3 balls where his stroke average is 68 on Thursday!

Key stat   167th (at 264.9 yards) for driving distance.

CHRIS SMITH

Age 31 **Born** Indiana **Lives** Indiana
University Ohio

BUY.COM tour wins 5, 1995 NIKE Gateway Classic, NIKE Dakota Dunes Open, 1997 NIKE Upstate Classic, NIKE Dakota Dunes Open, NIKE Omaha Classic **US tour** BEF 4th 1997 CVS Charity Classic

This year on the BUY.COM tour he posted no less than five 2nd-place finishes, in the BUY.COM South Carolina Classic, the BUY.COM Knoxville Open, the BUY.COM Richmond Open, the BUY.COM Dayton Open and the BUY.COM Inland Empire Open.

He made the cut in seventeen of his twenty starts with seven top 10s.

His stats are very interesting. 4th for driving distance, 3rd for greens in reg and top for par 5 birdies. However driving accuracy at 60% (111th) and sand saves, ranked 148th, are two areas needing improvement.

In 1997 he was the No. 1 player on the then NIKE tour after three wins and became the first player to achieve "battlefield promotion" to the main tour after three wins in a year.

> Although he didn't win this year he played consistently well to give him confidence for 2001. He'll be best suited by longer par 72 courses which do not place a premium on accuracy off the tee.

> Must not be opposed lightly in R1 and R2 3-ball betting as this year he was ranked top for present scoring at an impressive 69.85.

> He has the ability once he plays well to retain his form and go on to do well again. He's won back-to-back on the BUY.COM tour in 1997, and this year in late April-early May he finished 2nd in three successive weeks. So remember with Chris....when he's hot he's hot!

> His best tour finish (pre 1997) came when he was T8th in the 1993 BC Open so with a weak field (as this tournament plays alongside the British Open) this long hitter could do very well at New York in July.

Key stat No. 1 for stroke average (70.11) on the 2000 BUY.COM tour.

JERRY SMITH

Age 36 **Born** Iowa **Lives** Scottsdale, Arizona

Omega tour wins 1, 1998 Guam Open **US Tour** BEF 9th 2000 Byron Nelson Classic

Jerry who? earned his card when 7th at the 1999 Q School and in 2000 he's played fairly well, making 70% of his cuts and posting a top 10, and his best-ever finish, when 9th in the Byron Nelson Classic.

He also had top 25s in the Sony Open in Hawaii (T14th), the Tucson Open (T13th) and the BC Open (T15th).

Very, very short off the tee he's a relatively straight driver although his approach play off the fairways means he only hits 65% of his greens. Outside top 100 for putting.

> Yet to be in contention, with less than $3500 earned on the USPGA tour before this year and with only one top 10 it ain't easy to nominate him for success.

> However living in Arizona and having posted a top 15 in this year's Tucson Open he'll be looking forward to the 2001 renewal.

Key stat 175th (at 264.1 yards) for driving distance.

CRAIG A SPENCE D

Age 26 **Born** Victoria, Australia **Lives** Victoria, Australia
ANZ tour wins 1 1999 Australian Masters **US tour** BEF T4th 1999 BC Open

Craig earned his tour card after finishing T7th at Q School. Playing on the ANZ tour he finished 2nd (losing in a play off) in the Players Championship.

In the States he had one big finish when 5th at 150/1 in the International. He also posted top 25s when T13th in the Greater Greensboro Classic, and T12th in the Nissan Open.

Missed the cut in the US Open.

In an inconsistent year he's made only four cuts in every nine tournaments. Not surprisingly his stats are universally poor. Must now go to Q School.

> Inconsistent, yet the fact remains that in the last two years on the ANZ tour he's won and been 2nd, and in the States he's finished T4th and 5th.

> This year in the Greater Greensboro Classic he finished T13th after four inconsistent (73-66-75-69) rounds. Yet there was enough promise to note him at Forest Oaks in 3 balls next year.

Key stat 180th (!!) for greens in regulation.

CRAIG STADLER F

Age 47 **Born** California **Lives** Colorado
US Tour wins 11, 8 in the '80s, and 1991 Tour Championship, 1992 NEC World Series, 1994 Buick Invitational, 1996 Nissan Open **Majors wins** 1, 1982 US Masters **International wins** 4, **Ryder Cup** 1983, 1985 **Money list** BEF Top 1982, 2nd 1991

Craig lost over 50 lbs in weight (that's over 3½ stones in old money) during the winter so that this year the 'Walrus' is more like a porpoise!

He had a really big finish when 2nd at 100/1* in the Shell Houston Open losing the play-off to Allenby at the 4th extra hole after he missed holeable putts to win at the 18th, and on 3 of the play-off holes!

He also had high finishes in the AT&T (T15th), the Buick Invitational (T14th), the MCI Classic (T15th), the International (T14th) and the Canadian Open (T10th).

He missed the cut in the US Masters and the US Open, and finished T64th in the USPGA.

His driving accuracy (down 4%), greens in reg. (down 2%) and sand saves (down 2.5%) have all worsened this year. Although birdie conversion has risen (by 2%).

> Usually plays well fresh early in the year in California where he must be noted for matchbets in two tournaments.

   * AT&T. Form figures now read 15th-3rd-25th-4th-13th

   * The Buick Invitational. T14th-T26th-T13th-T2nd over the last four years and, of course, the Walrus won it in 1994.

> He must be noted for the MCI Classic where he's had ten of his last twelve rounds under par with finishing positions of T15th (2000), T12th (1999) and 9th (1997th).

Key stat   174th (!!!) for driving accuracy.

PAUL STANKOWSKI

Age 31   **Born** California   **Lives** Texas

College Texas

US Tour wins 2, 1996 Bell South Classic, 1997 Hawaiian Open **International wins** 1, 1996 Casio World Open **BUY.COM tour wins** 1, 1996 Louisiana Open **Money list** BEF 21st 1997

It's been a steady year for Paul after finishing 113th on the M/L in 1999.

He hasn't had a really big finish although he has posted nine top 20s, in the Phoenix Open (T10th), the Bell South Classic (T15th), the Shell Houston Open (T11th), the Compaq Classic (16th), the Byron Nelson Classic (T10th), the Kemper Open (T13th), the International (T11th), the Canadian Open (T10th) and the Invensys Classic in Las Vegas (T17th).

He finished T41st in the USPGA.

A 282-yard driver his stats show his key strength, namely his birdie conversion (up 3% and ranked 9th) and par 5 birdies (top 10) rankings. However his weakness shows in his driving accuracy stats still outside the top 150 although he's up 4% this year to 64%.

Second son born in August 1999.

> He is a good wind player. "I enjoy the wind. It makes you think".

> It would be no great surprise if 'Stanko' was to win or go very close in 2001. However without a win since 1997 he may be suffering from 'contention rust' judged by this year's Kemper Open, where he was T2nd after R3 only to shoot 3 over par in R4 to finish T13th.

> He has shown enough promise in the Byron Nelson Classic, when 5th in 1997, and with a 67-66-69 finish this year (when T10th) to merit serious consideration there in 2001.

> Trust me......he'll be a helluva bet at 50/1 in the Southern Farm Bureau Classic. In two starts he was T3rd in 1999 and T18th in 1998, and for his last six rounds

(three in '99 and his last three in '98) he is 27 under par for a stroke average of 67.5!

Key stat   17th (!) in the all-round ranking.

DAVE STOCKTON JR   V

Age 32 (Dad's 59)   **Born**   California   **Lives** California

US tour BEF T2nd 1995 Canon Greater Hartford Open **Money list** BEF 96th in 1994 (Rookie year).

Lost his card last year when 153rd on the M/L. He regained it when he finished 40th at the 1999 Q School.

In 2000 he posted three high finishes when T5th at 80/1 in the BC Open, T8th in the Air Canada, and T12th in his favourite tournament, the Canon Greater Hartford Open.

Short off the tee he is a good, if inconsistent, putter. His weakness has been inaccuracy off the tee and fairway.

His dad, Dave Senior, was US Ryder Cup Captain (remember Kiawah Island?) and currently plays on the Seniors tour. Must go to Q School.

> He simply cries out to be backed in the Canon Greater Hartford Open where his record, T12th (2000), T6th (1999), T2nd (1995) and T3rd (1994) is first class. He can be followed in R1 and R2 3 balls, and as an outsider with a genuine chance. His dad won the GHO in 1974 and his son could just do the same in 2001 as a 100/1 outsider.

> Played alongside the British Open the BC Open will provide a real opportunity (8th 1997: 5th 2000).

> He is a must R4 3-ball bet in the Air Canada Championship. Relaxed and 'off the pace' his final-round record (68 (2000), 68 (1999), 67 (1998) and 67 (1997)) is really awesome!

Key stat   157th (at 267 yards) for driving distance.

STEVE STRICKER   D

Age 33   **Born** Wisconsin   **Lives** Florida

US Tour wins 2, 1996 Kemper Open. 1996 Western Open **Presidents Cup** 1996 **The Dunhill Cup** 1996 **Majors** BEF 2nd 1998 USPGA **Money list** 4th 1996

After his two wins in 1996, when he was 4th on the Money list Steven Charles' (answers to Steve) form has been disappointing overall as he has clearly not progressed to 'the next level'.

In 1999 he posted two high finishes in the US Open (5th) and in the Players Championship (the fifth major) where he was T6th. In 2000 he changed to Ping clubs.

His big finish came when T4th at 80/1 in the Compaq Classic. He also had a top 25 in the Bob Hope (T23rd) and the Sony Open in Hawaii (T14th). In the majors he was T19th in the US Masters, T27th in the US Open, and he missed the cut in the USPGA and the British Open. In the WGC Match Play he beat Lee Janzen 2 and 1 before losing by the same score to Duffy Waldorf.

Long off the tee at 277 yards. His real problems are shown by his dreadful stats where he's outside the top 150 for both driving accuracy and greens in reg. His putting (6th in 1999) has also worsened in a poor year saved by one big finish.

> The big question is whether Steve can correct the flaws that are the root cause of his wayward approach play.

> Can suddenly spring into form after a bad run as he showed this year when he was T4th in the Compaq having missed four of his previous five cuts.

> If his stats show significant improvement he must be considered in the tournaments in which he's already shown form especially as his odds in 2001 will be large.

> If his stats show much improved accuracy he would be a player to note each way in the without Woods market for the 2001 US Open (T5th in 1998, and 5th in 1999). This major moves to the Southern Hills course in 2001 where Steve was 3rd in the 1996 Tour Championship when he was 2nd in that tournament's putting stats.

> He has sound recent form in the early season Hawaiian Open where he was 3rd 1996, T7th 1998 and T14th 2000.

> He can be backed for the 2001 Compaq Classic on the English Turn course where he found his form when T4th in 2000 having finished T20th in 1999.

> His 'personal major' is the Greater Milwaukee Open. His wife's family are deep into Wisconsin golf and this is the one he desperately wants to win. 3rd 1996: 12th 1997: 2nd 1998 and 10th 1999 he'll have a big chance if his stats show improvement.

> The other two tournaments in which he'll go well if he's in solid form will be

 * The Western Open. Coming from the adjacent state of Wisconsin he went to Illinois University, and was 5th in 1998 and he won it in 1996.

 * The Kemper Open. Provided him with his first win in 1996 and he's twice had top 10s (1998 and 1999) since.

Key stat   191st (!!!) for driving accuracy.

DAVID SUTHERLAND   V

Age   34   **Born**   California   **Lives**   California

US Tour wins BEF T2nd 1997 Greater Milwaukee Open **Money list** BEF 84th 1997

122nd on the M/L in 1998 and 120th last year. David continues to struggle in the "will I retain my card?" lower reaches of the Money list.

In 2000 he's had two top 10s, in the Shell Houston Open (T7th) and the NCR Classic at Disney (T8th), and four top 25s in the Buick Invitational (T14th), in the

Nissan Open (T12th on, "my favourite course"), in the Honda Classic (T19th including an albatross 2 on the par 5 14th) and in the Michelob (T15th).

Missed the cut in the British Open.

Improved his greens in reg. this year by 4 points to 67%. However his putting (64th last year) is now outside the top 130.

Younger, shorter and less successful than his brother Kevin.

> He does provide one betting opportunity. Back him in R4 of the Shell Houston Open if he's not in contention. His recent record on Sunday at Woodlands 69 (2000), 66 (1999) and 68 (1998) is first class, and he might just reward a 30/1+ place-only bet (7th this year and 33nd-22nd-20th before that) as well.

Key stat 52nd for greens in regulation.

KEVIN SUTHERLAND

Age 36 **Born** California **Lives** California

US tour wins BEF 2nd 1997 Shell Houston Open **Money list** 52nd 1997 **Money list** BEF 52nd 1997

He's older (by 19 months) and taller (only an inch) than his brother David and Kevin John continues to be the higher ranked player.

In 2000 he posted a top 5 in the Buick Invitational (T5th at 80/1*), top 10s in the Phoenix Open (T10th), the Canon Greater Hartford Open (T9th) and the Canadian Open (T10th), and top 25s in the Bob Hope (T23rd), the Nissan Open (T25th), the Shell Houston Open (T17th), the Byron Nelson (T25th), the Colonial (T20th), the Buick Classic (T19th) and the John Deere Classic (T23rd).

His consistency is based on his accuracy to the greens (top 40 last two years) and his fine bunker play (top 12 last two years). However he still finds it difficult to find that 'bit of brilliance' that turns a high finish into being in very serious contention. His birdie conversion ranking (124th last year: 80th this year to October) tells its own story.

> A first-time dad in very late August, 2001 will be Kevin's 'nappy factor' year and I would not be at all surprised if he were to post his first win at a tasty 100/1.

> His best chances will probably be in the following three tournaments:

   * Canon Greater Harford Open. T9th 2000: T17th 1999: T25th 1998: 13th 1997: 9th 1996 for a five-year eclectic score of 21 under which shows he could win. Worth a small each-way interest at 125/1.

   * Buick Invitational. T5th at 80/1* 2000: T4th at 80/1* 1999: T3rd 150/1 1998 for a three-year stroke average of 68.55! In 2000 his final three rounds were better than the winner Phil Mickelson. A born-and-bred Californian, with three consecutive top 5 finishes, raid your piggy bank and back him each way at 66/1+ for the 2001 Buick Invitational.

   * I think he could be a surprise packet in the Canadian Open where his 10th (2000)-29th-36th-23rd form figures are progressive. R1 leader this year, he could make the frame in, or even win, the 2001 Canadian Open at 100/1.

> His straight hitting is well suited to the Buick Classic, 19th 2000: 18th 1999: 7th 1998 for a 70.18 stroke average. With three successive top 20s he's a must match bet.

Key stat   T37th for greens in regulation.

HAL SUTTON   G ♣ F

Age 42   **Born** Louisiana   **Lives** Louisiana

US Tour wins 12, 6 in '80s, 1995 BC Open, 1998 Texas Open, 1998 Tour Championship, 1999 Canadian Open, 2000 Players Championship, 2000 Greater Greensboro Classic Majors 1, 1983 USPGA **Ryder Cup** 1985,1987,1999 **Presidents Cup** 1998 (W/D), 2000 **Money list** Top 1983, 4th 2000

It's been another superb year for Hal as he added two more wins to his already impressive tally. He landed the 'fifth major', the Players Championship at 40/1, and the Greater Greensboro Classic at 16/1. He also posted four top 5 finishes in the Bob Hope (T5th at 33/1), the Phoenix Open (T4th at 28/1), the Buick Open (3rd at 40/1) and the WGC NEC Invitational (T4th at 50/1*).

His other high finishes were in the Honda Classic (T7th), the Memorial (T8th) and the Canadian Open (T10th).

In the Andersen World Match Play he beat Ted Tryba (4 and 3), David Toms (1 up) and Duffy Waldorf (2 and 1), before he narrowly lost in the QF to the eventual winner, Darren Clarke (1 hole).

In the majors he played his best-ever US Masters, finishing T10th. He was T23rd in the US Open but missed the cuts in both the British Open and the USPGA (injured ankle). In the Presidents Cup he scored 3 points before losing to an inspired Carlos Franco (6 and 5) in the singles. T25th in the Tour Championship.

Hal is the classic 'fairways and greens' golfer. At 276 yards he's about average length. Top 20 for greens in reg and top 30 for fairways hit in each of the last two years is real accuracy and real consistency. This year his sand saves are up 6% although overall his putting has deteriorated (outside top 75). Very tough mentally (as discussed in Part 1). His weakness continues to be his chipping where he seems to lack 'feel' and so often over hits his shots.

> Hal is a superb player. A proven front runner who went head to head with the Tiger 'down the stretch' in the Players Championship and won. He's now won five times in the last three years and with his accuracy off both tee and fairway there's every reason to expect him to go on to further success.

> Last year I nominated him, inter alia, as 'the surprise winner' of the Players (won 40/1) and for the Buick Open (3rd at 40/1).

This year I suggest Hal can be supported in five tournaments in which he has proven form on courses suited to his game. An each-way bet in each should show a nice profit in 2001.

  * Phoenix Open. Recent changes emphasise accuracy and that's Sutton's stock-in-trade. T4th (2000) and 4th (1999) for a stroke average of 68.87. I can see him winning in 2001 at 25/1, so make Hal your Pal in Arizona.

* Honda Classic. T7th in each of the last two years Hal has a brilliant record on TPCs (Tournament Players' Courses).
* Shell Houston Open. Followed form figures of 2nd (1996), 6th (1998) and 4th (1997) with a flat T29th this year. However this came a week after his Greater Greensboro win when he had severe MLD so it's form best ignored. Expect normal service to be resumed, so back Hal at Houston in 2001.
* Buick Open. A three-year stroke average of 68.66 and progressive form figures of 12th (1998), 8th (1999) and 3rd (2000) give him an obvious chance.
* Canadian Open. 11th (1997), 4th (1998), Won (1999) and 10th (2000) make Hal a 'must' for match bets and on the spreads at Glen Abbey.

> His US Masters record before this year was on the really poor side of very bad i.e. twelve missed cuts in fourteen starts, no top 25 finish and a BEF of T27th in his halcyon days of 1983.

So his T10th finish in 2000 is surely significant. However it's not easy to see him winning although he may well continue his improvement in 2001 with another top 20 finish.

Key stat In each of the last two years Hal has hit 73-75% of fairways off the tee, and 69-70% of greens in regulation.

ESTEBAN TOLEDO

Age 38 **Born** Mexico **Lives** California
US Tour BEF T3rd 1998 BellSouth Classic **Money list** BEF 69th 2000

The Mexican born former boxer has secured his card for the third successive year thanks to one huge finish when he was 2nd at 125/1 in the BC Open winning $216K.

He also had top 25s in the Hawaiian Open (T14th), the Nissan Open (T25th), the Shell Houston Open (T17th), the Air Canada (T22nd), the NCR Classic at Disney (T13th) and the Southern Farm Bureau (T13th), and a top 10 in the Texas Open (T6th).

His stats are uniformly poor although his driving accuracy stats are once more very solid. His lack of length (ranked 190th) at 258 yards is a mega handicap.

> He can be followed in the opening round 3 balls in
* The Doral Ryder Open: 68 in R1 in each of the last two years
* Hawaiian Open: R1s of 67 (2000) and 65 (1999)

> Must be noted for match bets in the Hawaiian Open where he's posted consecutive top 20s in the last two years.

Key stat 26th for driving accuracy.

DAVID TOMS

🏇 **G**

Age 33   **Born** Louisiana   **Lives** Louisiana

US Tour wins 3, 1997 John Deere Classic, 1999 The International, 1999 Buick Challenge, 2000 Michelob Championship **Money list** BEF 10th 1999

Having won twice on the USPGA tour in 1999 he carried on the winning habit, in late 1999, when he won the Hassan Trophy beating Chris Perry in a play-off.

In 2000 he had three top 5s, in the Bob Hope (T3rd at 66/1), the Colonial (T4th at 50/1) and, most interesting of all, the British Open (T4th at 150/1) before he won his fourth US tournament in October when he beat Mike Weir (in a play-off) to land the Michelob Championship at 50/1.

He also had top 25s in the Mercedes (T19th), the Phoenix Open (T18th), the Buick Invitational (T14th), the Bell South Classic (T15th), the Fedex St Jude Classic (T15th) and the Texas Open (T19th).

In the World Match Play he beat Brian Watts (by 1 hole) in R1, before losing 4 and 3 to Hal Sutton. In the majors he posted that brilliant T4th in the British Open, finished T49th in the US Masters, T16th in the US Open and T41st in USPGA to make the cut in all four. T11th in the Tour Championship.

Average length off the tee at 276 yards. A straight driver (72% fairways hit) he's in the top 15 for greens in reg, top 40 for putting and top 15 for total driving.

> Toms is now a serious consistent player with very solid all round stats who knows how to win. Admittedly he let the pressure get to him on the back nine in the British Open although that was scarcely surprisingly. I expect that he'll go on to win more tournaments.

> He likes the John Deere Classic which gave him his first win in 1997. His record in the tournament, W 1997: 4th 1998: 12th 1999 was very good. This year on the new Deere run course he arrived from St Andrews jet lagged and without practice before shooting 74 in R1. So although he missed the cut we know he enjoys the new course because he shot 67 in R2. He can be backed with confidence, if he's not jet-lagged again, for the 2001 John Deere Classic.

> He must be a really strong contender for the 2001 Reno-Tahoe Open as he's got a two-year eclectic score of 16 (!) under par. T2nd in 1999 and T7th this year he won't be a big price but he will have a big chance.

> In his last four starts in the Kemper Open he's finished 4th in 1999 and 6th in 1996 (plus two missed cuts) and he's the joint course record holder with a 63. I can see him winning next year at the TPC at Avenel at 40/1.

> There are three other tournaments in which he can be followed in three different ways:-

   * The Texas Open. Three successive top 20s. I fancy he will do very well in the Lone Ranger state in 2001. Worth an each-way pop at 40/1.

   * The Bell South Classic. Match bets are called for after form figs. 15th-10th-MC-5th in the last four years.

* The St Jude Classic. He's shot a 65 in R1, R2, and R4 during the last four years so note him in the 3-ball betting.

> This year as defending champion in both the International and the Buick Challenge he missed the cut so in 2001 when he defends this year's Michelob title he may be worth opposing.

Key stat   He's now won three US tournaments in the last two years.

KIRK TRIPLETT

Age 38   **Born** Washington   **Lives** Scottsdale, Arizona

US Tour wins, 1, 2000 Nissan Open **Presidents Cup** 2000 **Money list** BEF 11th 2000

At last after 265 attempts Kirk finally made it to the winner's enclosure when he landed the Nissan Open at 100/1* in mid February. He also posted four top 5 finishes in the Phoenix Open (T4th at 125/1), the Buick Invitational (T5th at 100/1), the Canon Greater Hartford Open (3rd at 50/1) and the John Deere Classic (2nd at 28/1).

He also had top 10s in the Bob Hope (T10th), the Tucson Open (T7th), the Compaq Classic (T6th) and the Kemper Open (T10th), with top 25s in the Bay Hill (T22nd), the Colonial (T13th) and the Fedex St Jude Classic (T15th).

In the majors he missed the US Masters cut, finished 56th in the US Open, T60th in the British Open and T69th in the USPGA.

He finished a poor T33rd in the WGC NEC Invitational. Made a sensational Presidents Cup debut. Partnering Stewart Cink they won all three matches before Triplett halved with Michael Campbell in the singles. Kirk at 50/1 was 3rd top US points scorer. Subsequently finished T8th in the Tour Championship and T14th in the WGC American Express Championship.

Kirk is a player with a sound all-round game. Accurate off the tee and a good putter, his weakness has been an inability to clinch the deal. He had thirty-nine top 10s and five 2nd places before his first win this year. Fades the ball.

However this season he's in the top 10 for R4 scoring.

> He is a very consistent straight hitting pro who, now he's won for the first time, could go on to win again especially after his confidence boosting form in the Presidents Cup.

> In all tournaments from the start of 1999 (to 11th October this year) he's recorded twenty-four top 25s in fifty starts a staggering 48% record. So you can see he's always a candidate for match bets in which he must never be opposed.

> Well worth each-way support for the 2001 Compaq Classic. His game is tailor made for this Nicklaus designed course where in his last fourteen rounds he's had seven rounds at or under 68. His recent record (T6th 2000, T12th 1999 and 4th 1997) is good, so he's well worth supporting.

> He'll probably find it difficult defending his title in the Nissan Open. However he'll be a 'must' 3-ball bet in R1 where he's shot 67 (2000), 67 (1999), 69 (1997) and 69 (1996).

> An each-way bet on Triplett in his two 'home' desert tournaments, the Phoenix Open and the Tucson Open, should show a tidy profit. He lives in Arizona and has a superb record in each event.

* The Phoenix Open where the course changes suit his accurate style, and where he was the fastest finisher (11 under par for the last 54 holes) this year.

* The Tucson Open. In the last two years he's got a stroke average of 68.75 having finished T7th (2000) and T3rd (1999).

> He also enjoys the International tournament held in the desert in Colorado. He's made the final day in each of the last four years averaging 26 points per year. He's a must in match bets and on the spreads.

> He must be expected to play well in three tournaments where he's got a fine record.

* The Canon Greater Hartford Open. Made nine cuts in ten starts. Was 2nd in 1995 and 3rd in 2000 when he shot 61 in R3.

* The St Jude Classic. 9th-MC-7th-15th-15th in the last five years for a 68.6 stroke average.

* The Bob Hope. T10th-T18th-T10th in the last three years.

Key stat   From the start of 1999 to 11th October this year he'd posted a top 25 in 48% of all his tournaments.

BOB TWAY   D

Age 41   **Born** Oklahoma   **Lives** Oklahoma

US Tour wins 6, 4 in 80s, 1990 Las Vegas Invitational, 1995 MCI Classic **Major wins** 1, 1986 USPGA **Money list** 2nd 1986

It's been a season (as the Match of the day commentators would say) of two halves for Bob. Up to July he'd made twelve cuts from fifteen starts then from July he missed eight consecutive cuts!

His top 25 finishes were in the Buick Invitational (T14th), the Doral Ryder Open (T15th), the Compaq Classic (T24th), the Canon Greater Hartford Open (T12th), the Tampa Bay Classic (T10th) and the Southern Farm Bureau (T20th).

In the World Match Play he beat defending champion Jeff Maggert 6 and 5 in R1 before losing to Jim Furyk (2 and 1) in R2.

Missed the cut in the US Masters, the British Open and the USPGA.

An accurate iron player he stays in the top 30 for greens in reg, and the top 30 for par 3 birdies. Short off the tee at 269 yards his putting continues (outside top 65) to be his achilles heel.

> Bob's now gone almost 150 tournaments since his last win and his horrific loss of form in the second half of this year is most discouraging as he has always been a reliable cut making guy who's a must for match bets.

> So in 2001 we'll need to check out Bob's early season form and stats to see if 'normal service' has been resumed. If so he can be noted in match bets in two tournaments.

* The Doral Ryder Open where he's posted four consecutive top 15s (15th-15th-9th-9th).
* The Buick Invitational where he's had three top 16 finishes in the last four years.

> If the consistent straight hitting Bob of recent years returns in 2001 he must enter into calculations for the 2001 US Open in which he's posted three top 10s in the last six years (T10th 1995: T5th 1997: 3rd 1998), and he'll be really chuffed that it will be held in his home state of Oklahoma.   .

Key stat   His last win was over 140 tournaments ago in 1995.

JEAN VAN DE VELDE

Age 34   **Born** France   **Lives** Geneva

European tour wins 1, 1993 Roma Masters **US tour** BEF T2nd (lost in a play-off) 2000 Tucson Open, 2nd 2000 Reno-Tahoe Open **Dunhill Cup** 7 times, last 1999 **World Cup** 1989-1998 inclusive **Ryder Cup** 1999 **Majors** T2nd 1999 British Open **Money list** BEF 60th 2000

Yes, you're right, he was the one without the socks, and in 2000 he played mainly on the USPGA tour and he's retained his card in a successful first season.

He posted two really big finishes when T2nd at 100/1 in the Tucson Open and T2nd (after a play-off) in the Reno-Tahoe Open.

He also had high finishes in the Bell South Classic (T22nd) and the Michelob (T19th).

In the majors he was T19th in the US Masters, T31st in the British Open, T30th in the USPGA and he missed the US Open cut.

In Europe he was T3rd at 80/1 in the Deutsche Bank Open, T7th in the French Open, T14th in the Benson and Hedges, T11th in the German Masters (64 in R2) and T17th in the Volvo Masters. In the Seve Ballesteros Trophy he got just 1 point from five games.

Shortish at 275 yards he's outside the top 120 for greens in reg and driving accuracy. His putting and bunker play remain very good.

> He's always been at his best when the sun is out in bright dry conditions so it's not surprising that he's become a 'desert fox' in the States with his two really big tournaments being held in desert conditions.

> He would love to win the French Open (T7th 2000: T16th 1998). However returning from the States and adjusting to the greens is not easy and I can't see him succeeding.

> He's 15/8 to make the Ryder Cup side, and 8/1 to gain a wild card. If he's at the Belfry in 2001 it will surely be in the Benson and Hedges not the Ryder Cup!

Key stat   This year he won $540,000 in two desert tournaments.

SCOTT VERPLANK   G

Age 36   **Born** Texas   **Lives** Oklahoma

College Oklahoma

US Tour wins 2, 1985 Western Open, 1988 Buick Open, 2000 Reno-Tahoe Open
International wins No. 1 player in 1998 World Cup of Golf **Money list** 18th 1998

Scott has had a tremendous 2000 in which he gained his first win since 1988 when he landed the Reno-Tahoe Open at 66/1 winning at the 4th play-off hole.

In a most consistent season in which he's made over 80% of his cuts. He was T4th at 50/1 in the NCR Classic at Disney and he's posted four other top 10s, in the Doral Ryder Open (T6th), the Greater Greensboro Classic (T8th), the Canadian Open (T6th) and the Pennsylvania Classic (T8th), and six other top 25s in the Tucson Open (T17th), the MCI Classic (T11th), the Players Championship (T20th), the Byron Nelson Classic (T25th), the Colonial (T20th), the Memorial (T20th) and the Invenys Classic in Las Vegas (T15th).

In the US Open he was T46th, and he missed the USPGA cut. 14th in the Tour Championship.

His stats are impressive all round. Off the tee his fairways hit percentage is up from 71% to 79%, and his greens hit in reg up 4% to 69.9%. He's also top 30 for sand saves and a solid top 45 for putting. Short at 268 yards, par 5 birdies (130th) are not his forte.

Scott's a diabetic who, like Paolo Quirici in Europe, now uses a pump to control the condition.

> His consistency in 2000 was really superb as he posted four top 10s and twelve top 20s in twenty-one 'ordinary' tournaments up to October. The big challenge he now faces is to convert such consistency into another win. The two factors against him are his lack of length off the tee and his poor R4 scoring when in contention which (let's hope) he may have overcome.

> He showed his liking this year for new courses.

  * Pennsylvania Classic. T8th this year, and it moves to a new course in 2001 where in a weaker field I could see Verplank winning at 28/1.

  * John Deere Classic. 12th on this year's new course after three successive top 10s (1997-1999) in this event. Must go close again in 2001.

> Worth supporting in the NCR Classic in Walt Disney. T4th this year and T17th in 1999 are his only recent starts and give him an eclectic score of 67-67-65-65. Great Scott, what more do we want? So let's raid the bank to back Verplank.

> He can be followed in match bets and as a player with a serious chance in the outrights in three tournaments in which he has a good record.

  * The Buick Open. Won it in 1988, 2nd 1998 and 11th in 2000.

  * The Canadian Open. T6th 2000: T9th 1998

  * The Greater Greensboro: 8th 2000: 2nd 1998: 14th 1997 in a tournament in which you can see him winning at 33/1.

> When the 2000 US Open teed up Verplank was top of the driving accuracy stats. OK he finished down the field (T46th). However in 2001 the US Open will be held in his home state of Oklahoma and I can see Scott doing really well. His last five US Open form figs (46th-17th-49th-21st-18th) are sound but unexciting. Nevertheless I believe this straight-hitting Oklahoma resident will be worth an each-way bet at big odds in the 'without Tiger' market for the 2001 US Open.

Key stat   T2nd for driving accuracy and 13th for greens in regulation.

GRANT WAITE   G

Age 36   **Born** New Zealand   **Lives** New Zealand
College Oklahoma
US Tour wins 1, 1993 Kemper Open **International wins** 2, both in 1992 **Money list** 35th 1993 **Dunhill Cup** 1989, 1992, 1994-96, and 2000

This has been an unusual year for Grant in which he's played five times on the BUY.COM tour. However on the main tour he posted two successive high finishes in early September when he was 2nd at 100/1 in the Air Canada which he followed up the next week when he also finished 2nd at 100/1 in the Canadian Open, playing brilliantly in the final pair alongside Tiger, he shot 66 to Tiger's 65 in R4. Went on to finish T14th in the Buick Challenge and T6th in the Southern Farm Bureau.

He posted five top 25s, in the AT&T (14th), the Kemper (T16th), the Greater Milwaukee Open (T14th), the BC Open (T10th), the Michelob (T25th) and the NCR Classic at Disney (T24th). Won two of his three games in the Dunhill Cup to give him a very good career record of ten wins in fifteen games.

Grant is usually high for total driving as he's a very long, if not always accurate driver. However his putting often let's him down.

> His confidence will be sky high after he matched Tiger shot for shot down the stretch in R4 of the Canadian Open. With his putting improved this long hitter, who was twice Australian junior champ, can go on to post his first win for eight years in 2001.

> He's well suited to the Bell South Classic held on a driver's course. I suggest an each-way wager in both the top non-American market (T2nd at 40/1 in 1999) and in the outrights where 66/1+ will be on offer.

> He can be followed in match bets on the spreads and as a big priced outsider in the BC Open where in the last five years he's shot fourteen of his nineteen rounds under par with form figures of 10th (2000)-39th-40th-8th-20th.

> A good player in the fall he could well surprise in the 2001 Buick Challenge (T14th 2000: T20th 1999: T39th 1998: T9th 1997) where his four-year stroke average is a tad below 70. He certainly must be noted in match bets at Calloway Gardens.

> In the last three years he's finished T11th, missed cut and T6th (this year) in the Southern Farm Bureau Classic. He must have a fine chance at Annandale in 2001.

Key stat   33rd for greens in regulation.

DUFFY WALDORF

Age 38   **Born** California   **Lives** California
College California

US Tour wins 4, 1995 Texas Open, 1999 Buick Classic, 1999 Texas Open, 2000 NCR Golf Classic at Walt Disney **Money list** BEF 23rd 1992; 28th 1999

Duffy (who wears funny hats and flowery shirts) had a superb year in 1999 with two wins as he finished 28th on the Money list making over $1¼ million.

In 2000 he had not made a top 5 although he was T10th in Phoenix Open, and T7th in the Reno-Tahoe Open until he won the NCR Classic at Disney in October at 100/1 after a 62 in R4!

He also posted top 25s in Nissan Open (T25th), the Buick Classic (T13th) and the Mercedes (T19th).

In the WGC Match Play he collected $75,000 after beating Vijay Singh (at a tasty 7/4) by 2 and 1, and Steve Stricker 2 and 1 before he lost to Hal Sutton in R3. Played superbly to finish T3rd at 150/1* in the WGC American Express tournament at Valderrama in November.

In the US Masters he missed the cut for the first time on his fifth Augusta start and by just 1 shot. He also missed the cut in the US Open and he finished T46th in the USPGA.

In the Loch Lomond he was T15th.

In the top 30 for length off the tee at 281 yards. His strength is in greens in reg. (3rd last year, top 20 this year). His weakness is his putting which is outside the top 150 again.....although he sure putted well to win the NCR at Disney. Feels he's at his best on Bermuda greens because he doesn't spin the ball.

> Duffy is a long and accurate hitter, and when his putter works he sure knows how to win as he's had three wins in the last eighteen months.

> The tip (in his profile last year) to follow Duffy in the World Match Play certainly paid off with a tasty 7/4 R1 success against Vijay Singh followed up by a nice evens win in R2 over Steve Stricker. This year I suggest he should be given serious consideration in three US and one European tournament.

> He takes his family to Scotland for the Loch Lomond Invitational which he clearly enjoys. This year T15th overall he was T4th at 25/1 in the top US market. Remember him by the Bonnie Banks in 2001.

> He can be backed at 80/1 for the Buick Classic in the knowledge that he loves the Westchester course where he was 2nd in 1992, Won in 1999 and led after R3 before finishing T13th this year.

> In the two years of the Reno-Tahoe Open he's finished T7th this year and T24th in 1999 for an eclectic score of 11 under. He can be backed in match bets and as an 80/1 shot with a real chance

> If there's one tournament in which you back Duffy with total confidence it is surely in the Texas Open where his record in six starts is two wins (1995 and 1999), 4th (1997) and T6th (2000). A must for match bets he'll be worth a wager in the outrights at 33/1 or 40/1.

Key stat   19th for greens in regulation.

BRIAN WATTS   D V

Age 34   **Born** Quebec, Canada   **Lives** Oklahoma

College Oklahoma

US Tour BEF 3rd 1999 GTE Byron Nelson Classic **International wins** 14, latest 1998 Casio World Open **Majors** 2nd 1998 British Open **Money list** BEF 57th 1999

It's been a disappointing year for Brian Watts. Indeed he posted only one top 25 finish before September when he finished T22nd in the Bell South Classic. Then he earned $160,000 finishing T26th in the Canadian Open, T18th in the Pennsylvania Classic, T9th in the Texas Open and T18th in the Southern Farm Bureau.

In the World Match Play he lost in R1 to Dave Toms. He missed the cut in the US Masters and finished T51st in the USPGA.

After such an ordinary year his main stats are uniformly poor, although he remains a brilliant bunker player—9th in 1999 and still top 50 this year.

Short off the tee at 270 yards. A good shot maker.

Became a father of a first time daughter in November 1999.

> Let's remember this guy was 2nd in the 1998 British Open, made the cut in every 1999 major and posted four top 10s on the 1999 US tour. Back to form late in the season in 2000, I expect he'll be remotivated in 2001 when he'll be at 'value' prices because of his poor overall form this year

> I expect Brian Watts to return to form in 2001, and let's remember this guy knows how to win....after all he's done so fourteen times! Keep your eye on him in the New Year.

> In the last two years he has shown consistent form in only one event, the Buick Open (T9th 1999: T32nd 2000) with all eight rounds under par on the easy Warwick Hills course.

> His game is, I believe, well suited to the Kingsmill course where his final three rounds in 1999 were 10 under par when he finished T8th. He withdrew after R1 in 2000 so he'll be a big price in 2001. Watt's the tournament? The Michelob. And Watts the name? Brian!

Key stat   118th for driving accuracy.

MIKE WEIR   G

Age 30   **Born** Ontario, Canada   **Lives** Utah

US Tour wins 2, 1999 Air Canada Championship, 2000 WGC American Express Championship **Presidents Cup** 2000 **Money list** BEF 6th (!) 2000

Mike has not looked back since he earned his Tour card as top player at the 1998 Q School. In 1999 he had his first win, plus a 2nd, a 3rd and a T5th to finish 23rd on the M/L.

In 2000 he started well when T4th at 50/1 in the Mercedes, and he went on to post other top 4 finishes in the Memorial (4th at 66/1) and the Michelob (2nd at 50/1).

He had top 10s in the Phoenix Open (T10th), the Bay Hill (T7th) and the Colonial (T8th), and top 25s in the Honda Classic (T19th), the Buick Classic (T19th), the International (T19th) and the Invensys Classic in Las Vegas (T12th).

In the World Match Play he beat Carlos Franco 4 and 3 in R1, then lost (7 and 6) to Sergio Garcia. He made the cut in all the majors finishing T16th in the US Open, T28th in the US Masters, T52nd in the British Open and T30th in the USPGA. Made a sensational Presidents Cup debut finishing top points scorer for the Internationals at 12/1. He won two of his three paired games before he beat fellow lefty Mickelson (4 and 3) in the singles. 21st in the Tour Championship when suffering from food poisoning. However his big week came in early November at Valderrama when he was the impressive 66/1 winner of the WGC American Express Championship.

Not long at 274 yards he's a superb putter (top 25 last two years). This year his driving accuracy is down 2%, and his greens in reg is up by 3%. His birdie conversion ranking, top 25 both last year and this, shows he can take his chances.

Became a father of a second daughter just before the US Masters in March.

> He has been in serious contention and let winning chances slip in the 1999 USPGA and this year in the Buick Classic, the US Masters and the Bay Hill. However, those experiences have been deposited in his learning bank and they were drawn upon when he played superbly in the 'fall' in three events.

　* The Michelob. 2nd after a play-off, following 64 in R4.
　* The Presidents Cup. Top international points scorer at 12/1.
　* The WGC American Express. Champion at 66/1.

> His win at Valderrama was overshadowed by Tiger's defeat and Westwood's Order of Merit success, yet let's be clear this guy kept his head and played controlled golf under severe pressure. He's clearly going to be a very serious contender in 2001.

> His last five rounds at Muirfield Village average 68.4, so after his 4th place this year he can be supported for the 2001 Memorial in the 'without Tiger' market.

> He played the Canadian Tour for many years and was the Rookie of the Year there in 1993 so in the Autumn on 'the Canadian Swing' he can be supported and opposed in successive weeks.

　* In the Air Canada he's well worth a bet as his record Won 1999: 5th 1998: 5th 1996 is very good. His T38th as defending champion this year was understandable.

　* In the Canadian Open he can be opposed in match bets with some confidence as his record is abysmal as he's only made the cut once (when 78th this year) in ten starts.

> He'll be an outsider with a real chance in the US Masters. On his first visit to Augusta this year he was T5th after R3 and I can see him 'making the frame' in 2001 and being well worth backing to be the top Rest of The World player at Augusta.

> He must have a really good chance in the USPGA. He played very well on his debut in the tournament (T10th 1999) and had a top 30 (T30th) this year, and he

fits the profile of a guy in his thirties looking for his first major. He can be followed with some confidence at 50/1.

> He clearly has the game for the Kingsmill course where he's finished 3rd in 1999, and 2nd this year for a two-year stroke average (best of any player) of 68.25! Cries out to be backed for the 2001 Michelob.

> Mike lives in the adjoining state of Utah, so it's not surprising that he's building a good record in the Invensys Classic in Las Vegas (T12th 2000, including a 63 in R3, and T19th in 1999). Weir will be well worth a 'nibble' at Vegas in 2001.

Key stat   T25th for birdie conversion.

KEVIN WENTWORTH   D

Age 32   **Born** California   **Lives** California
College Oklahoma

US Tour BEF T4th 1999 St Jude Classic **BUY.COM tour** BEF T4th 1991 **Money list** BEF 98th 1999

Kevin Tyler is a tall (6 foot 2 in his slippers) Californian who has really struggled this year in which he's made the cut in only one third of his tournaments.

However he did have one mega week in March when he finished T2nd in the Honda Classic to earn $255,200. Outside of that he's not posted a single top 30!

So as you can imagine his stats are really poor apart from the interesting and notable exception of his high rating for par 3 birdies. His driving accuracy stays in intensive care at 55%. Left-handed player.

> His record in the Air Canada Championship before he missed the cut (by 7 shots!) this year is sufficiently solid (T8th 1999: T15th 1998 for a stroke average of 68.75) for him to be considered next year.

> He's posted a top 5 finish in two of his last three years on tour. However with him consistently missing four fairways in nine over the last two years it's not easy to support him with any confidence.

Key stat   193rd (!!!) for driving accuracy.

MARK WIEBE

Age 43   **Born** Oregon   **Lives** Colorado
US Tour wins 2, both in mid 1980s, last 1986 **Money list** BEF 25th 1986

Mark had one mega finish, at the end of September, when he secured his card when 2nd at 150/1 in the Texas Open to win $280,800.

Before then he'd managed only three top 25s, in the Tucson Open (T17th), the MCI Classic (T15th) and the Western Open (T23rd).

His greens in reg and putting are again outside the top 100 although his all-round ranking, 147th last year, has improved.

His strength is his driving accuracy which is still at 71% for the second successive year.

> He's not won for fourteen years nevertheless with my masters degree in hindsight from the University of the Blindingly Obvious I suggest that we mark Wiebe down as an each-way bet in the 2001 Westin Texas Open (2nd-T12th-T20th and T9th in five starts). At 66/1 he'll be a player with a genuine chance in a tournament that is ideal for course-specialist, experienced players like him.

Key stat   57th for driving accuracy (71.3%).

JAY WILLIAMSON

Age 33   **Born** St Louis, Minnesota   **Lives** Florida

USPGA tour BEF T4th 1999 AT & T Pebble Beach National Pro-Am (rain reduced)

In 1999 Jay lost his card when missing twenty of his thirty-two cuts. However he bounced back to regain it when he finished a fine 4th at Q School.

In 2000 he's had a top 10 in the Bay Hill (T7th), and top 20s in the AT&T (T11th), the Kemper Open (T20th) and the John Deere (T12th). He also had high finishes in the Buick Open (T21st), the Hawaiian Open (T26th) and the NCR Classic at Disney (T24th).

His strength is shown in his top 20 for total driving, his weakness by being outside the top 100 for greens in reg.

> Posted his best-ever finish when T4th in the AT&T in 1999 and followed up with T11th this year for a two-year stroke average of 69.85, so keep him in mind for 3 balls in that tournament.

> He's twice been the R1 leader of the Kemper Open in the last five years (64 in 2000: 66 in 1996). He led the tournament after R3 in 1996 before shooting a 79!

So back him at the TPC at Avenel in the early 3-ball betting and if he's to post a big finish it could well be there when coming from "off the pace".

Key stat   13th (!) for total driving

TIGER WOODS   **G F** 🐎

Age 25   **Born** California   **Lives** Florida

US Tour wins 15, 1996 Las Vegas Invitational, Walt Disney Classic, 1997 Mercedes, Byron Nelson Classic, Western Open, 1998 Bell South Classic, 1999 Buick Invitational, the Memorial, the Western Open, the National Car Rental at Walt Disney, and the Tour Championship, 2000 AT&T, 2000 Bay Hill Invitational, 2000 Memorial, 2000 Canadian Open **WGC wins** 3, the 1999 NEC Invitational at Akron, the 1999 American Express Championship at Valderrama, 2000 WGC NEC Invitational **European tour wins** 1, the 1999 Deutsche Bank Open **Majors** 5, 1997 US Masters, the 1999 USPGA, 2000 US Open, 2000 British Open, 2000 USPGA **Ryder Cup** 1997, 1999 **Presidents Cup** 1998, 2000 **Dunhill Cup** 1998 **Money list** Top 1997, 4th 1998, Top 1999, Top 2000

At the start of the new millennium Tiger had shown already what a brilliant player he was with an amazing eleven 'normal' US wins plus two majors. At the end of 1999 we had a foretaste of what was to come when he won the individual prize in the World Cup of Golf by 9 shots! This year there's no doubt he took his game to a new level and established himself not only as the world's best golfer by some distance but also as the most instantly recognised and revered sportsman on the planet.

Overall he won three majors, a world championship event and five 'normal' tournaments.

After finishing 5th at 5/2 in the US Masters he won the US Open by 15 (!!) shots at 3/1 and the British Open by 8 shots at 5/2 to complete a career Grand Slam in the majors. He then successfully defended his USPGA title (at 7/4) beating Bob May in a play-off.

In the Andersen World Match Play he beat Michael Campbell (5 and 4), Retief Goosen (1 up), Shigeki Maruyama (4 and 3), Paul Lawrie (1 up) in the QF, Davis Love (5 and 4) in the SF before, as the 7/2 ON favourite he was convincingly beaten by Darren Clarke 4 and 3 in the final. Finished T5th at 11/8 in the WGC American Express at Valderrama.

In the WGC NEC Invitational he once more ran away with a big tournament winning by 11(!) shots as the 11/8 favourite. In the Presidents Cup he won two of his four paired games alongside Notah Begay, and he beat Singh (2 and 1) in the singles.

Finished 2nd as 5/4 favourite in the Tour Championship.

On the 'normal' USPGA tour he won the season opening Mercedes Championship (at 10/3) beating Ernie Els in a play-off. It was his FIFTH consecutive PGA tour victory. Later he went on to win the AT&T (at 7/2) for his sixth consecutive victory, finishing the tournament eagle, birdie, par, birdie to come from way 'off the pace'. However his winning streak ended when he was T2nd at 7/4 to Phil Mickelson, when feeling tired, in the Buick Invitational.

His other wins came in the Bay Hill Invitational (at 9/2), the Memorial (at 7/2) when he successfully defended a title for the first time, and the Canadian Open (at 5/4).

He also finished T18th in the Nissan Open, 2nd at 7/2 to Hal Sutton in the Players Championship, T4th at 4/1 in the Byron Nelson Classic and 3rd at 5/4 in the NCR Classic at Walt Disney.

In 'The Law of the Tiger' in Part 1 I discuss his 'poor finishes' in the Western Open (T23rd after the US Open) and in the Buick Open (T11th after the British Open).

On the European tour most unusually he led after R3 in the Deutsche Bank Open and then finished only T3rd at 5/2.

With his phenomenal record it may seem odd to analyse his strengths and I almost said weaknesses! There are no weaknesses, yet he can still improve (heaven help the rest of 'em) in one or two areas.

Under the brilliant guidance of Butch Harmon he has a superb swing, he hits it 'miles' and now his distance control with his shorter irons is very good. His length enables him to 'murder' par 5s and to approach so many holes with more control from shorter clubs than so many of his opponents. His putting, in which he was ranked 128th in 1998, is now extremely good, possibly because he sees the lines better following laser eye surgery. Indeed if you had to select a player in the history of the game to hole a par-saving putt to save your life it'd be Tiger!

This year his greens in reg stats (still top) are up 3.4%, his driving accuracy up 0.1% (ranked 59th!), and he's No. 1 for putts per green in reg, par 4 birdies and par 5 birdies, while his birdie conversion is up 1.8%.

However the one area for improvement can still be made is his bunker play. Unlike Laurence of Arabia he's not at his best on sand. T39th at 56.8% (1999) he entered the Presidents Cup at 57.6% yet ranked 46th for sand saves!

The Tiger and his girlfriend Joanna will probably marry when Eldrick is 28 or 29 in three to four years time.

Overall one can only stand back in admiration of this fine player and fine man. Mature way beyond his years, Tiger, his brilliant (and oh so important) caddie Steve Williams and world-class coach Butch Harmon form 'Team Tiger', and they look set to continue to break all manner of golfing records.

> At his very best when fresh and on a par 72 course where he can exploit his massive length. Although he can, and has won on par 70 tracks, his comparative advantage is diminished in 'putting contests'.

> He has held the lead or a share of the lead after R3 in twenty-one USPGA tournaments and won nineteen of them. However this year he's TWICE led after R3 (Deutsche Bank Open and the Tour Championship) and not won!

> His whole year will be centred around the majors, the World Championships, and the very big tournaments like the Players and the Memorial.

* US Masters. Since he 'slaughtered' the course (18 under par) and the field (by 12 shots) in 1997 the course has, to some extent, been made Tiger-proof. His record since is 8th (1998), T18th (1999) and 5th (2000) for a three-year stroke average of 71.5. So they're not stats to make you want to lump on at odds of 6/5. However his final rounds this year (68-69) were his first in the 60s since 1997 and the best in the field. Certain to go very, very close in 2001, and if he beats Duval he'll win.

* US Open. I fully expect to see Tiger Woods retain his US Open Championship at Southern Hills. T3rd in 1999, runaway winner this year when his stats were awesome as he drove 7 yards further off the tee than anyone else and outdrove all but ten players by at least 20 yards. Top ranked for greens in reg at 71% his nearest challenger hit only 61%! Expect more of the same at Tulsa in 2001.

* The British Open. Of course he could walk away from his field at Royal Lytham as he did at St Andrews. However, I'm not convinced as a number of other players are long hitters well suited by links golf where the luck of the bounce is so important. Clearly he'll be thereabouts, but at the odds I'd prefer others.

* The USPGA. Tiger will be going for a threepeat in 2001. However although he could obviously get his hat trick it's worth remembering that his 1999 win was by a single shot, and his 2000 victory after a play-off. The wider fairways and the effects of a long season help some of the lesser players here as this tournaments' results over the years clearly show.

If he's going for a Grand Slam watch out for the biggest media hype in the history of the Universe!

> He looks 'past the post' in the 2001 WGC NEC Invitational which will be played for the last time at Firestone in late August. Winner in 1999 (by 1 shot) and runaway winner (by 12) this year he has a two-year stroke average of 66.12!!

> I give the full reasons in Part 2 for believing that Tiger will NOT win the Grand Slam in 2001. It's a poor non-value bet and one I would not recommend at the daft odds of 12/1 to 20/1 on offer.

> From Chapter One please remember the 'Law of the Tiger' which states that Eldrick Woods can be opposed in any 'ordinary' tournament he plays within three weeks following a victory in any major.

> The 2001 Ryder Cup will be Tiger's first experience of that 'biennial battle' in Britain and I'm not convinced he'll be any 'value' at all for three key reasons.

  Firstly, The Belfry will be changed to make it as 'Tiger proof' as possible.

  Secondly, it comes at the end of a long, hard season.

  Thirdly, his Ryder Cup record is not exactly awesome: Fourballs PL 2 L 2: Foursomes PL 2 W 1: Singles beat a very rusty Ryder Cup debutant Andrew Coltart. So PI 5 W 2!

> He must be seriously fancied for the Tour Championship. When it was last held at the Champions course he won by 4 shots in 1999.

Key stat   From his victory in the 1999 Memorial to the 2000 Presidents Cup he played in twenty-seven US tournaments, winning sixteen of them. A winning %age of fifty-nine equivalent to odds of almost 6/4 on per tournament.

STATISTICAL APPENDIX   PART 9

2000 EUROPEAN TOUR STATISTICS

AXA Performance Data is reproduced by kind permission of the European tour.

DRIVING ACCURACY (%)

1.	Richard Green	79.5
2.	Jose Coceres	78.7
3.	John Bickerton	78.0
4.	Gary Orr	76.3
5.	Pierre Fulke	75.6
6.	Andrew Oldcorn	73.4
7.	Peter O'Malley	73.1
8.	Mark McNulty	72.5
9.	Anders Hansen	72.3
10.	Miguel Angel Jiminez	72.0
11.	Simon Wakefield	71.8
12.	Jean-Francois Remesy	71.5
	John Senden	71.5
14.	Paul Eales	71.0
15.	Jorge Berendt	70.4
16.	Nick O'Hern	70.2
17.	Greg Owen	69.9
18.	Ian Garbutt	69.7
	Colin Montgomerie	69.7
20.	Gary Murphy	69.6

GREENS IN REGULATION (%)

1.	Gary Orr	77.8
2.	Colin Montgomerie	77.1
3.	Jose Coceres	76.4
4.	Ian Garbutt	74.4
5.	Greg Owen	74.3
6.	Padraig Harrington	74.0
7.	John Senden	73.6
8.	Angel Cabrera	73.3
9.	Miguel Angel Jiminez	73.1
10.	Andrew Coltart	73.0
	Retief Goosen	73.0
12.	Thomas Levet	72.2
	Gary Murphy	72.2
14.	Bernhard Langer	72.1
15.	Peter O'Malley	71.7
	Peter Baker	71.7
17.	Sergio Garcia	71.6
18.	John Bickerton	71.4
	Eduardo Romero	71.4
20.	Mats Lanner	71.3

DRIVING DISTANCE (YARDS)

1.	Emanuele Canonica	295.3
2.	Angel Cabrera	293.5
3.	Adam Scott	292.4
4.	Ricardo Gonzalez	291.4
5.	Stephen Allan	290.5
6.	Alberto Binaghi	290.2
7.	Sergio Garcia	287.9
8.	Paolo Quirici	287.0
9.	Mattias Eliasson	286.0
10.	Carl Suneson	285.8
11.	Des Terblanche	285.1
12.	Geoff Ogilvy	285.0
13.	Stephen Gallacher	284.9
14.	Ivo Giner	283.9
15.	Mathias Gronberg	283.5
16.	Ignacio Garrido	283.4
	Lee Westwood	283.4
18.	Kevin Carissimi	283.2
19.	Greg Owen	282.4
	Thomas Gogele	282.4

PUTTS PER GREEN IN REG.

1.	Lee Westwood	1.718
2.	Michael Campbell	1.719
3.	Pierre Fulke	1.726
4.	Jamie Spence	1.741
5.	Phillip Price	1.743
6.	Padraig Harrington	1.746
7.	Des Terblanche	1.753
	Jarmo Sandelin	1.753
9.	Brian Davis	1.755
	Fredrik Jacobson	1.755
11.	Darren Clarke	1.756
12.	Jean Van de Velde	1.762
13.	Paul Lawrie	1.763
14.	Dean Robertson	1.767
	Jose Maria Olazabal	1.767
16.	Olle Karlsson	1.769
17.	Daniel Chopra	1.770
	Raymond Russell	1.770
	Paul McGinley	1.770
20.	Nick O'Hern	1.771

AVERAGE PUTTS PER ROUND

1.	Lee Westwood	28.4
2.	Daniel Chopra	28.5
	Pierre Fulke	28.5
	Jamie Spence	28.5
5.	Michael Campbell	28.6
6.	Paul Lawrie	28.7
	Peter Senior	28.7
8.	Jeev Milkha Singh	28.8
	Dean Robertson	28.8
	Brian Davis	28.8
	Phillip Price	28.8
	Sam Torrance	28.8
	Raymond Russell	28.8
	Russell Claydon	28.8
15.	Des Terblanche	28.9
	Fredrik Jacobson	28.9
	Nick O'Hern	28.9
18.	Jean Van de Velde	29.0
	Joakim Haeggman	29.0
	Derrick Cooper	29.0

SAND SAVES (%)

1.	Tony Johnstone	78.9
2.	Ian Hutchings	77.9
3.	Mark Mouland	77.8
4.	John Senden	71.2
5.	Bernhard Langer	70.6
6.	Gustavo Rojas	70.1
7.	Jose Maria Olazabal	69.8
8.	Miguel Angel Martin	68.2
9.	David Park	67.5
10.	Pierre Fulke	66.2
11.	Seve Ballesteros	65.2
12.	Alberto Binaghi	64.3
13.	Nick O'Hern	63.3
14.	Jorge Berendt	63.3
15.	Sergio Garcia	63.0
16.	Raymond Russell	62.2
17.	Jean Van de Velde	61.7
	Daniel Chopra	61.7
19.	Ian Poulter	61.5
	Paolo Quirici	61.5

STROKE AVERAGE

1.	Lee Westwood	69.62
2.	Ernie Els	69.67
3.	Michael Campbell	70.25
4.	Colin Montgomerie	70.26
5.	Darren Clarke	70.29
6.	Padraig Harrington	70.33
7.	Bob May	70.38
8.	Pierre Fulke	70.51
9.	Eduardo Romero	70.69
10.	Thomas Bjorn	70.74
11.	Gary Orr	70.76
12.	Phillip Price	70.79
13.	Angel Cabrera	70.88
	Jose Coceres	70.88
15.	Sergio Garcia	70.89
16.	Adam Scott	70.92
17.	Bernhard Langer	70.95
	Nick Faldo	70.95
19.	Paul McGinley	70.97
20.	Jose Maria Olazabal	71.00
21.	Carlos Rodiles	71.08
22.	Retief Goosen	71.11
23.	Steen Tinning	71.17
24.	Fredrik Jacobson	71.22
25.	Miguel Angel Martin	71.24
26.	Des Terblanche	71.26
	Nick O'Hern	71.26
28.	Andrew Coltart	71.32
	Per-Ulrik Johansson	71.32
30.	Paul Lawrie	71.33
31.	Patrik Sjoland	71.34
32.	Mark McNulty	71.37
33.	Miguel Angel Jiminez	71.40
34.	Anders Hansen	71.41
35.	Dean Robertson	71.44
36.	Roger Chapman	71.45
	Ricardo Gonzalez	71.45
	Steve Webster	71.45
39.	Peter O'Malley	71.47
40.	Stephen Leaney	71.49

2000 VOLVO EUROPEAN ORDER OF MERIT

Final standings after WGC American Express Stroke-Play Championships. The top 115 qualify for a tour card for 2001.

1.	Lee Westwood	41.	Peter Senior	81.	Thomas Gogele
2.	Darren Clarke	42.	Nick O'Hern	82.	Roger Winchester
3.	Ernie Els	43.	Ignacio Garrido	83.	Tom Gillis
4.	Michael Campbell	44.	Anthony Wall	84.	Greg Turner
5.	Thomas Bjorn	45.	Niclas Fasth	85.	Maarten Lafeber
6.	Colin Montgomerie	46.	Alistair Forsyth	86.	Gary Evans
7.	Padraig Harrington	47.	Peter O'Malley	87.	Sam Torrance
8.	Phillip Price	48.	Geoff Ogilvy	88.	Thomas Levet
9.	J M Olazabal	49.	Mark McNulty	89.	J-F Remesy
10.	Gary Orr	50.	Dean Robertson	90.	Mark James
11.	M A Jiminez	51.	Gordon Brand Jr	91.	Andrew McLardy
12.	Pierre Fulke	52.	M A Martin	92.	Andrew Oldcorn
13.	Jose Coceres	53.	Anders Hansen	93.	Marc Farry
14.	Angel Cabrera	54.	Richard Green	94.	Peter Lonard
15.	Retief Goosen	55.	Ian Garbutt	95.	Wayne Riley
16.	Eduardo Romero	56.	Stephen Gallacher	96.	Richard S Johnson
17.	Andrew Coltart	57.	Peter Baker	97.	Gary Emerson
18.	Paul McGinley	58.	Rolf Muntz	98.	N Vanhootegem
19.	Bernhard Langer	59.	Jonathan Lomas	99.	Sven Struver
20.	Mathias Gronberg	60.	Carl Suneson	100.	Des Terblanche
21.	Sergio Garcia	61.	Stephen Allan	101.	Wei-Tze Yeh
22.	P-U Johansson	62.	John Bickerton	102.	Adam Scott
23.	Patrik Sjoland	63.	David Lynn	103.	Barry Lane
24.	Ian Woosnam	64.	Raymond Russell	104.	Joakim Haeggman
25.	Fredrik Jacobson	65.	Christopher Hanell	105.	Francisco Cea
26.	Paul Lawrie	66.	Soren Kjeldsen	106.	Diego Borrego
27.	Emanuele Canonica	67.	Markus Brier	107.	Bradley Dredge
28.	Stephen Leaney	68.	David Park	108.	Henrik Mystrom
29.	Brian Davis	69.	Steve Webster	109.	Olivier Edmond
30.	Steen Tinning	70.	Alex Cejka	110.	Massimo Scarpa
31.	Ian Poulter	71.	John Senden	111.	Des Smyth
32.	Jean Van de Velde	72.	Peter Mitchell	112.	Paul Eales
33.	Roger Chapman	73.	Soren Hansen	113.	Jose Rivero
34.	Ricardo Gonzalez	74.	Tony Johnstone	114.	Robert Karlsson
35.	Roger Wessels	75.	Van Phillips	115.	Daren Lee
36.	Jamie Spence	76.	David Carter		
37.	Lucas Parsons	77.	Jarrod Moseley		
38.	M Jarmo Sandelin	78.	Paolo Quirici		
39.	Greg Owen	79.	Santiago Luna		
40.	David Howell	80.	Raphael Jacquelin		

2000 USPGA TOUR STATISTICS

The position in eight key official PGA tour statistics for the 2000 season for each of the thirty players who qualified for the Tour Championship. References to other statistics may be found in the individual player profiles.

Up-to-date statistics can be found during the season at www.pgatour.com.

	DRIVING DISTANCE	DRIVING ACCURACY	TOTAL DRIVING	GREENS IN REGULATION
Robert Allenby	10th	65th	5th	68th
Stuart Appleby	8th	166th	76th	106th
Paul Azinger	50th	148th	115th	109th
Notah Begay	93rd	75th	65th	104th
Mark Calcavecchia	31st	55th	6th	31st
Stewart Cink	45th	164th	125th	26th
Chris DiMarco	48th	106th	45th	23rd
David Duval	18th	39th	2nd	9th
Ernie Els	38th	51st	7th	83rd
Steve Flesch	32nd	92nd	23rd	7th
Carlos Franco	68th	187th	162nd	125th
Jim Furyk	136th	14th	42nd	45th
John Huston	86th	103rd	92nd	81st
Franklin Langham	93rd	95th	90th	60th
Tom Lehman	103rd	51st	45th	10th
Justin Leonard	105th	45th	42nd	51st
Davis Love	3rd	136th	33rd	28th
Bob May	57th	105th	56th	12th
Phil Mickelson	3rd	125th	26th	42nd
Jesper Parnevik	93rd	66th	53rd	93rd
Chris Perry	75th	24th	11th	4th
Nick Price	97th	37th	29th	45th
Loren Roberts	192nd	4th	111th	85th
Vijay Singh	30th	112th	34th	5th
Hal Sutton	67th	29th	10th	15th
David Toms	68th	56th	23rd	11th
Kirk Triplett	90th	35th	25th	15th
Scott Verplank	143rd	3rd	38th	17th
Mike Weir	119th	83rd	120th	42nd
Tiger Woods	2nd	54th	1st	1st

EXPLANATORY NOTE Total driving is based on the aggregate of the player's rank in total driving and driving accuracy. Greens In Regulation is the percentage of greens hit in two shots less than par (or fewer). Putting Average is the number of putts per green hit in regulation. The All-Round ranking is computed by totalling the player's ranking in eight representative statistics (those shown here, excluding total driving, plus eagles per hole and birdies per round).

PUTTING AVERAGE	SAND SAVES	SCORING AVERAGE	ALL-ROUND RANKING	
97th	12th	35th	11th	Robert Allenby
37th	5th	23rd	19th	Stuart Appleby
4th	41st	5th	13th	Paul Azinger
174th	56th	47th	87th	Notah Begay
63rd	66th	32nd	25th	Mark Calcavecchia
43rd	10th	7th	22nd	Stewart Cink
37th	107th	40th	18th	Chris DiMarco
30th	48th	4th	2nd	David Duval
24th	22nd	3rd	5th	Ernie Els
20th	85th	8th	4th	Steve Flesch
35th	50th	57th	55th	Carlos Franco
45th	33rd	15th	39th	Jim Furyk
30th	69th	15th	36th	John Huston
13th	108th	64th	41st	Franklin Langham
139th	56th	9th	60th	Tom Lehman
45th	130th	18th	35th	Justin Leonard
24th	122nd	11th	10th	Davis Love
99th	104th	26th	33rd	Bob May
3rd	34th	2nd	3rd	Phil Mickelson
8th	154th	12th	28th	Jesper Parnevik
50th	195th	22nd	24th	Chris Perry
24th	32nd	6th	8th	Nick Price
17th	20th	10th	44th	Loren Roberts
99th	42nd	13th	19th	Vijay Singh
84th	145th	17th	17th	Hal Sutton
53rd	121st	19th	26th	David Toms
27th	84th	20th	12th	Kirk Triplett
41st	27th	26th	27th	Scott Verplank
8th	24th	28th	21st	Mike Weir
2nd	51st	1st	1st	Tiger Woods

2000 USPGA MONEY LIST

Final standings after WGC American Express Stroke-Play Championships. The top 125 golfers automatically retain their tour card.

1.	Tiger Woods	43.	Dudley Hart	85.	Brent Geiberger
2.	Phil Mickelson	44.	Scott Dunlap	86.	Bill Glasson
3.	Ernie Els	45.	Billy Andrade	87.	Steve Jones
4.	Hal Sutton	46.	Brad Faxon	88.	Bob Estes
5.	Vijay Singh	47.	Fred Couples	89.	John Cook
6.	Mike Weir	48.	Jim Carter	90.	Mark Brooks
7.	David Duval	49.	Blaine McCallister	91.	Brian Henninger
8.	Jesper Parnevik	50.	Skip Kendall	92.	Joe Ogilvie
9.	Davis Love	51.	Dennis Paulson	93.	Tom Byrum
10.	Stewart Cink	52.	Kenny Perry	94.	Mark Wiebe
11.	Kirk Triplett	53.	Frank Lickliter	95.	Craig Parry
12.	Tom Lehman	54.	Jeff Sluman	96.	David Sutherland
13.	Steve Flesch	55.	Andrew Magee	97.	Scott McCarron
14.	Justin Leonard	56.	Michael Clark II	98.	Olin Browne
15.	David Toms	57.	J P Hayes	99.	Brandel Chamblee
16.	Robert Allenby	58.	Fred Funk	100.	Woody Austin
17.	Jim Furyk	59.	Jerry Kelly	101.	Glen Hnatiuk
18.	Loren Roberts	60.	Jean Van de Velde	102.	Brian Gay
19.	Chris DiMarco	61.	Len Mattiace	103.	Bradley Hughes
20.	Notah Begay	62.	Lee Janzen	104.	Shaun Micheel
21.	Nick Price	63.	Stephen Ames	105.	Neal Lancaster
22.	Scott Verplank	64.	Carl Paulson	106.	Billy Mayfair
23.	Mark Calcavecchia	65.	Tim Herron	107.	Pete Jordan
24.	Stuart Appleby	66.	Kevin Sutherland	108.	Doug Barron
25.	John Huston	67.	Robert Damron	109.	Jay Williamson
26.	Franklin Langham	68.	Brad Elder	110.	David Peoples
27.	Paul Azinger	69.	Esteban Toledo	111.	Larry Mize
28.	Chris Perry	70.	Paul Stankowski	112.	Mark O'Meara
29.	Bob May	71.	Chris Riley	113.	Steve Stricker
30.	Carlos Franco	72.	Steve Pate	114.	Bob Tway
31.	Steve Lowery	73.	Joel Edwards	115.	Robin Freeman
32.	Duffy Waldorf	74.	Craig Stadler	116.	Jimmy Green
33.	Scott Hoch	75.	Glen Day	117.	Mathew Goggin
34.	Rocco Mediate	76.	Joe Durant	118.	Jerry Smith
35.	Tom Scherrer	77.	Edward Fryatt	119.	Gary Nicklaus
36.	Rory Sabbatini	78.	J L Lewis	120.	Brandt Jobe
37.	Shigeki Maruyama	79.	Harrison Frazar	121.	Paul Goydos
38.	Grant Waite	80.	Matt Gogel	122.	Tommy Armour III
39.	Jeff Maggert	81.	Greg Kraft	123.	Joe Ozaki
40.	Jonathan Kaye	82.	Jay Don Blake	124.	Doug Dunakey
41.	Greg Chalmers	83.	Russ Cochran	125.	Bob Burns
42.	Sergio Garcia	84.	Greg Norman		

2000 EUROPEAN CHALLENGE TOUR ORDER OF MERIT

The top 15 earn their European tour card for 2001. Those marked * have a player profile in Part 8

1.	Henrik Stenson*	6.	Tobias Dier	11.	Jose Manuel Lara
2.	David Higgins*	7.	Fredrik Henge	12.	Erol Simsek
3.	Carlos Rodiles*	8.	Christian Cevaer	13.	Jean Hugo
4.	Mikael Lundberg	9.	Johan Rystrom	14.	Andrew Raitt
5.	Michele Reale	10.	Trevor Immelman	15.	Marco Bernardini

2000 US BUY.COM TOUR MONEY LIST

The top 15 earn their US tour card for 2001. Those marked * have a player profile in Part 8

1.	Spike McRoy*	6.	Chris Smith*	11.	David Berganio Jr
2.	Mark Hensby*	7.	Kent Jones	12.	Jeff Gallagher
3.	Tim Clark*	8.	Tripp Isenhour	13.	J J Henry
4.	Briny Baird	9.	Paul Gow*	14.	Kelly Grunewald
5.	Ian Leggatt*	10.	John Riegger	15.	Jeff Hart

OFFICIAL WORLD GOLF RANKINGS

The top 64 in the world rankings qualify for the WGC Andersen Consulting Match Play. World rankings are arrived at by a complicated formula which gives points to each event based on the strength of the field. Points accumulated in the last fifty-two weeks are doubled, then each player's total is divided by the number of events in which they have competed. These are the rankings as of 12th November 2000.

1.	Tiger Woods	28.64	41.	Eduardo Romero	3.43
2.	Ernie Els	11.80	42.	Dudley Hart	3.40
3.	Phil Mickelson	11.07	43.	Steve Flesch	3.37
4.	David Duval	10.93	44.	Jose Coceres	3.35
5.	Lee Westwood	10.01	45.	Scott Hoch	3.30
6.	Colin Montgomerie	8.48	46.	Shigeki Maruyama	3.28
7.	Davis Love	7.88	47.	Joe Ozaki	3.23
8.	Hal Sutton	7.71	48.	Angel Cabrera	3.22
9.	Vijay Singh	7.32	49.	Pierre Fulke	3.18
10.	Darren Clarke	7.15	50.	Toshi Izawa	3.18
11.	Tom Lehman	7.10	51.	Mark Calcavecchia	3.17
12.	Jesper Parnevik	6.95	52.	Phillip Price	3.13
13.	Nick Price	6.85	53.	Scott Verplank	3.09
14.	Sergio Garcia	6.02	54.	Dennis Paulson	3.01
15.	Jim Furyk	5.74	55.	Gary Orr	2.94
16.	Michael Campbell	5.72	56.	Paul Lawrie	2.92
17.	Thomas Bjorn	5.48	57.	Hidemichi Tanaka	2.83
18.	Stewart Cink	5.30	58.	Bernhard Langer	2.83
19.	Justin Leonard	5.30	59.	Franklin Langham	2.81
20.	John Huston	5.00	60.	Tim Herron	2.73
21.	Mike Weir	4.96	61.	Jeff Sluman	2.70
22.	Loren Roberts	4.81	62.	Bob Estes	2.63
23.	David Toms	4.75	63.	Steve Pate	2.61
24.	Padraig Harrington	4.74	64.	Chris DiMarco	2.59
25.	Carlos Franco	4.68	65.	Paul McGinley	2.56
26.	Kirk Triplett	4.35	66.	Jumbo Ozaki	2.55
27.	Chris Perry	4.34	67.	Craig Parry	2.50
28.	Paul Azinger	4.32	68.	Toru Taniguchi	2.48
29.	M A Jiminez	4.29	69.	Mark O'Meara	2.47
30.	Stuart Appleby	4.27	70.	Brent Geiberger	2.38
31.	Rocco Mediate	4.17	71.	Scott Dunlap	2.38
32.	Bob May	4.15	72.	Andrew Coltart	2.33
33.	Notah Begay	4.02	73.	Andrew Magee	2.32
34.	J M Olazabal	3.91	74.	Fred Funk	2.25
35.	Duffy Waldorf	3.90	75.	Brad Faxon	2.22
36.	Jeff Maggert	3.88	76.	Per-Ulrik Johansson	2.22
37.	Fred Couples	3.72	77.	Skip Kendall	2.21
38.	Retief Goosen	3.70	78.	Steve Lowery	2.20
39.	Robert Allenby	3.47	79.	Jean Van de Velde	2.19
40.	Greg Norman	3.44	80.	Lee Janzen	2.18